FAIRNESS IN CONSUMER CONTRACTS

Markets and the Law

Series Editor:
Geraint Howells
Lancaster University, UK

Series Advisory Board:
Stefan Grundmann – Humboldt University of Berlin, Germany
Hans Micklitz – Bamberg University, Germany
James P. Nehf – Indiana University, USA
Iain Ramsay – York University, Canada
Charles Rickett – University of Queensland, Australia
Reiner Schulze – Münster University, Germany
Jules Stuyck – Katholieke Universiteit Leuven, Belgium
Stephen Weatherill – University of Oxford, UK
Thomas Wilhelmsson – University of Helsinki, Finland

Markets and the Law is concerned with the way the law interacts with the market through regulation, self-regulation and the impact of private law regimes. It looks at the impact of regional and international organizations (e.g. EC and WTO) and many of the works adopt a comparative approach and/or appeal to an international audience. Examples of subjects covered include trade laws, intellectual property, sales law, insurance, consumer law, banking, financial markets, labour law, environmental law and social regulation affecting the market as well as competition law. The series includes texts covering a broad area, monographs on focused issues, and collections of essays dealing with particular themes.

Other titles in the series

The Yearbook of Consumer Law 2007
Edited by Geraint Howells, Annette Nordhausen, Deborah Parry
and Christian Twigg-Flesner
ISBN 978- 0-7546-4733-1

Consumer Protection in the Age of the 'Information Economy'
Edited by Jane K. Winn
ISBN 978-0-7546-4709-6

European Fair Trading Law
The Unfair Commercial Practices Directive
Geraint Howells, Hans Micklitz and Thomas Wilhelmsson
ISBN 978-0-7546-4589-4

Fairness in Consumer Contracts
The Case of Unfair Terms

CHRIS WILLETT
De Montfort University, Leicester, UK

ASHGATE

Published by
Ashgate Publishing Limited
Gower House
Croft Road
Aldershot
Hampshire GU11 3HR
England

Ashgate Publishing Company
Suite 420
101 Cherry Street
Burlington, VT 05401-4405
USA

Ashgate website: http://www.ashgate.com

British Library Cataloguing in Publication Data
Willett, Chris
    Fairness in consumer contracts : the case of unfair terms.
    - (Markets and the law)
    1. Consumer protection - Law and legislation 2. Contracts
    3. Fairness 4. Service industries - Law and legislation
    I. Title
    346'.07

Library of Congress Cataloging-in-Publication Data
Willett, Chris.
    Fairness in consumer contracts : the case of unfair terms / by Chris Willett.
        p. cm. -- (Markets and the law)
    Includes index.
    ISBN: 978-1-84014-492-5
    1. Standardized terms of contract--Great Britain. 2. Immoral contracts--Great
Britain. 3. Contracts--Great Britain. 4. Conditions (Law)--Great Britain. 5.
Consumer protection--Law and legislation--Great Britain. I. Title.

    KD1554.W56 2007
    346.4102--dc22

                                                                    2007017562

ISBN: 978-1-84014-492-5

Printed and bound in Great Britain by TJ International Ltd, Padstow, Cornwall.

Contents

Preface vii

Chapter One 1
Introduction to Fairness Issues

Chapter Two 15
Freedom, Fairness and Testing for Unfairness

Chapter Three 75
Introduction to the Fairness Regimes

Chapter Four 119
Default Rules, Reasonable Expectations and Reasonableness
under UCTA

Chapter Five 161
The Unfair Terms in Consumer Contract Terms Regulations
(UTCCR)

Chapter Six 267
The General Fairness Reviews – UCTA, UTCCR and the New Test

Chapter Seven 377
A Broader View of the Fairness Regimes Described

Chapter Eight 395
The Transformation

Chapter Nine 411
Reviewing the Rules on Unfair Terms in Consumer Contracts and
Surveying the Bigger Picture

Index 459

Preface

The main aim of this book is to consider the law relating to unfair terms in consumer contracts. It looks at what we really mean when we talk about fairness; and at how this contrasts with the idea of freedom. It also examines the main existing legislation (the Unfair Contract Terms Act and the Unfair Terms in Consumer Contracts Regulations); and the backdrop to these pieces of legislation in terms of domestic and European law and policy.

A key goal is to develop a better understanding as to how we should understand the rules given the theoretical and policy backdrop. This is of particular importance as the Law Commissions have recently reported on this area and suggested a new unified regime. In addition, the European Commission is currently reviewing the law in this area.

Towards the end of the book I broaden out the discussion to include issues of fairness extending beyond the actual terms of consumer contracts and make a brief connection with the question of fairness in commercial contracts.

A number of people are due my thanks for helping in various ways during the writing of this book: Martina Adlington, Hugh Beale, Elisabetta Bergamini, Roger Brownsword, Martin Davis, Helen Davis-Hunt, Merav Doster, Geraint Howells, Owen Gallagher, Paul Gallagher, Sue Gallagher, Charo Gordillo, Mike McConville, Hans Micklitz, Andre Naidoo, Paolisa Nebbia, Annette Nordhausen, Aidan O'Donnell, David Oughton, Julie Prescott, Peter Rott, Martin Taylor, Joe Thomson, Richard Ward, Stephen Weatherill, Thomas Wilhelmsson and Geoffrey Woodroffe. Many thanks also to Ashgate for their enormous patience in relation to the completion of the book.

Chris Willett

Chapter One

Introduction to Fairness Issues

1.1 The Context

Notions of fairness and good faith have been given considerable academic attention in recent years.[1] The discussions have ranged over a variety of themes. So, for example, commentators have considered the nature of the underlying policies and philosophies associated with fairness and good faith;[2] the more concrete meaning of concepts such as fairness and good faith in various doctrinal contexts;[3] and whether legal recognition of general principles of fairness and good faith would be a positive thing.[4]

One factor, which must be considered when we talk about these issues, is the *stage* of the contractual relationship to which we are

---

[1]　See S. Whittaker and R. Zimmerman, Good Faith in European Contract Law, 2000; J. Beatson and D. Friedman (eds), *Good Faith and Fault in Contract Law*, Oxford, 1995; S. Smith, Atiyah's *Introduction to the Law of Contract*, 6th edn, Oxford, 2006, Ch. 12; T. Wilhelmsson *Social Contract Law and European Integration*, Dartmouth, 1995; C. Willett (ed.), *Aspects of Fairness in Contract*, Blackstone, 1996; D. Campbell and P. Vincent-Jones (eds), *Contract and Economic Organization*, Dartmouth 1996; Deacon and Michie, (eds), *Contracts, Cooperation, and Competition*, Oxford, 1997; J. Wightman, *Contract: A Critical Commentary*, Pluto Press, 1996; R. Halson (ed.), *Exploring the Boundaries of Contract*, Dartmouth, 1996; H. Collins, *The Law of Contract*, 4th edn, Butterworths, 2003, Chs 2, 12 and 13; A. Forte, *Good Faith in Contract and Property Law*, Hart, 1999; R. Brownsword, N. Hird and G. Howells, *Good Faith in Contract: Concept and Context*, Dartmouth, 1999; M. Furmston, (ed.), *The Law of Contract*, Butterworths, 1991, Ch. 1; R. Brownsword, G. Howells and T. Wilhelmsson, *Welfarism in Contract Law*, Dartmouth, 1994; J. Cartwright, *Unequal Bargaining*, Oxford, 1991; M. Chen-Wishart, *Unconscionable Bargains*, 1989.

[2]　See, T. Wilhelmsson, *ibid*; R. Brownsword, G. Howells and T. Wilhelmsson, *ibid*; R. Brownsword, N. Hird and G. Howells, *ibid*; H. Collins, *ibid*; J. Wightman, *ibid*.

[3]　R. Brownsword, N. Hird and G. Howells, *supra*, n. 1; C. Willett, *supra*, n. 1; J. Beatson and D. Friedman, *supra*, n. 1; and A. Forte, *supra*, n. 1.

[4]　R. Brownsword, N. Hird and G. Howells, *supra*, n. 1; A. Forte, *supra*, n. 1.

referring. First, there is the purely pre-contractual stage where the issue of fairness and/or good faith relates to the breakdown of negotiations.[5]

A second issue of fairness and/or good faith can arise in a situation where a contract has been concluded but concluded in circumstances and/or on terms which might in some way be said to offend against fairness or good faith. It is common in this context to speak of 'procedural' fairness, i.e. fairness in the process leading up to the agreement; and 'substantive' fairness, or fairness in substance, referring to fairness in the distribution of substantive rights and obligations under the contract. Sometimes an enquiry into procedural fairness and/or fairness in substance is simply referred to as an enquiry into the 'fairness' or 'unfairness' of *the terms*.

Thirdly, it may be possible to analyse rules of interpretation and gap filling from a fairness or good faith perspective. So we might question whether the interpretation or gap filling rules produce results which fairly balance the interests of the parties and/or which mean that the parties will be required to act fairly or in good faith.[6]

Fourthly, rules dealing with performance and changing contractual circumstances can be analysed from the perspective of fairness and good faith. Do these rules fairly balance the interests of the parties and require the parties to act in good faith?[7]

Finally the remedies set down by law for breach of contract can be analysed from fairness and good faith perspectives. Do these remedies

---

[5]   N. Cohen, Pre-Contractual Duties: Two Freedoms and the Contract to Negotiate, in J. Beatson and D. Friedman, *supra*, n. 1 at 25; J. Carter and M. Furmston, *Good Faith and Fairness in the Negotiation of Contracts*, 8 Journal of Contract Law pp. 1–15; H. Kotz, *Towards a European Civil Code: The Duty of Good Faith* in P. Cane and J. Stapleton (eds), *The Law of Obligations: Essays in Celebration of John Fleming*, Oxford, 1998 p. 243; and H.L. McQueen, Good Faith in the Scots Law of Contract, in A. Forte, (ed.), *supra*, n. 1, at 20–22.

[6]   T.D. Rakoff, Implied Terms: Of 'Default Rules' and 'Situation Sense' in Beatson and Friedman, *supra*, n. 1, at 191; R. Harrison, Good Faith in Sales, Ch. 3.

[7]   E.A. Farnsworth, Good Faith in Contract Performance, in J. Beatson and D. Friedman, *supra*, n. 1 at 153; E. McKendrick, The Regulation of Long-Term Contracts in English Law, in J. Beatson and D. Friedman, *supra*, n. 1, at 305; W. Lorenz, Contract Modification as a Result of Change of Circumstances, in J. Beatson and D. Friedman (eds), *supra*, n. 1 at 357; and G. Treitel, Alternatives and Frustration, in J. Beatson and D. Friedman, *supra*, n. 1 at 377.

fairly balance the interests of the parties? Do they allow the parties to behave in bad faith?[8]

1.2 The Core Purpose of the Book

The purpose of this book is to consider the *second* issue mentioned above i.e. the rules relating to the process leading to an agreement and the substance of that agreement. As indicated above, these rules are often simply summed up as being rules concerned with the 'fairness' or 'unfairness' of the terms. Of course the fairness of contract terms may be an issue in a variety of types of contract between different sorts of contractors. This book, however, is concerned with the fairness of terms in consumer contracts. In broad terms, this means contracts under which goods or services are supplied by a party operating in a business capacity to a party (the consumer) acting in a private capacity. The main rules considered are those of broad application which are contained in the Unfair Contract Terms Act (UCTA) 1977; and the Unfair Terms in Consumer Contracts Regulations (UTCCR) 1999.[9] First and foremost the book seeks to unpack what is meant by fairness in the context of consumer contract terms; to highlight the legal and policy influences that underpin these rules and which may influence the development of the rules; and to reflect upon current challenges and possible future developments in the regulation of consumer contract terms. However, towards the end of the book the discussion broadens out to consider issues of fairness in consumer contracts going beyond the actual terms of the contract and also (briefly) some issues as to fairness in commercial contracts.

1.3 Basic Freedom and Fairness Ideas

Chapter Two sets out competing philosophies of contract: a freedom-oriented approach and a fairness-oriented approach. In short, the

---

8 D. Friedman, Good Faith and Remedies for Breach of Contract, in J. Beatson and D. Friedman, *supra*, n. 1, at 399; R. Brownsword, *Retrieving Reasons, Retrieving Rationality*, 5 *Journal of Contract Law* 83–107; R. Brownsword, Bad Faith, Good Reasons and Termination of Contracts, in R. Bradgate, J. Birds and C. Villiers, *Termination of Contracts*, Chancery, 1995.

9 SI 1994/3159 and SI 1999/2083.

argument made is that a freedom-oriented approach tends to maximize the *self-reliant* freedom of the parties, both in relation to the process leading up to the bargain and in relation to the substantive terms which can be agreed to. If the parties are to have maximum procedural freedom in the making of an agreement this means that the law should define the basic idea of agreement fairly liberally and also that there should be limited scope to set the agreement aside on the grounds of procedural impropriety. If the parties are to have maximum substantive freedom this means that constraints on the substance of what can be agreed to should be kept to a minimum.

By contrast, a fairness-oriented approach seeks to balance the interests of the parties to the contract, and in particular to protect the substantive and procedural interests of the consumer. By the 'substantive interests' of the consumer I mean the interests affected by the substantive rights and obligations provided for by the terms. The rights and obligations stipulated for in the terms may affect important physical, proprietary, economic and social interests of the consumer. From a fairness-oriented perspective terms may be unfair where these consumer interests are unduly compromised. By the 'procedural interests' of the consumer I mean the interests that are affected by what happens in the process leading to the conclusion of the contract. Here, the consumer is affected by whether he is in a position to give 'informed consent' to the substantive terms (i.e. whether he is in a position to appreciate what he is agreeing to); whether he has a choice in relation to the substantive terms; and by his bargaining position relative to the trader. From a fairness-oriented perspective, if there is a lack of transparency (such that the consumer would find it difficult to give informed consent) then there may be an unacceptable compromise on the ability of the consumer to protect his interests at the pre-contractual ('procedural') stage. In addition, if there is a lack of choice for the consumer or if he is in a weaker bargaining position then, once again, there may be an unacceptable compromise on the ability of the consumer to protect his interests at the pre-contractual ('procedural') stage.

1.3.1 Possible Approaches to Testing for Unfairness

Chapter Two then goes on to further unpack exactly how we might test for unfairness; and the ways in which various unfairness issues relate to one another. Essentially, the argument is that we need to seek to base fairness standards around certain concrete norms such as default rules and reasonable consumer expectations. Terms that are detrimental to consumers by reference to benchmarks such as these should generally be the main focus of attention. The review of fairness might then potentially involve a full analysis of fairness in substance and fairness in procedure. Fairness in substance can be more fully assessed by considering such factors as the degree to which the term deviates from a default rule or allows for compromise of the reasonable expectations of the consumer; the particular types of interest affected by the term; whether the impact of the term could have been minimized by insurance cover; and whether any unfairness is counterbalanced by other terms that are especially favourable to the consumer.

In relation to the process leading to the contract, fairness means paying attention to factors that may prevent the consumer from protecting his interests in the agreement process. The first issue (and something that must be fundamental to fairness) is that the consumer should be in a position to give informed consent. This means that terms should be transparent; and if a term is not transparent this should strongly suggest that the term is unfair; and it is argued that this should be the case both where there is overall substantive unfairness and where a term is detrimental to consumers even although it is balanced out by another term and there is no overall substantive unfairness. It is also argued that where traders choose to include terms reflecting important legal rights these terms should be transparent and that sometimes it should be compulsory to include terms reflecting important legal rights as this may affect pre-contractual consumer understanding as to other terms and help consumers to protect themselves post-contractually against these other terms.

A further departure from a freedom-oriented approach (and therefore a more strongly fairness-oriented approach) involves taking account of other procedural factors (i.e. procedural factors other than transparency) which may affect the ability of consumers to protect their interests at the procedural stage. On this sort of approach where a term compromises the substantive interests of the consumer it will be relevant to ask whether alternative (and substantively fairer terms) were available. If no such alternative terms were available then the term agreed to is more likely to be viewed as unfair. Also, on this approach, if a term compromises the substantive interests of the consumer, it will be relevant to consider whether the consumer was in a weaker bargaining position when the term was agreed to. If so, then the term agreed to is more likely to be viewed as unfair. However, it is argued that lack of choice and the weaker bargaining position of the consumer are always secondary factors by comparison with lack of transparency. While it is feasible to say that a term that is significantly substantively detrimental to consumers is always unfair if there is a lack of transparency, it is not feasible to say that such a term is always unfair on the basis of a lack of choice or the weaker bargaining position of the consumer.

Finally, in Chapter Two, I consider the idea of a fairness regime within which there is protection of the substantive interests of the consumer, even where there has been a reasonable degree of procedural fairness and overall substantive fairness (or where terms are pre-emptively disallowed, there being no opportunity even to consider whether there is procedural fairness). These approaches move furthest along the fairness spectrum away from a traditional freedom-oriented approach. Various rationales for this are discussed: protection of the basic substantive interest; a presumption of procedural unfairness; an agenda to standardize substantive terms across a sector so as to enhance the practical usefulness of transparency; and the practical need to promote clear, effective consumer protection.

1.4 The Regimes: Overview and Background

Chapter Three sketches the basic nature of the two existing regimes: (UCTA) 1977 and (UTCCR) 1999 and the plans to create a single regime. (The UTCCR are an updated version of the UTCCR 1994 which were passed in order to implement The Directive on Unfair Terms in Consumer Contracts[10] – known as the Unfair Terms Directive, hereafter the 'UTD'). The chapter then considers the ways in which the law should and may be affected by the broader legal and policy background, by the European Court of Justice (ECJ) and by the fairness traditions of other Member States. ECJ jurisprudence thus far tells us that the test of unfairness should be approached by balancing the interests of the parties, i.e. by considering the respective benefits and detriments caused to the parties by the term. It is also clear that the ECJ will not interfere with the application of the test to the facts by national courts; although there does appear to be a readiness to take the view that a term should always be seen as unfair where there are no substantive benefits at all to the consumer (and this may well be the case whatever procedural fairness

---

[10]   93/13/EEC.

happens to exist). What is not clear is the extent to which the ECJ will be prepared to further flesh out the concept of unfairness; although it must be possible that any further fleshing out of the test would emphasize the importance of transparency as a fundamental requirement.

1.5 Default Rules, Reasonable Expectations and Reasonableness under UCTA

Chapter Four identifies the basic notions of fairness in substance underlying UCTA as default rules relating to the responsibilities of traders; along with 'reasonable expectations' that consumers may have as to the way in which traders will perform their obligations. Generally, if a term deviates from these fairness benchmarks the result is that the term is subject to a general 'fair and reasonable' test (in broad terms this involves a review of substantive and procedural factors and it seems to be accepted that – procedural fairness notwithstanding – terms can fail the test based on their substantive features/effects). However, the chapter also highlights those default rules that are treated as absolute fairness norms (deviation from which is always wholly ineffective); and considers the rationales for such an approach.

The chapter also considers the relationship between the UCTA fairness benchmarks and the proposed new regime. Essentially the point here is that the 'detriment' trigger proposed for the new regime would cover all of the terms already covered by the UCTA. However (being an 'open fairness norm') it would also cover forms of exclusion or restriction of the trader's responsibilities that would not necessarily be caught by UCTA (and, of course, it would cover those terms not caught by UCTA, but caught by the UTCCR, for example those terms that impose obligations and liabilities on the consumer).

1.6 The UTCCR

Chapter Five considers various issues surrounding the test of unfairness under the UTCCR and the way in which it has been approached by the courts. A term is unfair under the UTCCR where 'contrary to the requirement of good faith, it causes a significant imbalance in the parties' rights and obligations arising under the contract, to the detriment of the consumer'.[11] In contrast to UCTA, there is no statutory control trigger as such under the UTCCR. So a term does not need to satisfy a particular statutory formula in order to be subject to the good faith/significant imbalance test just outlined. Equally, there is no exclusive list of terms to which the test applies (although we shall see that the indicative list of terms that may be regarded as unfair[12] provides considerable guidance). The test applies to *all* terms that are not positively excluded. So, first of all Chapter Five discusses the exclusion of individually negotiated terms from the test of unfairness; why this is probably an undesirable exclusion; and the plans to remove it. However, the other exclusions are best understood in the context of the terms that the test is most focused on and we are in the best position to work out what the test is most focused on by first of all unpacking the test itself and the way in which it has been approached by the courts. Having done this, it does appear to be possible to discern that the test focuses on terms that deviate from default rules to the detriment of the consumer and terms that allow for compromise of the reasonable expectations of the consumer. (Essentially the point is that such terms will often cause a significant imbalance in the parties' rights and obligations and will therefore be subject to the broader review of unfairness under the good faith limb of the test. In other words, the significant imbalance concept can be viewed as the trigger for the broader review under the good faith element and there will normally be a significant imbalance where terms deviate from default rules or allow compromise of the reasonable expectations of consumers.) So, default rules and reasonable expectations appear to be the normal benchmarks of fairness under the UTCCR (as they are under UCTA). However, the UTCCR covers a broader range of terms dealing with the responsibilities of the trader than does UCTA. In addition, of course, UCTA does not cover any terms that *impose* obligations or liabilities on the consumer; so that the UTCCR are broader in this respect as well. All of the terms that are currently caught by the UTCCR will also be caught by the 'detriment' trigger under the proposed new regime.

Chapter Five also considers the exclusion from the test of unfairness of terms relating to the definition of the main subject matter of the contract and terms relating to the price or remuneration as against the goods or services supplied. It considers some of the arguments for and against these exclusions. However, assuming these exclusions remain, the

---

[11]   Regulation 5(1).
[12]   See Regulation 5(2) and Schedule 2.

argument is made that they are best understood as only covering main subject matter and price terms that genuinely reflect the reasonable expectations of consumers. This at least fits with the general idea (already outlined above) that the test focuses, inter alia, on terms deviating from reasonable consumer expectations. It is also the approach suggested by the Law Commissions for the proposed new regime.

Another issue dealt with in Chapter Five is a problem that is caused by the 'significant imbalance' concept. We have seen that where terms deviate from the default position or allow for compromise of the reasonable expectations of the consumer then there will normally be a significant imbalance and this will trigger a broader review of fairness under the good faith limb of the test. The problem is that in deciding whether there has been a significant imbalance it seems that we must take into account other terms that may be favourable to the consumer in various different ways. This could mean that, although term X is substantively detrimental to the consumer, the contract also contains term Y which, being a substantively favourable term, will cancel out the imbalance caused by term X. The overall result of this might then be that term X cannot be said to cause significant imbalance. If term X does not cause significant imbalance it cannot be unfair even if it violates the good faith requirement (e.g. based on there having been procedural unfairness). I suggest various ways around this problem and also point out that the proposed new approach removes the problem by removing the significant imbalance requirement and simply triggering a broad fairness enquiry where a term causes detriment.

Coming back to the test of unfairness itself, Chapter Five sketches the approach of the lower courts and the Office of Fair Trading (OFT) and provides a detailed analysis of the approach of the Court of Appeal and the House of Lords in the case of *Director General of Fair Trading* v. *First National Bank*.[13] In broad terms what emerges is a view that the significant imbalance concept focuses principally on the substantive features of terms; while the good faith concept facilitates a broad review of substance and procedure. The decision on the facts of *First National Bank* suggests that the House of Lords take a more freedom-oriented approach to the concept of unfairness than the Court of Appeal and the OFT (and possibly more freedom-oriented than would apply under a future – more developed – ECJ concept of unfairness). This more freedom-oriented approach applies both to the substantive features of

---

[13]   [2001] 3 WLR 1297.

terms and to matters of procedural fairness, in particular transparency. It is also unclear whether the House of Lords accept that a term can be unfair based on its substantive features irrespective of the level of procedural fairness. However, it remains difficult to draw definite conclusions at this stage due to the slightly quirky facts of the *First National Bank* case.

1.7 Drawing Together the General Reviews – UCTA, UTCCR and the Proposed New Test

Chapter Six builds upon what has already been concluded as to the general fairness reviews that exist under UCTA and the UTCCR. It draws upon the case law, the work of the OFT and other sources, in particular the legal and policy background to the Unfair Terms in Consumer Contracts Directive (UTD). It seeks to develop a fuller picture as to how fairness in substance and procedure are measured and how questions of substance and procedure interrelate. In particular, attention is paid to interests (in relation to services of general interest, human rights and 'mirror-image' balance) that may be given special attention by the good faith concept contained in the UTCCR test of unfairness. In particular, also, there is discussion of the distinction between a purely 'abstract' approach to unfairness and a more 'contextual' approach which takes account of the particular circumstances of the parties (and has the potential to reduce levels of protection in some cases but also to provide a greater level of protection for more vulnerable consumers).

The approach of the existing reasonableness and good faith tests to these various issues of substance and procedure is clearly of current importance. However, the approach of these existing tests would continue to be of relevance if the Law Commission proposals are adopted and we have a new 'fair and reasonable' test. Any such new test must be approached so as to offer at least the same level of protection as the unfairness concept under the UTCCR, so that the jurisprudence on the UTCCR unfairness concept would remain vital. In addition, the approach of the courts to the UCTA reasonableness test would be likely also to continue to be of assistance. However, the new regime would also include much more in the way of guidance than has been available before; and Chapter Six highlights these guidelines and what they would add to the picture.

1.8 Fairness and Other Broader Questions

Chapter Seven considers the relationship between the fairness rules discussed and other social, economic and theoretical issues. It is argued that there is a broad congruence with the values of the Welfare State. It is also argued that there is a connection with market values. So, for example, it is suggested that there is congruence with market values in that fairer terms are often more efficient terms and also in the sense that the unfairness concept deriving from the UTD aims at EC market integration. However, it is also argued that the actual content of 'fairness' is constructed more by reference to independent community based notions than trader dominated market norms. Finally, there is discussion of the relationship between the fairness rules discussed and the concepts of autonomy and expectation. It is clear that the rules deviate from traditional, self-reliant notions of autonomy and expectation. However, it is suggested that they remain connected to concepts of autonomy and expectation, albeit more fairness-oriented versions of these concepts.

1.9 Transformation

Chapter Eight identifies various ways in which the rules under discussion represent a transformation in the approach of the law to consumer contract terms. First of all, it is argued that there has been a transformation in terms of the basic suitability of the rules to deal with the issues. The courts did, of course, show some sensitivity to the problems of unfair terms in consumer contracts. However, common law and equity were limited in various respects. Essentially, the common law and equitable rules lacked one or more of three key features that are necessary: (1) a broad review of procedural and substantive fairness applicable to all or most terms that either exclude or restrict the obligations or liabilities that would otherwise be owed by the trader; add to those that would otherwise be owed by the consumer; or provide for either party to perform in a way that does not reflect the reasonable expectations of the consumer; (2) standards that (while they may sometimes be in congruence with the market) are not dominated by the market; (3) standards that do not allow a term to be made fair by the good conscience of the trader.

The second element of the transformation is connected to the first and relates to the style of legal reasoning. To a degree it can be argued that the rules under discussion represent a shift from rules based on formal reasoning to ones based on more substantive/discretionary type reasoning.

Finally, the UTCCR have brought a transformation for the UK in terms of enforcement. The proactive enforcement powers in the UTCCR have meant that the fairness standards have become more of a reality in practice than they would ever be within a wholly private law enforcement scheme. These powers have been a foundation for the OFT in particular to persuade traders to remove or amend large numbers of terms.

1.10 Review and the Bigger Picture

Chapter Nine reviews where we appear to be at and what are the key questions in relation to regulating unfair terms in consumer contracts. So, in particular, it emphasizes the remaining uncertainty as to exactly what level of fairness there is both in relation to procedure (in particular transparency); and in relation to substance. In relation to fairness in substance an important question is whether the House of Lords accept that certain terms can be unfair on essentially substantive grounds, irrespective of procedural fairness. If terms can be removed on purely substantive grounds then they can be removed more readily and without arguments as to levels of transparency (or other questions of procedural fairness). It is also possible to standardize the substantive features of terms across a trading sector, possibly allowing transparency to have more effect in practice. Disallowing terms on principally substantive grounds also represents a more radical version of fairness at a theoretical level. It is also of significance for our understanding of the theoretical trajectory of the overall EC consumer and contract law *acquis* (of which the UTD is a central part);[14] and, in relation to which there is an ongoing debate as to whether there should be reliance on an 'information paradigm', i.e. whether information is all that is needed to protect consumers or whether more is needed.

A further question is as to the appropriate role for a contextual approach to the concept of unfairness; and in particular one which seeks to give stronger protection to more vulnerable consumers.

It is suggested that the current review of the EC consumer *acquis* and the possible introduction of a new unified regime in the UK provide the

---

14   Most recently on the review see the Commission's Green Paper on the Review of the Consumer Acquis (8 February 2007) COM (2006) 744 final.

opportunity to address these difficult questions and to try to lay down clear markers.

A further question raised is as to the future prospects for development of the law at ECJ level. It is pointed out that it is as yet unclear as to how much further the ECJ will be prepared to go in fleshing out the meaning of the unfairness concept. In particular we do not know to what extent the ECJ will develop transparency as a vital part of the autonomous unfairness concept.

Finally, in relation to unfair terms in consumer contracts, it is suggested that there remain important questions as to the success or otherwise of the harmonization agenda that led to the UTCCR in the first place; and the extent to which there is (and will be) a cross-fertilization of fairness ideas as between the Member States. It is argued that the CLAB European Database on unfair terms[15] may be a significant resource in this regard; but that much will be dependent upon whether cases actually get referred to the ECJ and how prescriptive they choose to be in setting out an autonomous concept of unfairness. The House of Lords passed up a chance in the *First National Bank* case to obtain a view from the ECJ and at the same time to provide the ECJ with an opportunity to further develop the an autonomous EC notion of unfairness. At the same time, the *First National Bank* judgement did recognize the importance of interpreting the unfairness test in the light of the goals of the UTD. In addition, Lord Bingham chose to draw upon Article 138 of the German BGB in approaching the test. Both of these factors provide grounds for optimism in relation to harmonization prospects. At the same time, harmonization is always likely to be constrained in practice at least to some extent by the distinctive national legal cultural approaches that will inevitably influence interpretation of the unfairness concept.

Next I broaden out the discussion to consider fairness in other aspects of the trader-consumer relationship (i.e. beyond the actual terms). There is discussion of the Unfair Commercial Practices Directive,[16] which (in the same tradition as the UTD) uses a general clause on fairness applicable to both pre-contractual and post-contractual practices and to practices not necessarily related to a contract at all. There is analysis of the way in which this will broaden out the existing UK approach to these issues. This Directive only requires public law controls of such practices.

---

[15] http://europa.eu.int/comm/consumers/cons_int/safe_shop/unf_cont_terms/clab/index_en.htm.

[16] 2005/29/EC.

However, the DTI has suggested that new UK rules might attach private law sanctions and I seek to unpack what this might involve.

Finally, I consider the question of good faith/fairness in commercial contracts and the potential impact of the consumer regime in this regard. It is pointed out that arguments can be made to the effect that certain rationales for the instatement of fairness in consumer contracts apply also in the context of commercial contracts. I discuss various developments in relation to commercial contracts which may edge commercial contract law in the UK towards a general principle of fairness or good faith, e.g. the current Law Commission proposals to extend the UCTA reasonableness test in commercial contracts to terms other than exemption clauses; the good faith test (reflecting the one in the UTD) in the (non-mandatory) Principles of European Contract Law (PECL); the series of papers from the European Commission on harmonization of European contract law; the ongoing work towards the development of a 'Common Frame of Reference' for contract law at European level; and the 'spillover effect' of the general fairness clauses in consumer law.

Chapter Two

Freedom, Fairness and Testing for Unfairness

2.1 The Nature of Consumer Contracting

Some consumer contracts will be formed purely orally, or by conduct, or perhaps by a mixture of oral communication and conduct[1] In these kinds of scenarios it is possible (and indeed fairly common) for there to be no written terms. The obligations of the parties will be derived from the basic verbal and/or conduct-based agreement for the sale of a certain item at a particular price; along with the implied terms and other default rules deriving from the Sale of Goods Act 1979[2] and other legislation such as the Supply of Goods and Services Act 1982.[3] In some cases, however, there will be an attempt to add some written terms to the basic verbal and/or conduct-based agreement. There may be a notice on display at or near the point of contract that contains terms. Alternatively, there may be a ticket or some other document which is presented to the consumer and which either contains terms, or refers to the existence of terms that are to

---

[1] For example a consumer may verbally request a particular item from a shop assistant. This will normally be construed as an offer (see *Pharmaceutical Society of Great Britain* v. *Boots Cash Chemist (Southern) Ltd* [1953] 1QB 401). The shop assistant may then verbally indicate that he is prepared to sell the item (typically legally construed as acceptance of the consumer's offer). Alternatively, the consumer may have said nothing, but simply lifted the item from a shelf and presented it to the shop assistant (again, normally legally construed as an offer to buy); and the shop assistant may have acted in such a way as to indicate acceptance, e.g. by registering a sale on the cash till. Either of these alternatives can be varied slightly to produce a mix of oral and conduct based agreement. For example, the consumer may make a verbal offer to buy and the shop assistant may accept by conduct.

[2] Containing implied terms (applicable to contracts of sale) as to title, description, quality and fitness for purpose and default rules on passing of delivery, payment, acceptance and passing of property and risk.

[3] Containing default rules (applicable to other contracts for the supply of goods) on description, quality and fitness for purpose and (applicable to contracts for the supply of a service) on price, time of performance and the exercise of reasonable care in the provision of the service.

be found elsewhere. In other circumstances there will be full set of written terms at the point of contract, e.g. mortgage agreements, mobile phone contracts, credit agreements, many travel contracts, and most contracts relating to the membership of clubs and societies. These terms will almost invariably have been drawn up or adopted by the trader. The trader will intend that they should encapsulate the full extent of the binding agreement between the parties.

The standard form contract therefore represents the supplier's attempt to plan for the eventualities of the relationship, such as disputes as to mode/quality of performance, financial responsibilities, and the withdrawal of a service. There are obviously efficiency advantages in the use of such terms. This is because they are indeed standard i.e. they are used for all of the transactions of that type which a particular firm enters into with consumers. As such there is no need for time to be spent on individual negotiations with each consumer as to the range of issues and eventualities which must be covered. The efficiency advantages of standard form contracts were summed up in the following terms by Karl Llewellyn,[4]

> ... they save trouble in bargaining, they save time in bargaining. They infinitely simplify the task of internal administration within a business unit, of keeping tabs on transaction, of knowing where one is at, of arranging orderly expectations, orderly fulfilment, orderly planning. They ease administration by concentrating the need for discretion and decision in such personnel as can be trusted to be discreet. This reduces wear and tear, it cheapens administration, it serves the ultimate consumer.

Hugh Beale has also emphasized the benefits of standard form contracts which can provide us with '... a system of mass production which allows more and more people to obtain goods and services they might not otherwise be able to afford'.[5]

The essential point being made by both Llewellyn and Beale is that the use of standard terms reduces transaction costs for both the trader and the consumer. In particular, the reduction in transaction costs for the trader enables the trader to charge less than he would otherwise need to charge.

---

[4]   K. Llewellyn, 1939, 52 Harvard Law Review, 700, 701.
[5]   H. Beale, Unfair Contracts in Britain and Europe, 1989, Current Legal Problems 192.

2.2 The Basic Freedom/Fairness Distinction[6]

The above points by Llewellyn and Beale explain why standard terms are used and why their use is probably a good thing. However they do not in themselves tell us what sort of attitude to take to the particular types of terms that are used and the way in which they are used. One way of viewing the situation is to see there as being a choice between freedom-oriented and fairness-oriented philosophies of consumer contracting. We can apply rules that are more oriented towards freedom of contract (i.e. freedom of contract understood in a self-interested, self-reliant way) or rules that are more oriented towards fairness.[7] Of course, this is all a matter of degree. The best way of describing most rules is that they are *more* oriented towards freedom than fairness or vice versa. However, rules that are more oriented in one direction will still tend to have elements of the other approach. So, for example, there are rules that are, to an extent, oriented towards fairness but which do not provide 'full-blooded' fairness protection. A good example of this is provided by rules requiring a high level of transparency. It will be argued below that these are fairness oriented in the sense that they seek to enable the consumer to protect his interests in the bargaining process by improving the chances that he will understand what he is agreeing to. In addition, it will also be argued below that a full-blooded freedom approach would certainly not adopt rules requiring a high level of transparency as such rules interfere with the freedom of the parties in the bargaining process. They interfere with the freedom of the trader to present his terms as he chooses and the freedom

---

6   Generally on the distinction between freedom and fairness approaches see P.S. Atiyah, The Rise and Fall of Freedom of Contract, OUP, 1979; E. Hondius, The Protection of the Weaker Party in Harmonised European Contract Law: A Synthesis, 2004, Journal of Consumer Policy, 27: 245–251; T. Hartlief, Freedom and Protection in Contemporary Contract Law, 2004, Journal of Consumer Policy, 27: 253–267; R. Brownsword, Contract Law: Themes for the Twenty-First Century, 2nd edn, OUP, 2006, Ch. 3.

7   Freedom of contract can be viewed as a philosophy that held sway during a particular period in history (i.e. from around 1770–1870-see P.S. Atiyah, The Rise and Fall of Freedom of Contract, OUP, 1979, Ch. 16). Equally the focus can be on freedom of contract as a model that is not necessarily associated with a particular historical period (see H. Collins, The Law of Contract, Butterworths, 4th edn, 2003, Ch. 2 and R. Brownsword, Contract Law: Themes for the Twenty-First Century, 2nd edn, OUP, 2006, 46–48). Here, I am discussing freedom of contract more in the latter sense, although it does become clear in the following chapters that the rules on consumer contract terms were more freedom oriented until the Unfair Contract Terms Act (UCTA) 1977 and the Unfair Terms in Consumer Contracts Regulations (UTCCR) 1994 (now 1999).

of the consumer to choose whether or not to familiarize himself with these terms. So, in these senses, transparency rules are fairness-oriented. At the same time, they are not full-blooded fairness rules that reject any elements of freedom. A simple transparency rule is not as restrictive of freedom as a rule that disallows a term based on its substantive features. So, if we simply insist upon transparency and enforce terms as long as they are transparent, we retain the freedom of the parties to choose (based on a decent level of transparency) to agree to terms that are unfair in substance.

2.3.1 Freedom of Contract and Consumer Contract Terms[8]

At the outset it is useful to make a distinction between freedom *of* contract and freedom *from* contract. Both are concepts often associated with the classical law of contract.[9] However freedom *from* contract is best described as a negative freedom. This form of freedom can possibly be subdivided further. First, there is what might be described as 'party' freedom.[10] In the case of this kind of freedom from contract the idea is that parties should have freedom to choose *who* they enter into contracts with and, perhaps more aptly, freedom to choose *not* to enter into a contract with any given party. This form of freedom is most typically challenged by rules which prevent parties exercising racial or sexual discrimination in deciding who they will enter contracts with. The second type of freedom *from* contract is concerned with *whether* and *when* one chooses to contract rather than *whom* one chooses to contract with.[11] The

---

8   Generally on freedom of contract see P. Atiyah, The Rise and Fall of Freedom of Contract, 1979; J. Beatson and D. Friedman, From Classical to Modern Contract Law, in J. Beatson and D. Friedman, (eds), Good Faith and Fault in Contract Law, Oxford, 1995; H. Collins, The Law of Contract, Butterworths, 4th edn, Ch. 2; K. Zweigert and H. Kotz, An Introduction to Comparative Law, Oxford, 3rd edn, 1998, Ch. 24; and R. Brownsword, General Considerations, in M. Furmston (ed.), Butterworth's Common Law Series, The Law of Contract, 2nd edn, 2003, 1, at 24–41; R. Brownsword, Contract Law: Themes for the Twenty-First Century, 2nd edn, OUP, 2006, Ch. 3.

9   J. Beatson and D. Friedman, *ibid.*, at 7–8.

10 R. Brownsword, General Considerations, in M. Furmston (ed.), Butterworth's Common Law Series, *The Law of Contract*, 2nd edn, 2003, 1, at 1.45; R. Brownsword, Contract Law: Themes for the Twenty-First Century, 2nd edn, OUP, 2006, 50 and 57.

11 See Kessler and Fine, Culpa in Contrahendo, Bargaining in Good Faith and Freedom of Contract: A Comparative Study, 1964, 77 Harvard Law Review,401; E. Hondius, (ed.), Pre-contractual Liability: Reports to the XIII Congress International Academy of Comparative Law, 1991; N. Cohen, Pre-contractual Duties: Two Freedoms and the Contract to Negotiate, in J. Beatson and D. Friedman, 1995, Good Faith and Fault in Contract Law, Oxford, 1995, at 27; M. Hesselink, Pre-Contractual Good Faith, in H.

assertion of a discrete point at which contractual obligation arises is important to this second concept of freedom from contract. This discrete point may in some circumstances have been preceded by lengthy negotiations and a fairly high degree of expectation may well have been engendered in one or other of the parties that the contract would in fact come into existence. Indeed, one of the parties may have acted in reliance on the assumption that such a contract would come into existence. However the freedom *from* contract perspective firmly asserts that there is no contractual or contractual type liability unless and until such a contract has come into existence. Indeed a freedom from contract perspective may frown upon attempts to impose pre-contractual liability via *ex-lege* means such as tort or restitution; and a freedom from contract perspective will certainly frown upon attempts to impose pre-contractual liability via a good faith or fairness principle.

By contrast with freedom *from*, freedom *of* contract is a more positive concept, being about: 'the creative power of the participants in the contractual process to act as private legislators and to legislate rights and duties binding upon themselves'.[12]

Perhaps the most famous judicial expression of this positive freedom of contract philosophy was that of Sir George Jessell MR in *Printing and Numerical Registering Co* v. *Samson*[13] where he said:

> [if] there is one which more than another public policy requires it is that men of full age and competent understanding shall have the utmost liberty of contracting, and that their contracts when entered into freely and voluntarily shall be held sacred and shall be enforced by Courts of justice. Therefore, you have this paramount public policy to consider – that you are not lightly to interfere with this freedom of contract.

We can identify two closely associated elements here. First of all there is the idea of 'the utmost liberty of contracting' i.e. the notion that there should be maximum freedom for the parties to set the terms of their contract. By contrast with 'party freedom' as discussed above this has been described as involving 'term freedom'.[14] Secondly there is the idea

---

Beale, A. Hartkamp and D. Tallon, Contract (Common Law of Europe Series), Hart, 2002; and J. Gordley, The Enforceability of Promises in European Contract Law, Cambridge, 2001.

[12]   J. Beatson and D. Friedman, From Classical to Modern Contract Law, in J Beatson and D. Friedman, (eds), *ibid.*, at 7–8.

[13]   (1875) LR 19 EQ 462.

[14]   R. Brownsword, Contract Law: Themes for the Twenty-First Century, 2nd edn, OUP, 2006, 50; D.H. Parry, The Sanctity of Contract, 1965; and Baker, From Sanctity of Contract to Reasonable Expectation (1979) 32 Current Legal Problems 17.

that the parties' 'freely made agreements shall be enforced by the Courts'. This latter element seems to be what is often referred to as 'sanctity of contract'.[15]

This notion of freedom is, in broad terms, a libertarian notion which contains several elements. It is about the contract being based on the intention of the parties. This intention having been established this is what is enforced by the courts. The courts do not make the contract or review it on the basis of fairness; they simply enforce the intentions of the parties.[16] But what is the connection between this and freedom? First, there is the idea of the freedom of the parties to pursue *self-interest* through contracting; i.e. the idea that the parties should be free to reach enforceable agreements on terms that they consider to be in their own best interests, there being little or no obligation to consider the interests of the other party.[17] It is also about the freedom to choose what is in one's own self-interest. However, this freedom is essentially a *self-reliant, non-contextual*, form of freedom; i.e. it is about the freedom to understand, choose, bargain, agree, not agree etc depending wholly on one's own judgement, abilities etc.[18] It pays limited heed to context. First of all this means that it pays limited heed to restrictions on the ability to usefully exercise freedom to protect one's self-interest prior to conclusion of the contract (i.e. at the *procedural* stage). Here we are talking about personal weaknesses, power relationships, contractual processes etc that might in practice affect parties (and more likely consumers) in their ability to protect their interests prior to conclusion of the contract. The self-reliant approach to freedom is also unconcerned with context in the sense that it is unconcerned with the ways in which the *substantive* interests of the parties might be affected by the exercise of self-reliant freedom. In other words, the impact of the substantive terms is looked at in a non-contextual way. There is no concern that parties (such as consumers), who purchase goods and services for use in the private sphere of life, may be affected by

---

15 R. Brownsword, *ibid.*, 51.

16 P.S. Atiyah, The Rise and Fall of Freedom of Contract, OUP, 1979, 681.

17 This is part of what Brownsword (*supra*, n. 14 at 47) refers to as an 'adversarial ethic' and fits with Atiyah's characterization of the classical law as being based on the 'economic model of the free market' (P. S. Atiyah, The Rise and Fall of Freedom of Contract, OUP, 1979, *ibid.*).

18 This is the other dimension to Brownsword's adversarial ethic in the sense that if someone is my adversary I should rely not on them but on myself. Atiyah specifically refers to self-reliance, saying that a contractor is '[not] entitled to rely on the other except within the narrowest possible limits' (*ibid.*, 403).

terms in ways that differ from the way in which other contractors are affected.[19]

Another way of putting this lack of concern for context is that the focus is on the parties as 'abstract' persons.[20] They are viewed in the abstract from all of the factors mentioned that might, in reality, affect their ability to ability to pursue and protect their interests during the process leading to the contract; and they are viewed in the abstract from the ways in which their substantive interests might be affected.

This sort of approach will take a broad view as to the types of agreements which should be enforced. It will consequently frown upon restrictions on enforceability based either, a) on the sort of fairness criteria which are the subject of this book i.e. criteria concerned with doing some form of justice as between the parties by balancing their interests[21] or b) on the goal of protecting third parties[22] or c) on public interest criteria. By public interest criteria I mean criteria concerned to protect the broader public interest, for instance rules banning trading in certain items, based on moral or ethical concerns; or on the basis of public safety not directly related to the safety of one of the individual contractors e.g. bans on the sale of handguns.[23]

In broad terms the kind of freedom-oriented approach under discussion here is typically justified from one or both of the following two standpoints. First, there is the idea of respect for the individual right to

---

[19] For a discussion of term freedom and sanctity of contract in cases involving the fairness of terms included in the contract and also in relation to questions of renegotiated contracts and contracts that become more onerous to perform see R. Brownsword, Contract Law: Themes for the Twenty-First Century, 2nd edn, OUP, 2006, 51–57.

[20] T. Wilhelmsson, Critical Studies in Private Law, Dartmouth, 1992, Ch. 4 and T. Wilhelmsson, Social Contract Law and European Integration, Dartmouth, 1995, at 29–31.

[21] Note here that the focus is on balancing the interests/'doing justice' between the parties, the idea being that the issue is the extent to which the rights and obligations should be allowed to favour one over another. This is to be distinguished from rules (that would also be frowned upon from a freedom perspective) where the restriction of freedom might be said to be about the protection of both contracting parties from themselves, e.g. controls over gambling contracts or contracts for sexual favours – see R. Brownsword, Contract Law: Themes for the Twenty-First Century, 2nd edn, OUP, 2006, 52.

[22] For example, where there is a contract to harm a third party – see R. Brownsword, *ibid.*

[23] On c) see R. Brownsword, *ibid.*, and on the distinction between a) and c) see also S. Smith, In Defence of Substantive Fairness (1996) 112 Law Quarterly Review, 138 at 140.

make free and autonomous choices.[24] Second, there is the more utilitarian notion of maximization of overall welfare.[25] Here the general idea is that enforcing what the parties freely agree to (and not reviewing this on fairness or other grounds) is (a) 'good for' people in the sense that it enables them to 'learn to order their lives according to some definite plan [and] ... be encouraged to aim for particular goals'[26] and (b) the most effective way of serving the more general function of contract law in serving the market mechanism (agreements being presumed to be more efficient if they reflect individual preferences and market exchanges being presumed to be more stable and certain if they are based on what the parties agree and are not interfered with on the basis of some vitiating notion, whether this vitiating notion is fairness or some other independent criteria based on the public interest).

2.3.2 Freedom of Contract and the Process Leading to the Conclusion of the Contract

2.3.2.1 Procedural Factors Affecting Consumers

In order to fully understand the idea of allowing parties maximum freedom to make agreements, it is important to elaborate a little on the full significance of 'making an agreement'. It has become common to talk about the distinction between the process or procedure leading to the making of the agreement and the substantive terms of the agreement itself.[27] What happens in the course of the process leading to the agreement is, of course, closely linked with the substantive agreement itself. However, it remains possible, at least to some extent, to separate out

---

24 Generally see R. Dworkin, Taking Rights Seriously, 1978; R. Brownsword, Liberalism and the Law of Contract, in Bellamy (ed.), Liberalism and Recent Legal and Social Philosophy, ARSP, Beiheft, 36, 1986, 86; J. Raz, The Morality of Freedom, OUP, 1986; D. Kimmel, Neutrality, Autonomy and Freedom of Contract (2001) 21 Oxford Journal of Legal Studies, 473; and D. Kimmel, From Promise to Contract: Towards a Liberal Theory of Contract, Hart, 2005, Ch. 5.

25 See R. Brownsword, Contract Law: Themes for the Twenty-First Century, 2nd edn, OUP, 2006, 65–66.

26 P.S. Atiyah, Essays on Contract, OUP, 1986, at 16.

27 On this see A. Leff, *Unconscionability and the Code: The Emperor's New Clause*, 1967, 115, University of Pennsylvania Law Review 485; J. Gordley, *Equality in Exchange*, 1981, 69 California Law Review 1587; P. Atiyah, *Contract and Fair Exchange*, 1985, 35, University of Toronto Law Journal, 1; M. Eisenberg, *The Bargain Principle and its Limits*, 1982, 95, Harvard Law Review, 741; and S. Smith, *Atiyah's Introduction to the Law of Contract*, Ch. 12.

the issues. The essential point about the process leading to the agreement is that it is a way of describing the conditions/circumstances that exist up until the making of the agreement and which affect the expectations the parties have about the substance of the agreement and the extent to which the parties are able to protect their interests in relation to the substance of the agreement. This can be said to include the way in which the terms of the contract are presented to the consumer; or, putting this in another way, how 'transparent' the terms are. It is very common for terms to lack transparency. The terms may not actually be available at the time the contract is made. They may be expressed in unclear, possibly legalistic, language and in small, and otherwise difficult to read, text. There may be a considerable degree of complexity, poor structuring and poor cross-referencing. All of this may be compounded by the fact that consumers have little time to read the terms before making the contract; and may have little understanding of the legal context or how the term might affect them in practice. In some cases there may be a deliberate agenda to mislead and confuse the consumer or at least to deter the consumer from reading the terms. In many cases, however, it may simply be that lawyers draft from traditional models that were not drafted to be clear to non-lawyers and that are complex and lengthy in order to ensure that the interests of the client are as fully protected as possible.

The level of transparency obviously has the potential to influence what the consumer expects to get from the agreement and the ability of the consumer to protect his interests in relation to the substantive terms that are on offer. It may affect how well he is informed as to what is on offer; and what risks may be involved; whether he can rationally compare the terms on offer with those of other traders with a view to deciding who offers the best terms;[28] whether he can usefully seek to negotiate for better terms;[29] whether he enters the contract at all;[30] whether, if he enters the contract, he does so on the basis of a reasonable degree of knowledge as to the risks contained in the substantive terms; and whether, if he enters the contract, he takes steps to protect his interests, e.g. by insuring against some risk that the trader has excluded liability for using one of the standard terms.

The process leading to the agreement is not simply affected by the issue as to whether or not terms are transparent. Quite apart from whether terms are transparent there is also the question as to the *options* available to the consumer. So, for example, the consumer may have been under some pressure or influence affecting his ability to choose freely whether

---

[28] T. Wilhelmsson, Cooperation and Competition Regarding Standard Contract Terms in Consumer Contracts, (2006), European Business Law Review, 49, at 52.

[29] T. Wilhelmsson, *ibid.*

[30] T. Wilhelmsson, *ibid.*

or not to contract in the first place. However, more typically germane to our situation is that, while the consumer is under no such pressure or influence as to *whether* to contract, he is restricted in the choice of the *terms upon which* he can contract. This may be because the trader with whom he is dealing does not offer a choice and/or because other traders do not offer a choice. Clearly, the trader in question can make his own decisions as to whether to offer a choice. However, even if a market is competitive, other traders will not necessarily offer something different. If the terms are not transparent and consumers cannot understand and compare the offerings of different traders there will be no incentive for traders to compete with one another for the business of consumers.[31] The result, then, may be that traders simply compete over the elements of the contract that are in fact transparent to consumers. The consumer is likely to focus on the basic description and/or presentation of the goods or services. The signal is that certain fundamentals can be expected: goods or services of a certain type, at a certain price, perhaps (depending upon the type of contract) to be supplied at a particular time and place. These are the main issues on which there are likely to be specific signals and expectations. Consumers will understand what is on offer in relation to these fundamentals; and will be able to compare the offerings of different traders in relation to these issues. Assuming that the other conditions for a working market exist, there will be an incentive for traders to compete with one another to attract consumers. They will compete with one another in relation to their presentation of these fundamental or core issues. This should mean that the substance of what is put on offer to consumers on these issues is more favourable to the interests of consumers than it would otherwise be; as traders compete by seeking to offer more generous basic performance promises, and cheaper prices. There is also likely to be a degree of choice in the market on these issues. However, if the formal terms are not transparent to consumers there is little or no incentive for traders to compete on the ancillary issues that these terms deal with. Indeed there is an incentive for traders to use these other terms to load risks on to the consumer as a means offsetting the costs involved in the more 'pro-consumer' core provisions.[32] So, the non-

---

31 We should note here that even where terms dealing with ancillary matters *are* transparent there is often good reason to be sceptical as to how much impact this will have on consumers and therefore how effective it will be in creating a competitive market in these terms – see further below at 2.4.3.4(iv).

32 See H. Beale, The Directive on Unfair Terms in Consumer Contracts, in J. Beatson and D. Friedmann, Good Faith and Fault in Contract Law, 232 at 233; V.P. Goldberg, Institutional Change and the Quasi-Invisible Hand, 17 J Law & Econ 461 at 483 *et seq.* and M.J. Trebilcock, An Economic Approach to the Doctrine of

core terms are likely to be more unfair to the consumer and there is less likely to be a choice as between the offerings of different traders.

Of course, the non-core terms may be subjected to a degree of market discipline (possibly leading to choices being available) even where they are not particularly transparent. There may be a section of consumers who have the time, resources and education to overcome the lack of transparency and gain a good understanding of the terms and their implications. This so called 'active margin' of consumers may then exert market discipline on traders with the result that terms are more substantively fair and/or that there is improved choice.[33] However this all depends upon there being a sufficiently large margin of consumers that reads and digests terms and makes market choices on this basis.[34] It must be seriously questionable as to whether such a margin will often exist. It seems more likely that many of those who are ready and able to take positive steps to protect their interests will tend not to do so until there is a dispute. Such consumers may well scrutinize terms and/or seek advice as to their meaning when the trader seeks to rely upon the terms. This may enable such consumers to persuade traders to agree a compromise that is more favourable than what will be achieved by those who do not scrutinize and question the terms.[35] However, these will be individual victories and will not serve to discipline what traders offer in general.

Quite apart from consumer options being restricted by a lack of alternative terms, the options of the consumer may be restricted in another sense. Whatever choices are (or are not) available in relation to alternative terms, traders will usually refuse to *bargain* with consumers over the terms as it is not efficient to do so (the whole point of standard terms being to reduce transaction costs). Even if bargaining does take place, traders are usually in a strong enough bargaining position (relative to consumers) to enable them to avoid having to make significant changes to the terms.[36]

To summarize then, consumers may be faced with problems of lack of transparency, a lack of alternative terms and other bargaining problems (a

Unconscionability, B.J. Reiter and J. Swann, (eds), Studies in Contract Law (1980) at 379.

[33] See M.J. Trebilcock, *ibid.*

[34] See the discussion by W. Whitford, Contract Law and the Control of Standardized Terms in Consumer Contracts: An American Report (1995) 3 European Review of Private Law, 193, at 195–199.

[35] *Ibid.*

[36] The detailed nature of inequality of bargaining power and how a fairness-oriented approach might deal with it are both issues that are discussed below at 2.4.2.2 and 2.4.3.4(v).

refusal of the trader to bargain and – if bargaining does take place –being in a weaker bargaining position).

2.3.2.2 The Attitude of a Freedom-Oriented Approach to These Procedural Factors

We have seen, then, that consumers may face problems of transparency and lack of options at the procedural stage. However, an approach that is concerned to maximize self-reliant freedom to pursue self-interest in the making of agreements will seek first of all to maximize this type of freedom at the procedural stage; and to minimize the constraints that exist on the bringing about of a binding agreement. In other words self-reliant freedom to make a binding agreement should be maximized and minimal attention should be paid to restrictions on consumer information and consumer options.

So, minimal transparency should be required. From a self-reliant and self-interested freedom of contract perspective, as long as the level of transparency is such that the consumer has a basic awareness that terms exist[37] then the consumer is free to decide what to do. He is free to decide whether or not to enter the contract. He can make this choice based on having made no investigation as to the meaning and implications of the terms. In such circumstances he is free to choose not to enter the contract based on the risk of the unknown; and he is free to enter the contract while taking the risk that these terms are damaging to his interests. Equally, he can make the choice as to whether to enter the contract based on having acquired further information about the terms. This may result in the consumer having a fairly full understanding as to the risks; and he is then free to decide whether these are acceptable risks. Alternatively, his investigations may leave him little more the wiser; but, again, he is free to decide how to proceed. These are the freedoms that a self-reliant and self-

---

37 This often seems to be all that is required under common law incorporation rules (on which see below at 8.1.3). Where unsigned documents are concerned the provisions in question are usually treated as having been incorporated into the contract where the consumer is deemed to have had 'reasonable notice' of them; and this usually means no more than reasonable steps having been taken to make consumers aware of the *existence* of the provisions. It is not usually relevant to consider the type of language, print or overall contractual structuring, cross-referencing etc; whether there is time to read and understand them; or whether terms have been drawn to the attention of the consumer (although this is required where onerous or unusual terms are concerned). Provisions in signed documents are incorporated based on the signature; again without any of the above questions being asked (and with no requirement to draw the attention of the consumer to onerous or unusual terms).

interested based freedom-oriented perspective wishes to preserve. If a higher level of transparency is required, and if terms are set aside on the basis that this standard was not met, then these self-reliant and self-interested consumer freedoms have been overridden.

Of course, as we have already observed, these consumer freedoms are very much of a self-reliant, non-contextual, nature. The consumer is said to have the freedom to decide whether to read terms, seek advice on them, enter the contract etc. based on what he does or does not know. However, no attention is paid to whether the nature of the contracting process, the relationship between the parties or the personal weaknesses of the consumer make it reasonable to expect that the consumer can usefully make use of such freedoms in practice.[38]

Then, of course, there is the freedom of the trader. Maximization of trader freedom also requires limited transparency requirements. Imposition of too many such requirements restricts the freedom of the trader to pursue his self-interest. He is not required simply to make the consumer aware that terms exist, but also to ensure that they are drafted and presented in accordance with this higher standard.

As to procedural problems affecting the choices and bargaining options of the consumer, maximum freedom (and minimum intervention) seems to involve restricting intervention to cases where the choice of the consumer has been restricted by physical force and threats of physical force; and the will of the consumer has either been wholly overborne or at least his alternatives have been reduced to a significant extent.[39] Here, the substantial restriction on choice (caused by the force or threat) means that

---

[38] Of course, there is a considerable spectrum of what we might regard as 'freedom' or an exercise in 'voluntariness' – see A. Kronman, Contract Law and Distributive Justice, 1980, 89 Yale Law Journal, 472 and D. Kennedy, Distributive and Paternalist Motives in Contract and Tort Law, with Special Reference to Compulsory Terms and Unequal Bargaining Power (1982) 41 Maryland Law Review 563 at 582. So, the 'freedom' of a consumer can, of course, be read in a totally different way to that discussed in the text here. It can be said that consumers are not really 'free' unless they are free from restrictions at the procedural stage that obstruct their ability to protect their interests. However, this version of freedom is not the self-reliant, non-contextual version we are discussing here, but is a notion of freedom infused with fairness concerns. More generally on the relationship between the different 'ethics' with which we can infuse a concept such as freedom see R. Brownsword, Contract Law: Themes for the Twenty-First Century, 2nd edn, OUP, 2006, 65–66 and R. Barnett, A Consent Theory of Contract (1986) 86 Columbia Law Review 269, at 300–319 in particular. This issue is dealt with further below at 2.4.1 and 7.3.1.

[39] For example, the type of situation in a cases such as *Earl of Orkney* v. *Vinfra* (1606) Mor 16481; *Barton* v. *Armstrong* [1976] 1 AC 104 and *Hislop* v. *Dickson Motors (Forres) Ltd* 1978 SLT (Notes) 73.

there is very little real freedom left for the consumer. So, there is little of the freedom of the consumer to be preserved by enforcing the agreement. In addition, there is little in the way of a restriction on the freedom of the trader if all that is asked of him is that he does not use or threaten physical force. However, a freedom-oriented perspective will be increasingly uncomfortable with intervention as we move along the spectrum through cases where there is pressure but something less than physical pressure (e.g. economic pressure[40]) and where the restriction on consumer choice is less absolute; or indeed where there is no pressure as such, but simply a case of one party having entered the contract while under the undue influence of the other party, this influence deriving from the nature of the relationship between the parties.[41] There is a greater restriction on the freedom of the trader if we ask him to avoid not only physical threats and pressure, but also other forms of pressure such as economic pressure[42] and even to avoid contracting with a party over whom he has an undue influence.[43] In addition, if at least some form of choice is available to the

---

[40] Here I have in mind what is now known as 'economic duress' on which see *The Siboen and the Sibotre* [1976] 1 Lloyds Rep 293; *North Ocean Shipping Co. Ltd* v. *Hyundai Construction Ltd*, The Atlantic Baron [1979] QB 705; *Pao On* v. *Lao Yiu Long* [1980] AC 614; *Universe Tankships Inc. of Monrovia* v. *International Transport Workers Federation*, The Universe Sentinel [1983] 1 AC 366; *B & S Contracts & Design Ltd* v. *Victor Green Publications Ltd* [1984] ICR 419; *Atlas Express Ltd* v. *Kafco (Importers & Distributors) Ltd* [1989] 1 All ER 641; *DSND* v. *Subsea Ltd* v. *Petroleum Geo. Services ASA* [2000] BLR 530 and *R* v. *H.M. Attorney General for England and Wales* [2003] UKPC 22, [2003] EMLR, 24.

[41] Here, I have in mind the rules on undue influence on which see *Lloyds Bank* v. *Bundy* [1975] QB 326; *Nat West Bank* v. *Morgan* [1985] AC 686; *Barclays Bank* v. *O'Brien* [1994] 1 AC 180; and *Royal Bank of Scotland plc.* v. *Etridge* (No. 2) [2002] 2 AC 773.

[42] If economic pressure *is* stigmatized (as under the doctrine of economic duress) the question then arising is whether this should cover only pressure involving unlawful threats or whether it should extend to pressure that is lawful but exercised in bad faith (the latter clearly being a further infringement on the freedom of the party exercising the pressure). On these issues see *CTN Cash and Carry Ltd* v. *Gallagher Ltd* [1994] 4 All ER 714 and *GMAC Commercial Credit Ltd* v. *Dearden*, unreported, 28 May 2002.

[43] Where influence *is* stigmatized (as under the doctrine of undue influence) a question is whether a party must avoid only actions that could be positively shown to be in bad faith in the sense of intentionally wrongful or whether (and more restrictive of his freedom) he must always ensure that the other party makes a free and informed choice. On these issues see *Hammond* v. *Osborn* [2002] EWCA Civ 885, [2202] WTLR 1125; *R* v. *H.M. Attorney General for England and Wales* [2003] UKPC 22,

consumer (i.e. because there is no physical pressure or threat), then a robust freedom-oriented perspective (focusing on the pursuit of self-interest through self-reliance) might say that the consumer should be free to decide whether to enter the contract in these circumstances.[44]

Certainly, if there has been neither physical pressure or threats, economic pressure or undue influence, a freedom-oriented approach would not favour questioning the enforceability of terms on the grounds, for example, that no alternative terms are available to consumers, or that there is a disparity of bargaining strength.[45] In such circumstances the options of consumers may be restricted (by the lack of alternative terms or by the stronger bargaining position of the trader). However, the consumer remains free to try to bargain for the terms he wants (i.e. to act in a self-interested, self-reliant manner to protect his interests). He also remains free to choose not to enter the contract. Equally, he remains free to decide that, despite any dissatisfaction with the terms (or with fact that there are no alternative terms or that the trader refuses to bargain), he will nevertheless enter the contract.

[2003] EMLR, 24; *Macklin* v. *Dowset* [2004] EWCA Civ 9904, [2004] 2 EGLR 75; and *Watson* v. *Huber* [2005] All ER (d) 156 (Mar).

[44] Where the law *does* recognize the restrictions on choice caused by duress and undue influence not involving physical pressure or threats (as it does – see the preceding footnotes) the questions (on the 'plaintiff-side' of the equation) tend to focus on how much of a restriction on choice is required. So, in the case of duress, the question is whether the will of the plaintiff must have been 'overborne' or whether it is enough if the realistic alternatives of the plaintiff have been restricted (the latter approach being grounded in a less self-reliant based philosophy): see *Pao On* v. *Lao Yiu Long* [1980] AC 614; *Universe Tankships Inc. of Monrovia* v. *International Transport Workers Federation*, The Universe Sentinel [1983] 1 AC 366; *B & S Contracts & Design Ltd* v. *Victor Green Publications Ltd* [1984] ICR 419; *Atlas Express Ltd* v. *Kafco (Importers & Distributors) Ltd* [1989] 1 All ER 641.

In the case of undue influence the question revolves around the amount and quality of information and advice that must be furnished to the plaintiff before it can be said that the plaintiff has made a free choice and so not been influenced (the more information and advice that is required the more we move from a self-reliant philosophy): see the criteria set out in *Royal Bank of Scotland plc.* v. *Etridge* (No. 2) [2002] 2 AC 773.

[45] And this is broadly the position of English common law and equity which (while recognizing physical and economic duress and undue influence as vitiating factors) will not question a contract simply on the basis that there was no alternative set of terms available from the other party or that there was a disparity of bargaining strength (except where the disparity is extreme and has been taken advantage of to impose terms that are extremely unfair in substance (on which see 8.1.2 below).

From a freedom-oriented perspective based on the self-reliant pursuit of self-interest, these are consumer freedoms worth preserving. Again, of course, they are very much self-reliant, non-contextual freedoms. The consumer is viewed as free to choose to seek to bargain for better terms and (if this is not possible) to choose not to contract with the trader. However, no heed is paid to whether he has the bargaining strength to make this feasible and whether it is realistic to expect him to go without the goods or services.

Turning to the freedoms of the trader in the context of issues of choice and bargaining strength, maximization of self-interested trader freedom also requires that there should be limited intervention. Intervention in such cases restricts the freedom of the trader to pursue self-interest, more than in those cases where he is simply expected to avoid the positive application of pressure; or even those cases where he is expected to avoid taking advantage of the influence that he or another party has over a consumer. Intervention on the basis of a lack of alternative terms or on the basis that traders are in a stronger bargaining position has the following implications. Traders must check what else is on offer in the market to see if other traders offer a choice. If they do not, then the question is whether to offer terms with a built in alternative or to make the term in question fairer in substance (as we shall see below, on an approach that does take choice into account, any lack of choice is likely to be regarded as most unfair where the term is unduly detrimental in substance). As to being in a stronger bargaining position, if this is to be taken into account then (on the assumption that it becomes more significant the greater the substantive detriment caused by the term) the only realistic option for the trader is to offer terms that are fairer in substance. Yet again, however, this is a restriction on the freedom of the trader to enter into the agreements that he considers to be in his own best interest.

Intervention on the grounds that consumers have no alternatives or are in a weaker bargaining position seems to be even less acceptable from a freedom-oriented perspective than intervention on the grounds of lack of transparency. Knowledge seems to be a more fundamental element of free agency than choice or bargaining strength. It is fundamental to having freely made an agreement that there is at least the opportunity for a party to know what he is agreeing to. Having a choice of terms and/or being in a good bargaining position to obtain better terms are useless if a party does not know what is on offer in the first place. The point is that a certain threshold of actual or constructive knowledge is the minimum that must be acceptable if the consumer is to be said to have exercised any kind of freedom in entering the agreement. From a freedom-oriented perspective, it might be considered that the consumer has sufficient freedom when there is a basic knowledge as to the existence of terms and that a greater degree of transparency is unnecessary (see above). However, if a higher level of transparency is indeed required then (from a freedom-oriented perspective) there should be no further restriction on the self-reliant freedom of the consumer. The consumer should certainly now be free to choose whether to enter the contract, whether or not there is a choice of terms or the trader is in a stronger bargaining position.

Again, there are also 'trader sided' reasons why intervention on the grounds that the consumer had no alternatives or was in a weaker bargaining position is less acceptable (from a freedom-oriented perspective) than intervention on the grounds of lack of transparency. It may be restrictive of the freedom of the trader to ask him to present his terms in a transparent fashion. However, it is more restrictive of his freedom to ask that he offers alternative terms to consumers; or offers fairer substantive terms whenever the consumer has no choices or is in a weaker bargaining position.

2.3.3 Freedom of Contract and the Substance of the Contract

We now turn to the issue of substance. If the minimal procedural standards required by a freedom of contract approach are satisfied, the freedom of contract approach then demands that, as much as possible, the resulting terms should be enforced, irrespective of their substantive features and the extent to which these substantive features are fair to one of the parties. This is because the agenda of the freedom of contract approach is to maximize the freedom to agree and then to enforce what has been agreed to. These are the terms that have been agreed to and consequently they should be enforced without further enquiry as to their substance.[46] On the other hand, of course, if the minimal procedural standards set have not been met, then there is no satisfactory agreement and the apparent 'agreement' cannot be enforced. However, within the freedom of contract perspective, this is not because of the nature of the substantive terms. (Parties are to be free to agree to as broad a range of terms as they choose.) It is, rather, because the parties have failed at the procedural stage to make a satisfactory agreement. If the (minimal) procedural requirements are met, then the freedom of both parties demands that their freely chosen terms be enforced.

If, from a freedom-oriented perspective, it is undesirable to impose too many constraints at the procedural stage it is even less desirable to set aside terms on substantive grounds. If the procedural ground rules have been complied with it is wholly unacceptable (from a freedom-oriented perspective) to interfere with the freedom of the parties to agree to whatever substantive terms they choose. This is because it is through the

---

[46]   S. Smith, Atiyah's Introduction to the Law of Contract at 296–7.

process leading to the contract that the parties have had the opportunity to exercise their freedom. It is obvious that there need to be some basic restrictions on the way in which this freedom can be exercised. So, as we have said, the freedom to force the other to contract clearly places such an unacceptable limit on the freedom of the other party that it cannot be allowed. However, once a process is in place that enables some reasonable scope for the pursuit of self-interest through self-reliance, the parties have the freedom to decide what to agree to. In the exercise of this freedom, choices have been made as to the substantive terms to agree to. On an approach that prioritizes 'sanctity of contract' these substantive terms must now be enforced. In addition we must ignore the abilities of parties such as consumers to bear the consequences of the substantive terms. In this sense the freedom-oriented approach is, again, abstract and non-contextual. It is not concerned with the ways in which the parties (given their financial or other interests and position) might be affected by the substantive terms.

2.4 A Fairness-Oriented Approach[47]

2.4.1 General Concerns

A fairness-oriented perspective is less concerned with the freedom of the parties as this is understood within the kind of freedom of contract perspective described above. We said above that this is an essentially self-reliant, non-contextual, form of freedom; i.e. it is about the freedom to contract depending wholly on one's own judgement, abilities etc. It pays limited heed to context; i.e. restrictions (e.g. based on contractual form and processes) that might, in practice, affect the consumer. It is also unconcerned with context in the sense that it is unconcerned with the ways in which the substantive interests of consumers might be affected. I also

---

[47] On fairness generally see R. Brownsword, G. Howells and T. Wilhelmsson, Welfarism in Contract Law, Dartmouth, 1994; S. Smith, Atiyah's Introduction to the Law of Contract, 2006, Ch. 12; J. Beatson and D. Friedman, From Classical to Modern Contract Law, in J. Beatson and D. Friedman (eds), Good Faith and Fault in Contract Law, Oxford, 1995; J. Wightman, Contract: A Critical Commentary, Pluto Press, 1996; H. Collins, The Law of Contract, 4th edn, Butterworths, 2003; C. Willett, (ed.), Aspects of Fairness in Contract, Blackstone, 1996; R. Brownsword, N. Hird and G. Howells, (eds), Good Faith in Contract: Concept and Context, Dartmouth, 1999; A. Forte (ed.), Good Faith in Contract and Property Law, Hart, 1999; Tjittes, Unfair Clauses in H. Beale and D. Tallon (eds), Principles of European Contract Law, 2002; and S. Smith, Contract Theory, OUP, 2003, Ch. 9.

associated this with a view of the parties as 'abstract' persons.[48] They are viewed in the abstract from all of the factors mentioned that might, in reality, affect their ability to pursue and protect their interests; and they are viewed in the abstract from the ways in which their interests might be affected.

In contrast, a fairness approach *is* concerned with context and is not abstract in the sense described. It is more in line with what Wilhelmsson describes as a 'person-oriented' approach to contracts.[49] It views the parties other than as abstract persons, focusing rather on their *characteristics* as consumers and traders.[50] It is concerned with the way in which the physical, property, social and economic interests of such parties are affected by the substantive terms. It is also concerned with the factors that might affect the abilities of such parties to protect their interests in the process leading to the contract. The weaker party is perceived to be the consumer. Some substantive terms are viewed as having the potential to be especially damaging to the interests of consumers. The contractual process and broader market conditions are viewed as making it difficult for consumers to protect their interests (based on the problems of lack of transparency, choice and weak consumer bargaining strength mentioned above). Taking these elements into account, the agenda is to fairly balance the interests of the parties. Normally this means protecting the interests of the perceived 'weaker' party, i.e. the consumer.

This model can be viewed, in broad terms, as being connected to social justice or 'welfarism'. By 'welfarist' I mean that the agenda to protect the interests of the 'weaker' party (the consumer) is in broad congruence with the values of the welfare state.[51] Of course, there are different (and changing) notions of the overall 'big picture' view of the welfare state.[52] There is perhaps a broad consensus that it involves social and economic protection of those regarded as weaker in society. However, within a mixed economy, these welfarist goals might actually be achieved by a joint approach. On the one hand there might actually be a libertarian approach to contract, aimed at maximising wealth. At the same time there

---

[48] See above 2.3.1.

[49] See T. Wilhelmsson, Social Contract Law and European Integration, Dartmouth, 1995, at 29–31.

[50] *Ibid.*

[51] See R. Brownsword, G. Howells and T. Wilhelmsson, Welfarism in Contract Law, Dartmouth, 1994; H. Collins, Law of Contract, Butterworths, 4th edn, 2004, at 9; and for a broader discussion of the concept of 'consumer-welfarism' in contract law see J. Adams and R. Brownsword, Understanding Contract Law, Sweet and Maxwell, 4th edn, 2004, Ch. 8.

[52] See T. Wilhelmsson, Varieties of Welfarism in European Contract Law (2004) 10 European Law Journal, 712, at 714–5.

might be protective (welfarist) measures, but these might come from *outside* contract law. Alternatively, it might be achieved both by measures outside contract law *and* by fairness-oriented approaches to contractual relationships.[53] Clearly here we are dealing with the latter form of welfarism, i.e. rules, broadly reflecting the values of the welfare state, that protect consumer interests within contractual relationships with traders. Here it should be emphasized that when I refer to 'welfarist' protection of consumer interests I am not drawing any distinction between approaches that simply set standards of procedural fairness and approaches that go beyond this and disallow terms on primarily substantive grounds. I am using the phrase 'welfarist' broadly to encompass both such approaches.[54]

A further point should be made as to the relationship between the type of freedom-oriented approach described above and the type of fairness-oriented approach now described. I have pointed out that the fairness approach is contextual, person-oriented and less concerned with self-reliance; and, in this way, it is different from a freedom approach that is non-contextual, abstract and concerned with self-reliance. However, reference has already been made[55] to the idea (which will be developed further below)[56] that it remains possible to view such a fairness approach as representing a particular form of freedom. Of course, this is not the type of freedom described thus far. It is not about self-reliant, non-contextual freedom. It is about the idea that self-reliant, non-contextual freedom may not be effective or useful freedom in practice (at least for the consumer). So, for example, it may be about the view that there has only been *effective* freedom for the consumer where the terms are sufficiently transparent to enable an informed decision to be made. In other words it is a version of freedom inspired by sensitivity to context and concern with fairness.

A final point is that when we talk about rules being fairness-oriented (in the broad sense that they balance the interests of the parties and seek to protect the interests of a party such as a consumer) this actually encompasses a range of distinct (albeit sometimes overlapping) concepts

---

53 T. Wilhelmsson, *ibid.*, at 715.
54 Below at 7.1 I return to the concept of welfarism, distinguishing between 'maximal' welfarism which is concerned to protect the consumer as a weaker party within the relationship and 'minimal' welfarism which is concerned (more broadly) to redistribute resources within the overall social order. However, just as is the case here, the discussion at 7.1 does not seek to distinguish between procedural and substantive versions of welfarism. Of course, it *is* important to distinguish between fairness approaches that are more procedurally focused and approaches that are more substantively focused and this distinction is first discussed below at 2.4.3.5.
55 See above at 2.3.2.2.
56 See below at 7.3.1.

of fairness along with other agendas. For example, as Collins suggests, the rules on 'fair rents' may be partly about substantive fairness in the sense of a fair balance between the obligations of the parties;[57] but they are also about fairness in the sense of reducing the risk that tenants will be made homeless when they are faced by a rent increase that they cannot afford.[58] In addition, controlling the prices that can be charged for utilities may be partly about fairness in the sense of a fair balance as between all of the rights and obligations of the parties; but the main goals are to improve the *efficiency* of the utility operators and to achieve fairness in the sense of preventing consumers being socially excluded from these important services[59] (i.e. to make sure that the poorest consumers can afford to pay for them).

We shall see that the rules discussed in this book involve similar 'mixed motives' in terms of types of fairness and other goals. First of all, if we think at the fairly general policy level, we have already mentioned the way in which fairness rules can be viewed as being in congruence with broader *Welfare State* values. Secondly, we shall see that the Unfair Contract Terms Act controls exemption clauses (via outright bans and via a 'reasonableness' test) on the basis of a mixed concern with fairness and *efficiency*. Third, we shall also see that the UTCCR applies a fairness test but is based on an EC Directive that has the *constitutional* goal of *aiding completion of the internal market*. This is to be achieved by rules *eradicating competitive distortions, generating consumer confidence in cross-border shopping* and setting a *high level of consumer protection*. Drawing these points together then, we can see that when we talk about fairness and this being about the balancing of the interests of the parties, this often forms part of broader agendas such as welfarism, efficiency or EC market building. It also tends to include a notion that the party benefiting from the fairness rules has certain *particular* types of interest that should be given a degree of protection (that it is 'fair' to protect) even where protection of these interests cannot necessarily be equated with substantive fairness as such (substantive fairness, to reiterate, being about a fair balance as between all of the rights and obligations under the contract). So, when we look more closely at some of the terms that are controlled, we find that various specific fairness agendas can be found under the general 'fairness umbrella' (e.g. ensuring that terms are in line with reasonable consumer expectations, ensuring that traders are responsible for negligence, guaranteeing consumers the 'social right' to

---

[57] This is what many authors mean when they refer to substantive (un)fairness: see H. Collins, Regulating Contracts, OUP, 1999, 259–60; and S. Smith, Contract Theory, OUP, 2003, at 8.33 and 9.25.

[58] H. Collins, *ibid.*, at 257.

[59] *Ibid.*

goods of satisfactory quality, preventing consumers being denied access to justice or access to essential services[60]). The rules often protect consumers against terms that compromise these particular interests even where there is not overall substantive unfairness as described above. As we shall see below,[61] some of the interests just mentioned appear to be controlled whatever the position may be in relation to other terms. For example, terms excluding or restricting the trader's liability for breach of the implied term as to quality are wholly ineffective[62] and cannot be saved by other terms no matter how favourable they are and no matter to what extent there can be said to be overall fairness in substance. So, although the legislation containing this rule (the UCTA) refers to 'unfairness', the rule is not a rule against substantive unfairness in the sense substantive fairness is currently being described.

Having said this, we shall see below that notions of overall substantive fairness *do* nevertheless often play a significant role in the rules, e.g. in the context of the 'significant imbalance' element of the test of unfairness under the UTCCR.[63] When this is the case it becomes important to work out how exactly substantive fairness is being measured, e.g. by reference to market norms or by some other measure that gives more priority to the default position or to reasonable consumer expectations.

A final point is that the immediately preceding discussion illustrates an interesting similarity with freedom-oriented thinking. We noted above that a freedom-oriented approach can be justified from a rights based perspective (the right to freedom) and a more utilitarian perspective (including promoting efficiency and certainty in market transactions).[64] The immediately preceding discussion of fairness reveals something similar (albeit with different conceptions as to what rights are important and what amounts to broader utility). There is a concern with improving consumer rights, i.e. the entitlement to a certain level of (welfare state inspired) protection (whether of particular interests or of the more general interest in overall substantive fairness). However, there is also a utilitarian goal to serve the broader market (both generally in the sense of enhancing efficiency and more specifically in building the European single market).

---

60   See below at 4.2.7, 4.2.7.3, 4.6.1–2 and 6.3.4.
61   See below at 2.4.3.5, 4.2.7 and 6.5.
62   Unfair Contract Terms Act, ss 6(2) and 7(2) and below at 4.2.7.3.
63   See below at 3.5.4, 5.5.4.2, 5.7 and 5.9.
64   See above at 2.3.1.

2.4.2 Specific Conceptions of Unfairness

2.4.2.1 Consumer Interests Affected By Substantive Terms

As we have seen, a key element of a freedom-oriented approach is that there should be minimal restriction on the substantive terms that can be agreed to. No account should be taken of context, i.e. of the way in which terms might be damaging to the interests of types of contractors. By contrast, a fairness-oriented approach does take account of the way that terms affect the interests of the parties. An important aspect of the idea of fairness/protection of consumer interests in the context of consumer contracts seems to be the idea that consumers enter contracts in order to sustain and enhance the private sphere of life, rather than to make a profit. The terms of these contracts therefore affect the physical safety, proprietary, economic and social interests arising in, and affecting, the private sphere of life. The terms may be particularly harmful to these private interests. Consumer contracts may contain terms that seek to allow the trader to evade important responsibilities to the consumer; that impose undue burdens on the consumer; and/or that compromise particular expectations that the consumer may have based on the type of contract being entered into and other signals that he has received. These terms may affect the private interests of consumers in ways that are quite distinct from the way in which business entities would be affected by such terms. First of all, certain interests are only really relevant in relation to those acting as private citizens. So, the safety interests of the consumer may be affected by a term claiming that the trader is not liable when the goods or services cause injury or death to the consumer. Such a term simply does not have any impact upon a business entity that is subject to it as, patently, a business entity cannot itself be physically injured. Other terms may have the capacity to affect either business or private contractors (e.g. terms excluding liability for economic losses or damage to property or allowing for withdrawal of a service); but the way in which they impact on the *private* sphere of life may be distinctive. A business entity is often in a better position to insure against such losses. Even where this is not the case the business will still generally be better placed to absorb the loss. This can be done by,

> … making very small adjustments to prices, investments, dividends, or wages, especially where – as is probably most usual – the loss as a proportion of turnover is small. In other words, firms suffering losses which are small in terms of the scale of the firm, can act as their own insurers, and are in a position to make contracts of insurance when the scale of loss threatens to be

too large. The firm's position in a web of exchange relationships provides the means of coping with losses.[65]

Consumers, by contrast, generally do not have the capacity to distribute losses in these ways. They act in a private capacity and do not have the network of customers, investors, and employees who can share the losses. In addition the financial loss may loom large relevant to the overall 'turnover' of the private individual.[66]

However, terms that directly affect the economic interests of consumers may also indirectly affect their social interests. Again this can be illustrated by comparing the impact of terms on business entities with the impact on private consumers. The interest of a commercial entity in entering into a transaction is to secure the solvency and enhance the profitability of the business. Wightman sums up the nature of this interest in the context of the impact of a breach of contract:

> The loss caused by the breach – whether it be non-performance or defective performance of the obligation to deliver goods or render services – is ultimately a loss to the profit-making and asset-holding capacity of the firm. The performance is never wanted for its own sake, but because of its contribution to the economic wellbeing of the firm. It is wholly satisfactory to define a loss in pecuniary terms because it is only a loss of money or monetary value.[67]

The same point can be made in relation to the distribution of rights and obligations under a contract, and to an extent, in relation to any of the rights and obligations which favour one business over another, or a private party such as a consumer over a business. The business that is the loser is generally only the loser in financial terms. It must, for example, spend more money to insure against certain liability, or it must pay compensation in relation to a liability that it sought to exclude, but has now been told cannot be excluded. Of course, there may be a knock-on effect on the private lives of those who run businesses if the business consequently suffers financial difficulties or becomes insolvent. However, the primary interest affected is a financial, commercial one.

By contrast, when private individuals are affected by a breach of contract or by terms which are favourable to the other party, there is arguably a direct impact on, and possible damage to, the private sphere of life. This goes beyond the purely financial. Wightman points out that,

---

[65] J. Wightman, *A Critical Approach to Contract*, Pluto, 1996, pp. 98–9.
[66] Wightman, *ibid.*, at 98.
[67] *Ibid.*, at 97.

> The social relations centred on work, consumption and home, generate meaning in people's lives and they are fundamental to our identity and sense of membership of the disparate groups and communities which constitute civil society. Experiences such as being threatened with the sack or eviction or having nightmare experiences with defective cars, holidays, utility services, pensions, or endowment mortgages may vary in the sympathy they evoke, but all have the capacity to rupture lives beyond the impact on the pocket.[68]

So when goods or services are not provided or are defective, and/or when traders refuse to accept responsibility, or seek to impose liability of some kind on a consumer on the basis of a contract term, or assert power or dominion over a consumer on the basis of a contract term, consumers must deal with disruption in their private lives. In trying to resolve the issue, the individual consumer must make disruptive adjustments to private priorities. He must set aside what might otherwise be leisure time, rearrange work and career priorities etc. He must seek to acquire a sufficient grasp of the factual and legal issues and their interrelation with 'company policy'. The trader with whom the consumer is dealing may have a system that is designed (through structures, processes and the training and motivation of personnel) to systematically assert and impose the will and interests of the trader over those of the consumer. The process of 'doing battle' against this may be extremely draining in a social, emotional and financial sense for the consumer. Yet the consumer may stand to lose a lot if he does not stand his ground. In some cases e.g. where pensions, insurance, or life assurance are concerned, many years of planning and expectation may be frustrated. If a seller or supplier is able to withdraw banking or credit facilities, then in addition to suffering inconvenience, a consumer's essential human dignity and self-respect may be damaged. The same may occur, for example, if the seller or supplier is entitled to repossess goods.

2.4.2.2 Procedure

Thus far, we have discussed what appears to be relevant to questions of fairness in substance. However, a fairness-oriented approach also focuses upon the *process* leading to the conclusion of the contract. We have already noted that the process leading to the conclusion of the contract may affect what the consumer expects to get from the contract and the ability of the consumer to protect his interests in relation to the substantive terms of the agreement. So, if terms are not transparent (e.g. due to small

---

[68] *Ibid.*

print, unclear language, a badly structured contract etc.) then first of all there is a basic lack of informed consent (i.e. something that might be said to be problematic irrespective of the *substantive* features of the terms). Then there is the point that lack of transparency may mean that the consumer is not aware of the risks inherent in the substantive terms. This may mean that he cannot rationally compare the terms on offer with those of other traders;[69] that he is unaware of the need to seek to negotiate for better terms[70] or protect his interests in some other way; and that, if he enters the contract, he does so in ignorance of important risks to which he is exposed. In addition, the lack of transparency may mean that the consumer is unaware of the terms in the contract that are advantageous to him, so that he is less likely to take advantage of these when a dispute arises. A further problem is that consumers (by contrast with at least some commercial contractors) do not tend to have experience as to the types of standard terms used; nor do they tend to have experience as to the way in which these terms are interpreted and applied in practice by traders.[71] This compounds the problem of lack of transparency. Lack of transparency matters less where those affected by it have detailed background knowledge as to the terms used and how they are typically interpreted and applied. It matters more where this background knowledge does not exist.

Lack of transparency is not only a problem in the sense that it leads to lack of informed consent and prevents consumers from comparing terms, negotiating for improvements and protecting their interests post-contractually. It also undermines competition. As we saw above[72] if the terms are not transparent and consumers cannot understand and compare the offerings of different traders there will be no incentive for traders to compete with one another for the business of consumers.[73] This may be regarded as problematic in itself (i.e. to the extent that we regard competition as important in itself). However, it is also likely to mean that the level of choice and fairness in substance will be restricted (given that

---

[69]   T. Wilhelmsson, Cooperation and Competition Regarding Standard Contract Terms in Consumer Contracts (2006) European Business Law Review, 49, at 52.

[70]   *Ibid.*

[71]   J. Wightman, Beyond Custom: Contracts, Contexts and the Recognition of Implicit Understandings, in D. Campbell, H. Collins and J. Wightman, Implicit Dimensions of Contract, Hart, 2003, 169–70.

[72]   See above at 2.3.2.1.

[73]   We should note here that even where terms dealing with ancillary matters *are* transparent there is often good reason to be sceptical as to how much impact this will have on consumers and, in turn, in creating a competitive market in these terms – see further below at 2.4.3.4(iv).

strong competition may be expected to improve choice and to produce terms that better reflect consumer interests).

As already suggested, a fairness-oriented approach brings greater sensitivity to context than is allowed for in a freedom-oriented approach. This leads to recognition that it may not be realistic to expect consumers to overcome the problems of lack of transparency by self-reliant means. There are a number of reasons for this. First of all, there is the effect of pre-existing signals that are more powerful than the formal terms. These may have the effect of distracting consumers from the formal terms and conditioning consumers to believe that the formal terms are not important in practice. So, the power of advertising and the general 'consumption culture' may mean that many consumers are already heavily psychologically committed to the purchase,[74] and so may be disinclined to turn their attention to the formal terms. Apart from the influence of advertising and general consumption culture, there are other 'extra-contractual' signals influencing what the consumer can expect from entering contracts for goods and services. In particular there is the fact that in advanced capitalist societies (sector specific problems apart) performance does, in the vast majority of cases, reflect the basic expectations. The goods or services are *normally* supplied in accordance with the basic expectations generated by the initial description/presentation. The consumer *normally* adheres to his payment or other obligations. No recourse is *normally* had to the formal terms, so that there is more limited consumer experience of non-performance on either side and what the formal terms may actually allow the trader to do if this happens. There is, therefore, limited consumer experience of the terms being used to deprive the consumer of redress when the trader fails to perform properly. There is limited consumer experience of the terms being used to impose onerous obligations and liabilities on him (the consumer) when he is in some way in default. In sum, there is experience of, and an expectation of, successful, 'life enhancing' performance, reflecting the gist of what has been suggested extra contractually. By contrast there is much less experience of non-performance, and the social and economic disruption that this, and reliance on the formal terms, may cause. So, again, the consumer may not see much point in giving consideration to the formal terms; as these rarely have much to do with what actually happens.

Taking the initiative to become familiar with terms that are not transparent will also, of course, be made difficult by the lack of technical and legal expertise possessed by the average consumer. It may be that in order to obtain a full understanding of certain terms related to the product

---

[74] See generally here, I. Ramsay, Advertising, Culture and the Law, Sweet and Maxwell, 1996.

or service a degree of technical knowledge or expert knowledge of the product or service is required. It may also be that a degree of legal knowledge is required. For example, terms may employ legal jargon ('conditions', 'warranties', 'common law', 'statute', 'equity' etc). The problems caused for the consumer by lack of technical and legal knowledge and by generally unclear language, detail and complexity will not be easily overcome. It will not be realistic in most cases to seek legal advice. Many, if not most, consumer transactions will not be of high enough value to make it economical to seek such advice.

Another factor that may inhibit consumers from making a serious attempt to understand the meaning and implications of terms is that they may also have a range of complex decisions to make on the more basic question as to whether to buy the goods or services, e.g. decisions as to whether the goods are of good value in a basic sense, whether the consumer can afford to buy them, and how they might be made affordable (whether by altering general purchasing priorities and/or obtaining credit of some kind). In the light of these important considerations it may be difficult to focus on and 'get to grips' with the formal terms.

Also, consumers may not think to attain an understanding of the formal terms because they do not believe that they could ever persuade the trader to change them or that other traders will offer anything other than the same, or very similar, terms. In almost all cases it is of course a perfectly accurate assumption that traders will not negotiate over the terms. In many cases it is also accurate to assume that other traders will offer the same or very similar terms (for the reasons discussed above[75]). Another reason that consumers may not believe that terms can be changed is that they may believe that they have some form of official sanction, e.g. that they have been vetted in some way or possibly, in some way, represent 'the law'. This is not a ridiculous assumption for the lay person to make when dealing with businesses, who may be viewed as a form of officialdom.

Finally, consumers may not take the time to become familiar with terms simply because they are too lazy; or, to put it more charitably, there are simply better and more enjoyable ways to be spending one's time. The point has been made that this is could be argued to be entirely rational behaviour from an economic point of view.[76] It is accepted that economic behaviour is, quite rationally, constrained by 'transaction costs'. In this context we should not forget the transactions costs of consumers if we

---

[75] See above at 2.3.2.1.

[76] T. Wilhelmsson, Cooperation and Competition Regarding Standard Contract Terms in Consumer Contracts, (2006), European Business Law Review, 49, at 55.

expect them to invest time 'in very dull activities like reading standard form conditions instead of doing something more attractive'.[77]

Now we turn to the attitude of a fairness approach to problems of lack of consumer choice and the weaker bargaining position of the consumer. As we have already said, even if a consumer is aware of what a term provides for and he does not wish to agree to it (or is at best wary of agreeing to it), it may be that the trader in question does not offer any alternative package as standard. It may also be that there is no alternative package that is offered by other traders. From a freedom-oriented perspective, the consumer can now refuse to enter the contract or seek to bargain for better terms. However, a (more contextually sensitive) fairness approach recognizes that consumers can rarely realistically refuse to enter the contract – the goods or services are needed (not necessarily in that they are absolute necessities, but simply in that they are necessities by the standards of the type of society in which we live). A fairness-oriented approach also recognizes that it will usually also be unrealistic to expect the consumer to bargain for better terms. The trader will normally refuse to countenance any change in the standard terms. This, as already mentioned above, is often because it is simply inefficient to engage in bargaining over standard terms, the very purpose of which is to avoid such bargaining. Even if the trader *is* prepared to bargain the consumer is not likely to be in a sufficiently strong bargaining position to persuade the trader to amend or remove a term.[78] But what exactly does this mean? Despite the fact that judges have often made reference to supposed inequality of bargaining power;[79] and that the issue is relevant under the statutory regimes,[80] it has been pointed out that there has been relatively little work on what exactly we mean when we talk of 'bargaining

---

[77] T. Wilhelmsson, *ibid.*

[78] In general on bargaining power, see H. Beale, Inequality of Bargaining Power, 1986, 6 Oxford Journal of Legal Studies, 123; R. Brownsword, General Considerations, in Furmston (ed.), Butterworths Law of Contract, 2nd edn, 2003, Butterworths, 1, at 41–56; and R. Brownsword, Contract Law: Themes for the Twenty-First Century, OUP, 2006, Ch. 4.

[79] See Lord Reid in *Suisse Atlantique Societe d'Armement Maritime SA* v. *NV Rotterdamsche Kolen Centrale* [1967] 1 AC 361 at 406; Donaldson J in *Kenyon, Son and Craven Ltd* v. *Baxter Hoare and Co.* [1971] 2 All ER 708 at 720; Lord Diplock in *Schroeder Music Publishing Co.* v. *Macaulay* [1974] 1 WLR 1308 at 1316 and Lord Denning in *Lloyds Bank* v. *Bundy* [1975] 326 at 339.

[80] See, for example the Unfair Contract Terms Act 1977, Schedule 2, para. (a) and Unfair Terms in Consumer Contracts Directive (93/13/EEC), Recital 16 to the Preamble; on both of which see later chapters.

power'.[81] It has also been pointed out that references to bargaining power are sometimes to lack of market power and sometimes to lack of bargaining sophistication.[82] I am using the concept here in both senses. Another point that needs emphasis in relation to bargaining power is that we cannot sensibly speak of bargaining power in the abstract. It must either be talked of relative to some external ideal standard or relative to the other party to the contract. The bargaining power to which I am referring here is the bargaining power of consumers *relative to* traders.[83]

Let us begin, then, with market power dimension. The market power of consumers and traders is dependent partly on the degree of importance which the trader places on the custom of a particular consumer (the 'need to deal' as Brownsword calls it[84]). This in turn will depend on how well sales are going generally; whether this customer is likely to make further purchases; whether the customer is important to the supplier in some other regard; the value of the product or service being sold; and whether the value of this sale represents a small or large proportion of the supplier's overall turnover. It may also, of course, be that the trader is a monopolist who does not need to be concerned as to the custom of the consumer as he is in any event guaranteed this custom; and, clearly, this is a factor that is relevant to the question of market power. However, also relevant to the market power of both parties is how much the consumer 'needs to deal', i.e. whether he desperately needs to obtain the goods or services and to do so in a hurry; whether his needs in these respects are average or whether he can do without the goods or services or at least is in a less than average rush to obtain them.

It is clear that the ability of the consumer to use (market) bargaining power to obtain deletion or change of a term depends on the way that all of the factors interact in a particular bargaining encounter.[85] As such, the relative bargaining power may differ in each case. However, let us assume a (surely fairly typical) situation in which the consumer is in average need

---

[81] H. Beale, Inequality of Bargaining Power, 1986, 6 Oxford Journal of Legal Studies, 123, at 125.

[82] Law Commission Consultation Paper on Unfair Terms in Contracts, No. 166, 2002, para. 4.102.

[83] See discussion of inter-party relative bargaining power by R. Brownsword, Contract Law: Themes for the Twenty-First Century, OUP, 2006, 79–85; and see discussion of bargaining power relative to an external minimum standard in R. Brownsword, The Philosophy of Welfarism in the Modern English Law of Contract in R. Brownsword, G. Howells and T. Wilhelmsson (eds), Welfarism in Contract Law, Ashgate, 1994, 21.

[84] R. Brownsword, Contract Law: Themes for the Twenty-First Century, *ibid.*, at 78.

[85] See the discussion (and in particular the 'Smith and Jones' example) by R. Brownsword, *ibid.*, 79–81.

of the goods or services and has an average amount of time to secure a deal. Let us also assume (again surely fairly typical) that there are a fairly large number of consumers in a market and that the cost of each product or service is a small proportion of the overall turnover of the trader. In such circumstances individual consumers will be relatively unimportant to sellers or suppliers; and, given the general trader interest in adhering to the standardized terms already formulated, the trader will usually be in a position to refuse to bargain. The trader may not be abusing his position as such,[86] but nevertheless the consumer is limited in his ability to bargain in order to attempt to bring about a term or terms which he would prefer.

Now we turn to the matter of bargaining sophistication (which, I take, to be affected by knowledge and expertise, i.e. knowledge and expertise as to the terms and the product and knowledge and expertise in relation to negotiation). Here a key issue will often be the (typically) limited skill or expertise of the consumer. Of course it is true that which of the two contracting parties possesses the greatest bargaining skill and expertise will be a matter for enquiry in the particular circumstances. The trader will certainly not always have the upper hand in such circumstances. There may well be circumstances in which consumers are highly skilled. However, in the general course of things, it will tend to be difficult for the average consumer to match sellers or suppliers when it comes to the above issues. This will be particularly so, where technical knowledge is important, e.g. in the case of financial services, electrical products, mechanical products, etc. Then there are a number of problems which might affect either traders or consumers in individual cases and the extent to which any skill or expertise which does exist can be put to good use, e.g. depression, intoxication, pain etc. These could all affect the ability to bargain thoughtfully and skilfully and, of course, might affect either traders or consumers. However they seem more likely to have an impact on the bargaining abilities of consumers. This is because traders may be trained and/or practised at negotiating. As such, they may be better able to deal with any of the above afflictions. (Having said this, these constraints on the ability to bargain thoughtfully or skilfully are rather exceptional and do not represent any general pattern that is necessarily useful in drawing general conclusions in relation to consumer contracts.)

Finally, it seems arguable that, in addition to market power and bargaining sophistication, bargaining power is affected by resources, i.e. the resources that can be called upon to support the bargaining process. Again this will often (though, of course, not always) be more of a problem for the consumer; making him weak relative to the trader. Even if a consumer has something to offer the supplier and the skill to express this

---

[86] H. Beale, Inequality of Bargaining Power, 1986, 6 Oxford Journal of Legal Studies, 123 at 131.

positively, the negotiations may be protracted, requiring investment of time and/or money. Traders will often have the infrastructure which more readily enables them to engage in such protracted negotiations successfully.

2.4.3 Fairness Responses

2.4.3.1 Introduction

Within a fairness-oriented approach the agenda is to balance the interests of the parties and in particular to protect the interests of the consumer. This means being cognisant of the ways in which terms may (in substance) be damaging to consumer interests; and the problems of procedural fairness that may arise. However, we must go much further than this in properly understanding and regulating unfairness. Any rules need to be as clear as possible as to the type of problems being addressed and the way in which issues should interact. However, there is a particular issue with questions of fairness or unfairness. Fairness can be understood at such a level of generality and vagueness that it is unhelpful. Lack of certainty is a well-known concern in relation to assessments of fairness. This problem is affected in part by the kind of decision-makers and standard-setters involved in the process. Where adjudication takes place purely in the context of private law, after the fact, litigation a key problem is that there will always tend to be a shortage of precedent upon which to base the structuring and development of an assessment of fairness.[87] We shall see that in the case of some of the rules under discussion in this book this problem has been reduced by the fact that public law enforcement is also involved and this has contributed hugely to the development of the jurisprudence. Another factor contributing to clear and rational development of the law is the existence of specific guidelines for the application of the test. We shall see that the rules under consideration contain guidelines, but that they could be significantly improved and that this may happen in the future. However, before we even get to specific guidelines there needs to be a more general overview of what exactly we have in mind when we think of unfairness; the types of factors that we might regard as important; and how they should relate to one another. In other words we must take the fairness concerns discussed above and shape them into some kind of test. This is what we must seek to do now.

---

[87]   See H. Collins, *Regulating Contracts*, OUP, 1999, at 293.

2.4.3.2 Default Rules and Reasonable Expectations

We have seen that the general 'mischief' is represented by terms which allow the trader to avoid responsibility to the consumer or impose onerous obligations or liabilities on the consumer. However, it is useful to have a more concrete idea as to the types of substantive term that are targeted. One way to approach this issue is to use default rules (including implied terms) and remedies as benchmarks of fairness and to question the fairness of terms that are detrimental to the consumer by comparison with such default rules or remedies. The broad justification for such an approach is that default rules and remedies are often based on some kind of balancing of the interests of the parties. So, for example, the implied term as to satisfactory quality in contracts for the sale of goods is based on what 'a reasonable person would regard as satisfactory'[88] (i.e. it is not based solely on the perspective of traders or consumers). Remedies also tend to be based on a balancing of the interests of the parties. So, for example, rules on damages exist to compensate for the losses of the innocent party, but only insofar as these are not too remote[89] and the innocent party has taken reasonable steps to mitigate his losses.[90]

Of course, (and returning to default rules fixing primary obligations) not all default rules are necessarily based on an entirely independent balancing of interests. First of all, there is the general idea of implied terms that are implied in fact based on what the parties are presumed to have intended. What the parties may be presumed to have intended would not necessarily involve fairly balancing their interests. For example, the parties (based on the particular facts) might be presumed to have favoured one of their interests over the other on any given issue for all sorts of reasons. Second, there are those terms implied on the facts based on what is 'necessary on the facts' for 'business efficacy'. It is certainly clear that what is regarded as necessary for business efficacy can, depending on the factual context, elide with forms of fairness that involve balancing the interests of the parties.[91] However, just because implication of a term would fairly balance the interests of the parties or require some other form

---

[88] SGA, s. 14(2).

[89] *Hadley* v. *Baxendale* (1854) 9 Exch 341; *Victoria Laundries (Windsor) Ltd* v. *Newman Industries*, 2 KB 528, CA; *Koufos* v. *Czarnikow*, The Heron II [1969] AC 350; *Parsons (Livestock) Ltd* v. *Uttley Ingham & Co. Ltd* [1978] QB 791, CA.

[90] *Payzu Ltd* v. *Sanders* [1919] 2 KB 581, *CAPilkington* v. *Wood* [1953] Ch. 770; *Compania Financiera Soleada SA* v. *Hamoor Tanker Corp. Inc.*, The Borag [1981] 1 WLR 274, CA.

[91] See, for example, *Equitable Life Assurance Society* v. *Hyman* [2002] 1 AC 408 in which a term protecting the reasonable expectations of the policy holders was implied to give business efficacy.

of good faith or fairness will not necessarily mean that such a term will be deemed to be required for the purposes of business efficacy.[92] In addition, a term implied on the basis of business efficacy will not necessarily be one that is grounded in a balancing of the parties' interests. Third, where terms are implied based on trade custom or usage they may or may not be based on a balancing of the interests of the parties. The trade practice or usage may have been one that sought to balance the interests of the parties but it may not. Fourth, while terms implied *in law* by the courts (based on the type of relationship) seem to be based in part on interest balancing and fairness[93] they can also based on what is 'normal practice' in such contracts[94] (and, as we have just seen, this may or may not be fair). Fifth, in the case of some default rules there may be a serious question as to whether there is a fair balancing of interests. For example, the common law default position is that contractual interest 'merges' in the judgement,[95] so that (in the absence of contrary intention) contractual interest does not continue to apply to the amount owing after a judgement. However, in the only case so far to have reached the House of Lords on the UTCCR (*First National Bank* v. *DGFT*[96]) the House seem to have taken the view that this default position did not fairly balance the interests of the parties but was unfairly balanced against lenders. Whether or not one agrees with this, the point is that courts may not always make the assumption that a default rule is the obvious starting point for a fairness analysis. Finally, another situation in which default rules may not always fairly balance the interests of the parties is where they have been drawn up specifically to protect the interests of the supplier and this may be the case where many services of general interest are concerned.[97]

Subject to all of these caveats, if fairness is about balancing the interests of the parties, it still appears to make sense to use such default rules at least as an opening benchmark in many cases;[98] and we shall see

---

[92] See, for example, *Redwood Master Fund Ltd* v. *TD Bank Europe Ltd* [2002] All ER (D), 141, *The Times*, 30 January 2003 where a term requiring good faith in the making of lending decisions was not required.

[93] See E. Peden, Policy Concerns Behind Implication of Terms in Law (2001) 117 LQR 459 and *Crossley* v. *Faithful & Gould Holdings Ltd* [2004] 4 All ER 447, per Dyson LJ.

[94] *Spring* v. *Guardian Assurance plc.,* [1995] 2 AC 296, per Lord Woolf.

[95] In Re Sneyd; Ex p Fewings (1883) 25 Ch. D338, accepted without demur by the House of Lords in *Economic Life Assurance Society* v. *Usborne* [1902] AC 147.

[96] [2001] 3 WLR 1297 and see below at 5.5.

[97] See below at 5.7.3, 5.10 and 6.3.5.2.

[98] Another dimension to this issue is the normative question as to what default rules emanating from different sources *should* be based on (Presumed consent? The norms of the trading sector? Economic efficiency? Some combination of these criteria?

that UCTA, the UTCCR and the proposed new regime would all appear to give a central role to default rules.[99] However, there are not default rules dealing with every conceivable issue. For example, there is often no default rule dealing with whether and when the primary performance obligations of the parties can be altered or varied during the life of the contract. In such circumstances an alternative possible benchmark of fairness is a concept of reasonable expectations. Does the term allow the trader to perform, or require the consumer to perform, in a way that is different from what the consumer would reasonably have expected? So, in the absence of a default rule, we seek to determine reasonable expectations from all the circumstances. Of course, there remains a process of interest balancing. The focus may be on the expectations of the consumer, but these expectations must be objectively reasonable. We shall see that the regimes do indeed appear to use such expectations as a benchmark of fairness.[100]

2.4.3.3 Other Substantive Issues

So, the idea, then, is of regimes within which a term comes under suspicion where it deviates from a default rule or from the reasonable expectations of the consumer. However, this is potentially only the start of the analysis. At the very least there must also be consideration of the *type* of consumer interests involved. So, the assessment must take into account such questions as whether the term affects physical integrity (e.g. by denying responsibility for injury or death or exposing the consumer to a physical risk of some kind); property interests (e.g. by avoiding responsibility for damage to property or allowing interference with property rights of the consumer); economic interests (e.g. by denying responsibility for an economic loss suffered by the consumer or requiring the consumer to pay for something that has not been received); access to justice (e.g. by excluding or restricting self-help remedies such as set-off or seeking to prevent consumers taking claims to court); access to important services (e.g. by allowing withdrawal of these services at the

---

Some other criteria?). On these issues see C. Riley, Designing Default Rules in Contract Law, Consent, Conventionalism and Efficiency (2000) 20 Oxford Journal of Legal Studies, 367.

[99] See below at 4.2–3 and 5.7.3–5.

[100] See below at 4.4 and 5.7.6, where, of course, we shall see that the concept of reasonable expectations is by no means simple and could be interpreted in a variety of ways. Generally on this see C. Mitchell, Leading a Life of its Own? The Roles of Reasonable Expectation in Contract Law, Oxford Journal of Legal Studies, Vol. 23, No. 4 (2003), 639.

discretion of the trader); or consumer expectations (e.g. by allowing, contrary to such expectations, the trader to vary or terminate the contract at his discretion).

While the primary focus of a review of fairness would be on the effect of the term itself on the interests of the consumer, we might also look beyond this. So, for example, there is the question of insurance. It is clear that if insurance is available to the consumer there is at least some scope, in some cases, for the detrimental impact of a term to be reduced or extinguished. In such circumstances we may wish to view the term as fair on the basis that the consumer is in a position to self-protect against it. Equally, it may be that insurance is available to cover the losses that the trader seeks to avoid responsibility for. On this basis we may wish to view the term as unfair on the basis that it unduly compromises the interests of the consumer while not being necessary (given the insurance position) to protect the interests of the trader.

Then there is the question as to the interests of the trader. In very general terms, there is the trader interest in receiving full payment. This will be relevant in assessing the fairness of any term dealing with the consumer payment obligation, the remedies for breach of this obligation and the way this obligation can be enforced.[101] Then there is the trader interest in not being exposed to losses that are unduly onerous in cases where he fails to perform properly. This will be relevant in assessing the fairness of any term excluding or restricting liability.

However, the most comprehensive analysis of consumer and trader interests would (as we have already suggested[102]) look yet further. In particular, it would look to the issue of overall substantive fairness. This involves looking at the term under scrutiny in the context of other terms of the contract and of related contracts. As already indicated,[103] there is substantive fairness if there is a term that represents a 'fair price' and balances out any unfairness in the term under scrutiny. One way in which this might arise is that the other term in some way protects the consumer from the detriment caused by the term under scrutiny. So, for example, while one term allows the trader to change something to the detriment of the consumer (for instance to increase the price) another term may allow the consumer to protect his interests by withdrawing from the contract.[104]

---

101 See H. Collins, Regulating Contracts, Oxford, 1999, at 262–4.

102 See above at 2.4.2.1.

103 See above at 2.4.1.

104 Another example of this situation is where a term requires a consumer to pay for a service prior to commencement. This may be detrimental to the consumer in that the consumer (having paid) is in a weak bargaining position if the work is not completed or is defective. He is in a weak bargaining position as he is not in a position to withhold payment. However, this position may be strengthened if it is also provided

Alternatively, a term may exclude a particular liability, while there may be another term that is favourable to the consumer (e.g. in fixing a low price). Another possibility is that, while one term gives the trader rights against the consumer that are in some way detrimental to the consumer, another term gives the same ('mirror-image') rights[105] to the consumer against the trader in the same circumstances. In all these cases a key question is whether the favourable term might be said to represent a 'fair price' for the term that is detrimental to the consumer.[106] Collins shows that this requires a careful analysis as to the overall 'balance of advantage'.[107] This involves consideration (for our purposes) of the risk that the trader is seeking to protect himself against by use of the term under scrutiny and the degree of detriment or risk caused to the consumer by this term; and considering, in the light of these factors, whether any term that confers an advantage on the consumer can be said to represent a fair price for the term under scrutiny.[108] It may well sometimes be the case that the term conferring an advantage on the consumer does represent a fair price for the detrimental term, but this will not necessarily be the case.[109] Of course, this turns in large part on what measure we use to decide on the idea of 'fair price'. In some cases the measure to use will be reasonably obvious. So, if we take the example of the term allowing the consumer to cancel where there is a price rise, the obvious question is whether the right to cancel does protect the consumer from the price rise (in the sense that there is no liability to pay some part of the increased price) and also whether the consumer is in some way compensated for any inconvenience or other losses caused by the need to cancel. Indeed in any case where the purported feature of the 'beneficial' term is that it protects the consumer, or allows the consumer in some way to self-protect, against the consequences of the term under scrutiny, the obvious question is whether the beneficial term does in reality allow this.

However, this sort of formula is obviously not appropriate in other types of case. For example, where the purportedly beneficial term comes in the form of a price that is allegedly lower than it would otherwise be, this has nothing to do with *protecting* the consumer from the detrimental

---

that the trader must deliver to the consumer a Bank guarantee which would ensure that appropriate sums would be paid to the consumer in the event of non-performance or defective performance. This was the situation in a German case before the ECJ which is discussed below at 3.5.4.

[105] See E. Hondius, European Approaches to Fairness in Contract Law, in Willett, Aspects of Fairness in Contract, Blackstone, 1996, at 70–71.

[106] H. Collins, Regulating Contracts, OUP, 1999, at 259–260.

[107] *Ibid.*

[108] See the discussion and examples at *ibid.*, 258–266.

[109] *Ibid.*

term. The issue, rather, is whether the price in some way *compensates* the consumer for the detrimental term. Does the term fixing the price represent a 'fair price' for the detriment caused by the term under scrutiny and therefore balance out any unfairness we would otherwise say is caused by the term under scrutiny.[110] Putting this another way, the question is whether the degree of risk to which the consumer is exposed by the term under scrutiny is fairly balanced out by the fact that the use of such a term may have allowed the trader to charge a price that is lower than it would have been if the term under scrutiny had not been included.[111]

The problem (as indicated above[112]) is that there is scope for disagreement as to how to measure this. It is easy enough to identify the degree of risk to which the consumer is exposed by the term under scrutiny (and, on the other side) to which the trader would be exposed if it were not for the term. So, for example, we can see that if a trader is in breach of a particular term his liability (on general principles) will amount to X; and if this is excluded, then this is the risk which the trader avoids and the consumer bears. However, what is more difficult is to decide when the price charged is sufficiently beneficial to justify exposing the consumer to this risk. One measure of this might be whether the price has been subject to normal market discipline. It is fairly clear (and well accepted from an economic point of view) that in standard form contracting traders are able to load some of the risks on to consumers in relation to ancillary issues while (as a result of market discipline) being forced to be more competitive in relation to the core issues (including price[113]). In this sense it could be said that, as long as the price has been subject to market discipline, consumers are always getting a lower price in exchange for onerous ancillary terms.[114] However, it could also be said that the fact that the price is controlled by market discipline does not necessarily mean that there would have had to be a higher price if the term under scrutiny had not been used. On one view, this is the core question, i.e. whether without the term (and the protection it gives the trader against certain risks) the price would have needed to be higher in order to cover these risks and make such contracts economically viable for the trader. This being the case the price charged can be viewed as representing a fair

---

[110] This is what many authors mean when they refer to substantive (un)fairness: see H. Collins, *ibid.*, 259–60; and S. Smith, Contract Theory, OUP, 2003, at 8.33 and 9.25; and see above at 2.4.1.

[111] I am very grateful to Hugh Beale for discussions on this point.

[112] See above at 2.4.1.

[113] See above at 2.3.2.1.

[114] See H. Beale, Unfair Contracts in Britain and Europe, 1989, Current Legal Problems, 197, at 199–201.

price for the term and there can be said to be overall substantive fairness. One way of deciding whether (without the term under scrutiny) the price would indeed need to have been higher than that actually charged is to ask whether the price actually charged is the market typical price in contracts where such terms are used. The question as to whether the price and the overall balance of rights and obligations are fair by the typical standards of the market is in fact often suggested as a measure of substantive fairness.[115] This tends to be based on the idea that the typical market price should be assumed to be the best price that could be offered taking into account the other terms used; so that if the detrimental term (which protects trader interests at the expense of consumer interests) had not been used the trader would have had to charge a higher price. By definition, then, the price actually charged is lower than it would have been if the term was not used and, on this basis, it balances out any unfairness in the term under scrutiny.[116] So what this approach ends up saying is that as long as the price is typical for the market there is substantive fairness. Of course, this is assuming also that the term under scrutiny is typical for the market (if the term is harsher than normal at this price then it is clear that a lower price could have been offered and so there may not be substantive fairness). In sum, then, on this approach there is substantive fairness as long as both the term under scrutiny and the price are normal by the standards of the market. If the term is harsher than typical or if the price is higher than typical then there may not be substantive fairness.

However, a problem with this approach is that the typical market price is simply *assumed* to be the best price that could be offered taking into account the other terms used. Yet surely this does not necessarily follow. It is not really based on any evidence as to what exactly is economically feasible for the trader. All we know is that the price is typical and the ancillary term under scrutiny is typical. So, another approach might be to say that when a trader uses a term that is detrimental (but typical) the existence of a price that is also typical should only be accepted as creating a fair overall balance where it can be shown positively that the trader would have had to charge a significantly higher price if it was not for the detrimental term (i.e. that the trader should show the sort of costs or risks to which he is exposed if he does not use the term that is detrimental to the consumer, the amount extra that he would have to charge without protection against these costs or risks and why these costs or risks cannot

---

115 See S. Smith, Atiyah's Introduction to the Law of Contract, OUP, 2005, 297–8.

116 Of course, it follows, on this approach, that if the price is higher than is normal in the market for contracts in which the term under scrutiny is used (or if the price is a typical price but the term is unusual) then there is overall substantive unfairness. In these circumstances the consumer has not (by the standards of the market) been compensated for the term in question.

be absorbed in some alternative way). If the trader cannot make this case then there would only be substantive fairness where he charges a price that is actually lower than what is typical in the market. This latter approach obviously has the potential to offer a higher level of protection. Rather than making a conclusive presumption in favour of the norms of the market the trader is required to make a positive case to the effect that it is really necessary to use a terms that deviates significantly from the default position or from reasonable consumer expectations – that this is the only economically viable option if the price is not to be significantly higher. If this case cannot be made then the term that deviates significantly from the default position or from reasonable consumer expectations (but which is perfectly normal in the market) has not been balanced out by a market typical price. There is not overall substantive fairness in the case of the term unless there is a price that is lower than the market typical price.

Whichever of the above measures are being used there is surely a further issue in those cases where it is suggested that the price has in some way balanced out the unfairness caused by the term under scrutiny. Above we noted the possibility of the type of situation in which there is another term in the contract that *protects* the consumer against the detrimental features of the term under scrutiny. If the nature of the contract is such that a term of this type could be used then (assuming that the use of such a term does not impose an undue burden on the trader) surely there is only overall substantive fairness if such a term is indeed included. In other words, even if the balance between price and the risk allocation provided for by the term under scrutiny is shown to be fair, surely the overall substantive balance is only fair if the contract does indeed include the term protecting the consumer from the detrimental effects of the term under scrutiny. A fair balance as between the term under scrutiny and the price is surely insufficient if it would have been feasible to provide for concrete protection against the effects of the term under scrutiny.[117]

Another possible argument as to overall substantive fairness might revolve around whether it is economically efficient to provide goods or services at all without the term. There may be cases in which it is not. For example, it might be argued that powerful (and very detrimental) forms of security are needed by those lending to high risk consumers; otherwise they would find it economically inefficient to lend.[118] If this is so then it might be argued that the 'fair price' for being subject to the security in question (or whatever the term in question may provide for) lies in the basic access to the loan (or whatever the goods or services happen to be).

---

[117] On this issue see the ECJ case (referred by the German courts) mentioned above at n. 104 and discussed below at 3.5.4.

[118] See H. Collins, Regulating Contracts, OUP, 1999, 262–6.

Clearly, again, there is the question as to how to measure this issue, i.e. on what basis it should be decided whether the goods or services could be provided in the absence of the term. The more protective we wish to be the more it would need to be insisted that that the trader should show the sort of costs or risks to which he is exposed if he does not use the term that is detrimental to the consumer; and why these costs or risks cannot be absorbed in some alternative way, i.e. that the only options are to use the term or not to provide the goods or services.[119]

Apart from the above question as to how we might measure whether there is a fair balance in rights and obligations, there is also the question as to the *role* to be played by that measurement in the overall analysis. On one approach, if there is such a fair balance (however that is measured) the term is viewed conclusively as fair. However, an alternative approach (setting a higher standard) is to say that there should still be a review of matters of procedural fairness. The argument for such an approach is dealt with more fully below when we turn to the issue of transparency.[120] However, the essence of the argument is that, notwithstanding the existence of a fair balance of *substantive* rights and obligations, consumers have a legitimate interest in being able to make their own assessment of this package, i.e. that transparency remains vital.

2.4.3.4 Procedure

(i) Transparency: A Basic Requirement

Having set out the questions that we might wish to ask in relation to the *substance* of the terms the question is how this should relate to procedural issues. One possibility is to focus simply on transparency. Requiring a good level of transparency on matters such as size of print, clarity of language etc. is, as we have said, a departure from a traditional freedom-oriented approach. Such a freedom-oriented approach would require no more than that consumers are aware that terms exist. However, from a fairness-oriented perspective, a good level of transparency is fundamental. Where a term is significantly compromising of the substantive interests of the consumer, putting the consumer in a position to at least have the

---

[119] The question as to whether a loan could be offered without a term providing for interest to continue at the contractual rate after judgment arose in the only House of Lords decision so far under the UTCCR, on which see below at 5.5 and, in particular, at 5.5.4.2(iv).

[120] See below at 2.4.3.4(ii).

chance[121] of being able to exercise a reasonable degree of informed consent must surely be the first priority of a fairness-oriented approach. As we have also seen, transparency may be important in other respects for individual consumers – in allowing scope for negotiation, helping them to choose between traders and also in helping consumers post-contractually. In addition, transparency may improve the likelihood that competitive pressure will be brought to bear on the terms; thereby improving choice and fairness in substance.

(ii) Transparency, Substance and Overall Balance

Of course, to the extent that the agenda is to help the consumer protect his substantive interests (by making terms transparent where they are damaging to these substantive interests), the degree of transparency required should vary depending upon the degree of unfairness in substance. On this approach, we must begin by considering the degree of substantive detriment. This means considering the term itself and the broader questions of unfairness in substance, including, for example, the extent to which any detriment is balanced out by other terms of the contract that are favourable to the consumer. The greater the unfairness in substance the more should be required in the way of transparency, and vice versa.

On one approach to transparency we stop at this point. In other words, where there is no unfairness in substance, transparency (or lack of it) is not an issue. In one way, this appears to be a plausible approach, as a key reason for transparency is to enable consumers to protect their interests by being aware that there is substantive unfairness and making an informed choice as to whether to enter such a contract. So, if there is no substantive unfairness, it might be said that there is no need to be concerned about transparency. However, the issue is more complex than this. There is the possibility raised above[122] that the term under scrutiny *is* in fact in some way detrimental to the consumer (e.g. by excluding a particular liability or allowing for a price increase) and that the conclusion that there is not overall substantive unfairness is in fact based on a broader review of the substantive context, (e.g. there is another term that is favourable to the consumer and that can be said to represent a fair price for the detriment caused by the term under scrutiny[123]). In this situation there still appears to be a clear consumer interest in transparency (assuming that we wish to

---

[121] We shall see shortly that there are serious concerns as to how likely it is that consumers will take advantage of transparency even when it exists – see below at 2.4.3.5(iv).

[122] See above at 2.4.3.3.

[123] See discussion of this issue above at 2.4.3.3.

prioritize transparency as a value). Even although there may be *overall* balance the term under scrutiny remains in itself in some way problematic in deviating from the default position or from reasonable consumer expectations; and consumers surely have an interest in being aware of this prior to conclusion of the contract. In addition, even if an objective view of the overall situation is that the favourable term makes the overall substantive agreement fair, consumers are surely entitled (on an informed basis) to make this assessment (i.e. as to the benefits of the favourable term) for themselves. So, if there is a term excluding liability, but at the same time the price package is favourable, the consumer has an interest in being able to assess the risks posed by the exclusion clause; *and* an interest in being able to assess how beneficial the price package is, how it compares to what is offered by other traders and, in all the circumstances, whether the price package appears to be a worthwhile trade-off for the exemption clause. For all these purposes, the exemption clause *and* the price package needs to be transparent.

The conclusion, then, is that where a term is in some way substantively detrimental but is balanced out by a favourable term there remains a good argument for both the detrimental and the favourable term to be transparent. In other words, the regime should be such that a lack of transparency is capable of leading to the conclusion that the term under scrutiny is unfair. This would allow bodies charged with preventive control to say that if it is not transparent then it is unfair. Equally, it would allow courts (*ex post facto*) to take into account the lack of transparency. However, this does not necessarily mean that in after the fact litigation we would wish to hold the detrimental term to be unfair on the basis of the lack of transparency in all cases. It may well be that if the overall package had been transparent the consumer would have been happy to agree to it; and that, on this basis it is fair to enforce it.[124]

(iii) Transparency and Legal Rights

It is also arguable that where traders choose to include terms reflecting important legal rights (which terms will not be detrimental in substance) that these terms should be transparent. These terms should be transparent in particular because (as we saw above[125]) it is particularly in the interests of consumers to be aware of terms that are actually advantageous to them, so that they can take up these advantages in the context of a dispute. In the context of preventive controls the means of requiring transparency where terms reflecting important legal rights are concerned is to say that a lack

---

[124] I am grateful to Hugh Beale for discussions on this point; and for further discussion of this issue in the context of the UTCCR see below at 5.9.

[125] See above at 2.4.2.2.

of transparency makes such a term unfair (the term only being allowed to be used if it is transparent). However, where *ex post facto* action is concerned then there is no advantage to the consumer in such an approach. This is for the obvious reason that the term is actually substantively advantageous to the consumer, so that it is in the interests of the consumer at this stage for the term to be enforced. In such a case some other approach is required, e.g. a penalty for failure to make the term transparent.[126]

The immediately preceding discussion related to terms reflecting important legal rights that the trader has voluntarily included in the contract. However, it is also arguable that it should sometimes be compulsory to include terms reflecting important legal rights where this may affect pre-contractual consumer understanding as to other terms and help consumers to protect themselves post-contractually against these other terms. So, there might be a term having the effect of excluding or restricting liability for breach of the implied term to carry out a service with reasonable care and skill. One question is whether this is clearly and prominently expressed. However, it is arguable that another aspect of the transparency of such a term is whether consumers can really understand what is being taken from them. In order to understand this it is arguable that they need to be made aware of the rights that they would have in the absence of the exemption clause. Being aware of such rights may also mean that (at the dispute stage) a consumer is more likely to challenge the trader over reliance on the exclusion clause. We shall see later that in the only case so far to have reached the House of Lords[127] on the UTCCR a slightly different version of this issue arose. The term in question (in a loan agreement) provided for contractual interest to continue to accrue in addition to the amount payable by the consumer under the judgement. It is certainly arguable that the Bank should have been required to make consumers aware of the background legal regime which allows consumers to ask the court to review the amounts payable and the time over which payments must be made. Awareness of this regime might mean that many consumers would request and obtain such a review. At the very least they would then be more likely to be aware of the separate accrual of interest and in many cases the amounts payable might be reduced. The Court of Appeal took the view that the Bank should make consumers aware of the regime; while the House of Lords took the view that there was no such obligation. This raises questions as to exactly where the law stands on transparency of background legal rights. We shall return to these issues below.

---

[126] For discussion of these issues under the UTCCR see below at 5.10.

[127] *Director General of Fair Trading* v. *First National Bank* [2001] 3 WLR 1297.

(iv) The Limits of Transparency and the Implications for the Approach Taken

It is well recognized that there are limits as to how effective transparency can be. Above we mentioned a number of factors that would be likely to inhibit consumers overcoming problems of lack of transparency.[128] However, even if terms are transparent, it seems likely that these factors may still cause difficulties for consumers.[129] First of all there is the basic disinclination to read detailed contract terms. Then, there is the effect of the powerful pre-existing expectations suggesting a successful relationship and that the terms will not come into play. The result may be that the consumer may not see much point in giving consideration to the formal terms dealing with ancillary matters;[130] as these rarely have much to do with what actually happens.[131] Another factor that may get in the way of consumers reading terms is that they may also have a range of complex decisions to make on the more basic question as to whether to buy the goods or services, e.g. decisions as to quality, affordability and financing. In the light of these important considerations it may be difficult to focus on and 'get to grips' with the formal terms.

In addition, consumers may not think to attain an understanding of the formal terms because they know that traders will be unlikely to be prepared to change them; possibly because they believe that the terms have some form of official sanction,[132] e.g. that they have been vetted in some way or possibly, in some way, represent 'the law'; and because, even if they realize that they can be challenged, they have no idea as to the type of legal criteria that will be applied to determine the enforceability of the term.

Then there is the fact that, even if terms are transparent, it may still be difficult for consumers to understand the legal context, e.g. what exactly is being taken away by the term. It may also be difficult for consumers to understand the way in which the term could affect them in practice. This

---

[128] See above at 2.4.2.2.

[129] Generally on the limits of information as a means of consumer protection see G. Howells, The Potential and Limits of Consumer Empowerment by Information, 2005, 32(3), Journal of Law and Society, 349; and see C. Scott and J. Black, Cranston's Consumers and the Law, Butterworths, 2000, at 372–5.

[130] The specific reference to 'ancillary' matters should be noted. It has already been argued that the main problems arise with these terms. The 'core' issues of main subject matter and price are much more likely to be focused on, understood and subjected to competitive discipline – see above at 2.3.2.1; and see below at 4.4.8.2 and 5.8 for the particular way these are approached in the regimes.

[131] See discussion above at 2.4.2.2.

[132] See above at 2.4.2.2.

makes it difficult for consumers to assess how much of a risk is involved in agreeing to the term; and whether it is worthwhile seeking to have the term removed or amended, or seeking to compare the term with those used by other traders. It may, for example, be very difficult for the (typically non-expert) consumer to work out how likely it is that circumstances will arise which will bring the term into play. So, for instance, the consumer may be faced with a term which he can clearly see excludes the liability of the trader for a certain type of breach of contract. However, the consumer will probably find it very difficult to work out how likely it is that this type of breach of contract will occur. He will also find it hard to work out how much he will stand to lose if this type of breach does occur, and therefore how much the term in question stands to deprive him of.[133]

Then there is the question of whether the trader will rely upon the term in practice. Consumers often do not have sufficient experience as to how traders behave in the context of disputes to be able to be sure whether the trader will actually rely upon the term, or whether he will pay out as a matter of goodwill.

A final problem relates to the role that might be played by transparency in enabling consumers to choose between terms and (through these choices) to exert competitive pressure on traders to offer something better.[134] Even if terms reach a certain level of transparency, different traders may be dealing, in their standard terms, with slightly different substantive issues and the manner of expression may be different. As such, it may be very difficult, in practice, for consumers to make a rational comparison that helps them in the immediate context or that contributes to an accumulation of competitive pressure on traders.[135]

Various implications seem to flow from the above observations as to the limits of transparency. First of all, the rules requiring transparency should place a strong emphasis on *standardization* of the way in which the terms should be presented.[136] This does not address all (or even many) of the above problems. So, for example, it does not make it more likely that consumers will even think about reading terms or that they will be able to weigh up the risks of the event covered occurring or that they will have any better idea as to the approach of the trader to the term in practice. However, standardized presentation does at least mean that if terms are read they may be slightly easier to understand as consumers are used to

---

[133] See M.J. Trebilcock, An Economic Approach to Unconscionability, in B. Reiter and J. Swann (eds), Studies in Contract Law, Butterworths, 1980, 416–7.

[134] See above at 2.4.2.2.

[135] See T. Wilhelmmson, Cooperation and Competition Regarding Standard Contract Terms in Consumer Contracts, (2006), European Business Law Review, 49, at 55.

[136] *Ibid.*, at 56.

seeing the information presented in this way. It may therefore mean that there is a greater possibility of informed consent and that it is easier to make comparisons and therefore more likely that competitive pressure will result.

Second, the above problems may show that (although transparency must be a basic right so that the opportunity for understanding is there) it will often be little more than a vain hope that consumers will ever really make much real *pre-contractual* use of it. We should surely search for (and give particular emphasis to) situations in which consumers could make real use of knowledge. This brings us back to the discussion at heading (iii) above. We talked there of making consumers aware of legal rights that they can use to protect themselves against the standard terms *post-contractually*. This is information that the consumer can actually make use of as it is information about rights in law. It is arguable, then, that this is a form of transparency that should be given particular emphasis. Of course, this is largely a matter for specific disclosure rules in relation to legal rights; and such rules exist in many sector-specific regimes.[137] However, in the context of general rules on fairness (the subject of this book) my point is that these general fairness rules should insist on disclosure of legal rights where these rights affect the way in which the standard terms impact the consumer (or to put this in another way, when these rights might help to protect the consumer against the effects of the standard terms). Unfortunately, as we have already seen, the House of Lords has not shown itself to be sympathetic to such an approach.[138]

The final implication of the limited usefulness of pre-contractual transparency is that there seems to be a greater case for legal standardization of the *substantive* features of the terms.[139] This is partly about the immediate transparency agenda. It is about accepting that there will never really be much chance of consumers identifying differences, choosing between traders and stimulating competition over these terms. One of the reasons (apart from all the other factors inhibiting consumers from making use of transparency) is that (quite apart from differences in presentation – see above) differences in *substance* may make matters even more confusing for consumers. So, if the terms are standardized in

---

[137] The most common requirements to disclose legal rights are focused on the cancellation rights available in many sectors. See, for example, Consumer Credit Act, 1974, s. 64; Consumer Protection (Distance Selling) Regulations 2000 (SI 2000/2334) (Regulation 8(2)(b)); Timeshare (Cancellation Information) Order 2003 (SI 2003/2579) (Article 3(1)(a)).

[138] See further below at 5.5.4.2(iv)(d).

[139] See T. Wilhelmmson, Cooperation and Competition Regarding Standard Contract Terms in Consumer Contracts, (2006), European Business Law Review, 49, at 56.

substance there is a better chance that transparency will at least lead to a better level of informed consent. (Of course, there is another reason for standardising the substance of the terms. If transparency cannot really be expected to work in many cases then we may wish to set a basic level of substantive protection. We shall return to this issue below.[140])

(v) Broader Procedural Fairness

Whatever is done on transparency, a procedural approach may then go further and consider questions of choice and bargaining power whenever there is a term that is significantly compromising of substantive consumer interests. Where there is such a term, then a lack of choice and/or the fact that the consumer was in a weaker bargaining position might be said to count against a finding of fairness; while the existence of choice and/or the fact that the consumer was in a sufficiently strong bargaining position to have protected his interests should count in favour of a finding of fairness. As we have already indicated, this involves a further departure from a freedom-oriented approach by comparison with an approach that simply requires transparency. At the same time it represents a stronger form of fairness. It recognizes that even where a term is transparent, such that the consumer is aware of the risks, the lack of choice and/or weak bargaining position of the consumer may mean that he could not have done anything to protect his interests – other than not entering the contract.

However, there are various important points about the role that should be played by enquiries into choice and bargaining power. First, we should emphasize that (while there may be reasons to require transparency even where terms are advantageous to the consumer) the same cannot be true of choice and bargaining power. In both cases there is only surely an issue that the law can become involved in when the term is in some way substantively disadvantageous to the consumer. In a free market economy it is surely unrealistic to expect there to be choices to be on offer for all terms. It is clear that this will never be the case. As we saw above,[141] most competition will tend to take place in relation to the core terms of the contract; the issues they deal with being sufficiently important and transparent to consumers to create a working market in the terms in question. In addition, the fact that all traders offer the same term may or may not mean that the terms do not fairly balance the interests of the parties. It may be that all traders get away with offering terms that are unbalanced because there is little competitive pressure in relation to these terms (as will often be the case in relation to the non-core terms of the

---

[140] See below at 2.4.3.5.
[141] See 2.3.2.1 above.

contract). However, it may be that the terms in question are common because traders have an understandable interest in using them and they do indeed reflect a fair balance as between the interests of the parties. In relation to bargaining power there will surely *usually* be inequality of bargaining power in consumer contracts in the sense that the individual consumer will usually not be important enough to the trader to give him any leverage and will be unlikely to have the skill, expertise or resources to bargain as effectively as the trader. So, if lack of choice and inequality of bargaining power is usual it becomes unrealistic to use them as sole measures of fairness. It is necessary to juxtapose them to another factor, i.e. that the terms are in some way detrimental to the consumer in substance. The agenda is not to stigmatize lack of choice or inequality of bargaining power *per se*, but only where it may prevent consumers from protecting their interests against terms that are detrimental in substance.

The issue, in relation to choice, then, is whether the term is significantly detrimental in substance. If so, the idea is to enquire as to whether this trader or a competitor offers a choice in the form of an alternative package of some kind that does not involve the degree of risk as is involved in the term under scrutiny. The consumer is, for example, offered services by trader X subject to a term excluding all liability for defective performance. At the same time trader X or another trader, Y, offers the same services while accepting some liability as long as the consumer pays a higher basic price. If this happens the first advantage in terms of fairness is that the alternative package (whether from trader X or from trader, Y) enhances the basic transparency of the no liability package in that this no liability package is put into some perspective. Then there is the choice issue itself. The consumer can now choose whether to take the risk of agreeing to the no liability package, or pay a higher price in exchange for the trader accepting more liability. In other words there is a procedural means of the consumer protecting their interests in the face of the detrimental term. In summary, then, such a choice would count in favour of fairness; while the lack of such a choice would count against fairness.

The issue in relation to bargaining power is, as with choice, whether the term is significantly detrimental in substance. If so, then the inequality of bargaining power that will usually exist will now be stigmatized as preventing consumers from protecting their interests in the face of the detrimental substantive term. This said, if the consumer is actually in a strong bargaining position so that he could have protected his interests in the face of the harsh term then this may count in favour of fairness.

Of course, it is logical that the approach to the issues of choice and bargaining power should be dictated by the *degree* of unfairness in substance. If the question is whether the consumer has an opportunity, at the procedural stage, to protect his substantive interests then clearly it is relevant to consider the extent to which these substantive interests are affected. So, while limits on consumer choice or bargaining power should count against a finding of fairness whenever a term is significantly detrimental to the interests of the consumer, the degree to which such procedural unfairness should count against the term should (logically) vary with the degree of substantive detriment.

There is a final issue is as to how the role of the enquiries into choice and bargaining power compares to the role played by the transparency enquiry. We have already said that if a term compromises the substantive interests of a consumer and is not reasonably transparent then this should often be enough for a finding of unfairness. This is because understanding the relevant risks and being able to give informed consent is fundamental to fairness. Of course, if we are concerned with broader fairness, then transparency is not necessarily enough. On the procedural front, this implies an enquiry into the choice and bargaining power issues (at least where the substantive terms in question are significantly detrimental). However, unlike with transparency, it cannot be said that either choice or equality of bargaining power are fundamental to fairness. As a matter of principle, the ability to give informed consent must be more fundamental than the existence of choice as to what to agree to or the opportunity to bargain for an improvement. In addition it is more practical to expect terms to be transparent in all cases, as all that is required is careful attention to drafting. Choice is much more problematic for traders. A trader has to work out which of his terms significantly compromise consumer interests to such an extent that a choice might be expected. He must then work out whether other traders who are reasonably accessible offer a choice. If such a choice does exist the trader must work out whether this choice is likely to be treated as sufficient to make his term fair. If no other trader does offer a choice on the issue in question then the trader must then either develop an alternative package which is likely to be regarded as adequate or make the term fairer in substance. It would therefore place an intolerable burden on traders if choice was a prerequisite of enforceability. Equally, as we have already said, it is not usually efficient for traders to bargain over terms. This is why they are standardized in the first place. Even if a trader is prepared to bargain most traders are in a stronger bargaining position than consumers as a matter of economic reality. So it would be unrealistic to hold a term to be unfair quite as readily on the basis of inequality of bargaining power as should be the case where lack of transparency is concerned.

So, the most that can be expected is that choice and bargaining power issues should be taken into account. Of course, there can be cases in which the term is transparent but the term is unfair on the basis of either a lack of choice or weak consumer bargaining strength, especially where the term is very unfair in substance (otherwise these are not additional tools of protection on top of transparency). However, the point simply is that, as a matter of general principle, the issues of choice and bargaining strength are not as fundamental as transparency.

Finally, there are some issues specifically as to the way in which we might approach the question of inequality of bargaining power. It has already been emphasized that the fact of the consumer being in a weaker bargaining position should only matter where the result is a term that is significantly detrimental in substance. However, one further question seems to be whether this should only count against the term where there is something particularly unconscionable about the transaction (whether on the basis that the unfairness in substance is extreme, the bargaining disparity is extreme or there is some sense in which the trader has acted unconscionably). These sorts of requirements may well have a place to the extent that inequality of bargaining power is to be allowed as a vitiating factor for contracts in general.[142] However, if there is an agenda to control more routine unfairness in consumer contracts then such requirements arguably have no place at least as standard requirements.[143]

2.4.3.5 Disallowing Terms with Certain Substantive Features

(i) Introduction

In one way, the most radical form of fairness involves disallowing terms with certain substantive features (whether in after the fact litigation or pre-emptively) irrespective of questions of overall substantive fairness and irrespective of whether there is procedural fairness. In after the fact litigation the scenario I am describing involves a term being held to be unfair based on its substantive features alone and ignoring (i) the existence of a beneficial term and whether this means that there is overall substantive fairness,[144] and (ii) the transparency of the term, the existence of choices for the consumer and the fact that the consumer was in a

---

[142] See Thal, The Inequality of Bargaining Power Doctrine (1988) 8 Oxford Journal of Legal Studies 17 at 29–30 on extremes of inequality of bargaining power; see J. Cartwright, Unequal Bargaining, OUP, 1991 generally on the need for there to be unconscionable advantage taking by the party in the stronger position; see R. Brownsword, Contract Law: Themes for the Twenty-First Century, OUP, 2006 at 81–85; and see below at 8.1.2 on the role played by such factors in the equitable doctrine of unconscionability.

[143] On how such requirements might hinder the goals of the Unfair Contract Terms Directive see below at 3.4.2 and on the attitude of the House of Lords see below at 5.5.4.2(iii).

[144] On the different possible ways of measuring substantive fairness see above at 2.4.3.3.

position to bargain for a better term. In relation to pre-emptive control a term displaying certain substantive features might simply be banned, declared ineffective etc by legislation. The result then is that it will be ineffective in whatever circumstances it is used (i.e. whether it is used in a contract that is substantively fair overall – because it contains a beneficial term – or it is used in circumstances that involve procedural fairness). Alternatively, a regulatory body such as the OFT might require a trader not to use a term even though it is used in a contract containing a beneficial term, is presented transparently, and there is a choice between this and another term (and even although it might conceivably be used in some circumstances in which the individual consumers have sufficiently strong bargaining strength to protect their interests).

From a freedom-oriented perspective, this is the least acceptable form of fairness. This sort of approach restricts the freedom of the trader to the greatest extent. It says that even if there is overall contractual balance and even if the trader seeks to enable the consumer to protect his own interests (by making the term transparent and possibly also by offering a choice) the trader is nevertheless not free to use the term. Such an approach would also be seen from a freedom-oriented perspective as being corrosive of the freedom of the consumer. The freedom of the consumer is restricted, even although the consumer may have been in a position to know what he was agreeing to, may have had a choice (whether from this trader or another), and could perhaps have bargained for a more favourable term;[145] and even although he may benefit from other favourable terms by agreeing to the term.[146] From a fairness-oriented perspective there seem to be several interconnected reasons for taking this type of approach.

(ii) The Purely Substantive Focus

First and foremost, there is the idea that consumers should be given absolute protection where certain substantive interests are concerned – that consumers have certain 'irreducible' rights.[147] This idea has also

---

[145] See S. Grundman, W. Kerber and S. Weatherill, introductory chapter in S. Grundman, W. Kerber and S. Weatherill (eds), Party Autonomy and the Role of Information in the Internal Market, De Gruyter, 2001, at 1.

[146] The favourable term he may have benefited from could have been a lower price. See, for example, Atiyah, who points out that to ban a term that excludes certain rights is to deprive the consumer of his freedom to choose – he is forced 'to buy certain rights as a sort of compulsory extra', P.S. Atiyah, Essays on Contract, OUP, 1988, 375.

[147] See discussion by H. Beale, Legislative Control of Fairness, in J. Beatson and D. Friedmann, Good Faith and Fault in Contract, 1995, 231, 236–7; and generally on the relationship between guaranteeing certain rights and paternalism see D. Kennedy, Distributive and Paternalist Motives in Contract and Tort Law with Special Reference

been expressed as being about the creation of a 'social market', i.e. one in which certain social rights are seen as guaranteed, even within a market exchange.[148] The protection of these rights is the priority and these rights cannot be traded for other beneficial terms, i.e. they cannot be taken away on the basis that the overall balance of the contract is substantively fair. In addition, they cannot be taken away on the basis that there has been procedural fairness. We do not care whether there is procedural fairness that might enable consumers to protect their own substantive interests. Neither do we care about the fact that protection of the interest in question means that the consumer may lose the chance of a lower price (or some other favourable term). The substantive interests affected by the term are interests that *the law* should protect irrespective of questions of procedural fairness or broader substantive fairness.

(iii) The Presumption of Procedural Unfairness

However, an alternative way of viewing things is to say that there *is*, in fact, a concern with procedural fairness. This line of thought runs as follows. Ideally, we would hope that consumers were in a position to take advantage of procedural fairness to protect their interests against terms compromising their substantive interests. However, the nature of the unfairness in substance is so serious that we cannot take the risk that any procedural fairness could or did work in practice. It might be said that the degree to which the term compromises the substantive interests of consumers is such that it is *presumed* that consumers may not, in practice, take the opportunities that may have been available to protect their interests pre-contractually.[149] In other words, although there may have been (or be the prospect for) procedural fairness in the sense that the terms were (or could be) reasonably transparent and a choice or bargaining opportunities were (or could be) available, it is presumed that this was not or may not be taken advantage of in practice. This must be the case. Surely, the argument runs, no consumer would really want to agree to this sort of term.

This approach seems to be most appropriately based upon the recognition that there are serious doubts as to how effective procedural fairness can be in reality in helping consumers to protect their interests.

---

to Compulsory Terms and Unequal Bargaining Power (1982), Maryland Law Review, 563.

[148] H. Collins, Good Faith in European Contract Law, 1994, 14 Oxford Journal of Legal Studies, 228 at 246.

[149] On the idea of a presumption of procedural fairness see R. Bradgate, R. Brownsword and C. Twigg-Flesner, Report to the DTI on A General Duty to Trade Fairly, 2003, at 39–44.

For example, within the constraints of the typical consumer contract context, we have already seen that there is a limit to the impact which transparency can actually have on the consumer; and, consequently, a limit to the extent to which transparency is likely to stimulate competition and produce greater choice and fairness in substance.[150] So, it may be that, even where terms are transparent, consumers will not necessarily read them so that there will not necessarily be any real informed consent. If this is the case, then there will be a knock-on effect on the usefulness of the other elements of procedural fairness that may exist. If consumers are unaware of the detrimental nature of terms they will not see any need to take up any choice that may be available or use the bargaining power they may have to bargain for better terms.

If a consumer *has* made himself aware of the terms and risks involved and if a choice is theoretically available or the consumer, in theory, has the bargaining power to bargain for better terms, there may also be understandable reasons why the consumer does not take up these opportunities. First of all, just as habit and poor consumer education may militate against consumers paying attention to standard terms these facts may also mean that many consumers are unlikely to notice that choices are available. Secondly, it may be difficult, in practice, to make a rational comparison between the alternatives. The alternative may have to be paid for with a higher price or some other less favourable term. The consumer's limited ability to assess how much of a risk the term poses in practice[151] may make it difficult to assess whether it is worth doing so. Finally, as we have already said,[152] consumers may believe that terms have some kind of official sanction, either because they believe that the terms have been vetted in some way or because they believe that traders have some kind of quasi-governmental authority to set standards. To the extent that this is perceived to be the case, the consumer may not bargain for a change in terms even if he may, in theory, have had the bargaining power to do so.

As already suggested, all of these points about the limits of procedural fairness can then be juxtaposed to the fact that the term is very prejudicial in substance. Given the degree of fairness in substance we must assume that if a consumer was to agree to such a term then it must be because the procedural opportunities that existed are not being taken advantage of for the understandable reasons mentioned.

The idea of unfairness in substance raising a presumption of procedural unfairness is a common one in contract law thinking.[153] The

---

[150] See above at 2.4.3.4(iv).

[151] See above at 2.4.3.4(iv).

[152] *Ibid.*

[153] See S. Smith, Atiyah's Law of Contract, OUP, 2006, p. 289.

suggested approach here is loosely analogous to that taken in cases of undue influence where the existence of a substantive provision that is 'manifestly disadvantageous' raises an evidential presumption that the contract was brought about in circumstances of undue influence.[154] In our present unfair terms context the idea is that the substantive detriment caused by the term is such that it is presumed that whatever procedural opportunities for self-protection may be available to consumers these were/will not be taken advantage of for understandable reasons. However, there are differences between the presumption of procedural unfairness in the undue influence situation and the current situation. Where undue influence is concerned the presumption is rebuttable. It is rebutted where it is shown that there was no undue influence and this is usually shown by establishing that the plaintiff was provided with sufficient information and advice to enable him to self-protect.[155] By contrast, in our current situation (at least in those cases were terms are pre-emptively banned) we are thinking of an *irrebuttable* presumption that the procedural opportunities existing were not taken advantage of. So, the focus is not on what the trader did to give the consumer the chance to self-protect; but on whether the consumer could have taken advantage of these opportunities (and the presumption against this is irrebuttable). Of course, this is a perfectly logical distinction to make. In the case of undue influence the opportunities for self-protection come in the form of legal advice as to the risks involved in entering the transaction, and it is perfectly reasonable to suppose that many consumers will learn enough from this advice to make an informed choice (and therefore not be acting under the influence of the other party). However, legal advice is not practical as a matter of routine in relation to standard terms (unless the core of the transaction is inherently risky as in the case of the guarantees that are typically involved in undue influence cases). So when we talk of procedural opportunities for protection in the case of standard terms we are really talking about whether the terms are transparent, choices are available and the consumer is in a strong bargaining position. However (for the reasons set out above), it may not be reasonable to expect consumers to take advantage of these opportunities. These points also illustrate a further difference between the undue influence approach and the approach here. The fact that the presumption is rebuttable in the case of undue influence shows that the primary focus of the test really *is* procedural fairness. The conclusion will not always be reached that there is procedural unfairness and if there is not, there will not be relief. However, here the problems facing consumers (in self-protecting during the pre-contract process) always exist. There is *always* procedural unfairness in this sense. Yet we do not always find the

---

[154] See *Royal Bank of Scotland* v. *Etridge* (No. 2) [1998] 2 AC 773.

[155] See *Royal Bank of Scotland* v. *Etridge, ibid.*

terms to be unfair. We do this when they are particularly substantively detrimental. So, in fact, this must tell us that the core problem being regulated relates to the substantive features of the term. Yes it is possible to provide further rationalization for disallowing the term by alluding to the likelihood that opportunities for self-protection were (quite reasonably) not taken advantage of. However, the real reason we are taking action in the circumstances must be because of the substantive features of the term.

(iv) Making Transparency More Useful

Another reason for setting substantive standards that apply irrespective of matters of procedural fairness is to actually get more benefit from procedural fairness. We have already discussed the various limitations on transparency being of use to consumers in the context of ancillary terms; and suggested that these problems are actually exacerbated by the differences in the substantive terms used by different traders.[156] As far as the pre-contractual stage is concerned, we may therefore want to abandon the idea of using transparency to enable consumers to identify differences, choose between traders and stimulate competition over these terms; and focus simply on hoping that transparency at least helps consumers know what they are agreeing to, i.e. that it facilitates informed consent. The chances of this may be improved by standardizing the *substantive* features of the terms.[157] However (and this brings us to the current point) this necessarily involves setting substantive standards which are to apply irrespective of matters of procedural fairness.

(v) The Clear and Effective Protection Dimension

However, quite apart from nice arguments about the relative extent to which disallowance of terms is about substantive unfairness and procedural fairness, there is another very important element in actually *banning* certain terms proactively. This is the need to promote clear, effective consumer protection. Given the degree to which certain terms do compromise the substantive interests of consumers (and perhaps also the fact that consumers will often not really be able to take advantage of procedural fairness to self-protect) an outright ban may be imposed on the grounds that if the issue is left open, the interests of consumers will, in practice, be compromised. What I mean by this is that traders may routinely raise (and consumers accept) the argument that the term is

---

[156] *Ibid.*

[157] See T. Wilhelmmson, Cooperation and Competition Regarding Standard Contract Terms in Consumer Contracts, (2006), European Business Law Review, 49, at 56.

justified, whether on the grounds that the term is not in fact unfair in substance; or on the grounds that, even if it is unfair in substance, there is a beneficial term making for overall substantive fairness; or that there has, in the circumstances, been sufficient procedural fairness to justify its use. Even if such arguments may be valid in certain circumstances, they will not be valid in most cases. However, they will be used routinely if the issue is left open, and many consumers will suffer detriment as a result. In other words, a significant factor in banning certain terms is to secure the practical and effective protection of the majority of consumers; who, in practice, would not usually want to agree to the term in question.[158]

(vi) Freedom of Contract

Whatever the rationales for disallowing terms despite the existence of a reasonable level of procedural fairness, there is no doubt that such an approach is more restrictive of the freedom of the trader than an approach that allows terms to be justified on the basis of a reasonable degree of procedural fairness being established. There is also no doubt that it is more restrictive of the self-reliant form of freedom of *the consumer* that is favoured by a freedom-oriented approach. From a freedom-oriented perspective, if there is a reasonable level of procedural fairness the consumer remains free to overcome any difficulties that may exist and take advantage of the opportunities for self-protection that have been presented; while here we are saying that overcoming these difficulties is not realistic.

2.4.3.6 Abstract and Contextual Fairness[159]

I have already characterized the freedom approach as 'abstract' in the sense that it views parties in the abstract from the impact that terms may have on them and from their abilities to protect their interests in the contracting process.[160] Having ignored these elements, the view is that

---

[158] See the apparently similar view of Atiyah to the effect that the justification for disallowing certain substantive terms in all cases may be that it is only likely to be the minority of consumers who would really wish to 'trade in' the rights in question and that such wants might be able to be justifiably compromised in the interests of the majority who would prefer the rights on question to be absolutely protected in all cases, P.S. Atiyah, Essays on Contract, OUP, 1988, 376.

[159] On abstract and contextual approaches to fairness see P. Nebbia, Law as Tradition and the Europeanization of Contract Law: A Case Study, (2004) Yearbook of European Law, 363.

[160] See above at 2.3.1.

there is no need for protection. By contrast, I have characterized a fairness-oriented approach as being 'person-oriented' or 'contextual' in the sense that it takes into account these factors.[161] However, *within a fairness approach* it is possible to describe some approaches as abstract and other approaches as contextual. Of course, 'abstract' and 'contextual' now have different connotations. One way of characterising abstract and contextual fairness is as follows. On an abstract approach to fairness we set the same standards of fairness for all of those falling into the consumer and trader categories; these standards being abstract in the sense that they are applicable to all consumers and traders irrespective of their particular characteristics, strengths and weaknesses; and irrespective of the particular circumstances of a case.

There are advantages in adhering to such an abstract approach. One important advantage is that an abstract approach retains a greater degree of certainty and calculability in assessing unfairness. Following the suggested model set out above[162] an abstract approach would focus purely on matters such as the extent to which a term deviates from the default position; the ways in which such a term would affect the interests of the typical consumer; whether there is another term that is beneficial to consumers in general; and whether the term is sufficiently transparent to be able to be understood by the typical consumer.[163] By contrast, a contextual approach to unfairness would add to all of this consideration of the particular weaknesses, strengths and general circumstances that might arise after the contact is drafted.[164] Inevitably, this involves less

---

[161] See above at 2.4.1.

[162] See above at 2.4.3.2–2.4.3.5.

[163] This type of abstract approach to fairness is similar to that described by Nebbia (see P. Nebbia, Law as Tradition and the Europeanization of Contact Law: A Case Study, (2004) Yearbook of European Law, 363, at 367) in that the factors described as relevant are all matters than can be assessed when the contract is drafted. So, for example, the focus is on the type of substantive term and its impact on the typical consumer; the clarity of the term from the point of view of the typical consumer; and whether in general a choice is available to consumers. However, Nebbia's abstract approach would also take into account another factor that can be assessed when the contract is drafted, i.e. the particular position of the trader in the market, e.g. whether he is a monopolist and (logically) his more general bargaining strength. I am excluding this latter factor from my notion of abstract fairness.

[164] In general, where preventive control mechanisms are being used (and there is therefore no particular consumer) the approach will inevitably be mainly abstract as there will be no particular consumer and therefore no possibility to assess his particular circumstances. However, as already indicated, my notion of abstraction involves ignoring the particular circumstances of the trader as well. Yet these could plausibly be taken into account where preventive control is concerned, so that

predictability. A second advantage in taking an abstract approach is that (to the extent that consumer protection is an important agenda) the standard of protection will often be higher in that there is no scope to reduce the level of protection based on the particular weaknesses of the trader in question. Finally, to the extent that the rules (as is the case with the UTCCR) aim to harmonize laws across the EC, an abstract approach might be argued to make this goal more secure than a contextual approach; at least in the sense that it involves the same standard being applied to all irrespective of particular circumstances.

However, there are also advantages in a more contextual approach. First of all, taking account of the particular circumstances affecting the parties could be argued to amount to a purer form of individual justice. Second, it allows a more protective approach to be taken to particularly vulnerable consumers (i.e. for terms that might otherwise be fair to be found to be unfair based on the particular weaknesses of the consumer).

We shall see that the picture in practice is mixed. Of course, there is limited scope for a contextual approach in preventive control in any case. In *individual* litigation the rules under consideration are expressed in a broad enough manner to take account of contextual factors (and some guidelines seem to point strongly in this direction). However, the very breadth and openness of the standards provides scope to minimize any contextual emphasis of the tests (or, indeed, to pick and choose as to which contextual factors to focus on at the expense of others). Courts and regulators retain a fair degree of choice, therefore, as to how to proceed.

---

preventive control does not necessarily involve a wholly abstract approach. Where a particular consumer challenges a term for unfairness the choice between an abstract and a contextual approach is more significant. In such cases it is possible to take an abstract approach that ignores the particular strengths and weaknesses of both trader *and* consumer and focuses purely on the abstract factors mentioned above or a contextual approach that takes these particular strengths and weaknesses into account.

Chapter Three

Introduction to the Fairness Regimes

3.1 Introduction

This chapter sets out the basic features of the fairness-oriented regimes contained in the Unfair Contract Terms Act (UCTA) 1977 and the Unfair Terms in Consumer Contracts Regulations (UTCCR) 1999. It also explains the proposal to repeal these pieces of legislation and replace them with a single piece of legislation. It then considers the ways in which the law should and may be affected by the broader legal and policy background, by the ECJ and by the fairness traditions of other Member States.

3.2 The Existing Law and the Future – in Brief

The UCTA regulates only terms affecting the obligations and liabilities of the trader to the consumer (so called 'exemption clauses').[1] By contrast the UTCCR[2] regulates these terms as well as terms affecting the obligations and liabilities of the consumer to the trader. The UCTA was passed after the Law Commissions reports of 1969 and 1975.[3] These reports had been a response to the obvious problems caused by exemption clauses and the limited ability of the common law to address these problems.[4] The UTCCR are an updated version of the UTCCR 1994. These were passed in order to implement the EC Directive on Unfair Terms in Consumer Contracts of 1993.[5] At present the two regimes exist

---

[1]   It is mainly concerned with terms 'excluding or restricting liability' – see s. 13 for a definition; and also catches terms allowing the trader to offer a contractual performance substantially different from that reasonably expected or no performance at all (s. 3(2)(b)).

[2]   SI/99/2083.

[3]   See Exemption Clauses in Contracts, First Report (1969) Law Com No. 24 and Exemption Clauses in Contracts, Second Report (1975) No. 69.

[4]   On which see below at Ch. 8.

[5]   93/13/EEC; for a recent overview of the Directive, its implementation across the EU and various remaining questions and problems see M. Ebers, Unfair Contract Terms Directive, in H. Schulte-Nölke, EC Consumer Law Compendium – Comparative

side by side. However, the Law Commissions have proposed that the two regimes should be repealed and replaced by a new regime.[6] A key reason for this is to remove the uncertainty that may be caused by the existence of two regimes that overlap, but also differ, in terms of scope of application, effects, concepts and terminology.[7]

In terms of application, there are differences in relation to the contracts and terms covered. For example, UCTA applies to all types of contract (including both consumer and business to business contracts) except those positively excluded (those excluded include insurance contracts and contracts relating to the creation, transfer or termination of an interest in land).[8] By contrast, the UTCCR appear to apply to any consumer contract[9] (including insurance and land contracts[10]), although they do not apply to business to business contracts. In relation to terms covered, UCTA does not positively exclude individually negotiated and main subject matter terms, while UTCCR does exclude these terms from the assessment of fairness.[11] On the other hand, as we have already seen, UCTA only covers terms dealing with the obligations and liabilities of the trader, i.e. excluding or restricting trader liabilities[12] or allowing for a

---

Analysis, University of Bielefeld, 2006, 324–415 (available at http://ec.europa.eu/consumers/cons_int/safe_shop/acquis/comp_analysis_en.pdf); and on the Directive in the particular context of European law and a comparison between England and Italy see P. Nebbia, Unfair Contract Terms in European Law, Hart, 2007.

[6] See Law Commission No. 292, at p. 8 and for a discussion see H. Beale, Unfair Terms in Contracts: Proposals for Reform in the UK, 2004, 24 Journal of Consumer Policy, 289.

[7] *Ibid.*, at 1.4.

[8] UCTA, Schedule 1, 1(a) and (b).

[9] Regulation 4(1); and on the notion of the 'consumer' in EC law generally, under the Unfair Contract Terms Directive and traditionally in UK and Italian law see P. Nebbia, Unfair Contract Terms in European Law, Hart, 2007, Ch. 5.

[10] See (on land contracts) *London Borough of Newham* v. *Khatun EWCA* Civ 55 and (on insurance contracts) *Bankers Insurance Co. Ltd* v. *South* [2003] Lloyds Rep IR 1; and see discussions by H. Collins, Good Faith in European Contract Law, 1994, Oxford Journal of Legal Studies, 229; and S. Bright and C. Bright, Unfair Terms in Land Contracts: Copy Out or Cop Out? 1995, 111 Law Quarterly Review 655.

[11] Regulations 5(1) and 6(2). In the case of main subject matter terms this is only if they are in plain and intelligible language – Regulation 6(2).

[12] See ss 2, 3(2)(a) and 5–8.

performance by the trader that is substantially different from that reasonably expected by the consumer or no performance at all.[13]

The UTCCR is generally broader, covering all terms except those positively excluded.[14] Significantly, this means that it covers not only exemption clauses but also terms imposing obligations and liabilities on the consumer. The UTCCR is narrower than UCTA in not covering individually negotiated terms,[15] although these are of very limited significance in practice in consumer contracts.[16] In addition, as we have seen, the UTCCR also does not cover terms relating to the definition of the main subject matter; and neither does it cover the question as to the adequacy of the price as against the goods or services supplied in exchange.[17] In fact UCTA does not seem generally to apply to main subject matter terms and certainly does not apply to price terms. However, in the case of UCTA this is not as such because such terms are positively excluded. There is no mention of such terms in UCTA. It is simply that main subject matter terms do not generally (and price terms definitely do not) fall within the UCTA criteria that define what *is* covered. UCTA covers terms excluding or restricting certain types of liabilities described in the Act.[18] A main subject matter term will be one that defines the *core primary* obligation of the trader.[19] The UCTA provision dealing with excluding or limiting liability for general breaches of contract is focused on exclusion or restriction of the *secondary remedies* and not primary obligations.[20] There is also control of terms excluding or restricting liability for breach of the implied terms as to description, quality and fitness in contracts for the sale and supply of

---

[13] See s. 3(2)(b); UCTA also covers another category of term allowing a party to avoid responsibility, i.e. a clause requiring another party to indemnify the party in question in respect of any liability that may arise – see s. 4.

[14] Terms reflecting mandatory statutory or regulatory provisions or the provisions or principles of international conventions to which the Member States or the European Community is party are excluded from any coverage by the UTCCR (Regulation 4(2)). Excluded from the test of unfairness are individually negotiated terms (Regulation 5(1)); terms defining the main subject matter (Regulation 6(2)(a)); and the adequacy of the price or remuneration as against the goods or services supplied in exchange (Regulation 6(2)(b)).

[15] Regulation 5(1).

[16] For a full discussion of individually negotiated terms see below at 5.2.

[17] Regulation 6(2), although in both cases such terms are only exempted from the test of unfairness if they are in plain and intelligible language.

[18] See ss 2, 3(2)(a) and 5–8.

[19] See below at 5.8.3.

[20] Section 3(2)(a) and see below at 4.2.1.

goods.[21] This does cover restrictions or exclusions of the relevant primary obligations.[22] However, it is only the implied term as to description that might be said to be a main subject matter provision, so that it might be said that control of terms excluding or restricting this implied term involves controlling a term that defines the main subject matter.[23] Apart from this, as we have seen, UCTA also covers terms allowing the trader to offer a contractual performance substantially different from that reasonably expected.[24] Yet, as we shall see below, a term is probably only a main subject matter term for the purposes of the UTCCR if it genuinely reflects the expectations of the consumer as to the main subject matter.[25] Such a term will not be covered by UCTA because it will not be offering a contractual performance substantially different to that reasonably expected.[26] Finally, price terms are not positively excluded from UCTA; but they do not need to be. UCTA only covers the various types of term already mentioned that deal with the responsibilities of the trader to the consumer. Patently, a term stipulating the price to be paid by the consumer is not such a term.

Turning to the effects of the legislation, both UCTA and UTCCR provide for terms to be set aside in the context of private litigation.[27] However, there are differences in the precise effects. For example, under UCTA most terms can only be set aside once it has been concluded that the term was not a fair and reasonable one to have included in the contract;[28] while some terms are ineffective purely on the basis of their substantive features (i.e. they are banned outright[29]). In contrast no terms are banned in this way by the UTCCR. A term can only be set aside where, on an application of the full test of unfairness, it is found to be unfair.[30] Another difference in effects is that there may be a more liberal approach to severance (severing the fair and unfair parts of a term and allowing the fair elements to stand) under the UTCCR than there is under

---

[21] Sections 6(2) and 7(2) and see below at 4.2.1.

[22] Section 13 and see below at 4.2.2.

[23] See below at 5.8.3.1.

[24] Section 3(2)(b)(i).

[25] See below at 5.8.3.1.

[26] See below at 4.4.8.2.

[27] In the UTCCR this is provided by the single provision in Regulation 8(1) to the effect that an unfair term shall not be binding on the consumer. Under UCTA the formula is (under each distinct section) to provide that a term cannot exclude or restrict the liability in question or to provide that the term cannot do this except in so far as it satisfies the requirement of reasonableness (see, for example, ss 2(1) and (2)).

[28] See, for example, ss 2(2) and 3(2)(b).

[29] See, for example, ss 2(1), 6(2) and 7(2) and see below at 4.2.6.

[30] See Regulations 5 and 6.

UCTA.[31] The biggest difference of all is that private litigation is the only means of enforcement under UCTA, while UTCCR provides for a range of bodies who can, *inter alia*, seek injunctions to prevent the continued use of unfair terms.[32]

As to differences in concepts and terminology, many such differences are obviously generated by the above differences in application and effects. However, particularly significant differences exist in relation to the central control mechanisms. UCTA uses a test of 'reasonableness',[33] while the UTCCR use a test of 'unfairness' which turns on questions of good faith, significant imbalance and consumer detriment.[34] There is obviously a terminological difference here. Conceptually, (as we shall see), the tests undoubtedly share many features (being concerned in broad terms with a review of both procedure and substance); but there are certainly also differences. As we shall see, the concepts of imbalance and good faith may well bring nuances that do not come with the test of reasonableness.[35] In addition, the good faith, significant imbalance and consumer detriment concepts (and the overall test of unfairness) must be read in the light of the distinctive requirements of the Unfair Terms in Consumer Contracts Directive (UTD) and its underlying goals.[36] Another important difference is that the UTCCR contain a requirement to the effect that written terms be in plain and intelligible language and that if there is doubt as to the meaning of a term then the interpretation most favourable to the consumer should prevail.[37] UCTA contains no such rule.

---

[31] See the discussion in the Law Commission Report on Unfair Terms in Consumer Contracts (No. 292) at 49–50.

[32] See Regulations 10–16 and Schedule 1.

[33] See s. 11.

[34] See Regulation 5(1); this comes from Article 3(1) of the UTD. Good faith was previously used as a concept for controlling unfair contract terms in Germany and Portugal (respectively, German Standard Contracts Act, 1976, Article 9 and Portuguese Law of 1985 on Unfair Terms, Article 16). Imbalance seems to have roots both in Germany (where the 1976 Act referred – along with good faith – to 'unreasonable disadvantage' a concept that seems similar to imbalance) and France (where the travaux preparatoires to Loi Scrivener of 1978 referred to an 'evident imbalance in parties' rights and obligations'). See, on these issues, and on the other tests proposed in previous drafts of the UTD, P. Nebbia, Unfair Terms in European Law, Hart, 2007, 143–4.

[35] See below at 6.3.5.2–3 and 6.3.6.2.

[36] On which see further below at 3.4.

[37] See Regulation 7.

Of course the complex picture described is not helpful in promoting certainty and making it easy for consumers to ascertain their rights.[38] The Law Commission proposal is to repeal both UCTA and UTCCR and adopt a new model for the new regime.[39] The idea is that this new regime will eliminate overlaps and, where possible, eradicate the existing minor differences in concepts, terminology and definitions, so as to avoid over complexity.[40] There is also an agenda to promote clarity and accessibility in terms of language and structure.[41] The view is that this cannot be achieved by legislation essentially modelled on UCTA or UTCCR.[42] Of course it is recognized that the new legislation must give proper effect to the UTD.[43] It is also proposed that there should be no reduction of existing levels of protection.[44] Of course, this is necessary in the case of the UTCCR which itself reflects the requirements of the UTD. This means that the new regime would cover all of the contracts and terms currently covered by the UTCCR.[45] Indeed, the proposal is that the new regime would also cover individually negotiated terms,[46] which are not currently covered by the UTCCR. It also means that the test of unfairness should be of such a nature that it is capable of providing the same level of protection offered by the test in the UTCCR. The new test would provide that where a term is 'detrimental to the consumer, the business cannot rely on the term unless the term is fair and reasonable'.[47] The view of the Law Commission is that this does, indeed, provide at least as high a level of protection as the existing test in the UTCCR.[48] As we shall see below,[49] although there is the possibility that EC law requires the precise language of the Directive to be used in implementing measures, on

---

[38] See Law Commission, No. 292 at 8–10; the argument has even been made that the confusion caused could be viewed as improper implementation of the UTD – see F. Reynolds, (1994) Unfair Contract Terms, 110 Law Quarterly Review, 1.

[39] Law Commission Report, No. 292, at p. 8.

[40] *Ibid.*, at 1.4.

[41] Law Commission Consultation Paper, 2002, 4.12 and 4.18–19; 9.4; Law Commission Report No. 292, 2.44–2.46, 3.2.

[42] Law Commission Consultation Paper, *ibid.*, 4.18.

[43] Law Commission, Consultation Paper, *ibid.*, 4.22–4.29; Law Commission Report, 2.3.

[44] Law Commission Report, 3.10–13.

[45] See the various provisions of the Draft Bill, contained in the Law Commission Report, No. 292, Appendix A.

[46] Law Commission Report at 3.50–3.55.

[47] Draft Bill, Clause 4(1), Law Commission Report, p. 144.

[48] Law Commission Consultation Paper, 4.7–4.10 and 4.87–4.106 and Law Commission Report, 3.84–3.91.

[49] See below at 9.3.

balance the use of the 'fair and reasonable' test is probably acceptable[50] (as well as possibly aiding the achievement of clarity and accessibility by making the position easier to understand and apply in the UK). In addition, maintaining the level of protection required by the UTD means that the powers to obtain injunctions to prevent the use of unfair terms would be retained.[51]

Retaining existing levels of protection also means that where UCTA provides a higher level of protection than is required by the UTD this would generally be maintained. So the outright ban on certain terms would remain.[52]

More generally, the agenda to promote greater clarity and accessibility will arguably be fostered by provision of significantly more guidance than is provided by either piece of legislation at present; and by expressing the descriptions on the indicative list in a manner more understandable to UK lawyers and providing examples.[53]

3.3 The Background to UCTA

The Law Commission first reported on exemption clauses in 1969[54] and then again in 1975.[55] It is clear that the Law Commissions were alert to the problems caused by standard contracts, both in relation to procedural fairness and in relation to the substance of exemption clauses themselves. In the 1975 Report it was said that:

> … it is clear the exemption clauses are much used in dealings with private individuals and in purely commercial transactions. We are in no doubt that in many cases they operate against the public interest and that the prevailing judicial attitude of suspicion, or indeed of hostility, to such clauses is well founded. All too often they are introduced in ways which result in the party affected by them remaining ignorant of their presence or import until it is too late. That party, even if he knows of the exemption clause would often be unable to appreciate what he will lose by accepting it. In any case, he may not have sufficient bargaining strength to refuse to accept it. The result is that the risk of carelessness or of failure to achieve satisfactory standards of

---

50 Although see the view of P. Nebbia, Unfair Contract Terms in European Law, Hart, 2007, 147 to the effect that more needs to be done to prove that the effect of the fair and reasonable test is the same as the good faith/significant imbalance test.

51 See Law Commission Report, 3.143 and Draft Bill, Schedule 1.

52 See Law Commission Report, 3.41–3.49; Draft Bill, Clauses 1(1) and 5.

53 See Law Commission Report 3.115–6 and 3.117–9.

54 Law Commission Report No. 24.

55 Law Commission Report No. 69.

performance is thrown on to the party who is not responsible for it or who is unable to guard against it. Moreover, by excluding liability for such carelessness or failure, the economic pressures to maintain high standards of performance are reduced there is no doubt that the misuse of these clauses is objectionable. Some are unjustified. Others may operate fairly or unfairly, efficiently or inefficiently depending on the circumstances; for example the cost and practicability of insurance may be factors in determining how liability should be apportioned between two contracting parties.[56]

Specifically then, the law Commission were concerned that 'terms [might be] introduced in ways which result in the party affected by them remaining ignorant of their presence or import until it is too late', i.e. that they might lack transparency. There was also a concern over the inequality of bargaining power existing between the parties and the likelihood that the consumer would not be in a sufficiently strong bargaining position to influence the trader. The result, according to the Law Commissions, was that the substantive terms could impose the risks of defective performance on the party (for our purposes the consumer) who was not responsible for the defective performance or who cannot guard against it. In broad terms this accords with the fairness-oriented concerns over procedure and substance that I outlined above – a concern that the substantive terms of the contract might be damaging to the interests of the consumer and that these damaging terms might be agreed to in circumstances in which the consumer had been prevented (due to procedural unfairness) from protecting his interests. The Law Commissions took the view that some exemption clauses might be fair or unfair depending upon the circumstances. It was these types of clause that it was thought should be subjected to the test of reasonableness referred to above. As we shall see, this test allows for a review of all the circumstances, including the type of procedural and substantive issues mentioned. By contrast, the Law Commissions took the view that certain terms were 'unjustified' in all circumstances. This thinking led to the outright ban on certain terms that we also mentioned above.[57]

We should notice also that this excerpt does not merely talk about the problems of exemption clauses in terms of fairness, but also in terms of efficiency. The two issues are not necessarily treated as entirely synonymous, however they are treated as being very closely associated. This is not so surprising if we think back to the discussion above.[58] It was argued there that many standard terms dealing with ancillary (i.e. non-core) issues may escape market discipline. If this is the case, then not only

---

[56] Paragraph 11.
[57] See above at 3.2 and see further below at 4.2.7.
[58] See above at 2.3.2.1.

would this enable the seller or supplier to use terms which unfairly favour his own interests over those of the consumer; but these terms may not represent efficient allocations of risk. So improving on the fairness of terms need not be very different from making them more efficient. Transparency provides a good example of this. Greater transparency may bring greater procedural fairness in the sense that consumers may make more fully informed, autonomous decisions to agree to the terms. But transparency also increases the chances that terms will be efficient. If terms are more transparent then this increases the chances that they will be subject to market discipline of some kind. This is because the more transparent the terms are the more chance there is that a margin of consumers will become aware of their significance and will exert pressure upon suppliers to change things which they do not approve of.[59] Terms that reflect the preference of a reasonable margin of consumers can usually be assumed to be more efficient. A connection between fairness and efficiency can also be seen if we look directly at the substance of terms. A term may unfairly compromise the interests of the consumer by exonerating the supplier of a certain type of liability for breach of contract. It may be that the term is not only unfair, but also inefficient in that the supplier is in a better position than the consumer to insure against the loss in question. Indeed we will see that the question as to who is the best insurer is an important one in the Unfair Contract Terms Act.[60]

Next, it is important to emphasize that the Law Commissions did not see the main issue as being about the use of terms that displayed some form of extreme unfairness in substance, e.g. the restriction the liability of the trader to a much greater extent than would be normal in the market sector in question. The problem, rather, was *routine* unfairness in substance, i.e. the very common use of terms that were unfair (and that were not prevented from being unfair by the fact that they were common). In addition, the issue was about more than simply regulating the most extreme forms of procedural fairness, e.g. by protecting those consumers in a particularly weak bargaining position. It was also about *routine* procedural unfairness. These exclusions and restrictions routinely lacked transparency. All consumers were faced by these terms and most would tend not to have the bargaining power to persuade the trader to remove or amend them. This all suggests a notion of fairness that is not strongly tied to market norms.[61] Finally, there was no mention by the Law

---

[59] See M. Trebilcock, An Economic Approach to the Doctrine of Unconscionability, B.J. Reiter and J. Swann, (eds), Studies in Contract Law (1980) at 379.

[60] See below at 4.6.1 and 4.6.2.1.

[61] On the general relationship of fairness standards to market norms see above at 2.4.3.3 and below at 7.2.2 and on the approach of the reasonableness test under UCTA see below at 4.6.2.

Commissions of any kind of 'good conscience defence'. There was no suggestion that the substantive and procedural problems related to exemption clauses were to be assessed anything other than objectively. Exemption clauses were being used to enable traders to avoid responsibility for defective performance; and this was usually allied with the procedural problems described. This problem is not diminished (and there was no suggestion that it should be excused) by the fact that traders had not deliberately or recklessly acted unfairly or might not believe themselves to be acting unfairly.[62]

The Unfair Contract Terms Act started life as a private member's Bill, called the Avoidance of Liability Bill. This was undoubtedly a more appropriate name than its final name given that the Act does only cover terms which in some way exclude or limit the responsibilities of the trader. It does not cover other terms which may be unfair to the consumer, for example by way of the trader imposing obligations or liabilities upon the consumer. This is in contrast with the approach taken by some other countries when they enacted legislation to deal with unfair terms in the 1970s. For example the German Standard Contacts Act of 1976 covered all non-individually negotiated terms.[63] The French Loi Scrivener of 1978 covered 'any clause dealing with a determined or determinable price, or its payment, with the quality of the thing or its delivery, with the allocation of risks, or with termination or modification of the agreement…'.[64]

3.4 The Background to the Unfair Terms Directive and its Significance for the UTCCR and any New Regime

3.4.1 Introduction

The UTCCR were introduced in order to implement the Unfair Terms in Consumer Contracts Directive (UTD) of 1993.[65] The background to the UTD is of even greater significance then the background to UCTA. This is because measures (such as the UTCCR) implementing EC Directives should be interpreted so as to give effect to the purpose of the

---

62 This approach can be contrasted with the equitable doctrine of unconscionability which generally requires that there be extreme unfairness and that there be bad conscience or exploitation of some sort – see below at 8.1.2.

63 Sections 1(1) and (2).

64 Article 35(1).

65 93/13/EC; on the history of the UTD see P. Nebbia, Unfair Contract Terms in European Law, Hart, 2007, 6–8.

Directive.[66] This purpose can only be fully understood by considering the legal and policy background to the UTD. The UTCCR are in fact a virtual 'copy-out' of the UTD; so that what matters is to read the text of the UTCCR (which follows the UTD) in the light of the purpose of (and the legal and policy background to) the UTD. For example, the test of unfairness in the UTD and the UTCCR is whether 'contrary to the requirement of good faith, it causes a significant imbalance in the parties' rights and obligations arising under the contract, to the detriment of the consumer'. This, as indicated, must be read in the light of the purpose of/legal and policy background to the UTD.[67] If, as we saw above is planned, new legislation does indeed introduce a new 'fair and reasonable' test this test will need to be interpreted so as to reflect the protective effects of the above test from the UTD. If a term would, contrary to good faith cause significant imbalance to the detriment of the consumer, then it will need to be held to fail the proposed fair and reasonable test. Of course, as we have already said, the test from the UTD must itself be understood in the light of the purpose of/legal and policy background to the UTD.

3.4.2 The Preamble – Routine or Extreme Unfairness?

The Preamble to the Directive is a useful starting point. It seems to show that the Directive is aimed at regulating both procedural unfairness and unfairness in substance. It refers to 'abuse of power' and to 'one-sided standard contracts'.[68] It seems likely that 'abuse of power' refers to procedural unfairness. The trader might be said to be abusing power if he obtains the agreement of the consumer when there is a lack of transparency, lack of choice or weak consumer bargaining strength. Then we turn to unfairness in substance. The concern with unfairness in substance seems to be revealed by the reference to 'one-sided standard

---

[66] *Marleasing SA* v. *La Commercialde Alimentacion* [1992] 1 CMLR 305; Faccini Dori [1995] All ER (EC) 1.

[67] For earlier work that analyses the unfairness test and other aspects of the UTD in the light of the EC legal and policy background see S. Weatherill, Prospects for the Development of European Private Law (1995), European Review of Private Law, 3, 307; C. Willett, Good Faith in Consumer Contracts: Rule, Policy and Principle, in A. Forte (ed.), Good Faith in Contract and Property Law, Hart, 1999, 181; S. Whittaker, Unfair Contract Terms, Public Services and the Construction of a European Conception of Contract, (2000), 116 Law Quarterly Review, 95.

[68] Recital 9; and on the history of this thinking in the broader context of EC consumer policy see P. Nebbia, Unfair Contract Terms in European Law, Hart, 2007, 4–7.

contracts'. Terms that (in substance) unduly favour the interests of the trader over the consumer might be said to make the contract one-sided.

However, without closer consideration, the reference to 'abuse of power' might be troubling. The reference to 'abuse' might suggest that there is something out of the ordinary. This might come in the form of extreme unfairness in substance, e.g. terms that are significantly less fair in substance than is normal in the market sector in question.[69] It might also suggest extreme forms of procedural fairness, e.g. the use of onerous terms against those consumers in a particularly weak bargaining position. It might even suggest a need to establish positively that the trader had knowingly or recklessly taken advantage of the weaker position of the consumer.

However, it does seem that 'abuse of power' can be read in a different way. It can be said that there may be 'abuse' simply when the terms do not represent a fair balancing of the interests of the parties (this being measured by reference to independent standards, rather than trader dominated market norms); and where there is the procedural unfairness (i.e. lack of transparency, lack of consumer choice and disparity of bargaining strength) that routinely arises in consumer contracts. Indeed, the broader policy background to the UTD surely suggests that this must be the case. This point needs further explanation.

3.4.3 The Broader Constitutional Context and the General Level of Fairness

The UTD was adopted under Article 100(a) (now Article 95) of the Treaty of Rome. Article 95 provides, '... for the approximation of such provisions laid down by law, regulation or administrative action in Member States as directly affect the establishment or functioning of the internal market'.

The broad rationale for harmonising consumer protection laws under Article 95 is that market integration is hindered by the existence of variations between the consumer protection laws of the Member States.[70] There is the idea that variation as between certain consumer protection laws causes competitive distortions. This is expressed in the preamble to the UTD itself, where it is said that:

---

[69] Generally on using the market norm as a measure of fairness see above at 2.4.3.3 and on the approach under the UTCCR see 3.5.4, 5.5.4.2(ii) and (iii) and 7.2.2.

[70] For more on the constitutional background to the UTD, including its relationship to the famous free movement of goods case, Casis de Dijon case (*Rewe-Zentral* v. *Bundesmonopolverwaltung fur Brantwein* [1979] ECR 649), see P. Nebbia, Unfair Contract Terms in European Law, Hart, 2007, 8–12.

Whereas the laws of the Member States relating to the terms of contract between the seller of goods or supplier of services, on the one hand, and the consumer of them, on the other hand, show many disparities, with the result that the national markets for the sale of goods and services to consumers differ from each other and that distortions of competition may arise amongst the sellers and suppliers, notably when they sell and supply in other Member States.[71]

The idea, then, is that competition is distorted if different laws apply to sellers and suppliers depending upon which Member State they operate in. Let us suppose that state X has more rigorous control of unfair contract terms than state Y. In such circumstances sellers and suppliers in State Y might be viewed as having a competitive advantage over those in state X. In addition suppliers in State Y may well be deterred from doing business in state X as they will be subject to more rigorous controls. The reasoning is that such competitive distortion undermines the achievement of a single market. This sort of reasoning has been used to justify a number of other harmonising Directives in the consumer protection area, e.g. on consumer credit, doorstep selling, package travel, timeshare, distance selling and consumer sales.[72]

In these contexts, and in the context of unfair contract terms, the idea has been to create a so called 'level playing field' i.e. a set of rules which are common to all Member States.[73] There can, of course, be common standards (capable of eradicating competitive distortions) based on market norms. There can also be common standards (also capable of eradicating competitive distortions) based on the avoidance of extreme unfairness in substance or procedure. However, these standards would surely need to be objective standards. There would be no room for subjective questions such as whether the trader intended to positively exploit a weak consumer or to be unfair or whether or not he realized that he was being unfair. It would be impossible to build a common standard,

---

[71] Recital 2.

[72] 87/102, 85/577, 90/314, 94/47, 97/7 and 99/44 respectively.

[73] For a full discussion of this rationale for harmonization see S. Weatherill, EU Consumer Law and Policy, Elgar, 2005, Chs 2–5 and for a discussion and empirical analysis as to whether businesses are deterred from cross-border trade by differences in rules see S. Vogenauer and S. Weatherill, The European Communities Competence to Pursue the Harmonisation of Contract Law – an Empirical Contribution to the Debate, in S. Voganauer and S. Weatherill, The Harmonisation of European Contract Law, Hart, 2006, 105. Most recently, raising serious questions as to whether the minimum harmonization formula of the UTD can really eradicate competitive distortions see P. Nebbia, Unfair Contract Terms in European Law, Hart, 2007, 13–19.

capable of eradicating competitive distortions, around such subjective criteria.

However, the establishment of a 'level playing field' is not the only rationale for regulating unfair terms. The UTD was the first Directive to make play of the idea that harmonization of consumer protection rules can also lead to market integration by giving consumers the confidence to purchase goods and services in Member States other then their own. This idea seems to have originated in the Sutherland Report of 1992 which identified lack of consumer confidence as a major obstacle to market integration.[74] The argument is that if consumers are not confident and do not engage in cross-border shopping then the market is only really a single one for sellers and suppliers. Since the UTD the same idea has been used as a justification for other Directives, e.g. the Consumer Sales Directive;[75] and the idea continues to flourish in Commission thinking.[76] What is distinctive about this sort of approach is that it views the consumer as more than just a passive beneficiary of a single market which is erected by a combination of liberalization and positive protection (via the law) and viewed a market player whose action (or inaction) is vital in determining whether an integrated single market is realized. The consumer must be nurtured and cajoled to be active: to confidently 'shop abroad'.[77]

In the UTD this thinking is summed up by the following extract from the Preamble:

> Whereas, generally speaking, consumers do not know the rules of law, which, in Member States other than their own, govern contracts for the sale of goods or services; whereas this lack of awareness may deter then from direct transactions for the purchase of goods or services in other Member States.
>
> Whereas, in order to facilitate the establishment of the internal market and to safeguard the citizen in his role as consumer when acquiring goods and services under contracts which are governed by the laws of Member States other than his own, it is essential to remove unfair terms from those contracts.[78]

---

[74] The Internal Market after 1992: Meeting the Challenge; and see S. Weatherill, Prospects for the Development of European Private Law (1995), European Review of Private Law, 3, 307, at 315.

[75] 1999/44/EC, Recital 5 to the Preamble.

[76] See, for example, the Report from the Commission on the Action Plan for Consumer Policy1999–2000 and on the General Framework for Community Activities in Favour of Consumers 1999–2003, COM(2001) 486, 23 August 2001, p. 11.

[77] See S. Weatherill, Prospects for the Development of European Private Law (1995), European Review of Private Law, 3, 307, at 315.

[78] Preamble, Recitals 5 and 6.

Of course this links with the four freedoms and with competition in the internal market. The freedoms are intended to develop the internal market. The freedoms (backed by negative law) are supposed to enhance competition and the efficiency/effectiveness of the internal market, which in turn should enhance trader and consumer freedom and choice. However, on the 'consumer confidence' reasoning outlined, if there is no consumer confidence and no cross-border purchases then there will be fewer customers and less business to compete over. So, positive law is needed to generate consumer confidence, and make for a more integrated and competitive market. This in turn is supposed to make it more likely that the benefits of the freedoms will actually be achieved.

But if we follow the consumer confidence line of reasoning then this appears to have consequences for the level of protection that the UTD should be interpreted to provide. In order to ensure that consumers have the confidence to be active cross-border consumers it has been argued that the provisions of the UTD should be interpreted in a 'determinedly pro-consumer fashion.[79] On this approach it is not enough to base the standards on the avoidance of extreme unfairness or even on trader dominated market norms. Such standards are hardly likely to engender consumer confidence. Surely what is required is an independent standard that balances the substantive interests of the parties and addresses routine problems of lack of transparency, lack of choice and disparity of bargaining power.

We should note that the consumer confidence argument has been vigorously challenged by Wilhelmsson. He argues that consumer confidence is much more likely to be affected by lack of access to justice.[80] This seems clearly to be correct. However, this issue apart, what of the possibility of differing rules on unfair terms nevertheless damaging consumer confidence? Essentially, Wilhelmsson argues that consumer ignorance of the laws of their own Member States does not deter them from buying in their own Member States so that there is little reason to suppose that ignorance of the law of other Member States should deter them from buying in these other Member States.[81] He does, however, accept that there may be some force in the consumer confidence argument

---

[79] S. Weatherill, Prospects for the Development of European Private Law (1995), European Review of Private Law, 3, 307, at 317.

[80] T. Wilhemsson, The Abuse of the Confident Consumer as a Justification for EC Consumer Law (2004) 27 Journal of Consumer Policy, 317 at 329–332; for a discussion see also P. Nebbia, Unfair Contract Terms in European Law, Hart, 2007, 12, and see also Nebbia at 19–21 on whether, if the UTD is not really needed to eradicate competitive distortion on the trader side, it can be justified on the consumer confidence argument alone.

[81] *Ibid.*, at 325.

(for the purposes of minimum directives such as the UTD) on the basis that although consumers may be ignorant of their own law they may assume that it is more protective than that of other countries;[82] although he takes the view that this argument may be overstated and have serious geographical and temporal limitations.[83] The question, then, is whether the consumer confidence agenda should be given any relevance in interpreting what level of protection is intended by a directive such as the UTD. Wilhelmsson seems to take the view that it should not.[84] Although I find his cynicism as to the significance of the consumer confidence argument fairly convincing, I still cannot agree with this conclusion. Surely if we are seeking to discover what purpose was intended to be achieved by a rule, if the legislator declares that a particular purpose was intended and if there is at least some prospect of this purpose being achieved (consumers are surely likely to be more confident where there is a higher level of protection than they will with a lower level) then it is valid to take this into account when interpreting the level of protection intended.

The consumer confidence issue apart, there is another element of the background to the UTD that goes to the level of protection that might be expected. Article 95(3) says that: 'The Commission, in its proposals ... will take as a base a high level of protection.'

Article 153 says that the Community should: '... contribute to the attainment of a high level of consumer protection through ... measures adopted pursuant to Article 95.'

Why is a high level of consumer protection to be taken as a base in consumer protection measures under Article 95? The principal reason seems to be that otherwise there is a risk that the harmonized standard will lead to a reduction in the levels of protection in some Member States.[85] Where, as in the case of the UTD, the Directive is a minimum one,[86] Member States are entitled to provide for a higher level of protection than that contained in the Directive. However, the risk, perhaps, is that some states might reduce standards previously existing by simply copying out a directive and repealing national law on the issue.

The other possibility is that, without a high level of protection, the minimum clause in a given directive might lead to too much variation in approach between Member States and therefore undermine the market integration agenda. The danger is that if the Directive only demands a

---

82   In support of this view see P. Nebbia, Unfair Contract Terms in European Law, Hart, 2007, 12.

83   *Ibid.*, at 326–7.

84   *Ibid.*, at 328 (n. 23).

85   See S. Weatherill, EU Consumer Law and Policy, Elgar, 2005, at 65.

86   Article 8.

relatively low level of protection state X may offer nothing more than is required by the Directive, while state Y may offer a much higher level of protection (but still one which does not operate as a barrier to trade). If a high level of protection is required by the Directive there is less scope for variation between the floor (provided by the Directive) and the ceiling (provided by negative law).

A high level of protection may also be required if the harmonization measure is to have the effect of generating consumer confidence and encouraging consumers to shop across national borders. We should recall that the consumer confidence agenda is to overcome the uncertainty felt by consumers as to the protection which they will receive in countries other than their own. If the harmonized level of protection is low then there will be a risk that it is pitched at a lower level than the pre-existing domestic laws of some states. Consumers from these states will not be confident to purchase good and services in Member States which have done no more than to implement the minimum (and low) level of protection required by the Directive.

Of course it must be recalled that Article 95(3) does not in itself demand that Directives will actually achieve a high level of protection, nor does it guarantee that they will. It simply says that the 'Commission in its proposals ... will take as a base a high level of protection'. As Weatherill points out this could be taken to mean that while the Commission should aspire to a high level of protection it may be legitimate to compromise on a lower level after negotiation.[87] Certainly, it has been held that no provision in the Treaty requires harmonization at the highest level to be found in a Member State.[88] It is also true that the 'high level of protection' concept is fairly vague and imprecise making it 'more political aspiration than independently enforceable legal norm'.[89]

So, where a provision in a directive clearly does not offer a high level of protection there is no prospect of it being challenged on the basis that it is in conflict with the aspiration to achieving a high level of protection. However, it certainly seems reasonable to suggest that, where there is doubt as to the level of protection intended by a provision in the Directive, national courts would be expected to assume that a high level of protection was intended and to interpret the provision accordingly. This surely adds greater weight to the view that the standard of fairness intended is one aimed at addressing the routine unfairness in substance and procedure that arises in relation to consumer contract terms; rather than one based on trader dominated market norms or the avoidance of

---

[87] S. Weatherill, EU Consumer Law and Policy, Elgar, 2005, at 66.

[88] The Deposit Guarantee case (Case C–233/84) and see discussion by S. Weatherill, *ibid.*

[89] S. Weatherill, *ibid.*

extreme unfairness. The concept of unfairness is a classic broad standard that surely does invite some interpretive input from a provision such as Article 95(3).

3.4.4 The Legal and Policy Background and More Specific Conceptions of Fairness

As we have seen, the UTD aims at eradicating competitive distortions, generating consumer confidence and achieving a high level of protection; and that these goals suggest an agenda to address routine unfairness in substance and procedure. However, if we set these goals in the context of broader EC consumer policy it becomes possible to argue that these goals suggest more specific fairness norms. For example, transparency has been a powerful theme in EC consumer law and policy.[90] This thinking can be seen in Article 153 (the old Article 129a) which talks of the 'attainment of a high level of protection through ... specific action ... to provide adequate information to consumers'. Further evidence as to the importance of transparency comes from the various soft law measures produced over the years; and the influence these have had on the Directives adopted. By 'soft law' I mean the various resolutions and action plans which have emanated from the European Commission and the Council of Ministers in relation to consumer policy. The first of these was the Council Resolution of 14 April 1975 which contained an Annex entitled a 'Preliminary Programme of the European Economic Community for a Consumer Protection and Information Policy'.[91] Five basic rights were asserted here: (a) the right to protection of health and safety; (b) the right to protection of economic interests; (c) the right of redress; (d) the right to information and education; and (e) the right of representation (i.e., the right to be heard). This Resolution has been followed by a series of other Resolutions and Action Plans.[92] These have, in varying ways, reasserted the five basic rights from the 1975 Resolution. One thing which is particularly noticeable, and relevant to our discussion, is that consumer information and education seem to have been given an increasingly high priority over the years. The second and third Three Year Action plans begin by citing information and education as top priorities.

---

[90] S. Weatherill, The Role of the Informed Consumer in EC Law and Policy, 1994, 2 Consumer Law Journal, 49; S. Weatherill, EU Consumer Law and Policy, Elgar, 2005, Ch. 4; and G. Howells and T. Wilhelmsson, Has EC Consumer Law Come of Age? 2003, 28 European Law Review, 370.

[91] OJ 1975 C91/2.

[92] Three Year Action Plan 1993–95, COM(93) 378, Three Year Action Plan 1996–98 COM(95) 519.

Such soft law provisions do not have binding legislative effect. However, these soft law consumer initiatives, and their particular emphasis on transparency, have had a very direct effect upon the legislative process. Various Directives have imposed transparency requirements on sellers and suppliers of goods and services. Such requirements are contained in the directives on consumer credit, doorstep selling, package travel, timeshare and distance selling.[93]

Most importantly, in our present context, the 1975 resolution is cited in the Preamble to the UTD.[94] The general idea of transparency in European Community law and policy seems to be that it is a fundamental requirement. The consumer should always be 'conscious of his rights and responsibilities'.[95] The belief is that this will help individual consumers to give informed consent and to enforce their rights; and, further, that it will improve competition between sellers and suppliers.[96] This relates to the market integration agenda. We said above that the development of consumer confidence is viewed as being necessary if consumers are to engage in more cross-border shopping, and therefore contribute to increased market integration. Consumers are more likely to be confident if the terms they are presented with are reasonably transparent. As indicated above, this transparency may also result in improved competition as between traders. The knock-on effect of this may be that there is greater choice as between the terms on offer in the market. It may also be that improved competition forces traders to make some terms fairer in substance. Improved choice and improvements in substantive fairness may also contribute to greater consumer confidence.

It must therefore be arguable that very good levels of transparency are fundamental to the concept of fairness in the UTD (and the UTCCR and any new legislation replacing the UTCCR). In addition, however, the aspiration to a high level of protection and the generation of consumer confidence surely suggest that while transparency is vital it is not necessarily sufficient. We have already seen that transparency cannot necessarily be relied upon to deliver strong protection. There are a number of reasons why consumers may not read terms even where they are transparent.[97] So transparency may not really result in informed consent in many cases. If it does not do this then it may not result in

---

[93] 87/102, 85/577, 90/314, 94/47 and 97/7 respectively and see the discussion in S. Weatherill, EU Consumer Law and Policy, Elgar, 2005, Ch. 4.

[94] Recital 8.

[95] OJ 1975 C91/2.

[96] S. Weatherill, The Role of the Informed Consumer in EC Law and Policy, 1994; C. Willett, Good Faith in Consumer Contracts: Rule, Policy and Principle, in A. Forte, Good Faith in Contract and Property Law, Hart, 1999, 181.

[97] See above at 2.4.2.2 and 2.4.3.5(iii).

improved market discipline either, so that it may not have the planned effect of improving the substantive fairness of terms. In addition, even if transparency does mean that consumers read terms, problems of lack of choice and weaker bargaining power are often likely to mean that they can do little to get them changed. So, to the extent that there is an aspiration to a high level of protection, the appropriate way to read the test of unfairness may be that broader procedural fairness is often required; and that a term can be unfair on substantive grounds even where there has been a reasonable level of procedural fairness.[98]

These arguments notwithstanding, there are ways of viewing the UTD that lead some commentators to the conclusion that the core aim is the avoidance of 'unfair surprise' (with the possible conclusion that the main emphasis should be solely on transparency). Smith makes various arguments to this effect.[99] First of all he focuses on the fact that the UTD only applies to business to consumer contracts.[100] He argues that the terms in such contracts will be subject to strong competitive pressures and will therefore tend to be fair in substance; but that they still may not be understood by consumers. As such, the argument appears to be, the main aim of the UTD is probably to defeat unfair surprise by requiring transparency.[101] However, the problem here is surely that there will be very little competitive pressure on ancillary terms if they are not transparent[102]; and there may be limited competitive pressure on such terms even where they are transparent.[103] To the extent that this was recognized by those drafting the Directive, it may well have been thought that a test of unfairness would need to focus not only on transparency, but also on questions of fairness in substance. A second argument made by Smith relates to the Directive's indicative list of terms that may be regarded as unfair.[104] He points out that this list is largely made up of terms (such as exclusion clauses, penalty clauses, and terms allowing for variation and termination of the contract) that the average consumer is unlikely to understand as they deal with 'temporally distant, low probability' issues.[105] This is undoubtedly correct.[106] However, it does

---

[98] C. Willett, Good Faith in Consumer Contracts: Rule, Policy and Principle, in A. Forte, Good Faith in Contract and Property Law, Hart, 1999, 181, at 184–199.

[99] S. Smith, Atiyah's Introduction to the Law of Contract, OUP, 2005, at 319–20 and 323.

[100] See Articles 1(1) and 2(b).

[101] Smith, *supra*, at 323.

[102] See above at 2.3.2.1.

[103] See above at 2.4.3.4(iv).

[104] See Article 3(3) and the Annex to the UTD (implemented by UTCCR, Regulation 5(5) and Schedule 2.

[105] Smith, *supra*, at 323.

not necessarily follow that those including the indicative list did not also view some of the terms there described (or some versions of such terms) as being unfair in substance.[107]

Smith also points out that the UTD aims at encouraging cross border shopping;[108] and that such cross-border shopping will be deterred if consumers are unfairly surprised by terms.[109] If the conclusion then is that all that is required is transparency, then this seems to miss the point that consumers are also likely to be deterred[110] by other forms of procedural unfairness and by unfairness in substance.[111] Smith then points out that the UTD does not apply to individually negotiated terms.[112] He argues that this demonstrates an agenda to defeat unfair surprise (as a negotiation will not necessarily result in a term being fairer in substance but will at least ensure that the consumer is aware of the term).[113] There is certainly no doubt that negotiation will be likely to enhance consumer understanding of the term in question but that (due to the generally stronger bargaining position of the trader) such negotiation will not necessarily improve fairness in substance.[114] On this basis Smith's argument is convincing. One plausible response seems to be that (as we shall see below) for a term to be treated as having been individually negotiated there must have been an opportunity for the consumer to influence the substance of the term. Of course, an opportunity to influence the substance of the term is not the same as saying that the substance of the term is influenced to the extent that it is now fair in substance. However, if the purported negotiation does not result in the term being (in at least some way) more substantively fair than

---

[106] See the various other reasons that terms are likely to be difficult for consumers to understand – above at 2.3.2.1 and 2.4.2.2.

[107] Of course, it may be that Smith is not actually disputing this. His point may be that such terms *should* generally be viewed as unfair because they are unfair in substance and that this is particularly important because consumers are never likely to understand them.

[108] On this see above at 3.4.3.

[109] Smith, *supra*, at 323.

[110] That is, consumer confidence is likely to be damaged – on consumer confidence see above at 3.4.3.

[111] Again it may be that Smith's point is that the only way to prevent unfair surprise is by eradicating the unfair substantive features of terms as (due to the limitations on the effectiveness of transparency) consumers are likely to be unfairly surprised even where terms are transparent.

[112] Smith, *supra*, at 323; see Articles 3(1) and (2); and see below at 5.2 for discussion of this under the UTCCR.

[113] Smith, *ibid.*

[114] See 5.2 below.

it was before then it may be difficult to establish that the consumer really did have an opportunity to influence its substance.[115] So, it may be that it is implicit in the exclusion of individually negotiated terms that such terms will usually be fairer in substance than they were before. This being the case it would be reasonable to suppose that, in the case of those terms that are subject to control (i.e. those that have not been negotiated), the agenda is also to improve fairness in substance in addition to improving transparency.

Smith's final argument relates to the exclusion from the test of unfairness of terms (insofar as they are in plain and intelligible language) relating to the definition of the main subject matter of the contract or the adequacy of the price or remuneration as against the services or goods supplied in exchange.[116] He points out that exclusion of such terms must mean that the UTD is not concerned solely with unfairness in substance as unfairness in relation to these core obligations is the main type of unfairness in substance. However, Smith argues, if the agenda is transparency it makes sense to exclude these terms as they are likely to be known of and understood anyway.[117] It is certainly true that unfairness in the context of these issues is likely to be the most significant type of unfairness for consumers in most cases given that consumers will be affected by the price and main subject matter in all cases, while they will only be affected by ancillary terms in the less frequent circumstances where these ancillary terms are called into play. It is also true that part of the reason that they are excluded is that they are more likely to be known of and understood. However, it seems likely that they are also excluded because to test them for fairness is perceived to be too much of an incursion into freedom of contract (given that they are indeed the core obligations under the contract). In addition, because such terms are likely to be known of and understood, then, as long as they are in plain language, they are more likely to be subject to strong market discipline. This may result in them being fairer in substance than can be expected in the case of the ancillary terms.[118] So the exclusion of these terms may well be based on the idea that they are likely to be transparent to consumers. However, it is only partly based on this (being based also on a freedom of contract philosophy being thought to be appropriate in the case of such terms). In addition, the transparency of such terms is intended to produce fairer substantive terms. Viewed in this way it does

---

[115] See below at 5.2.2.

[116] See Article 4(2), UTCCR, Regulation 6(2) and see discussion below at 5.8.

[117] Smith, *supra*, 319–20.

[118] See above at 2.3.2.1 and below at 5.8.

not seem that the exclusion of these terms leads to the conclusion that the only agenda in relation to ancillary terms is a transparency agenda.

3.5 The Role of the ECJ

3.5.1 Introduction

Thus far I have emphasized the immediate legal and policy context to the UTD and what this suggests about the way in which the unfairness concept should be understood. However, a key issue is the extent to which the ECJ is prepared to take a view as to the test of unfairness (possibly developing an autonomous EC interpretation of the unfairness concept) and how it should be applied.

3.5.2 Expression and Limitation Issues

Thus far there have been a handful of cases before the ECJ dealing with the test of unfairness itself. First of all, there have been two cases about the manner of expression of the concept of unfairness in implementing measures. There is the case taken by the Commission against the Netherlands.[119] Here, it was stated that Member States, in implementing the UTD, must make the position sufficiently precise and clear so as to enable individuals to be fully aware of their rights under the Directive; and that it was insufficient for Member States to rely on a 'schematic' interpretation of their existing legislation. The issue in the case was whether the Netherlands had failed to properly implement the UTD by not adding to its legislation provisions equivalent to Article 4(2)[120] and 5.[121] The argument of the Dutch government was that 'settled case law' interpreted pre-existing legislation in a way that conformed to the requirements of Articles 4(2) and 5. However, the ECJ rejected this, saying that such an approach was not sufficient.

Then there is *Commission* v. *Spain* dealing with the failure of Spain to repeat (in implementing provisions) the part of Article 5 which says

---

[119] Case C–144/99 [2001] ECR I–3451.

[120] The provision excluding from the test of unfairness terms defining the main subject matter and excluding from the test of unfairness the adequacy of the price in both cases only insofar as the term in question is in plain and intelligible language (see above at 3.2 and below at 5.8.3.1).

[121] The provision requiring terms to be in plain and intelligible language and requiring that if there is doubt as to the meaning of a term it should be interpreted in the way that is most favourable to the consumer.

that the 'most favourable interpretation' rule does not apply in the context of preventive proceedings under Article 7.[122] The ECJ reiterated the point that in such preventive proceedings Article 5 does indeed provide that the 'most favourable interpretation' rule does not apply and that in such cases there should be an 'objective' approach to interpretation. It was explained that interpreting the term in a favourable way in individual proceedings was of immediate benefit to the consumer (the Court's point – presumably – being that in individual proceedings a 'favourable' interpretation for the consumer could involve the term being interpreted not to have the most unfair effect or possibly to have no unfair effects at all). By contrast, the Court pointed out that in preventive proceedings it is not this type of favourable interpretation as such that produces the fairest result for the consumer. (An interpretation that involves the term being substantively fair means that a regulatory body – such as the OFT – cannot demand removal of the term.) What is needed, rather, is an objective approach making it easier in more cases to find a term to be unfair (the Court's point, one imagines, being that such an interpretation may highlight the unfair features of the term and then enable the conclusion that it is unfair and should be removed). Although the Spanish government contended that in preventive proceedings an objective approach to interpretation was indeed taken, the ECJ decided that this requirement of the UTD was not made sufficiently clear and precise as a result of the failure of Spanish law to say expressly (following Article 5) that the most favourable interpretation does not apply in preventive proceedings.[123]

Next, there was the case brought by the Commission against Sweden.[124] In this case the ECJ had to decide whether Sweden had failed to properly implement the Directive by failing to include the indicative list of terms that may be regarded as unfair[125] in the main body of the legislation implementing the UTD. The Court emphasized the principle that directives must be implemented in national law in a sufficiently clear and precise manner as to enable individuals to be able to ascertain their rights under the directive in question.[126] However, it was also emphasized that the 'indicative and non-exhaustive' nature of the list meant that the terms on the list were not necessarily always unfair (and

---

[122] *Commission* v. *Spain* Case C–70/03, 9 September 2004; and for the full content of Article 5 see *ibid*.

[123] For further discussion of this case and its implications within the UK system see 5.10 below.

[124] C–478/99.

[125] Referred to in Article 3(3) of the UTD and set out at the end of the UTD and referred to in Regulation 5(5) of the UTCCR and set out in Schedule 2.

[126] C–478/99, para. 18.

equally that terms other than those on the list could be unfair). As such, the list was found not to create rights that were additional to the test of unfairness itself. In consequence, failure to include it in the main body of the law in question did not mean that the law failed to convey clearly and precisely the full extent of consumer rights under the UTD.[127] The Court also dealt with the fact that Recitals 5 and 8 to the Preamble say that the UTD also aims to improve consumer information as to their rights under the Directive and accepted that the list was a valuable source of such information.[128] However, the Court also accepted the argument of the Swedish government that its inclusion in the preparatory work was satisfactory for these purposes as this is common in the Swedish and broader Nordic tradition, and the preparatory work can be consulted by the public.[129]

Next there is the Cofidis case[130] which was an Article 234 reference from a French court dealing with a limitation rule in French law. Here, the ECJ decided that the requirement to interpret national law in accordance with the wording and purpose of directives meant that the national court should set aside a rule applicable to credit contracts in France preventing terms in such contracts being set aside any later than two years after the contract. Such a restriction made it excessively difficult for consumers to obtain the benefit of the Directive.[131]

So, none of the above cases actually go directly to the criteria for assessing unfairness. We now turn to cases that do go directly to this matter.

3.5.3 The *Oceano* Case

First of all, there is *Oceano Grupo Editorial SA Quintero*.[132] This was another reference under (at that time Article 177 and now) Article 234. The core question in the case does not actually go to the criteria for assessing unfairness. The question was whether the protection provided for by the Directive is such that a national court has the power to declare '*ex officio*' that a term is unfair. It was decided that this was indeed the case. The Court emphasized that the system of protection under the Directive is based on the idea that the consumer is in a weaker position both in terms of bargaining power and knowledge; meaning that he has to

---

127 *Ibid.*, para. 21.

128 *Ibid.*, para. 22.

129 *Ibid.*, para. 23.

130 C–473/00.

131 See paras 35–38.

132 Joined cases C–240/98 and C–244/98 of 27 June [2000] ECR 1–4941.

agree to terms without being able to influence their content.[133] It was said that the aims of Article 6 of the UTD (which provides that unfair terms are not to be binding on the consumer) would not be achieved if courts did not have *ex officio* powers and the issue of unfairness could only be raised by the consumer. This was because legal costs and consumer ignorance would often deter consumers from raising the unfairness of a term.[134] It was also pointed out that Article 7 requires Member States to ensure the existence of adequate and effective means to prevent the continued use of unfair terms and that such means are to include consumer bodies being empowered to seek a decision as to unfairness and an order for removal of such terms from contracts.[135] The Court said that it would be inconceivable to have a system within which such preventive action could be taken and yet, in cases involving a specific contract, only to consider the fairness of a term where the issue was raised by the consumer.[136] The final conclusion, then, was that the Directive requires that national courts must be able to make an *ex officio* assessment as to the unfairness of a term.[137]

Important as this issue is, it does not actually go to the core criteria for determining unfairness. However, the Court did have something separate to say that appears to go to this core issue. It was stated that the term in question 'satisfies all the criteria enabling it to be classed as unfair for the purposes of the Directive'.[138] The term gave exclusive jurisdiction to a court in an area with which the consumers had no connection but which was the principal place of business of the trader. It was said that this might make it difficult for the consumer to make an appearance and that, especially where the claim involved a limited amount of money, the cost of making an appearance might deter the consumer and cause him to forego any remedy or defence. The Court said that such a term therefore fell within para. 1(q) of the indicative list (which refers to terms excluding or hindering the consumer's right to take legal action).[139] The court contrasted the position of the consumer with that of the trader who, by being able to deal with any litigation where he has his principal place of business, could more easily put in an appearance.[140] However, it was at this point that the analysis seemed to

---

[133] Paragraph 25.

[134] Paragraph 26.

[135] On the powers given to the Office of Fair Trading and other bodies in pursuance of Article 7 see below at 5.4.1.

[136] *Oceano, supra*, paras 27–28.

[137] Paragraph 29.

[138] Paragraph 21.

[139] Paragraph 22.

[140] Paragraph 23.

break down. It was said to follow from the foregoing that if, contrary to good faith, such a term caused significant imbalance to the detriment of the consumer then it would be unfair. Of course, if any term has this effect it is unfair. So, this latter statement is superfluous. What is missing is a full explanation as to why a term with the characteristics described 'satisfies all the criteria enabling it to be classed as unfair'. However, we might surmise that what the ECJ was getting at was the idea of a balancing of interests; more particularly a balancing of the relative benefits and detriments accruing to the parties as a result of the term and the way in which these benefits and detriments affect the interests of the parties. This seems to be what the ECJ was doing when referring to the difficulties for the consumer in making a court appearance in a place with which he has no connection and the contrasting ease of making an appearance for the trader. In other words, the term was to the considerable disadvantage of the consumer and the considerable advantage of the trader. On this basis it caused a significant imbalance to the detriment of the consumer and violated the good faith requirement.

3.5.4 The *Freiburger* Case

The other important case on the test of unfairness is *Freiburger Kommunalbauten GmbH Baugesellschaft & Co. K.G.*[141] This case arose out of an Article 234 reference concerning a contract under which a husband and wife had agreed to buy a parking space from Freiburger Kommunalbauten (FK) in a car park to be constructed by FK. The term in question provided that full payment was due by the couple (before the work had even started) on delivery of a security by FK and that in the event of late payment the couple would be required to pay default interest. The security to be delivered by FK was in the form of a guarantee to the effect that the guarantor would guarantee any claims that the couple might have against FK (e.g. for failure to complete the work or for other breaches). The couple had refused to pay until the space was ready and they had accepted it free from defects. The dispute was over their liability to pay default interest under the term as described. The question for the Court was whether such a term was unfair under the test of unfairness in the Directive. It should be noted that the term certainly deviated to the detriment of the consumer from the general default rule in the German Civil Code (the 'BGB'). Paragraph 641 of the BGB provides that payment is only due when the work is accepted by the customer. This is particularly significant. This is because the case was taken under the German Standard Contracts Act of 1976 (the 'AGBG') (which was

---

[141] C–237/02, 1 April 2004.

viewed as adequately reflecting the requirements of the Directive[142]). Under Article 9(1) of the AGBG a term was unfair if 'contrary to the requirement of good faith' it places the other party at an 'unreasonable disadvantage'. Under Article 9(2) an 'unreasonable disadvantage is deemed to exist if … a provision … cannot be reconciled with the essential basic principles of the statutory rule from which it deviates'.

The couple argued[143] that the clause offended the general principle in civil law systems that mutual obligations should be performed contemporaneously. It upset the 'equality of arms' between the parties, placing the consumer in a weak position particularly in cases where there was a defect in the construction. (The view that the position of the consumer is weakened is, of course, based on the fact that if the payment has already been made then it cannot be withheld in cases where there is a complaint as to the work done. This weakens the bargaining position of consumers in resolving the issue, making it more likely that they will need to take the matter to court.) These arguments were expressly linked to paras 1(o) and (b) of the indicative list. Paragraph 1(o) focuses on the matter of contemporaneousness and describes a term 'obliging the consumer to fulfil all his obligations when the seller or supplier does not perform his'. Paragraph 1(b) focuses on the legal rights of consumers in cases of total or partial non-performance by the trader. It refers to terms 'inappropriately excluding or limiting the legal rights of the consumer' in such circumstances 'including the option of offsetting a debt owed to the seller or supplier against any claim which the consumer may have against him'.

It was also argued by the couple that the term was unfair on the basis that it was unusual, that it was unclear and that the supplier was in a monopoly position.[144]

FK argued that the term was not unfair. They argued that the disadvantage of paying the price before performance (which, it was accepted, changed the order of performance laid down in the default rule in BGB Article 641) was counterbalanced by the Bank guarantee which would ensure that appropriate sums would be paid to them in the event of non-performance and defective performance. In addition, it was argued that the provision for early payment reduced the need for the builder to finance the work through borrowing and thereby allowed the builder to charge a lower price.[145]

---

142 The German law on unfair contract terms is now contained in the updated BGB, Articles 307–310.

143 At para. 17.

144 *Ibid.*

145 At para. 16.

First the Court emphasized the point already made in the *Commission v. Sweden* to the effect that a term is not automatically unfair on the basis that it is on the indicative list;[146] and that the criteria for assessing unfairness is the general test in Article 3(1), i.e. the significant imbalance/good faith test.[147] Second, the Court emphasized that, in making this assessment, it is provided in Article 4(1) of the Directive that account should be taken of the nature of the goods or services and all the circumstances at the conclusion of the contract.[148] In this context, the Court said that it was necessary to consider the consequences of the term under the law applicable to the contract and that this involved consideration being given to the national law.[149] From this it was said to follow that, although the Court could interpret the general criteria for unfairness in the Directive (i.e. significant imbalance/good faith test), it should not rule on the application of these criteria to a particular term, this being a matter which should be considered in the light of the particular circumstances of the case in question.[150] This, in other words, was a matter for the national courts to decide.[151]

However, the Court, in reaching this conclusion, did have some explaining to do in relation to the decision in *Oceano*. In that case, as we saw, it was essentially decided that the term in question was unfair. The Court in *Freiburger* explained this on the basis that (as was said in the *Oceano* case itself) the term in *Oceano* satisfied all the criteria to be viewed as unfair by the ECJ. It was suggested above that this appears to have been based on the idea that the term in *Oceano* operated to the considerable disadvantage of the consumer and the considerable advantage of the trader. In *Freiburger* the Court said that the term in *Oceano* was solely to the benefit of the trader and contained no benefit to the consumer. As such, whatever the nature of the contract, the term undermined the effectiveness of the legal protection of the rights granted to consumers by the Directive. It was therefore possible to conclude that the term was unfair without having to consider all the circumstances and without having to consider the advantages and disadvantages that the term might have under the national law applicable to the contract.[152] The Court said that it was clear from the submissions that this was not the case here in the *Freiburger* case. We must presume that the Court was

---

146 At para. 20.
147 At para. 19.
148 At para. 20.
149 *Ibid.*
150 At para. 22.
151 At para. 25.
152 At para. 23.

referring here to the benefits claimed to accrue to the consumer in the provision of the security and in a lower price.

Apart from anything else, then, the decision tells us that the ECJ will interpret the meaning of the test of unfairness; but that it will not interfere with the application of the test to a particular term – such an assessment of all the circumstances, including the relationship of the term to the broader national legal framework, is for the national courts (unless, it seems, as in a case like *Oceano*, the term is solely to the benefit of the trader and contains no benefit to the consumer). It is certainly understandable that the ECJ are cautious about getting involved in relation to application of the law to the facts and dealing with the relationship of the unfairness concept with the broader national legal context. At least three plausible justifications for such an approach had been given by the Advocate General in his initial opinion on the case: maintenance of a clear demarcation of powers between the national courts and the ECJ; economical use of remedies; and sensitivity to the distinctive national legal context of the term.[153]

We are therefore left with some uncertainty as to the prospects for the ECJ to interfere with a national decision as to the application of the test to a term. The Court will not do so unless the term is solely to the benefit of the trader and contains no benefit to the consumer. The first instinct might be to think that the Court will only take such a view in exceptional circumstances. However, it is submitted that this is not so clear. It depends, self-evidently, on when exactly the Court views a term as being solely to the benefit of the trader, there being no benefit to the consumer. Of course, it is very difficult to assess this without actually discussing the approach taken to interpreting the test itself. So we now turn to the question as to the interpretation of the test; and, in due course, to the way in which this might affect the immediately preceding question as to the meaning of 'benefit' within the test.

As in the *Oceano* case, the Court did not deal in any systematic way with the meaning of good faith and significant imbalance and the relationship between these concepts; with the question as to whether these are separate elements under the test; with the relationship between questions of procedural and substantive unfairness; or with what factors might be relevant to procedural fairness (the focus of the discussion was purely on the substantive features of the term and the substantive advantages that might counterbalance any disadvantage caused by the term). It seems that we can discern the following from the *Freiburger* case as to the ECJ notion of unfairness:

---

[153] Opinion of the Advocate General, 25 September 2003.

1. It does seem to be confirmed by *Freiburger* that this sort of term (i.e. one altering the order of performance from that provided for under a default rule) is at least suspect.
2. It also seems to be confirmed that balancing of interests is relevant (i.e. that the less the detrimental features of the term are balanced out by some benefit – whether in the term itself or in another term – the more likely it should be to be unfair and vice versa). This particular approach to interest balancing clearly involves what has already been described as an assessment as to overall substantive fairness. Above it was pointed out that that such an assessment involves considering whether the term under scrutiny is balanced out by a benefit provided by another term that can be said to amount to a 'fair price' for the detriment caused by the term under scrutiny; and that there are various different ways in which this might be measured.[154] The Court did not specify whether this assessment was relevant to the significant imbalance/detriment issue, the good faith issue or both; indeed, as we have seen already, the Court did not specify whether significant imbalance/detriment and good faith are separate elements under the test. What was clear was that if there is no benefit for the consumer the ECJ seems to be prepared to go beyond interpreting the test and to actually find the term to be unfair; while if there is such a benefit the ECJ are not prepared to do this. So, the ECJ appears to be prepared to make a preliminary assessment as to overall substantive fairness. This involves considering whether there are benefits to consumers that might counterbalance the detriment caused by the term under scrutiny. The lack of any such benefits conferred by other terms leads the ECJ to the conclusion that the term is conclusively unfair; but the existence of such benefits leads the Court to pass the matter back to the national courts to decide more precisely on how to measure the worth of these benefits in deciding whether there is overall fairness in substance. So, it is then up to the national courts to decide between the various models suggested above and how the chosen model should apply to the term in question.[155]

As already indicated, it seems that the ECJ found the existence of benefits in the guarantee provided to the couple and/or in the fact that the price may have been lower as a result of the provision for prepayment. What was not clear from the judgement is exactly how the ECJ went about measuring the issue. In the case of the guarantee provided to consumers the obvious approach is to ask whether it genuinely enables consumers to be protected against the detrimental

---

[154] See above at 2.4.1 and 2.4.3.3.
[155] See above at 2.4.3.3.

effects of the term requiring prepayment.[156] The problem with prepayment (apart from having to find the money to pay at an earlier stage and – from this point – not earning interest on this money in one's own bank account) is that the consumer is in a weak bargaining position if the work is not performed or is defective. The consumer is not in a position to withhold payment and may be required to go to court to obtain a refund and/or compensation. So, the question should probably be whether the guarantee means that the consumer's position is improved by comparison with this situation, e.g. because it requires payment of appropriate sums to the consumer whenever the consumer asserts that the work has not been done or is defective, it then being for the supplier of the service to take action against the consumer to recover the money if the supplier believes that the consumer's claim is invalid. There is insufficient information in the report to assess whether the guarantee in question was of this nature. If it was, then the suggestion might be that the general ECJ approach in relation to this type of alleged benefit would be to insist that it genuinely cancels out at least some of the negative effects that the term under scrutiny would otherwise have on the consumer.

It is also not clear what kind of assessment the ECJ made in relation to the claim that the price of the service was lower than if prepayment had not been required. Above it was suggested that there are various ways in which such a claim might be measured.[157] So, it could be concluded (a) that the price must be lower than it would otherwise have been simply because the price is subject to market discipline; (b) that the price must be lower than it would otherwise have been because the price reflects the average market price for the goods or services in question; or (c) it might only be accepted that price is lower than it would otherwise have been where the trader can (i) identify specific costs or risks to which he is exposed if he does not use the term that is detrimental to the consumer, (ii) identify the amount extra that he would have to charge without protection against this risk and (iii) explain why the costs or risks cannot be absorbed in some alternative way. Certainly, there is no evidence to suggest that the ECJ proceeded on either of the first two possible measures (i.e. (a) or (b)). What of approach (c)? It will be recalled that it was argued that the provision for early payment reduced the need for the builder to finance the work through borrowing and thereby allowed the builder to charge a lower price. So, the trader had actually made a plausible argument as to costs that he would need to incur in financing the work where prepayment was not received. To the extent

---

[156] See the discussion above at 2.4.3.3.

[157] *Ibid.*

that the Court took this argument into account, the suggestion seems to be that the Court favours something closer to approach (c). Having said this it is not apparent that the trader explained how much higher the price would have been if the trader had faced these costs or why these costs could not be absorbed in some alternative way. So, it may be that the ECJ view is that these latter two elements ((c)(ii) and (c)(iii)) are not required.

What is not clear is what the attitude of the ECJ would be where the only alleged benefit comes in the form of a lower price. Is the ECJ view that such a benefit (established on the (c)(i) criterion) is sufficient in its own right to lead to the conclusion that the issue should be passed back to the national court? Alternatively, was the guarantee the important benefit for the ECJ in this case? Did the possibly lower price simply count as a potentially additional benefit; a benefit that would not be viewed as sufficient in its own right? Certainly, in view of the consumer confidence and protection goals of the Directive, it is arguable that the ECJ should not accept an argument that the price represents a benefit in its own right unless a strong case has been made to the effect that not using the term would involve specific extra costs or risks that could not be absorbed; and that the use of the term therefore can be viewed as having significantly reduced the price. Even if such a case can be made, it is arguable that the price should not be regarded as a sufficient benefit in its own right in cases (such as *Freiburger*) where the nature of the contract is such that it could also have included a term offering concrete protection against the detrimental effects of the term under scrutiny (assuming that the use of such a term does not impose an undue burden on the trader).[158] Such an approach would surely be in keeping with the consumer confidence and protection goals of the Directive.

It is also unclear what the attitude of the ECJ would be to an argument that the benefit to a consumer comes in the form of basic access to goods or services, i.e. the argument that it would be uneconomical to provide goods or services at all without the term.[159] This argument was not raised on the facts of the case and neither did the facts of the case suggest such a benefit; so that it is simply unclear as to what the view of the ECJ might be. The ECJ could refuse to recognize this form of benefit. If they were to accept that, in principle, this form of benefit could be recognized they might take a restrictive approach. So, as in relation to the argument that the price is lower as a result of the term, it might be that the least that would be

---

[158] See the discussion above at 2.4.3.3.
[159] See the discussion above at 2.4.3.3.

expected by the ECJ is an explanation as to the costs and risks associated with supplying the goods without the term and why these costs and risks are significant. Then there is the question as to whether, even if the consumer is now deemed to be receiving a benefit, the ECJ would view this as being negated if the trader could have, but has not, used a term that could have provided concrete protection against the term.

3. A further point as to the *Freiburger* approach to balance is that it is not clear (and at present it is left for the national courts to work out) exactly what role transparency should play and how this should interact with the substantive features of the terms. From what the ECJ has said we might take the impression that it is working with a purely substantive model of unfairness (at least in terms of what it is prepared to dictate to the national courts). As we have seen, the view in *Freiburger* was that the ECJ was only prepared to 'interpret' the test and that it was for the national courts to apply it, except where there were no benefits at all for the consumer, in which case the ECJ would say that the term was unfair. If this refers simply to substantive benefits (i.e. benefits in relation to the substantive rights and obligations) then the suggestion is that the ECJ interpretation of the test is, in fact, one in which only such substantive factors are relevant (or at least that the ECJ is only prepared to assert control over aspects of the test dealing with the substantive features of the terms).

Of course, one clear implication of this sort of approach is that that a term offering no benefit to the consumer (in a contract that does not contain any other provision that could be said to counterbalance this) can be unfair on these grounds alone. In other words this would be an approach within which a term can be unfair on the basis of its substantive features irrespective of whether there has been what would be a reasonable level of procedural fairness (this taking us a step further away from a freedom-oriented approach and arguably being entirely appropriate in the light of the goals of the Directive[160]). There does not appear to have been any consideration of the issue of transparency in *Oceano*. In other words there does not seem to have been any suggestion that transparency of the term could have justified this term which contained no substantive benefit for the consumer. The suggestion, then, may be that transparency cannot save a term that is sufficiently substantively unfair at least where there is no countervailing substantive benefit for the consumer.

However, if transparency is not a factor that the ECJ will consider then, this could surely also place limits on the level of protection. The argument was made above that even if there is overall substantive balance

---

[160] See above at 2.4.3.5 and 3.4.4.

there is surely a legitimate consumer interest in being aware of the overall substantive picture (the detrimental term and the favourable term[161]). The ECJ did not say anything expressly on this issue. However, as we know, transparency is arguably fundamental to EC consumer policy and the goals of the Directive. In addition, as we shall discuss further below,[162] it is arguable that transparency should be regarded as a fundamental element of good faith (i.e. just as important to 'interpretation' of the test as is the concept of a substantive benefit). So, if the ECJ can conclude that where there is no substantive benefit to the consumer the term is definitely unfair, should it not also be possible to say that that where there is significant substantive detriment (even although there are some substantive benefits) but no transparency, then the term is unfair.

Freiburger does not really rule this out. In *Freiburger* the key element of the contract that the ECJ accepted might balance out the early payment provision (the guarantee) would probably be transparent to the consumers given that it was handed over specifically at a point after the contract. It may then have been that the ECJ did not feel the need to emphasize what they might insist upon if required, i.e. that overall substantive balance without transparency is unacceptable. It may even have been that the ECJ viewed the concept of a 'benefit' as including transparency. In other words, if there is no transparency this cancels out any countervailing substantive benefit (there being transparency in *Freiburger*, the issue did not arise). The fact is that the position remains unclear.[163] What *is* clear is that an approach within which transparency is insisted upon as a fundamental requirement (i.e. as being *necessary*) need not be an approach within which transparency is regarded as always being *sufficient*. Transparency can be regarded as a requirement. At the same time we can hold to the position suggested above (which appears to emerge from *Oceano* and be confirmed in *Freiburger*) to the effect that where there is no substantive benefit to the consumer the term is unfair irrespective of transparency.[164]

---

[161] See above at 2.4.3.4(ii).

[162] See below at 3.5.5.2.

[163] Further on this problem under the UK law see 5.7.1 and 5.9 below.

[164] Further on the Freiburger case see P. Rott, What is the Role of the ECJ in EC Private Law? (2005) 1 Hanse Law Review 6 at 11–12; M.W. Hesselink (2006) 2 European Review of Contract Law, 366; N. Reich (2006) Protection of the Consumer's Economic Interests by EC Contract Law – Some Follow Up Remarks, 28 Sydney Law Review 37 at 50.

3.5.5 The Prospects for Further Development of an Autonomous EC Interpretation of Unfairness

3.5.5.1 Introduction

Now it is appropriate to consider whether the ECJ is likely to show an appetite to further develop an autonomous EC interpretation of the test of unfairness; what the content of any such interpretation might be; and the extent to which it would draw upon the good faith and fairness traditions in the Member States.[165]

There are certainly reasons to suppose that there may be limited prospects for the development of a *comprehensive* autonomous ECJ notion of unfairness. First, it depends on the ECJ having an opportunity to deal with cases that raise the core issues as to the test of unfairness. They have already been denied an opportunity by the UK House of Lords, who have refused to make a reference to the ECJ on the test in the first and only case so far to be heard by the House of Lords[166] (an issue which we shall be returning to later). (As we have seen, there have only been two cases before the ECJ from other Member States that went directly to the test of unfairness.) A further factor that must be borne in mind is that the ECJ may be cautious about being overly prescriptive in relation to guidance on a test of unfairness (and we have just noted that nothing has been said expressly on transparency so far and there is uncertainty as to whether it is regarded as a core issue under the test). As we have seen, the ECJ will not interfere with the application of the law to the facts by national courts.[167] Of course, this is understandable but one might argue that we could legitimately expect a more interventionist approach in relation to the interpretation of the test itself.[168] After all, in the *Freiburger* case, as we saw, the Court did emphasize that, while it would not rule on application of the test to a particular term, it would interpret the test itself. There might be a considerable temptation to do so in the future given its core importance in the Directive and the fact that the agenda of the Directive is to have a harmonized approach to consumer contract terms. There are significant differences in the national traditions in dealing with such terms. As such, the ECJ might view itself as having a responsibility to make a significant contribution to the development of a

---

165 Generally on the likely reluctance of the ECJ to play a significant role in developing autonomous private law concepts and why this might be a good thing see C.U. Schmid (2006) The ECJ as a Constitutional and a Private Law Court, ZERP DP (Centre for European Law and Politics, University of Bremen) 4/06.

166 *DGFT* v. *First National Bank* [2001] 3 WLR 1297.

167 See the *Freiburger* case discussed at 3.5.4 above.

168 See P. Nebbia, Unfair Contract Terms in European Law, Hart, 2007, 169–171.

convergent EC jurisprudence on the concept of unfairness; effectively mediating between the traditions in the development of an autonomous concept. Putting this in another way the ECJ might facilitate what Weatherill describes as 'an indirect channel [of communication] between national courts in different states'.[169]

At the same time, we may find the ECJ conscious of the difficulties that national systems might find in transplanting notions of fairness that have not come from within the national tradition, but have come from the ECJ and from other countries with different social and economic systems and expectations[170] and different terminological and conceptual approaches to fairness. In addition, it has been suggested that the ECJ may view the UTD more as a consumer protection measure and (following this) take the view that 'consumer protection, effectiveness and uniformity of remedies are far more important than the uniformity of substantive concepts [such as the test of unfairness]'.[171]

With these caveats in mind, we can now consider (to the extent that the ECJ *is* inclined to develop an autonomous approach to unfairness) what the sources and content of this might be.

3.5.5.2 Transparency

In particular, as we have seen, it is noticeable that the ECJ has said nothing on the role of transparency within the test; so that it is simply not clear whether the ECJ regards – or might in the future regard – transparency as fundamental to fairness. We have already noted that the goals of the Directive could be viewed as arguing for an interpretation that views transparency as being fundamental to fairness;[172] and clearly any autonomous EC interpretation of the unfairness test should draw strongly on the legal and policy goals of the UTD. However, as has also been suggested above, the ECJ might also seek to construct an autonomous EC interpretation of unfairness by reference to the traditions of the various Member States. It is clear that transparency is a core requirement in the good faith traditions of many Member States. This was

---

[169] S. Weatherill, EU Consumer Law and Policy, Elgar, 2005, at 122.

[170] G. Teubner, Legal Irritants: Good Faith in British Law or How Unifying Law Ends Up in New Divergences (1998) 61 Modern Law Review 11; P. Legrand, Against a European Civil Code (1997) 62 Modern Law Review 44; and N. Cohen, The Effect of the Duty of Good Faith on a Previously Common Law System: The Experience of Israeli Law, in R. Brownsword, N. Hird and G. Howells, Good Faith in Contract: Concept and Context, Ashgate, 1999, 189–212.

[171] P. Nebbia, Unfair Contract Terms in European Law, Hart, 2007, 171.

[172] See above at 3.4.4.

highlighted for an English audience in *Interfoto Picture Library Ltd* v. *Stilleto Visual Programs*.[173] Bingham LJ (as he then was) said that,

> ... in many civil law systems good faith does not simply mean that they should not deceive each other, a principle which any legal system must recognize; its effect is perhaps most aptly conveyed by such metaphorical colloquialisms as 'playing fair, coming clean' or 'putting ones cards face up on the table'. It is in essence a principle of fair and open dealing.

This description of the importance of transparency to good faith could relate to a whole host of pre- and post-contractual situations in which 'coming clean' about something could be significant. In Scandinavian law a duty of disclosure is viewed as an important element of the general good faith principle.[174] 'Coming clean' certainly covers being open about the terms themselves, i.e. making them transparent. Transparency is certainly relevant to the German concept of good faith as it applies to the control of standard terms[175] (although it does not appear to be as important as the substantive features of the term).[176] Indeed, in the only House of Lords decision so far on the UTCCR, Lord Bingham has continued to draw upon the idea that transparency is relevant to good faith in the context of the fairness of terms.[177] We will deal with the case in more detail below, but, in essence, he has said that good faith (in the context of the test of unfairness) is about 'fair and open dealing'; and that open dealing is about the terms being transparent in various ways.[178]

'Coming clean' might have implications other than in relation to the presentation of the terms of the contract. For example, good faith as a general principle in France has been used as the basis for the doctrine of obligations d'information which requires disclosure of important *facts*.[179]

---

[173] [1989] QB 433 at 439.

[174] See T. Wilhelmsson, Good Faith and the Duty of Disclosure in Commercial Contracting – The Nordic Experience, R. Brownsword, N. Hird and G. Howells, Good Faith in Contract: Concept and Context, Ashgate, 1999, 165–187.

[175] N. Reich, La Principe de la transparence des clauses limitatives relatives au contenudes prestations dans le droit allemande des conditions generales des contrats, in J. Ghestin (ed.), Les Clauses Limitatives on exoneratoires de responsabilitie en Europe (1990), 77–93.

[176] See H.-W. Micklitz, The Politics of Judicial Co-operation in the EU, CUP, 2005, 374.

[177] *DGFT* v. *First National Bank* [2001] 3 WLR 1297.

[178] *Ibid.*, at 1308.

[179] See M. Hesselink, The New European Private Law, Kluwer, 2002, at 205; R. Sefton-Green, Duties to Inform Versus Party Autonomy, in G.A. Janssen and R. Schulze (eds), Information Rights and Obligations, Ashgate, 2005, 171; J. Ghestin, The Pre-

Disclosure of important facts could be relevant in various contractual contexts. However, as we shall see below, if it was developed in the context of rules on unfair terms it might require disclosure of information as to facts affecting the risks provided for by the terms and the likelihood that the terms will be relied upon.[180]

Another question as to the role of transparency in any autonomous interpretation of unfairness is as to the *level* of transparency that might be required. We have already seen that the goals of the Directive suggest that a high level of transparency should be required. However, there is, in fact, another dimension to the EC context which *might* be taken to suggest a lower level of transparency. This is the ECJ jurisprudence on consumers as it has been developed in the variety of other contexts in which EC law bears on the consumer interest. What has emerged is that the ECJ holds the average consumer to be 'reasonably well-informed and circumspect'[181] (a notion of the consumer that has now found its way into the recently adopted Unfair Commercial Practices Directive[182]). It is well-known that this notion of the consumer is less protective than certain models that arise at national level in other Member States, including, for example, the notion of the consumer as the 'casual observer'.[183] The 'reasonably well-informed and circumspect' model has led to the view, for example, that a '10% Extra Free' sticker on a Mars Bar would not mislead consumers[184] and that use of the word '*clinique*' in relation to a cosmetic product would not mislead consumers into believing that the cosmetic had medicinal properties.[185]

The question is whether the 'reasonably well-informed and circumspect consumer' model might suggest a consumer who does not need such a high level of protection in order to understand the terms.[186] It

---

contractual Duty to Disclose Information, in D. Harris and D. Tallon (eds), Contract Law Today, OUP, 1989; and J.H.M. Van Erp, The Pre-Contractual Stage, in A. Hartkamp *et al.*, (eds), Towards A European Civil Code, (Kluwer), 363.

[180] See further below at 6.4.2.9 where it is suggested that this could be argued to be required in certain circumstances under the unfairness test in the UTCCR.

[181] Case C–210/96, *Gut Springheide GmbH* v. *Oberkreisdirektor des Kreises Steinfurt* (1998) ECR I–4657 (para. 37).

[182] 2005/29/EC, Recital 18.

[183] Case C–210/96, *Gut Springheide GmbH* v. *Oberkreisdirektor des Kreises Steinfurt* (1998) ECR I–4657 (para. 37); and contrast the approach of the Belgian Cour de Cassation in the Judgement of 12 October 2000 and the German Bundesgrichtshof in the Judgement of 20 December 2001: I ZR 215/98.

[184] *Verein gegen Unwesen in Handel und Gewerbe* v. *Mars BmbH*, C–470/93 [1995] ECR 1–1923.

[185] C–315/92 [1994] ECR 1–317.

[186] See P. Nebbia, Unfair Terms in European Law, Hart, 2007, 140.

is certainly possible that in assessing the appropriate level of transparency in the context of contract terms the ECJ might draw upon the 'reasonably well-informed and circumspect consumer' model and determine the appropriate level by balancing this notion against the consumer confidence and high level of protection policies. In fact we shall see below that the House of Lords may not have required a particularly high level of transparency in the first case that they have heard under the UTCCR. It has been suggested that this might be viewed as being in line with the ECJ approach.[187] However, three points must be borne in mind here. First, the consumer confidence and high level of protection policies are much more directly related to the UTD itself and might arguably be given precedence on this basis. Secondly, it has been accepted that a higher level of transparency can be required where local 'social, cultural or linguistic' factors suggest it is necessary;[188] so that, if the ECJ takes the view that such factors (as they apply in any particular country) mean that consumers might not be so well-informed and circumspect in relation to contract terms, then a higher standard of transparency (than would otherwise be expected) might be applied. Third, and very importantly I would suggest, the 'reasonably well-informed and circumspect consumer' model has tended to be relied upon in cases where the issue is significantly different from that arising in relation to standard terms. The 'reasonably well-informed and circumspect' model has been developed partly in the context of cases dealing with whether domestic measures are incompatible with Article 28 EC;[189] so that the approach must be seen in the context of the goal of furthering market integration, and the 'ambition to open national markets and de-crystallize consumer habits'.[190] By contrast, while the UTD aims at market integration, it seeks to achieve it by positive regulation. This is at least partly on the assumption that Community law needs to take positive protective and confidence building steps. A good level of transparency can be argued to be necessary for this protection and confidence. It is true that some cases in which the 'reasonably well-informed and circumspect' model has been developed the law in issue has been the Misleading Advertisements Directive[191] which is (in common with the UTD) a measure of positive EC law.

---

187 R. Bradgate, R. Brownsword and C. Twigg-Flesner, The Impact of Adopting A General Duty to Trader Fairly, Report for DTI, 2003, 38.

188 C–2220/98 [2000] ECR 1–117; this 'social, cultural or linguistic' element has also found its way into the consumer concept in the Unfair Commercial Practices Directive – see 2005/29/EC, Recital 18.

189 See, for example, *Estee Lauder* v. *Lancaster* C–220/98.

190 See P. Nebbia, Unfair Terms in European Law, Hart, 2007, 140.

191 84/50/EC; see, for example, the *Nissan* case (Criminal Proceedings against X [1992] ECR I–131.

However, two differences can be suggested. First, in misleading advertisement cases the issue is the extent to which a consumer is likely to be misled by a form of communication that consumers are bombarded with and engage with all the time. This form of communication tends to be used to convey a message on core (price and main subject matter) issues that consumers would always be likely to focus on. In this light it is likely that quite a lot of consumers may in fact be quite circumspect/cynical etc. But the issue in the context of unfair terms is different. Here we have terms expressed via an essentially intransparent medium, on ancillary issues that are not normally focused on/thought about. It is at least possible that the ECJ would take the view that even the reasonably well-informed and circumspect consumer (who can understand that 'X% Extra Free' stickers should not be taken too seriously) will need a fairly high level of transparency in order to help him in the context of standard terms. A second difference that has been suggested is that the Misleading Advertisement Directive is more concerned with facilitating parallel imports and that the approach taken may have been strongly influenced by the desire to encourage cross-border competition.[192]

The suggestion, then, is that if the ECJ were to take a view on transparency within the test (rather than leaving this to national courts) that a contextual distinction could be argued for as between the barrier to trade and misleading advertisement cases on the one hand and those on unfair terms on the other hand. In short, a reasonably high level of transparency could be argued to be needed in the case of unfair terms. However, there is a final caveat here. The ECJ could opt for an approach within which it insists upon at least some basic transparency and says that without this a term should always be unfair; while refusing to get involved in determining the level of transparency (i.e. leaving this as a question for the national courts). This might be attractive to the Court in minimising its involvement and allowing national courts to apply the test in the context of local conditions.[193] However, it is arguable that if there is a real ambition to have a high level of protection, consumer confidence and at least a reasonably similar approach to presentation of terms (that can help remove competitive distortion), then there should be a more ambitious approach to transparency. In other words, there should be an attempt to set a reasonably high level of transparency. (Whether the level

---

[192] See P. Nebbia, *Unfair Terms in European Law*, Hart, 2007, 140.

[193] And there may be support for this in the *Buet* decision (*Buet* v. *Ministere Public* [1989] ECR 1235) and see discussion by P. Nebbia, *Unfair Terms in European Law*, Hart, 2007, 141.

of transparency thought to be appropriate by the House of Lords matches up is an issue to which we shall return below.[194])

3.5.5.3 Other Values

In constructing an autonomous interpretation of the test of unfairness the ECJ might also draw upon values other than transparency from the traditions of other Member States. In other Member States where good faith in particular has a very significant pedigree it is used to import all sorts of loosely fairness-oriented functions into the law.

Quite apart from being used to control unfair contract terms[195] good faith is used to supplement contracts as well as to set standards of behaviour pre-contractually and in relation to performance and enforcement.[196] The common denominator in relation to good faith seems to be that parties should limit the pursuit of their own interests in some way and respect the interests of the other party. The Dutch Hoge Raad, for example, has equated good faith with taking account of the legitimate interests of the other party.[197] In fact this formulation found its way into the 'definition' of good faith in the Preamble to the Directive where it is said that 'the requirement of good faith may be satisfied by the seller or supplier where he deals fairly and equitably with the other party whose legitimate interests he has to take into account'.[198] This, of course, is broadly in congruence with the idea expressed above that fairness is about balancing the interests of the parties.[199] However, the literature and jurisprudence show that, depending on context, this general idea can trigger a whole variety of values. These include respect for the legitimate expectations of the other, avoidance of opportunism, avoidance of

---

[194] See below at 5.5.4.2(iv)(f).

[195] For example, in the German AGB 1976, Article 9 (now BGB, Article 307).

[196] See M. Hesselink, Good Faith, in A. Hartkamp *et al.*, (eds), Towards a European Civil Code, Kluwer, 2004, 471; and see Chen-Wishart, Contract Law, OUP, 2005, 386–7.

[197] HR, 15 November 1957; and in civil law generally good faith is thought of as requiring that one party does not take advantage of the other's trust by securing an unduly advantageous contract (on this see H. Collins, Good Faith in European Contract Law (1994) 14 OJLS 229, 250 and H.-W. Micklitz, The Politics of Judicial Co-operation in the EU, CUP, 2005, 372–3).

[198] Recital 16.

[199] See above at 2.4.1. At this very general level the only difference from fairness as a balancing of the interests of the parties is that good faith has a slightly more moralistic flavour in that it focuses not so much on the role of the law in balancing interests but on the *obligation of the parties* to respect the interests of each other.

backsliding, avoidance of encouraging misplaced reliance, acting with good motive, acting cooperatively and acting proportionately.[200] It is quite plausible that values such as these could develop into forms that have relevance in the context of the fairness of the substantive terms of a contract and the process leading to the contract; and could find their way into an autonomous ECJ concept of fairness.

Apart from these general values deriving from other Member States we should recall that the legal and policy background to the UTD also suggests going beyond transparency (e.g. in considering other matters of procedural fairness and, where appropriate, in focusing principally on the substantive features of the term).[201] We have already noted that the autonomous notion of unfairness that has emerged thus far seems to recognize that terms can be unfair on principally substantive grounds.[202] The good faith traditions of other Member States would also appear to support an approach that takes into account procedural factors other than transparency. So, for example, the Dutch concept appears to take into account whether one party has been prepared to negotiate with the other;[203] while German law considers whether any choice was available to the customer.[204] In addition, the good faith traditions of other Member States would appear to support an approach in which terms can be viewed as unfair on principally substantive grounds. This has been emphasized by a German scholar;[205] who, in commenting on the approach to the UTD in English law, has criticized what he views as an undue fixation in English

---

[200] See M. Hesselink, Good Faith, in A. Hartkamp *et al.*, (eds), Towards a European Civil Code, Kluwer, 2004, 471; F. Martinez-Sanz, Good Faith of the Parties, in H. Schulte-Nölke and R. Schulze, European Contract Law in Community Law, Bundesanzeiger, 2002,127; H.-W. Micklitz, The Politics of Judicial Co-operation in the EU, CUP, 2005, 372–3; and D. Friedmann, Good Faith and Remedies for Breach of Contract, in J. Beatson and D. Friedmann (eds), Good Faith and Fault in Contract Law, OUP, 1995, 399, 400–1.

[201] See 3.4.4 above.

[202] See 3.5.3 and 3.5.4 above.

[203] See H. Beale, Legislative Control of Fairness, in J. Beatson and D. Friedman, Good Faith and Fault in Contract Law, OUP, 1995, 231, 244.

[204] See N. Reich, Le Principe de la Transparence des clauses limitatives relatives au contenu des prestations dans le droite Allemande des conditions general des contrats, in Gestin (ed.), les clauses limitatifs ou exoneratoire des responsabilites en Europe 1990, 77–93; H.-W. Micklitz, La Loi Allemand relative au régime fundique des conditions générades des contrats du 9 Decembre 1976 (1989) Rev. Int. Droit Comparé 101 at 109; J.P. Dawson, Unconscionable Coercion; The German Version (1976) 89 Harvard Law Review 1041, 1114.

[205] H.-W. Micklitz, The Politics of Judicial Co-operation in the EU, CUP, 2005, 374.

law with the procedural aspects of good faith at the expense of the substantive aspects.[206]

3.6 Non-Mandatory Convergence and the Role of CLAB

ECJ interpretations of the unfairness concept under the Article 234 reference procedure are, of course, binding not only on the Member State making the reference but also on other Member States. By contrast, interpretations of the unfairness concept by national courts are not binding on courts in other Member States. However, there is nothing to prevent academics, lawyers and ultimately judges drawing inspiration from such decisions; with the result that the unfairness concept in (for example) UK courts comes to be influenced and shaped by some of the approaches taken in other Member States. This is made more feasible by the existence of the CLAB database on national case law on unfair terms.[207] At the time of writing there does not appear to be any evidence of material from CLAB emanating from other Member States being cited in the UK courts. Indeed, a study of the CLAB database suggests that very limited use has been made of it by practitioners generally across Europe.[208] However, the database is currently under review and it is possible that this may result in more use being made of it in the future.[209]

---

[206] Micklitz, *ibid.*, generally 355–423.

[207] See:

http://europa.eu.int/comm/consumers/cons_int/safe_shop/unf_cont_terms/clab/index_en.htm.

[208] See H.-W. Micklitz and M. Radeideh, CLAB Europa – The European Database on Unfair Terms in Consumer Contracts (2005) 28 Journal of Consumer Policy, 225–260.

[209] *Ibid.*

Chapter Four

Default Rules, Reasonable Expectations and Reasonableness under UCTA

4.1 Introduction

First of all this chapter seeks to identify the basic notions of fairness in substance underlying UCTA. Essentially, the argument is that the key benchmarks of fairness are default rules relating to the responsibilities of traders; along with 'reasonable expectations' that consumers may have as to the way in which traders will perform their obligations. In most cases if a term deviates from these fairness benchmarks the result is that the term is subject to a general 'fair and reasonable' test. However, the chapter also highlights those default rules that are treated as absolute fairness norms in the sense that deviation from them is wholly ineffective; and considers the rationales for such an approach.

The chapter also considers the relationship between these fairness benchmarks and the approach suggested for the proposed new regime. Essentially the point here is that the 'detriment' trigger proposed for the new regime would cover all of the terms already covered by the UCTA. However (being an 'open fairness norm') it would also cover forms of exclusion or restriction of the trader's responsibilities that would not necessarily be caught by UCTA (and, of course, it would cover those terms not caught by UCTA, but caught by the UTCCR, for example those terms that impose obligations and liabilities on the consumer).

Finally, we consider the way in which the reasonableness test has been approached by the courts, considering what guidance has emerged in relation to procedural and substantive unfairness.

4.2 Default Rules and Fairness Standards under UCTA

4.2.1 The Basic Provisions, Default Remedies and Interest Balancing

In order to understand the notions of fairness existing under the UCTA we need to begin by focusing on the types of term that are regulated by UCTA. This provides the first indication as to the types of unfairness in substance that the Act is aimed at. As we have seen, UCTA covers terms excluding and restricting various types of liability. Most importantly, the Act controls terms excluding or restricting liability for negligence (including the tort of negligence and breach of contractual duties to take reasonable care);[1] terms excluding or restricting liability for breach of contract;[2] terms excluding or restricting liability for breach of the implied terms as to title, description, quality and fitness for purpose in contracts for the sale and supply of goods;[3] and terms excluding or restricting liability for terms excluding or restricting liability for misrepresentation.[4] So, where a term excludes or restricts a remedy that would otherwise arise based on the commission of the tort of negligence or for breach of a contractual obligation to take reasonable care, then the term is controlled. Where a term excludes or restricts a remedy that would otherwise arise based on breach of any other type of contractual obligation then the term is controlled. Where a term excludes or restricts a remedy that would otherwise arise based on breach of one of the implied terms in contracts for the sale or supply of goods then the term is controlled. Finally, where a term excludes or restricts a remedy that would otherwise arise based on the existence of a misrepresentation then the term is controlled. In other words these various default remedies are seen as benchmarks of fairness or reasonableness.

It seems possible to explain this on the basis that the default remedies for breach of contract, for breach of a tortious duty to take reasonable care and for misrepresentation are based on a balancing of the interests of the parties (balancing the interests of the parties being core to the idea of fairness). So, the compensatory remedy of damages for breach of contract is intended to put the innocent party (in this case the consumer) in the position he would have occupied had the contract been performed and no more, i.e. not to punish the trader or enable the consumer to make a profit. In addition, the innocent party (in this case the consumer) can only recover losses that are not too remote;[5] and then only if he has taken reasonable steps to mitigate his losses.[6] Where damages for negligence and misrepresentation are concerned the agenda is to compensate the consumer for losses that have been caused by the negligence or misrepresentation, and not to punish the trader or allow the consumer to

---

1   Section 2.
2   Section 3(2)(a).
3   Sections 6(2) and 7(2).
4   Section 8.
5   *Hadley* v. *Baxendale* (1854) 9 Exch 341, the Heron II (1969) 1 AC 350.
6   *British Westinghouse Electric and Manufacturing Co. Ltd* v. *Underground Electric Rlys of London Ltd* (1912) AC 673.

make a profit. Again, what the consumer can recover is restricted by rules on remoteness.[7]

Turning to other remedies, the right of the consumer to reject goods and terminate a contract for breach only arises where there is a breach of a condition or a sufficiently serious breach of an innominate term.[8] Even where the right to reject and terminate does arise, the law protects the interests of the trader. This is done by removing the right to reject and terminate in certain circumstances (e.g. on the basis of waiver, estoppel[9] affirmation[10] or acceptance.[11] The consumer can rescind the contract for a misrepresentation, but again, this right is curtailed by various bars to rescission that protect the interests of the trader.[12]

4.2.2 Default Obligations and Interest Balancing

So, the remedies available to the consumer when the trader is in breach of a contractual obligation or a tortious duty or where there has been a misrepresentation seek to balance the interests of the parties and this seems to explain why they are viewed as benchmarks of fairness; and why terms offering something less favourable to the consumer are controlled. However, the Act also judges terms defining *primary obligations* against fairness norms. In some cases (where there is no default rule as such) the Act uses a concept of reasonable expectations. So, the Act not only covers terms excluding or restricting liabilities for breach of a primary contractual obligation; it also covers terms defining a contractual obligation in such a way as to allow for a contractual performance substantially different from that reasonably expected or no performance at all.[13] We shall deal with this further below.[14] However, for the moment we will stay with situations in which there *are* default rules dealing with primary contractual obligations and tortious duties. In at least some cases where there are default rules fixing duties and primary obligations these are treated as benchmarks of fairness. Section 13(1) of the Act says, *inter*

---

[7]   Wagon Mound No. 1 [1961] AC 388.

[8]   *Photo Production Ltd* v. *Securicor Transport Ltd* (1980) AC 827 and *Hong Kong Fir Shipping Co. Ltd* v. *Kawasaki Kisen Kaisha Ltd* (1962) 2 QB 26.

[9]   *Panchaud Frere SA* v. *Establishments General Grain Co.* (1970) 1 Lloyds Rep 53.

[10]   *Peyman* v. *Lanjani* (1985) Ch. 457, *Farnworth Finance Facilities Ltd* v. *Attryde* (1970) 1 WLR 1955.

[11]   Sale of Goods Act, ss 11(4) and s. 35.

[12]   For a review of these see E. McKendrick, Contract Law, Palgrave Macmillan, 6th edn, 2005, 285–8.

[13]   Section 3(2)(b)(i) and (ii).

[14]   See below at 4.4.

alia, that ss 2, 6 and 7 also prevent 'excluding or restricting liability by reference to terms and notices which exclude or restrict the relevant obligation or duty'. Section 2 is the provision dealing with exclusion/restriction of liability for negligence and ss 6 and 7 are the provisions dealing with exclusion/restriction of liability for breach of the implied terms as to title, description, quality and fitness etc in contracts for the sale and supply of goods. The effect of s. 13(1) then, is that terms are treated as excluding/restricting liability (and are therefore controlled) when they exclude or restrict the scope of the primary duty or obligation. So, s. 2 covers a term excluding or restricting the duty to take reasonable care in tort or the implied term in contracts for services to the effect that the supplier will take reasonable care.[15] In other words the duty to take care is viewed as a benchmark of fairness. In the case of ss 6 and 7 a term excluding or restricting the obligations as to title, description, quality and fitness is covered. So, these obligations are also viewed as benchmarks of fairness.

On the whole, it makes perfect sense for a fairness regime based on interest balancing to treat these contractual and tortious duties and obligations as benchmarks of fairness in the same way as remedies are viewed as benchmarks of fairness. As with the remedies, these primary obligations and duties are already based on a balancing of the interests of the parties. For example, the basic idea of imposing the implied term as to satisfactory quality seems to be that consumers will often have insufficient knowledge to be able to properly assess the quality of products; to assess the kinds of issues that they should seek assurance on; and insufficient knowledge or power to obtain any assurances that they do seek. The agenda then is to consider a range of criteria that are relevant to quality; and, taking into account the interests of both parties, along with the way the goods were priced and described, to assess what it is reasonable for the consumer to have expected in relation to these different criteria.[16] Moving to tort, the imposition of a duty of care is based on the conclusion that there is a *sufficient degree of proximity* in the relationship between the parties, that the *trader can reasonably foresee* that his negligence would cause loss to the consumer, and that it is *fair and reasonable* to impose a duty.[17] The trader will be in breach of this duty if he does not exercise a *reasonable* standard of care.[18] The trader will be liable to compensate the consumer if the breach of duty has caused

---

[15]   See *Smith* v. *Bush* [1990] 1AC 831.

[16]   C. Willett, Fairness in Quality Obligations and Remedies, in C. Willett (ed.), Aspects of Fairness in Contract, Blackstone, 1996, 123, 125–9.

[17]   *Caparo* v. *Dickman* [1990] 2 AC 605.

[18]   *Bolton* v. *Stone* [1951] AC 850 and *Bolam* v. *Friern Hospital Management Committee* [1957] 1 All ER 118.

damage which is not regarded as being too *remote*.[19] At every point here the interests of the parties are balanced and those of the trader taken into account.

Not only are the default remedies and default duties and obligations both based on a process of interest balancing, but the *practical* effect of terms that exclude or restrict them is also the same. In the case of terms excluding or restricting liability for breach of a primary obligation or duty the consumer is being deprived (to a greater or lesser degree) of a remedy which he would otherwise have as a matter of law based on the trader's breach of a primary obligation or duty. In the case of terms which bite at the earlier stage and restrict the scope of the trader's primary obligation or duty (so as to enable the trader to do something less than that which the law would otherwise dictate), the result of this may be that there will not be a breach in cases where there would otherwise have been a breach. The result of this will be that the remedy which would have been available if there had been a breach will not be available (just as it would not have been available if it had been directly restricted or excluded).[20]

4.2.3 Default Obligations and the Transfer of Information

However, there is a complication with the particular default rules that define the primary obligations and duties as to reasonable care and the primary obligations as to description, quality and fitness of goods. In both cases information exchanged between the parties may be relevant to the interest balancing process that the makeup of the obligation or duty is based on. In deciding, for example, whether there should be a duty of care in tort in relation to advice given by the trader a key question is whether the trader has 'assumed responsibility' for the advice and whether there has been concomitant reliance by the consumer on the advice.[21] As such, information provided by the trader as to his attitude towards the advice is usually relevant. Such information may help to indicate whether he should be taken to have assumed responsibility for the advice and whether it is reasonable for the consumer to rely on the advice. Moving to the implied terms, let us take the implied term as to satisfactory quality as an example. The obligation does not apply to defects specifically drawn to

---

[19]   Wagon Mound No. 1 [1961] AC 388.

[20]   See B. Coote, Exception Clauses, 1964, Chs 1 and 10 and the discussion by E. MacDonald, Exemption Clauses and Unfair Contract Terms, Butterworths, 1999, at 91; and for a comparative view of English and Italian law on this issue see P. Nebbia, Unfair Contract Terms in European Law, Hart, 2007, 125–129.

[21]   *Henderson v. Merrett Syndicates Ltd and Others* [1994] 3 All ER 506.

the attention of the consumer before the contract is made.[22] So, if a seller draws the attention of the consumer to specific defects the obligation will be restricted accordingly and will not apply to these defects.

This raises the question as to whether information on the above issues *provided through the medium of the formal terms* can and should have the effect of circumscribing the scope of the obligation. Now it is one thing for a term to provide information that could not be regarded as sufficiently nuanced to be relevant to the interest balancing process. So, for example, if a term simply denies that there is any obligation as to quality then it is hard to see how this would really influence the expectations as to quality of a consumer; these expectations being affected by a host of other factors such as the price paid, the way the goods have been described etc. Even if a term makes a general reference to the consumer being 'deemed aware of all defects' this clearly does not draw the attention of the consumer specifically to any particular defects. It is clear that when s. 13 refers to 'excluding or restricting liability' by reference to terms and notices which 'exclude or restrict the relevant obligation or duty' that these sorts of terms are covered. These terms have not provided information that has genuinely influenced the expectations of the consumer in any real way that is required by the default rule in question. Clearly these sorts of terms are intended to be treated by s. 13 as not playing a genuine (or 'fair') role in constructing the obligation or duty, but as simply trying to exclude or restrict the obligation or duty as legitimately constructed in the absence of the term.

However, a term might make reference to particular defects. In these types of situation does the reference to specific defects reduce the scope of the satisfactory quality obligation? Equally, if a term or notice makes it clear that no responsibility is taken for advice, should this prevent a duty of care in tort arising? Does the term then cease to be treated as one that is excluding /restricting the respective obligations/duties and come to be viewed as having played a legitimate role in circumscribing the obligation /duty (and therefore escape the coverage of s. 13, and therefore the Act)? The answer, on the whole, seems to be in the negative. In *Smith* v. *Bush* it was held that the effect of s. 13 was that the question as to whether a duty to take reasonable care arises is to be assessed by ignoring the term – the question is whether 'but for' the term there would be a duty.[23] It is generally assumed that the same approach would be taken in relation to the implied terms.[24]

---

[22]   SGA, s. 14(2C).

[23]   *Smith* v. *Bush* [1989] 2 All ER 514, Lord Griffiths at 30 and *Phillips* v. *Hyland* [1987] 2 All ER 620, Slade LJ at 625.

[24]   See E. MacDonald, Exemption Clauses and Unfair Contract Terms, Butterworths, 1999, at 92–3.

Of course, if the *broader circumstances* displace or restrict the scope of the obligation or duty in question then this is surely quite legitimate.[25] Suppose that a seller of goods makes it clear verbally that a car has particular defects and the term also makes reference to these defects. In this case the quality obligation will not extend to these defects,[26] but this will be because of what was said verbally. As a result of this, the obligation will not cover the defects. Section 13 arguably does not prevent this result as it is concerned with the ability of *the term* to circumscribe the obligation or duty.[27] Here, *the term* is not circumscribing the obligation – it has been circumscribed by the verbal statement. The term is simply repeating what we already know, i.e. that the obligation does not cover these defects. The same analysis is presumably correct even if there is no verbal statement as such but the attention of the consumer is drawn to the provision in the contract that identifies specific defects. Here, to all intents and purposes, the seller has pointed out the defects. The real difficulty is whether a formal term should be able to have some force *in its own right* in determining the scope of the duty or obligation. As we have seen, the authority seems to suggest that it cannot.

This might be regarded as harsh on the trader in those cases where the term in question is '*uber* transparent' i.e. where it is extremely clear, goes directly to a matter that would otherwise affect the obligation and where there is even evidence that the consumer has read the term.[28] However, there is good reason for caution about allowing scope for any argument that a formal term has legitimately circumscribed the scope of an obligation or duty. Even in cases where the term is extremely clear (as described above) it may be that, in practice, many consumers will not read the contract and become aware of the term. (As we have already observed, it is often perfectly understandable that consumers do not read terms even where they are transparent.[29]) Yet, if the term is treated as having legitimately circumscribed the scope of the obligation it will not

---

25   Yates, Exclusion Clauses in Contracts, 2nd edn, 1982, at 78 and E. MacDonald, Exemption Clauses and Unfair Contract Terms, Butterworths, 1999, at 93.

26   SGA, s. 14(2C).

27   But see Yates, Exclusion Clauses in Contracts, 2nd edn, 1982, at 78 and E. MacDonald, Exemption Clauses and Unfair Contract Terms, Butterworths, 1999, at 93 who seem to take the view that the term is still covered by s. 13 in such a case.

28   Especially as a term is wholly invalid and there is no opportunity to seek to justify it under the reasonableness test where it is treated as excluding/restricting the obligations/liabilities based on the implied terms or excluding/restricting an obligation or duty to take reasonable care where the breach might lead to personal injury or death (see ss 2(1), 6(2) and 7(2).

29   See above at 2.4.3.4.

be controlled. Indeed, if the argument is left open as a possibility there is the risk that traders will routinely raise the argument and consumers will routinely be put off even where a court would not have held it to be a genuine alteration of the obligation. So, if we want to protect consumers from this then there is justification for taking a strict approach and never allowing the term itself to play any role in altering the obligation.

4.2.4 Misrepresentation and the Transfer of Information

The strict approach described above does not seem to have been taken in relation to misrepresentation. Although the default *remedies* for misrepresentation are benchmarks of fairness (there being control whenever a term excludes or restricts a remedy that would otherwise exist[30]) it seems that the same is not necessarily true in relation to the essential ingredients that must be established for there to be liability for misrepresentation in the first place. In order for there to be a misrepresentation the accepted view is that there must be a false statement of existing fact (which may have come from the trader or his agent) that has induced the consumer to enter the contract.[31] The provision in question simply refers to exclusion/restriction of 'any liability to which a party may be subject by reason of any misrepresentation ... or any remedy available to another party to the contract by reason of such a misrepresentation'.[32] The provision is not subject to the rule in s. 13 which, as we have seen, defines exclusion/restriction of liability as including excluding/restricting the primary obligation or duty. It is clear that this leaves uncertain the question as to whether the section covers terms denying the existence of an essential ingredient of misrepresentation. This has led to the courts taking a confused and inconsistent approach. On the one hand the provision has been interpreted to cover terms denying the existence of an essential ingredient for a misrepresentation action such as the existence of a statement of fact or inducement, e.g. where a so called 'entire agreement' clause asserts that the formal agreement represents the full extent of the trader's responsibility and that the consumer has not been induced to enter the contract by any pre-contractual statements.[33] On the

---

[30] See above at 4.2.1.

[31] See discussion by E. McKendrick, Contract Law, Palgrave Macmillan, 6th edn, 2005, 273–4.

[32] UCTA, s. 8.

[33] See *Cremdean Properties* v. *Nash* (1977) 244 EG 547 *Walker* v. *Boyle* [1982] 1 WLR 495; *Thomas Witter Ltd* v. *TBP Industries* [1996] 2 All ER 573; and *Inntreprenneur Pub Co.* v. *East Crown Ltd* [2000] 2 Lloyds Rep 611.

other hand, it has been held not to cover a term that denies that an agent has authority to make a representation.[34] Equally, there seems to be some confusion over the status of an entire agreement clause that asserts that there has been no reliance on any pre-contractual statements. It appears that the provision may not apply to such a clause on the basis that the effect of the clause is that the innocent party is estopped from claiming reliance; although it may be that this is only the case as between commercial contractors of equal bargaining power (i.e. not where consumers are concerned).[35] Yet surely whether an agent has authority is a matter that should be assessed based on the normal criteria applicable to this issue and without consideration of the formal term. If such authority would exist in the absence of the term then a fairness review should be triggered.[36] Equally, surely whether there has been reliance is something that should be assessed based on the normal criteria applicable to this issue and without consideration of the formal term. As suggested, this may well be the position where consumers are concerned, but it is simply not clear. Such an approach to the authority of agents and to the question of reliance would follow the same logic as that applied to primary tortious duties of reasonable care and primary contractual obligations as to reasonable care, title, description, quality, fitness etc; i.e. that there is a serious risk that there will be no real substantial consent to the formal terms and so the law should make an assessment (independent of the formal terms) as to whether the criteria for liability exist.

This problem would have been prevented by simply providing that whether any necessary ingredient for liability for misrepresentation exists is something that should be worked out in the absence of the term. On this approach if there would have been liability but for the term then the reasonableness test would be triggered. However, the issue ceased to be of practical importance since the UTCCR were passed, as they clearly do control terms that seek to deny the existence of basic ingredients of misrepresentation (see further below). In addition, as we shall see, such terms would be controlled by the new regime.

---

34   *Overbrooke Estates Ltd* v. *Glencombe Properties Ltd* [1974] 1 WLR 1335, Ch. D.

35   *Watford Electronics Ltd* v. *Sanderson CFL Ltd* [2001] 1 All ER (Comm) 696 and see the discussion by E. Macdonald, Exemption Clauses and Unfair Terms, Butterworths, 2nd edn, 2006, 70–77..

36   This argument can be put in terms of looking at the 'substance' of the situation – see E. Peel, Reasonable Exemption Clauses, 117 LQR, 545.

4.2.5 The Limits of UCTA

We have seen, then, that UCTA controls terms that exclude/restrict a variety of obligations/liabilities that would otherwise exist under default rules. Of course, a key limitation of UCTA has always been that it does not control terms that *add to the obligations or liabilities of the consumer* by comparison with default rules. There is only control where a term in some way limits or excludes the responsibility of the trader to the consumer. This problem is addressed by the UTCCR which *do* cover both terms that exclude/restrict the obligations/liabilities that the trader would otherwise owe *and* terms that add to the obligations/liabilities that the consumer would otherwise owe.[37] The same would, of course, be true of the new regime,[38] given the need to ensure proper implementation of the Unfair Terms Directive.

4.2.6 The Two UCTA Approaches

In some cases the control comes in the form of a test of reasonableness. This happens in the case of terms that exclude or restrict secondary liability for breach of contract (other than breach of the implied terms as to title, description, quality and fitness);[39] terms that exclude or restrict liability for negligence causing loss other than death or personal injury;[40] and terms that exclude or restrict liability for misrepresentation.[41] The reasonableness test, as we shall see, considers the term in the context of the broader substantive picture and matters of procedural fairness.[42] So, the view of terms deviating from these default rules is that they may or may not be fair depending upon the specific interests affected by the term, the overall substantive picture and whether there was procedural fairness.[43]

However, terms that exclude or restrict obligations and duties to take reasonable care or liability for breach of these obligations or duties where

---

[37] See above at 3.2.

[38] See below at 5.7.5.

[39] Section 3(2).

[40] Section 2(2); as we have seen, this covers exclusion or restriction of either the primary obligation or duty or the secondary liability for breach of the primary obligation or duty – see discussion of the effect of s. 13 above.

[41] Section 8.

[42] The test is contained in s. 11; see below at 4.6.

[43] See the discussion above at 2.4.3.2–4 outlining what a comprehensive analysis of substantive and procedural fairness issues might involve and see below at 4.6 for the way in which the UCTA reasonableness test is approached in practice.

the result is death or personal injury are wholly ineffective;[44] as are those terms that exclude or restrict the obligations created by (or liability for breach of) the implied terms as to description, quality, fitness etc in consumer contracts.[45] So the default rules on these issues are not triggers for a broader assessment of reasonableness. They are, rather, absolute fairness or reasonableness norms. In other words, where these default rules are concerned the interests that they protect are protected without any enquiry as to broader substantive fairness or as to procedural fairness. So, for example, where a term excludes or restrict liability for negligence there is no enquiry as to whether the price of the goods or service was sufficiently low as to make the overall balance of rights and obligations substantively fair; and neither is there any investigation as to whether the term was sufficiently transparent to enable the consumer to exercise an informed choice.[46] This approach would continue to be the case under the proposed new regime.[47] In particular, this is in pursuance of the policy not to reduce existing levels of protection.[48]

4.2.7 Rationales for Making Certain Terms Wholly Ineffective

4.2.7.1 Introduction

From a freedom-oriented perspective, this is the least acceptable form of fairness. As we saw above,[49] this sort of approach restricts the freedom of the trader to the greatest extent. The trader is not free to use the term even if the trader seeks to enable the consumer to protect his own interests by making the term transparent and possibly also by offering a choice; and neither does it matter that the overall balance of the counteract may be fair as a result of other terms that are beneficial to the consumer. Such an approach is also, from a self-reliant freedom-oriented perspective, restrictive of the freedom of the consumer, who cannot agree to the term even although he may have been in a position to know what he was agreeing to, may have had a choice (whether from this trader or another), could perhaps have bargained for a more favourable term; and even although he may benefit from other favourable terms by agreeing to the term.

---

[44] Section 2(1).

[45] Sections 6(2) and 7(2).

[46] See above at 2.4.3.2–4 outlining what a comprehensive analysis of substantive and procedural fairness issues might involve.

[47] Consultation Paper, 4.34–4.35, Report, 3.42–3.45 and Draft Bill, Clauses 1(1) and 5.

[48] Consultation Paper 4.22–4.29, Report, 3.42–3.45.

[49] See above at 2.4.3.5(i).

Above[50] it was suggested that there seem to be several interconnected reasons for taking this type of approach. These include the idea that consumers should be given absolute protection where certain substantive interests are concerned – that consumers have certain 'irreducible' rights.[51] These are substantive interests that *the law* should protect irrespective of questions of procedural fairness or broader substantive fairness. However, it was also suggested above that there might sometimes be said to be a latent concern with procedural fairness.[52] The argument is roughly thus. In an ideal world consumers would always be in a position to take advantage of procedural opportunities to protect their interests against terms that are very substantively unfair. However, the nature of the unfairness in substance is so serious that we cannot take the risk that this will happen in practice. Even if the level of procedural fairness is as high as can reasonably be expected, it cannot necessarily be expected that consumers will take advantage of the opportunities presented. So, as has already been argued above,[53] even where a term is reasonably transparent this may not really mean that the consumer reads the terms or makes an informed decision even if he does read them. If this is the case then the consumer will not see any need to take up any choice that may be available or use the bargaining power he may have to bargain for better terms. If consumers *do* make themselves aware of the terms and risks involved and if a choice *is* theoretically available or consumers, in theory, have the bargaining power to bargain, consumers might still not take up these opportunities. They may not realize that choices are available;[54] they may find it difficult to make a rational comparison between the alternatives;[55] and they may not realize that the terms are, in theory, negotiable.[56]

The idea then is that even where the term was transparent and choices were available or the consumer, in theory, had a chance to bargain for a better term, the unfairness in substance is such that it is *presumed* that consumers did not, in practice, take up these opportunities to protect their interests pre-contractually.

---

50   *Ibid.*, (i)-(v).
51   See *ibid.* (ii) and see discussion by H. Beale, Legislative Control of Fairness, in J. Beatson and D. Friedmann, Good Faith and Fault in Contract Law, 1995, 231 at 236–7.
52   See above at 2.4.3.5(iii).
53   *Ibid.*
54   *Ibid.*
55   *Ibid.*
56   *Ibid.*

It was also suggested above that another reason for banning certain terms outright is to promote clear, effective consumer protection.[57] Given the degree to which certain terms do compromise the substantive interests of consumers (and perhaps also the fact that consumers will often not really be able to take advantage of procedural fairness to self-protect) an outright ban may be imposed on the grounds that if the issue is left open, the interests of consumers will, in practice, be compromised as traders raise (and consumers accept) the argument that the term is justified, whether on the grounds that the term is not in fact unfair in substance or on the grounds that, even if it is unfair in substance, there is a beneficial term making for overall substantive fairness; or on the grounds that there has, in the circumstances, been sufficient procedural fairness to justify its use. Even if such arguments may be valid in certain circumstances, they will not be valid in many cases where the term is particularly unfair in substance. However, these arguments will be used routinely if the issue is left open, and many consumers will suffer detriment as a result. In other words, a significant factor in banning certain terms (whether bans by regulatory bodies or by legislation) is to secure the practical and effective protection of the majority of consumers.

4.2.7.2 Exclusion of Liability for Negligence

It is arguable that we can identify all of these rationales in the case of the terms that are actually banned by UCTA. In the case of the ban on terms excluding or restricting liability for death or injury caused by lack of reasonable care the Law Commissions did not initially propose a ban other than in certain cases (e.g. in car parks) where the view was that the consumer had no effective choice but to enter the contract.[58] In other cases, where such a choice was thought to exist, the Law Commissions did not initially support a total ban on exclusion or restriction of liability.[59] So, in these cases the Law Commissions believed that, as there was a choice as to whether to proceed, there should not be a ban. So, in one sense, the Law Commissions might be said to have viewed the issue as turning on questions of procedural fairness – when there was a choice of some kind there should not be a ban. However, ultimately Parliament chose a total ban. It may have been that Parliament did see such terms as very unfair in substance, based on the idea that the physical safety of contractors should always be protected. However, it has been suggested the ban can be associated with an indirect concern with procedural

---

[57] See above at 2.4.3.5(v).
[58] See Law Commission Report, No. 69, paras 88–9.
[59] *Ibid.*, paras 72–74.

fairness.[60] The reasoning here is that in relation to exclusion or restriction of liability *not* causing death or personal injury (where the reasonableness test applies[61]) the courts (in applying the reasonableness test) focus on procedural matters such as the relative bargaining strength of the parties;[62] it therefore being plausible that the courts assume that the outright ban on terms excluding or limiting liability for negligently caused death or injury is based on the likely weaker bargaining position of the consumer.[63] It is certainly possible to rationalize that the *risk* of such procedural unfairness (or at least parties not taking advantage of opportunities for self-protection) is at least part of the explanation for the ban. However, it must be noted that, in applying the reasonableness test in relation to exclusion or restriction of liability *not* causing death or personal injury, the courts also appear to consider matters related to the substantive features of the term and its consequences for the consumer.[64] This might suggest that the courts assume that the outright ban on terms excluding or limiting liability for negligently caused death or injury is based on the particularly detrimental *substantive impact* of such terms. Of course, another good reason for banning this sort of term proactively is the need to promote clear, effective consumer protection. The degree of unfairness in substance (along with the high risk that consumers will not have taken the opportunities available to self-protect) means that such terms will be unfair in most cases – so we should not take the risk that traders will use the terms in many cases where they cannot be justified and routinely argue that they are fair when in most cases they will not be.

4.2.7.3 Exclusion of Liability for Breach of the Implied Terms

We now turn to the ban on terms excluding/restricting liability for breach of the implied terms as to description, quality, fitness etc. Again, there appears to be a blend of rationales. The core concern for the Law Commission appears to have been as to the substantive effect of such terms. There was agreement with the view of the Molony Committee to the effect that the result of such exclusions was that 'heavy and irrecoverable loss may fall upon the consumer who is unlucky enough to

---

[60] R. Bradgate, R. Brownsword and C. Twigg-Flesner, The Impact of Adopting a General Duty to Trade Fairly, DTI, 2003, 41.

[61] See above at 4.2.6.

[62] On which see further below at 4.6.

[63] R. Bradgate, R. Brownsword and C. Twigg-Flesner, The Impact of Adopting a General Duty to Trade Fairly, DTI, 2003, 41.

[64] *Ibid*; and see below at 4.6.1 and 4.6.2.1.

get a defective article'.[65] It must be said as well, however, that the Law Commission also referred to the fact that the Molony Committee had said that consumers would not usually know how he was being treated and, if he did know, could not have done anything about it.[66] So, there is clearly a nod here to the procedural problems that will usually exist. In addition, it has been suggested that the ban could be viewed as based on concerns as to procedural fairness on the basis that it is only aimed at consumers.[67] The logic here is that the restriction of the ban to consumer sales must be based on the assumption that consumers are always likely to be procedurally weak and are unlikely to have given real consent, while business buyers are more likely to be able to self-protect procedurally.[68] However, it might also be said that the ban is only aimed at consumers because they are less able to bear the substantive loss (in other words that the ban shows sensitivity to the particular impact of poor quality goods on the private sphere of life[69]). Indeed, the Law Commission did seem to veer in this direction when they said that the biggest difference between consumer and commercial buyers was the ability to absorb the loss via insurance, costings, servicing and other means (the view was that this was more of a difference between consumer and non-consumer buyers than any difference in ability to protect pre-contractually by detecting defects, for example).[70]

Again however, certainty and effective consumer protection were also important factors. In the context of discussions as to whether there should be any cases in which there should not be a ban, much was made of the difficulty of creating exceptions for this case and the uncertainty and reduction in the bargaining power of the consumer in disputes that might be caused.[71] Let us take an example. Where there is a breach of the implied term as to satisfactory quality the consumer has a short term right to reject and obtain a full refund ('short term' because it is lost by lapse of a reasonable time – usually a few weeks or months – under the acceptance rules in the Sale of Goods Act[72]). In addition the consumer has a right to ask for a free repair or for replacement (subject to these

---

[65]   Law Commission, First Report on Exemption Clauses, para. 68, citing the Molony Committee, Cmnd 1781, 1962, para. 427.

[66]   Law Commision, *ibid.*, para. 68.

[67]   See R. Bradgate, R. Brownsword and C. Twigg-Flesner, The Impact of Adopting a General Duty to Trade Fairly, DTI, 2003, 41.

[68]   *Ibid.*, 41–2.

[69]   See above at 2.4.2.1.

[70]   Law Commission First Report, para. 82.

[71]   *Ibid.*, para. 73.

[72]   Sale of goods Act, s. 35(4).

being possible and proportionate).[73] If neither repair or replacement is possible or proportionate, or if they are not effected in a reasonable time or without significant inconvenience to the consumer, the consumer has a right to rescind the contract and obtain a refund subject to a deduction for beneficial use of the goods[74] (this being a fresh right that exists even where the initial short term right to reject has been lost). Let us suppose that traders were allowed to exclude the short term right to reject goods of unsatisfactory quality in cases where the contract provides expressly for a right to repair that is more beneficial to the consumer than the right existing in law, e.g. that the goods will be repaired even where the cost is disproportionate. Such a right may well be very beneficial in the sense that repair may often be what most consumers want in practice and there is now an assurance that it will be carried out whatever the cost. However, there would be scope for considerable argument, e.g. as to whether the consumer was really fully aware of the right to reject that he was giving up and as to whether the repair has been carried out quickly enough and without significant inconvenience (this being relevant because, as we have seen, if these conditions are not satisfied the consumer is entitled to rescind – the only opportunity to rescind that would exist if it was permissible to exclude the short term right to reject). The consumer's position is simpler and stronger where (at least in the short term) he can choose to insist on a complete refund in those cases where he has any reason to doubt the ability of the trader to repair quickly, effectively and without inconvenience.

4.3 Default Rules under the Proposed New Regime – a Comparison with UCTA

4.3.1 The General 'Detriment' Trigger

Under the proposed new regime there would be a general 'fair and reasonable' test to which terms causing 'detriment' would be subject.[75] So when exactly does a term cause 'detriment' and how will the detriment concept relate to the existing control triggers under UCTA? There is no definition of detriment in the Draft Bill. However, it seems clear that if a term is *substantively* prejudicial to the consumer then it can be said to cause detriment. It then seems logical to suppose that assessment as to whether a term should be treated as being substantively prejudicial should be based on whether the term offers something less beneficial than the

---

73   Sale of Goods Act, s. 48B(2)(b).
74   Sale of Good Act, s. 48B(2)(a) and SGA s. 48C(1) and (2).
75   Draft Bill, Clause 4(1).

default position. So, any term that excludes or restricts a *remedy* that would otherwise exist for breach of a primary obligation or duty will surely cause detriment. As we have seen, those terms that exclude or restrict liability for breach of contract or for misrepresentation are currently subject to the UCTA reasonableness test. Such terms would surely cause detriment under the new regime and, on this basis, be subject to the new fair and reasonable test. However, the detriment trigger is broader than the UCTA triggers. For example, we have seen that the UCTA concept of excluding or restricting liability for misrepresentation has been held not to cover terms denying the authority of an agent.[76] Such a term will surely, however, cause detriment under the new regime. If, in the absence of the term, the agent would (under the general law) have authority such that the trader would be liable for statements made by the agent, then a term denying this surely causes detriment by denying the consumer the right (that would otherwise exist) to a claim for misrepresentation.

What of terms offering a primary contractual obligation or tortious duty that is less favourable to the consumer than what is provided for under the general law (whether under the law of tort or under a default rule or implied term)? Currently, under UCTA, as we have seen,[77] a term is caught if it seeks to restrict or exclude a duty to take reasonable care or one of the obligations provided for by the implied terms as to description, quality etc. The new regime would not, in fact, deal with these under the 'detriment' concept but separately and we will turn to this shortly. However, it is interesting to note that UCTA does not in fact have a *general* rule subjecting to control (i.e. to the reasonableness test) any term that offers something less favourable than would be the position under a contractual or tortious default rule. It only catches terms seeking to exclude or restrict the specific default obligations and duties as to reasonable care and the implied terms. However, the proposed new regime *would* appear to catch such *any* term that offers something less favourable than would be the position under a contractual or tortious default rule. Such a term surely causes detriment (if we assume that detriment is simply a threshold requirement that is satisfied whenever the term has some negative substantive effects for the consumer).

---

[76] See above at 4.2.4.
[77] See above at 4.2.3.

4.3.2 Exclusion of Liability for Negligence and the Implied Terms under the New Regime

Under UCTA, as we have seen,[78] a term is caught if it seeks to restrict or exclude a duty to take reasonable care or one of the obligations provided for by the implied terms as to description, quality etc. As I have just indicated, such terms would not be dealt with via the 'detriment' concept in the new regime. These terms would not be subject to control on the basis that they cause detriment as such. They would simply continue to be controlled on the basis of the current model. In other words, the question would remain simply whether a term excludes or restricts an obligation or duty to take reasonable care or liability for breach of such an obligation or duty. Where death or personal injury is involved the term would be wholly ineffective and where other losses are concerned the term would be subject to the new fair and reasonable test.[79] Equally, in relation to the implied terms, the question would continue simply to be whether the term excludes or restricts the relevant obligation or liability for its breach. In consumer contracts such a term would continue to be wholly ineffective.[80]

4.4 Reasonable Expectations under UCTA

4.4.1 Introduction

Another benchmark of fairness under UCTA is the concept of reasonable expectations. Section 3(2)(b)(i) of the Act controls terms that enable the trader to offer a contractual performance substantially different from that reasonably expected. Such terms are subject to the reasonableness test. Putting this in another way, the reasonableness test is triggered by terms allowing the trader to perform in ways that substantially differ from what the consumer would reasonably have expected. This catches situations in which there is no default rule to use as a benchmark, i.e. where there is no default rule against which the trader's performance obligation can be measured (see initial discussion of this above at 2.4.3.2). In some cases where there *is* a default rule (i.e. the implied terms as to description, quality and fitness of goods) UCTA, as we have seen, asks whether the formal term provides for a performance that is in some way more limited or less favourable to the consumer than the default rule.[81] As indicated, s.

---

78   See above at 4.2.3.
79   Draft Bill, Clauses 1(1) and 1(2).
80   *Ibid.*, Clause 5.
81   See ss 2, 6, 7 and 13.

3(2)(b)(i) seems to be aimed at cases in which there is no default rule against which the term can be measured. In the absence of a default rule s. 3(2)(b)(i) uses the idea of reasonable expectations as a benchmark.

But how are we to determine what are the reasonable expectations of the consumer? Lord Steyn (speaking generally about the idea of reasonable expectations in contract law) has said that 'reasonable expectations' are those expectations that are 'objectively reasonable' based on 'community values'.[82] In the context of consumer contract terms, this could be simply another way of saying that terms should be fair in the sense that they should (according to community values) balance the interests of the parties and properly protect the interests of the (weaker) consumer. But this does not take us very far in a concrete sense. How do we identify more specific expectations for the purposes of this provision and what is the connection of such expectations with 'community' values?

4.4.2 Terms Providing the Trader with Discretion

The idea of reasonable expectations is probably best understood by first of all highlighting the type of term that s. 3(2)(b)(i) is generally accepted to be aimed at. The consensus is that the provision is aimed mainly at the sort of terms that provide for one of the parties (here the trader) to have some form of discretion in the way that he performs his obligations.[83] In the Law Commission Report that led to UCTA the following well-known example was given: 'Steamers, Sailing Dates, Rates and Itineraries are subject to change without notice'.[84]

Then there are more recent examples from OFT work under the UTCCR.[85] First of all, we have a term used by a shipping company: 'Stenna Sealink reserves the right to alter, amend, or cancel any of the arrangements shown in this publication'.[86]

---

[82] J. Steyn, Fulfilling the Reasonable Expectations of Honest Men, (1997) 113 Law Quarterly Review 433 at 434.

[83] See E. Mc Kendrick, Contract Law, 6th edn, Palgrave Macmillan, 2005, 244; and see discussion by H. Collins, Discretionary Power in Contracts, in D. Campbell, H. Collins and J. Wightman, Implicit Dimensions of Contract, Hart, 2003, 233–237.

[84] From *Anglo-Continental Holidays* v. *Typaldos (London) Ltd* [1967] 2 Lloyds Rep 61, CA, 462, cited in the Law Commission Report, No. 69 (1975) at paras 143–6.

[85] As we shall see below (at 5.7.6) the UTCCR concept of unfairness also has a strong focus on reasonable expectations and terms that allow for compromise of the reasonable expectations of the consumer.

[86] Stenna Line, OFT Bulletin 1.

Then we have a term used by a health club which gives the management, 'the right to refuse access to the club without giving any reason for doing so' and 'the right to change the training days or to alternate the training days for men and ladies' if they felt it was 'to the benefit of the club ... without any refund or reimbursement of any kind'.[87]

What we can see, then, are terms giving the trader the right to make changes in the way he performs his obligations. Indeed, in the Stenna Sealink example there is a right to cancel the contract; and it has been held that a term giving a party the right to terminate is indeed covered by s. 3.[88]

So, in what way do such terms deviate from reasonable expectations (or more specifically, allow the trader to perform in a way that is substantially different from that reasonably expected by the consumer)? What reasonable expectations are we talking about? Where do they come from?

4.4.3 Reasonable Expectations: Sources, Contracting Communities, Unilateral Expectations and Community Values

It seems likely that the reasonable expectations in question are viewed as being constructed (at least in part) by a source or sources *other than* the formal term in question. Whitford talks of US conceptions of reasonable expectations under which the question is whether a term reflects the 'pre-existing expectations of the parties'.[89] Similar ideas appear in other US literature which is focused more on good faith *performance* of contracts. So, for example, Nehf refers to good faith performance involving parties acting consistently with the 'justified expectations' of the parties.[90] However, questions remain as to where exactly these expectations come from, what these expectations are and why it is more 'reasonable' to rely on them than it is to rely on expectations created by the formal terms.[91]

---

87 Falkirk Sunbed, Solarium and Ladies Health Club, OFT Bulletin 1.

88 *Timeload Ltd* v. *British Telecommunications Plc*. [1995]3 EMLR 459, CA.

89 W.C. Whitford, Contract Law and the Control of Standardised Terms in Consumer Contracts: An American Report (1995) 3 European Review of Private Law, 193, at 201.

90 J. Nehf, Bad Faith Breach of Contract on Consumer Transactions, in R. Brownsword, N. Hird and G. Howells, Good Faith in Contract: Concept and Context, Ashgate, 1999, at 124.

91 See H. Collins, Discretionary Power in Contracts, in D. Campbell, H. Collins and J. Wightman, Implicit Dimensions of Contract, Hart, 2003, 233–237, where he points out the challenges of talking about 'reasonable expectations' as to what the other

Also, in what way do these discretion giving terms compromise these expectations?

To get the beginnings of an answer to these questions we need to go back to the Law Commission Report upon which UCTA is based. The mischief that the Law Commissions viewed as being caused by such terms (and which s. 3(2)(b)(i) was intended to address) was said to be that in the case of these types of term there was a 'likelihood that in the light of surrounding circumstances including the way in which the contract was presented the consumer might reasonably have misunderstood the extent of the obligation'.[92] So, for the Law Commissions, pre-existing expectations might come from two sources: the surrounding circumstances and the way in which the contract is presented.

The general idea, then, seems to be as follows. The surrounding circumstances generate an expectation to the effect that the trader will essentially perform his core or other obligations in a particular way and possibly also (e.g. where an ongoing service is concerned) that it will continue to be supplied indefinitely unless the consumer wishes to discontinue or the consumer is in serious breach or some extraordinary circumstances arise. This expectation may then be fortified by the fact that the most prominent terms of the contract do not contradict it in any way. They simply refer in simple terms to the basic performance obligation and nothing is said of a right to vary or terminate. However, we then find that there is a term which gives the trader rights to vary or perhaps even to terminate his performance, i.e. not to perform as was expected based on the surrounding circumstances and possibly also the most prominent formal terms.

We must now unpack this a little further to see some of the specific ways in which surrounding circumstances and the prominent terms of the contract might generate expectations, why these are 'reasonable' expectations and what connection there is to 'community values'. In many commercial contracts when we talk about 'surrounding circumstances' we may really be talking about shared understandings as to how contracts will be performed and what will happen where there is a problem of some type. A shared understanding (as to what it is reasonable to expect in the sense of what the terms actually provide and what it is reasonable to expect in terms of practical resolution of the matter) is possible in many commercial contracting contexts. It is possible in those cases where the parties form a part of the same contracting community and have dealt with each other (or at least in this community) sufficiently often to develop common understandings as to what terms say and what it

---

party can do, when there is express contractual provision as to what he can do; and see also M. Chen-Wishart, Contract Law, OUP, 2005, 461.

[92]   Paragraph 146.

is reasonable to expect in practice where disputes arise as to the performance of one of the parties. These shared understandings and expectations will come from factors such as trade usage, custom, past dealings etc.[93] The shared understandings and expectations may be, for example, that it is the formal terms of the contract (read as a whole) that determine what happens. So, if the formal terms allow for variation or arbitrary termination, then this is what can be expected. However, it is quite possible that the shared understandings and expectations are not really based on what the formal terms provide.[94] It may be that the shared understandings and expectations are that (whatever the formal terms read as a whole may say) parties perform according to the *gist* of what was agreed; that there is no right to deviate from this (at least not without some form of sanction); and that (again whatever the formal terms may say) the parties will not withdraw the service (or discontinue supply of goods) arbitrarily. In this situation, then, this shared understanding and expectation translates (for the purposes of s. 3) into a reasonable expectation held by the promisee that there will not be variation or termination. The 'reasonableness' of having expectations that are out of step with what the formal terms may actually say, lies in the fact that these expectations are grounded in practice and experience and are shared by the parties. These reasonable expectations are grounded in 'community values' in the sense that they are based on membership of the particular contracting community. In addition, it might be said that the community in general (i.e. the broader community) would regard it as appropriate that terms should be measured by reference to the norms of the particular contracting community. Expectations grounded in the shared experiences and understandings of particular contracting communities have been described as having an 'empirical' basis, i.e. they are based on the observations of contractors from their past experience.[95] This can be contrasted with an 'institutional' approach to expectations, i.e. one that determines expectations by reference to what is provided for in the institution that is the formal contract.[96] Of course, notwithstanding the

---

[93]   These are all factors that have a role to play in some US approaches to reasonable expectations – see J. Nehf, Bad Faith Breach of Contract in Consumer Transactions, in R. Brownsword, N. Hird and G. Howells, Good Faith in Contract: Concept and Context, Asgate, 1999, 125–6.

[94]   See J. Wightman, Beyond Custom: Contracts, Contexts and the Recognition of Implicit Understandings, in D. Campbell, H. Collins and J. Wightman, Implicit Dimensions of Contract, Hart, 2003, 149–160.

[95]   C. Mitchell, Leading a Life of its Own? The Roles of Reasonable Expectation in Contract Law, Oxford Journal of Legal Studies, Vol. 23, No. 4 (2003), 639, at 655–657.

[96]   C. Mitchell, *ibid.*

validity of this way of characterizing the distinction it can be argued that a *normative* choice is also involved. Surely the choice to focus on these particular empirically based expectations (rather than insisting on focusing purely what is contained in the formal terms) is a normative (i.e. fairness-oriented) choice. In other words it is regarded as fairer to prioritise expectations based on shared past experience over expectations based on the formal contract.

Reasonable expectations in relation to *consumer* contracts will not usually be determinable by reference to the same type of 'surrounding circumstances' as are applicable in commercial contracts. In consumer contracts there may be much less of a *shared* understanding as between the parties as to what it is reasonable to expect.[97] There may be a shared understanding as to what normally *happens* in the routine supply of particular goods and services, i.e. that they are routinely supplied according to the general gist of what has been agreed to. However, there is much less of a sense of a shared understanding as to what the terms actually say and what will happen in practice in those cases where the terms themselves actually come into play,[98] i.e. those cases where there is some form of dispute as to the performance/liabilities of either of the parties. In other words, consumers are often not sufficiently frequent buyers of goods or services from particular categories of traders so as to enable them to develop an experience based understanding as to what the terms actually say on matters such as variation and termination by the trader. This compounds the fact that the terms are unlikely to be sufficiently transparent for consumers to gain this understanding in specific cases. In addition, consumers are often not sufficiently frequent buyers of goods or services from particular categories of traders so as to enable them to develop an understanding that is shared with the trader as what happens *in practice* in relation to the trader seeking to vary or terminate the contract. So, when we talk of measuring terms (e.g. those dealing with variation and termination by the trader) against a notion of reasonable expectations based on 'surrounding circumstances' we are very often really talking about the unilateral expectations[99] of the consumer as to the scope of the obligations (and in particular here, the trader's performance obligations).

For consumers, these expectations are likely to be formed by the basic description of the goods or services at the point of sale or in advertising; and by the perceptions of the consumer as to what normally happens in transactions of this type (these perceptions being formed by personal experiences of buying these goods or services from this trader or other

---

[97] J. Wightman, *supra*, n. 94, 160–172.

[98] *Ibid.*

[99] *Ibid.*, 177–184.

traders and/or by observation of what normally happens to others when they purchase such goods and services).

So, as we have seen, (by contrast with many commercial contractors) consumer expectations are not really based on 'community values' in the sense that they are based on membership of the particular contracting community and the shared values and understanding of that community. Consumer expectations are of a more unilateral nature. However, they are *reasonable* to the extent that they are based on the way the goods or services are presented and what normally happens (none of this being reasonably contradicted for the consumer by the formal terms as these are unlikely to impinge sufficiently on the consciousness of the consumer). Here, then, if we wish to tie these reasonable expectations of the consumer to 'community values' we are not talking about the values of a *contracting* community. We are talking, rather, of the broader community who (we might say) would think it reasonable, in all the circumstances, to have such expectations.

4.4.4 The Content of the Reasonable Expectations

So, what will these expectations relate to and what will be their substance? It seems that the primary expectations of the consumer will relate to the core elements of the trader's performance and the core elements of his own (the consumer's) performance.[100] So the consumer will have expectations as to the basic nature of the goods or services to be provided and the price that he will have to pay for these goods or services (goods or services of a certain type, at a certain price, perhaps – depending upon the type of contract – to be supplied at a particular time and place). These expectations, as already suggested, will come from the basic presentation of the goods or services at the point of sale and/or in advertising or other promotion. The consumer will expect to receive goods or services that accord with the basic way in which they have been described at the point of sale and/or in promotional material; and to pay the price as it has been described at the point of sale and/or in promotional material. These expectations are typically fortified by the fact that this is what normally happens.[101] The consumer may not buy

---

[100] See R. Brownsword, G. Howells and T. Wilhelmsson, Between Market and Welfare: Some Reflections on Article 3 of the EC Directive on Unfair Terms in Consumer Contracts, in C. Willett (ed.), Aspects of Fairness in Consumer Contract, at p. 41.

[101] See F. Kessler, Contracts of Adhesion (1943) 43 Columbia Law Review, 629 at 637, W.D Slawson, Binding Promises, 1996, Princeton University Press, at 65 and B.J. Reiter and J. Swan, Contracts and the Protection of Reasonable Expectations, in B.J. Reiter and J. Swan (eds), Studies in Contract Law, 1980, Toronto: Butterworths, at

frequently from this trader. Indeed he may never have bought from this trader before. However, his experience of buying from other traders and his experience of observing others will tell him that goods or services are normally supplied in accordance with the basic expectations generated by the initial description/presentation; and the price to be paid is normally as per the initial description/presentation. There is not normally variation or early termination. In sum, there is experience of, and an expectation of, successful performance, reflecting the gist of what has been suggested outwith the formal terms); and experience of, and an expectation of, paying the price that was suggested outwith the formal terms. There is less experience of variation and early termination. Also, of course, it is possible that other factors come into play, like past experience of this trader, which may further justify an expectation that what was expressed in the basic encounter will be received or may perhaps suggest that there *is* in fact scope for variations etc.

Pre-existing expectations are not necessarily confined to core aspects of the contract. There may also be signals and expectations on other issues related to the contract (because the trader has chosen to emphasize, and/or the consumer has shown an interest in, these particular issues).[102]

In sum, then, the 'surrounding circumstances' will usually (although not necessarily always) generate an expectation in the consumer that traders will perform the gist of what was promised and that there will be no variation of this and that the trader will not arbitrarily terminate the relationship.

Another point requires emphasis here. If, in constructing a notion of what it is reasonable to expect, we were to focus purely on *consumer* experience (i.e. on the consumer experience of uninterrupted performance according to the gist of the contract), this (empirical) model might be a rather weak justification for a legal entitlement (in this case the entitlement being the setting aside of formal terms). It might be viewed as weak by comparison with the empirical basis of expectation existing in commercial contracts (i.e. *shared* experience).[103] The argument has been made that some other justification is needed – some normative justification.[104] The difficulty is that some normative justifications – e.g. simply that 'fairness' demands that a term not allow too much discretion

---

65; all of whom share the same broad view of expectations emerging from life experiences of dealing with traders.

[102] M.I. Meyerson, The Reunification of Contract Law: The Objective Theory of Consumer Form Contracts (1993) 47 University of Miami Law Review, 1263, at 1301.

[103] C. Mitchell, Leading a Life of its Own? The Roles of Reasonable Expectation in Contract Law, Oxford Journal of Legal Studies, Vol. 23, No. 4 (2003), 639, at 656.

[104] *Ibid.*, at 656–7.

for a trader – seem to reduce or negate the need to focus on reasonable expectations in the first place. Why talk of reasonable expectations if we simply mean a more general notion of fairness? However, if we say that the normative justification for 'enforcing' the expectation is connected to the 'moral' position of the trader in relation to the expectation, then the expectation itself remains at the core of the analysis *and* the expectation is also given greater legitimacy. The way in which the moral position of the trader enters the equation here seems to be through the notion of '*encouraged* expectations'.[105] I would explain this in the following way. The expectations we have been discussing have, on the whole, been induced by the trading community in general. This community supplies goods and services on the basis of a general gist of an agreement. It knows perfectly well that consumers will expect the type of performance suggested by this gist agreement. It knows that this is expected because it is what normally happens. It knows that it is using formal terms which are likely to have very little real impact on the consciousness of the consumer and do very little to alter consumer expectations. As such, it can surely be argued that traders play a role in encouraging consumers to expect smooth performance with a limited discretion to change things. On this basis the concept of reasonable expectation retains relevance and the legitimacy and 'reasonableness' of the expectation is fortified.

4.4.5 Reasonable Expectations and Transparent Formal Terms

In consumer cases these expectations are likely to be reasonable (despite the fact that they may be contradicted by the formal terms) not only because of the surrounding circumstances described and the strength of the signals received in the context of these surrounding circumstances; but also because, as we saw above, the formal terms may not be particularly transparent to the average consumer. There may be a main term that suggests that there will be routine performance without variation or termination. This may be much more transparent than any term allowing for variation or termination. This, as we saw, was part of the Law Commission's concern. Not only might there be background expectations from the surrounding circumstances, but the structure of the formal terms themselves may tend to reinforce these background expectations. However, even where this is not the case (i.e. even where the term allowing for variation or termination is reasonably prominent in the formal terms) this may have limited impact in practice on the average consumer. As we have already suggested, even where the terms are fairly transparent there will often be limited time to read them; and most

---

[105] *Ibid.*, at 660–663.

consumers may be unlikely to read them even where there is time.[106] So, the consumer is likely to have given a very insubstantial degree of consent to the formal terms and they are likely to have a fairly limited role to play in forming the expectations of the average consumer. The expectations generated by the surrounding circumstances are likely to have a much more significant impact on the consciousness of the consumer than do the formal terms.[107] As such, it is arguable that there should be a strong presumption in consumer cases to the effect that the formal terms have played no significant role in determining the expectations of the consumer.[108] Of course, this is not to say that it may not have been made genuinely clear to the consumer outwith the formal terms that there is a real possibility of variation in performance (and that this is reflected in a formal term). In such a case the pre-existing expectations of the consumer will genuinely have been altered and the term may now reflect these expectations. However, this is not because of what the term says, but because of what has been said outwith the formal terms.

There is another problem with saying that if a formal term provides (transparently) for the trader to have discretion of some kind then this should be treated as having altered the expectations of the consumer; so that trader discretion is now what the consumer reasonably expects. The problem is that there is then no further possibility of control on any other

---

[106] See above at 2.4.3.5(iii).

[107] Focusing on the surrounding circumstances and what is 'normally expected' given the nature of the contract and what is normal (more than on the way the deal was presented in the formal contract document) seems to reflect the Italian approach – see P. Nebbia, Unfair Contract Terms in European Law, Hart, 2007, 131–2.

[108] If such an approach is not taken there is a risk that the provision becomes weakened and gets closer to a rule of construction such as the main purpose rule, which construes the term in light of background expectations but enforces the term as long as its effect is clearly expressed by the formal terms, even where the formal terms do not genuinely reflect the reasonable expectations of the consumer – see further below at 8.1.4. Of course, it may be that in commercial contracts it is appropriate to place greater emphasis on the overall presentation of the formal terms (at the expense of the 'surrounding circumstances) in determining the reasonable expectations of the party affected by the discretion. On this see E. McKendrick. (Contract Law, 6th edn, Palgrave Macmillan, 2005, 244) who suggests that insufficient attention may have been paid to the terms in a commercial case involving a term allowing the provider of a service to terminate the contract 'at any time' (*Timeload Ltd* v. *BT plc.*, [1995] EMLR 459). See also the discussion by C. Mitchell, Leading a Life of its Own? The Roles of Reasonable Expectation in Contract Law, Oxford Journal of Legal Studies, Vol. 23, No. 4 (2003), 639, at 647–654 which characterizes a reasonable expectations model that is focused on what the formal terms provide for as 'institutional', i.e. based on the institution of the contract.

fairness grounds. If the term is held *not* to allow for a contractual performance substantially different from what was expected (on the basis that the term is transparent enough to have altered the expectations of the consumer, or on any other basis) the term is not subject to the reasonableness test. This means that there is no scope to consider matters of fairness in substance (e.g. as to the breadth of the discretion) or other issues of procedural fairness (e.g. as to whether a choice was offered). If, on the other hand, a term providing for discretion to be exercised by the trader is found to allow for a contractual performance substantially different from what was expected the term is subject to the reasonableness test. Under the auspices of the reasonableness test the question as to the transparency of the term can be taken into account; but this will not be at the expense of other procedural and substantive factors that may indicate that the term is unreasonable – these factors will also be able to be taken into account.

4.4.6 The UCTA Concept Compared with Other Reasonable Expectations Concepts

The idea, then, is that the reasonable expectations benchmark described is applied to the term itself. The question is whether the term would allow the trader to perform in a way that is out of step with the reasonable expectations of the parties (these being constructed in the way described above). If this is the case, the term is subject to the reasonableness test. This can be contrasted with other approaches to discretion giving terms (applied to terms before UCTA was enacted, or still applied to terms falling outside UCTA). One such approach is seen in a rule of construction such as the so called 'main purpose' rule. Here, the scope for the exercise of discretion is construed narrowly in the light of the main purpose of the contract (this being determined by looking at least to some extent beyond what is said by the formal term).[109] Of course, where such a rule is concerned, there is a limit to the control available. If the term clearly enough provides for the discretion then ultimately it overrides the background expectation.

The approach of s. 3 is also different from other techniques for controlling contractual discretion. One such approach is to imply a term to the effect that the discretion must be *exercised* according to certain standards, e.g. that it must be exercised by reference to fiduciary

---

[109] See *Glynn* v. *Margetson* [1893] AC 351, in particular Lord Halsbury at 357; see discussion by B. Coote, Exception Clauses, Sweet and Maxwell, 1964, 94–98; and see below at 8.1.3.

standards, fairly, not capriciously etc.[110] Another approach is to insist upon good faith *exercise* of the discretion under the auspices of a *good faith in performance* rule such as that existing in the US.[111] Here, again, the idea is often that the discretion be exercised in accordance with background expectations;[112] and not capriciously. These approaches focus on the *exercise* of the discretion, rather than whether the *term* is problematic itself in *allowing* for such a discretion. (Of course, there is a very similar agenda in that the more the *term* allows for unfair or capricious exercise of the discretion the more objectionable it will be as a term in *allowing* for compromise of reasonable consumer expectation; while unfair or capricious *exercise* of the discretion would be likely to be viewed as being in violation of good faith and at odds with the reasonable expectations of the consumer.)

However, these approaches which focus on the *exercise* of the discretion are often weaker (in terms of protecting the party affected by the discretion) than an approach that focuses on whether the term itself is valid. Such an approach is concerned purely with the objective question as to what the term allows to happen. By contrast, the approaches focusing on exercise of the discretion sometimes excuse the way in which the discretion has been exercised as long as there was subjective good faith in the sense of a genuine or honest approach to its exercise.[113]

4.4.7 The 'No Performance at All' Rule

Section 3 also allows for control of terms allowing the trader 'in respect of the whole or part of his contractual obligation, to render no performance at all'.[114] This has always been a curious provision. First of all, it must surely be the case that it is not aimed at terms that allow the trader not to perform all or part of his obligation in cases where the law would (in any event) give him this right based on the serious breach of the consumer. It must surely be aimed at cases in which the right not to

---

[110] See H. Collins, Discretionary Power in Contracts, in D. Campbell, H. Collins and J. Wightman, Implicit Dimensions of Contract, Hart, 2003, 219 at 238, 241, 245; and T. Daintith, Contractual Discretion and Administrative Discretion: A Unified Analysis (2005) 68 Modern Law Review 554, at 567–575.

[111] See J. Nehf, Bad Faith Breach of Contract in Consumer Transactions in R. Brownsword, N. Hird and G. Howells (eds), Good Faith in Contract: Concept and Context, Ashgate, 1999 at 125–6 and 128–131.

[112] J. Nehf, *ibid.*, 124, 130.

[113] See H. Collins, Discretionary Power in Contracts, in D. Campbell, H. Collins and J. Wightman, Implicit Dimensions of Contract, Hart, 2003, 219 at 238, 241, 245.

[114] Section 3(2)(b)(ii).

perform would not exist 'but for' the term. This being the case, it has been pointed out that it may not add anything to the common law to the extent that it allows for *no performance at all* (i.e. of the entirety of the trader's obligation under the contract); as in such a case there would be a total failure of consideration.[115] To the extent that it is aimed at terms allowing the trader not to perform *part* of his contractual obligation, such terms will surely often be covered in any case by the reasonable expectations standard we have been discussing. A term allowing for part of the trader's contractual obligation not to be performed could often be said to be allowing for a contractual performance substantially different from that reasonably expected by the consumer. Perhaps, however, the idea was to ensure coverage of terms allowing a distinct element of the obligation not to be performed whether or not this would represent a contractual performance substantially different from that reasonably expected.

4.4.8 The Limits of UCTA in Relation to Reasonable Expectations

4.4.8.1 Only Terms Dealing with the Performance of the Trader

We must, of course, also remember that (in keeping with the general approach under UCTA and the approach taken to terms deviating from default rules[116]) s. 3(2)(b) is only focused on terms dealing with the performance of the party using the term (for our purposes, the trader). It does not catch terms allowing the trader discretion in fixing or varying the obligations of *consumers* (e.g. the right to vary the interest rate or price due from the consumer). Such a discretionary power relates to the performance of the consumer and not that of the trader.

By contrast, as we shall see, the UTCCR covers not only those terms allowing the trader to perform in ways that are out of step with the reasonable expectations of the consumer, but also terms fixing *consumer* obligations that are out of step with such reasonable expectations.

4.4.8.2 Reasonable Expectations, the Core Performance Obligation of the Trader and a Comparison with the UTCCR

Even within the ambit of what is covered by UCTA, it must also be emphasized that the essence of s. 3(2)(b)(i) is that a term is only caught if

---

[115] See D. Oughton and J. Lowry, Textbook on Consumer Law, OUP, 2000, 395 and M. Chen-Wishart, Contract Law, OUP, 2005, 461–2.

[116] See above at 4.2.5.

it allows for a contractual performance substantially *different* from that reasonably expected by the consumer. As I have suggested, the main pre-existing expectations of the consumer are likely to relate to the core aspects of the contract, i.e. the essential nature of the goods or services being supplied and the basic price obligation. So, if the background expectation of the consumer is that the trader will supply particular goods or services and that there will be no change or variation in this, then a term allowing for such change or variation will be caught by s. 3(2)(b)(i). However, if a term simply reflects what the consumer would reasonably have expected then it is not controlled. So, if the term (whether dealing with the core performance obligation of the trader or any other performance obligation of the trader) does not allow for a variation, or if it does allow for such a variation but this reflects the background expectations, then the term is not controlled. So, although UCTA does not positively exclude terms defining the core performance obligation of the trader, it only covers such terms where they do not reflect the reasonable expectations of the consumer. The UTCCR *does* positively exclude terms defining the 'main subject matter' of the contract,[117] which means terms defining the core performance obligation of the trader.[118] However, as we shall see, this probably only means those terms that genuinely reflect the background expectations of the consumer as to the core performance obligation of the trader.[119] In other words, the result seems to more or less the same under both pieces of legislation: a term genuinely reflecting the reasonable expectations of the consumer as to the core performance obligation of the trader will not be caught, while a term allowing for deviation from these expectations will be covered.

4.4.8.3 Reasonable Expectations, Pre-Contractual Statements, Entire Agreement Clauses and a Comparison with the UTCCR

The above discussion has focused on reasonable expectations that are formed from 'surrounding circumstances' and the way in which the formal terms are presented (i.e. a combination of the way in which things are described in general and by formal terms that are likely to be focused on by consumers; along with what consumers might expect from past experience and general life experience). The idea has been that (taking these various factors into account) consumers may not reasonably expect that traders will be entitled to vary or terminate the contract at their

---

[117] Regulation 6(2)(a).
[118] See below at 5.8.1.
[119] See below at 5.8.3.1.

discretion. It is terms that allow for traders to exercise such discretion that most of the commentary and case law on s. 3(2)(b)(i) has focused on.

However, very little thought seems to have been given to the prospects for using this provision to control terms that deny responsibility for the specific expectations created by pre-contractual statements. So there may be a so called 'entire agreement clause' in the formal contract which asserts that the formal contract represents the full extent of the trader's contractual obligation and that nothing said pre-contractually can be viewed as forming the basis of a contractual obligation on the trader. Let us suppose that, ignoring such a clause, a pre-contractual statement would otherwise satisfy the criteria for being treated as a contractual term, e.g. because it relates to an important matter that the consumer had enquired about and appears to have been strongly influential in persuading the consumer to enter the contract. It is surely then arguable that the consumer now has a reasonable expectation to the effect that the performance of the trader will reflect the statement. It is surely also arguable that a term denying contractual effect to such a statement is covered by s. 3(2)(b)(i) on the basis that it is allowing for a contractual performance substantially different from that reasonably expected. Such an approach would surely fit with the idea that consumer expectations are created by factors (such as pre-contractual statements) arising outside the formal terms; and that the formal terms (including entire agreement clauses) will rarely be sufficiently transparent to consumers to alter these expectations. There now appears to be judicial support for such an approach;[120] although there is generally considerable doubt as to the status of entire agreement clauses and the position under UCTA, s. 3 was certainly less clear prior to the *SAM Business Systems* case.[121]

This is in contrast to the position under the UTCCR. We shall see below that there is little doubt that entire agreement clauses denying the contractual effect of pre-contractual statements are certainly an important target under the UTCCR;[122] and will very often be viewed as unfair.[123]

4.5 Reasonable Expectations under the Proposed New Regime – a Comparison with UCTA

As we have seen, the proposed new regime would catch any term causing 'detriment'; this being caused by any term that is substantively

---

[120] *SAM Business Systems* v. *Hedley & Co.*, [2003], All ER (COMM) 465.

[121] For a general discussion of entire agreement clauses see E. Macdonald, Exemption Clauses and Unfair Terms, Butterworths, 2nd edn, 2006, 70–77.

[122] See below at 5.7.6.1–2.

[123] See below at 6.3.2.2(b).

detrimental to the consumer.[124] In terms of a comparison with UCTA, this, as we saw above, covers terms excluding or restricting obligations or liabilities that would otherwise be owed as a matter of law by the trader. However, it would also seem to cover terms defining the performance obligation of the trader in ways that are substantially different from that reasonably expected by the consumer (based on the background expectations of the consumer). In other words it covers the terms discussed above that are currently covered by UCTA, s. 3(2)(b)(i). However, it may go further than this in relation to terms dealing with the performance of the trader. First of all, it removes any formal need for the term to allow for a performance that is *substantially* different from that reasonably expected by the consumer. In this respect it may set a higher level of protection than UCTA (although it is likely that the courts would interpret 'detriment' so as to require that the scope for variation is in some way material). The second way in which the proposed new 'detriment' trigger may go further than s. 3(2)(b)(i) in relation to the performance of the trader is that it presumably catches any scope for variation that would not be caught by the reasonable expectations formula under UCTA. So, first of all it should cover entire agreement clauses denying contractual effect to pre-contractual statements. As we have seen, these may not be covered by s. 3(2)(b)(i), but are covered by the UTCCR. If they are covered by the UTCCR they will need to be deemed to cause detriment under the new regime, so that the new regime properly covers what is covered by the UTD/UTCCR. In addition, terms allowing the trader to not to perform all or part of his contractual obligation (i.e. those terms caught by s. 3(2)(b)(ii)) presumably cause detriment whether or not they can be related to the expectations of the consumer as such.

Of course, the detriment trigger is clearly also broader in another sense. UCTA, s. 3(2)(b) only covers terms dealing with the performance obligation of the trader. However, the new regime (like the UTCCR) also covers terms dealing with the performance obligations of the consumer. So, if a term requires the consumer to perform in a way that is out of step with the reasonable expectations of the consumer, it seems likely that it will cause detriment and be subject to the proposed new fair and reasonable test.

---

[124] Draft Bill, Clause 4(1) and see above at 4.3.1.

4.6 The UCTA Reasonableness Test

4.6.1 Introduction to Procedural and Substantive Criteria

We now turn to consider the approach of the courts to the test of reasonableness under UCTA.[125] UCTA only applies in the context of private litigation between the parties to a particular contract. As such, the decision-makers are the lower and higher courts. A number of cases involving consumers (and some involving commercial customers that provide useful insights) have reached the courts over the years. The basic substance of the term and its implications for the consumer has, of course, always been regarded as being of relevance. Sometimes this has been essentially about financial losses. So, for example, one case involved assessing the reasonableness of a term limiting a carrier's liability to a sum calculated by reference to the weight of the item (a suitcase).[126] However, this meant liability of only £27 when the actual value of the item was £320. This difference (and the large loss that would be suffered

---

[125] The test of reasonableness is set out in UCTA, s. 11. The basic test is whether the term is 'a fair and reasonable one to be included having regard to the circumstances which were, or ought reasonably to have been, known to or in the contemplation of the parties when the contract was made' (s. 11(1)). The only other guidance in the Act that is technically applicable to consumer contracts is the guidance in s. 11(4). There it is provided that that if a contract term or notice restricts liability to a specified sum of money regard shall be had to '(a) the resources which he could expect to be available to him for the purpose of meeting the liability should it arise; and (b) how far it was open to him to cover himself by insurance'. Further guidelines are supplied in Schedule 2 to UCTA. These are technically only relevant in commercial contracts in relation to exclusion or restriction of the implied terms as to description, quality and fitness in contracts of the sale and supply of goods (s. 11(2)). However, the courts have drawn upon these in consumer cases. The guidelines are: (a) the strength of the bargaining positions of the parties relative to each other, taking into account (among other things) alternative means by which the customer's requirements could have been met; (b) whether the consumer received an inducement to agree to the term, or in accepting it had an opportunity of entering into a similar contract with other persons, but without having to accept a similar term; (c) whether the customer knew or ought reasonably to have known of the existence and extent of the term (having regard, among other things, to any custom of the trade and any previous course of dealing between the parties); (d) where the term excludes or restricts any relevant liability if some condition is not complied with, whether it was reasonable at the time of the contract to expect that compliance with that condition would be practicable; (e) whether the goods were manufactured, processed or adapted to the special order of the customer'.

[126] *Waldron-Kelly* v. *BRB* [1981]3 Curr Law 33.

by the consumer if the clause were to be upheld) influenced the court in deciding the term was unreasonable. In other cases the effect of the substance of the term on other interests of the consumer has had an influence. So, for example, *Woodman* v. *Photo Trade Processing*[127] concerned the liability of a shop for loss or damage to photographs they were developing for the customer. A notice limited the liability of the shop to the cost of the film. This was unreasonable in part because it fell far short of compensating the customer for the loss of wedding photos that were of considerable sentimental value.

A further point about the approach of the courts to the substantive terms is this. It is noticeable that there has been no pattern of the courts considering the overall balance of rights and obligations, i.e. there has not been a pattern of the courts looking at the question of overall substantive fairness. In other words, the focus has been on the particular interest affected by the term and not whether it is justifiable to compromise this interest based on other terms that might be favourable to the consumer.[128]

Procedural matters have also been regarded as relevant. So, for example, in the *Woodman* case the shop did not offer a choice of another service that accepted liability albeit at a higher price; and this counted against the reasonableness of the notice.[129] The transparency of a term and whether the customer could have known of and understood it has also been identified as relevant in some commercial cases; although, interestingly never seems to have been raised as an issue in consumer cases.[130]

Unsurprisingly, there has not been any sort of comprehensive analysis by the lower courts of what factors should be taken into account and how they should interact, e.g. how procedural and substantive matters should be weighed against one another.

4.6.2 Reasonableness in the Higher Courts

4.6.2.1 Discretion, Substance and Procedure

Moving to the higher courts, the House of Lords has only heard a few cases of any relevance to consumer contracts. *Smith* v. *Bush*[131] is the only

---

[127] (1981) 131 New Law Journal 935.
[128] On the distinction between focusing on the particular interest affected by the term and focusing on broader substantive fairness see above at 2.4.3.3.
[129] *Ibid.*
[130] *AEG (UK) Ltd* v. *Logic Resource Ltd* [1996] CLC 265.
[131] [1989] 2 All ER 514.

actual consumer case; while *George Mitchell* v. *Finney Lockseeds*[132] (a commercial case) has some relevance. *Smith* was a case about exclusion of a surveyor's liability in negligence for a valuation report which the consumer had relied upon. The report missed various problems and the consumer ended up with a house that was worth considerably less than it would have been if the report had been accurate. The term in question had the effect of excluding liability for negligence. The exclusion was held to have failed the reasonableness test. The House of Lords identified various factors (to which we shall turn shortly) that they considered should be taken into account at least in cases involving exclusion of liability for negligence. However, it seems clear that (beyond this guidance) the lower courts are free to consider other factors. In *George Mitchell* the House of Lords indicated that the first instance decision should be treated with the 'utmost respect' unless it was based on some 'erroneous principle or was plainly or obviously wrong'.[133] This seems to be referring, *inter alia*,[134] to whether it is wrong in law to take certain factors into account, the idea being that any factor that could be described as relevant in any way to process or substance can be taken into account. It seems as if a factor would only be regarded as based on an 'erroneous principle' or being 'plainly and obviously wrong' if no rational connection could be made between the issue and the reasonableness of the term. The latitude to be allowed to the lower courts in deciding what factors are relevant is then emphasized by the statement that the courts should 'entertain a whole range of considerations, put them on the scales on one side or the other, and decide at the end of the day on which side the balance comes down'.[135] This emphasizes that the lower courts are free to consider a wide range of factors. However, if a court actually misunderstands the meaning of a particular factor then the higher courts will intervene.[136]

Some of the factors identified in *Smith* related to the substance of the term. First of all, there was 'the sums of money potentially at stake and the ability of the parties to bear the loss involved', this being viewed in the context of the 'the availability and cost of insurance'.[137] These issues

---

[132] [1983] 2 AC 803.

[133] *Ibid.*, at 810.

[134] It also seems to be a reference to the application of the law to the facts – see below at 4.6.2.4.

[135] At 816.

[136] See for example *AEG (UK) Ltd* v. *Logic Resource Ltd* [1996] CLC 265 where the first instance judge thought that the question as to whether a party knows or should know of the existence of a term (see UCTA Schedule 2 guidelines, (c), *supra*) could be equated with the common law test of incorporation. The Court of Appeal made it clear that this was not the case and that more is expected under Schedule 2, para. (c).

[137] Lord Griffiths at 530–1.

are related to substance in that it is the substance of the term that determines how much liability is being excluded and therefore what sums are involved and whether insurance would be available to cover these losses. Essentially it was thought that the surveyor was better placed to absorb the loss. A huge loss would be involved for the consumer if the exclusion of liability was effective; while the surveyor could accept liability and insure accordingly without a significant increase in premiums. Another factor regarded as relevant was the degree of difficulty of the task being carried out by the surveyor.[138] This is related to substance in that what the court was saying was that if there was a high risk of failure because the task was difficult or dangerous then this would make it more reasonable for the substantive term to exclude liability. In the circumstances, the view was that a valuation was at the 'lower end of the surveyor's field of professional expertise' and only requiring 'a fairly elementary degree of skill and care'.[139] This made exclusion of liability less reasonable.

Again, as with the lower courts, the focus was on the specific way in which the term affected the interests of the consumers involved. There was no particular focus on overall substantive fairness, i.e. whether there was a favourable term that balanced out the detriment caused by the exclusion of liability. Certainly the House of Lords did not make any suggestion that the price of the valuation must be assumed to be lower than it would have been without the exclusion (based on the fact that the term and the price seem to have been fairly typical for the market[140]); and that there could therefore be said to be overall substantive fairness.

Then there were factors related to procedural fairness. First, there was the relative bargaining power of the parties. The clause would be more likely to be reasonable if it had been agreed to in a 'one-off situation between parties of equal bargaining power', as opposed to this situation in which the consumer had 'no effective power to object'.[141] Secondly, there was the question as to whether (taking into account questions of cost and time) it would have been practicable for the consumer to have protected himself by obtaining the advice from an alternative source.[142] It should be remembered that the lender is obliged to have the valuation carried out and the consumer is required to pay for this in any event. The question, then, was whether it would be reasonable for the consumer to seek a second opinion (i.e. from a surveyor independently commissioned

---

[138] Lord Griffiths at 530.

[139] *Ibid.*

[140] This is one of the ways in which substantive fairness might be assessed – see above at 2.4.3.3.

[141] Lord Griffiths at 530.

[142] *Ibid.*

by the consumer). Such a second opinion would protect the consumer. If this second opinion picked up on the faults then the consumer would know of the risks of buying the house, would not suffer the losses in question and the defendant's exemption clause would be irrelevant. If the second opinion did not pick up on the faults then the consumer would have an action against the party that he paid for the second opinion. However the House of Lords took the view that young first time buyers who were buying at the lower end of the market would be under 'considerable financial pressure without the money to go paying twice for the same advice'.[143]

4.6.2.2 Fairness and Freedom[144]

The first general point here is that (in broad terms) the House of Lords seems to be more inclined to a fairness-oriented approach than a freedom-oriented approach. Obviously, simply by having a reasonableness test in the first place there is a rejection of the most fundamental version of a freedom-oriented approach which would reject any enquiry into reasonableness or fairness. However, once such a test is in place there are clearly choices as to how freedom- or fairness-oriented the approach to this test should be. In *Smith* v. *Bush* the approach seems to incline more towards fairness rather than freedom instincts. For example, a freedom-oriented approach to analysing the *substance* of an exclusion clause would start from the position that in the normal course of things there should be the freedom to determine the extent of one's liability – the basic assumption should be that exclusion of liability is legitimate, the impact of this on the consumer being of very limited concern. However, the premise in *Smith* v. *Bush* was much more fairness-oriented than this – if a surveyor is carrying out a routine task then he should accept and insure against liability for negligence, especially given the consequences of holding otherwise for the consumer. In addition, a more freedom-oriented approach might consider whether the detrimental features of the term were balanced out by other favourable provisions. In particular, there might be an inclination to the view that if the term and the price paid were normal in the market in question then the price must be lower than it would have been without the exclusion clause; so that this could be said to make the contract substantively fair. However, as we have seen, no such approach was taken in the case.

---

[143] *Ibid.*

[144] On the contrast between freedom-oriented and fairness-oriented approaches see 2.3–4 above.

In relation to *procedural* matters one of the issues was whether the consumer should protect his interests by seeking a second opinion as to the property. The freedom-oriented instinct would be that the consumer should be expected to take such self-reliant action and that, if he does not, the law should be disinclined to provide alternative protection by making the surveyor liable. However, the more fairness-oriented approach taken was that such self-reliance (involving paying twice for the same advice) could not be expected of these relatively poor consumers.[145]

4.6.2.3 Limitations in Guidance

We can see, then, that certain key substantive and procedural criteria emerge from the *Smith* v. *Bush* case and that, in broad terms, the House of Lords were inclined towards fairness-oriented values rather than freedom-oriented values. However, in other respects the guidance is more limited. First of all, the factors set out in *Smith* v. *Bush* were not being prescribed as such in cases involving exclusion or restriction of liability other than negligence. Secondly, the House of Lords did not undertake any significant analysis of the relationship between procedural and substantive fairness e.g. there was nothing on transparency, what role it might play and how this might interact with the substance of the term.[146] In addition, although there was discussion of choice in the sense of a second opinion, there was nothing on whether a lack of choice (in the sense of a lack of better terms being available from this or another trader at a higher price) should count against a finding of reasonableness.[147] It *was* noted that all lenders tended to use the term in question but this lack of choice was not articulated as a positive reason for the finding that the term was not reasonable. Still on the relationship between substance and procedure, we noted that the House of Lords made reference to whether the consumer had the bargaining power to object to the term in question. On the facts, the weaker bargaining power of the consumer clearly counted against the term. However, it was not made clear (although probably it was implicit) that the issue is connected to substance – the greater the unfairness in substance the more the weaker bargaining position of the consumer will count against the term.[148] Finally, on the relationship between substance and procedure, there was nothing on

---

[145] On a 'consumer-welfarist' versus a 'market-individualist approach generally in UCTA case law see J. Adams and R. Brownsword, The Unfair Contract Terms Act: A Decade of Discretion, 1988, 104 Law Quarterly Review, 94.

[146] On the general issue see above at 2.4.3.4 and see below at 6.4.2.3.

[147] On the general issue see above at 2.4.3.4 and see below at 6.4.4.

[148] On the general issue see above at 2.4.3.4 and see below at 6.4.5.

whether terms can fail the reasonableness test on purely substantive grounds.[149]

So, the guidance on offer from the House of Lords is useful but also has limitations. As we have seen, beyond the guidance provided, the lower courts are free in terms of the criteria that are applied. Of course, while it might be better if there was fuller, more rigorous guidance from the House of Lords the lower courts are as free to develop a rational approach to the issues as they are to develop an irrational one.

4.6.2.4 Lower Court Discretion in Application of the Law to the Facts

Turning now to the application of the law to the facts by lower courts, we should recall that in *George Mitchell* the House of Lords indicated that the first instance decision should be treated with the 'utmost respect' unless it was based on some 'erroneous principle or was plainly or obviously wrong'.[150] As we said, this seems to refer at least in part to whether it is wrong *in law* to take certain factors into account. However, it seems also to give latitude in relation to the application of the law to the *facts* of the case. The idea in *George Mitchell* of treating the original decision with the utmost respect (as well as referring to the factors that it is *legally* relevant to consider) clearly also refers to the way in which the law is applied to the particular facts. The reference to whether something is 'plainly or obviously wrong' (as well as referring to what it is *legally* relevant to consider) also seems to relate to the application of the law to the facts. It is clear then that the idea is that the higher courts should leave considerable scope for differences of opinion as to how the law should apply to the facts and interfere very sparingly. This approach is understandable to an extent as individual circumstances can differ so much. Now, there are certainly debates as to the extent to which a fairness regime should take a contextual approach that concerns itself with individual circumstances as opposed to an approach that focuses on more abstract questions, e.g. the substance and transparency of the term itself.[151] For good or ill, the UCTA test seems to be contextually inclined and from this premise it is clear that it is logical for decisions to vary with varying facts.[152] However, it is a cause for more concern if the provision

---

[149] On the general issue see above at 2.4.3.5 and see below at 6.5.

[150] At 810.

[151] See above at 2.4.3.6 and below at 6.3.9, 6.4.2.1, 6.4.4.4 and 6.4.5.3.

[152] Rather ironically the Court of Appeal has recently criticized a first instance judge for not taking sufficient account of the particular circumstances of a case in deciding whether there was or should have been knowledge of a term – see Mance LJ in *Britvic Soft Drinks* v. *Messer* [2002] 2 Lloyds Rep 368 at 375–6. For a case in which

of latitude to lower courts in application of the law to the facts means that they are in fact free to take significantly different views on application of the law to what are essentially similar facts, so that the same term, exhibiting the same level of transparency used in similar circumstances is viewed differently in different cases.

---

the Court of Appeal took the view that the first instance court had not applied the law properly to the facts in not recognising that there were two separate clauses rather than one that excluded two types of liability see *Watford Electronics* v. *Sanderson CFL Ltd* [2001] EWCA Civ 317, on which see E. Peel, Reasonable Exemption Clauses, (2001) 117 Law Quarterly Review 545.

Chapter Five

The Unfair Terms in Consumer Contract Terms Regulations (UTCCR)

5.1 Introduction

This chapter considers the test of unfairness under the UTCCR and the way in which it has been approached by the OFT and the courts. Unlike with UCTA there is no statutory control trigger as such. In other words there is no exclusive list of terms to which the test applies (although the indicative list of terms that may be regarded as unfair[1] provides considerable guidance). The test is applicable to all non-excluded terms.[2] The chapter begins by considering one category of terms that are positively excluded, i.e. terms that have been individually negotiated.[3] There is discussion as to the rationales and problems associated with this exclusion. Of course, there is no such exclusion under UCTA where consumer contracts are concerned. We shall see that the Law Commissions have recommended that no such exclusion should apply under the proposed new regime.

Next the chapter considers the indicative list of terms that may be regarded as unfair and some of the types of unfairness that this seems to show the test to be concerned with.[4] We then turn to the general role that is played by the OFT and the courts in applying the test of unfairness.[5] The sheer volume of work done by the OFT means that this is a very significant role in practice. There is discussion of the apparent attitude of the OFT to various key elements of unfairness. In particular it is pointed out that the OFT view transparency as vital to fairness and appear to set quite high standards of transparency. However, the OFT certainly do not appear to view transparency as necessarily being sufficient. Terms appear to be viewed routinely as unfair on substantive grounds. In setting fairly high levels of transparency, but also in not viewing transparency as

---

[1] See Regulation 5(2) and Schedule 2.
[2] See above at 3.2 for an overview.
[3] See below at 5.2.
[4] See below at 5.3.
[5] See below at 5.4.

necessarily sufficient, the OFT appear to take an approach that is more fairness-oriented than freedom-oriented.

Next the chapter considers in detail the approaches taken to in the case of *First National Bank* v. *DGFT*.[6] Views emerge from the Court of Appeal and House of Lords judgements that broadly associate the 'significant imbalance' element of the test with unfairness in substance and the good faith element both with matters of substance and procedure; although, both in relation to substance and procedure, the Court of Appeal (like the OFT) may be more inclined to a fairness-oriented approach, while the House of Lords may be more inclined to a freedom-oriented approach. Transparency is emphasized as important by both higher courts (under the auspices of the good faith element of the test). However, the Court of Appeal seem to be closer to the OFT in apparently setting a higher standard of transparency. This is demonstrated, in particular, by the Court of Appeal view that consumers are entitled to be given post-contractual information that may help to protect them from the detrimental impact of the term (a view that – at least on the particular facts of the case – was not shared by the House of Lords). The point is made that it is possible that the ECJ would take an approach more in line with the Court of Appeal in relation to the transparency issue. In relation to the substance of the term being considered, the more freedom-oriented approach of the House of Lords also emerges. In the broadest terms it seems that the House of Lords (in contrast to the Court of Appeal and the OFT) prioritized the trader interest in being free to stipulate for recovery of all interest on a loan both before and after judgement over the consumer interest in being protected from the detrimental effects of such a term. Again, it is suggested that the ECJ might be more inclined to the Court of Appeal approach; based, in particular, on the idea that the ECJ might not regard the term in question (or the rest of the contract) as containing the type of 'benefit' to the consumer that may be required under the ECJ approach.[7]

The chapter goes on to consider whether the House of Lords should have made a reference to the ECJ in relation to the unfairness test; arguing that such a reference possibly should have been made. Next there is discussion of the extent to which the higher courts do (and are likely to) interfere with decisions of the lower courts and 'decisions' of regulatory bodies such as the OFT (and there is comparison with the approach taken under UCTA that was discussed in Chapter Four).[8]

The final part of the chapter deals with the question as to what exactly is needed under the UTCCR in order to trigger a broad review of

---

6   [2001] 3 WLR 1297 and see below at 5.5.
7   On the ECJ approach see above at 3.5.4.
8   See below at 5.6.

procedural and substantive issues.[9] This may appear to be a strange question. The point has already been made that any term that is not positively excluded is subject to the significant imbalance/good faith test. However, first of all this begs the question as to what types of term are most likely to fall under suspicion, thereby causing their substantive features and effects to be scrutinized more closely and questions to be asked about procedural fairness.[10] Essentially the conclusion reached is that this will generally be terms that reduce the obligations or liabilities that would otherwise be owed by traders under default rules; define the obligations of the trader in ways that are less favourable to the consumer than would reasonably be expected; increase the obligations or liabilities that would otherwise be owed by consumers under default rules; or define the obligations of the consumer in ways that are more onerous for the consumer than would reasonably be expected. The first two categories cover very similar ground to UCTA, although there may be terms in these first two categories that would not be caught by the UCTA concepts of 'excluding or restricting liability' and 'reasonable expectations'. The second two categories are clearly not covered by UCTA (as it is focused on terms dealing with the performance and liabilities of the trader and not the consumer). It is also concluded that all four categories are likely to be viewed as causing 'detriment' for the purposes of the proposed new regime. The discussion also deals with a particular issue arising in relation to the second and fourth categories, i.e. those terms allowing for compromise of the reasonable expectations of consumers. Some of the terms that appear to allow for compromise of the reasonable expectations of consumers appear to deal with 'core' obligations (i.e. the main subject matter obligation of the trader and the price obligation of the consumer). These terms appear to allow for compromise of reasonable expectations by allowing for the trader to vary his own core performance obligation or to vary the core price obligation of the consumer (e.g. by allowing for a price increase). So, how does control of such terms square with the fact that core terms are excluded from the test of unfairness?[11] The answer, it is argued, is that core terms are only generally excluded if they do actually reflect the reasonable expectations of consumers.

The next issue in relation to when a broad review of substantive and procedural issues is triggered relates to the role of terms *other than* the term under scrutiny.[12] We have already noted that if a contract contains terms that are favourable to the consumer then we may wish to enquire as to whether these favourable terms balance out any unfairness in the term

---

[9] See below at 5.7–10.
[10] On which see below at 5.7.2–6.
[11] See below at 5.8.
[12] See below at 5.9.

under scrutiny.[13] Under a completely open textured test such as the UCTA reasonableness test this factor can be weighed in the scales along with other factors including, in particular, whether or not there has been procedural fairness.[14] It has already been argued that consumers may have a legitimate interest in transparency even where there is overall substantive fairness.[15] However, the significant imbalance/good faith test may not be as open textured and flexible as the reasonableness test under UCTA. In particular we need to consider whether the need for significant imbalance means that a term cannot be unfair where there is overall substantive fairness (even although there is a lack of transparency). The conclusion reached is that this may well be the case; although there are ways of reading the overall test in order to avoid this result. What is certainly true is that the proposed new test seems to avoid this result much more simply. The 'detriment' requirement will usually be satisfied whenever a term deviates from a default rule to the detriment of the consumer or allows for compromise of reasonable consumer expectations. The term will then be opened up to an open textured review of substantive and procedural issues; so that even if there is overall substantive fairness this will not necessarily be enough if there is procedural unfairness.

The final issue in relation to what triggers a broad review of fairness relates to achieving transparency in cases where the term (in substance) does not actually deviate from the default position.[16] Such a term may not be able to be said to be causing a significant substantive imbalance. Indeed in some cases such a term may actually reflect a mandatory statutory or regulatory provision and so may not be subject to the controls of the UTCCR at all.[17] Yet, as has been argued above, consumers have a legitimate interest in such terms at least being transparent (so that they can take advantage of the important rights that these terms may grant).[18] The discussion considers ways in which the test of unfairness can be understood (on its own and in conjunction with the interpretation rule in the UTCCR) in order to enable bodies (such as the OFT) exercising preventive powers to reach the conclusion that such terms are unfair

---

13 See above at 2.4.3.3 and see also at 2.4.3.3 the various ways in which overall substantive balance/fairness might be measured; and see at 3.5.4 for the approach of the ECJ to these issues.

14 Although, as we saw above (at 4.6.1), the courts do not seem to have chosen to give much prominence to the question of overall balance/substantive fairness in applying the UCTA reasonableness test.

15 See above at 2.4.3.3 and 2.4.3.4(ii).

16 See below at 5.10.

17 See above at 3.2.

18 See above at 2.4.3.3 and 2.4.3.4(iii).

purely on the basis of their lack of transparency. Ultimately, however, it is argued that the point requires clarification.

5.2 Individually Negotiated Terms

5.2.1 The Basic Concept

Regulation 5(1) (following Article 3(1) in the Directive) excludes from the test of fairness terms that have been individually negotiated. This exclusion was not included in the initial drafts of the directive;[19] but was inserted after the intervention of the Council between the 1992 draft and the adoption of the final Directive in 1993.[20] This can be seen as veering towards the German tradition as originally contained in the German Standard Contracts Act of 1976.[21] The German legislation actually goes further in that it excludes terms which are not 'standard',[22] so that it will not regulate a term which has been produced on the spot by the trader (as this is not a standard term) even although the term may not have been the product of any negotiation between the parties but may still simply have been imposed by the trader. Notwithstanding this distinction, the approach of German law and the Directive share a common theme. The idea of the Directive seems to be that if a term has been negotiated then the transactions costs which standard terms seek to avoid have actually been incurred and that the result should be a term which is fair and efficient. The assumption of German law seems to be that even if a term has not been negotiated, the fact that it is non-standard suggests that it could have been. As such there was an opportunity to negotiate a fair and efficient term and the law should not interfere.[23] However, the German legislation, while only applying to standard terms, applies to both consumer and commercial contracts. The Directive, in only applying to consumer contracts (while restricting the application to individually negotiated terms), seems to have been an attempt to strike a compromise between the German and French traditions. The French legislation of

---

[19] See OJ 1990 C243/2 and OJ 1992 C73/7.

[20] For a fuller history of the position taken in different drafts see M. Teneiro, The Community Directive on Unfair Terms and National Legal Systems (1995) 3 European Review of Private Law 273.

[21] The rules are now contained in the revised German Civil code ('BGB'): see Articles 305(1) and 307.

[22] BGB, Article 305(1).

[23] See Tenreiro and Karsten, Unfair Terms in Consumer Contracts: Uncertainties, Contradictions and Novelties of a Directive, European Commission, The Unfair Terms Directive Five Years On, 1–3/7/99, pp. 8–9.

1978 applies only to consumer contracts but applies to terms whether or not they are standard or individually negotiated.[24] The position in the UK under the Unfair Contract Terms Act is in fact somewhere between these two positions. All of the controls we have discussed above in relation to consumer contracts apply whether or not the term is individually negotiated. However, in commercial contracts certain controls only apply where the contract was on one party's written standard terms of business.[25]

Regulation 5(2) following Article 3(2) of the Directive says that 'a term shall always be regarded as not having been individually negotiated where it has been drafted in advance and the consumer has therefore not been able to influence the substance of the term'. The text of Article 3(2) of the Directive actually then goes on to give pre-formulated standard contract terms as specific examples of terms which will always be regarded as non-individually negotiated. A standard term which has not been influenced by the consumer *is* obviously the most typical example of an individually negotiated term. However, it is also clear that a non-standard written or non-written term which has not been the subject of negotiation will not be treated as a term which has been individually negotiated and will be subject to the unfairness test.

Regulation 5(3) (following the second para. of Article 3(2)) is badly drafted and causes some confusion. It says that 'notwithstanding that a specific term or certain aspects of it in a contract has been individually negotiated, these Regulations shall apply to the rest of a contract if an overall assessment of it indicates that it is a pre-formulated standard contract'. This of course could be taken to suggest that if there are some negotiated terms in a contract, then the question as to whether other terms in this contract are to be excluded from the fairness test is no longer whether these other terms have been individually negotiated or not; but whether, overall, the contract is a pre-formulated standard one. It is clear, however, that the intention of the Directive, as indicated by Article 3(1) and Recital 12 to the preamble (which also refers to non-individually negotiated terms and not to standard contracts), was only to exclude individually negotiated *terms* and not to exclude terms simply on the basis

---

[24] Law of 10 January 1978, Article 35 and see now the legislation implementing the UTD, i.e. the Law of 1 February 1995. On the UTD striking a balance between the French and German traditions and on the approaches in English and Italian law see P. Nebbia, Unfair Contract Terms in European Law, Hart, 2007, 34–401 and on the Italian approach contrasted with the UK approach see Nebbia, *ibid.*, 116–8.

[25] These are the controls under s. 3 of terms excluding or restricting liability for breach of contract and terms allowing a party to offer a contractual performance substantially different from that reasonably expected or no performance at all.

that they are not contained in pre-formulated standard contracts.[26] So, if the exclusion is not to be removed in the UK, then the current law should at least be amended to make this point clear (however it seems likely that the exclusion will be removed – see below).

Regulation 5(4) places the burden of proof on the trader to show that a term has been individually negotiated. So, for example, the trader may be able to introduce evidence to show that the parties worked from a blank sheet of paper towards an agreed term; or from the initial starting point of a term suggested by one of the parties, through negotiation, to a finally agreed term which differs from this initially suggested term; or from a standard term, through negotiation, to an amendment of this standard term by handwriting or otherwise. However what is quite clear from Article 3(2) and Regulation 5(2) is that if the finally agreed term is a pre-formulated standard term which has not been in any way amended then it cannot be treated as having been individually negotiated. So it cannot be said, for example, that there has been negotiation simply because the consumer has studied the term and indicated contentment with it;[27] or even where the consumer has chosen the set of terms on which he wishes work done but has not actually influenced the substance of any term therein.[28] The possibility that an unmodified standard term *could* in some circumstances be treated as individually negotiated had been left open by the text of the third paragraph of Article 3(2) of the directive which says that where a seller or supplier 'claims that a standard term has been individually negotiated, the burden of proof in this respect shall be incumbent on him'. This could be taken to imply that it would be possible to prove that an unmodified standard term had nevertheless been individually negotiated. However the UK provision in Regulation 5(4) avoids this problem by simply referring to the burden of proof being on

---

26   See T. Wilhelmson, The Scope of the Directive: Non Negotiated Terms in Consumer Contracts, European Commission, The Unfair Terms Directive Five Years On, 1–3/7/1999 at p. 3.

27   As may be believed by the Royal Institute of British Architects who have guidance to the effect that terms should be explained and that consumers should then be asked to confirm that the terms have been negotiated – see *Picardi* v. *Cuniberti* [2002] EWHC 2923, para. 51.

28   In *Bryen & Langley Ltd* v. *Martin Boyston* [2004] EWCA 2450 TC it was however, suggested (obiter) by the High Court that that in such latter circumstances it was 'at least arguable' that there has been individual negotiation. However, this simply cannot be correct and seems to have been dismissed by the Court of Appeal (see [2005] EWHC Civ 973. See also on this C. Twigg-Flesner, The Implementation of the Unfair Contract Terms Directive in the United Kingdom in H. Collins, L. Tichy and S. Grundmann, Standard Contract Terms in Europe, Kluwer, forthcoming.

the seller or supplier to establish that the term is individually negotiated, and making no reference to the standard term issue.

5.2.2 Critique and Protective Interpretation

The exclusion of individually negotiated terms seems to miss the point that even if a term has been individually negotiated between the consumer and the trader this does not mean that there has necessarily been overall procedural fairness.[29] For example, although the term resulting from the negotiation may be more transparent than would be normal for the typical standard term, the consumer may not have fully understood what he was giving up by agreeing to the term in question; and he may not fully understand the rules to which he is exposed by the negotiated term. In addition, although the process of negotiation no doubt implies that there was some element of choice, it does not necessarily mean that the choices were reasonable. Further, the fact that the consumer negotiated does not mean that he was in a strong enough bargaining position to protect his interests. In addition, individual negotiation will not mean that the resulting term is fair in substance.[30]

Notwithstanding these points, it may be that it is possible to approach the concept of individual negotiation in such a way as to minimize the detrimental effects on consumers and the extent to which fairness is undermined. We know that the Directive aims to assure consumer protection and consumer confidence and in particular to do so via the enhancement of transparency.[31] In the light of these goals it can be argued that even where a consumer has had some input in relation to a term then the term should only be treated as having been individually negotiated if this input is both informed and substantial. For the consumer's input to be informed the consumer should have some knowledge of what rights and remedies he will be giving up by agreeing to the term. This sort of approach to the concept of individual negotiation would mean that if individually negotiated terms are to continue to be excluded from the test of fairness then at least the consumer will have been well-informed at the stage of agreeing to the term as to what he stood to gain and what he stood to lose.

As to whether the consumers input was substantial there may have to be some evidence that the process was more than a mere formality, i.e. that the trader and consumer did actually 'engage' with each other in a meaningful way. There appears to be some support for this approach in

---

29 On which see 2.4.3.4 above.
30 On which see 2.4.3.2–3.
31 See 3.4.3–4 above.

the German courts. In a German Court of Appeal decision it has been held that 'negotiation' should involve the consumer, with reasonable efforts, being able to recognise the available choices, and that there should be some opportunity to influence the substance of the term.[32] The fact that the resulting term is, in substance, unfair to the consumer will not of course prove that there was no meaningful consumer input. However it may help to establish that there was not. If the result of the purported negotiation is that the term is no fairer in substance than it was before then it may be difficult to establish that the consumer really did have an opportunity to influence its substance.

5.2.3 The Future

The question now is whether or not the exclusion of individually negotiated terms should be retained. The first significant point in this connection is that the vast majority of terms will be standard terms and therefore will not be individually negotiated. We could therefore conclude that the individually negotiated term exclusion does not cause significant problems for consumers and therefore there is no real need to remove it; and indeed that to do so might unfairly prejudice traders who have quite genuinely negotiated a fair term and then later find themselves faced with a vexatious claim to the effect that the term is unfair. However a genuine negotiation on the principles which I have outlined above will usually weigh heavily in favour of a finding of fairness so that the consumer will not normally succeed with such a claim. In addition, in a case where has been genuine negotiation but there are still reasons for finding the term to be unfair, it is arguable that a mechanism for reaching such a conclusion should be available. A further reason for removing the exclusion is that its presence, and the uncertainty as to its precise scope, may cause confusion which can be exploited by traders to the detriment of consumers. Traders may develop techniques to give the impression to consumers that negotiation has taken place; and even if these techniques do not represent genuine individual negotiation within the meaning of the UTD/UTCCR, the trader may be able to persuade the consumer that they do. In the 2000 report by the Commission on the UTD[33] there are two examples of such practices already being used. One example involves contracts including terms by virtue of which the consumer declares that he has negotiated and accepted the trader's terms and conditions. When the parties are in dispute, the trader is then in a position to refer back to this term and claim that its effect is that the terms are indeed individually

---

[32] CLAB Database, No. DE002814.

[33] EC Commission 2000 (COM)2248 final at p. 14.

negotiated. Another example involves the use of terms which are in fact standardized terms but which do not exist in a pre-printed form. They are then reproduced on a case by case basis for each individual consumer. The intention is to give the impression that they are tailor made for that consumer; and possibly then to lead to the argument that they have therefore been the subject of negotiation between the trader and that consumer. In order to avoid the possible detriment to consumers that might be caused by such practices it might be wise to remove the individually negotiated terms exclusion.

It is also important to remember the point made above to the effect that the existence of individual negotiation will not necessarily prevent there being procedural unfairness or unfairness in substance. It is true that if there has been negotiation, this will at least mean that the consumer is aware of the existence of the term. However, as noted above, the consumer may not appreciate what he has given up by agreeing to the term; and in addition, the likely impact of the term may remain intransparent to the consumer. Negotiation may imply some form of choice, e.g. in the way of one price for term X and another lower price for the less favourable term Y. However, even if this is the case, neither alternative may be reasonable in the particular circumstances. In addition, although bargaining of a sort will have taken place where there has been negotiation, it will still often be the case that many consumers will lack the expertise or experience to effectively protect their interests. The result may be that substantively unfair terms are sometimes the result of the negotiation. This is even more likely to be the case where the most vulnerable consumers are concerned.

The Law Commissions propose that the new regime should not exclude individually negotiated terms.[34] One reason given by the Law Commissions relates to the uncertainty as to exactly when a term has been individually negotiated.[35] Another reason is that consumers may not appreciate the implications of having negotiated a term.[36] A further reason is that the OFT provided evidence to the effect that some traders are seeking to exploit the exclusion,[37] i.e. by arguing that terms are negotiated when they are not. Then there is the fact that the protection already given by UCTA is to be preserved. This means that the exemption clauses which are controlled by UCTA, (whether or not they have been individually negotiated), would still be controlled under the new regime

---

[34] Consultation Paper, 4.52, 9.9; Report, 3.50–3.55; and see discussion by H. Beale, Unfair Terms: Proposals for Reform in the UK (2004) 27 Journal of Consumer Policy, 289, 292–3.

[35] Report, 3.52.

[36] *Ibid.*

[37] *Ibid.*

whether or not they have been individually negotiated. So, although such clauses are only controlled by the UTCCR where they have not been individually negotiated, they would be controlled by the new regime whether or not they have been individually negotiated. Confusion might then be caused if terms imposing obligations/liabilities on the consumer (the other category of term controlled by the UTCCR) were only controlled if they were not individually negotiated.[38]

The result of removing the exclusion may be marginal in practice. However, it will mean a more full-blooded fairness approach, i.e. one that recognizes that, even where there has been individual negotiation, there is still the possibility of unfairness procedurally and in substance. If the exclusion is not to be removed then (as suggested above) the very least that should happen is that precise criteria for a term to qualify as having been individually negotiated should be laid down, so as to remove uncertainty that may be exploited to the detriment of consumers. Important among these criteria should be the need for the input of the consumer to have been both informed and substantial. This would at least guarantee a modicum of procedural fairness. In addition there might be an impact on fairness in substance if a lack of fairness in substance was treated as evidence that consumers could not have had a substantial input.

5.3 The Indicative List and an Initial View of Terms Targeted

As we have seen, the test applies to all terms not positively excluded. There is no formal trigger mechanism. In other words it is not like UCTA where we know that certain terms are targeted because these are the only terms that are actually covered. Nevertheless, as already suggested,[39] it is clearly helpful if we can identify the types of unfairness in substance which the test is most focused on. The list of terms that may be regarded as unfair[40] provides some help in this regard. It contains a variety of different forms of exemption clause[41] and terms giving the trader the

---

[38] See Consultation Paper, 4.43 and H. Beale, Unfair Terms: Proposals for Reform in the UK (2004) 27 Journal of Consumer Policy, 289, 293.

[39] See above at 5.1.

[40] Regulation 5(5) provides that Schedule 2 to the regulations contains an indicative and non-exhaustive list of the terms that may be regarded as unfair. This replicates Article 3(3) to the Directive and the annex attached to the Directive. The idea of a list such as this to support a general fairness clause derives from continental tradition – see for example, the pre-existing Austrian Konsumentenschutzgesetz, Article 6; Belgian Loi sur les pratiques du commerce, Article 32; Dutch Civil Code, Articles 6:236 and 237; German AGB-Gesetz, Articles 9 and 10; and the Italian Codice Civile, Article 1341.

[41] See paras 1(a), (b), (n) and (q).

right to vary or terminate his performance under the contract;[42] various examples of terms imposing liability on the consumer and allowing the price to be varied;[43] and various terms that appear to be viewed as potentially unfair on the basis that they give rights to the trader but do not give similar rights to consumers in similar circumstances.[44] However, terms on the list are simply examples of what is often unfair. In addition, the list is not exhaustive, so that being on the list is not a requirement of unfairness. Neither is the list a 'blacklist' (it is simply 'indicative' as to terms that 'may' be regarded as unfair[45]); so being on the list does not necessarily mean that the term is unfair. As such, the list does not provide a definitive indication as to the types of substantive term that are targeted. Indeed, the list can only really be understood in the light of the test of unfairness; and it is only really after some discussion of the test that we can develop a clearer picture as to the types of substantive terms targeted. Essentially what will emerge[46] on this point is that the significant imbalance limb of the test seems to be the closest to being a trigger mechanism dealing with the substantive features of terms and identifying those terms that are then opened up to a broader review of fairness under the good faith test. Terms will often (although not always) cause significant imbalance where they (like UCTA) exclude or restrict obligations or liabilities that would otherwise arise as a matter of law under default rules; add to the obligations or liabilities of the consumer by comparison with default rules; or provide for a performance by either of the parties that is out of step with the reasonable expectations of the consumer.

---

42 See paras 1(g), (j) and (k).

43 See paras 1(c), (e), (h) and (l).

44 See paras 1(d), (f) and (o).

45 The list will often describe a term quite broadly, e.g. para. 1(b) refers to 'inappropriately' excluding or limiting liability, so that whether there is 'inappropriateness', i.e. unfairness will depend on the precise degree of the exclusion/restriction and possibly the procedural circumstances. This sort of approach is best described as a 'greylist' as it points to terms that may be fair depending on the precise circumstances. In some countries (Austria, Germany and the Netherlands) there is a tradition of having both such a greylist and a so called 'blacklist', i.e. a list of terms that are always unfair (see the discussion by E. Hondius, European Approaches to Fairness in Contract Law, in C. Willett (ed.), Aspects of Fairness in Contract, Blackstone, 1996, 69–72.

46 See below at 5.7.2–6.

5.4 The Sources of Interpretation of the Test of Unfairness

5.4.1 An Overview

Under the UTCCR the courts obviously have a role to play in normal after fact litigation. Unfair terms are not binding on the consumer, although the remainder of the contract continues to bind the parties if this is possible without the unfair term.[47] However, along with the after the fact role of the courts, various regulatory bodies have a huge role to play. This is because the UTCCR also allow for proactive control by various regulatory bodies. The various bodies are empowered to seek injunctions to prevent the continued use of terms that are unfair.[48] However, the UTCCR also allow for the bodies to seek undertakings as to the use of terms.[49] In support of these powers the bodies are required to investigate complaints as to unfair terms in certain circumstances.[50] The vast bulk of this work is done by the OFT. The OFT investigates a huge number of terms and take a view as to their fairness.[51] In particular, the OFT has also taken time in some bulletins to identify trends of unfairness in certain specific trading sectors, i.e. to identify terms which are typical (and perhaps unfair) in the sectors in question.[52] In other words, the work of the OFT is a very significant element of the jurisprudence on the fairness concept in the UTCCR.

So, in practice, most of the 'decisions' as to when a term is unfair are at regulatory level. If a term is considered to be unfair the regulatory bodies seek to persuade the trader to stop using it; and traders give informal undertakings to this effect. In all but one case[53] (where an injunction was sought and challenged) this is what has happened. In other

---

[47] Regulation 8, following Article 6(1) of the Directive.

[48] See Regulation 12 which gives powers to the OFT and a variety of 'Qualifying bodies'. These bodies are set out in Schedule 1 to the UTCCR.

[49] Regulation 10(3).

[50] Regulation 10(1).

[51] The work is published regularly in routine OFT Bulletins recording the work being done and there has also been special guidance setting out an overall view of the OFT's approach to unfairness and drawing on examples from work done over the years since the UTCCR were passed (OFT Guidance on Unfair Terms, 2001).

[52] See, for example, Guidance on Unfair Terms in Consumer Entertainment Contracts, OFT, 2003, Guidance on Unfair Terms in Care Home Contracts, OFT, 2003, Guidance on Unfair Terms in Package Holiday Contracts, 2004, and Guidance on Unfair Terms in Home Improvement Contracts, OFT, 2005.

[53] *Director General of Fair Trading* v. *First National Bank* [2001] 3 WLR 1297.

words, in all but this one case, the view of the regulatory body as to the fairness of a term has, in practice, prevailed.

5.4.2 The Significance of OFT Involvement

This contribution of the OFT to the jurisprudence on unfairness is a very significant factor. As we have seen, the unfairness concept comes in the form of a general clause based around significant imbalance and violation of good faith. It has been pointed out by various commentators[54] that there are serious limitations on the role that can be played by courts in after the fact litigation in unpacking such general clauses; such that there emerges a well-developed jurisprudence that can provide certainty and calculability and assist framing of actions, compliance and future adjudication. Even if courts give a meaning to a general clause, if this is in the context of a particular set of facts (as it will be in private litigation) it will not necessarily be clear how it will apply to other fact situations.[55] This is exacerbated by the fact that only a relatively small number of cases will be privately litigated, so that the potential for a comprehensive and rigorous jurisprudence based on private litigation will be extremely limited.[56] The consequence may be that there is limited guidance for consumer advisers in framing actions, for traders in seeking to comply and for the courts in future (isolated) cases. The conclusion is often that regulation by private law means simply will not work.[57]

However, where bodies have the proactive power to investigate unfair terms and this enables production and dissemination of a considerable jurisprudence on fairness, this has the potential to aid the framing of actions, compliance and adjudication. Private litigation then becomes slightly less important at least as a source of jurisprudence and guidance; its role remaining vital, of course in providing for corrective justice.

---

54 See T. Bourgoigne, New Patterns of Consumer Protection Under Warrant law: Lessons from the US Magnusson-Moss Warranty Act, (1979), 3 Journal of Consumer Policy 266, at 268; H. Collins, Regulating Contracts, Oxford, 1999, 293–295; R. Bradgate, R. Brownsword and C. Twigg-Flesner, The Impact of Adopting a General Duty to Trade Fairly, Report for the DTI, 2003, 67–68.

55 H. Collins, Regulating Contracts, Oxford, 1999, at 293.

56 T. Bourgoigne, New Patterns of Consumer Protection under Warrant law: Lessons from the US Magnusson-Moss Warranty Act, (1979), 3 Journal of Consumer Policy 266, at 268.

57 H. Collins, Regulating Contracts, Oxford, 1999, 295.

5.4.3 An Introduction to OFT Attitudes to Unfairness

We shall be considering the OFT jurisprudence in greater detail below. However, in broad terms we can say the following about the OFT's concept of unfairness. First, that great importance is placed on the transparency of terms. Detailed guidelines have been given as to what amounts to transparency,[58] fairly high levels of transparency seem to be expected and transparency is viewed as a fundamental requirement.[59] Second, little mention tends to be made of questions of choice or bargaining power. This may simply reflect an assumption that there is often not a choice and that the vast majority of consumers are in a weaker bargaining position than the trader using the terms; and these factors may be implicitly counted against the terms. However, there certainly does not appear to be any attempt to investigate whether, in the market in question, a choice is in fact available or those consumers tend to have greater than average bargaining strength. So, there is little sense of a belief that terms might be justified on these grounds. A third, and key point, is that while, as we have seen, transparency seems to be viewed as fundamental by the OFT, neither transparency nor any other form of procedural fairness can necessarily justify terms that are viewed as unfair on substantive grounds. *Some* terms are 'made fair' by insisting that they be more transparent.[60] However, very many terms are revised or deleted on the basis of their substantive effect, there being no suggestion that they would be acceptable as long as they were made transparent.[61] (We have seen above that the idea of terms being able to be unfair on purely substantive grounds appears to have support from the ECJ.[62]) A fourth point is that the key guide to unfairness in substance for the OFT has been the indicative list of terms that is attached to the UTCCR.[63] A large volume of the work of the OFT has focused on comparing terms to those described on the list.[64] A fifth point is that, while the OFT does often consider the issue of overall substantive fairness, this is usually only in relation to terms allowing the consumer to protect his interests by cancelling the contract in response to actions taken by the trader under the term in question. However, it does not appear more generally that there is

---

[58] See, for example, Unfair Contract Terms Bulletins 2 (1996) (8–13), 4 (1997) (12–18) and 5 (1998) (14–17).

[59] See below at 6.4.2.

[60] *Ibid*; and see H.-W. Micklitz, The Politics of Judicial Co-operation in the EU, CUP, 2005, 395.

[61] See below at 6.5.

[62] See above at 3.5.4.

[63] Schedule 2; and see below at 6.3.

[64] See, for example, the 2001 OFT Guidance on Unfair Terms, and see below at 6.3.

a routine assessment as to overall substantive fairness. Certainly the OFT do not routinely ask whether term and the price are typical for the market (such a question is sometimes connected to the issue of overall substantive fairness in the sense that if the term and price are indeed typical then – on one approach to measuring substantive fairness – it is assumed that the price is lower than it would have been without the term and that, therefore, there is substantive fairness).[65]

Finally, in very broad terms, the approach seems more grounded in fairness instincts than freedom instincts. As we have seen, a high level of transparency is required. Even more significantly, as we have also seen, it seems that terms are readily disallowed on essentially substantive grounds irrespective of procedural fairness. As we saw above this is a fairly radical departure from a freedom-oriented approach which would view interference on substantive grounds as being more of a compromise on the freedom of the parties than interference on procedural grounds.[66]

5.4.4 First Instance Cases

There has been a small amount of case law in the lower courts. One case[67] involved a term in an insurance contract which made it a condition precedent to the cover being valid that the consumer report full details of an incident as soon as possible and also forward, immediately on receipt, any relevant legal documentation. Buckley J said (obiter) that the term was unfair in so far as it allowed for invalidation of the claim even where the delay caused no prejudice to the insurer. In effect, he suggested an approach that severed this element from the term, so that what was left was a term that only allowed for invalidation of the claim where the delay caused prejudice to the insurer. This conclusion was arrived at on the basis of the significant imbalance concept (there being no consideration of the good faith element of the test). The approach to significant imbalance involved balancing the interests of the parties. The judge looked on the one hand at the prejudice that might be caused to a consumer by the fact that the term allowed a claim to be defeated on technical grounds. At the same time the judge considered the fact that placing a time limit on claims was necessary for the insurer in order to protect his own right of subrogation and his prospects of claiming from third parties. These considerations were weighed against one another. The conclusion, as we saw, was that the interests of the insurer could be

---

65   See above at 2.4.3.3.
66   See above at 2.4.3.5.
67   *Bankers Insurance Co Ltd* v. *South* [2003] Lloyds Rep IR 1.

protected by enforcing the term only to the extent that it allowed for invalidation on the basis of a delay causing actual prejudice to the insurer.

Unsurprisingly, there was no broader discussion of questions of unfairness in substance or procedure or of the relationship between substance and procedure. As we have seen, there was no discussion of good faith at all.

What *is* of interest is that it was decided that the term was in plain and intelligible language; and the term also appears to have been made reasonably prominent in the contract. However, there was no suggestion that this should or could prevent the term from being unfair. In other words the implication is that a term can be unfair on the basis of its substantive features irrespective of whether it there is procedural fairness. In addition, there was no analysis as to whether the contract also contained beneficial terms (e.g. a low price) that would make it substantively fair overall.[68] The focus was on the specific consumer interest in being protected from a term allowing the insurer to avoid a claim on the basis of delays that cause the insurer no prejudice.

Another case is *Westminster Building Co.* v. *Beckingham.*[69] This is hardly a paradigm consumer case as it involved the terms of the contract for renovation of the consumer's property being put forward by chartered surveyors on behalf of the consumer. As such, it does not involve the paradigm situation in which the terms come from the supplier. It is hardly surprising, then, that the term was held not to be unfair. The term was an adjudication clause which did not significantly exclude or hinder the right of the consumer to take legal action; and, as the builder in this case had done no more than accept the clause put forward by the agent of the consumer, there was no duty to point out to the consumer any pitfalls contained in the clause. As such there was no violation of the good faith requirement. This being such an unusual set of facts it is difficult to draw any useful general conclusions.

5.5 The *First National Bank* Case

5.5.1 Introduction

Only one case has reached the House of Lords and this same case is the only one to even have got as far as the Court of Appeal. The case is *First National Bank* v. *Director General of Fair Trading.*[70] It arose out of OFT action against a term in a consumer loan agreement requiring consumers

---

68 See above at 2.4.3.3.
69 [2004] EWHC 138 (TCC), 94 Con LR 107.
70 [2001] 3 WLR 1297.

to continue to pay the contractual rate of interest on sums owing both before and after any judgement. This was achieved by stipulating that the obligation to pay interest under the contract would not 'merge' in any judgement that there might be. The default position at common law is that the contractual interest *does* merge in the judgement,[71] so that the term was stating a contrary intention, i.e. that the contractual interest would not merge in the judgement and would continue to be payable after the judgement. The effect of this term is that if the lender obtains judgement on an outstanding debt and the consumer is bound under the judgement to pay by instalments, interest on the amounts remaining outstanding on the judgement debt continues to accrue at the contractual rate. Put another way, the amount that the court orders the consumer to pay will not be the full extent of the consumer's liability – interest at the contractual rate continues to accrue on (and will be owed in addition to) the outstanding component of the judgement debt.

5.5.2 The OFT View

The OFT argued that the term was unfair. The argument was as follows. The term would be unlikely to be noticed by consumers at the time of the agreement. The result would be that, at the time of any judgement, the average consumer would expect that if all instalments due under the judgement were paid the debt would be extinguished (when, as we have seen, contractual interest would, in fact, be continuing to accrue). In addition, the OFT viewed the term as unfair on the grounds that it deprived consumers of advantages conferred by the County Courts (Interest on Judgements) Order 1991 which prevents courts awarding *statutory* interest on judgement debts in relation to this type of 'regulated agreement' (i.e. an agreement regulated under the Consumer Credit Act (CCA) 1974); and also provides that, where a judgement debt is to be paid by instalments, interest does not accrue on the amount of any instalment until it falls due.[72] So, the argument of the OFT in relation to the 1991 Order was effectively that the 1991 Order reflected a policy against consumers being required to pay interest in addition to the amount being awarded by the court. This policy was viewed as being manifested in the fact that the Order prevents the court itself awarding *statutory* interest and also makes it clear that interest will not be payable on the judgement debt as long as the consumer pays the instalments within the time period specified. The effect of the *term*, of course, is that the lender

---

[71] In Re Sneyd; Ex p Fewings (1883) 25 Ch. D338, accepted without demur by the House of Lords in *Economic Life Assurance Society* v. *Usborne* [1902] AC 147.

[72] Articles 2(3)(a) and 3.

is entitled to *contractual* interest in addition to the amount due under the judgement debt and even although the consumer pays the amounts due under the judgment debt on time. So, although the 1991 Order does not actually ban provision being made for *contractual* interest to be payable after judgement, the OFT view was that the 1991 Order reflects a general policy against interest being added to the amount payable under a judgement debt. So, by making consumers liable to pay interest (albeit contractual interest) in addition to the amount payable under a judgement debt, the term departed from this protective policy.

It should be noted also that the OFT did not seem to consider the possibility that the term might be justified on the basis of overall substantive fairness. We shall see below that the House of Lords seem to have adopted a kind of substantive fairness argument. The House of Lords argument was that the Bank would find it uneconomical to lend without being guaranteed the recovery of interest until the full capital sum has been paid off.[73] Based on this argument it can be said that the consumer benefits from the term in the sense that the term allows the Bank to be able to lend money in the first place. However, the OFT clearly did not believe that such a benefit existed; presumably taking the view that Banks would not find it so difficult to absorb the cost of lost interest on the amounts outstanding on those minority of debts on which a judgement has been issued.

5.5.3 The Court of Appeal View

5.5.3.1 Introduction

The *First National Bank* did not accept that the term was unfair and fought the OFT case for an injunction in the High Court and won (it being held that the term was not unfair).[74] The Director General of Fair Trading appealed to the Court of Appeal. The Court of Appeal overturned the High Court decision and found in favour of the OFT, i.e. that the term was unfair.[75]

5.5.3.2 The Test of Unfairness

As to the test of unfairness in general the Court of Appeal view was that the,

---

[73]   See below at 5.5.4.2(iv)(a)-(c).

[74]   [2000] I WLR 98.

[75]   [2000] QB 672.

'good faith' element seeks to promote fair and open dealing, and to prevent unfair surprise and the absence of real choice. A term to which the consumer's attention is not specifically drawn but which may operate in a way which the consumer might reasonably not expect and to his disadvantage may offend the requirement of good faith. Terms must be reasonably transparent and should not operate to defect the reasonable expectations of the consumer. The consumer in choosing whether to enter the contract should be put in the position where he can make an informed choice.

The element of significant imbalance would appear to overlap substantially with that of the absence of good faith. A term which gives a significant advantage to the seller or supplier without a countervailing benefit to the consumer (such as a price reduction) might fail to satisfy this part of the text of an unfair term.

Finally the element of detriment must be present for the term to be unfair (at 687).

So, for the Court of Appeal, a term causes significant imbalance (which must of course be to the detriment of the consumer, i.e. not the trader) where it gives a 'significant advantage' to the trader; and one imagines that the Court of Appeal generally contemplates such advantage being caused by the substantive features of the term, although they do not expressly say so. The Court of Appeal also appear to see a role for an enquiry as to overall substantive fairness. We can see that it was said that there might be no significant imbalance where there was a countervailing benefit such as a reduced price. As to good faith, the Court of Appeal vision appears to be of a blend of procedural factors (such as transparency and choice) and factors related to the substance of the term. The relevance of factors related to the substance of the term seems to be emphasized by the reference to the term operating to the 'disadvantage' of the consumer; and by the notion that significant imbalance and good faith overlap (this presumably meaning that the substantive features of terms – which are relevant to significant imbalance – are also relevant to good faith).

As to the reference to 'reasonable expectations' there is some sense of confusion as to whether this is viewed as a concept essentially related to the substantive features of the term, or a concept strongly influenced by questions of transparency. The idea that a sufficient degree of transparency is able to determine what it is reasonable to expect might be suggested when it is said that good faith might be violated by 'a term to which the consumer's attention is not specifically drawn but which may operate in a way which the consumer might reasonably not expect'. On the other hand it is also said that terms 'must be reasonably transparent *and* should not operate to defeat the reasonable expectations of the consumer' (my italics).

More generally on the relationship between substance and procedure the Court of Appeal did appear to take the view that some terms might be sufficiently unfair in substance as to be unfair even where there had been procedural fairness. The following excerpt from Hugh Beale was cited with approval:

> I suspect that good faith has a double operation. First, it has a procedural aspect. It will require the supplier to consider the consumer's interests. However, a clause which might be unfair if it came as a surprise may be upheld if the business took steps to bring it to the consumer's attention and to explain it. Secondly, it has a substantive content: some clauses may cause such an imbalance that they should always be treated as unfair.[76]

We now turn to the application of the law to the facts by the Court of appeal. As already indicated the Court of Appeal decided that the term was unfair.

5.5.3.3 Application of the Test

In relation to application of the test, the first element of the Court of Appeal view (in common with that of the OFT) was that consumers would expect that the judgement debt represented the full extent of their liability and would not expect interest to be accruing separately (especially as this is not drawn specifically to his attention at the conclusion of the contract, prior to the making of the judgement or in the judgement itself). It has been suggested that this represented a normative approach to reasonable expectation.[77] Essentially the point being made here is that when the Court of Appeal says that consumers would not reasonably expect contractual interest to continue to accrue, the Court is not basing this on consumer experience (a basis for expectation that can be characterized as 'empirical'). Rather, the Court is simply proceeding as an independent (normative) value judgement as to what is fair. In other words the Court is simply making an independent value judgement that consumers should not suffer the burden of the extra interest that has built up, especially when the term is not drawn to their attention. One can also

---

[76] At p. 686, citing H. Beale, Legislative Control of Fairness: The Directive on Unfair Terms in Consumer Contracts, in J. Beatson and D. Friedmann, Good Faith and Fault in Contract Law, OUP, 1995, 245.

[77] C. Mitchell, Leading a Life of its Own? The Roles of Reasonable Expectation in Contract Law, Oxford Journal of Legal Studies, Vol. 23, No. 4 (2003), 639, at 659. The distinction between empirical and normative approaches to reasonable expectation was first discussed above at 4.4.

tie the other aspects of the Court of Appeal's reasoning into this analysis. Below we shall see that two other reasons for viewing the term as unfair were (i) that courts do not usually review the amount of interest payable at the time of the judgement and (ii) that the default rule is that interest is not payable on a judgement debt. On the view that the Court of Appeal's approach to reasonable expectation is purely normative, the Court can be characterized as finding further normative justification for their approach in these two factors. Factor (i) means that the unfair burden is unlikely to be prevented from occurring; while factor (ii) is taken to give added legitimacy to the Court's normative view as to fairness (in that this view is argued to reflect the default position in law).

The argument that the Court of Appeal's approach to reasonable expectation is normative could be said to lead to the conclusion that the idea of reasonable expectations (at least as used by the Court of Appeal here) adds nothing to our understanding of unfairness. The argument in effect is that if, in deciding, whether a term reflects reasonable expectations we simply mean whether it is fair, then the idea of reasonable expectations does not add anything to our understanding of fairness.[78] Of course I have already argued that there is an empirical basis for some reasonable expectations, i.e. the reasonable expectation that traders will not have undue scope to vary or terminate the contract.[79] I believe that a similar argument can be made here. Surely (empirically) many consumers *would* expect that the judgement debt represented the full extent of their liability and would not expect interest to be accruing separately. They would expect this based on life experience and observation, which would tell them that the role of courts is to make a final judgement on the matter at hand; a judgement that determines, in full, the future extent of the relevant liabilities. Of course, there may (empirically) be other consumers who do not view matters in this way and who would imagine that the contractual interest would continue to be payable in addition to the amount awarded in the judgement. Indeed, we shall see below that the House of Lords made this latter empirical assumption in relation to consumer expectations.[80] The point is that, in the absence of a proper empirical study that determines which expectations are most common, the decision to prefer one set of expectations over another is probably strongly influenced by underlying normative judgements. In other words, the Court of Appeal probably chose the expectations of some consumers over the expectations of others based on a normative preference; a preference for protecting consumers

---

[78] *Ibid.*

[79] See the discussion above at 4.4.3–4.

[80] See below at 5.5.4.2(iv)(a).

from the consequences of the term over allowing lenders to recover full contractual interest in all cases.[81]

However, this does not seem to alter the fact that there is at least some empirical basis for the Court of Appeal's notion of reasonable expectation; just as there may be a competing empirical basis for the approach to the House of Lords. What we *can* see is that the choice between such empirical positions is of course influenced by normative judgements (the more protective, fairness-oriented standpoint of the Court of Appeal versus the more freedom-oriented standpoint of the House of Lords). Of course if we wished to have a wholly empirical approach there would need to be a rigorous empirical study as to exactly what are the experiences and assumptions of consumers.

We now turn to other aspects of the Court of Appeal approach. In focussing on the issue as to the lack of consumer awareness as to the separate accrual of interest, the Court of Appeal added a separate dimension to that described above. This related to the provisions in s. 129 and ss 136–9 of the CCA.[82] These provisions allow the court, at the time of judgement, to allow an appropriate time to pay given all the circumstances and to review (and possibly reduce) the actual amount payable. As already mentioned above, the view of the Court of Appeal was that part of the reason that the term was unfair was that it allowed the lender to obtain judgement without the court considering whether to exercise their powers under these provisions.[83] What the Court of Appeal was getting at is that the law does not provide for these powers to be exercised automatically by the court. The consumer must ask the court to exercise them. However, the law does not provide for it to be automatically made known to the consumer that the court has these powers and that consumers might like to consider asking the court to exercise them. So, for the Court of Appeal, this compounded the problem of consumers being caught unaware. Consumers may not realize that the term will have the effect of making them liable to pay a (continually accruing) sum in addition to the amount specified in the judgement. As such, they would not think to ask the court at the time of judgement to exercise their powers under the CCA to provide some form of relief. They are unlikely in any case to know that such relief is available and the law is not such that provision of such relief is considered automatically. So, drawing everything together, consumers may be left with a debt that they did not realize was accruing and which they did not realize they could ask

---

81   See above at 4.4.4 on the UCTA reasonable expectations concept and the normative and empirical elements it arguably contains.

82   See now the new provisions on 'unfair relationships' in s. 140(A)-(D) added by ss 19–22 of the Consumer Credit Act 2006.

83   [2000] QB 672 at 688.

the court to review (whether by adjusting the time for payment or actually reducing the amount).[84] For the Court of Appeal, this all meant that the term caused 'unfair surprise' and on this basis the term violated the good faith aspect of the test.[85]

The next element of the Court of Appeal view (in common with the OFT view on the same point) was that it was unfair that the lender should be able to obtain interest via a contractual term when (as a result of the 1991 Order discussed above) statutory interest cannot be awarded by the court on a judgement debt. For the Court of Appeal, this went to the other limb of the test. The term, in providing for contractual interest (when the 1991 Order prevents statutory interest being awarded), caused a significant imbalance in the rights and obligations of the parties to the detriment of the consumer.[86]

A further point is that, in common with the OFT (and in contrast with the House of Lords), the Court of Appeal did not seem to consider the possibility that the term might be justified on the basis of overall substantive fairness. We saw that the Court of Appeal did say that one form of substantive fairness might be relevant, i.e. where in exchange for the term the consumer has received a reduced price. However, the Court clearly did not consider that this had happened. We shall see below that the House of Lords view may have been that consumers benefited from the term in the sense that the Bank might not lend at all without being guaranteed the recovery of interest until the full capital sum has been paid off.[87] However, in common with the OFT, the Court of Appeal clearly did not view things in this way; presumably taking the view that Banks would be able to absorb the cost of lost interest on the amounts outstanding on those minority of debts on which a judgement has been issued.

Despite taking the view that (as it stood) the term was unfair, the Court of Appeal did not grant an injunction. Instead, undertakings from the bank were accepted. First of all the Bank undertook to amend the term so as to oblige the Bank to bring to the attention of consumers the powers of the court under s. 129 and ss 136–9 of the CCA (i.e. the powers to make a time order and to review the amounts due and possibly reduce or extinguish the debt). Secondly, the Bank undertook not to enforce a claim to post-judgement interest unless the attention of the court had indeed

---

84 See discussion by E. MacDonald, Scope and Fairness of the Unfair Terms in Consumer Contracts Regulations: *Director General of Fair Trading* v. *First National Bank* (2002) 65 Modern Law Review 763, at 770–2 on this informational deficit in relation to the term and the legal/statutory context surrounding it.

85 [2000] QB 672 at 688.

86 *Ibid.*

87 See below at 5.5.4.2(iv)(a)-(c).

been drawn to the powers under s. 129 and ss 136–9 of the CCA and the court had considered whether to exercise these powers.[88]

So what was the Court of Appeal really saying about unfairness? As we have already seen, in the absence of the undertakings described, the Court of Appeal view was that the term caused a significant imbalance in rights and obligations to the detriment of the consumer (on the basis that it allowed for contractual interest to be payable after judgement when – as a result of the 1991 Order – interest would not otherwise be payable). The Court of Appeal also considered that, as the term stood, it violated the requirement of good faith. This was because of the unfair surprise issue. This related to the issue of information and transparency (or lack of it). Consumers would not be likely to expect interest to accrue in addition to the judgement sum; they were not adequately warned of this; they would be unaware of the review powers of the court or (indeed) of the need to ask for a review (being unaware of the issue of the contractual interest in the first place). However, the Court of Appeal clearly took the view that, with the undertakings, the term was no longer unfair. But on what precise basis was this the case? Why did the undertakings make a difference?

As we have seen, one undertaking was to the effect that the lender should inform consumers at the stage of court action that they could ask the court to exercise its powers under the CCA to, *inter alia*, review the amount payable. The result of providing such information to the consumer may then be that the consumer is no longer unfairly surprised by the term.[89] Either the court reduces or extinguishes the amount payable as contractual interest; or even if it is left in place the review has made the consumer aware of the issue.

Provision of information is often associated with procedural fairness. However, the information to be provided here is certainly not about purely *pre-contractual* procedural fairness. The Bank is not promising to make *the term* spell out more clearly that contractual interest will continue to accrue after a judgement; nor is it promising to make any other form of pre-contractual explanation to this effect. So, the agenda is not to enable the consumer to make a more fully informed decision as to the terms *before* entering the contract. The Bank, rather, is promising to

---

[88]   [2000] QB 672 at 688–9 in the Court of Appeal and see the House of Lords judgement reported at [2001] 2 All ER (Comm) 1000.

[89]   Support for this approach to good faith is provided by German commentator, H.-W. Micklitz, The Politics of Judicial Co-operation in the EU, CUP, 2005, 418 (the significance of such support being that the good faith concept in the UTD seems to have derived from the provision originally contained in the German Standard Contracts Act 1976 (now Article 310 of the new German Civil Code, the 'BGB'). On the significance of other legal traditions in developing an autonomous EC approach to unfairness see above at 3.5.5.

provide information to the consumer at a later stage, i.e. at the time when the matter is about to reach court. As was suggested above[90] this may be a particularly useful form of transparency which can help the consumer to self-protect post-contractually by enabling the consumer to seek protection against the *consequences* of the term (in the form of the review under the CCA powers). However, action taken by the Bank after conclusion of the contract (including provision of the type of information in question) is not, in itself, relevant to the question of fairness. Fairness is to be assessed in the light of the circumstances existing at the time when the contract is concluded.[91] Post-contractual information only becomes relevant if the obligation to provide it is in existence at the time when the contract is concluded. In other words, the provision of the later information must be something which the Bank is obliged to do by a practice adopted in all cases or under an actual term of the contract. It is not entirely clear from the judgement, but it may have been that the undertaking of the Bank was in fact to amend the terms of the contract so as to provide for this post-contractual obligation as to the provision of information to the consumer. If this is the case then, for the Court of Appeal, what would help to justify the term allowing for interest to be payable after judgement was a *substantive term* requiring the Bank to provide the relevant information (about the possibility of having the term reviewed) to the consumer at the time of the judgement. The result may be that the consumer is no longer surprised by the term (either the court reduces or extinguishes the amount payable as contractual interest; or even if it is left in place the review has made the consumer aware of the issue). The Court of Appeal did not actually articulate how this related to the specific components of the test of unfairness. However, it seems logical to suppose that their view was that the obligation to provide the information means that there may no longer be a violation of the good faith requirement (it being recalled that the Court of Appeal view was that it was the unfair surprise that caused there to be a violation of the good faith requirement).

Certainly, it seems that the fact that the obligation to provide information derives from a substantive term does not prevent such an obligation being relevant to the good faith issue. Good faith appears to be related to both pre-contractual procedural issues and matters related to the substance of the terms.[92] Notwithstanding that the obligation to provide information may go to the issue of good faith, it may also go to the issue of significant imbalance. It appears that whether a term is found to cause significant imbalance can be affected not only by what it provides for

---

[90] See above at 2.4.3.4.

[91] Regulation 6(1).

[92] See below at 5.5.4.2(iii) and 6.2.

itself but also what is provided for by other substantive provisions.[93] So, the view of the Court of Appeal may have been that the obligation to provide information as to the review powers of the court helped prevent there being a violation of good faith and/or helped to prevent there being a significant imbalance.

The other undertaking was to the effect that the lender would not rely on the term where such a review had not taken place. Again, this could be described as a form of post-contractual procedural fairness. However, unlike above, this is not about procedural fairness in the sense of being transparent with the consumer as to his rights so as to enable the consumer to take action to protect his interests. Here, the procedural fairness lies in the lender not taking full advantage of his own rights during the process of enforcement, i.e. his right to contractual interest in addition to the amount due under the judgement (it being fair that the lender does not take advantage of this right because, for whatever reason, the court has not reviewed the situation and in particular has not reviewed whether or not it is fair for the consumer to continue to pay interest at the contractual rate). However, once again, we come back to a *substantive* obligation that arises at the time of the contract. The undertaking not to rely on the interest after judgement term can only properly be viewed as a matter going to the fairness of the interest after judgement term if the undertaking relates to an obligation that will be in existence at the time the contract is concluded, e.g. if the obligation derives from a substantive term of the contract. Again it is not entirely clear from the judgements that the undertaking was indeed to amend the actual term in this way. If it was then it must be that what the Court of Appeal was really saying was this. The fairness of the interest after judgement term was enhanced by provision in the contract for a substantive obligation; this substantive obligation being to the effect that the Bank would not rely on the interest after judgement term where the court had not exercised its powers of review under the CCA. So, again the idea is that the fairness of the interest after judgement term is enhanced by another substantive provision providing that the Bank has a substantive obligation to exercise post-contractual procedural fairness. However, this time the post-contractual procedural fairness is not about the provision of information, but about the Bank not relying on the interest after judgement term in certain circumstances.

Again, the Court of Appeal did not articulate exactly in what way the substantive promise (not to rely on the term where a review had not taken place) related to specific components of the test. However, this promise not to rely on the term where such a review has not taken place (being a

---

93   This was confirmed by Lord Bingham in the House of Lords at [2001] 3 WLR 1297 at 1308; and see further below at 5.5.4.2(ii).

substantive obligation) seems to be capable of being linked to both the good faith and significant imbalance components of the test. The view of the Court of Appeal may have been that the obligation not to rely on the term where there had not been a review by the court helped prevent there being a violation of good faith and/or helped to prevent there being a significant imbalance.

5.5.3.4 Conclusions on the Court of Appeal Approach

To conclude on the approach of the Court of Appeal, it can be said that it is reasonably protectively and fairness-oriented. It shows the kind of fairness-oriented sensitivity to context described above,[94] i.e. sensitivity to the impact of terms on consumers and to the procedural difficulties they may face in self-protecting against such terms. A key idea seems to be that the 1991 Order suggests a general policy against post-judgement interest. When we look further at the approach of the Court of Appeal, we begin to see more clearly why the Court of Appeal is in sympathy with such a policy and in it being applied to post-judgement contractual interest. In part, it is about the idea that if the situation has got to court then circumstances have clearly changed from the time the contract was made. The consumer is in difficulty. Sure, the lender has an interest in recovering the expected principal and interest. However, there is a competing interest. The consumer is in difficulty and may be unduly prejudiced if the court awards interest on top of the basic award. In addition, where contractual interest is payable, the consumer may be unduly prejudiced unless there is a review by the court at this stage in order to determine what the consumer can afford to pay and/or the way in which these payments should be structured and/or the period over which the payments should be made. This seems to explain why, ultimately for the Court of Appeal, the term should not be relied upon unless such a review had taken place. In other words, the Court of Appeal favoured the consumer interest in avoiding undue hardship over the lender interest in having an untrammelled right to recover the full amount of interest contracted for until the principal sum had been completely repaid. In particular, the Court of Appeal certainly did not take the view that consumers could be viewed as benefiting from use of the term (on the basis that Banks would not lend without it and that therefore use of the term enabled consumers to obtain a loan in the first place).

Then there is the approach to information and unfair surprise. Again, there was a broadly fairness-oriented approach. First of all the assumption was made that the term in question would be unlikely to alert consumers

---

[94]   See 2.4.1–2 above.

to the fact that there is liability for interest in addition to the amount payable under the judgement. Consumers were not blamed for this. There was no suggestion that consumers should exercise more self-reliant autonomy and familiarize themselves with such a term and its implications. Further, it was thought appropriate to impose a responsibility on the lender to make consumers aware of the how to obtain protection against the term by asking for a court review. This was not viewed as being unduly restrictive of the freedom of the trader. In the light of the consumer interest in being placed in a better informed position to protect his interests, this restriction on the freedom of the trader was viewed as necessary.[95]

5.5.4 The House of Lords View

5.5.4.1 The European Context

On appeal to the House of Lords[96] the term was found not to be unfair. The House of Lords, and Lord Bingham in particular, began by setting out a view as to the meaning of the test of unfairness. This was prefaced by recognition of the EC context[97] and the need to approach the fairness concept accordingly. Lord Bingham acknowledged that the UTCCR had been passed to give effect to the UTD.[98] Lord Bingham also made reference to the general aim of the UTD to partially harmonize the law on unfair terms among the Member States of the EU;[99] and said that the test of unfairness must be interpreted in the light of the objective they were intended to promote[100] (i.e. implementation of the UTD). Lord Steyn also stressed the importance of interpreting the UTCCR so as to give effect to the goals of the UTD.[101] However, he gave more detail as to his view of these goals than had Lord Bingham. He referred to promoting fair standard contract terms in order to improve the functioning of the European market and protecting consumers.[102] He also emphasized that the Directive was aimed at 'take it or leave it contracts' and treated

---

[95] See above at 2.3.2.2 for the typical freedom-oriented approach to such procedural issues.

[96] [2001] 3 WLR 1297.

[97] See discussion above at 3.4–5.

[98] [2001] 3 WLR 1297, Lord Bingham at 1307.

[99] *Ibid.*

[100] At 1308.

[101] At 1311.

[102] *Ibid.*

consumers as 'presumptively weaker parties and therefore fit for protection from abuses by stronger contracting parties'.[103]

Of course, we can see from the above sketch that Lord Bingham referred to harmonizing the law. The suggestion, then, is that there should be a concept of unfairness that is very similar if not exactly the same for all Member States. Indeed Lord Steyn went further and actually said that 'the concepts of the Directive must be given autonomous meanings so that there will be uniform application of the Directive so far as is possible'.[104] Lord Bingham and Lord Hope acknowledged that the Member States have no pre-existing common concept of fairness or good faith. [105] However, Lord Bingham took the view (which the others did not express disagreement with) that the meaning of the test of unfairness as expressed in the Directive was clear and not likely to give rise to different interpretations at least insofar as it applied to the facts of this case; and that, therefore, there was no need to make a reference to the ECJ for guidance as to the meaning of the unfairness concept.[106] This seemed to be based partly on the view that the test was not supposed to reflect the pre-existing position in any one Member State but to be a new test to be applied, whatever the pre-existing law, in each country. Lord Bingham said that:

> The Member States have no common concept of fairness or good faith, and the Directive does not purport to state the law of any single Member State. It lays down a test to be applied, whatever their pre-existing law, by all Member States. If the meaning of the test were doubtful, or vulnerable to the possibility of differing interpretations in differing Member States, it might be desirable or necessary to seek a ruling from the European Court of justice on its interpretation. But the language used in expressing the test, so far as applicable in this case, is in my opinion clear and not reasonably capable of differing interpretations.[107]

I shall return to comment properly on this conclusion having unpacked what the House of Lords actually said about the test of unfairness and how they applied it to the term in question.

---

[103] *Ibid.*

[104] At 1312.

[105] See Lord Bingham at 1307 and Lord Steyn at 1312.

[106] See Lord Bingham, *ibid.*

[107] *Ibid.*

5.5.4.2 Interpreting and Applying the Test of Unfairness

(i) Breaking Down the Test

We now turn to the interpretation of the test taken by the House of Lords. In broad terms, it appears that the House of Lords took the view that for a term to be unfair there would need to be a significant imbalance in rights and obligations to the detriment of the consumer *and* a violation of the requirement of good faith; these being separate, if connected, requirements.[108]

(ii) Significant Imbalance to the Detriment of the Consumer

So, dealing first with significant imbalance/detriment, the House of Lords related this to the substantive features of the term; there being a significant imbalance where the term is 'so weighted in favour of the supplier as to tilt the parties' rights and obligations under the contract significantly in his favour'.[109] This would be the case where terms give unduly beneficial rights to the trader or impose undue burdens on the consumer. Lord Bingham said that:

> The requirement of significant imbalance is met if a term is so weighted in favour of the supplier as to tilt the parties' rights and obligations under the contract significantly in his favour. This may be by the granting to the supplier of a beneficial option or discretion or power, or by the imposing on the consumer of a disadvantageous burden or risk or duty.[110]

Lord Bingham said that the indicative list of terms provided guidance as to unfairness in substance.[111] He also said that whether a term caused a significant imbalance to the detriment of the consumer was a question that involved looking not only at the term in question but also at the contract as a whole, i.e. at the other terms of the contract.[112] The other significant discussion of the test of unfairness came from Lord Steyn. He shared the view of Lord Bingham that the 'significant imbalance' element of the test related to matters of substantive unfairness,[113] although he did not elaborate as to what form such substantive unfairness might take.

---

[108] Lord Bingham at 1307–8, Lord Steyn at 1313.

[109] Lord Bingham at 1307.

[110] *Ibid.*

[111] *Ibid.*

[112] At 1307–8.

[113] At 1313.

These views on significant imbalance are helpful, but leave some unanswered questions. First of all, is there a more specific way to concretize the concept of significant imbalance than by simply saying that it relates to the substance of the terms and involves, in Lord Bingham's words, beneficial options, discretions or powers for the trader or disadvantageous risks, burdens or duties for the consumer? So, for example, can it be said (as with UCTA) that deviation from default rules to the detriment of the consumer or allowing for compromise of reasonable consumer expectations have a role to play? Indeed, can it be said that the significant imbalance concept is a kind of substantive trigger mechanism (in a broadly similar way that the 'excluding or restricting liability' concept under UCTA is a trigger) for a broader review of fairness in substance and fairness in procedure? Certainly, we shall see shortly that the good faith element of the test appears to involve assessment of both substantive and procedural issues, so it is plausible that the significant imbalance element is the trigger mechanism for this broader review. Then there is a further issue as to significant imbalance. We have seen that the House of Lords seemed to take the view that, in determining whether there is significant imbalance, it is also relevant to consider the other terms of the contract. In other words, the view may have been that in deciding whether there is significant imbalance there should be consideration as to whether there are favourable terms that can be said to represent a 'fair price' for the term under scrutiny. Such an approach equates significant imbalance with overall substantive unfairness. However, as we have seen, there are various ways in which we might measure whether a beneficial term does indeed cancel out the imbalance caused by the term under scrutiny;[114] and it is not clear what measure the House of Lords would use to assess this. The House of Lords did not need to develop this issue on the facts of the case as no argument was made as to the existence of a favourable term. However, as we shall see below, there was a hint at a particular model of substantive fairness. This did not relate to the relationship between the term under scrutiny and another term as such. Rather it related the idea that the Bank would not lend if it could not charge interest after judgement;[115] possibly suggesting that the 'fair price' for the detriment caused by the term was access to the loan.

A final question about the approach of the House of Lords to the concept of significant imbalance is whether they viewed it as being entirely and exclusively concerned with fairness in substance? If it is, then if, (taking into account other terms of the contract or any other benefit such as basic access to the goods or services) there is not deemed

[114] See above at 2.4.3.3 and 3.5.4.
[115] See below at 5.5.4.2(iv)(a).

to be overall substantive unfairness, a term cannot be unfair despite the existence of procedural unfairness. This is because procedural unfairness would only be relevant to the good faith element of the test and (given that *both* significant imbalance and a violation of good faith seem to be required for unfairness) it would not matter that there might be a violation of good faith as long as there was no significant imbalance. This would be problematic. As was suggested above,[116] consumers surely have a legitimate interest in terms being transparent whenever there is substantive detriment, even where there is overall fairness in substance. We shall, however, return to these issues below.[117] First of all we must consider the approach taken to good faith and to the application of the test as a whole to the term in the *First National Bank* case.

(iii) Good Faith

Turning to good faith, Lord Bingham equated good faith with 'fair and open dealing'.[118] The emphasis on 'openness' carries forward from the previous views expressed by Lord Bingham (and already referred to above[119]) as to the meaning of good faith in civil law. We saw that he referred to good faith in civilian jurisdictions as being, *inter alia*, about 'coming clean' and 'laying one's cards face upwards on the table'[120] (i.e. as being about transparency). In the *First National Bank* case Lord Bingham said that 'openness' meant that terms should be 'expressed fully, clearly and legibly'; not containing 'concealed pitfalls or traps'; and being given 'appropriate prominence' where they might 'operate disadvantageously' to the consumer.[121]

As well as basing these views about the relationship between good faith and transparency on civilian traditions, Lord Bingham may also have been influenced by his understanding of a particular aspect of the historical role that has been played by good faith in English law. Lord Bingham referred to Lord Mansfield's judgements in the eighteenth century, describing Lord Mansfield as a 'champion' of good faith.[122] In fact the statement for which Lord Mansfield may be most famous in relation to good faith was to the effect that: 'The governing principle is applicable to all contracts and dealings. Good faith forbids either party

---

[116] At 2.4.3.4.
[117] At 5.7.
[118] [2001] 3 WLR 1297 at 1308.
[119] At 3.5.5.2.
[120] *Interfoto Picture Library* v. *Stiletto Visual Programmes Ltd* [1989] QB 433, at 443.
[121] [2001] 3 WLR 1297 at 1308.
[122] *Ibid.*

from concealing what he privately knows, to draw the other party into a bargain, from ignorance of that fact, and his believing to the contrary'.[123]

This equates good faith with not inducing the other to contract when one knows *facts* that the other does not. In other words it is associated with *disclosure of important or material facts*. Despite Lord Mansfield's broad view as to the applicability of this concept, it did not (over the next 250 years) develop as a principle applicable to 'all contracts and dealings'. Rather, situations in which such a duty of disclosure was recognized became understood as exceptions to the general rule; the general rule being that no such duty is owed.[124] However, the point for present purposes is that Lord Bingham may have viewed (Lord Mansfield's notion of) *disclosure* of material facts as being central to the notion of good faith. This, of course, further emphasizes the idea that good faith is about 'openness' in general, i.e. that the parties should also be 'open' in relation to the *terms of the contract*. So there should be clear expression of the terms, avoidance of traps and disclosure of disadvantageous terms.

Two points can be made then as to what Lord Bingham seems to be saying about transparency. First of all, he seems to be saying that transparency is generally important. Second, he appears to be saying that transparency is particularly important the more detrimental in substance a terms is. He says that prominence should be given to 'disadvantageous terms' and this must surely be a reference to terms that are disadvantageous in a substantive sense. He also refers to 'concealed pitfalls or traps'. The implication, surely, is that the term is a 'trap' or 'pitfall' on the basis that it is particularly substantively detrimental.

We then turn to the second aspect of Lord Bingham's concept of good faith –'fair dealing'. Lord Bingham said that fair dealing: 'requires that the supplier should not, whether deliberately or unconsciously, take advantage of the consumer's necessity, indigence, lack of experience, unfamiliarity with the subject matter of the contract [or] weak bargaining position ...'.[125]

So, while 'open dealing' for Lord Bingham is about procedural fairness in the form of transparency, 'fair dealing' appears to be about other forms of procedural fairness, i.e. not taking advantage of these various possible consumer vulnerabilities. This formulation appears to be loosely based on Article 138[126] of the German BGB which referred to a situation in which: 'someone exploiting the necessity, lack of experience,

---

[123] *Carter* v. *Boehm* [1766]3 Burr. 1907, 97 Eng. Rep. 1162 (K.B.).

[124] *Keates* v. *Cadogan* (1851) 10 CB 591; and see discussion by E. Mc Kendrick, Contract Law, Palgrave Macmillan, 2005, at 259–264.

[125] [2001] 3 WLR 1297 at 1308.

[126] The new German Civil Code repeats this provision in slightly amended form.

lack of discernment or lack of willpower of another, obtains monetary advantage or a promise to be granted monetary advantage out of proportion to his own performance.'

We can see that both Lord Bingham's approach and the German provision have in common the 'necessity' and 'lack of experience' criteria. There are differences in relation to the other factors mentioned, although perhaps not huge differences. Lord Bingham refers to indigence, while Article 138 refers to 'lack of discernment'. He also refers to the 'weak bargaining position' of the consumer. This is a very broad criterion that could encapsulate, *inter alia*,[127] all of the other factors that he mentions and all of the factors that are mentioned by Article 138 (including 'lack of willpower' which is the final Article 138 criteria).

Lord Bingham's formulation for the 'fair dealing' element of good faith is also comparable to Article 138 in that it refers to the trader 'taking advantage' of the various vulnerabilities, while Article 138 refers to the vulnerabilities being 'exploited'. So, in both cases there is a focus not simply upon the vulnerability of the consumer, but also (possibly) on the way in which the trader 'deals with' this vulnerability.

So, precisely what is the nature of the procedural fairness that Lord Bingham is discussing here? One possibility is that the trader is viewed as 'taking advantage' of these various consumer weaknesses simply by entering any contract with consumers who are weak in these sorts of ways, i.e. that there is no need to establish any form of unfairness or detriment in relation to the substance of the terms. There might be said to be some support for this in the fact that in the case of Article 138 the strong party must end up with a monetary advantage (or promise of such) that is out of proportion to his own performance, i.e. the result must be some form of unfairness in substance; while, by contrast, there is no express mention of unfairness in substance in Lord Bingham's formulation. However, it seems wholly implausible that Lord Bingham could have intended to suggest that a term could be unfair without any need for it to be in any way substantively detrimental to the consumer. As we said above, although we might wish to demand pure procedural fairness in the form of transparency, it is unrealistic to be concerned with other forms of pure procedural fairness.[128] In other words, other forms of procedural fairness (e.g. lack of choice and the weaker bargaining position of the consumer, including the various vulnerabilities referred to in Article 138 and by Lord Bingham) should only matter where the result is that there is a degree of unfairness in substance.

---

127 See further at 2.4.3.4 for the various issues that seem to be relevant to bargaining power.

128 See above at 2.4.3.4.

We can reach this conclusion by relating the notion of 'advantage taking' to the substantive features of the terms. Traders may be viewed as having 'taken advantage' of these weaknesses by using terms that are unduly detrimental in substance. The question as to whether there has been advantage taking depends upon the extent of the substantive detriment caused by the term. Putting this another way, the weaker position of consumers (in terms of bargaining position and the other weaknesses mentioned) counts more against the term – there is more likely to be deemed to be advantage taking – the more detrimental the term is in substance. This seems a much more plausible way to read what Lord Bingham said than the first possibility above.

Then, there are various possible readings of what Lord Bingham said connected to the need for bad conscience by the trader and/or extreme unfairness in substance and/or extreme bargaining weakness on the part of the consumer (i.e. not simply weakness relative to the trader but relative to other consumers). So, one possibility is that when Lord Bingham referred to 'advantage taking' he was referring to a requirement of bad conscience (i.e. some form of intentional or reckless exploitation) on the part of the trader. Certainly the phrase 'advantage taking' could have these connotations.[129] In addition, the formulation appears to be modelled on BGB Article 138 and the 'advantage taking' phrase seems to have been used as a substitute for 'exploitation' in Article 138.

Another possibility, which seems close to what is required under the doctrine of unconscionability,[130] is again to say that advantage taking is equivalent to bad conscience but that this bad conscience need not be established *per se* but can be established by showing not simply that there is a degree of unfairness in substance, but that the terms are *extremely* unfair in substance by comparison with the market norm[131] (possibly with the added requirement that the consumer is particularly weak, i.e. weaker than the average consumer[132] – the requirement of the consumer being especially weak possibly being suggested not only by the reference to 'advantage taking' but also by the reference to such concepts as 'necessity', possibly suggesting a more than normally vulnerable consumer).

However, as we have already said,[133] the goals of the Directive would surely be frustrated by any requirement of bad conscience. In

---

[129] See H.-W. Micklitz, The Politics of Judicial Co-operation in the EU, CUP, 2005, 420.

[130] On unconscionability see further below at 8.1.2.

[131] On using market norms as a measure of fairness see above at 2.4.3.3 and below at 7.2.2.

[132] See 8.1.2 below.

[133] See above at 3.4.3.

addition, the Directive certainly seems to be aimed at routine unfairness, i.e. it is not simply aimed at extreme unfairness in substance or procedure;[134] and there is no evidence that the ECJ considers that such extreme unfairness is required.[135] It is to be hoped, then, that the reference to 'advantage taking' was simply (as suggested above) a reference to the idea that the terms are unduly (although not necessarily extremely) unfair in substance. It is to be hoped also that Lord Bingham did not intend to suggest that there is only advantage taking where the consumer is in a particularly weak bargaining position, i.e. not simply weak relative to the trader but weak relative to other consumers. Indeed, it does not seem that when Lord Bingham referred to taking advantage of the weak bargaining position of the consumer that he had in mind extreme weakness, but simply weakness relative to the position of the trader. In discussing the facts of the *First National Bank* case itself he said that: 'It may ... be assumed that any borrower is in a much weaker bargaining position than a large bank contracting on its own standard form.'[136]

In conclusion, then, it is not entirely clear what Lord Bingham was getting at in relation to his 'fair dealing' criteria. In particular it is not entirely clear what implications of this criteria are for questions of unfairness in substance and procedure. However, the preferable interpretation (especially in the light of the goals of the UTD) is that consumers are presumptively treated as suffering from the various weaknesses listed (i.e. these are weaknesses *relative* to the trader); and that traders are to be viewed as taking advantage of these if they use terms that are unduly (although not necessarily extremely) detrimental in substance to consumer interests.

Lord Steyn considered that there was 'a large area of overlap' between the significant imbalance and good faith limbs of the test.[137] This seems to have been based on his view that violation of good faith was also concerned with unfairness in substance (as well as being concerned with procedural unfairness – see below). He drew, in particular, on the indicative list to reach the conclusion that good faith related to matters of substance.[138] What he seems to have been getting at is that the list generally describes terms by reference to their substantive features. From this he seems to have reasoned that, as the list describes terms that are potentially unfair and as violation of good faith is a requirement of unfairness, then violation of good faith must be based (at least in part) on a conclusion as to the unfairness in substance of the term.

---

134 *Ibid.*

135 See above at 3.5.4.

136 [2001] 3 WLR, 1297 at 1305.

137 [2001] 3 WLR 1297 at 1313.

138 *Ibid.*

Indeed, he rejected the idea that good faith is primarily concerned with procedural matters, saying that: 'Any purely procedural or even predominantly procedural interpretation of the requirement of good faith must be rejected.'[139]

At the same time it seems clear that he did view procedural matters as being relevant to good faith. He approved Lord Bingham's statement that good faith was about 'fair and open dealing';[140] and, as we have seen, this, for Lord Bingham (and we must assume also for Lord Steyn) connoted procedural fairness (i.e. transparency and not taking advantage of the various vulnerabilities discussed above). So, it appears that, for Lord Steyn, procedural fairness was relevant, but that consideration of the substantive features of the terms was at least (if not more) important than such procedural matters. Lord Steyn's other relevant comment about good faith was a more general one, i.e. an approval of the view that the aim of the good faith standard is to 'enforce community standards of decency, fairness and reasonableness in commercial transactions'.[141]

In relation to procedural fairness, we have already discussed what the House of Lords had to say about transparency and not taking advantage of various consumer weaknesses including the weaker bargaining position of the consumer. However, there is no discussion of the role of choice (in the sense of whether the lender or other lenders offered more favourable terms that might have been available at a higher price). It was noted that this was a common term for lenders to use.[142] However, as we shall see, if anything this seemed to have weighed in favour of the term in that it was viewed as confirming the view that no lender would lend without such protection.[143] This does not necessarily mean that in other circumstances lack of choice might not count against a term. The point for now is simply that the House of Lords did not expressly indicate any such approach.

Finally, there was no explicit discussion as to whether a term can be unfair on purely substantive grounds, i.e. irrespective of the existence of a reasonable level of procedural fairness. The Court of Appeal did suggest that this was possible,[144] but the House of Lords said nothing expressly on the issue. Lord Steyn, as we have seen, indicated that good faith was

---

[139] *Ibid.*

[140] *Ibid.*

[141] Here he was citing (at 1313) the commentary to O. Lando and H. Beale, Principles of European Contract Law, Kluwer, 2000, p. 113. See below at 7.2.2 for discussion of the idea of a 'community standard' and the extent to which this suggests a standard not tied to market norms.

[142] See Lord Millett at 1319.

[143] Lord Bingham at 1308–9.

[144] See above at 5.5.3.2.

not 'wholly or even predominantly procedural'. This may have meant no more than the possibility suggested above to the effect that in assessing procedural fairness the substantive features of the term must be taken into account. However, it might suggest that terms can be unfair based on their substantive features even where there is significant procedural fairness.

(iv) Applying the Test to the Facts

(a) Significant Imbalance As to the application of the law to the term in question, the House of Lords, as indicated, took the view that it was not unfair to provide that contractual interest would not merge in the judgement and that it would therefore continue to be payable in addition to the amount awarded in the judgement. The view was that the essence of a loan agreement was that the principal sum and interest would be paid back to the lender and that lenders would not lend if they did not believe that they would be able to recover both the principal sum and all of the interest for as long as some portion of the principal sum was outstanding.[145] It was also pointed out that it was perfectly normal for lenders to use a term ensuring this result.[146] In addition, on the consumer side of the equation, the House of Lords defended the term on the basis of reasonable expectation. Lord Millet said that: 'If [the borrower's] attention were drawn to the impugned term … he might well be surprised at the need to spell this out, but he would surely not be at surprised by the fact. It is what he would expect.'[147]

So, for the House of Lords, the term did not cause significant imbalance to the detriment of the consumer. There was nothing unbalanced or detrimental in providing for the contractual interest not to merge in the judgement and to continue to be payable in addition to the sum payable under the judgement debt.[148] Without such a provision there would be an imbalance to the detriment of *the lender*.[149] The House of Lords rejected the Court of Appeal view that the interest after judgement term caused significant imbalance to the detriment of the consumer by allowing for contractual interest after judgement when the 1991 Order prevented county courts awarding statutory interest on a judgement debt.[150] In other words, they rejected the idea that the ban on awarding statutory interest was indicative of a policy against interest being payable

---

[145] See Lord Bingham, at 1308–9, Lord Steyn at 1313–14, Lord Hope at 1316 and Lord Millett at 1319.

[146] Lord Millett, *ibid.*

[147] Lord Millett, *ibid.*

[148] *Ibid.*

[149] See Lord Bingham at 1309.

[150] *Ibid.*

after judgement; a policy that, in turn, suggested that it would be unfair for the contract to provide for interest to be so payable. The House of Lords reasoning as to why there was no general policy against the payment of post-judgement interest was based on a particular interpretation of the regulatory context. The argument was that the CCA 1974 was passed to protect consumers and contained a range of protective measures; and that, if there had been a general policy agenda against payment of post-judgement interest then the 1974 Act would have prohibited terms having this effect.[151] Indeed, the ban on awarding statutory interest was viewed as being a reason that lenders would legitimately feel the need to provide for contractual interest.[152] A solution, for some of their Lordships, was to allow for courts to award interest on the judgement. The idea was that provision for contractual interest would not then be necessary; there would be a single judgement award for principal and interest (not an award only for the principal that allowed interest to accrue separately); and in making the award the court would have considered the liability of the consumer for interest in deciding whether to make an instalment order.[153]

(b) Significant Imbalance, Fairness and Freedom This approach to significant imbalance seems (by contrast with the approach of the Court of Appeal) to sit quite firmly at the freedom-oriented end of the spectrum in terms of the way that a fairness test can be approached. We saw that the Court of Appeal was fairly protectively inclined. First of all, by contrast with the Court of Appeal, the House of Lords view was that lenders would not lend at all if they could not use such a term. In making this point the House of Lords may also have been taking a view on overall substantive fairness and concluding that consumers benefited from the term in the sense that it enabled access to funds that would not otherwise be available.[154] Whether we view the approach as simply being about the entitlement of the Bank to full interest until the full capital amount is repaid or also being about the benefit to consumers of obtaining access to loan funds, the point about a freedom-oriented approach is the same. The House of Lords prioritized the freedom of the Bank to obtain recovery of interest until the full capital sum was repaid; supporting this freedom by the argument that, without this freedom, they would not lend. By contrast, the Court of Appeal prioritized the consumer interest (in being protected against the consequences of the term) over this freedom (presumably on the basis of the assumption that the issue would only arise in a small

---

[151] *Ibid.*

[152] See Lord Steyn at 1314.

[153] See Lord Hope at 1316 and Lord Millett at 1320.

[154] On this approach to substantive fairness see above at 2.4.3.3.

minority of cases, so that the sums involved in lost interest would be small enough for the Bank to absorb[155]).

The more freedom-oriented approach of the House of Lords then logically also applied to the attitude to reasonable consumer expectation. The approach of the Court of Appeal to reasonable expectation was arguably based at least in part on the idea that consumers generally expect that a court decision provides the full and final word on the extent of one's liabilities.[156] For this reason (for the Court of Appeal) it was not reasonable to expect the separate accrual of contractual interest after the judgement. I argued above that this approach to reasonable expectation is 'empirical' to the extent that it can be said to be based on the life experience and observation *of some consumers*, to the effect that the role of courts is to make a final judgement on the matter at hand; a judgement that determines, in full, the future extent of the relevant liabilities.[157] Of course, perhaps not all consumers hold this view. So, choosing this consumer expectation over the expectations of others that expect to have to pay the contractual interest even after judgement is probably based on a normative judgement. The normative judgement of the Court of Appeal was that the effect of the term was unfair based on the large additional amount of liability building up in interest; the failure to highlight the term at the conclusion of the contract; the fact that court usually does not consider reduction in interest at the time of the judgement; and the fact that the default position is that interest is not payable post-judgement. By contrast, the House of Lords (Lord Millet in particular) took the view that consumers *would* always expect to pay all of the interest on a debt. This approach has been characterized as empirical.[158] It may well be that many consumers *do* hold this view and, in this sense, the approach is indeed empirical. However, as there is no evidence that this is the predominant view, it seems that the House of Lords must have preferred this view on normative grounds. In other words, the House of Lords prioritized the freedom of the Bank to obtain recovery of interest until the full capital sum was repaid over an agenda to protect consumers from the consequences of this.

Then we turn to the Court of Appeal view that there was a general policy against interest being payable after judgement. This, as we have seen, can plausibly be said to be based on a concern that the consumer is now in a vulnerable position; that it should not be made worse by the court adding interest to the award; and that there should be a general

---

[155] See above at 5.5.3.3.

[156] See above at 5.5.3.3.

[157] See above at 5.3.3.3.

[158] See C. Mitchell, Leading a Life of its Own? The Roles of Reasonable Expectation in Contract Law, Oxford Journal of Legal Studies, Vol. 23, No. 4 (2003), 639, at 658–9.

review of the situation and the position of the consumer which should take account of any provision for contractual interest that exists. We might add to all of this that not only does the 1991 Order ban awarding statutory interest but that the common law default position is that contractual interest is not payable. This might also be taken to lend support to the idea that there might be something unfair about interest being payable after judgement. However, the House of Lords started from a much more freedom-oriented premise. It was naturally right that lenders should be free to stipulate for, and expect recovery of, interest until the principal sum had been paid off. The regulatory framework (the common law position and the 1991 ban on courts awarding interest) is read in this context. The common law default position and the 1991 Order are simply out of step with what is naturally right. Indeed, the 1991 Order is viewed as troublesome in not doing the job (i.e. providing for interest after judgement) that is so clearly justified. This idea of the 'natural rightness' of interest after judgement being available is so strong that the argument is even made that it is supported by the fact that it is not outrightly banned. It might be said that there would be no need for a general test of fairness if we believed that everything that was not actually banned was fair! It is true that the CCA does represent a very focused regime for credit contracts and the failure to choose to ban such a term outright may suggest that the UK Parliament did not view such a term as unfair. However, it does not follow from this that such a term was not intended to be viewed as unfair under the UTD. The suggestion has been made that the ECJ might well wish to challenge the idea that pre-existing national norms should determine what is unfair.[159] Of course, the ECJ, as we have seen, *has* made it clear that it is for the national courts to decide on fairness in the particular factual and national legal context.[160] However, this does not apply where there is no benefit at all to the consumer.[161] So, we must now turn to the question as to what view the ECJ might have taken in relation to this particular term.

(c) Significant Imbalance and the European Court What we know for sure at the moment is that as long as the ECJ regards there as being some form of benefit to the consumer it will then be up to the national courts to make an overall assessment as to whether the term is unfair.[162] So, where such a benefit is present the national courts will, for example, be free to take the more fairness-oriented approach of the Court of Appeal to the

---

[159] H.-W. Micklitz, The Politics of Judicial Co-operation in the EU, CUP, 2005, 422.

[160] See above at 3.5.4.

[161] *Ibid.*

[162] It is of course possible that the ECJ, at some later stage, will impose other fundamental requirements such as, in particular, transparency – see above at 3.5.4–5.

various issues in a case such as *First National Bank*; or to take the more freedom-oriented approach of the House of Lords to the various issues. However, this licence does not appear to be available where the ECJ considers that there is no benefit for the consumer. In such a case the ECJ will apparently view the term as unfair. We saw above that we can only draw limited conclusions from the *Freiburger* case as to the ECJ's notion as to how to measure whether there is a 'benefit' to consumers from the use of the term. One possible measure of this[163] involves focusing on the fact that in the *First National Bank* case both the term and the price paid (here the interest) are normal for the market in question. Based on this it is assumed that the price (here interest rate) would need to have been higher if the lender had not been protected against the loss of income from interest on judgement debts. Therefore, runs this argument, the interest rate actually charged is a benefit in the sense that it is lower than it would otherwise have been.[164] This argument was not actually raised in the *First National Bank* case. In any event it is not clear whether the ECJ would recognize this form of benefit. It is true that one of the alleged benefits in the *Freiburger* case was the fact that the price was lower than it would have been without the term (a term requiring the consumer to pay the trader before the commencement of building work). However, first of all, there was another alleged benefit in *Freiburger*, i.e. that the consumer received a Bank guarantee possibly ensuring return of monies where the work was not carried out or was defective. So it is possible that this guarantee was the real benefit recognized by the ECJ (or at least that the allegedly lower price was only regarded as a benefit because it came along with the guarantee). In addition, even if the allegedly lower price in *Freiburger* was regarded as an independent benefit by the ECJ, the case for concluding that there is a lower price as a result of the term (and that, therefore, there is a benefit) seems to be stronger in *Freiburger* than it is in *First National Bank*. In *Freiburger* the result of the prepayment was that the trader would not have to borrow money to finance the work. This is a clearly identifiable outlay that might well need to be made if prepayments are not received. In this sense it contrasts with the future risk of losing income from interest payments. It is more obvious that prices would need to be increased in the former situation than in the latter situation.

So, the conclusion must be that it is not clear that the ECJ would have concluded that the interest rate charged in *First National Bank* represented a benefit to consumers. If they would not, then (assuming they would have viewed the term as being sufficiently detrimental and assuming that they could not see any other benefit) their conclusion

---

[163] See above at 2.4.3.3.
[164] *Ibid.*

would have been that the term was unfair. The only other conceivable benefit that might be said to exist in the *First National Bank* case is that of basic access to lending services.[165] This is the argument that could be said to flow from the view of the House of Lords in *First National Bank*. The House of Lords view was that lenders would not lend without the term in question.[166] It could be then that the House of Lords was saying that use of the term provided a benefit to consumers in allowing them to have access to lending services.[167] Would the ECJ regard this as a benefit? No argument as to this type of benefit was raised on the facts of the *Freiburger* case and neither did the facts of the case suggest such a benefit; so that it is simply unclear as to what the view of the ECJ might be.[168] The ECJ could refuse to recognize this form of benefit. Even if they did accept that, in principle, this form of benefit could be recognized they might take a restrictive approach. It was suggested above that it is arguable that the least that might be expected by the ECJ is an explanation as to the costs and risks associated with supplying the goods without the term and why these costs and risks are significant.[169] So, for example, the ECJ might expect some explanation from the Bank as to how many customers would be likely to go into default and have a judgement issued against them (and therefore how much money in interest is at stake); whether Banks can adequately cover loss of such interest by insurance; or whether the 'writing-off' of such debts is routinely built into the Banking system and easily absorbed. Without such a case being made the ECJ conclusion might be that the availability of the loan had not been proven to be dependent on the use of the term and that the availability of the loan could not therefore be said to be a sufficient benefit.

Of course, another point is that it is also not clear whether, even if the ECJ did recognize a benefit of this type to exist on the facts, the ECJ would view this as having been negated in cases where trader could have, but has not, used a term that could have provided concrete protection against the term.[170] As we have seen it is indeed arguable that a term or terms could have been used in *First National Bank* that would have provided some such protection. This would have been the sort of provision insisted on by the Court of Appeal requiring the Bank to inform consumers of the right to ask the court to review the amounts to be paid and the time for payment and obliging the bank not to rely on the term if

---

[165] Generally on this form of benefit see above at 2.4.3.3.

[166] See above at 5.5.4.2(iv)(a).

[167] See above at 5.5.4.2(iv)(b).

[168] See above at 3.5.4.

[169] *Ibid.*

[170] *Ibid.*

this review has not taken place.[171] It is conceivable that the ECJ would take the view that without such a term there is no benefit to consumers; and that therefore the term is unfair.

Of course the benefit arising from such a term is in the form of transparency; and it is possible that when the ECJ referred to benefit it was thinking of matters related to the substantive features of the term. However, even if this was the case, the point has already been made above that what we are talking about here *is*, in fact, a substantive term, albeit one that provides for a particular form of transparency later in the relationship.[172] Of course, it may well be (even if the current ECJ approach *is* focused only on substantive benefits) that at some point in the future the ECJ will insist upon pre-contractual transparency as a fundamental requirement in addition to benefit (or view such pre-contractual transparency as a necessary form of benefit).[173] However, even if the ECJ does not do this, it is clear that transparency is a key element of EC consumer policy and is surely fundamental to the consumer protection and confidence goals underlying the UTD. With these points in mind, it would seem strongly arguable that the ECJ would at least take significant account of transparency. In other words, there seems a reasonable chance that the ECJ would take the approach suggested here, i.e. to look, in particular, for substantive terms that are beneficial in the sense that they provide for post-contractual transparency enabling the consumer to protect his interests.

(d) Good Faith We now turn to application of the good faith requirement to the term. It will be recalled that the Court of Appeal took the view that consumers may be left with a debt that they did not realize was accruing and which they did not realize they could ask the court to review (whether by adjusting the time for payment or actually reducing the amount).[174] For the Court of Appeal, this all meant that the term caused 'unfair surprise' and on this basis the term violated the good faith aspect of the test. However, the Court of Appeal view was that this unfair surprise could be removed by an obligation on the Bank to inform consumers of the power of the court to review matters at the time of the judgement along with an obligation not to rely upon the term if this review had not taken place. I have already made the point that this form of transparency

---

[171] See above at 5.5.3.3.

[172] See above at 5.5.3.3.

[173] On which see further below at 5.5.4.2(iv)(f).

[174] See discussion by E. MacDonald, Scope and Fairness of the Unfair Terms in Consumer Contracts Regulations: *Director General of Fair Trading* v. *First National Bank* (2002) 65 Modern Law Review 763, at 770–2 on this informational deficit in relation to the term and the legal/statutory context surrounding it.

may be particularly useful.[175] However, the House of Lords disagreed with the approach of the Court of Appeal. For the House of Lords, the term did not violate the requirement of good faith. The House of Lords accepted that consumers might be unpleasantly surprised by the effect of the term.[176] However, they did not believe that the lack of an obligation on the bank to inform consumers as to the powers of the court meant that the term was unfair; or that the Bank should be obliged not to rely on the term where such a review had not taken place.[177] In other words, they did not believe that it was the Bank's responsibility to inform the consumer as to the possibility of asking the court to review matters; or that the Bank should be prejudiced by the fact that a review had not taken place.

The idea that the Bank could not be expected to inform consumers as to the review powers of the court seems to have been based, in part, on the view that the real source of the problem was *the law*, i.e. the failure of *the law* to ensure consumers were aware of the review powers or to ensure that they were exercised automatically. Various suggestions were made as to how the legal position might be improved. One of these, as we have seen, was that the ban on the award of statutory interest by county courts be lifted – this removing the unfair surprise problem by meaning that there would be a single judgement award for principal and interest and allowing the court to consider the liability of the consumer for interest in deciding whether to make an instalment order.[178] Another suggestion was that administrative arrangements be made to ensure that where an instalment agreement leaves an outstanding contractual liability it is automatically referred to the district judge for consideration.[179] Another suggestion was that provision be made to ensure that the debtor is aware of the potential for review under the CCA.[180]

Of course, the fact that the existing state of the law is an important part of the problem (which is undeniable) would not, in itself, necessarily lead to the conclusion that there should be no responsibility on a lender (as the price of using a term that is to his advantage and that he knows may have surprising and onerous consequences for consumers) to give consumers notice of the review powers of the court. It is perfectly logical to say that the law should have better safeguards for the consumer; and also to say that (while the law does not have those safeguards) if a lender wishes to use a term that he knows is likely to prejudice the consumer (and where this prejudice is in part due to the lack of a guaranteed process

---

[175] See above at 5.5.3 and 2.4.3.4.
[176] Lord Bingham at 1310.
[177] *Ibid.*, and Lord Rodger at 1321.
[178] Lord Hope at 1316.
[179] Lord Millett at 1320.
[180] Lord Rodger at 1322.

of review) then the lender should be required to give notice as to the possibility of such a review. However, Lord Bingham gave specific reasons for the view that the failure to give such notice should not make the term unfair. The first two reasons were that it is not customary for such notice to be given;[181] and that it is not a requirement of the CCA that such notice is given.[182] A third reason was that the test is whether it is unfair to include a term not whether it is unfair to use it in a particular way.[183] The implication here seems to have been that to impose a duty to inform as to the review powers would, if such a duty arose post-contractually, be tantamount to saying that the fairness of the term depended on whether the term was used in a particular way i.e. whether it was used with or without such a warning. However, as we have already seen, if the post-contractual obligation to inform is based on an obligation that arises at the time the contract is made, then fairness does not depend upon the way the term is used but on this obligation – an obligation that existed from the outset.

The final reason given by Lord Bingham for refusing to insist that the Bank should give consumers notice of the review powers of the court was that the Bank already took steps to prevent unfair surprise. The evidence was that, at the time of the judgement, the Bank sends a letter reminding the consumer that contractual interest continues to accrue; and that the consumer should consider increasing the instalment paid in order to avoid a much greater balance than the judgement debt quickly building up.[184] So, this warning does indicate that interest continues to accrue in addition to the judgement debt, although it does not inform consumers as to the possibility of obtaining a review of his liability. Of course, this letter is sent post-contractually; so that it should only be a factor to be taken into account if it is based on an obligation arising at the time of the contract or, possibly, if it is a standard practice, so that it can be said to be a factor that is 'permanently' in existence and therefore is in existence at the time of the conclusion of the contract.[185]

(e) Good Faith, Fairness and Freedom Again, we can see that there is a freedom-oriented flavour to the approach of the House of Lords to the transparency/unfair surprise/good faith issue. The Court of Appeal approach was that, in the light of the consumer interest in being placed in a better informed position to protect his interests, it was not unduly restrictive of the freedom of the lender to expect him to inform consumers

---

[181] At 1310.

[182] *Ibid.*

[183] *Ibid.*

[184] *Ibid.*

[185] See further discussion of this issue at 6.4.2.11.

of the powers of the court to review matters. By contrast, for the House of Lords, this was too much to ask of traders. The sole responsibility for informing consumers of the review powers of the court should lie with the law. This (arguably) rather indulgent attitude towards lenders was also evident in the idea that they should not be expected to provide information on this matter as it was not customary; and was not already positively required by the law. As benchmarks of what can be expected of a trader, these seem remarkably undemanding. Asking only what is customary appears to align fairness with trader dominated market norms rather than independent, high standards of fairness.[186] Also, requiring no more than what is already required may well set a low standard of fairness (as well as failing to reflect what the ECJ might conceivably say is required under the UTD – on which see immediately below at para. (f)). This is comparable to the idea that post-contractual interest is not unfair *in substance* because it is not already banned. Here we have the idea that failing to do something *procedurally* is not unfair if doing it is not positively required already. If applied more generally, this approach seems to leave little for a fairness test to do.

Of course, all of this must be viewed in the light of the fact that Lord Bingham did place some emphasis on the letter that the Bank sends warning of the additional liability to pay interest.[187] It is hard to know how important this factor was as only Lord Bingham raised it and he said very little about it. So we do not know whether he took the letter to be making a large contribution to informing consumers and whether, without the letter, he would have regarded the term as unfair. If this *is* the case this, at least, indicates a sense of there being some responsibility on the bank to inform consumers of the risks of the term. However, given the limited discussion of the letter and the lack of evidence about how much impact it appears to have on consumers, it is hard to say whether it represents a useful form of transparency. Certainly there must be some doubt as to whether it does. The OFT brought the case due to significant problems of consumers being surprised by the impact of the term. This might suggest that the letter does not register at all. Alternatively, it might suggest that although the letter makes consumers generally aware that interest continues to accrue separately, it does not do enough to spell out the full implications of this, i.e. exactly how much is being added every month in interest. The suspicion, at least, must be that without specific examples being given many consumers (not really understanding how interest works) might considerably underestimate the amounts involved.

We should note that s. 17 of the new Consumer Credit Act 2006 provides that creditors must give notice after a judgement (and at six

---

[186] See further discussion of this at 7.2.2.

[187] See above at 5.5.4.2(iv)(d).

month intervals thereafter) of the continuing accrual of contractual interest.[188] This, in other words, puts on a statutory footing the Bank's practice of sending a letter. However, as we have seen, an issue about such a letter is whether in substance it makes the position clear to the consumer. Section 17 provides for regulations to be passed on the form and content of such notice.[189] So, these regulations may go some way to addressing the 'unfair surprise' issue in relation to post-judgement contractual interest. The question is whether these regulations will provide that the notice must explain fully (with examples) the amounts being added every month. This, as we have seen, would be of some help. However, this may still come too late. At best, it makes the consumer aware of the contractual interest and puts them in a position to try to 'manage' the debt sensibly. As suggested above, one aspect of the Court of Appeal approach was that the lender should be required to inform the consumer prior to the judgement of the right to ask for a review by the court. This of course provides the consumer with information that may actually result in a lower sum being payable or may result in the terms of the repayment being more favourable in terms of time. Of course, the other aspect of the Court of Appeal approach was that the provision for post-judgement contractual interest should not be enforceable if a review does not take place. The alternative is the approach suggested by Lord Millett to the effect that where there is an outstanding contractual liability the matter is automatically referred to the district judge for review.[190] These approaches, of course, go beyond addressing the unfair surprise issue, i.e. putting the consumer on notice as to the issue and the possibility to seek protection. We go beyond this by actually ensuring that a review takes place.

Unfortunately, there is nothing in the new legislation either about informing the consumer of the right to ask for a review or about ensuring that a review takes place in all cases.

(f) Good Faith and the European Court of Justice It is important at this point to ask what the ECJ might have said on the issue of transparency. The answer, in short, is that it is very difficult to say. First of all, we saw above that it is simply not clear whether the ECJ would interfere with the approach of a national court other than where there is no substantive benefit for the consumer.[191] However, it was also noted that the ECJ might well regard there as being no substantive benefit where, as here, there was no substantive provision in the contract requiring the Bank to

---

[188] Section 17 inserts a new s. 130A(1) into the Consumer Credit Act having this effect.

[189] See the new s. 130A(6).

[190] See above at 5.5.4.2(iv)(d).

[191] See above at 5.5.4.2(iv)(c).

inform consumers at the judgement stage that they are entitled to ask the court to review matters[192] (a form of transparency that has already been argued to be particularly useful[193]). If the ECJ did take this view, then, as already noted,[194] the conclusion would be that the term was unfair. So such an approach would not only be a rejection of the House of Lords view that there was no significant imbalance in the *First National Bank* case. It would also be a rejection of the specific view taken by the House of Lords in relation to the good faith question and whether (in this context) there should have been a term obliging the Bank to inform consumers at the judgement stage that they are entitled to ask the court to review matters (the Court of Appeal having viewed such a provision as necessary for good faith while the House of Lords did not). However, if the ECJ was to take such an approach it would also represent a further restriction of the idea that pre-existing national norms should determine what is unfair.[195] (I say this because, it will be recalled, one of the reasons given by the House of Lords for not thinking that lenders should be required to oblige themselves to provide such information is that they are not currently required to do so by UK law.)

A closely related issue is the letter sent by the Bank at the time of judgement warning consumers that they are liable for contractual interest in addition to the amount owing on the judgement debt. Lord Bingham regarded this as an important reason that the Bank could be said to have done enough in the way of transparency; an important reason for not requiring anything more (such as telling the consumer of the right to have matters reviewed). It was argued above that there must be some doubt as to whether the letter represents a sufficiently effective form of transparency. The OFT brought the case due to their perception that significant numbers of consumers are affected by the term and this might suggest either that the letter does not register at all or that it does not do enough to spell out the full implications, for example by giving specific examples to consumers as to the potential impact of the continuing accrual of contractual interest. In the light of these points it must be doubtful as to whether the ECJ would regard the letter as being a 'benefit'. There must at least be some doubt as to whether the ECJ would take the view that even the 'well informed and reasonably circumspect

---

[192] *Ibid.*

[193] See above at 5.5.3 and 2.4.3.4.

[194] See above at 5.5.4.2(iv)(c).

[195] The argument has been made that the relationship between the good faith concept and national legal norms is something that is ripe for fuller consideration by the ECJ – see H.-W. Micklitz, The Politics of Judicial Co-operation in the EU, CUP, 2005, 422.

consumer' (who can certainly deal with advertising 'puffery'[196]) would necessarily be able to appreciate (from the letter sent by the Bank) the large amounts of interest that might accrue (without this being spelt out via the use of examples as mentioned above). If the ECJ were not to regard the letter as a sufficient benefit and if they find no other benefit then, as we have seen, the ECJ is prepared to find the term to be unfair.

The final question in relation to good faith is what attitude the ECJ might take to *pre-contractual* transparency, i.e. transparency of the terms at the time of the conclusion of the contract. This form of transparency cannot be said to be a benefit deriving from the substantive terms of the contract. As such it may not be the type of benefit that the ECJ was referring to when it said that if there was no benefit to the consumer it was prepared to find a term to be unfair. It may well be the ECJ views, and will continue to view, matters of pre-contractual transparency as questions of fact which it will not get involved. On the other hand, it is possible that transparency *is* (or *will* ultimately come to be) regarded as fundamental to fairness; with a lack of transparency leading the ECJ to the view that a term is unfair.[197] If this is the case, we need to look at another aspect of the approach of the House of Lords, i.e. the attitude to the way in which the term itself was expressed. The term provides that: 'Interest on the amount which becomes payable shall be charged in accordance with Condition 4, at the rate stated in para. D overleaf (subject to variation) until payment after as well as before any judgement (such obligation to be independent of and not to merge with the judgement).'

According to Lord Bingham:[198] '[T]he obligation to pay the principal sum in full with interest … is very clearly and unambiguously expressed in [the above] condition.'

It is arguable that this view suggests that Lord Bingham is not setting a particularly high standard of transparency. The basic idea that the consumer must pay the principal sum with interest may be fairly clear from the clause. However, it must be doubtful that the average consumer would understand the idea that contractual interest will accrue separately from the amount awarded in any judgement. Would the average consumer fully appreciate what is meant by a 'judgement'? Would he fully understand what 'obligation' is being referred to'? Would he realize what is meant by the idea that this obligation does not 'merge' with the judgement? Even if a consumer would realize that he must continue to pay interest is it possible that he might believe that this would be included

---

[196] See cases C–470/93 [1995] ECR 1–1923 and C–315/92 [1994] ECR 1–317 and see above at 3.5.5.2.

[197] See 3.5.5.2.

[198] At 1309.

in the sum he is ordered by the court to pay? Would it not be much clearer if it was simply stated that if a court makes an order for the consumer to pay arrears then, in addition to this sum, the consumer will also be liable to pay interest on this sum until it is paid off (this being supported with an example)?

The question then is whether the term would satisfy any transparency standard that might be set by the ECJ. This seems to depend, in part, on whether the ECJ would simply set a basic transparency standard or whether there would be a readiness to set a higher standard. The consumer protection and confidence goals of the UTD would certainly support the argument for a reasonably high standard; and it must be at least questionable as to whether the term would satisfy such a standard. We must also bear in mind the general ECJ jurisprudence that characterizes the consumer as being 'well informed and reasonably circumspect'. Even although it is often thought that this does not set a particularly high standard in relation to advertising claims,[199] the different context here is surely important.[200] Advertising is a form of communication that consumers are bombarded with and engage with all the time. It is used to convey a message on core (price and main subject matter) issues that consumers would always be likely to focus on. In this light it is likely that quite a lot of consumers may in fact be quite circumspect/cynical etc. Here the issue is entirely different. The term comes as one of a number of terms dealing with complex but ancillary issues that are not normally focused on or thought about; and the consumer is unlikely to take time to read them unless certain issues are highlighted as important. Then there is the fact, as suggested, that the meaning of the term itself may not be entirely obvious to the average consumer. It is at least possible that the ECJ would take the view that even the reasonably well-informed and circumspect consumer (who can understand that 'X% Extra Free' stickers should not be taken too seriously[201]) would need a better level of transparency in the circumstances.

(g) Fairness, Freedom and Omission Aside from the more freedom-oriented approach that emerges from the approach of the House of Lords to the issues that were expressly dealt with, it might also be said that such an approach seems evident from what they chose not to consider. We saw under UCTA that a key factor considered by the House of Lords in *Smith* v. *Bush* was the question of the sums of money involved for both of the

---

[199] See cases C–470/93 [1995] ECR 1–1923 and C–315/92 [1994] ECR 1–317 and see above at 3.5.5.2.

[200] See above at 3.5.5.2.

[201] See case C–470/93, *supra*.

parties and their abilities to bear these losses (i.e. who stands to lose most and who will be most affected) and the availability of insurance to cover these losses.[202] These issues (going to the impact on the substantive interests of the parties of allowing or disallowing the term) might be said to go both to the significant imbalance and good faith issues under the test of unfairness in the UTCCR. Interestingly, however, there was very little focus in *First National Bank* on the sums involved and the relative abilities to bear the losses. There was recognition that large debts could build up as a result of consumers being unaware of the accrual of post-judgement interest.[203] However, this problem was not viewed as being as important as the basic right of lenders to receive this interest. Of course, this may have been simply because, on the facts, the House of Lords thought the issue was straightforward. What is interesting more generally is whether the view of the House of Lords is that there should be a careful analysis of the interests of the two parties and their abilities to bear the losses involved, and in particular (as in *Smith* v. *Bush*) a sensitivity to the large losses that may fall on consumers; or whether *First National Bank* is indicative of an approach that is less concerned with this.

Then we turn to the question of insurance. This was not mentioned at all in *First National Bank*. In one way, this is not so surprising as the question of insurance is traditionally associated with the situation in which the trader is excluding or restricting liability; the question being whether the trader could have obtained insurance against the liability.[204] The view here may have been that the question as to whether the trader should be expected to insure should only be raised where the trader is seeking to avoid responsibility that would otherwise arise; not where he is simply making provision for recovery of interest. However, given that the provision for post-judgement interest is, in a way, detrimental to the consumer, one might argue that it would be legitimate to ask whether insurance is available to lenders to cover what they lose in terms of the principal sum and interest when the consumer defaults. If such insurance is available then it might at least be open to argument that this makes it less fair for the trader to provide for post-judgement interest to be payable by the consumer. However, this point notwithstanding, the more general question remains as to whether the House of Lords regard the insurance question as being relevant in other situations.

(h) Reference to the European Court It is clear that the House of Lords missed an opportunity by not making an Article 234 reference to the ECJ

---

[202] See above at 4.6.2.1.

[203] See Lord Bingham at 1310.

[204] See, UCTA, 11(4)(b) and above at 4.6.2.1.

for authoritative guidance as to the meaning of the unfairness test;[205] an opportunity to provide a more solid foundation for future case law – a foundation upon which the UK courts could confidently build in the interpretation and application of the unfairness concept. Certainly, such a reference may have clarified whether what was said as to the test was correct; and what the position is on the various questions that the ECJ has not, as yet, been clear on. When would the ECJ regard there as being a benefit to the consumer? Would they have regarded there as being a benefit in the *First National Bank* case? Is transparency regarded as fundamental by the ECJ (whenever a term is detrimental, even where there is overall substantive balance[206])? If so, what level of transparency? Is it the case (as it appears to be[207]) that (for the ECJ) a term can be unfair on substantive grounds irrespective of procedural fairness?

Clarification on such matters would have provided a solid foundation not only for the development of future case law, but also for the vast amount of work done by the OFT on the unfairness concept. Given the sheer quantity of this work it is surely important that the OFT can proceed with confidence that it is approaching the concept in the correct way. Indeed, this is of particular importance given that the decision of the House of Lords in *First National Bank* actually overturned an OFT 'decision'.

A reference to the ECJ might also arguably have aided the harmonization cause. The goal of the UTD, after all, is to harmonize the law in this area. Now it may not be possible (or desirable) to achieve exactly the same approach to the test of unfairness in the different Member States.[208] However, the cause of harmonization might have been advanced by a reference to the ECJ in this case. There was at least the opportunity to make a contribution to a convergent EC jurisprudence on the concept of unfairness;[209] as Weatherill puts it, '[to cut] ... an indirect

---

[205] See S. Whittaker, Assessing the Fairness of Contract Terms: The Parties' Essential Bargain, its Regulatory Context and the Significance of the Requirement of Good Faith [2004] Zeitschrift fur Europaisches Privatrecht 75; H.-W. Micklitz, The Politics of Judicial Co-operation in the EU, CUP, 2005, at 422–3 and S. Weatherill, EU Consumer Law and Policy, Elgar, 2005, at 123.

[206] See above at 3.5.4.

[207] *Ibid.*

[208] Due to differing background legal and social conditions, on which see, in particular, G. Teubner, Good Faith in British Law or How Unifying Law Ends Up in New Divergences, 1998, 61 Modern Law Review, 11.

[209] M. Dean, Defining Unfair Terms in Consumer Contracts – Crystal Ball Gazing? *Director General of Fair Trading* v. *First National Bank plc.*, (2002) 65 Modern Law Review 773, at 776.

channel [of communication] between national courts in different states'.[210]

It is also arguable that the House of Lords was actually *obliged* to refer the issue to the ECJ.[211] If the issue has not already been considered by the ECJ (which it arguably had not at that time[212]), and there is no consistent ECJ jurisprudence on the issue, courts of final instance are obliged to make such a reference unless the proper interpretation is so obvious that there is no room for reasonable doubt as to how it should be interpreted.[213] In deciding on this, account is to be taken of the fact that EC legislation is printed in eleven different languages and that concepts do not necessarily have the same meaning in different Member States.[214]

The House of Lords argument was that a reference was not needed as (although it was acknowledged that there is no common meaning of unfairness or good faith in the Member States) in the opinion of Lord Bingham, 'the language used in expressing the test, so far as applicable in this case, is in my opinion clear and not reasonably capable of differing interpretations'.[215] But surely this view is difficult to sustain. First of all, there are indeed different approaches to good faith and fairness more generally among the Member States,[216] so that it is not at all obvious that, in building an autonomous concept of unfairness, the ECJ would agree with the approach of the House of Lords. Secondly, as we have seen, there remain a number of important questions as to exactly what concept of unfairness the House of Lords was working with, so that it must be possible that the ECJ would think it correct to focus on some issue that

---

[210] S. Weatherill, EU Consumer Law and Policy, Elgar, 2005, at 122.

[211] M. Dean, Defining Unfair Terms in Consumer Contracts – Crystal Ball Gazing? *Director General of Fair Trading* v. *First National Bank plc.*, (2002) 65 Modern Law Review 773, at 779–80.

[212] The only ECJ case decided at the time of the *First National Bank* case that went to the actual meaning of the test of unfairness was the *Oceano* case ([2000] ECR 1–4941 – on which see above at 3.5.3). However, in *Oceano* all that was said was that the term in question fell within one of the paragraphs on the indicative list of terms that may be regarded as unfair, was very disadvantageous to consumers and advantageous to traders and 'satisfies all the criteria enabling it to be classed as unfair for the purposes of the Directive'. However, there was no actual explanation as to what these criteria were exactly (apart from what one can surmise to the effect that it is about whether there is an unfair balance of advantage); so that it must be doubtful as to whether this can be treated as a real consideration of the nature of the test.

[213] CILFIT – Case 238/81 [1982] ECR 3415.

[214] *Ibid.*

[215] [2001] WLR 1297, at 1307.

[216] See R. Zimmerman and S. Whittaker, Good Faith in European Contract Law, CUP, 2000.

the House of Lords did not address. Third, the existence of interpretative uncertainty in relation to the test appears to be further confirmed by the fact that the House of Lords came to a different decision from the Court of Appeal.[217] It is true that the ECJ has indicated that it will not interfere with the application of the test to particular terms unless the view is taken that the term is solely to the benefit of the trader and there are no counterbalancing benefits for the consumer.[218] However, the argument has already been made above[219] that the ECJ could have taken the view that this was indeed a case in which there were no benefits to the consumer.

5.6 The House of Lords, Lower Courts and the Regulatory Bodies

A further point about the House of Lords decision in *First National Bank* is that nothing was said as to the attitude of the House of Lords to decisions of the lower courts and regulatory bodies. Of course, the *First National Bank* decision arose out of the OFT seeking an injunction to prevent the continued use of the term in question.[220] In *First National Bank* the House of Lords did in fact overturn an OFT 'decision', so there is an apparent willingness to interfere with application of law by the OFT. This does not, in itself, indicate that there is a more or less interventionist approach than under UCTA. However, there are reasons that, in general, the higher courts may need to be more prepared to intervene than they have been under UCTA. One reason is that there is a particular EC context to the test in the UTCCR; and the higher courts will need to ensure that lower courts and regulatory bodies interpret the test in the light of this. Another reason may be that the test of unfairness in the UTCCR is actually more concrete than the fair and reasonableness test in

---

[217] S. Weatherill, EU Consumer Law and Policy, Elgar, 2005, at 123 and P. Nebbia, Annotation, (2003) 40 Common Market Law Review 983.

[218] See above at 3.5.4.

[219] See above at 5.5.4.2(4)(c).

[220] OFT 'decisions' are obviously made on the basis of their view of the law applied to facts, but the facts are obviously more limited than in cases involving specific individuals. The facts will tend to be made up of the substantive features of the term and the general prospects for it to prejudice consumers (but not its impact between particular parties); its presentation and whatever other standard information is provided with it (but not particular explanations, obfuscations or other communications arising between particular parties); choice in the market (but not particular deals that might be on offer in individual cases); the bargaining conditions generally in the sector, including the market power of the supplier (but not particular strengths and weaknesses of the consumer).

UCTA. Apart from the nuances that should be given to it in order to give effect to the goals of the UTD, the idea of significant imbalance might suggest a particular approach to the substantive features of the term under scrutiny and the relationship of this term to the other terms of the contract. Good faith, as we have already seen, may suggest particular approaches to both substance and procedure, given its pedigree in various legal systems.[221] These points will continue to be valid if the proposed new regime is brought into force. Although the new test would use different terminology than the test in the UTCCR (a term that causes 'detriment' being unfair if it is not 'fair and reasonable'[222]) this test will need to be approached so as to give at least as much protection to the consumer as the significant imbalance/good faith test in the UTCCR. So, the new test would need to consider when there might be said to be significant imbalance and a violation of good faith; and to continue to understand these concepts in the light of the goals of the UTD.

Specifically in relation to regulatory bodies, another reason (which would obviously apply under the proposed new regime too) for the House of Lords being prepared to interfere with decisions by such bodies on the facts is that there is a more limited factual matrix than in individual cases. As such, higher courts may feel that there is less scope for argument as to how the law should apply to these facts; and that it is more legitimate to question certain such applications.

But (surely very importantly) also, a generally closer eye would need to be kept on the approaches of regulatory bodies than on the decisions of the lower courts, as many more parties are affected by decisions of the regulatory bodies than are affected by court decisions in individual litigation. The only parties affected by a decision in the context of individual litigation are the immediate parties to the case (and others who happen to come before the courts with exactly the same factual matrix). However, a decision of a regulatory body will affect all the consumers in future affected by that term if it remains in use (or who will in future be protected against it if it is removed). It will also affect the trader who will or will not be able to use the term in all future dealings. Possibly also affected will be other traders and consumers. This could happen because the injunction is applied to other traders using that term.[223] It could also happen because (even although the injunction is not aimed at other traders) the decision in practice means that the OFT will target other traders using the same term or an equivalent type of term. Finally, it could

---

[221] See above at 3.5.5.3.

[222] Draft Bill, Clause 4(1), Law Commission Report No. 292, at 144.

[223] Regulation 12(4) provides that an injunction 'may relate not only to use of a *particular* contract term drawn up for general use but to *any similar term, or a term having like effect, used or recommended for use by any person*'.

happen because the term is found to be fair and no one is prevented from using it.

So, these factors will affect the approach of the higher courts under the existing regime and under the proposed new regime. Having said all of this, there is no general statement of policy in *First National Bank* as to the attitude to OFT decisions. So, there is no general indication as to the House of Lords attitude to the question as to whether an interventionist or more hands-off policy is to be pursued. In addition, what was very important in the case was the particular type of term and the fact that the default position (i.e. that interest was not payable after judgement) was viewed as not being fair on lenders. So, in this sense it is not possible to draw the certain conclusion from the case that the House of Lords are generally planning to be particularly interventionist in relation to OFT decisions or that the House of Lords has an obviously different view of fairness in general from that of the OFT. Another important factor is that the High Court/Court of Appeal/ House of Lords may not interfere too readily when given the chance, due to the possible inclination to support the OFT (and its regulatory authority) in the interests of effective regulation. Also, in practice, the higher courts only get a chance to take a different view if cases are appealed; and so far only this one OFT decision in 12 years has actually got to court.

With some caution then (given the points made above about why intervention might sometimes be thought to be desirable), it might be said that (under the existing regime and under the proposed new regime) intervention from higher courts is likely to be quite rare. So, the practice is likely on the whole to be that most of the law will continue to be interpreted and applied by the OFT who are likely to deal with a lot more cases than the lower courts even; and therefore, effectively, have a more significant role to play. Indeed, in a sense, the role of the OFT will increase after unification of the regimes, as there will be no separate stream of UCTA case law from the lower courts under a piece of legislation that the OFT has no jurisdiction over. There will simply be a single test of fairness, backed by court and OFT interpretation/application/enforcement powers; but with the interpretation/application/enforcement powers of the OFT continuing (in practice) to be in use more often.

What is not clear is the attitude of the House of Lords to the interpretation of the unfairness test by the lower courts or the application of the law by these courts to the particular facts of a case. No positive statement was made in the *First National Bank* case on these questions. As to the proper interpretation of the law, we saw that with UCTA there were fairly limited guidelines along with a statement to the effect that there would be no interference unless an 'erroneous principle' had been applied.[224] However, we have seen that fuller guidance has been given by the House of Lords in *First National Bank* (this may be for the reasons set out above, i.e. that there is more to the test in the UTCCR on its face and in terms of its EC context). So, at least to this extent, there is more for the lower courts to follow. In addition, the higher courts may be particularly keen to keep the lower courts to these guidelines in view of the need to comply with the UTD. What is less clear is the extent to which the House of Lords/Court of Appeal will seek to develop the legal criteria more fully in the future and then seek to hold the lower courts to these criteria. This may depend upon developments at ECJ level in relation to how the test should be approached. It may also depend upon developments in other Member States and how strongly the courts are urged by counsel to take a similar approach.

It is also unclear whether the House of Lords and Court of Appeal will take the same hands-off approach to applying the law to the facts as is adopted under UCTA. Again, there may be some pressure to be more interventionist, for some of the reasons cited above. Although this is not always true, if it is clearer exactly what the legal criteria are than in the case of UCTA, then it may often be more obvious how these legal criteria should be applied to a set of facts. Of course, there will still be many cases in which legitimate differences of opinion will be permissible. However, sometimes it *will* surely be clearer. For example, if the legal position in the view of the House of Lords (as it seems to be) is that terms should be clearly expressed in order to satisfy the requirement of good faith, it is hard to see how it could be correct for a first instance court to hold that this is satisfied by a term relying heavily on legal jargon.

5.7 Stepping Back – Establishing Benchmarks of Fairness

5.7.1 Introduction

In the following chapter we shall seek to build upon what we have already concluded as to the general fairness reviews that exist under UCTA and the UTCCR. All of these factors would continue to be of relevance under the proposed new 'fair and reasonable' test, but we will also consider the extra guidance that would come with the proposed new test. This discussion will draw upon the case law, the work of the OFT and other sources, in particular the legal and policy background to the UTD. However, before turning to the broad reviews of fairness there are several threshold issues to be dealt with. First of all, there is the question as to

---

[224] See above at 4.6.2.1 and 4.6.2.4.

what types of terms are under most suspicion, i.e. what substantive features of a term are most likely to raise questions as to unfairness. This issue is dealt with at 5.7.2–5.7.6 below. Essentially the conclusion is that the terms under most suspicion are generally those that deviate (to the detriment of the consumer) from default rules and that are out of step with the reasonable expectations of consumers. These terms are the ones most likely to cause significant imbalance. However, giving a central role to the reasonable expectations concept raises another issue (dealt with at 5.8 below). Some terms appear to allow for compromise of reasonable expectations by allowing for the trader to vary his own main subject matter obligation or to vary the core price obligation of the consumer (e.g. by allowing for a price increase). So, how does control of such terms square with the fact that main subject matter and core price terms are excluded from the test of unfairness? The answer, it is argued, is that terms only count as main subject matter and core price terms in the first place if they do actually reflect the reasonable expectations of consumers.

The next threshold issue (dealt with at 5.9 below) relates to the role of terms *other than* the term under scrutiny. We have already noted that if a contract contains terms that are favourable to the consumer then we may wish to enquire as to whether these favourable terms balance out any unfairness in the term under scrutiny.[225] Under a completely open textured test such as the UCTA reasonableness test this factor can be weighed in the scales along with other factors including, in particular, whether or not there has been procedural fairness.[226] It has already been argued that consumers may have a legitimate interest in transparency even where there is overall substantive fairness.[227] However, the significant imbalance/good faith test may not be as open textured and flexible as the reasonableness test under UCTA. In particular we need to consider whether the need for significant imbalance means that a term cannot be unfair where there is overall substantive fairness (even although there is a lack of transparency). The conclusion reached is that this may well be the case; although there are ways of reading the overall test in order to avoid this result. What is certainly true is that the proposed new test seems to avoid this result by focusing simply on consumer detriment rather than the overall balance of the rights and obligations under the contract.

---

[225] This is one way of approaching the question of fairness (see above at 2.4.3.3). If this approach is being taken there are then choices as to how to measure whether there has been overall balance (again see 2.4.3.3 and on the approach of the ECJ see above at 3.5.4).

[226] Although as we saw above (at 4.6.1) the courts do not seem to have chosen to give much prominence to the question of overall balance/substantive fairness in applying the UCTA reasonableness test.

[227] See above at 2.4.3.3 and 2.4.3.4(ii).

The final threshold issue (dealt with at 5.10 below) relates to achieving transparency in cases where the term under scrutiny is not in itself substantively detrimental. A term that does not actually deviate from the default position may not be able to be said to be causing a significant substantive imbalance. Indeed in some cases such a term may actually reflect a mandatory statutory or regulatory provision and so may not be subject to the controls of the UTCCR at all.[228] Yet, as has been argued above, consumers have a legitimate interest in such terms at least being transparent (so that they can take advantage of the important rights that these terms may grant).[229] The discussion considers ways in which the test of unfairness can be understood (on its own and in conjunction with the interpretation rule in the UTCCR) in order to enable bodies (such as the OFT) exercising preventive powers to reach the conclusion that such terms are unfair purely on the basis of their lack of transparency. Ultimately, however, it is argued that the point requires clarification.

5.7.2 Significant Imbalance as a Substantive Trigger Mechanism

By contrast with UCTA (which only applies to terms that exclude or restrict particular, positively defined, obligations or liabilities and terms allowing for a performance that is substantially different from that reasonably expected), the unfairness test in the UTCCR applies to all terms not explicitly excluded.[230] However, as we noted above,[231] this raises the question as to what substantive terms the test is most focused on; or, to put this in another way, what terms are most likely to trigger a broad enquiry into fairness. We already know that the UTCCR contain the indicative list of unfair terms, so that this is clearly a useful starting point in identifying types of unfairness in substance.[232] This also seems to have been the view of the House of Lords who, as we have seen, referred to the list as providing guidance as to when a term causes significant imbalance to the detriment of the consumer and is unfair.[233]

However, as already indicated,[234] the list has limitations in helping us to determine which terms the test is most focused on, which terms fall under the greatest suspicion. First of all, the list is not exhaustive. It does not cover every conceivable type of unfairness in substance; rather it

---

[228] See above at 3.2.
[229] See above at 2.4.3.4(iii).
[230] See above at 3.2.
[231] See above at 5.1, 5.3 and 5.7.1.
[232] *Ibid.*
[233] See above at 5.5.4.2(2).
[234] See above at 5.3.

provides examples. This leaves open the question as to what the position is with terms that fall outside the list. In addition, the list is not a 'blacklist' (it is simply 'indicative' as to terms that 'may' be regarded as unfair[235]); so being on the list does not necessarily mean that the term is unfair. As such, the list does not provide a definitive indication as to the types of substantive term that are targeted. Indeed, the list can only really be understood in the light of the test of unfairness.

We know that the view of the House of Lords in *First National Bank* was that there is a two limb test which requires there to be significant imbalance to the detriment of the consumer *and which also* requires there to be a violation of the requirement of good faith.[236] We also know that the view was that the significant imbalance/detriment question is essentially focused on the substantive features of terms;[237] and that, at least if we read the views of Lord Bingham and Lord Steyn together, both substantive and procedural factors seem to be relevant to good faith.[238] We must pause briefly at this point to confirm that this is a valid way to view the test. Certainly, there is very little doubt that (whatever else it may involve[239]) significant imbalance involves an enquiry as to the

---

[235] The list will often describe a term quite broadly, e.g. para. 1(b) refers to 'inappropriately' excluding or limiting liability, so that whether there is 'inappropriateness', i.e. unfairness will depend on the precise degree of the exclusion/restriction and possibly the procedural circumstances. This sort of approach is best described as a 'greylist' as it points to terms that may be fair depending on the precise circumstances. In some countries (Austria, Germany and the Netherlands) there is a tradition of having both such a greylist and a so called 'blacklist', i.e. a list of terms that are always unfair (see the discussion by E. Hondius, European Approaches to Fairness in Contract Law, in C. Willett (ed.), Aspects of Fairness in Contract, Blackstone, 1996, 69–72.

[236] See above at 5.5.4.2(i).

[237] See above at 5.5.4.2(ii).

[238] See above at 5.5.4.2(iii) and see discussion of these matters by H. Beale, Legislative Control of Fairness, in J. Beatson and D. Friedmann (eds), Good Faith and Fault in Contract Law, OUP, 1995, 231, 245; M. Tenreiro, The Community Directive on Unfair Terms and National Legal Systems (1995) 3 European Review of Private Law 273, 279; R. Brownsword, G. Howells and T. Wilhelmsson, Between Market and Welfare: Some Reflections on Article 3 of the EC Directive on Unfair Terms in Consumer Contracts, in C. Willett (ed.), Aspects of Fairness in Contract, Blackstone, 1996, 25, 30–33; C. Willett, Good Faith in Consumer Contracts: Rule, Policy and Principle, in A. Forte (ed.), Good Faith in Contract and Property Law, Hart, 1999, 181, 195–9; S. Bright, Winning the Battle Against Unfair Contract Terms (2000) 20 Legal Studies 331; M. Chen-Wishart, Contract Law, OUP, 2005, 475–6.

[239] There is the possibility of reading a procedural element into significant imbalance by saying that whether a substantive imbalance is significant can be determined in part

substantive features of the term. The imbalance concept has a long history of being used as a measure of fairness in substance among jurists and in various legal systems.[240] In addition, the literature on the significant imbalance concept in the UTD/UTCCR is all very clear at least on the general idea that significant imbalance is concerned with the substantive features of terms.[241] There is perhaps less certainty as to the role of good faith. There is a view to the effect that it has no role that is independent from significant imbalance, i.e. that the only question is whether there is a significant imbalance and that if there is such a significant imbalance then there is also automatically a violation of good faith.[242] There is a huge difficulty with this view given that there are positive guidelines on good faith in the UTD.[243] It would seem strange to have such guidelines if

---

by whether there has been procedural fairness. One way of doing this is to say that whether a substantive imbalance is 'significant' is determined by reference to the good faith concept and that procedural fairness is relevant to good faith. On this issue see the text immediately following here. Another possibility is to say that (whatever the role of good faith) the degree of procedural fairness affects the 'significance' of a substantive imbalance. On this see S. Bright, *ibid.*, 348.

[240] See Zweigert and Kotz, An Introduction to Comparative Law 3rd edn, Oxford p. 329; R. Zimmerman, The Law of Obligations 1990 at p. 259; in relation to Austria see P. Kolber, Report on the Practical Implementation of Directive 93/13/EEC in Austria, in European Commission *The Unfair Terms Directive Five Years on Evaluation and Future Perspectives*, Brussels 1–3/7/1999); and in relation to Italy, see P. Nebbia, Law as Tradition and the Europeanization of Contract Law: A Case Study (2004) Yearbook of European Law, 363, at 381.

In addition, imbalance (specifically as a test for the fairness of consumer contract terms) seems to have roots both in Germany (where Article 9 of the 1976 Act referred – along with good faith – to 'unreasonable disadvantage' a concept that seems similar to imbalance (the new Civil code, Article 310 uses the same language)) and France (where the travaux preparatoires to Loi Scrivener of 1978 referred to an 'evident imbalance in parties' rights and obligations').

[241] H. Collins, Good Faith in European Contract Law (1994) 14 Oxford Journal of Legal Studies 229 at 249; R. Brownsword, G. Howells and T. Wilhelmsson, 1996, Between Market and Welfare: Some Reflections on Article 3 of the EC Directive on Unfair Terms in Consumer Contracts, in C. Willett (ed.), Aspects of Fairness in Contract, Blackstone, 25, at 45; H. Beale, 1995, Legislative Control of Fairness, in J. Beatson and D. Friedmann (eds), Good Faith and Fault in Contract Law, OUP, 1995, 231, 243.

[242] M. Tenreiro, The Community Directive on Unfair Terms and National Legal Systems (1995) 3 European Review of Private Law, 273, 279; and S. Smith (1994) 47 Current Legal Problems, 1, 8.

[243] Recital 16 to the Preamble to the Directive says that 'the assessment ... of the unfair character of terms ... must be supplemented by a means of making an overall

good faith was to have no positive and distinctive role to play.[244] However, it might be that whether there is a violation of good faith could be regarded as relevant to the 'significance' of any substantive imbalance that is caused by the term.[245] On this view we get to consider questions of good faith as part of the significant imbalance enquiry as opposed to the two questions being separate. However, the practical result of this alternative approach seems to be the same as the practical result of the approach taken by the House of Lords. On the approach of the House of Lords that treats the significant imbalance and good faith issues as two separate aspects of the test, one question is whether (based on the

---

assessment of the different interests involved; whereas this constitutes the requirement of good faith; whereas in making an assessment of good faith, particular regard shall be had to the strength of the bargaining position of the parties, whether the consumer had an inducement to agree to the term and whether the goods or services were sold or supplied to the special order of the consumer; whereas the requirement of good faith may be satisfied by the seller or supplier where he deals fairly and equitably with the other party whose legitimate interests he has to take into account'.

[244] It is certainly true that the 1990 proposal (COM/90/322 final OJ C243, 28 September 1990) contained incompatibility with good faith as an independent criterion for a finding of unfairness. This was accompanied by three other criteria (that the term caused significant imbalance in rights and obligations to the detriment of the consumer, that the term caused the performance of the contract to be unduly detrimental to the consumer and that the term caused the performance of the contract to be significantly different from that legitimately expected). A term could be unfair on either of these independent grounds. It is clear, then, that the test in the adopted UTD was intended to move away from this position and not treat a term as unfair purely on the basis of a violation of good faith. Indeed it seems to have been deliberately deprived of this status due to the 'visceral aversion' to it of representatives of certain Member States, including the UK (see M. Tenreiro, The Community Directive on Unfair Terms and National Legal Systems (1995) 3 European Review of Private Law, 273, 277–8).

It appears that violation of good faith was nevertheless included in the adopted test to take account of those traditions more used to working with good faith (see P. Nebbia, Unfair Contract Terms in European Law, Hart, 2007, 143). As we saw above (at 3.2) in the particular context of unfair contract terms this included Germany and Portugal. At the same time the criteria laid down in the Preamble explaining good faith (*ibid.*) were drawn from UCTA, Schedule 2 as a means of giving more meaningful content to good faith for UK lawyers.

[245] On other approaches that read significant imbalance as containing elements that would normally be thought only to be relevant to good faith see C. Willett, Good Faith in Consumer Contracts: Rule, Policy and Principle, in A. Forte, Good Faith in Contract and Property Law, Hart, 1999, 181, 197–9 and below at 5.9–10.

substantive features of the terms) there is a *significant imbalance*; while another question is whether there has been a violation of good faith. On the alternative approach we ask whether (based on the substantive features of the terms) there is an *imbalance* and then whether (based on there being a violation of good faith) this imbalance is significant. Given that the results appear to be the same we will proceed on the basis of the generally accepted two stage test: i.e. there being a need for significant imbalance *and* a separate need for a violation of good faith.

This brings us to a further issue. We have said that although Lord Bingham and Lord Steyn may have placed differing degrees of emphasis on procedure and substance, the view seems to have been that both were relevant to good faith.[246] This certainly appears to make sense, given that guidance on good faith in the preamble to the UTD refers to taking into account the 'legitimate interests' of the consumer and involving an 'overall evaluation of the different interests involved'.[247] Of course, this does not wholly exclude the possibility of other models, i.e. models that focus purely on process or focus purely on substance.[248] The reference to the 'interests' of the parties might be understood as a reference to purely procedural or purely substantive interests. However, it is submitted that the natural impression is that the broad reference to 'interests' is a reference to procedural and substantive interests (albeit, that there is scope for a difference of view – as there may have been between Lord Bingham and Lord Steyn – as to which, if either, of these elements is most dominant[249]).

Overall, then we seem to be in a position in which the significant imbalance/detriment limb of the test comes closest to being a kind of trigger concept, i.e. if there is significant imbalance to the detriment of the consumer based on substantive factors, there is then a broad review of substantive and procedural matters under the good faith limb of the test.[250] We also know Lord Bingham's formulation for significant

---

[246] See above at 5.5.4.2(iii).

[247] Recital 16.

[248] See R. Brownsword, G. Howells and T. Wilhelmsson, 1996, Between Market and Welfare: Some Reflections on Article 3 of the EC Directive on Unfair Terms in Consumer Contracts, in C. Willett (ed.), Aspects of Fairness in Contract, Blackstone, 25, at 31–33 on purely procedural and purely substantive approaches to good faith.

[249] Lord Bingham seemed to focus more on procedural issues, while Lord Steyn may have viewed substantive issues as being the most important part of the good faith concept – see above at 5.5.4.2(iii).

[250] This approach may answer a question raised by commentators as to how good faith has any independent value to the extent that it deals with fairness in substance (given that significant imbalance also deals with matters of substance) (see P. Nebbia, Unfair Terms in European Law, Hart, 2007, 149–50). If we view significant imbalance as

imbalance ('granting to the supplier of a beneficial option or discretion or power, or imposing on the consumer of a disadvantageous burden or risk or duty'[251]). However, this is where we run into difficulties. This formulation is fairly unspecific as a trigger mechanism. When exactly does a term having these effects cause a significant imbalance? How beneficial does the option, discretion or power granted to the trader need to be? How disadvantageous does the burden, risk or duty imposed on the consumer need to be? Is it a question, for example, of whether the term deviates from a default rule to the detriment of the consumer, or compromises the reasonable expectations of the consumer? This is a tempting approach. It provides an element of certainty. It reflects the approach of UCTA under which the trigger concept is whether a term 'excludes or restricts' a liability that would otherwise exist or allows the trader to perform in a way that is substantially different from that reasonably expected by the consumer (although of course it goes further by applying to terms imposing obligations and liabilities on the consumer).

However, the *First National Bank* case is very far from clear on this issue. Nothing is said positively to the effect that this is the case. In addition, the decision on the facts could positively suggest to the contrary. The term in question *did* deviate from a default rule, i.e. the common law default position to the effect that post-judgement interest does not automatically apply under the contract. It also, deviated more indirectly from the approach under the 1991 Order which is to ban the court from awarding statutory interest. Nevertheless the term was held not to cause significant imbalance.[252]

---

being the trigger (or threshold) concept on matters of substance we are not necessarily saying in all cases that there is sufficient substantive detriment for a finding of unfairness. As such the substantive wing of the good faith concept still has some work to do in determining whether the substantive detriment is in violation of good faith.

Of course, this does not mean that good faith will not often be an ancillary issue (a view apparently having support from the European Commission – see M. Tenreiro, The Community Directive on Unfair Terms and National Legal Systems (1995) 3 European Review of Private Law, 273, 279; and M. Tenreiro and E. Ferioli, Examen Comparatif des legislation nationals transposant le Directive 93/13/EEC in H.-W. Micklitz, The Unfair Terms Directive: Five Years On, Office for Official Publications of the European Communities, 2000); in the sense that where there is significant imbalance in many cases this will also amount to a violation of good faith – see further below at 6.5.

[251] See above at 5.5.4.2(ii).

[252] See above at 5.5.4.2(4).

5.7.3 Significant Imbalance and Default Rules

It is certainly clear that terms reflecting a default rule (whether a mandatory rule or one that applies in the absence of contrary agreement) are excluded from the test of unfairness.[253] This exclusion originated in the UTD[254] and is based on the presumption that such terms are fair,[255] i.e. it is based on the presumption that the default rules themselves are fair.[256] Of course, this only tells us that if a term reflects a default rule

---

[253] Regulation 4(2).

[254] Article 1(2).

[255] Recital 13 to the Preamble.

[256] It should be emphasized that, while such terms will *usually* be fairer than terms drafted by the trader, this does not mean that they will always be substantively fair (see above at 2.4.3.2). The mandatory provision may not actually be fair to the consumer. Indeed the exclusion of 'mandatory terms' from the test of unfairness is particularly problematic in the context of services of general interest. This is because not only are such 'mandatory' provisions (and terms reflecting them) particularly common in the context of services of general interest; but there is evidence that very large numbers of such terms may be unfair in substance. On this see the study by the French Institut National de Consommation (INC) and the UK National Consumer Council (NCC), 'Application de la directive 93/13 aux prestations de service public', at: http://europa.eu.int/comm/consumers/cons_int/safe_shop/unf_cont_terms/uct02_fr.pd f; and see also the discussion of the German Standard Conditions on both Electricity and Natural Gas, by P. Rott, Regulation of Services of General Economic Interest in the EC (2005) European Review of Contract Law, 323, at 331–2. In other words, the presumption (at least where services of general interest are concerned) that such terms are fair may well be misplaced. There is, in fact, some question as to whether the Directive intended that is presumption can be rebutted where it is established positively that the default position in question is not fair. The waters seem to be somewhat muddied by Recitals 13 and 14 of the Preamble to the Directive which say that:

13. Whereas the statutory or regulatory provisions of the Member States which directly or indirectly determine the terms of consumer contracts are presumed not to contain unfair terms; whereas, therefore, it does not appear to be necessary to subject the terms which reflect mandatory statutory or regulatory provisions and the principles or provisions of international conventions to which the Member States or the Community are party; whereas in that respect the wording 'mandatory statutory or regulatory provisions' in Article 1(2) also covers rules which, according to the law, shall apply between the contracting parties provided that no other arrangements have been established;

14. Whereas Member States must however ensure that unfair terms are not included, particularly because this Directive also applies to trades, business or professions of a public nature'.

Of course Member States are not actually expressly obliged by the text of the UTD to review default provisions for fairness or to make them fair. At the same time the text of the UTD should be interpreted in the light of the Preamble. What then are we to make of Recitals 13 and 14 and their relationship with the Article in the text (1(2)) which excludes terms reflecting mandatory statutory and regulatory provisions from the Directive's controls? As we have noted already, Recital 13 explains the exclusion of such terms on the grounds that they 'are presumed to [be] fair'; while Recital 14 says that Member States 'must ensure that unfair terms are not included'. It is possible that the presumption in Recital 13 is not rebuttable, being no more than an explanation as to why Article 1(2) excludes such terms. Equally it is possible that the statement in Recital 14 is no more than a non-binding encouragement to Member States to review their default provisions for fairness. On the other hand Recital 13 could be read as saying that Article 1(2) only excludes default provisions if they are fair, but that there is a stronger than normal (while nevertheless rebuttable) presumption that they are fair. If this is the case Recital 14 begins to sound like a binding instruction to Member States to empower regulatory bodies and courts to analyse the fairness of such provisions albeit (perhaps) in the context of a strong presumption in favour of fairness. At the 1999 European Commission conference on the implementation of the UTD, Mario Tenreiro (Head of the Legal Matters Unit at the Consumer policy section of the European Commission) and Jens Karsten expressed the view that the effect of Recital 13 is indeed to make the exemption from review of mandatory statutory and regulatory provisions subject to the 'condition that those regulations are themselves fair' (Tenreiro and Karsten, Unfair Terms in Consumer Contracts: Uncertainties, Contradictions and Novelties of a Directive, p. 14). They go on to express the view that Recital 14 places Member States under an 'obligation' to 'remove unfair terms from public services' (*ibid.*). This reference to public services makes it difficult to know whether Tenreiro and Karsten are confining their comments on the issue to the public service context (and this is not really made much clearer by the text which precedes or follows the comments which I have cited). It is true that Recital 14 refers specifically to public services, but these seem only to be viewed as contracting contexts in which there is most likely to be a problem (no doubt for the reasons mentioned above). The obligation to ensure that unfair terms are not included arises 'in particular' to cover the public service context, but it seems to arise in any event. Whether Tenreiro and Karsten are referring to all contracts or just to public sector contracts, they go on to say that there are two ways to read the obligation imposed on Member States in relation to terms reflecting mandatory statutory or regulatory provisions. One is to say that they are not exempted by Article 1(2) where they are 'plainly unfair'. If this is the case then the new legislation should recognize this by saying that the mandatory statutory and regulatory based terms can

then it can be taken to be fair; and that default rules are therefore something of a fairness benchmark. It does not, however, tell us conclusively that if a term deviates from a default rule to the detriment of the consumer that it causes a significant imbalance in rights and obligations to the detriment of the consumer.

However, there does seem to be a lot of evidence to the effect that default rules have a key role to play. It seems that this 'threshold' significant imbalance requirement will indeed very often be satisfied whenever the term deviates to the detriment of the consumer from a default rule that would otherwise apply. Support for this can be found in the idea that both significant imbalance and default rules are linked to interest balancing. Hugh Beale has suggested that whether a term causes a significant imbalance should be determined by reference to a process of interest balancing. He has said that the concept of imbalance can be seen as being about an overall balancing of the interests of the parties and that there may be imbalance where the term causes the consumer to be fixed

---

in fact be found to be unfair in certain circumstances. The question then, becomes how to determine when these terms should be subject to review. Perhaps it could be said that there is a strong presumption in favour of fairness and/or that they can only be challenged if there is *prima facie* evidence of unfairness.

The other possibility suggested by Tenreiro and Karsten is that terms reflecting mandatory statutory or regulatory provisions are wholly exempted from the UTD by Article 1(2), but that, '... the Commission could control directly the 'fairness' of the Member States legal provisions and if appropriate, take Member States to Court under (the) Article 169 (now 226) EC Treaty procedure' (*ibid.*, at p. 15).

There are at least three other issues as to the scope of Article 1(2) which there is no space to deal with here. First, there is the question as to whether it only covers terms directly inserted by legislation or whether it also covers terms approved for use by regulatory bodies; second, there is the question as to it covers terms inserted by secondary as well as primary legislation; and finally, there is the question as to whether the word 'mandatory' should be interpreted narrowly only to cover provisions that are based on an overall balancing of the interests of consumers suppliers and the market. Clearly all of these issues affect the scope of Article 1(2) and therefore the range of terms in public service relationships that are covered by the UTD. On all of these issues see Whittaker, Unfair Contract Terms, Public Services and the Construction of a European Conception of Contract (2000) 116 Law Quarterly Review, 95, at 117–9.

See generally on the application of the UTD to public services P. Nebbia, Unfair Contract Terms in European Law, Hart, 2007, Ch. 6. We shall return to the issue of mandatory terms below when there is a detailed discussion of the application of the unfairness test to services of general interest – see below at 6.3.5.2.

with a risk of some kind; a risk that is considered to be unacceptably high for those consumers for whom it will materialize.[257]

If a term causes a significant imbalance when it does not properly balance the interests of the parties then it seems quite plausible that default rules should often serve as a benchmark. It has already been suggested that default rules are often based on a balancing of the interests of the parties.[258] So, if a term reduces the obligations/liabilities of the trader by reference to the default position or adds to those of the consumer by reference to the default position then it would seem plausible to suggest that it causes a significant imbalance to the detriment of the consumer. There may be support for this approach in the *First National Bank* case. As we have already said, Lord Bingham has said that,

> The requirement of significant imbalance is met if a term is so weighted in favour of the supplier as to tilt the parties' rights and obligations under the contract significantly in his favour. This may be by the granting to the supplier of a beneficial option or discretion or power, or by the imposing on the consumer of a disadvantageous burden or risk or duty.[259]

The language used by Lord Bingham is undoubtedly fairly open-ended. It does seem possible, however, to relate the language used to terms that deviate from default rules. A term that excludes or restricts an obligation or liability that the trader would otherwise owe to the consumer could certainly be said to be granting to the trader a '*beneficial* option or discretion or power'. The trader has the option, discretion or power to offer something less than the law would otherwise demand of him. Equally a term that adds to the obligations or liabilities that the consumer would otherwise owe could be said to be imposing on the consumer a 'disadvantageous burden or risk or duty'. The scope of the obligations or liabilities of the consumer is greater than it would be as a matter of law; and in this sense might be said to be imposing a *disadvantageous* burden, risk or duty.

This approach is also consistent with the German approach to unfairness which tests for fairness terms that deviate from the legal rule that would otherwise apply.[260] This seems to flow naturally from the idea

---

[257] H. Beale, 1995, Legislative Control of Fairness, in J. Beatson and D. Friedmann (eds), Good Faith and Fault in Contract Law, OUP, 1995, 231, 243.

[258] See above at 4.2.1.

[259] [2001] 3 WLR 1297, 1307

[260] The German approach, originally contained in the Standard Contracts Act of 1976 (and now in the German Civil Code, Article 310) is known to have influenced the test used in the UTD. As already indicated (at 3.2 above), the German test (under the

(common in civilian codes) that the background default rules represent what is 'fair' or in good faith.[261]

Another important factor in forging a link between the significant imbalance concept and terms deviating from default rules is the indicative list of terms that may be regarded as unfair. Immediately following his analysis of significant imbalance as being about whether the trader has a 'beneficial option or discretion or power' or a 'disadvantageous burden or risk or duty' is imposed on the consumer, Lord Bingham goes on to say that, 'The illustrative terms set out in Schedule 3 to the Regulations provide very good examples of terms which may be regarded as unfair …'.[262]

The implication is that the terms described on the list may cause significant imbalance. We have seen already that the list is ambiguous in certain respects. However, it does tell us something about the connection between significant imbalance and default rules. Certainly in the context of the terms on the list dealing with the responsibilities of the trader, the basic default rules would seem to have a role to play. Paragraph 1(a) describes a term 'excluding or limiting the legal liability of the … [trader]' for death or injury. Paragraph 1(b) describes a term 'inappropriately excluding or limiting the legal rights of the consumer' where there has been total or partial non-performance. How are we to determine the 'legal liability' of the trader or the 'legal rights' of a consumer other than by reference to the relevant default rules?

The idea that terms deviating from default rules may cause significant imbalance also seems to be supported by the OFT. It has been said that:

> The OFT's starting position in assessing the fairness of a term is … normally to ask what would be the position for the consumer if it did not appear in the contract … . Where a term changes the normal position seen by the law as striking a fair balance it is regarded with suspicion.[263]

1976 Act and now the Civil Code) refers to whether a term causes an 'unreasonable disadvantage', a concept that appears to be close to 'significant imbalance'.

[261] See M. Tenreiro, The Community Directive on Unfair Terms and National Legal Systems (1995) 3 European Review of Private Law, 273, at 279; see the position in Greece, (CLAB, 000302) where the measure of fairness said to be deviation from substantive and basic evaluations of the law; and see the approach in Italy where the typical measure is also deviation from default rules ('dispositive' provisions) (see P. Nebbia, Unfair Contract Terms in European Law, Hart, 2007, 154).

[262] [2001] 3 WLR 1297, 1307.

[263] Office of Fair Trading, Unfair Contract Term Guidance (2001) (Introduction), p. 2; for further support for the idea that default rules are the basic benchmark of fairness under the test of unfairness see S. Grundman, The General Clause or Standard in EC

It therefore does seem to be the case that there will often be a significant imbalance where a term deviates from the default position to the detriment of the consumer.

But how does this analysis square with the fact that there was held to be no significant imbalance in the *First National Bank* case despite the fact the term deviated from the default position to the detriment of the consumer. The default position, we should recall, is that the contractual interest merges in the judgement and that it does not continue to accrue in addition to the judgement debt (this default position being arguably 'supported' by the fact that the 1991 Order prevents courts awarding statutory interest on the judgement debt). Yet the term deviating from this position and providing that the contractual interest did not merge in the judgement was found not to cause significant imbalance. As we saw from the discussion of the case above it was very clear that the House of Lords did not view the particular default rule as being fair or balanced. The view was that *not* being allowed to provide for post-judgement contractual interest would cause an imbalance in favour of the consumer. In addition, a particular reason was given as to why this whole regulatory context could not be viewed as indicating that it was in any way unfair to provide for contractual interest to continue to accrue after judgement; this reason being that the regime did not outrightly ban provision for contractual interest.

The key question now is whether this rather freedom-oriented approach provides any broader indication as to the attitude of the House of Lords to the relationship between default rules and fairness; or whether the approach can be viewed as very much dependent on the facts of the particular case. Certainly, if the idea that there is only an indication of unfairness where there is an outright ban was to be applied more broadly this would be extremely alarming. A default rule would be no form of fairness benchmark. Deviation from a default rule would mean nothing. Indeed, there would be little point in having a fairness test. A term does not cause significant imbalance unless it is already banned! Clearly this would be out of step with the consumer protection and confidence goals of the UTD and would put at risk the vast swathe of OFT jurisprudence that has developed and that is much more inclined to use default rules as benchmarks of fairness.[264]

So it is simply not plausible that the House of Lords would take this approach more generally. But, short of this extreme position, does the *First National Bank* case suggest that the House of Lords do not generally view default rules as significant benchmarks of fairness? I would suggest

---

Contract Law Directives, in S. Grundman and D. Mazeaud (eds), General Clauses and Standards in European Contract Law, Kluwer, 2006, 141, at 144–8.

[264] See below at 6.3.2.

that it is simply very difficult to say unless and until the House of Lords has the opportunity to hear other cases. However, it does seem plausible to suggest that no general lack of respect for default rules can be read into the House of Lords decision. First of all, there were no statements as to the attitude of the court to default rules in general. Second, the court approved of the general idea that there should be a review of the position of the consumer at the stage of the judgement and lamented the fact that this was not guaranteed by the current law. So, the court approved of the idea of consumers, where appropriate, not being required to pay the full interest provided for. They just did not believe that it was the responsibility of the lender to ensure protection of consumers by not providing for post-judgement interest in the first place. Third, this was a term that arguably came as near as it is possible to come to being a core term. It involved the basic obligation to pay interest, albeit it escaped being viewed as a core term on the grounds that it was (in this situation) operating in a post-default situation.[265] However, it may be that the House of Lords felt particularly uncomfortable about saying that any part of the basic obligation to pay interest (which did not involve any problem of there being undue scope for a variation or increase that might be said to be compromising of the reasonable expectations of the consumer[266]) should be treated as unfair.

In sum, then, it may be that *First National Bank* is very much a case about the particular type of term involved and that, on the whole, it remains valid to say that terms allowing for deviation from a default position to the detriment of the consumer will be viewed as causing significant imbalance and triggering the broader good faith enquiry (subject, of course, to the question – to be discussed at 5.9 below – as to whether this significant imbalance can be negated by favourable terms).

---

[265] See below at 5.8.3.1.

[266] We shall see below that terms allowing undue scope for variation (whether in relation to interest rate or other matters) will usually be viewed as causing significant imbalance on the basis that they allow for compromise of the reasonable expectations of the consumer – see below at 5.7.6. Of course, the Court of Appeal in *First National Bank* thought that the term allowing for post-judgement contractual interest also compromised reasonable expectations while the House of Lords disagreed. My point, then, is that the House of Lords view may be that, where a term deals with the basic interest to be paid and does not even allow undue scope for variation of the interest rate, such a term is so close to being a core term that it is to be strongly presumed to be fair. On when a term is actually a core term see below at 5.8 and, in particular, on the approach to the term in *First National Bank* on the core term issue see below at 5.8.3.1.

5.7.4 Default Rules under UCTA and UTCCR: A Comparison

5.7.4.1 Exclusion and Restriction of Trader Obligations and Liabilities

This brings us to a comparison with UCTA in relation to the terms targeted and the precise means of control. We saw above[267] that UCTA subjects to the test of reasonableness terms excluding or restricting liabilities that would otherwise arise for negligence or breach of a contractual duty to take reasonable care where the loss is something other than death or personal injury; terms excluding or restricting liabilities that would otherwise arise for breach of contract (other than the implied terms as to title, description, quality and fitness); and terms excluding or restricting liabilities that would otherwise arise for misrepresentation. These terms (in deviating from the default remedies that would otherwise arise) almost certainly also cause significant imbalance under the UTCCR and are then subject to a general review of fairness under the good faith test. We also saw above[268] that UCTA renders wholly ineffective terms excluding or restricting liabilities that would otherwise arise for negligence or breach of a contractual duty to take reasonable care causing death or personal injury along with terms excluding or restricting liability for breach of the implied terms as to title, description, quality and fitness. Clearly such terms cause significant imbalance under the UTCCR. However, they are not actually banned under the UTCCR, but simply subject to the good faith test. In another sense, though, the UTCCR provide much more effective control of such terms. They will virtually always be held to be unfair under the UTCCR, thereby allowing the OFT to order that they are removed[269] – a sanction that is not available under UCTA.

Of course, we also saw above[270] that under UCTA terms are treated as excluding/restricting liability (and are therefore controlled) when they exclude or restrict the scope of the primary duty or obligation. So, in the case of s. 2 covers a term excluding or restricting the duty to take reasonable care in tort or the implied term in contracts for services to the effect that the supplier will take reasonable care. So the duty to take care is viewed as a benchmark of fairness. Sections 6 and 7 cover terms excluding or restricting the obligations as to title, description, quality and fitness in contracts for the sale and supply of goods. Here, these

---

[267] See above at 4.2.1.

[268] See above at 4.2.6.

[269] See below at 8.3.

[270] See above at 4.2.2.

obligations are viewed as benchmarks of fairness. As we saw above,[271] this makes sense as the primary obligations and duties are based on interest balancing just as the remedies are and the practical effect of excluding or restricting the primary obligations or duties is the same as excluding or restricting the remedies. In addition, there is a serious risk that consumers will not really digest information conveyed via a formal term as to the scope of the duty or obligation in the same way as if the information was conveyed outwith the formal terms. As such, the same approach must surely be appropriate under the UTCCR, with a term being treated as causing a significant imbalance when it excludes or restricts primary obligations or duties in relation to negligence and the implied terms. It also seems fair to assume that there will usually also be a significant imbalance when terms exclude or restrict obligations that would arise under other default rules; although the *First National Bank* case shows that where the default rule itself is regarded as unfair to the trader then this will not be the case.

It seems clear that the UTCCR do indeed treat exclusion and restriction of primary obligations in the same way as exclusion or restriction of remedies. The indicative list describes terms having the 'object or effect' of excluding or restricting the 'legal rights' of the consumer in relation to breach of contract.[272] This surely means that, even if 'legal rights' only refers to remedies, if the same 'effect' is achieved by excluding or restricting the primary obligations then the term may be unfair; suggesting that such a term does indeed cause significant imbalance.

However, to the extent that there is significant imbalance whenever a term excludes or restricts the obligations or liabilities of the trader by comparison with the default position, this facilitates coverage of a broader range of terms than UCTA. Under UCTA, terms must fall into the specific categories in order to be covered. No such restrictions apply in the case of the UTCCR. So, for example, the OFT have targeted terms which deny the authority of an agent to make representations on behalf of the trader. These are viewed in some circumstances as causing significant imbalance and violating good faith.[273] Yet, as we saw above,[274] these terms have been held not to be covered by the relevant section of UCTA. This illustrates the greater breadth of coverage that can be achieved by using a general principle such as significant imbalance; rather than relying on the narrower, more specific UCTA triggers.

---

[271] See above at 4.2.3.

[272] Schedule 2, para. 1(b).

[273] See 6.3.3.2(b) below.

[274] See above at 4.2.4.

5.7.4.2 Adding to Consumer Obligations and Liabilities

The most significant advance on UCTA is that the test is focused on terms *adding to* the obligations and liabilities that the consumer would otherwise owe according to the default position. The default rules fixing consumer obligations are also generally based on a process of interest balancing; as are the remedies for breach. As such, deviation to the detriment of the consumer from these default rules should generally amount to a significant imbalance and trigger the good faith test. So, for example, this would cover terms imposing a strict liability standard on consumer hirers of goods when the default position is a reasonable care standard (this reasonable care standard being based on the idea that this is generally all that can reasonably be expected of a consumer); imposing a more onerous duty of disclosure in insurance contracts than would otherwise be imposed by law, e.g. requiring disclosure of non-material facts;[275] requiring an earlier performance than would be required by the default position (e.g. requiring payment before delivery in contracts of sale[276]); or expanding a consumer's obligation from a warranty (that does not give trader a right to terminate if it is broken) to a condition (which does give such a right).[277]

We now turn to terms imposing *liabilities* going beyond the default position. For example there are terms requiring the consumer to pay sums when he is in breach (or allowing the trader to retain sums) which sums exceed a reasonable pre-estimate of the loss likely to be caused to the trader by the breach. The default position is that damages should only compensate for the foreseeable losses resulting from the breach. Terms allowing for recovery of significantly more than this are expressly mentioned by para. 1(e) of the indicative list which refers to a term 'requiring any consumer who fails to fulfil his obligation to pay a disproportionately high sum in compensation'. Under the proposals of the

---

[275] The duty of disclosure only covering *material* facts.

[276] The default position is that the consumers must only accept and pay for the goods when they have been delivered (SGA, s. 27), this being a fair balance given that it allows the consumer to withhold payment if the goods are defective. Consumers are particularly compromised by full payment in advance terms as they have to part with the money and are in a weaker position if the trader is in breach later. Of course it is true that they can claim some or all of the payment back as damages but they need to take initiative to do so. See the (ECJ) *Freiburger* case, illustrating the type of counterbalancing protection that might make such a term fair – above at 3.5.4; and see below at 6.3.3.2(2)(a) for the approach of the OFT.

[277] Classification as a warranty is based on a balancing of interests in the sense that it is based on the idea that the term does not go to the root of the contract so that a right to terminate for its breach would be disproportionate.

Law Commissions for the new regime the language of the list would be simplified to describe a 'term requiring A, when in breach of contract, to pay B a sum significantly above the likely loss to B'.[278] The Law Commission would (in the new regime) exemplify this with the following:

> A term of a contract (other than a loan agreement) which requires the consumer, when late in making any payment, to pay a default rate of interest which is substantially more than the business has to pay when borrowing the money.
>
> A term of a loan agreement which requires the consumer, when late in making a payment, to pay a default rate of interest which is substantially above the rate payable before default.[279]

Of course, although such terms are not covered by UCTA, a term providing for damages exceeding a reasonable pre-estimate of the loss has long been viewed as an unenforceable penalty at common law, so the UTCCR overlap with this control in relation to the situations described above.

Then there are terms (again applicable when the consumer is in breach) allowing the trader to obtain or retain sums that do not take into account the duty of the trader to mitigate his losses. This is a duty that arises under the general law and operates as a limitation on the losses that can be claimed by a party who is the victim of a breach. Terms allowing the trader to claim losses that do not take this duty into account are certainly not covered by UCTA; and it is unclear as to whether they would be covered by the common law rules on penalties. However, they would certainly appear to cause a significant imbalance under the UTCCR. The Law Commissions would treat such terms as covered by the same provision on the list as that covering penalties, i.e. under the heading of a 'term requiring A, when in breach of contract, to pay B a sum significantly above the likely loss to B'. This would then be exemplified as follows:

> A term of a contract for the sale of goods which requires the consumer, if he wrongfully terminates the contract, to compensate the business for the full loss of profit it suffers, without making any allowance for the amount which the business should be able to recover by taking reasonable steps to resell the goods.[280]

---

[278] Law Commission Report at p. 188.
[279] Law Commission Report at p. 189.
[280] *Ibid.*

Next there are terms allowing the trader to terminate the contract for a breach (e.g. a breach of a warranty) that would not (under the general law) give the trader a right to terminate. So, for example, the OFT dealt with the following term: 'If the customer shall commit any breach of this agreement ... the company shall be at liberty to treat this agreement as repudiated and accordingly may terminate it forthwith by notice in writing to the customer.'

The OFT obtained the agreement of the trader to amend the term so that it only allowed termination where there was a 'serious breach' by the customer.[281] This reflects the default position which is that there cannot be termination for a non-serious breach (i.e. for breach of a warranty or for a breach of an innominate term where this does not deprive the innocent party of substantially the whole benefit of the contract).[282]

Finally, there are terms allowing for a form of enforcement that would not otherwise be allowed. For example the OFT has required removal of terms allowing the trader to enter the premises of the consumer in order to repossess goods (a remedy that does not exist under the general law).[283]

Noticeably missing from above discussion are so called 'disguised penalties'. These are terms which impose some form of charge on the consumer in circumstances where the consumer acts (or fails to act) in a certain way; this being a charge that exceeds any loss that the act or omission would cause to the trader. However, the act or omission triggering the charge is not characterized by the term as a default or breach by the consumer. Rather it is simply characterized as an option or choice that the consumer has under the agreement. The intended consequence of this is that the sum now payable by the consumer is owed under a primary obligation rather than being secondary liability for breach of a primary obligation. The original purpose of such terms was to avoid the penalty jurisdiction at common law. This jurisdiction only catches situations in which the amount payable is triggered by an actual breach, the sum now payable representing an agreed damages provision, i.e. secondary liability for breach of a primary obligation.[284] It does not cover cases where the sum payable is technically payable under a primary obligation.

What is the approach of the UTCCR to such terms? One approach is to look at the substance (rather than the form) of the term and to say that, despite what is said by the term, the act or omission of the consumer that

---

281 OFT Unfair Contract Terms Guidance, February 2001, p. 141 (Caledonia Motor Group).

282 *Hong Kong Fir Shipping Co. Ltd* v. *Kawasaki Kisen Kaisha* [1962] 2 QB 26.

283 OFT, Unfair Contract Terms Guidance, February 2001, p. 142 (Moben Kitchens).

284 See for example *Bridge* v. *Campbell Discount Co. Ltd* [1962] AC 600.

triggers the payment is in fact a breach. The result of such a construction of the term is that the sum now payable is not treated as a primary obligation but is, rather, treated as an agreed damages provision, i.e. as secondary liability for breach of a primary obligation. If, then, the sum exceeds a reasonable pre-estimate of the loss likely to be caused to the trader then it causes a significant imbalance on the basis of the above analysis, i.e. that it deviates from the default position on damages to the detriment of the consumer.

However, if it is accepted that the act or omission triggering the responsibility to pay the sum is not a breach then a different analysis has to be applied. In such a case (as we have already seen) the responsibility to pay the sum does not arise on the basis of an agreed damages provision, but, rather, must simply be viewed as a primary obligation. For this reason we cannot base any notion that there is significant imbalance on the idea that that the term deviates from a default rule to the detriment of the consumer. This is because there *is* no default rule dealing with primary payment obligations of this type. However, the answer seems to lie in a notion of reasonable expectations. I will argue below that, where no default rule exists, there is a significant imbalance where the term allows for a performance by the trader that does not reflect the reasonable expectations of the consumer, or allows the trader to impose an obligation on the consumer that exceeds what would be reasonably be expected by the consumer. It is, therefore, based on such a reasonable expectations benchmark that a 'disguised penalty' can be said to cause a significant imbalance.[285]

5.7.5 Default Rules under the Proposed New Regime

Under the proposed new regime, as we have already seen, the general review of fairness will be triggered when the term causes 'detriment'. We have already seen that there is probably detriment when a term deviates from a default rule to the detriment of the consumer and that this clearly covers all of the terms already covered by UCTA.[286] It clearly also covers all of the terms that would cause significant imbalance under the UTCCR, i.e. any term that deviates from the default position by excluding or restricting trader obligations or liabilities that would otherwise arise or imposing on the consumer obligations or liabilities that would not otherwise be imposed.

There is an interesting question as to whether the replacement of the 'significant imbalance causing detriment' trigger with the 'detriment'

---

[285] See below at 5.7.6.2.
[286] See above at 4.3.1.

trigger would make any difference to the decision in *First National Bank*. A requirement of significant imbalance/detriment is clearly more difficult to establish than a requirement simply of detriment. In particular, a concern of the House of Lords in *First National Bank* was that not allowing for post-judgement contractual interest would unbalance the contract against the interests of the trader.[287] But if we remove significant imbalance from the equation it might be hard to resist the conclusion that the term in question does cause detriment to the consumer. However, this does not mean that the final decision would be any different. In order to be unfair a term under the proposed new regime a term causing detriment will need to fail the proposed 'fair and reasonable' test. The House of Lords did not take the view that the term was sufficiently problematic in substance or that there was sufficient procedural unfairness for it to violate the good faith requirement. If we assume that the 'fair and reasonable' test is no more protective than the good faith requirement then we must assume that the House of Lords would reach the conclusion that the term is 'fair and reasonable'.

5.7.6 Significant Imbalance and Reasonable Expectations

5.7.6.1 The Basic Idea

So, we have seen that terms deviating from default rules (to the detriment of the consumer) will usually cause significant imbalance under the UTCCR and trigger a broader assessment of fairness under the good faith test. Under UCTA, as we have seen, reasonable expectations are also viewed as a benchmark of fairness. If a term allows the trader to perform in a way that is substantially different from what the consumer would reasonably expect the term is subject to the reasonableness test.[288] We also saw that under UCTA the reasonable expectations are largely based on the pre-existing expectations of the consumer, so that terms allowing for the trader to vary or terminate his performance are typically viewed as allowing for a performance substantially different to what was reasonably expected (given that the pre-existing expectation will often be that there will not be variation or termination). It appears that the same approach is taken by the test under the UTCCR, i.e. that a term allowing the trader discretion to vary, terminate etc will often be viewed as causing a significant imbalance and will therefore be subject to general review under the good faith test. However, the UTCCR also apply to terms

---

[287] See above at 5.5.4.2(4).

[288] UCTA, s. 3(2)(b)(i); see above at 4.4.

imposing obligations on the consumer, so that terms allowing for variation (usually in the form of increases or extensions) of consumer obligations will also be viewed as causing significant imbalance and will be subject to general review under the good faith test.

How do we reach these conclusions? It will be recalled that according to Lord Bingham in the *First National Bank* case a significant imbalance can be caused by a term 'granting to the supplier ... a beneficial option or discretion or power' or a term imposing 'disadvantageous burden or risk or duty' on the consumer.[289] This seems to cover terms relating to either the obligations of the trader (a beneficial option, discretion or power), or those of the consumer (a disadvantageous burden, risk or duty) that allow compromise of the reasonable expectations of the consumer. Indeed the indicative list confirms this, containing examples both of terms allowing the trader to vary or terminate his performance or to add to the obligations of the consumer. So (in relation to trader obligations), paras 1(j) and (k) describe terms enabling alteration of terms and the product/service without a valid reason that is specified in the contract.[290] Paragraph (f) describes a term enabling the trader to dissolve the contract on a discretionary basis. Paragraph (g) describes terms enabling termination of contracts of indeterminate duration without either reasonable notice or serious grounds.[291]

This fits with the reasonable expectations analysis already outlined above.[292] The consumer may have pre-existing expectation as to how the trader will perform and to the effect that this will not be changed without a valid reason; and paras (j) and (k) describe terms allowing for the trader to do something different without a valid reason. The consumer may also reasonably expect that the trader will not terminate the contract at his discretion at least without reasonable notice or serious grounds; and paras (f) and (g) describing terms that allow expectations to be compromised.

As to *consumer* obligations, para. 1(l) describes terms enabling the trader to increase the price to an amount that is too high in relation to the initially agreed price.[293] Paragraph (h) describes a term automatically extending a contract of fixed duration where the consumer does not indicate otherwise when the deadline for the consumer to express his desire not to extend the contract is unreasonably early.[294] Again, this fits with the reasonable expectations analysis. The consumer may have pre-existing expectations as to how much he will have to pay and how long

---

[289] See above at 5.5.4.2(2).
[290] Schedule 2.
[291] *Ibid.*
[292] See above at 4.4.
[293] Schedule 2.
[294] *Ibid.*

the obligation will last; while the terms described allow (respectively) price increases and extension of the length of time when the consumer owes obligations.

5.7.6.2 Reasonable Expectations: A Comparison Between UCTA and the UTCCR

In relation to terms dealing with the performance of the trader, the ground covered by the significant imbalance concept is much the same as that covered by UCTA, s. 3. However, as we saw above[295] there was until recently some doubt as to whether UCTA s. 3 covers entire agreement terms denying contractual effect to pre-contractual statements.[296] It now appears that it does cover such clauses.[297] There is little doubt that entire agreement clauses denying the contractual effect of pre-contractual statements will usually be regarded as causing a significant imbalance under the UTCCR;[298] and will very often be viewed as unfair.[299] This clearly makes sense. If the statement would be important and influential enough to satisfy the normal criteria for having contractual effect then there is surely a reasonable expectation that it will be binding. In addition, the formal terms (including entire agreement clauses) will rarely be sufficiently transparent to consumers to alter these expectations.

Then we turn to terms imposing obligations on the consumer (which of course are not controlled by UCTA). In relation to such terms, it seems reasonable to assume that the indicative list in the UTCCR simply provides examples of a general principle, i.e. that terms allowing for imposition of obligations on the consumer that exceed the reasonable expectations of the consumer will be treated as causing significant imbalance and therefore be subject to the general review under the good faith test. This being the case, this general principle catches terms providing for price increases and extra charges generally. This will include, for example, those 'disguised penalty' cases discussed above where the responsibility to pay the sum is not technically triggered by a breach and therefore is not technically a sum payable as damages; but is a primary obligation.[300] If it is nevertheless an obligation that the consumer would not have reasonably expected to owe in the due performance of the

---

[295] See above at 4.4.8.3.

[296] *Watford Electronics Ltd* v. *Sanderson CFL Ltd* [2001] 1 All ER (Comm) 696 generated some such doubt although it did not go directly to the point.

[297] *SAM Business Systems* v. *Hedley & Co.*, [2003], 1 All ER (Comm) 465.

[298] See OFT Guidance on Unfair Terms, 2001, para. 14.

[299] See below at 6.3.2.2(b).

[300] See above at 5.7.4.2.

contract then it presumably causes a significant imbalance and is subject to the general review under the good faith test.

5.7.6.3 Reasonable Expectations and Transparent Terms

When discussing reasonable expectations under UCTA we addressed the issue of the transparency of the term giving the discretion to the trader.[301] The argument was that no matter how transparent a formal term is it will rarely have much real impact on the expectations of a consumer, so that we should be very cautious about saying that a term giving discretion reflects consumer expectations simply because it is transparent. The point was also made that if a term is found to reflect reasonable expectations then it is not subject to the UCTA reasonableness test so there is no scope to consider matters of fairness in substance (e.g. as to the breadth of the discretion) or other issues of procedural fairness (e.g. as to whether a choice was offered). If, on the other hand, a term providing for discretion to be exercised by the trader is found to allow for a contractual performance substantially different from what was expected, the term is subject to the reasonableness test. Under the auspices of the reasonableness test the question as to the transparency of the term can be taken into account; but this will not be at the expense of other procedural and substantive factors that may indicate that the term is unreasonable – these factors will also be able to be taken into account.

The same issues seem to arise here. A term providing for exercise of discretion by the trader should surely rarely, if ever, be said not to cause a significant imbalance simply on the basis that it is transparent. It will not normally really have affected the expectations of the consumer, so it will usually still be allowing for something that the consumer does not really expect. In addition, if the term is held not to have caused a significant imbalance there is no scope for consideration of other fairness issues under the auspices of the good faith test (or at least such assessment is irrelevant as a term cannot be unfair unless it fails both limbs of the test). The good faith test allows for consideration of the various substantive and procedural issues, including whether the term is genuinely transparent. Indeed the argument for ignoring the transparency of a term in reaching the conclusion that a term should be subject to a broader review of fairness is even stronger where the significant imbalance trigger is concerned. This is because the significant imbalance formula looks more like a purely substantive question than the broader reasonable expectations formula under UCTA. If the question as to whether there is

---

[301] See above at 4.4.5.

scope to deviate from the reasonable expectations of the consumer is part of the question as to whether there is a significant imbalance in rights and obligations this looks especially like a test that is concerned with the *substantive* effect the term has on pre-existing expectations (not a test concerned with the possible effect of transparency in altering the expectations of the consumer).

Indeed, the Court of Appeal in *First National Bank* seems to have taken the view that the place for considering the relationship between expectations and transparency is under the auspices of the good faith test. It was said (and the House of Lords did not say anything to contradict this) that: 'A term to which the consumer's attention is not specifically drawn but which might operate in a way which the consumer might not reasonably expect and to his disadvantage could offend the requirement of good faith.'[302]

Of course, even although this sets the relationship between transparency and reasonable expectation issues in the context of the good faith test it might also suggest that a term allowing for compromise of the reasonable expectations of the consumer will pass the good faith test as long as it is transparent. This may not in fact be the full picture; however, this is an issue for later.[303] The point for now is simply that the question as to whether there is a significant imbalance based on the discretion provided for should probably ignore the fact that the term was transparent (this apparently being a matter for the good faith test).

5.7.7 Reasonable Expectations under the Proposed New Regime

As we have seen the trigger for the new 'fair and reasonable' test under the proposed new regime will be that a term is 'detrimental' to the consumer. A term will be detrimental where it is substantively beneficial to the trader and prejudicial to the consumer. We have seen that a term deviating from the default position to the detriment of the consumer will be detrimental in this sense. It must also surely be the case that, under the new regime, terms will be viewed as 'detrimental' and will therefore fall to be assessed under the broad fair and reasonable test where they allow for a trader performance that does not reflect the reasonable expectations of the consumer or impose obligations on the consumer that do not reflect his reasonable expectations.

---

[302] [2000] 2 All ER 759, at 769.

[303] See below at 6.5.

5.8 The Core Exclusion and Reasonable Expectations

5.8.1 The Basic Idea

Regulation 6(2) (following Article 4(2) of the UTD) excludes from the test of fairness (in so far as they are in plain and intelligible language) terms relating: '(a) to the definition of the main subject matter of the contract, [and] (b) to the adequacy of the price or remuneration, as against the goods or services supplied in exchange.'

When Regulation 6 refers to terms defining the 'main subject matter' this clearly refers to terms defining the core element of the trader's performance obligation, i.e. the basic *nature* of the goods or services being supplied (and not to any other elements of the primary obligation, e.g. obligations as to quality, delivery or as to *when* performance will take place). In addition, it clearly does not cover terms determining secondary liability for breach of the primary obligation. When it refers to the '*adequacy* of the price or remuneration, as against the goods or services supplied in exchange' it means the *amount* of the price being paid for the goods or services (not *when* or *how* it is payable and certainly not secondary liability for failure to honour primary obligations).

5.8.2 Rationales for (and Arguments Against) Exclusion of Core Terms

The exclusion of the core obligations from the test of unfairness in the UTD is resonant of civilian tradition, which seems to have traditionally distinguished between ancillary terms and core terms.[304] The distinction appears to have been based upon the idea that there is rarely true consent to the ancillary terms; while there *is* true consent to the core terms.[305]

---

[304] A. De Moor, Common and Civil Law Conceptions of Contract and a European Law of Contract: the Case of the Directive on Unfair Terms in Consumer Contracts (1995) 3 European Review of Private Law, 257, at 268–8; and if the core elements of the parties' obligations are viewed as representing the main element of the consideration provided by the parties to each other, then the exclusion of these elements from review also fits with the common law notion of not being concerned with the adequacy of the consideration. The exclusion of core terms from the UTD (Article 4 (2)) was as a result of pressure from the German government and appears to be based on the provision to this effect in Article 8 of the German Standard Contracts Act of 1976 – see H.-W. Micklitz, The Politics of Judicial Co-operation in the EU, CUP, 2005, 360.

[305] *Ibid.*

Certainly (as has already been suggested[306]), the consumer is much more likely to focus on the core performance promise of the trader and his own core price obligation than he is to focus on terms dealing with ancillary matters. In addition, we must remember that under the UTCCR (following the UTD) core terms are only excluded from review if they are in plain and intelligible language; so that this also increases the chances that there will be genuine understanding of, and consent to, these terms. As such there is, from one point of view, a greater argument for adhering to a freedom-oriented approach in relation core terms. Indeed, the issue may go beyond the fact that there is a purer form of consent to these terms. Because consumers focus on these issues, it may also be that the deal (on main subject matter and price) is more likely to be disciplined by market forces.[307] This, in turn, may mean that some of the other unfairness problems are reduced. First of all, there may be more choice on offer in the market in relation to these issues, as traders compete for business by reference to what they offer on these issues. This, in turn, may mean that the terms dealing with these issues are more substantively favourable to consumers than is the case where ancillary terms are concerned. If there is no competition over the ancillary terms, traders can use them to load risks onto the consumer, while the competition in relation to the issues dealt with by core terms may prevent this happening.[308]

Having said all of this, there is no doubt that exclusion of these terms from the test of fairness means that there cannot be said to be the facility to ensure overall substantive fairness or to use contract law as a means of redistribution of wealth. Traders can, for example, increase prices in order to compensate for having to meet fairness standards in relation to ancillary terms. In addition, from one point of view, the result may be that consumers are, on the whole, worse off. This is because the risk of being adversely affected by ancillary terms is only a fairly small one that will materialize in a few isolated cases in which there is a dispute of some kind; while higher prices will affect consumers in every case. Another potential problem with excluding core terms from the test of fairness is that, in practice, the argument may be routinely raised by traders that terms fall into this category, even when they do not; but that lack of

---

[306] See above at 4.4.4.

[307] See above at 2.3.2.1 and see H. Beale, The Directive on Unfair Terms in Consumer Contracts, in J. Beatson and D. Friedmann, Good Faith and Fault in Contract Law, 232 at 233; V.P. Goldberg, Institutional Change and the Quasi-Invisible Hand, 17 J Law & Econ 461 at 483 *et seq*; and C. Willett, Good Faith in Consumer Contracts: Rule, Policy and Principle, in A. Forte, Good Faith in Contract and Property Law, Hart, 1999, 181 at 185.

[308] V.P. Goldberg, *ibid.*, and H. Beale, *ibid.*

consumer knowledge means that they readily accept this argument and do not take the issue further.

Of course, the UTD does not require Member States to have these exclusions. The directive is a minimum directive and Member States are free to offer a higher level of protection than that provided for by it.[309] In other words they are free, in this context, to subject core terms to the test of unfairness. Indeed, English law already has rules on unconscionability that can catch the more extreme types of unfairness, including where this comes in the form of an unfair price.[310] Extremely unfair interest rates can also be controlled under the 'extortionate bargain' provisions of the CCA.[311] However, both of these examples deal with extremes of unfairness.[312] This said the recent Consumer Credit Act contains provision for a fairness test that would be applicable to interest rates and may well set a higher standard of fairness than is applicable under general unconscionability rules or the existing extortionate bargain provisions in the CCA.[313]

However, UK law does not contain a rule controlling more 'routine' unfair prices in consumer contracts generally. Some countries do contain such a control, having chosen not to implement the exclusion of core terms in their laws which implemented the UTD. This is the case where the Nordic countries are concerned; and this appears to be based on the idea that the price should at least be in line with the norm in the sector in question.[314]

However, the Law Commissions are against removal of the exclusion of core terms from the new fairness regime that will exist here. In relation to main subject matter terms, the Law Commissions give three arguments in favour of this position. First of all, they take the view that such terms will rarely be unfair (presumably this view is based on the points made above as to consent and the likelihood of market discipline). Second, the Law Commissions argue that testing such terms for fairness would unduly interfere with freedom of contract (presumably the idea is that there should at least be freedom in relation to the core elements of the contract and, again, that consumers give genuine consent to such terms). Finally, the Law Commissions argue that if the exclusion is removed traders will

---

[309] Article 8.

[310] See further below at 8.1.2.

[311] See ss 137–140 CCA.

[312] At the very least there needs to be a price or interest rate that is extremely unfair by comparison with the market norm – see further below at 8.1.2.

[313] See further below at 9.5.

[314] See T. Wilhelmsson, *Social Contract Law and European Integration*, Ashgate, 1995, at 199.

have little incentive to make it clear to the consumer what the main subject matter is.[315]

In relation to the exclusion of price terms the view of the Law Commissions is that most consumers are reasonably alert to price, and that, given variation in market prices, even where markets are competitive (based on factors that might not be obvious to consumers) there could be large numbers of challenges. In addition the Law Commissions make the argument that there would be a lot of scope for argument, e.g. on issues such as the costs faced by traders and whether the market is competitive. The conclusion is that these factors would create too much uncertainty.[316]

5.8.3 Core Terms and Reasonable Expectations

5.8.3.1 The Current Approach

But whatever view one holds as to whether core terms should be subject to the test of unfairness the exemption raises a further question. How does the exclusion of core terms from the test of fairness square with some of the terms that we have already said are controlled? We have seen that terms allowing for the trader to perform in ways that are out of step with the reasonable expectations of the consumer cause significant imbalance and are subject to the good faith test; and that terms imposing obligations on the consumer that are out of step with the reasonable expectations of the consumer will also cause significant imbalance and be subject to the general review of fairness under the good faith test.[317] But how does this square with the fact that so called 'core terms' are excluded from the test of unfairness altogether if they are in plain and intelligible language? Some of the terms allowing the trader to perform in ways that are different from that reasonably expected by the consumer clearly cover performance of the trader's core performance obligation. For example, we talked of terms allowing the trader to vary the product or service provided;[318] yet the obligation to provide the product or service is clearly the core obligation of the trader. Equally, some of the terms allowing for imposition of obligations on the consumer that are out of step with the reasonable expectations of the consumer clearly cover the core consumer obligation to pay the price and relate directly to the amount payable. So, for example, we talked of a term providing for the price to be

---

[315] Law Commission Report, para. 3.57.

[316] Law Commission Consultation Paper, 3.27–3.34.

[317] See above at 5.7.6.

[318] *Ibid.*, and see the indicative list, para. 1(k).

increased;[319] and clearly this relates to the core payment obligation of the consumer. So, there appears to be a conundrum. These terms are clearly covered by the test of fairness (being listed on the indicative list); yet they deal with core issues.

The House of Lords in *First National Bank* certainly indicated in general terms that a 'restrictive interpretation' should be taken to what counts as a main subject matter term.[320] This was said to be because otherwise the regime will be 'frustrated by endless formalistic arguments ...'.[321] Equally, in relation to price, it was said that there should be a 'restrictive interpretation';[322] and that only those terms 'falling squarely within' the exclusion should be interpreted as excluded.[323] Specifically, in *First National Bank* it was held that the term providing for contractual interest not to merge in the judgement and to continue to be payable in addition to the judgement debt was not an excluded price term within the meaning of the UTCCR.[324] However, this generally 'restrictive approach' to the core term exclusions does not directly answer the question as to why some terms apparently dealing with core issues are not viewed as core terms.

The answer seems to lie in the notion of reasonable expectations itself. The exemption, although it does not say so expressly, only seems to be intended to cover terms genuinely reflecting reasonable consumer expectations on these core issues. So, the idea appears to be that, as we have already said,[325] consumers will typically have pre-existing expectations as to the basic nature of the goods or services to be provided and the price that he will have to pay for these goods or services. These expectations will come from the basic presentation of the goods or services at the point of sale and/or in advertising or other promotion. The consumer will expect to receive goods or services that accord with the basic way in which they have been described at the point of sale and/or in promotional material; and to pay the price as it has been described at the point of sale and/or in promotional material. These expectations are typically fortified by the fact that this is what normally happens.[326] The consumer may not buy frequently from this trader. Indeed he may never

---

[319] *Ibid.*, and see the indicative list, para. 1(l).

[320] [2001] 3 WLR 1297, Lord Steyn at 1312.

[321] *Ibid.*

[322] *Ibid.*

[323] Lord Bingham at 1304–5.

[324] [2001] 3 WLR 1297.

[325] See above at 4.4.3.

[326] *Ibid.*, and see M.I. Meyerson, The Reunification of Contract Law: The Objective Theory of Consumer Form Contracts (1993) 47 University of Miami Law Review, 1263, at 1301.

have bought from this trader before. However, his experience of buying from other traders and his experience of observing others will tell him that goods or services are normally supplied in accordance with the basic expectations generated by the initial description/presentation; and the price to be paid is normally as per the initial description/presentation. In sum, there is experience of, and an expectation of, successful performance, reflecting the gist of what has been suggested outwith the formal terms); and experience of, and an expectation of, paying the price that was suggested outwith the formal terms.

What the core exclusions really intend to exclude, then, are terms that genuinely reflect these pre-existing expectations. There does not appear to be an intention to exclude terms that allow the trader to offer something different in terms of his own core performance from that reasonably expected by the consumer; or terms that allow prices or charges to be imposed that extend beyond what the consumer really expected in terms of his core payment obligation. Of course, this makes perfect sense in terms of the basic logic of excluding core terms in the first place. The consumer gives real consent to what is presented to him and what he agrees to in the basic encounter with the trader; this is what genuinely goes to the core of the bargain; this is what is subject to market discipline; and this is what has the strongest claim to be exempt from a review of fairness. These arguments will simply rarely be able to be made in relation to the formal terms whatever issues they formally deal with (the only exception will surely be where it is made genuinely clear to the consumer in the basic encounter with the trader that, not only do the formal terms allow it, but that in the normal course of things there is a real possibility of changes, extra charges, etc[327]).

An important point to emphasize is that when we talk about pre-existing expectations as to core obligations this is restricted to what happens in the normal performance of the contract, i.e. in the normal and due course of things. So, for example, if (under a particular term) the trigger for a sum to be payable by the consumer is a default (or anything that does not arise in the due performance of the contract) this is surely not a core term as the reasonable expectations of the consumer as to his core obligation will not extend to what happens outwith normal performance of the contract.[328]

---

[327] See the example given in the Law Commission Report at paras 3.58 and 3.60.

[328] See the approach taken in *Bairstow Eves* v. *Smith* [2004] EWHC 263 and see the discussion by P. Nebbia, Unfair Contract Terms in European Law, Hart, 2007, 129–132 and C. Twigg-Flesner, The Implementation of the Unfair Contract Terms Directive in the United Kingdom, in H. Collins, L. Tichy and S. Grundmann (eds), Standard Contract Terms in Europe, Kluwer, forthcoming.

It seems that the same approach is correct in any case where the terms allow for the obligation of the consumer to be increased from what he would reasonably have viewed as his basic payment obligation to some higher amount; even if the initial payment obligation is expressed technically as a concessionary rate, with the 'ordinary' rate being triggered when there is a default. This is because the consumer reasonably expected that the so-called concessionary rate was the rate he would have to pay in the due performance of the contract. Now that the consumer is in default, another rate is applicable, but this is not the rate that the consumer reasonably expected to have to pay and therefore does not represent the core payment obligation from the point of view of the reasonable expectations of the consumer.

Indeed, it seems also that the same approach is correct *in any circumstances* where the extra or different charge can be imposed in a situation that is not (from the point of view of the reasonable expectations of the consumer) the due performance of the contract, i.e. even where the event triggering the extra or different charge is not technically a default as such. This explains why the 'disguised penalties' described above[329] are subject to the test of unfairness. The sum is not technically triggered by a breach and therefore is not technically a sum payable as damages; but is a primary obligation. Nevertheless it is usually an obligation that the consumer would not have reasonably expected to owe in the due performance of the contract and so it is not a core term.

Returning to the issue of payments that *are* applicable at a time when a consumer is indeed in default, it seems that even if a term does not provide for an obligation to *change* when the consumer is in default, but only allows for it to continue, such a term will usually not be treated as a core term that is excluded from the test of unfairness. In other words it seems that if an obligation applies in post-default circumstances then its application in those post-breach circumstances is not to be treated as the basic price obligation of the consumer. So, in *First National Bank* it was held that the term providing for contractual interest not to merge in the judgement and to continue to be payable in addition to the judgement debt was not an excluded price term within the meaning of the UTCCR. This was because it was not a payment that arose in the due performance of the contract, but in circumstances of default by the consumer.[330] One might quibble with this and say that the payment does in one way *arise* in the due performance of the contract – it simply *continues to be payable* in circumstances that no longer involve the due performance of the contract. However, the underlying point probably is that the consumer would not really be contemplating *anything* that is payable at the default stage when

---

[329] See above at 5.7.6.2.
[330] [2001] 3 WLR 1297.

he thinks of what his core performance obligations are (whether such post-default payments are only *triggered* by default or judgement or simply *continue* after default or judgement).

To summarize, then, terms dealing with core issues are only excluded from the test of unfairness where they genuinely reflect the reasonable expectations of the consumer in relation to what will happen in the due performance of the contract. Where a term does not reflect such expectations it will be subject to control; will probably be treated as causing significant imbalance (detriment under the new regime); and will then be subject to the broad review of fairness under the good faith test (fair and reasonable test under the new regime). In fact, in relation to terms dealing with the performance of the trader, the effect seems to be much the same as under UCTA. Under UCTA there is no positive exclusion of terms dealing with the core performance obligation of the trader. However, it seems that there are only two types of term that *are* caught by UCTA and that could relate to the core performance obligation of the trader. First of all, there are those terms that allow for performance substantially different from that reasonably expected.[331] So, as already suggested,[332] if a term reflects the reasonable expectations of the consumer on a core issue it will not usually be caught by the UCTA test, just as it will not be caught by the test under the UTCCR. The second type of term caught by UCTA that relates to the core obligation of the trader is a term describing the basic nature of goods being sold to the consumer. Such a term could certainly be argued to be a core or main subject matter term, yet it will be caught by UCTA, s. 6(2) if it seeks to qualify any descriptive statement as to the essential identity of the goods that has been made to the consumer outwith the formal terms. This is because a descriptive statement as to the essential identity of the goods that has been made to the consumer outwith the formal terms will form the basis of an implied term (under s. 13 of the Sale of Goods Act) to the effect that the goods will comply with this description; and any attempt to restrict the scope of the obligation created by this implied term is wholly ineffective.[333] However, such a term will surely also be covered by the UTCCR. This is because it will not be reflective of the reasonable expectations of the consumer as to the essential identity of the goods (these expectations having been formed by the description given outwith the formal terms). Of course a description given outwith the formal terms *will* be an excluded core term under the UTCCR. But such a description will be unaffected by UCTA as well. It will not be excluding or restricting anything. Rather, it will, itself, be forming the basis of the implied term as

---

[331] UCTA, s. 3(2)(b)(i).

[332] See above at 4.4.8.2.

[333] See above at 4.2.1 and 4.2.3.

to description (and will not be able to be excluded or restricted by a formal term).

5.8.3.2 The Proposed New Regime

The new regime will make it clear that the criteria for a core term to be excluded is that it must be one reflecting reasonable expectations. The Law Commissions propose that the new legislation should exclude terms defining the main subject matter from the test of fairness; but only in so far as they are substantially the same as the definition the consumer reasonably expected, and are transparent.[334] In relation to price, the Law Commissions proposal[335] is to say that the adequacy of the price should not be subject to review where it is, (1) payable in circumstances substantially the same as the consumer reasonably expected; (2) calculated in substantially the same way as the consumer reasonably expected; (3) not payable under a default or subsidiary term of the contract;[336] and (4) transparent.

This is a considerable improvement on the formula currently adopted. First, it makes it clear that the issue is whether the term reflects the reasonable expectations of the consumer. The current rule, as we have said, says nothing expressly about this. Secondly, in relation to core price terms, it is made clear that both the circumstances of payment and the means of calculating the payment must reflect the reasonable expectations of the consumer. Third, also in relation to core price terms, it is made clear that a sum payable under a default or subsidiary term cannot be a core term. Finally, the requirement would no longer simply be that the term must be in plain and intelligible language,[337] but that it must be transparent. This will require not only plain language, but also that the term be legible, be presented clearly and be available to the consumer.[338] The Law Commission considered that it was wise to expand the requirement in this way as it may be that the Directive actually requires this. The actual provision in the Directive on main subject matter and

---

[334] Law Commission Report, 3.65; Draft Bill, Clause 4(2).

[335] Law Commission Report, 3.66; Draft Bill, Clause 4(3).

[336] This is arguably already covered by (1) above in that the consumer would surely not reasonably expect his core payment obligation to arise in circumstances of default, however, the idea here seems to be to avoid any arguments by emphasising that financial obligations arising in the context of default or subsidiary terms are never core terms.

[337] See above at 5.8.1.

[338] Law Commission Report, para. 3.63 and Draft Bill, Clauses 4(3) and (5).

price terms only refers to plain and intelligible language.[339] However, as the Law Commissions point out,[340] Recital 20 to the Preamble, in discussing plain and intelligible language, says that 'the consumer should actually be given the opportunity to examine all the terms'. So, it may be that in the Directive 'plain and intelligible language' is to be viewed as being language that is not only plain and intelligible language in a linguistic sense but also in the sense that it is available, legible and clear. Whether or not this was required by the Directive, such a change means that even if a term, in substance, reflects pre-existing reasonable expectations as to core issues it will not escape the test of fairness unless the consumer is in a position to be able to look at the formal contract and easily identify these core obligations.

5.9 Significant Imbalance, Default Rules, Reasonable Expectations and the Role of Favourable Terms

We have seen that under the UTCCR there will often be a significant imbalance, triggering a broad review of fairness under the good faith test, where a term deviates from a default rule to the detriment of the consumer or allows for compromise of the reasonable expectations of the consumer.[341] However, above[342] it was suggested that this may not be the full story. There is ambiguity as to whether a broad enquiry as to process and substance is triggered simply on the basis that a term deviates from a default rule to the detriment of the consumer or allows for compromise of reasonable expectations; or whether there is no broad review of fairness where (taking into account provisions that are favourable to the consumer and represent a 'fair price' for the term that is detrimental to the consumer) there is no overall substantive unfairness. The result of this latter approach is that procedural fairness is ignored in cases where there is deemed to be overall substantive fairness.

The difficulty is caused by the fact that the question as to whether a term causes a significant imbalance in the parties' rights and obligations clearly involves consideration not only of the detrimental features of the term in question, but also any beneficial features of this (or another) term of the contract. This has been confirmed by the House of Lords in the *First National Bank* case.[343] The issue might arise in various ways. First,

---

[339] Article 4(2).
[340] Report at 3.63.
[341] See above at 5.7.2.
[342] See above at 5.7.1.
[343] [2001] 3 WLR 1297, Lord Bingham at 1307–8.

there is the so-called 'mirror-image' scenario [344] in which a term gives the trader the right to retain sums when the consumer is in breach (these sums possibly exceeding the losses actually caused to the trader); but also provides (or another term provides) that the consumer can claim an equivalent sum in compensation in circumstances where the trader is in breach.[345] Secondly, there is the situation in which the other term in some way protects the consumer from the detriment caused by the term under scrutiny. So, for example, there may be a term allowing for a price increase; while it also provides (or another term provides) for the consumer to have a right to withdraw from the contract in response.[346] Third, there is the situation in which a term is detrimental in any way (e.g. by excluding or limiting a liability of the trader); but there is another term that is particularly favourable to the consumer (e.g. the price is lower than normal).

In all of these cases there does, of course, need to be an assessment of the particular circumstances in order to assess whether it could be said that the favourable term is sufficiently favourable to count as a fair price for the detrimental term and consequently to lead to the conclusion that there is no overall significant imbalance in rights and obligations. We have already seen that there are various ways in which this could be measured;[347] and that it is not entirely clear exactly what measure is used by either the House of Lords or the ECJ (although it may be that the ECJ might use a measure that is more protective of consumers than the House of Lords[348]). The current point is that, however this is measured in relation to the substantive features of the terms, if it is possible to reach the conclusion that there is no overall significant imbalance *purely on the basis of the substantive rights and obligations in question* then, in a case where this conclusion is reached, the term causing detriment could not be found to be unfair under the current regime. This is because if there is no significant imbalance then the term cannot be unfair. Significant imbalance and violation of good faith are distinct requirements for a finding of unfairness.[349] If there is no significant imbalance then it does not matter whether there is a violation of good faith. The problem with this is that it excludes any concern with procedural fairness (or more significantly, procedural unfairness). Yet surely, as has already been

---

[344] See E. Hondius, European Approaches to Fairness in C. Willett (ed.), Aspects of Fairness in Contract, Blackstone, 1996, 61 at 71.

[345] Schedule 2, indicative list, para. 1(d).

[346] *Ibid.*, para. 1(l).

[347] See above at 2.4.3.3.

[348] See above at 5.5.4.2(iv)(c).

[349] See above at 5.5.4.2(i).

argued,[350] consumers have a legitimate interest in being in a position to assess the overall package in order to assess whether it is a package that they wish to agree to. In the case of the first situation cited above, surely the consumer is entitled to expect the terms in question to be sufficiently transparent so that he can assess whether his right to claim equivalent compensation in cases where the trader is in breach is a benefit that makes it worthwhile taking the risk of forfeiting excessive sums in a case where he (the consumer) is in breach. In the second situation (taking the example of the price variation clause) the consumer is surely entitled to expect the term allowing for the increase to be transparent so that he knows that this is a possibility; and to expect the term giving him the right to cancel to be transparent so that he can assess whether this makes entering the contract less risky; and also so that he is actually in a position to exercise the cancellation right if the price is increased. In the third situation cited surely the consumer is entitled to expect the term excluding the liability of the trader to be sufficiently transparent so that he can assess whether the risk involved in agreeing to it is balanced out by the lower price.

In other words, a lack of transparency should be capable of leading to the conclusion that the term under scrutiny is unfair. This allows a lack of transparency (whether in the term under scrutiny or the favourable term) to lead to a finding of unfairness in the context of preventive control and for the lack of transparency to be considered in after the fact control. Of course, the point has already been made that in after the fact litigation we would not necessarily wish to hold the detrimental term to be unfair on the basis of the lack of transparency in all cases. It may well be that if the overall package had been transparent the consumer would have been happy to agree to it; and that, on this basis it is fair to enforce it. The point, however, is that the question of transparency should be able to be taken into account.

The ECJ have not provided a clear view on the issue.[351] We know that the ECJ take the view that benefits provided by other terms are relevant to the overall assessment of fairness. However, the ECJ did not explain where transparency does (or does not) fit in. Neither did the ECJ break down the test into its two components. (Doing so brings the problem into sharp focus because – as we have seen – it highlights the fact that there cannot be unfairness without significant imbalance and that significant imbalance – if viewed in purely substantive terms – might be prevented from arising where there is a beneficial term.) As such we do not know whether the view of the ECJ is that overall fairness in substance (based on the existence of a beneficial term) is sufficient; or whether

---

[350] See above at 2.4.3.4, 3.5.4 and 5.7.1.
[351] See the discussion above at 3.5.4.

transparency is also (at least sometimes) required. The House of Lords decision did not really go to this issue either. The House of Lords *did* break the test down into the significant imbalance and good faith components.[352] They also said that other terms of the contract were relevant in assessing whether there was significant imbalance.[353] Further, it may be that they reached the conclusion that there was no significant imbalance partly on the basis that there was a benefit to the consumer (not in the form of another term as such but in obtaining access to the loan in the first place[354]). However, they did not say whether the issue as to significant imbalance is to be determined purely on the basis of substantive elements of the contract. So it is not possible to say whether, for the House of Lords, if there is overall substantive fairness there is automatically no significant imbalance. Certainly we shall see below[355] that, while OFT practice in applying the overall test does seem to involve (sometimes) considering the question of overall balance, there is certainly (in addition) a requirement of transparency. So, for the OFT, there does not seem to be a notion that the existence of overall substantive balance prevents an enquiry into procedural fairness.

Of course, this does not mean that the courts will not take such an approach. Now it may well be that, in practice, a court would always find a way of insisting on transparency before saying that a substantively 'beneficial' provision of the type described could result in a finding of fairness. One way of approaching the issue is to say that even if there is not strictly a substantive imbalance there is often *in practice* an imbalance in cases where the terms are not transparent, as the consumer is not in a position to understand the substantive position.[356] Another approach is to say that, although significant imbalance in the rights and obligations under the contract is *usually* about the *substantive rights and obligations under the contract*, there is also a *legal* consumer *right* to transparency (implied into the contract) and a concomitant trader *obligation* to be transparent. So, even although there may be substantively beneficial terms, the lack of transparency may still mean that there remains a significant imbalance in rights and obligations (caused by the consumer having been deprived of his 'right' to transparency). There seems to be support in German law for reading the UTD test often to require transparency, whatever the substantive position. Article 307(1) of the new German civil code provides that: 'Provisions in standard business terms

---

352 See above at 5.5.4.2(i).

353 See above at 5.5.4.2(ii).

354 *Ibid.*

355 See below at 6.3.3–6 and 6.4.2 and see 6.3.6 in particular.

356 See S. Bright, Winning the Battle Against Unfair Contract Terms (2000) 20 Legal Studies 331 on giving a practical reading to significant imbalance.

are invalid if, contrary to the requirement of good faith, they place the contractual partner of the user at an unreasonable disadvantage. An unreasonable disadvantage may also result from the fact that the provision is not clear and comprehensible.'[357]

It is fairly obvious that this provision is supposed to reflect the test in the UTD, with the 'unreasonable disadvantage' concept being used instead of the significant imbalance concept. As we can also see, the 'unreasonable disadvantage' can be caused by lack of transparency. This appears to allow (possibly on the basis of an assumption that the UTD test requires this) a term to cause an 'unreasonable disadvantage' on the basis of a lack of transparency either where it is not in itself detrimental in substance or (and this is its importance here) where the term is substantively detrimental but the substantive disadvantage caused by this is balanced out by a favourable term so that there is no longer substantive disadvantage.

Certainly, in the light of the consumer protection and confidence goals of the UTD (and the clear importance of transparency to EC consumer policy), it would be desirable to interpret the test in any way possible so as to ensure terms are always transparent. However, it is clear that the position will be more satisfactory if the significant imbalance trigger is replaced (as we have said is suggested) by simply a requirement of 'detriment'. There can clearly be detriment on the basis of the detrimental substantive effect of the term in question[358] and the fact that this term or other terms contain provisions that may be substantively favourable does not negate this. The benefits of any such provisions can then be assessed under the general review of fairness along with matters of procedural fairness.

5.10 Terms Not Deviating From the Default Position but Lacking Transparency

We have seen that terms which, in substance, deviate from the default position or allow for compromise of reasonable expectations will often be subject to the general review of fairness to which we shall turn shortly.

---

[357] And see the approach previously taken in German case law, for example in BGH 17 January 1989 NJW 1989 Westpapier Mitteilungen, 1989, 126; although, we should note that the German statutory provision does in fact refer to the fact that 'an unreasonable disadvantage *may* also result from the fact that the provision is not clear and comprehensible', the use of the word 'may' suggesting that this will not always be the case – see P. Nebbia, Unfair Contract Terms and European Law, Hart, 2007, 139.

[358] See above at 4.3.1 and 5.7.5.

(This is currently on the grounds that they cause significant imbalance and would, under the new regime, be on the basis that they cause detriment.) This regime allows for a review of substantive and procedural matters. This, in particular, means that the terms in question must be transparent,[359] which as we said, is a key priority of any fairness regime. However, what is the position in relation to terms that actually give useful rights to the consumer (possibly reflecting the default position or improving on it)? It was argued above that there is a case for these to be transparent as well; so that consumers know of the rights which they have and can make use of these when there is a dispute.[360] So what of terms that are technically at least as favourable to the consumer as the default position but lack transparency, e.g. terms that are unclear, in small print or are misleading as to the rights in question, perhaps even being capable of giving the impression to the consumer of a position that is *not* as favourable as the default position? If we were (notwithstanding how the consumer might interpret the term) to treat the term as having the effect that it technically has (i.e. as being reflective of the default position) then it will often not be subject to the test of unfairness as it will often be a term reflecting a mandatory provision; and such terms are excluded from the test of unfairness.[361] Even if the term does not reflect any particular mandatory rule, if it is beneficial (in substance) to the consumer it might be said not to cause a significant imbalance. So, in either case, the term is not subject to the general review of fairness under the good faith test (and therefore is not subject to the transparency requirement that comes with good faith). In after the fact litigation this does not matter as such. By the time the case has got to this stage the consumer has already been prejudiced by the lack of transparency. What matters now is that he is not prejudiced by a term that is unfair in substance. However, if the term is actually fair in substance then the consumer is not prejudiced by the fact that the term cannot be tested (because it reflects a mandatory provision). Neither is the consumer prejudiced by the fact that (because the term is fair in substance) the term does not cause significant imbalance and therefore cannot be found to be unfair. The term is fair in substance and so there is no problem. Of course, the consumer *will* be prejudiced if the reason that the term is not covered by the test of unfairness is that it

---

[359] See Lord Bingham, in particular on good faith requiring 'open dealing' above at 5.5.4.2(iii) and see below at 6.4.2.

[360] See above at 2.4.3.4(iii).

[361] See above at 3.2 and 5.7.3. This exclusion (although referring to terms reflecting 'mandatory' provisions) covers terms reflecting default rules that would apply in the absence of contrary agreement – see Preamble, Recital 13; although note the arguments above at 5.7.3 about the precise status of the rule excluding mandatory terms.

reflects a mandatory provision and this is a mandatory provision that is not actually fair in substance. However, this is an issue to which we shall return below. For the moment let us concentrate on the position in relation to terms that lack transparency but (in substance) reflect the default position (which is a fair default position) and (because of this) do not cause significant substantive imbalance and terms lacking transparency that not only reflect the default position but also reflect mandatory provisions (which are fair mandatory provisions) and are therefore not subject to the provisions of the UTCCR at all.

The question is whether the existing rules are actually capable of being understood in such a way as to deal with this problem. In other words is it possible to read the rules in such a way as to say that such terms are required to be transparent? To the extent that this is not possible what changes are required? First of all, in the context of after the fact litigation it is clear that if a term is not in plain language and if this gives rise to interpretation difficulties the court is able to impose the interpretation most favourable to the consumer.[362] So it might be that, notwithstanding what was intended by those drafting the term, the term can (on the facts) be interpreted as being *less* favourable than the default position. On the basis of this interpretation it no longer reflects any mandatory provision (so it is covered by the rules) and it may also now (in being less favourable than the default position) be said to cause a significant substantive imbalance. As such it is opened up to the good faith element of the test and (because it is not transparent) it may be unfair. In other words, a route has been found to the conclusion that such a term must be transparent otherwise it will be unfair. However, this approach is, in fact, of no help whatsoever. The result of such an approach in the immediate circumstances of the case is that the term is not binding. But this is not to the advantage of the individual consumer. The term was intended to reflect the default position which is in fact fair and therefore beneficial to the consumer.

Another possible scenario (again using the interpretation rule) is that the term is capable of an interpretation that makes it *more* beneficial to the consumer than the default provision it was intended to reflect. So the ambiguity caused by the lack of transparency is exploited to put the consumer in a better position than he would otherwise have been in. This might serve as an incentive to traders to make such provisions more transparent. However, it seems likely that the exclusion from the controls of the UTCCR of terms reflecting mandatory provisions means that this type of approach cannot be taken where the term (on whatever interpretation) is at least as favourable as a mandatory provision. This is because such a term is excluded from the controls of the UTCCR

---

[362] Regulation 6(2), following Article 5 of the Directive.

(including the interpretation rule). A further problem is that even if the term does not reflect a mandatory provision, the transparency problem may not give rise to an interpretation problem as such. It may simply be that the term is in small print, insufficiently prominent in the overall contract etc. In these cases where the term does not cause significant substantive imbalance (because it reflects the default position) the interpretation rule is of no help in achieving an even more substantively fair interpretation (and thereby encouraging traders to be more transparent in the future).

What may be needed in after the fact litigation is a quite distinct sanction where terms are seriously lacking in transparency. So, compensation might be available to the consumer if the lack of transparency has caused the consumer not to take up the rights contained in these beneficial (but non transparent) terms; and this has caused inconvenience or other losses. Another possible sanction would be for the other terms of the contract not to be enforceable against the consumer.

Of course, what we really want is for traders to be prevented (before the fact) from presenting terms that reflect the default position in a way that is not transparent. What is required is that such terms are controllable under the proactive powers of the regulatory bodies. In order for this to be possible they have to be able to be viewed as unfair. The 'most favourable' interpretation rule does not apply to action taken by the regulatory bodies against unfair terms.[363] Indeed, interpreting such terms so that they *do not* have unfair substantive effects does not help in proactive control. Such an interpretation means that the term is less likely to be found to be unfair and if the term is not unfair then the trader cannot be prevented from using it. Indeed, (as we have already noted) if the interpretation is to the effect that the term is no less favourable than the default position then the term often cannot even be reviewed for unfairness. This is because, in being no less favourable than the default position, the term often reflects mandatory statutory or regulatory provisions and is excluded form the test of unfairness on this basis.

The OFT approach seems to be to interpret such terms in the way that is *least* favourable to the consumer and that the consumer might reasonably understand them.[364] The OFT reasoning (although not spelt out) appears to be that if the consumer would reasonably understand the term to be providing something less favourable than the default position then (if we adopt this interpretation) we have a term that no longer reflects a mandatory statutory provision (or more generally is not substantively beneficial to the consumer). It is therefore covered by the test. Presumably, then, this reasoning is followed through to say that as

---

[363] Regulation 7(2), following Article 5 of the Directive.

[364] OFT Guidelines, 2001, Plain and Intelligible Language, 19.6.

the term *appears to consumers* to deviate from the default position then it causes a significant imbalance (even although it does not technically have this substantive effect[365]). This would then allow the OFT to say that the term is unfair under the good faith test (based on the lack of transparency). This is probably a valid approach to take in the light of the goals of the UTD. This approach may have support in the German approach referred to above[366] under which a term can be said to cause an 'unreasonable disadvantage' (analogous to a significant imbalance) on the basis of lack of transparency. This appears to be aimed at the same result, i.e. that a term should be able to be viewed as causing significant imbalance (whatever its technical substantive effect) where it lacks transparency. The ECJ has actually reiterated the point that in preventive proceedings under Article 7 of the UTD (the provision which the OFT powers are intended to be in fulfilment of) the 'most favourable interpretation' rule does not apply and that in such cases there should be an 'objective' approach to interpretation.[367] Of course, the question then is as to whether an 'objective' interpretation is an interpretation based on how the average consumer might reasonably understand the term. If this is the case it would seem that the OFT approach has support from the ECJ. However, an 'objective' interpretation could refer to the way in which a court or decision making body would interpret the term. If this is the case the OFT approach may be less stable. The latter form of objective interpretation might result in the conclusion that (notwithstanding the confusion that might be caused to a consumer) the term does in fact reflect the default position (so that it does not in fact cause significant substantive imbalance and therefore the lack of good faith resulting from the lack of transparency is not enough to make the term unfair); and possibly that the term actually reflects a mandatory provision, so that it is no longer able to be tested for unfairness at all and therefore cannot be found to be unfair.

The approach based on interpretation is also limited in the sense that the transparency problem may not give rise to an *interpretation* issue as such. There may be no way of interpreting the term to be less fair in

---

[365] This is another instance of the practical approach to significant imbalance discussed above at 5.9. The term may not technically cause an imbalance in the substantive rights and obligations, but, in practice, it causes an imbalance as consumers are likely to be misled as to its substantive effect. Alternatively, this approach could be grounded in the idea (also discussed at 5.9) that there can be a significant imbalance in rights and obligations based on the trader not fulfilling his (procedural) transparency *obligation* and consumers not benefiting from their (procedural) *right* to transparency.

[366] See above at 5.9.

[367] *Commission* v. *Spain*, Case C–70/03.

substance than the default position (and possibly a mandatory provision). The transparency problem may lie in small print, a lack of prominence within the contract etc.[368] In other words, what seems to be needed is an approach that deems terms to be causing a significant imbalance (whatever their substantive effects, i.e. whether they reflect a default rule or even a mandatory provision) whenever they lack transparency in any significant way (such terms will, in consequence, probably be unfair once the good faith test is applied). This avoids any restrictions in the interpretation approach inherent in the 'objective' interpretation approach) and also covers cases where there is no interpretation issue at all. The German approach described above certainly appears to extend beyond interpretation problems. It refers to whether the term is 'clear and comprehensible' and is not dependent on any lack of clarity or comprehensibility causing the consumer (or being likely to cause consumers) to understand or interpret the term in any particular way. Having said this both 'clarity' and 'comprehensibility' might both be taken to refer only to the language used and not to problems of small print or lack of prominence within the contract.

The desired result can possibly be achieved within the existing UK test without any reference to the interpretation rule by taking one of the two approaches to significant imbalance already discussed above. So it might be said that (even where there is technically no deviation from the default position and no other reason to say there is a substantive imbalance) a significant imbalance can arise *in practice* whenever there is any transparency problem that might affect the ability of consumers to understand the effect of the term. Alternatively, it might be said that any such transparency problem causes a significant imbalance in rights and obligations because it is in breach of the consumer *right* to transparency and the trader *obligation* to be transparent.[369]

However, neither of these approaches will help if the test cannot be applied in the first place because the term (substantively) reflects a mandatory provision. Does the answer to this now lie in the new regime? The new position will be that a term will only excluded if it reflects the default position (or as the new legislation would say, 'leads to substantially the same result as would be produced as a matter of law if

---

[368] Although small print, lack of prominence etc have (quite plausibly) been argued to go to whether language is 'plain and intelligible' (see M. Hetherington and S. Brothers, Unfair Terms in Consumer Contracts Regulations, (1995), International Insurance Law Review, 263 and P. Nebbia, Unfair Contract Terms in European Law, Hart, 2007, 136–6) it does not follow that the lack of 'plain and intelligible' language will necessarily lead to an interpretation problem as such.

[369] See above in this paragraph and above at 5.9.

the term were not included') *and* the term is transparent.[370] This will mean that even if a term reflects the default position (and even a mandatory provision) it will be subject to the test of unfairness where it is not transparent. 'Transparency' under the proposals involves availability, plain language, legibility and clear presentation.[371] Probably, the ability to insist on availability, plain language, legibility and clear presentation will cover the various transparency problems including most (if not all) ways in which a term might lead consumers to believe that the term is less favourable than the default position. However, to be absolutely sure that this problem is addressed it might be better to include 'not misleading to the average consumer' as a component of transparency. This point notwithstanding, the point is that once the term is deemed to be subject to the test of unfairness (on the basis that it lacks transparency) it can then be found to fail the test. This involves a further two stage process. First, (assuming the term is fair in substance) it needs to be accepted that the term causes a significant imbalance based on its lack of transparency. This depends at present on the arguments made above (i.e. either that the term causes a practical imbalance or that there is imbalance as a result of the failure to respect the consumer right to transparency). However, as these approaches have not been given judicial approval they are not entirely stable and it would be better if it was made clear that terms can cause significant imbalance (or under the proposed new regime that they can cause detriment) purely on the basis of a lack of transparency. Once we get over this hurdle, the issue is simpler as the term can be found to be unfair on the basis that the lack of transparency violates the good faith requirement.

Of course, the Law Commission proposal also deals with another problem in relation to terms reflecting mandatory provisions. It has already been pointed out that mandatory provisions are not necessarily always fair to consumers in substance.[372] At least, under the proposals, such provisions will need to be transparent or they will be subject to the full test of fairness.

Quite apart from the above issues in relation to express terms that may technically reflect legal rights but that are misleading, there are questions as to whether (and when) traders should *disclose* legal rights in order to make more fair the express terms that they use (express terms that clearly *do* deviate from the default position and cause substantive detriment to the consumer). We have already touched on this issue in the context of the *First National Bank* case where one of the issues was whether a condition of using the term in question should have been that

---

[370] Report, 3.70–3.72 and Draft Bill, Clause 4(4).

[371] Draft Bill, Clause 14(3).

[372] See 5.7.3 above.

the Bank drew the attention of consumers to the legal regime that might result in the amount payable under the term being reviewed. This seems to be part of a broader question as to the circumstances in which the fairness of a term should depend on disclosure of relevant aspects of the legal context. However, this issue is not properly dealt with here. The issue in this section has been about whether a term technically reflecting a default rule can itself be tested for fairness. This is quite separate from the question as to whether a term that clearly does not reflect the default position is more likely to be unfair where background legal rights are not disclosed and the consumer is thereby prevented from making use of knowledge of these rights to self-protect against the prejudicial express term. This latter question is relevant to the overall review of fairness (whether under the UCTA reasonableness test, the UTCCR good faith test or the proposed 'fair and reasonable test) to which we turn in the next chapter.[373]

A separate issue, again, is whether traders should be required to include in the formal contract terms reflecting important independent legal rights; not (as above) based on any particular link with any term that has been included, but simply on the basis that consumers should be made aware of important rights granted to them by law. Now it is clear that this is not required under the unfairness test. This test is a vitiation measure that is concerned with the fairness of terms that the supplier chooses to put in the contract. It is not a supplementation measure that can be used to insist upon the trader including summaries of key rights emanating from default rules (except, as discussed already, to the extent that it can be said that making these rights known – or not – could be said to affect the fairness of terms that have been included).

Of course, certain sector specific measures do insist upon information on legal rights being provided to consumers; although this tends to be restricted to information as to cancellation rights.[374] However, the point has been made already that the most important form of transparency for consumers may be transparency in relation to rights that can be made use of post-contractually. So, it is arguable that more work should be done on identifying other important rights (e.g. in relation to quality and fitness of goods and quality of services) that should be set out in all contracts of this type.

---

[373] This specific issue as to the disclosure of background legal rights is dealt with at 6.4.2.8 below.

[374] See, for example, Consumer Protection (Cancellation of Contracts etc) Regulations 1987, Regulation 4 and Consumer Protection (Distance Selling) Regulations 2000, Regulation 7(1)(a)(vi).

Chapter Six

The General Fairness Reviews – UCTA, UTCCR and the New Test

6.1 General Introduction

This chapter builds upon what we have already concluded as to the general fairness reviews that exist under UCTA and the UTCCR. It draws upon the case law, the work of the OFT and other sources, in particular the legal and policy background to the UTD. It seeks to develop a fuller picture as to how fairness in substance and procedure are measured and how questions of substance and procedure interrelate. These issues are obviously of current relevance. However, they will continue to be of relevance if the Law Commission proposals become law. The proposed test, as we have seen, is whether the term is 'fair and reasonable'.[1] This must be approached so as to offer at least the same level of protection as the unfairness concept under the UTCCR, so that the jurisprudence on this would remain vital. In addition, the UCTA case law would be likely also to continue to be of assistance. However, the new regime would also include much more in the way of guidance than has been available before.[2] So it is important to highlight these guidelines and what they would add to the picture.

6.2 Introduction to the General Fairness Reviews

We have seen that the broad assessments of fairness take place under the auspices of the reasonableness test (UCTA)[3] and the good faith limb of the unfairness test (UTCCR)[4]; and that under the proposed new regime

---

[1] Draft Bill, Clause 4(1).

[2] The proposed test contains explicit reference to (and guidance on) transparency (Clause 14(1)(a) and 14(3)); along explicit reference (and guidance on) the 'substance and effect' of the term and 'all the circumstances existing at the time it was agreed'(Clause 14(1)(b), and 14(4)).

[3] UCTA, s. 11(1).

[4] See UTCCR, Regulation 5(1).

the broad assessment will take place under the 'fair and reasonable' test.[5] We know for sure that under these tests there is a review of the substantive features of the term and a review of matters of procedural fairness. This has been accepted by the House of Lords in UCTA case law.[6] As to the UTCCR, the preamble to the UTD refers to an 'overall evaluation of the different interests involved' and taking into account the interests of the consumer.[7] These interests are clearly both substantive and procedural and the idea of considering both substantive and procedural issues seems to have been accepted by the House of Lords.[8]

Indeed the proposed new test would make it even clearer that both substantive and procedural factors must be taken into account. It would refer explicitly to the 'substance and effect of the term'; 'transparency'; and the circumstances in existence at the time the contract was made.[9] The latter 'circumstances' include matters relating to the broader substantive interests of the parties and matters relating to choice and bargaining power.[10] Clear identification of these factors is, in itself, an important move forward; as is the fact that there would be guidelines on all of these matters[11] (to which guidelines we shall return below).

6.3 Criteria Related to the Substance of the Terms

6.3.1 Introduction

The first thing which we need to do is to try to unpack the various ways in which the law seems to look at substantive issues and how this will be developed under the proposed new regime. We have already dealt with the first element of the way in which the law approaches unfairness in substance (i.e. by targeting terms that deviate from default rules to the detriment of the consumer or provide for trader or consumer obligations that do not reflect the reasonable expectations of the consumer). So where do we go from here? A full review of substance would also surely look at the *extent* to which the term deviates from the default position or allows for compromise of reasonable expectations; and then at the *type* of consumer and trader interests that are affected (including the insurance context); and the broader substantive context (including, for example, the

---

5   See Law Commission Report No. 292, p. 41 and Draft Bill, Clause 4(1).
6   See *Smith* v. *Bush* [1990] 1 AC 831 and above at 4.61–2.
7   Recital 16.
8   See above at 5.5.4.2(3).
9   Law Commission Report, p. 42 and Draft Bill, Clause 14(1)(a) and (b).
10 *Ibid.*, Clause 14(4).
11 *Ibid.*, Clause 14(3) and (4).

way in which the other terms of the contract affect the interests of the parties).[12] Of course, this latter point as to the role of other terms (the issue of overall substantive fairness) is already a familiar theme that we have returned to on various occasions. We know that (for the ECJ) it is a relevant factor to the test of unfairness under the UTD/UTCCR. We know that for the House of Lords it is relevant, in particular, to the significant imbalance element. We do not know for sure whether, for either the ECJ or the House of Lords, overall substantive fairness will prevent there being a significant imbalance and therefore make issues arising under good faith (e.g. transparency) irrelevant. However, it certainly remains possible that questions as to overall substantive unfairness are relevant under the good faith element of the test (whether in addition to or instead of under the significant imbalance element). In addition, it is clear that if the new regime was in place such matters would fall to be considered under the general 'fair and reasonable' test. This is because the trigger for this test to apply is simply whether the term causes 'detriment' and this is clearly only concerned with the effect of the term itself, leaving questions of overall substantive fairness to be considered under the general fair and reasonable test.

6.3.2 The Extent of Deviation from Default Rules or Reasonable Expectations

We begin, then, by considering the *extent* to which the term in question actually does deviate from the default position or compromise the reasonable expectations of the consumer. Neither UCTA nor the UTCCR make any express reference to such a criterion. However, it is fairly easy to conclude that it must have been anticipated that it would be relevant. It also seems clear that the courts regard the issue as relevant. Under UCTA the question is whether it is fair and reasonable to include terms that exclude or restrict various liabilities or allow for a performance that compromises the reasonable expectations of the consumer. It must surely then be relevant to consider the *extent* of the exclusion or restriction or the *extent* of scope that there is for compromise of the reasonable expectations of the consumer.

This certainly seems to fit with good faith as it is often understood; with the general default positions of the law being thought of as fair and reflective of good faith.[13] It also fits with the reference made by the House of Lords to whether there has been a significant imbalance 'to an

---

12 See above at 2.4.3.3.
13 See above at 5.7.3.

extent' as to be contrary to good faith.[14] This seems to mean that the *extent* of the significant imbalance is relevant to good faith. Given that significant imbalance is caused when a term deviates from default rules to the detriment of the consumer or allows for compromise of reasonable consumer expectations, it seems clear that the extent of this deviation is the first question related to substance that is relevant to good faith. This also fits with the idea expressed in the preamble to the UTD that good faith involves respect for the legitimate interests of the other party.[15] The interests of a consumer are clearly increasingly compromised the more that the term departs from the general default position in ways that are favourable to the trader and detrimental to the consumer. The OFT recognize this approach. In particular in a guidance note from 2001 it is stated that,

> The OFT's starting position in assessing the fairness of a term is ... normally to ask what would be the position for the consumer if it did not appear in the contract. Where a term changes the normal position seen by the law as striking a fair balance it is regarded with suspicion.[16]

It seems clear, also, that the greater the deviation from the default position the more likely that the OFT will view the term as being unfair. So, terms that completely exclude a particular liability that would otherwise arise are generally viewed as unfair by the OFT.[17] Indeed, any significant restriction or limitation of liability is very often viewed as unfair by the OFT, e.g. limitation of the damages claimable so as not to cover consequential losses.[18] The extent to which a limitation is acceptable also appears to depend upon whether the effect is to allow the trader to escape liability in cases where there is an element of fault. So, limitation of liability for delays seems generally to be viewed as unfair if the limitation applies in circumstances that were within the control of the trader.[19] This reflects a general 'anti-fault' policy that appears to be applied by the OFT under the UTCCR[20] and by the courts under UCTA[21] Case law from

---

14 *First National Bank* case, [2001] 3 WLR 1297, Lord Bingham at 1307.

15 Preamble, Recital 16.

16 Office of Fair Trading, Unfair Contract Term Guidance, 2001, (Introduction), p. 2.

17 Office of Fair Trading, Unfair Contract Terms Guidance, 2001, para. 1.3 and para. 2.2.2.

18 *Ibid.*, paras 2.3.1 and 2.3.3.

19 *Ibid.*, paras 2.6.5.

20 See below at 6.3.8.

21 See *George Mitchell* v. *Finney Lockseeds* [1983] 2 All ER 737, Lord Bridge at 744; *Smith* v. *Bush* [1990] 1 AC 831, Lord Griffiths, at 831; and see Collins, Law of Contract, 4th edn, 2004, 259–260, and see below at 6.3.8.

other countries also indicates a tendency to find terms unfair where the effect is to exclude or limit liability for fault.[22]

The Law Commission would refer expressly to deviation from default rules. In determining fairness under the new regime it is proposed that we should have regard to: 'The extent to which the term (whether alone or with others) differs from what would have been the case in its absence.'[23]

As obvious as it may seem that this factor should be relevant it must be an improvement to indicate its relevance expressly in the statute.

There is also support for the idea that the assessment of good faith must involve consideration of the extent to which the term compromises the reasonable expectations of the parties. Indeed, in general jurisprudence (and in particular in the jurisprudence of EC consumer law) objective good faith and reasonable consumer expectations can be viewed as being closely related and interdependent; good faith by the trader requiring respect for the reasonable expectations of the consumer.[24] The Court of Appeal made this connection explicit. It was said that: 'A term to which the consumer's attention is not specifically drawn but which might operate in a way which the consumer might not reasonably expect and to his disadvantage could offend the requirement of good faith.'[25]

The House of Lords also made reference to expectations. As we saw Lord Millett discussed whether a consumer would expect to have to pay all of the agreed interest on the loan. His view was that this would be expected.[26] This, of course, was a different view from that of the Court of Appeal, which had decided that consumers would not reasonably expect to pay a sum in addition to that set out in the judgement debt.[27] However, this difference of approach is not the concern here. The point simply, is that there is support from both the Court of Appeal and the House of Lords for the idea that reasonable expectations are a relevant factor. So under the auspices of the good faith question it seems right to ask just how much scope the term gives for compromise of the reasonable expectations of the consumer. This seems to be supported also by the approach of the OFT. They appear inclined very much to view as unfair those terms giving the trader a broad discretion to determine or change his own obligations or those of the consumer, i.e. those terms allowing for

---

22 See for example, cases reported in the CLAB database from Portugal (000001, 000002, 000067 and 000068) and from France (000524).

23 Draft Bill, Clause 14(4)(g).

24 See G Howells and T. Wilhelmsson, European Consumer Law, Ashgate, 1999, 99.

25 [2000] QB 672 at 687.

26 See above at 5.5.4.2(iv)(a).

27 See above at 5.5.3.

compromise of the reasonable expectations of the consumer.[28] Such terms are less likely to be viewed as unfair where they are limited in scope, e.g. by the right to vary only being exercisable for clearly stipulated reasons; or where the consumer has a right to respond to the variation by cancelling the contract.[29] Neither UCTA nor the UTCCR currently mention as relevant the extent to which the term allows for compromise of the reasonable expectations of the consumer. The Law Commissions make no mention of this factor as something that should be spelt out in the legislation; but it would surely be a good idea to do so.

Indeed, the good faith concept may be particularly sensitive to the idea of reasonable expectations. Putting this in another way, it may be that a term allowing for compromise of the reasonable expectations of the consumer is especially likely to violate good faith. There is a contrast here with default rules. These arise as a matter of law and not on the basis of any positive action on the part of the trader. However, reasonable expectations have often been raised consciously by the trader by advertising and/or basic presentation of the goods/services.[30] From these sources comes the suggestion that a certain type of performance is expected from the trader and/or the consumer; while a formal term allows for some variation by the trader to his advantage. It can be argued that there is an element of moral blameworthiness in sending very positive signals to consumers and raising certain expectations while at the same time using a term allowing for compromise of these expectations. The focus on moral blameworthiness may accord with German conceptions of good faith which concentrate on 'good morals'.[31]

It seems clear even from the above brief discussion that the OFT jurisprudence at least does not simply target the more extreme forms of unfairness in substance. There is no suggestion of any need for an extreme deviation from the default position or for a term to allow for extreme compromise of reasonable expectations. Any such requirement would of course seriously undermine the agenda of the UTD to generate consumer confidence and provide a high level of protection. Indeed, as we have seen, the OFT will often regard a term as being unfair where it does not fully reflect the default position.

But what of the idea that deviation from the default position – perhaps even quite an extreme deviation – is acceptable as long as such a term is

---

28　OFT, Unfair Contract Terms Guidance, 2001, 311 (Analysis of Unfair Terms in Schedule 2), at paras 10.1, 11.1, 12.1.

29　*Ibid.*, at paras 10.3, 11.5, 11.6 and 12.4.

30　See the discussion above at 4.4.4 of 'encouraged expectations'.

31　See BGB Article 138 and U. Reifner, Good Faith: Interpretation or Limitation of Contracts, in Brownsword, Hird and Howells, Good Faith in Contract: Concept and Context, 271 at pp. 277–286.

normal or common in the market in question? As we have already seen,[32] such an approach may be associated with a particular vision of overall substantive fairness – in gist the idea being that if a term is normal for the market and the price is also normal this suggests that this is the fairest term/price balance that was economically viable and therefore this balance can be regarded as substantively fair. However, it has been argued that the problem with this approach is that the typical market price is simply *assumed* to be the best price that could be offered taking into account the other terms used. The conclusion is not really based on any evidence as to what exactly is economically feasible for the trader. It has been argued that the trader should at least have to show positively that he would have had to charge a significantly higher price if it was not for the detrimental term. Certainly an approach based too closely on market norms would tend not to be very protective and would surely not be in keeping with the consumer confidence and high level of protection goals of the UTD. There is no evidence that the ECJ favour such an approach.[33]

Of course, it is true that a term may be very common because it is so obviously fair. However, it is equally true that terms may be very common, but still very disadvantageous to consumers. In particular we should bear in mind that in general the terms are likely to fairly intransparent to consumers and play a very limited role in determining their expectations.[34] So, it is not as if a term that is in common use can be said necessarily to reflect the reasonable expectations of consumers (these expectations being more likely to be based on other factors such as the basic nature of the goods or services, the way in which they have been advertised and presented and what typically happens when such goods or services are supplied).[35] In addition (to reiterate), it would hardly generate consumer confidence or amount to a high level of protection to treat terms as fair simply on the grounds that they are normal in the market (especially if they are not only detrimental in a general sense, but do not reflect reasonable consumer expectations).

Of course, if a term is actually harsher than is normal, then this should obviously count against the term (and perhaps this should be in the guidance). A key aspect of good faith (and a factor consistently recognized by the OFT[36]) is that a term should do no more than protect the legitimate interests of the trader. However, in the case of a term that is harsher than is normal in the sector in question there must be a suspicion

---

32   See above at 2.4.3.3 and see below at 6.3.6 where the question of overall substantive fairness is considered further.
33   See above at 3.5.4.
34   See above at 4.4.3–5.
35   See above at 4.4.3.
36   OFT Guidance on Unfair Standard Terms, 2000, at 3.

that the trader is going further than is required (or at least than is thought necessary by other traders) to protect his legitimate interests. In addition, even although formal terms may play little role in determining the reasonable expectations of consumers, it is arguable that consumers reasonably expect traders at the very least to match up to industry norms of fairness. So, to the extent that reasonable expectations are important to fairness and good faith, it must again be arguable that a term not even matching up to industry norms is particularly likely to unfair. (It stands to reason, also, that any other approach undermines consumer confidence and aspirations to a high level of protection.) Of course, if a term is harsher than normal it might be that this genuinely balanced out by a price that is significantly lower than normal (or by some other beneficial provision) so that it can be said that the consumer really has been paid a fair price for the harsh term.[37] But, this possibility apart the general point surely stands, i.e. that if a term is harsher than normal this is usually suggestive of unfairness.

In *First National Bank*, Lord Millett did make reference to whether the term was a standard one not only in non-negotiable consumer contracts but also freely negotiated commercial contracts.[38] To the extent that he seems to have been referring to whether it was normal for traders in general to use such a term (i.e. rather than simply whether it was a standard one for that trader) there is a suggestion that this normality might count in favour of the term. However, it seems that Lord Millett was actually addressing a slightly different question as to normality. His core concern was not so much whether it was normal to use such a term in consumer contracts (although it clearly was in this case) but whether the term was also a standard one (and I again assume he meant normal) in *freely negotiated commercial contracts*. So this is not really about saying that a term in a non-negotiated consumer contract is likely to be fair because it is normal. Indeed, he seems in a sense to accept implicitly that common use of such terms in such contracts does not mean that the term is fair, precisely because of the lack of negotiation. His point seems to be that if such a term is routinely accepted by lawyers negotiating commercial contracts as being fair then *this* suggests that the term is fair. This perspective has its own problems, but these relate to the way in which the test of fairness should conceive of the consumer interest, a matter to which we will turn below. The point for present is that his comments may not have been intended to indicate that a term is very likely to be fair simply because it is in common use in *consumer* contracts.

---

[37]   See above at 2.4.3.3 and below at 6.3.6.
[38]   [2001] 3 WLR 1279, 1318.

6.3.3 Types of Consumer Interests Affected

6.3.3.1 Introduction

It is clear then that the first question relates to the *extent* to which the term deviates from default rules or the extent to which it allows for compromise of reasonable expectations. However, the degree to which the term deviates from the default position or allows for compromise of the reasonable expectations of the consumer does not provide a full picture as to the impact of the term on the substantive interests of the consumer. Aside from the *degree* to which the term deviates from default rules or compromises the reasonable expectations of the consumer, a fairness-oriented approach must also surely be sensitive to the *type* of substantive consumer interests that are affected by the term in question; and the extent to which the term is detrimental to these interests.[39]

Neither the reasonableness test nor the good faith test, as laid down in the legislation, actually expressly articulate the idea that terms can affect different types of consumer interest and that it is relevant to consider the extent to which such interests are affected by the term in question. However, both tests are very open-textured and clearly allow for such an analysis; and such an analysis seems, in practice, to be undertaken in application of the tests. If it was not obvious that it was appropriate to do this under any test concerned with the fairness of terms, then there is also the fact that under the UCTA test the court is directed to the 'circumstances that were, or ought reasonably to have been, in the contemplation of the parties when the contract was made'.[40] When a trader makes a contract with a consumer he can clearly be expected to contemplate at least some of consumer interests that are affected by the way in which he performs the contract and therefore the losses that a consumer might suffer if he does not perform properly. It therefore follows that when he uses an exemption clause he can see the type and extent of loss that he is seeking to avoid liability for. This, then, must be relevant to the assessment of reasonableness. In actually applying the reasonableness test the House of Lords have put the matter slightly differently, but, it seems, with the same conclusion. It has been said that regard should be had to the 'practical consequences' of the decision.[41] This surely involves consideration of the type of consumer interest affected by the exclusion or restriction of liability. Indeed in *Smith* v. *Bush* (as we have seen) the size of the economic loss falling on the consumer as a result of having relied on the negligent valuation was

---

[39] See above at 2.4.3.3.
[40] UCTA, s. 11(1).
[41] See above at 4.6.2.1.

clearly a significant factor in deciding that clause excluding liability was unreasonable; and the argument that the consumers could have obtained alternative protection by obtaining an independent survey was rejected on the basis of the cost to the consumer of having to pay twice for the same advice.[42] In Woodman, the sentimental significance of wedding photos was a factor in deciding that it was unreasonable to allow exclusion of liability for their loss.[43]

Under the UTCCR there is also reference to the 'circumstances attending the conclusion of the contract'.[44] There is no mention, as under UCTA, of what the parties might 'contemplate' in these circumstances. It might therefore be said that this provision does not so obviously push for a consideration of (what the trader should have known as to) the types of consumer interests affected by the term. However, the UTCCR also say that regard should be had to the 'nature of the goods or services for which the contract was concluded'.[45] Consideration of the *nature* of the goods or services must surely include consideration of the types of losses that will be caused if there is a failure to perform properly; and therefore the effect of a term that seeks to exclude or restrict liability for failure to perform properly. More generally, the concepts of 'fairness' and 'good faith' in the UTCCR are clearly very open-textured, surely requiring consideration of the type of consumer interests affected by the term. In particular, also, the tests must be read in the light of the UTD. The preamble to the UTD says expressly that good faith requires that the trader have regard to the interests of the consumer and also that good faith involves an 'overall evaluation of the different interests involved'.[46] In *First National Bank* we saw that the House of Lords did recognise that where interest at the contractual rate continued to accrue after judgement consumers might quickly be saddled with large and unexpected debts. Equally, the view was that traders had a legitimate interest in using the term (indeed that they would not lend otherwise). There is, then, a recognition that the impact of using or not using the term on the interests of both parties needs to be taken into account. However, the House of Lords did not perhaps engage in the rigorous process of interest balancing called for. They did not ask whether the level of debt that might typically be built up and the way that this might affect the average consumer was outweighed by the losses that would be suffered by traders if they did not provide for interest after judgement. Indeed, they did not really produce any evidence for the view that trader interests would be seriously

---

42 See above at 4.6.2.1.
43 See above at 4.6.1.
44 Regulation 6(1).
45 *Ibid.*
46 Recital 16.

damaged by not being able to use the term (i.e. that they would not lend).[47] So we are left wondering as to whether this is indicative of a general approach to be expected by the House of Lords in relation to the good faith concept, i.e. one that is not especially sensitive to the size of the loss that might be caused to a consumer; or whether the approach in *First National Bank* does not indicate any broader policy.

The proposed new regime would focus on these issues via references to 'the substance and effect of the term'[48] (the reference to 'effect' clearly focusing attention on the types of losses that the term enables the trader to avoid liability for or the types of obligations and liabilities that the term imposes on the consumer); 'the balance of the parties' interests'[49] (including, obviously, the way in which the term affects the economic or other interests of the consumer, the extent to which the term or broader contract contains some countervailing benefit for the consumer and the trader interest in using the term); 'the risks to [the consumer]'[50] (e.g. a clause excluding or limiting liability will expose a consumer to differing degrees of risk depending on the types of losses that could flow from a breach in the circumstances and which cannot be recovered if the term is upheld); and as with UTCCR the 'nature of the goods or services'.[51]

We will now seek to identify a range of particular types of interest that appear to be recognized in current practice. Of course, the vast bulk of the evidence as to the current approach does not come from the courts but from the work of the OFT. This means that, to the extent that the OFT takes a fairly protective approach (as it appears to do), we cannot be entirely sure how stable this is, given the limited sensitivity to consumer interests shown by the House of Lords in *First National Bank*.

Clearly a huge variety of interests can be affected by terms excluding or restricting obligations and liabilities, adding to those of the consumer or allowing for compromise of the reasonable expectations of the consumer. A major aid in identifying these interests for the purposes of the UTCCR is the indicative list of unfair terms;[52] and this will hopefully become even more useful if any new regime includes the Law Commission proposal to reformulate the list to make it more accessible to UK readers and to provide more examples.[53] It should also provide a more dynamic representation of relevant interests in the future if the

---

[47]   See above at 5.5.4.2(iv)(c).
[48]   Draft Bill, Clause 14(1)(b).
[49]   *Ibid.*, 14(4)(c).
[50]   *Ibid.*, 14(4)(d).
[51]   *Ibid.*, 14(4)(j).
[52]   Regulation 5(6) and Schedule 2.
[53]   Report, 3.117–3.123.

proposal is taken up to allow the list to be updated by ministerial order so as to add appropriate terms to it.[54]

6.3.3.2 Specific Consumer Interests

(i) Terms Excluding or Limiting Liability

Let us begin with terms excluding or restricting the obligations and liabilities of the trader to the consumer and the consumer interests that can be affected by such terms. Sometimes the indicative list is quite specific as to the types of exclusions with which it is concerned and this section draws strongly on the list and the way it is approached by the OFT.

(a) Restricting Access to Justice There are various ways in which terms may hinder consumer access to justice. One particular example is a term excluding or limiting the right of a consumer to offset a debt owed to the seller or supplier against any claim the consumer may have against the seller or supplier.[55] The right to set off is clearly important as a practical self-help remedy in the face of superior trader bargaining power in the context of a dispute. In addition, the OFT have emphasized that if a term excludes the right to set off (or subjects the consumer to a penalty of some kind if such a right is exercised[56]) consumers will believe that they have no choice but to pay the sum demanded. Their only option then is to take court action to seek to recover it; and the costs, delays and uncertainties of such action may deter them from doing this, so that they are then deprived of their rights.[57] It might also be added that, quite apart from being deterred from going to court, there is surely a legitimate consumer interest in not being forced into doing so. Why should the consumer be forced in to the inconvenience and stress of a court action?

A further point is that, if the contract is one in which there is a right to reject goods when there has been a breach, then this may to some extent mitigate the effects of there being no right of set-off. This is because, if the goods have been handed back, then the seller might be more inclined to return the price paid by the consumer. This means that

---

[54]   *Ibid.*, 3.110–3.112.

[55]   Schedule 2, para. 1(b).

[56]   Unfair Contract Terms Guidance, 2001, para. 2.5.6.

[57]   *Ibid.*, 2.5.2; so terms effectively excluding a right of set off by, for example, demanding full payment on completion of work have been revised to provide for full payment on 'satisfactory completion' (OFT Bulletin 3 at 60 and OFT Bulletin 4 at 72).

the right to set-off is of particular importance where there is no such right to reject[58] (e.g. where the contract is for a pure service). However, even where there is a right to reject goods, the right of set-off is usually still very important. First of all, the consumer may legitimately wish to exercise remedies other than the right to reject. So, for example, it may be too much trouble to go back to square one (as it were) and have to make a fresh purchase. The consumer may prefer to have price reduction or to have the goods repaired by a third party and recover the cost from the seller. If this is the case, and the consumer does not return the goods, the seller may refuse to grant a price reduction and proceed to demand full payment. Exclusion of the right to set-off will mean that the consumer cannot reduce what he pays back to take account of the defects[59] or the cost of repair or indeed to reflect other losses that he has suffered. Secondly, even if the consumer wishes to reject the goods, the seller may refuse to take back the goods and if the consumer has not yet paid for them he may demand payment; so that, if there is no right to set-off, then the consumer cannot deduct an amount from what he gives back to take account of the defects, repair costs or other losses.

Exclusion of the right to set-off can be achieved indirectly by providing for all or most of the payment to be made at an early stage, i.e. before the consumer has a chance to assess whether the trader is in breach. There are also other ways in which provision for early payment can compromise consumer interests. However, as (technically) terms making such provision deal with *imposition* of obligations on the consumer (rather than exclusion of the rights of the consumer), we shall deal with such terms below.

Thus far we have been focusing on the attitude to the right to set-off under the UTCCR. However, it is clear that UCTA also shows sensitivity to the problems caused by terms that make practical enforcement of rights more difficult. Section 13(1) (the provision determining which terms count as exclusions or restrictions that are covered by the Act) covers terms making a liability or its enforcement subject to restrictive or onerous conditions; excluding or restricting a right or remedy; subjecting a person to any prejudice in consequence of pursuing a remedy; or excluding or restricting rules of evidence or procedure. This has been held to cover terms excluding a right of set-off.[60] The effect of this is that such terms are generally subject to the reasonableness test. However,

---

58   *Ibid.*, 2.5.4.

59   *Ibid.*, 2.5.5.

60   *Stewart Gill* v. *Horatio Meyer Ltd* [1992] QB 600; of course, s. 13 clearly extends beyond terms excluding set-off rights and covers a much broader range of ways in which terms might place obstacles in the way of consumers enforcing their rights – see further below.

where the exclusion affects any remedy that would otherwise arise under the implied terms as to description, quality or fitness the exclusion would be wholly ineffective under UCTA;[61] and under the proposed new regime which would continue to apply this outright ban.[62] So, there would be no scope at all under UCTA to argue that the right to reject arising for breach of these implied terms should mean that the exclusion of the right of set off is more acceptable (see the discussion above). Any exclusion of the right of set-off affecting the right to claim damages or price reduction for breach of these implied terms will be wholly ineffective.

The UTCCR also specifically recognizes other ways in which consumer access to justice may be hindered. So, the indicative list refers to a term excluding or hindering the consumer's right to take legal action or exercise any other legal remedy.[63] The paragraph then goes on to refer to terms requiring consumers to go exclusively to arbitration not covered by legal provisions.[64] The idea here is that this may compromise the consumer interest in not being dragged though a process which may or may not be as protective of his interests as the courts. Such terms are not covered by UCTA but where the sum in question is less than £5,000 they are wholly ineffective under s. 91 of the Arbitration Act 1996.

There is also reference on the indicative list to terms restricting the evidence available to the consumer or imposing a burden of proof that would otherwise not apply.[65] The problem here, of course, is twofold. First, if the case actually gets to court the consumer cannot rely on the sort of evidence that would normally be available to establish his claim. However, much more significant in practice is the ability such a term gives to the trader to 'fob-off' a consumer and discourage them taking further action. This might be done by reference, for example, to a term that provides that refunds will not be given or other remedies will not be

---

[61] Sections 6(2) and 7(2).

[62] See above at 4.3.2.

[63] See the indicative list, para. 1(q). As we have seen, s. 13(1) of UCTA refers to excluding or restricting a right or remedy as being something that counts as 'excluding or restricting liability' for the purposes of the legislation and this would continue in the proposed new legislation (Draft Bill, Clause 30(1)(b)). See also, the Law Commissions proposed slight amendment to the proposed new indicative list, which would also refer to terms excluding or restricting the consumer's right to *defend* any action (Report No. 292, p. 190, example 20(a)).

[64] Paragraph 1(q).

[65] *Ibid*; as we have seen, such terms are currently also identified as being covered by the UCTA definition of 'excluding or restricting liability' (s. 13(1)(c)) and this would continue to be the case in the proposed new regime (Draft Bill, Clause 30(1)(d)); and the proposal is that the indicative list would refer to a term restricting the evidence on which the consumer can rely (term 21, p. 190).

available unless the original receipt or invoice is produced as proof of purchase.[66] This may well succeed in putting off many consumers who will, as a result, give up pursuing their rights.[67] So, for example, the OFT has viewed as unfair a term providing that only documents issued by the trader would be accepted as evidence of the existence of the contract.[68]

The list (by contrast with UCTA, s. 13(1)) does not currently refer to terms making a liability or its enforcement subject to restrictive or onerous conditions or subjecting a person to any prejudice in consequence of pursuing a remedy, although such terms are clearly covered as the list applies to terms having the 'object or effect' of excluding or limiting liability. It is clear that this is the object of such terms and will certainly often be their practical effect. Consumers will often be put off by the need to fulfil conditions (e.g. making a claim within a very short time period) or the suggestion that his failure to do so means that he has no rights; and they will also often be put off by terms threatening some negative consequence if further action is taken (e.g. a term providing for loss of a deposit if the consumer pursues a remedy). As we have seen, such terms are expressly classed as terms 'excluding or limiting liability' under UCTA and this would continue in the proposed new regime.[69]

(b) Limiting the Seller's Responsibility for Statements from his Agent[70]
The issue here in terms of protection of the consumer interest is that consumers are likely to place a reasonable degree of reliance on such

---

[66] See proposed example 21, p. 191.

[67] Very closely associated (and possibly covered also by UCTA, s. 13(1)(c)) are terms (described on the indicative list) allowing the trader to decide whether goods or services are in conformity or to interpret any term of the contract (para. 1(m)). Clearly the consumer is entitled to an objective assessment as to matters such as these that affect his rights. In a new regime the Law Commissions would give an example of a term providing that a suppliers decision is final on the question as to whether services have been provided properly; and that it is for the supplier to determine the appropriate extent of any deduction in refund to make to take account of the use that a consumer has had from goods (p. 191, heading 15 examples).

[68] See OFT Bulletin 3 at 79 (David Cover & Son Ltd) and at p. 78 (Town and Country Driveways plc.).

[69] UCTA, s. 13(1)(b) and s. 13(1)(c); and see Draft Bill, Clause 30(1)(a) and Clause 30 (1)(c).

[70] See indicative list, para. 1(n); and see the examples given by the Law Commission whereby a an agent or employee is deemed to have no authority to make a promise or statement or any such promise or statement is not binding unless authorized in writing by Head Office (Law Commission Report, p. 191, example 16).

statements. They should not be able to be misled with impunity;[71] and the consumer should be able to claim for the losses caused by buying goods and services that do not do what was promised. It is, of course, of particular significance that the UTCCR pay special attention to this issue. As we saw above, in one UCTA case a term denying that an agent had authority to bind the trader to statements was held not to be covered by UCTA.[72] There is also some uncertainty as to whether UCTA covers entire agreement clauses denying reliance on a pre-contractual statement (for the purpose of misrepresentation).[73] However, it is clear that (for the OFT at least) such terms will often cause significant imbalance[74] and will often also violate good faith and be unfair.[75]

(c) Non Return of Consumer Payments when the Trader Does Not Perform Paragraph 1(f) of the indicative list refers to a term permitting the seller or supplier to retain the sums paid for services not yet supplied by him where it is the seller or supplier himself who dissolves the contract. This issue may overlap with others. First, to the extent that we are talking here of a right to cancel the contract at the trader's discretion, part of the problem is the scope of the discretion (and this is discussed below at 6.3.5.2 in the context of a discussion of services of general interest). However, we are not concerned here as such with the way in which a right to cancel affects a consumer and whether and when the trader should be allowed to cancel. The key issue here is simply the right to retain sums paid by the consumer when the contract *is* cancelled. There is an obvious consumer interest in not paying for something that has not been received and, whatever justifications there may be for a trader right to cancel at his discretion, and whatever is required in the way of specification of grounds for cancellation, the consumer interest in not paying for something that has not been received is surely wholly undiminished. Secondly, a completely separate possibility is that the right to dissolve or cancel is in response to *consumer* breach, in which case the issue is one as to the liability which it is legitimate to impose on the consumer for breach of an executory contract. This is probably not the situation contemplated by para. 1(f) and will be dealt with further below[76] when discussing para. 1(d) (which is probably the one focused

---

71 OFT Guidance, 2001, 14.1.1.

72 See above at 4.2.4.

73 See above at 4.2.4.

74 See above at 5.7.4.1 and 5.7.6.2.

75 OFT Guidance, 2001, para. 14, and note that the Outer House of the Court of Session in Scotland has recently held that a form of entire agreement clause was unfair – Office of Fair Trading v. MB Designs (Scotland) Ltd, 2005, SLT 691.

76 See below at 6.3.6.2.

on cases where it is the consumer who is in breach). It suffices to say for now that in a situation in which the trader right to dissolve arises from *consumer* breach, even although the supplier has not supplied any service there may still be some legitimate interest in retaining sums as compensation for expenses, although possibly no more than this. However, if we assume that we are currently simply dealing with a case in which the seller is exercising a right to cancel which is unconnected with anything the consumer has done, and provides for retention of a sum for services not supplied, then the issue is more straightforward. The problem is simply that there is an obvious consumer interest in not paying for something that has not been received; and this interest is not in any way diminished as the consumer is not in any way responsible for the cancellation issue arising.

Paragraph 1(f) suggests that under the UTCCR the right to keep a sum that the consumer has paid when no goods or services have been provided will, in itself, strongly suggest that the term is unfair. This is obvious from the inclusion of such a term on the indicative list. The common law may be able to achieve the same effect on the basis that there has been a total failure of consideration. Such a term would often probably be caught by UCTA. If the term provides that the trader can retain the sum even when he is in breach this appears to be exclusion of liability under s. 3 which refers to exclusion or restriction of 'any liability of his in respect of the breach'. The trader would often be liable to return the sum in question if he does not perform, so that a term providing the will not do so is apparently caught by this provision. Alternatively, if the trader simply provides that he can cancel at his discretion without being in breach then this is normally covered by s. 3(2)(b) (whether as offering a contractual performance substantially different from that reasonably expected or no performance at all).

(d) Unilateral Variation of Terms Paragraph 1(j) refers to a term enabling the seller or supplier to alter the terms of the contract unilaterally without a valid reason which is specified in the contract.[77] There is an obvious interest in the consumer receiving the performance originally agreed and therefore reasonably expected. In particular, problems arise with terms allowing sellers to vary delivery dates, the consumer having an obvious interest in receiving goods when expected (the issue not only being that the goods may be needed, but also that special arrangements may need to

---

[77] Such terms clearly fit the reasonable expectations analysis. See above at 5.7.6 for discussion of the general idea under the UTCCR. The term described in para. 1(j) is also clearly targeted by the UCTA provision dealing with terms allowing for a contractual performance substantially different from that reasonably expected (s. 3(2)(b)(i)); and more generally on this see above at 4.4.

be made to take delivery, e.g. staying at home between certain hours on the promised delivery date). There is also an obvious consumer interest in knowing exactly in what circumstances the delivery might be delayed, in the language of para. 1(j) having any 'valid' reason 'specified in the contract'.

We saw above that the OFT is particularly likely to view as unfair a term allowing for delivery delays or excluding liability for them where the term covers situations in which the seller is at fault.[78] The OFT have emphasized that seller fault includes shortage of stock, labour problems, machinery problems etc.[79] (in the language of para. 1(j) these are not regarded as 'valid reasons'). In other words, the consumer is viewed as having an interest in receiving goods when promised in all cases; other than where the delay is wholly outside the control of the seller. The OFT also take the view that such terms should perhaps provide that in cases of substantial delay the consumer has a right to cancel the contract.[80] This is presumably based on the view that there is a limit to the time with which the consumer should go without use of the goods and suffer the inconvenience of both this and the making of arrangements to receive delivery. Interestingly, the general OFT guidance on terms dealing with delivery delays says nothing of the reasons being specified in the contract and this is clearly important. Interestingly, also, there is no mention of any further requirement to the effect that any term should require the seller to inform the consumer when it is clear a delay will in fact take place and explain which of the reasons provided for under the contract applies. The OFT do, in fact, consider that terms should provide for such notification where a trader is actually exercising a right to *cancel*.[81] However, given what has been noted already as to the need to make special arrangements to receive delivery, it is surely arguable that the consumer has a legitimate interest in being given such notice where delivery is going to be *delayed*.

The Law Commission proposal is that the following example be included in the Explanatory Notes to the proposed new regime:

> A term giving a business an unqualified right to alter the date by which it is to deliver goods rather than (a) limiting the right, for instance, to cases in which the delay is caused by reasons outside its control and (b) stating in the contract the circumstances in which it can defer delivery.[82]

---

78 See above at 6.3.2.
79 OFT Guidance, 2001, at 2.6.5.
80 *Ibid.*, at 2.6.6.
81 *Ibid.*, at 11.6.
82 Law Commission Report, p. 191, example 11.

We can see, then, that there is the same idea as the OFT; to the effect that there should always be liability where the reason is within the control of the seller. The Law Commission also emphasizes that there should be specification of the precise circumstances that are outside his control and which he seeks to excuse himself from liability for. This emphasizes the other aspect of para. 1(j), i.e. that valid reasons should be specified in the contract. However, there is no mention by the Law Commission of either a consumer right to cancel or an obligation to inform the consumer (at the time) as to the delay and the reasons for it. It would arguably be beneficial if mention was made of these important aspects of the consumer interest.

(e) Unilateral Variation of Product and Service Characteristics   The indicative list refers to terms enabling the seller or supplier to alter unilaterally without a valid reason any characteristics of the product or service to be provided.[83] Similarly to above, there is an obvious interest in the consumer receiving the performance originally agreed and therefore reasonably expected. In particular, consumers have an obvious interest in receiving the *type* of goods expected. There is also an obvious consumer interest in knowing exactly in what circumstances the there might be changes. Interestingly, para. 1(k) (the relevant provision on the list) does not refer to such reasons being 'specified in the contract'. The OFT certainly take the view that a 'valid reason' must be something beyond the trader's control. One term was revised to restrict the right to supply a different item to cases where the reason was 'beyond the company's control'.[84] However, in their general guidance, they suggest that there must be a greater degree of specification.[85] This recognizes that consumers have a legitimate interest in knowing of the reasons that there might be for a change, so as to be in some way prepared for it; and a separate interest in not accepting something different from what they were originally promised.

The revisal of this same term also involved specifying that the change could only take place where the consumer agreed. Presumably, by implication, if the consumer does not agree, then he can cancel the contract. However, it is surely better to require that such a cancellation right be specified. For the new regime, the Law Commission would exemplify as unfair a term allowing for a change of colour to a car; unless the right to change is restricted to cases in which the original colour is no

---

[83]   Paragraph 1(k).
[84]   See OFT Bulletin 1 (Moben Kitchens), at 25.
[85]   OFT Guidance 2001, paras 11.5 and 11.6.

longer obtainable *and* the consumer is given the right to cancel without charge.[86]

The right to cancel seems to be vital as otherwise the term is likely to be wholly ineffective in any case under UCTA (and the proposed new regime) in cases where goods are concerned and the term provides for a change to characteristics that go to the essential identity of the goods – such a right (without a consumer right to cancel) would be a (wholly ineffective) restriction on the implied term as to description and the rejection remedy available for breach of it.[87] Where the change allowed for is to other characteristics of the goods or to characteristics of a service, the term is, of course, subject to the general unfairness test under the UTCCR. It is currently also caught by UCTA, s. 3(2)(b)(i)[88] and subject to the UCTA test of reasonableness. The lack of a right to cancel makes it more likely to fail these tests.

(f) Transfer of Rights Paragraph 1(p) on the list describes a term allowing the seller to transfer his rights under the contract where this may reduce the guarantees for the consumer without his agreement'. There seem to be several consumer interests at stake here. There is an interest in having the same rights as originally agreed; an interest in having a clear idea as to who these can be enforced against; and an interest in being able to veto any proposed change. Paragraph 1(p) suggests that assignation terms may be regarded as acceptable (even where the consumer's rights may be reduced) as long as the consumer consents. The Law Commission proposal seems to be to follow this approach. Under the Law Commission proposal, the description of the term on the list would refer only to the need for consent.[89] However, the example provided is in fact one in which the consumers rights are reduced,[90] so the implication may be that where the term allows for a reduction in rights this may be acceptable as long as it provides that the consumer must consent. In fact, the OFT take the view that where services and payments are of a continuous nature (as with a club or bank account), a more practical approach may be to say that an assignment provision is only fair if the consumer has a right to cancel in response to its exercise.[91] Indeed the OFT also suggest a more protective approach to the effect that assignment terms should *never* be

---

[86] Law Commission, p. 191, example 12.

[87] Ineffective under ss 6(2) and 7(2) of UCTA, which will be replicated in the new regime.

[88] By allowing for a contractual performance substantially different from that reasonably expected – see above at 4.4.

[89] Law Commission Report, example 18, p. 190.

[90] *Ibid.*, example 18, p. 191.

[91] OFT Guidance, 2001, para. 16.2.

fair where they reduce the rights of the consumer.[92] There appears to be a decent case for this approach or at least for saying that there must be a right to cancel *and* to be compensated for any inconvenience caused by the need to cancel and find an alternative supplier.[93]

(g) More General Exclusion and Restriction   In other cases the list is more general. So, for example, para. 1(b) refers to terms excluding or limiting the legal rights of the consumer vis-a-vis the seller or supplier or another party in the event of total or partial non-performance or inadequate performance of any of the contractual obligations. The agenda obviously is to catch cases in which the term takes away consumer rights and remedies that would otherwise arise for breach of contract. The OFT has shown a particular concern with the general notion of consumers not getting what they were promised[94] or that the law intended.[95] However, this is at a very general level. So the issue may be that goods or services are not provided, are delivered late, are of poor quality etc; and the term in question seeks to exclude or restrict the obligations relating to these matters and/or to exclude or restrict the remedies normally available when there is a breach of such obligations. However, in order to know what the consumer 'loses' in these contexts (or putting this in another way, what consumer interests are affected) we will need to look to the subject matter of the contract.

Non-performance or defective performance of a contract may affect a range of different consumer interests. So, for example, a failure to properly repair a washing machine (or the supply of a defective washing machine) will mean that the consumer suffers a pure economic loss in the sense that he has received a performance that is worth less than what he paid. However, the failure to repair it properly (or its defective state when sold) may also result in the washing machine flooding the consumer's kitchen, thereby causing property damage. It might be wrongly wired such that it is dangerous and causes injury. In addition, a range of other problems may result: the hassle and inconvenience of being without a washing machine, the cost of hiring or buying a replacement, the time spent in trying to resolve the dispute, money spent in trying to resolve it (whether on legal advice or on 'often premium rate' phone calls to the company).

---

[92]   *Ibid.*

[93]   Terms allowing for assignment may be covered by UCTA in allowing the trader to offer a contractual performance substantially different from that that reasonably expected or no performance at all (see s. 3(2)(b)). However, this is unclear and in any case there is no case law illustrating the approach of the courts to such terms.

[94]   OFT Guidance, 2001, at para. 1.2.

[95]   *Ibid.*, at para. 1.3.

The exemption clause in question may actually identify the losses for which liability is limited or excluded. Alternatively there may be a broad clause simply excluding or limiting liability for all losses. In this instance we will need to consider what losses might be caused in order to work out what types of loss the trader seeks to avoid liability for. In either case (having identified the *type* of loss that the clause seeks to avoid liability for) we must then work out what the extent of the liability for this loss would be in the absence of the clause. It is then possible to see the extent to which the clause affects different types of interest be they economic, property or otherwise.

As we have already seen, any significant restriction or limitation of liability is very often viewed as unfair by the OFT.[96] This obviously includes the basic difference in value between what was contracted for and what was actually received, so that the right to a refund or appropriate price reduction should generally not be excluded. However, it also includes limitation of the damages claimable so as not to cover consequential losses[97] (in other words it will normally be regarded as appropriate that consumers should be able to obtain full recovery for the types of loss summarized above as long as they are foreseeable).

(ii) Terms Imposing Obligations or Liabilities on the Consumer

We now turn to terms allowing the trader to *impose* obligations and liabilities on the consumer. These terms may also affect a range of consumer interests.

(a) Terms Requiring Full Prepayment One example is provided by terms requiring full prepayment by the consumer. Such terms are not exemplified on the indicative list. However, they will often cause significant imbalance on the basis that they deviate from the default position (the default position in relation to goods at least being that there is no obligation to pay until delivery of the goods[98]). Thinking more broadly about the way such terms affect consumer interests, it seems they can affect the consumer in several ways. First, there is the basic point that the consumer has to make early arrangements to make money available, perhaps by obtaining finance or at least using available money for this rather than something else. Secondly, there is the potential impact on the ability to self-protect by set-off when goods or services are discovered to be defective or are not delivered. We saw above[99] that, without a right of

---

96 See above at 6.3.2.
97 See 2.3.6.
98 Sale of Goods Act, s. 27.
99 See above at 6.3.3.2(i)(a).

set off, the consumer may be deterred from taking court action to assert his rights. Clearly if there has been full prepayment there is, in practice, no right of set-off.[100] Finally, receipt of full payment in advance may remove an incentive to do the work properly.[101] The OFT have tended to encourage the use of terms that balance the interests of the parties by allowing for staged payments with a substantial sum not being payable until the contract is concluded and the consumer is in a position to assess whether the there has been proper performance.[102] Of course, we saw earlier that another possible way of redressing the balance (and one that appears to have some approval by the ECJ) is by requiring the trader to deliver (at the time when the advance payment is made) some form of security guaranteeing the completion and quality of the work.[103]

(b) Price Variation Clauses Then, there are price variation clauses where the obvious problem (and arguably the initial basis of the significant imbalance) is that the consumer will end up paying more than he initially expected.[104] Paragraph 1(l) describes a term enabling the trader to increase the price to an amount that is too high in relation to the initially agreed price without giving the consumer a corresponding right to cancel the contract. This catches purely discretionary rises (obviously the most unacceptable means of compromising the expectations of the consumer and imposing a higher price). However, unlike in the case of some of the other variation terms discussed above, there is no allowance here for 'valid reasons', e.g. that there can be increases for reasons that are outside the control of the trader such as his supplier increasing prices. The OFT cite two reasons for this. First, the trader is in a better position to control factors such as increased costs imposed by his supplier.[105] Secondly, consumers have no real way of knowing whether increases actually reflect increased costs faced by the trader.[106] Of course, these points could be made in relation to other changes. However, there is arguably still a difference in that a price increase will always, by its nature, prejudice the consumer, while many consumers may often be indifferent to other changes.

Provision for an increase will, however, normally be fair where the term is a 'price indexation' clause,[107] i.e. one linking the price to a

---

[100] OFT Bulletin 3, at 2.14.

[101] *Ibid.*

[102] OFT Bulletin 5, at 12.

[103] See the *Freiburger* case above at 3.5.4.

[104] See the analysis at 5.7.6.1 above.

[105] OFT Guidance 2001, at 12.3.

[106] *Ibid.*

[107] See para. 2(d) on the list.

published price index such as the Retail Price Index.[108] This is because the potential increase is readily identifiable and applicable to all consumers. Even where this is not the case, para. 1(l) (as we have already seen) expressly contemplates that an increase may be acceptable where the consumer can respond by cancelling the contract. This is obviously because the consumer need not then be prejudiced by the increase. However, the OFT rightly acknowledge that consumers may still be prejudiced if, as a result of cancellation, they suffer financial loss (such as forfeiture of a deposit[109]), serious inconvenience or any other adverse consequences.[110] So, it is arguable that a cancellation right should only be able to justify a term providing for an increase where there is also provision for the trader to compensate the consumer for such losses.

Of course, a final point is that para. 1(l) only contemplates that the right to cancel should be operative where the final price is 'too high' in relation to the price initially agreed. So, the extent of the actual increase may become an issue in individual litigation. However, the Law Commission seem to suggest that this would no longer be an issue in any new legislation. Their reworked list would simply refer to a right to cancel 'if the business increases the price' (saying nothing of the extent of the increase).[111] Equally, their example simply refers to a right to cancel when the price is 'higher than that stated in the contract or quoted to the consumer'.[112]

(c) Automatic Contract Extensions Then there are terms 'automatically extending a contract of fixed duration where the consumer does not indicate otherwise, when the deadline fixed for the consumer to express his desire not to extend the contract is unreasonably early' (as exemplified on para. 1(h) of the indicative list). Here the problem is that (if the consumer even realizes the provision is in the contract) because the time for notification is so early, the consumer may forget that he needs to act and consequently he may end up being committed to the contract (and to pay the price due under the contract) for longer than he expected or wanted.[113] In addition, the need for an early decision may mean that he has not had a proper opportunity to assess his future needs.[114] Periods of more than a month prior to the end of the initially agreed term appear, often, to be viewed as unfair. So, for example, three month 'notice to

---

[108] OFT Guidance 2001, at 12.4.
[109] Or, one might add, a financial layout necessary under the contract.
[110] OFT Guidance, 2001, 12.4.
[111] Draft Bill Schedule 2, part 2, list term 13.
[112] Example 13, p. 191.
[113] See the analysis at 5.7.6.1 above.
[114] OFT Guidance, 2001, 8.3.

terminate' periods have been viewed as too long by the OFT in internet and mobile phone contracts.[115]

(d) Unreasonable Charges for Consumer Default   Then we turn to terms imposing liabilities for breach that exceed the real losses of the trader; or, in response to consumer actions that are not technically breaches, imposing (via primary obligations) charges and costs that are not reasonably expected in the circumstances. We have already seen that both such types of term are likely to cause significant imbalance under the UTCCR.[116] The former type of term is mentioned expressly on the indicative list (requiring a consumer who fails to fulfil his obligation to pay a disproportionately high sum in compensation[117]); and large numbers of such terms are dealt with by the OFT.[118]

The latter types of term are those 'disguised penalty' provisions that allow the trader to obtain some form of extra payment from the consumer based on an action or omission of some type by the consumer. This action or omission is not defined as a breach and the extra payment is technically owed under a primary obligation rather than as damages for breach. However, the amount payable exceeds the real losses of the trader and does not represent what the consumer would reasonably expect to pay in the due performance of the contract. So, there might be a term requiring a consumer in a hire purchase contract to make a minimum payment where he exercises an option to surrender goods. This minimum payment may actually be well in excess of any loss that the trader suffers in the circumstances. However, as we saw, such a term is not caught by the penalty rules as the payment in question is not technically triggered by breach.[119] Terms of this type are not mentioned on the indicative list.

---

[115] *Ibid*; and see the example proposed by the Law Commission: 'A term in a contract for an annual subscription to a magazine stating that the contract will be renewed for the following year, and the consumer will have to pay the subscription or a cancellation charge, unless the consumer sends a notice that he does not wish to renew by a date which is several months before the end of the current subscription period' (Report, No. 292, example 9, p. 191).

[116] See above at 5.7.4.2 and 5.7.6.2.

[117] Paragraph 1(e), under the auspices of which, for example, the OFT view terms in holiday contracts that compensate the supplier when the consumer cancels as fair only when there is a 'sliding scale' approach making the degree of compensation depend on how late the booking is and therefore how likely it is that the holiday will be able to be resold (see ABTA Travel Law Seminar (A talk by Ray Wooley, OFT Unfair Contract Terms Unit, 25 March 1999, http://www.oft.gov.uk/html/researchsp-arch/spe13-99.htm)).

[118] OFT Guidance, 2001, Group 5.

[119] *Bridge* v. *Campbell Discount* [1962] 1 All ER 385 and see above at 5.7.4.2.

However, it is clear that such terms are targeted by the OFT and often regarded as unfair.[120]

(e) Other Unreasonable Remedies   We have just been discussing terms that impose some onerous obligation or liability of a financial nature on the consumer. However, another possibility (in cases of consumer breach) is a term allowing for undue compromise of consumer interests that go beyond the purely financial. In this context, the OFT have looked beyond what is exemplified on the list by recognising the importance of consumer property interests and targeting forms of unfair enforcement by the trader, especially where these involve entry onto the premises of the consumer. So, a term allowing a landlord to enter the premises and immediately terminate the tenancy has been viewed as unfair;[121] as has a term allowing for entry onto the consumer's premises and repossession of goods.[122]

6.3.4 Insurance

We now turn to the question of insurance. This can clearly affect the consumer interest. So, for example, consumers are more at risk from certain terms (e.g. terms preventing them from claiming for losses caused by trader breach) where insurance is not available; and less at risk if insurance is available. We should recall here that, prior to UCTA being passed, the Law Commissions were concerned that exclusion clauses may be inefficient, imposing losses on parties not best placed to protect against them;[123] so in this light it makes sense to ask who is the best insurer. UCTA expressly says that, where liability is limited to a specific sum, attention should be given to how far it was open to the party limiting the liability to cover himself by insurance.[124] However, there was no mention of whether *the consumer* could obtain insurance. Again, in *Smith* v. *Bush* the focus appears to be on the insurance position of the trader. It *was* said to be relevant to consider the availability and cost of insurance in considering which of the *two* parties should be required to bear the risk of a loss.[125] However, the discussion then focused on the fact that surveyors could obtain insurance cover for a negligent survey without an

---

[120] OFT Guidance 2001, 5.8.

[121] OFT Guidance, 2001, 18.3.2.

[122] *Ibid.*

[123] See above at 3.3.

[124] UCTA, s. 11(4).

[125] [1989] 2 All ER 514, per Lord Griffiths at 531–532 and see above at 4.6.2.1.

unacceptable increase in the insurance premiums of surveyors.[126] There was no mention as to whether the consumer could have obtained insurance cover. The focus, then, seems to be on whether the loss is an unacceptable one for the consumer to bear and whether, if so, there is any excuse for the trader using the term based on the cost of insurance.

The insurance issue is not mentioned at all in the UTD or the UTCCR. Also, as we have already noted,[127] it was not mentioned by the House of Lords in *First National Bank*. Its absence from the UTD is probably explained by the fact that it is not an issue that is traditionally seen as having the same degree of relevance in continental notions of fairness as it has in UK notions of fairness. Then there is the agenda in the UTD to generate consumer confidence and a high level of protection. This appears to have mixed implications for the question as to whether the insurance issue should be regarded as relevant. On the one hand, if we are concerned to promote consumer confidence and set a high level of protection then it is certainly plausible to argue that if the trader could have obtained insurance (or if the consumer could not have obtained insurance) then this should help confirm that the term is unfair.[128] However, just as the goals of the Directive might push for such an approach where insurance is available for the trader or unavailable for the consumer, in the light of the same goals it must be questionable as to whether a term should be able to be saved on the basis that traders *cannot* obtain insurance or that consumers *can* obtain insurance. This would tend to lower the level of protection being provided.[129]

Beyond making these points as to what the goals of the UTD seem to suggest, we can say little more as to the current position under the good faith test. Not only has the House of Lords said nothing on the issue, but the OFT do not appear to have considered the issue in analysing terms. However, the proposed new test does make reference (under the auspices of the 'matters relating to the substance and effect of the term, and all the

---

[126] *Ibid.*

[127] See above at 5.5.4.2(iv)(g).

[128] However, as we have seen, nothing was said in *First National Bank* as to whether lenders could insure against the inability to recover post-judgement contractual interest from consumers. Of course, it is very difficult to know how much to read into this, given that the issue does not appear to have been raised by the OFT in their arguments and, as we have said already, the case does involve a rather distinctive factual matrix. It clearly remains possible that the House of Lords would take the view that in general where terms place risks or costs on the consumer the availability of insurance for traders to insure against these risks or losses (or the unavailability of insurance for consumers to protect against these risks or losses) should count against a finding of fairness.

[129] See further below, at 6.3.9.

other circumstances existing at the time it was agreed') to 'the possibility and probability of insurance'.[130] This will clearly highlight the issue and the courts and regulators will need to decide how to approach the issue (hopefully in the light of the points made above as to the goals of the Directive).

6.3.5 Good Faith and the Particular Type of Goods or Services

6.3.5.1 Introduction

Those consumer interests discussed above that are affected by terms imposing obligations and liabilities on the consumer are only protected by the UTCCR (as they will be in the new regime) as such terms are not covered by UCTA. However, quite apart from this stark contrast between UCTA and the UTCCR it may be that the use of the good faith concept in the UTCCR also brings recognition and protection of certain consumer interests that were not so obviously recognized and protected under UCTA (even where it formally applied). First of all, the test of unfairness in the UTCCR may be particularly sensitive to the particular type of goods and/or services involved. It is clear that both the UCTA reasonableness and the good faith tests are very open textured; allowing attention to be given to a wide range of factors related to process and substance, and the breadth of what can be taken into account under UCTA has been emphasized by the House of Lords. However, it is also true that the UTCCR (following the UTD and by contrast with UCTA) specifically refer to the need to take account of the 'nature of the goods or services for which the contract was concluded'.[131] So, it appears to be thought to be particularly important in applying this test to take into account the type of goods or services being contracted for, given that different interests (both consumer and trader) might exist depending on the type of goods or services. This is interesting as a general observation, although there is no space in a work of this nature to seek to be comprehensive in relation to the types of interests that arise in relation to different goods and services. However, it does seem that some attention should be given to particular consumer interests in relation to services of general interest and also particular human rights interests that might arise in relation to services of general interest and contracts more generally.

---

[130] See Draft Bill, Clauses 14(1)(b) and 14(4)(e).

[131] Regulation 6(1), Directive, Article 4(1).

6.3.5.2 Good Faith and Services of General Interest

The good faith concept may bring with it a particular concern with certain types of term in contracts for the supply of services of general interest.[132] In Recital 16 to the Preamble the concept of good faith is explained as being based on an 'overall evaluation of the different interests involved' and requiring that the supplier 'deals fairly and equitably with the [consumer] whose legitimate interests he has to take into account'. However, this standard is also said by Recital 16 to have been chosen 'in particular' to take account of 'sale and supply activities of a public nature providing collective services which take account of solidarity amongst users'. Whittaker has argued that argued that the reference to 'collective services which take account of solidarity among users' indicates that, at least where public services are concerned, the 'overall evaluation of the different interests involved' may involve account being taken not only of the interests of the supplier and the consumer but also the broader public interest.[133] In particular, in this context, he has argued that the reference to 'solidarity among users' may allude to the notion in French administrative law that users of public services should have equal access and be treated equally.[134] This equality principle may have a variety of

---

[132] For a discussion of such services and the European Commission plans to develop a general framework of protection for consumers of these services see the Commission's Communications on 'Services of General Interest in Europe', COM(96) 443 final and COM(2000) 580 final; the Green Paper on Services of General Interest, COM(2003) 270 final; the White Paper on Services of General Interest, COM(2004) 374 final; C. Scott, Services of General Interest in EC Law: Matching Values to Regulatory Technique in the Public and Privatised Sectors (2000) European Law Journal, 310 at 313; T. Wilhelmsson, Services of general interest and European private law, in C.E.F. Rickett and G.W. Telfer, International Perspectives on Consumers' Access to Justice, CUP, 2003, 149; P. Rott, Regulation of Services of General Economic Interest in the EC (2005) European Review of Contract Law, 323; and C. Willett, General Clauses on Fairness and the Promotion of Values Important in Services of General Interest (forthcoming, 2007) Yearbook of Consumer Law.

[133] S. Whittaker, Unfair Terms in Consumer Contracts, in H. Beale (ed.), Chitty's Law of Contract, at 15–059.

[134] *Ibid*; and see generally S. Whittaker, Public and Private Law Making: Subordinate Legislation, Contracts and the Status of 'Student Rules' (2001) 21 Oxford Journal of Legal Studies, 103 and S. Whittaker, Judicial Review in Public Law and in Contract Law: The example of 'Student Rules' (2001) Oxford Journal of Legal Studies, 193 for discussion of the relationship between contract and administrative law in the context of University-Student relationships.

implications under the UTD general clause.[135] In the particular context of price, Whittaker argues that, in keeping with the principle of equal treatment, the use of differential tariffs may be viewed as unfair.[136] He suggests that this would not be prevented by the provision excluding the price from the test of fairness. As he points out,[137] if we question the price on the basis that it is *different from the price charged in relation to other consumers* this is surely quite different from questioning the price on the basis of its 'adequacy … *as against the goods or services sold or supplied*'.[138] The issue of *differential* pricing goes to equality of treatment; while the issue of adequacy *as against the goods or services supplied* goes to the question as to whether the price is a fair one *measured by reference to what is promised in exchange*.

Equality might also be said to be relevant to the control of terms allowing the supplier to vary or terminate the contract on a discretionary basis. The above discussion of variation terms focused on the problem of these terms allowing for compromise of reasonable expectations.[139] Such terms are more likely to be unfair the greater discretion they allow the trader to exercise (this allowing for greater compromise on the expectations of the consumer). However, there is also an *equality* dimension to the exercise of trader discretion. The broader the discretion, the more scope there is for traders to treat consumers differently, i.e. to act in a discriminatory and arbitrary way, withdrawing or changing services where some consumers are concerned, but not others. So, if we take seriously the reference in the preamble to the idea of 'solidarity among users' (and the equality this requires) we should be particularly restrictive in terms of the degree of discretion that a trader is entitled to provide for where the service is one of general interest. We saw from the above discussion of variation terms that the idea generally is indeed to restrict the degree of discretion available to traders to vary the contract.[140]

What about terms allowing the trader to terminate? The general approach in the UTD seems to depend on whether termination is based on the discretion of the supplier or on the breach of the consumer. In the first

---

[135] It should be noted also that equal treatment is an important principle of the European Commission's approach to the development of a framework for protection of consumers of services of general interest – see White Paper on Services of General Interest, COM(2004) 374 final.

[136] S. Whittaker, Unfair Terms in Consumer Contracts, in H. Beale (ed.), Chitty's Law of Contract, at 15–059.

[137] *Ibid.*

[138] The sort of assessment of the price that is excluded under Regulation 6(2).

[139] See above at 6.3.3.2(i)(d) and (e) on variation terms.

[140] *Ibid.*

situation (a discretionary supplier right to cancel) the question appears to be whether the consumer has an equivalent discretionary right to cancel. Paragraph 1(f) of the indicative list refers to a term allowing the supplier to dissolve the contract on a discretionary basis where the same facility is not granted to the consumer. This appears to be an inadequate model to the extent that equality of treatment is regarded as important. A discretionary consumer right to cancel may not be of much practical benefit and is certainly no concrete protection against the supplier's discretionary right to cancel. In other words the supplier remains free to exercise termination rights in an arbitrary, discriminatory and unequal fashion. Much more effective in fostering equality is to insist that a term is only fair if the supplier right to cancel is restricted to circumstances in which continued provision of the service has become impossible or impractical for reasons outside the control of the supplier; and also to insist that the term in question specifies that consumers are entitled to be compensated where loss or inconvenience are suffered. This appears to be the approach *in practice* of the OFT[141] and the new regime could usefully be amended along these lines.

Turning to situations in which the consumer is in breach, para. 1(g) describes a term enabling the supplier to terminate a contract of indeterminate duration without reasonable notice except where there are serious grounds. The idea, in other words, is that a contract can be terminated without reasonable notice for serious consumer breach. This paragraph has been used by regulators to target terms that allow termination by the supplier for non-serious breaches.[142] This is important in pursuit of the equality agenda. If the supplier is restricted in his scope to terminate to cases of serious breach then he is restricted in his ability to treat consumers unequally, e.g. by choosing to terminate for non-serious breaches where some consumers are concerned, while choosing to overlook the breach in other cases.

Two final points need to be made as to the relationship between good faith and services of general interest. First, we have focused here on the reference in the Preamble to 'solidarity amongst users' and the equality agenda that this suggests is inherent in the good faith concept. However, the good faith concept is clearly also capable of paying heed to other values that might be important in services of general interest. For example, 'choice' and 'continuity' are also regarded as important by the

---

[141] OFT Guidance, 2001, para. 6.

[142] See, for example, a term used by UK Online allowing termination without notice for any breach. The view of OFCOM was that a serious breach should be a requirement. This can be found at:

http://www.ofcom.org.uk/bulletins/comp_bull_index/comp_bull_ccases/closed_all/cw_887/#content (term xix).

European Commission in their plans to develop a framework for services of general interest.[143] 'Continuity' is clearly affected by terms allowing for termination by the supplier. In addition choice (in the sense of the choice to change providers) is affected by terms restricting the *consumer right* to terminate and by terms that provide for automatic contract extensions.[144]

The second point is that there is a particular limitation on any agenda to focus on terms that are particularly damaging to values of importance in relation to services of general interest. This is the fact that, as we have seen, the UTD/UTCCR do not apply to terms reflecting mandatory provisions.[145] This exclusion may be particularly problematic in the context of services of general interest. This is because not only are such 'mandatory' provisions (and terms reflecting them) particularly common in the context of services of general interest; but, as we have already seen, there is evidence that very large numbers of such terms may be unfair in substance.[146] In other words, the presumption that such terms are fair may well be particularly misplaced (at least where services of general interest are concerned). This may well explain the view that has been expressed that such terms may well be able to be tested for unfairness where it can be shown that the presumption of fairness is inappropriate and that this is most likely to be possible in the case of public services.[147] However, the fact is that it remains unclear as to whether the UTD does ever require such terms to be tested for fairness; and the UTCCR in the UK contain an outright exclusion (there being no plans to change this except where the terms in question are not transparent[148]).

---

[143] White Paper on Services of General Interest, COM(2004) 374 final.

[144] On the latter type of term see above at 6.3.3.2(2)(c) and on the use of the UTD in promoting all of the values important in services of general interest see C. Willett, General Clauses on Fairness and the Promotion of Values Important in Services of General Interest (forthcoming, 2007) Yearbook of Consumer Law.

[145] See above at 3.2, 5.7.3 and 5.10.

[146] See the study by the French Institut National de Consommation (INC) and the UK National Consumer Council (NCC), 'Application de la directive 93/13 aux prestations de service public', at:
http://europa.eu.int/comm/consumers/cons_int/safe_shop/unf_cont_terms/uct02_fr.pd f; and the discussion at 5.7.3 above.

[147] Tenreiro and Karsten, Unfair Terms in Consumer Contracts: Uncertainties, Contradictions and Novelties of a Directive, European Commission, 1999, p. 14.

[148] See above at 5.10; and see also generally on the application of the UTD to public services P. Nebbia, Unfair Contract Terms in European Law, Hart, 2007, Ch. 6.

6.3.5.3 Good Faith and Human Rights

Next we turn to another possible form of consumer interest that may be recognized by the good faith concept in particular – protection of human rights. Whittaker has argued that the good faith test is able to take into account both the extent to which the term respects the human rights of the consumer and (given the relevance of the broader public interest) the extent to which it takes account of the human rights of third parties.[149] It is certainly the case that in other jurisdictions general clauses have been used as vehicles to import constitutional values (including human rights) into to the private law of contract.[150] The Human Rights Act (HRA) 1998 places the obligation to respect the rights deriving from the European Convention on Human Rights ('Convention Rights') on 'public authorities'.[151] However, it may be that (contrary to the view of some[152]) this does not mean that these Convention rights cannot be applied in contracts between contractors who are not public bodies (whether two commercial contractors, a business and a consumer or even, perhaps, two private parties). There is support for such so called 'horizontal effect' from the Court of Appeal and, although the position of the House of Lords is not clear, it may be that they would also be prepared to countenance such a notion.[153] (This is presumably on the basis that *the court* – as a public body – must respect the Convention rights in the way they deal with contractual relationships.[154]) A 'full' horizontal approach

---

[149] S. Whittaker, Judicial Review in Public Law and in Contract Law: The Example of 'Student Rules' (2001) 21 Oxford Journal of Legal Studies, 193 at 213.

[150] S. Whittaker, *ibid.*, and B. Markesinis, Privacy, Freedom of Expression and the Horizontal Effect of the Human Rights Bill: Lessons from Germany (1998), 115 LQR 47 at 52–58.

[151] Human Rights Act, s. 6(1); of course, when a contractor is a public authority will not necessarily always be straightforward. See *R (on the application of Heather)* v. *Leonard Cheshire Foundation* [2002] 2 All ER 396; *Poplar Housing and Regeneration Community Association Ltd* v. *Donoghue* [2001] 4 All ER 604; N. Bamforth, The Application of the Human Rights Act 1998 to Public Authorities and Private Bodies (1999) 58 Cambridge Law Journal 159 and R. Brownsword, Contract Law: Themes for the Twenty-First Century, OUP, 2006, 265–70.

[152] See R. Buxton, The Human Rights Act and Private Law (2000) 116 Law Quarterly Review 48.

[153] *Wilson* v. *Secretary of State for Trade and Industry*, sub nom *Wilson* v. *First County Trust (No2)* [2001] 3 All ER 229, [2003] UKHL40, [2003] 3 WLR 568.

[154] See G. Phillipson, The Human Rights Act, 'Horizontal Effect' and the Common Law – A Bang or a Whimper? (1999) 62 Modern Law Review, 824; N. Bamforth, The True 'Horizontal Effect' of the Human rights Act 1998 (2001) 17 Law Quarterly Review 117, 34; W. Wade, Horizons of Horizontality (2000) 116 Law Quarterly

might imply the idea that Convention rights should, in themselves, give rise to free standing causes of action. However, the gathering support appears to be for a form of indirect horizontality.[155] There are various shades of opinion as to the appropriate model.[156] However, the idea appears to be that (in keeping with the approach taken in other jurisdictions, e.g. Canada,[157] Italy, Spain and Japan[158]) the courts should approach accepted law applicable to contracts in a way that is in keeping with the Convention rights.[159] Open textured norms such as good faith (and reasonableness) could then be interpreted in such a way as to reflect the Convention rights. In the main, this would involve the Convention rights of the consumers that are party to the contract and subject to the term in question (so, courts should ask whether the term in question compromises the Convention rights of the consumer). However, Whittaker's suggestion seems to be that the Convention rights of third parties could also be taken into account.[160] It seems likely that he is not referring here to such parties gaining enforceable rights as such, as it is hard to see how this could be achieved under the auspices of the good faith concept that we have here. This is a concept that has the (potentially vitiating) function of determining whether a term is fair and should be used or enforced as against consumers in general or this consumer in particular. It is not a concept that has a supplementation function. In other words it does not provide extra rights for the consumer as such, and certainly not for third parties.[161] However, the idea may be that if a term

---

Review, 217; Beyleveld and Pattinson, Horizontal Applicability and Direct Effect (2002) 118 Law Quarterly Review 623.

[155] See N. Bamforth, *ibid*; G. Phillipson, *ibid*; and H. Beale and N. Pittam, The Impact of the Human Rights Act 1998 on English Contract and Tort Law, in D. Friedmann and D. Barak-Erez (eds), Human Rights in Private Law, 2001, Hart, 131.

[156] See A. Lester and D. Pannick, The Impact of the Human Rights Act on Private Law: The Knights Move (2000) 116 Law Quarterly Review 380 and Barak, Constitutional Human Rights and Private Law, in D. Friedman and D. Barak-Erez, *ibid.*, 22.

[157] *Retail Wholesale and Department Union Local 580* v. *Dolphin Delivery Ltd* (1986) 33 DLR (4th) 174.

[158] Barak, Constitutional Human Rights and Private Law, in D. Friedman and D. Barak-Erez (eds), Human Rights in Private Law, 2001, 22.

[159] See G. Phillipson, *ibid*; Barak, *ibid*; A. Lester and D. Pannick, The Impact of the Human Rights Act on Private Law: The Knights Move (2000) 116 Law Quarterly Review 380; or at least underlying human rights *values* (see *Retail Wholesale and Department Union Local 580* v. *Dolphin Delivery Ltd* (1986) 33 DLR (4th) 174).

[160] S. Whittaker, Public and Private Law Making: Subordinate Legislation, Contracts and the Status of 'Student Rules' (2001) 21 Oxford Journal of Legal Studies, 103, 112.

[161] Although, having said this, there are views as to the horizontal effect of the Human Rights Act that do edge towards creation of entirely new contractual rights – see

might affect third party Convention rights (e.g. an unrestricted right to terminate a tenancy which deprives the tenant *and a family member* of their right to shelter, the protection of family life and the protection of property[162]) then this might strengthen the case for the term being viewed as unfair in *ex casu* assessments and in litigation as between the parties to the contract.

I have not discovered any express reference to human rights considerations in case law or the work of the OFT. However, to the extent that human rights considerations were to be taken into account, they might not add a huge amount to the protective norms; given that, as Adams and Brownsword point out, the Convention rights are mainly 'first generation' civil and political rights[163] (i.e. the sort of rights that, even if we did not call them human rights as such, we would tend to think should not be unduly encroached upon by a term and that if they were the term would be likely to be unfair). As in the case of services of general interest, one is inclined to think of access rights in particular, e.g. rights of access to education or to private life and home. Such rights might be affected by terms allowing for withdrawal of education; eviction from property; entry on to, interference with, forfeiture of property etc. So, for example, a human rights lens might focus in particular on terms allowing a university to prevent a student sitting examinations where there is a very small debt; terms allowing for forfeiture of a home (with added concern for the rights to private life and home of family members); and terms providing for excessive enforcement rights, e.g. rights to enter and repossess property. These, as already suggested, are the sort of terms that are likely to come under heavy suspicion even without any thought to human rights. However, it is conceivable that the human rights dimension might convince a court that an otherwise 'borderline' term is unfair.

6.3.6 Balance and the Role of other (Favourable) Terms

6.3.6.1 The General Issue

We have already seen that the significant imbalance concept causes some difficulties in relation to terms other than the term under scrutiny where these other terms are in some way favourable to the consumer.[164] The

---

Barak, Constitutional Human Rights and Private Law in D. Friedman and D. Barak-Erez, (eds), Human Rights in Private Law, 2001, 22 at 30.

[162] See European Convention on Human Rights, Article 8(1) and Article 1 of the First Protocol.

[163] Understanding Contract Law, at 122.

[164] See above at 5.9.

problem is that if significant imbalance is viewed as a matter purely related to the substantive features of terms, then a favourable term might sometimes mean that the term under scrutiny no longer causes significant imbalance. If this was the case then the term could not be unfair even where there was procedural unfairness (as even if procedural unfairness causes there to be a violation of good faith, there can be no unfairness without there also being a significant imbalance). This would be problematic because, even if there is a fair balance in substance, the consumer surely has an interest in transparency, so that he can assess the overall package.[165] The solution suggested (while significant imbalance remains a requirement) was that if terms lack transparency this should also be relevant to the question of significant imbalance, so that even where there is a favourable term there is always a significant imbalance as long as there is a lack of transparency. The result, then, is that the term is opened up to the general review of fairness under the good faith test.[166] In fact it is unclear what attitude the courts take to the whole issue, i.e. it is unclear whether the courts think that significant imbalance is to be viewed as a purely substantive matter that does not exist where there are favourable terms or whether the view is that procedural factors can be taken into account in assessing significant imbalance.[167] All we know is that (for the ECJ) other terms (and whether they provide a benefit to the consumer) are relevant to the overall question of unfairness;[168] and that (for the House of Lords) other terms are relevant to the question of significant imbalance.[169] As far as the OFT is concerned it certainly seems that they do not (as a matter of routine) view overall substantive balance as sufficient in itself. Although they do take this into account, there is, in addition, an insistence on transparency.[170]

We now turn to consider the role of favourable terms in general reviews of fairness such as the reasonableness test, the good faith test and the proposed 'fair and reasonable' test.

What provision is there for an analysis of other favourable terms under the existing broad reviews and under the proposed new test? Consideration of this element under the good faith concept does seem to be provided for. The Preamble refers to an 'overall evaluation of the different interests'.[171] This clearly includes assessment of the broader distribution of rights under this and other contracts. The preamble also

---

165 *Ibid.*

166 *Ibid.*

167 *Ibid.*

168 See above at 3.5.4 and 5.9.

169 See above at 5.5.4.2(ii) and 5.9.

170 See, generally, OFT Guidance on Unfair Terms, 2001.

171 Recital 16.

refers to whether the consumer received an 'inducement' to agree to the term.[172] Such an inducement may well come in the form of other terms that are favourable to the consumer. Consideration of the other terms of the contract is also expressly called for by Regulation 6(1) which says that the assessment of unfairness should involve consideration of 'all the other terms of the contract or of another contract on which it is dependent'. The House of Lords do not appear to have said expressly that other terms are relevant to the good faith element of the UTCCR test. However, there is evidence that this was implicit. Lord Bingham referred to the relevance of Regulation 4(1) of the 1994 Regulations.[173] This is the provision that is now Regulation 6(1) (of the 1999 Regulations) which, as we have just seen, requires consideration of 'all the other terms of the contract or of another contract on which it is dependent'. He also said that this 'lays down a composite test, covering both the making and the substance of the contract'.[174] The reference to 'the contract' suggests consideration of all the terms. The ECJ also appear to view the issue as relevant.[175] Under UCTA the question as to whether there was an inducement to agree to the term is mentioned in Schedule 2.[176] Although the criteria in Schedule 2 are only strictly relevant to the reasonableness of certain terms in commercial contracts, it is accepted that they can be drawn upon in consumer contracts. Having said this there has been no particular development of the issue in consumer cases and there was no mention of it in the guidance provided in the *Smith* v. *Bush* case.[177]

Consideration of other terms would be expressly provided for in the proposed new law. It would be provided that it is relevant to consider 'the substance and effect of the term, and all the circumstances existing at the time it was agreed'.[178] This, following the language of the current UTCCR, would be defined to include 'the other terms of the contract' and the 'terms of any other contract on which the contract depends'.[179]

The general question in relation to favourable terms should surely be whether the benefit provided to the consumer by such a term represents a

---

[172] *Ibid.*

[173] [2001] 3 WLR 1297 at 1308.

[174] *Ibid.*

[175] See above at 3.5.4. We should recall that the ECJ did not break down the test of unfairness under the UTD into components. The point was simply made that other terms were relevant to the overall question of unfairness. This seems to leave scope for this question to be taken into account under the auspices of the significant imbalance and the good faith limbs of the test.

[176] Schedule 2, para. (b).

[177] See above at 4.6.2.1.

[178] Draft Bill, Clause 14(1)(b).

[179] *Ibid.*, 14(4)(a) and (b).

'fair price' for the risks being borne by the consumer as a result of the term under scrutiny.[180] We have already seen that terms allowing the consumer to cancel the contract in response to a price rise may indeed amount to such a 'fair price' for the price increase; but that (at least in OFT practice) there may also need to be provision for the consumer to be compensated for any loss caused.[181] The issue will arise in different ways depending upon the type of favourable term. Where it is of the type just described (i.e. a term that helps the consumer to protect himself from the effects of the term under scrutiny) the obvious approach is to ask whether the beneficial term does in reality protect the consumer from the adverse consequences of the term under scrutiny.[182] In cases where the purportedly beneficial term comes in the form of the price we have seen that there are different ways to measure whether this there is indeed overall substantive fairness.[183] It can be assumed that this is the case in any case where the market is working properly. It can be assumed that this is the case where the term and the price are typical in the market. Alternatively, it can be said that if the price is a normal one for the market there is only substantive fairness where the trader produces positive evidence (based on costs, risks etc.) to show that he would have needed to charge a significantly higher price if it was not for the detrimental term because the relevant costs or risks cannot be absorbed in some alternative way. If the trader cannot make this case then there would only be substantive fairness where he charges a price that is actually lower than what is typical in the market. Indeed, a more protective approach would involve saying that even where such a case can be made in relation to the price there should not be taken to be overall balance if it would also have been possible to provide for some concrete way in which the consumer could be protected.

We have seen that the House of Lords have not given any real indication as to how they would measure this issue, but that there has certainly been no suggestion that there is generally balance simply on the basis that the term and price are normal.[184] In addition, there is no such indication from the lower courts and certainly not from the OFT. The OFT do not appear to routinely raise the question as to whether the terms they view as unfair have been counterbalanced by low prices;[185] so it appears that they must take the view that (at best) only an unusually low price can balance out the detriment caused by the term under scrutiny.

---

[180] See above at 2.4.3.3.

[181] See above at 6.3.3.2(2)(b) and 2.4.3.3.

[182] See above at 2.4.3.3.

[183] *Ibid.*

[184] See above at 5.5.4.2(ii).

[185] See, in particular, OFT Guidance on Unfair Terms, 2001.

We do know that the ECJ will pass the matter back to national courts where there is some form of benefit. We also know that there was found to be a benefit in the *Freiburger* case.[186] The argument in that case in relation to the price was at least based on the trader making a specific connection between early payment and the fact that this meant that the trader did not need to borrow money to finance the work. So there was no suggestion that there was substantive fairness simply because the term and price were normal or the market was competitive. It seems that the least expected by the ECJ is that the trader makes a specific case of the type in that case in relation costs, risks etc. However, it is not clear if this is enough for the ECJ or whether the benefit for the ECJ came with the cumulative effect of the lower price and the security provided to the consumer guaranteeing protection where the work was unsatisfactory.

Finally, it was suggested that another possible argument as to 'benefit' might be that it is not economically efficient to provide goods or services at all without the term.[187] If the case can be made that this is genuinely the case, then it might be said that the detrimental features of the term are balanced out by the fact that goods or services are available which would not otherwise be available. On this issue, there does appear to be a difference in approach between the OFT and the House of Lords. As we saw, the House of Lords in *First National Bank* did not take the approach I have suggested. It was accepted, without any particular evidence, that Banks would not lend in the first place without the assurance that they would be able to recover all of the interest, including in a post-judgement situation.[188] No consideration was given, for example, as to how many customers would be likely to go into default and have a judgement issued against them (and therefore how much money in interest is at stake); whether banks can adequately cover loss of such interest by insurance; or whether the 'writing-off' of such debts is routinely built into the Banking system and easily absorbed. By contrast, the OFT clearly did not consider that loans would not be available without such a term and that, therefore, the term was compensated for by the availability of the loan. The point has been made above that it is questionable as to whether the ECJ would take the view that the availability of the loan is a sufficient benefit to counterbalance the detriment caused by the term in question. The ECJ might not regard this (by its very nature) as the type of benefit that can be taken into account. Another possibility is that the ECJ might at least expect the Bank to make a more detailed case as to why they would find it uneconomical to lend without the protection of this term, i.e. to make the sort of case outlined

---

[186] See above at 3.5.4.

[187] See above at 2.4.3.3.

[188] See above at 5.5.4.2(iv)(c).

just above as to the numbers of customers likely to have judgements issued against them, and whether the Bank could insure against the problem or otherwise absorb any losses caused.

Even if this sort of case was made the ECJ might expect more. It might be said that there can only be a sufficient benefit if (in addition to any benefit the consumer gets in the sense of access to the loan) there is also a term providing concrete protection to the consumer against the term in question. In this case such a term could have been used. It would have come in the form of the term suggested by the Court of Appeal which would have obliged the Bank to explain to consumers at the time of the judgement that they (consumers) are entitled to ask the court to review the amounts owing and the time for payment.

6.3.6.2 Mirror-Image Balance

Then we turn to so called 'mirror-image' terms. Paragraph 1(d) of the indicative list describes a situation in which a term gives the trader the right to retain sums when the consumer is in breach; while there is no provision for the consumer to claim an equivalent sum in compensation in circumstances where the trader is in breach.[189] This seems to suggest a type of overall substantive unfairness that we have already mentioned briefly.[190] The idea appears to be that the term giving the trader the right to retain sums is unfair unless the contract expressly provides for the consumer to have the same rights in the 'mirror-image' situation of trader breach. Of course, the suggestion is also that if there *is* such provision for mirror-image consumer rights then the term providing for the trader to retain sums when the consumer is in breach might be viewed as fair on this basis alone, i.e. that the term is fair on the basis of this mirror-image form of overall substantive fairness.[191] Generally in relation to substantive fairness it has been suggested that the question should be whether the purportedly favourable term represents a 'fair price' for the term under scrutiny.[192] On this approach it would be arguable that in the situation described by para. 1(d) the term allowing the consumer to retain equivalent amounts when the trader is in breach only has the potential to amount to a fair price for the trader right to retain the amounts in question

---

[189] See above at 5.7.1.

[190] See above at 2.4.3.3.

[191] Of course it must be remembered that the list is only indicative and in particular it does not provide *exclusive* notions of unfairness, so the term allowing the trader to retain sums can still be viewed as unfair on the general unfairness test even where there is a mirror-image consumer right.

[192] See above at 2.4.3.3.

if, in the circumstances, there is at least as much risk that the trader will cancel as there is that the consumer will cancel.[193] If the risk that the consumer will cancel is greater than the risk that the trader will cancel, then providing for the consumer to obtain compensation if the trader cancels certainly does not seem to be a fair price for the risk borne by the consumer of having to pay compensation if he (the consumer) cancels. It is not clear whether such an approach is implicit in para. 1(d) or whether para. 1(d) should be taken at face value to be concerned solely with whether there is an equivalent consumer right to compensation (and not whether there is an equal chance that the consumer will benefit from this right). Certainly the consumer protection and confidence goals of the UTD would push for the former interpretation. This former interpretation seems to be supported by the OFT.[194]

What the ECJ might say is unclear. We know that for the ECJ there needs to be a 'benefit' of some kind for the consumer[195] and the question is whether they would regard a mirror-image right to be such a benefit even where there is less of a chance of this right being taken advantage of by a consumer than there is of the trader taking advantage of his own compensation right.

Another question is whether para. 1(d) contemplates that the mirror-image term could potentially balance out the term allowing the trader to retain sums in all cases (i.e. even where the sums being retained by the trader exceed his real or estimated losses) or whether it is only aimed at situations in which the term allows the trader to retain a sum that would not be excessive (excessive compensation being left to be dealt with under para. 1(e) which focuses on whether compensation is disproportionate and does not provide any express scope for this to be justified by a mirror-image term[196]). If the latter approach is correct then in *any* case where a term allows a trader to retain a deposit (even where it does not represent a sum that exceeds his real losses), there should be a term allowing the consumer to claim equivalent compensation in mirror-image circumstances (i.e. where the trader cancels). This would represent quite a novel approach for UK law. A term providing for a deposit to be retained by the trader could be unfair even although the amount is not excessive in a concrete sense; the basis of the unfairness being the more abstract one that consumers do not have *equal rights* (at least in the sense

---

[193] This appears, in broad terms, to be the approach taken to mirror-image balance in Italy and Germany – see the discussion by P. Nebbia, Unfair Contract Terms in European Law, Hart, 2007, 160–1.

[194] OFT Guidance, 2001, para. 4.4 (n. 17).

[195] See above at 3.5.4.

[196] See above at 6.3.3.2(ii)(d).

of a right to an equivalent amount of compensation) in the reverse situation.

However, para. 1(d) could certainly be read in this way. It does not make any reference to the trader retaining an *excessive* amount, but simply to the trader retaining the deposit, so it is plausible that it contemplates *any* non-excessive deposit (leaving excessive deposits to be dealt with under para. 1(e)). Further, it would arguably accord with the consumer protection and confidence goals of the UTD to take such an approach. It would hardly be conducive to consumer protection and confidence to allow traders to retain an excessive amount simply because consumers have mirror-image rights. Even if we do insist (as suggested above) that the mirror-image right must be just as likely to be exercised as the trader's right, the mirror-image right still provides no concrete protection against the trader's right to retain an excessive amount. Apart from this point, there seem to be good reasons for insisting on mirror-image balance where the trader stipulates for the right to retain even a non-excessive sum. The right to retain *any* sum puts the trader in a strong bargaining position in cases where the consumer cancels; and this may be thought to be potentially unfair especially where the consumer may be claiming that the reason for the cancellation is trader breach. The idea of insisting on a mirror-image consumer right to compensation being provided for in the contract may be to highlight such a right to the consumer and thereby provide a type of balance. Alternatively, the idea may be to provide a kind of deterrent to the trader. Traders may be less inclined to insist on non-returnable deposits if they are required (as a *quid pro quo*) to provide expressly for consumer rights to compensation in mirror-image situations.

There also appears to some support from the OFT for this approach. Their practice suggests that they generally take the view that the compensation that it is provided that the consumer must pay should not exceed the reasonably estimated losses of the trader; *and* that *any* provision for retention of a deposit should be balanced by a term providing for the consumer to be compensated for his losses where the trader is in breach.[197]

The proposed redraft of para. 1(d) simply refers to 'a term entitling [the trader], if [the consumer] exercises a right to cancel a contract or if [the trader] terminates the contract as a result of [the consumer's] breach, to keep sums that [the consumer] has paid, the amount of which is unreasonable'.[198] So, the focus will be purely on the reasonableness of the sum in its own right. This is a positive move to the extent that it emphasizes that a mirror-image term cannot justify a term allowing the

---

[197] See OFT Bulletin 3, at 35 (Maples Stores).
[198] Draft Bill, Schedule 2, part 2, term 4.

trader to retain an *excessive* deposit. However, there remains the possibility (just canvassed) that a mirror-image term is in fact required as a matter of fairness whenever there is a term allowing the trader to retain any form of deposit. Arguably the new legislation should make it clear that this is the case.

6.3.7 Concluding Comment on Consumer Interests

We can see, therefore, that the general criteria laid down in the legislation (reasonableness in the case of UCTA and good faith in the case of the UTCCR) are capable of showing sensitivity to different types of consumer interests as well as the extent to which terms actually affect these interests. The types of interest protected by good faith should be given particular attention in the new test in order to ensure that the requirements of the UTD continue to be complied with. We have seen that the new legislation would provide a variety of guidelines related to consumer interests – the balance of interests, the risks, the substance and effect of the term etc. However, it would arguably be preferable if any new legislation was to focus more specifically on the distinctive nature of the consumer interest, including those aspects of the consumer interest that may be particularly important to good faith. So, for example, courts and regulatory bodies might be directed by the legislation to consider in general whether the term is damaging to, or will cause significant disruption to, the private sphere of life. More particularly they might be required to consider whether large financial losses are involved; whether physical welfare is at stake; whether important property interests at stake; whether, in appropriate cases, a term is balanced by a mirror-image term; whether the principle of equal treatment in services of general interest is compromised; whether human rights or other important personal, family or domestic interests are at stake; and whether there is likely to be significant and/or long term hardship.

6.3.8 Trader Interests

So far we have been talking of factors affecting the interests of the consumer and how these might weigh against (or in favour of) enforcement. We now turn to factors focused more on trader interests that may help to justify enforcement. It is clear that, in general, the interests of the trader are relevant under the general UCTA reasonableness criteria. For example, in *Smith* v. *Bush*, Lord Griffiths made reference to the 'ability of the parties to bear the loss involved',[199] this clearly referring to both parties. Trader interests are also obviously relevant under the UTCCR. The preamble to the UTD, as we know, refers to good faith as 'an overall evaluation of the different interests involved'[200] (clearly including the interests of the trader). Trader interests would also be relevant under the new regime. It would refer (under the auspices of the 'matters relating to the substance and effect of the term' and 'all the other circumstances') to 'the balance of the parties' interests'.[201]

So what types of trader interest are significant? First of all, there is clearly a general interest in not facing a risk of liability that is too large to bear. So, in this context, it must be relevant to consider what would be the extent of the liability without the term. However, this has to be seen in the context of the question of fault. It was recognized in the UCTA case law[202] that there should be less sympathy with the position of the trader where the exclusion covers liability for negligence. In *Smith* v. *Bush* the question was asked as to how difficult the task was that was being performed.[203] The idea here seems to have been that there might be greater sympathy where the exclusion covered negligence if the task was a particularly difficult one (where falling below the required standard of care might be more likely and understandable than normal). However, where, as in *Smith* v. *Bush*, the task was viewed as being 'at the lower end of the surveyor's field of professional expertise'[204] the view was that there was less excuse for an exclusion of liability in such a case.

As we have already seen,[205] the OFT also seem to take the view that a term is less likely to be fair where it enables the trader to avoid liability for fault. The 'anti-fault' policy certainly fits with the UCTA focus on efficiency, it being usually most efficient to impose liability on the party at fault; but it also fits with the broader fairness agendas of both UCTA and the UTCCR, the idea being probably that it is not fair to expect the consumer to bear risks that the trader could have avoided by reasonable care.

We now turn to some more specific types of scenario. We have seen[206] that there is a difference of view between the OFT and the House of Lords as to whether traders are entitled to basic interest on whole

---

[199] *Smith* v. *Bush, supra* at 531–532.

[200] Recital 16.

[201] Draft Bill, Clause 14(4)(c) (and see the discussion above as to the question of insurance).

[202] See above at 4.6.2.1.

[203] *Supra* at 531–532.

[204] *Ibid.*

[205] See above at 6.3.2.

[206] See above at 5.5.2–5.5.4.

amount of a loan even where this applies after default and after judgement. Of course, the House of Lords have not been involved other than in this case; the key views having come from the OFT. For the OFT at least there does not appear to be a legitimate interest in providing for an increase in the price or changing the goods or services supplied without the consumer having a chance to withdraw. At least where price variation is concerned, this seems to apply even where the trader could not control the factors that have made the change necessary.[207] Equally, where building work is concerned it is recognized that the trader has a legitimate interest in obtaining some prepayment and some ongoing payments, but not full prepayment as this compromises the bargaining position of consumer in cases where there is a dispute over the work done.[208]

6.3.9 Abstract and Contextual Approaches to the Substantive Interests of the Parties

6.3.9.1 Introduction

Earlier we have seen that a freedom-oriented approach to contract can be viewed as abstract in the sense that it ignores the characteristics of contractors that might affect their abilities to protect their interests and absorb certain losses.[209] A fairness approach, by contrast, is contextual in that it recognizes the context within which parties such as consumers enter contracts and are affected by contracts, i.e. it recognizes factors affecting the ability of consumers to protect their interests at the procedural stage and affecting their abilities to absorb the losses that may be caused by certain terms.[210] However, once we move into a fairness arena a different 'abstract versus contextual' dichotomy arises.[211] Within a fairness approach the interests of consumers and traders can be analysed in a purely abstract manner. By this I mean that they can be assessed as at the time when the contract is drafted. The question is how the interests of the typical or average consumer or trader would be affected by such a term and no attention is paid to the way in which the interests of particular consumers and traders would be affected by the term.[212] So, for

---

[207] See above at 6.3.3.2(ii)(e).

[208] See above at 6.3.3.2(2)(a).

[209] See above at 2.3.2.

[210] See above at 2.4.1.

[211] See above at 2.4.3.6.

[212] See P. Nebbia, Law as Tradition and the Europeanization of Contract Law: A Case Study, (2004) Yearbook of European Law, 363, at 367; but note the point made

example, this form of analysis involves asking to what degree does the term deviate from the default rule or allow for compromise of reasonable expectations (i.e. the reasonable expectations of an imaginary – average – consumer); what type of consumer interests are affected (i.e. what type of obligations or liabilities is the term imposing or excluding and how would this affect the consumer interest in general); whether the term allows traders (in general) to escape liability when they are at fault; how much traders (in general) would stand to lose if such a term could not be used; whether insurance is available against the risks in question; and whether, when drafted, the contract contains provisions that reduce or negate the compromise of consumer interests caused by the term under scrutiny.[213]

By contrast, within a fairness approach, the interests of the parties can include sensitivity to context. By this I mean that the interests can be assessed in the context of the potential impact on the *particular* consumers and traders of the presence or absence of the term in question. So, for example, we ask whether the task is particularly difficult for this trader as a result of his own limitations or the particular needs of this consumer; how well placed the particular consumer is to bear the loss that might arise from the term;[214] how well placed this particular trader is to bear the loss that might be involved if the term is not included; whether either of these particular parties has the resources or practical opportunities to insure; how much of a burden it would be for this trader to offer particular counterbalancing benefits to the consumer; and how beneficial such benefits would be for this consumer (all of these matters being viewed in the light of the particular circumstances surrounding the contract in question). Private litigation is the forum in which there is most scope to take such contextual factors into account.[215] However, they might also be taken into account in a 'quasi-abstract' way by a body carrying out proactive control – what would be the position for the particular trader (not just any trader) using the term and what would be the position for particular types of consumers in the market where these terms are used?

---

above at 2.4.3.6 to the effect that Nebbia's notion of abstraction would include taking into account the particular position of the trader in the market.

[213] Nebbia associates an abstract approach with Kelsenian principles which avoid 'metalegal' considerations: *ibid.*, at 379. On abstract and contextual approaches under the UTD and in English and Italian tradition see P. Nebbia, Unfair Contract Terms in European Law, Hart, 2007, 65–67.

[214] On understanding the ways in which consumers may be disadvantaged see the discussion paper by George and Lennard, At a Disadvantage, Leicester University, Centre for Utility Consumer Law, October 2006.

[215] Equally, of course, in private litigation a court could ignore contextual factors and focus purely on the kind of abstract factors described.

6.3.9.2 The Approach Taken

In broad terms the actual picture seems to be as follows. The two existing regimes and the proposed new regime seem to allow for contextual factors to be taken into account although this may only happen to a limited extent in practice. Under the two existing regimes and the proposed new regime the test refers to 'the circumstances' at the time of conclusion of the contract.[216] Clearly these 'circumstances' could be read to include the ways in which the term (or the contract without the term) would affect the particular parties given their particular characteristics and the particular circumstances of the contract. The same can be said of the other broad criteria that are used: 'the abilities of the parties to bear the loss'[217]; 'the availability and cost of insurance'[218]; 'an overall evaluation of the different interests involved'[219]; 'the substance and effect of the term' and 'the balance of the parties' interests'.[220] These could all be read to call for consideration of the particular circumstances of the parties in question. In other words, they could all be taken to be referring not only to the position of traders and consumers in general, in relation to the types of interests and losses involved and the availability of insurance; but also to the interests and loss bearing abilities of the particular traders and consumers involved; along with the particular circumstances affecting the availability of insurance in the case in question (and thereby leaving scope for a more contextual approach).

However, this does not mean that such an enquiry will always be carried out. For example, in both existing regimes it is clear that there is a policy against exclusion of liability for fault, and whether a term covers liability for fault is an abstract question. However, there is also the further development of this policy; to the effect that there should be consideration as to whether the task in question is particularly difficult.[221] In *Smith* v. *Bush* this was probably only intended to refer to how difficult the task is in general for members of the trade in question.[222] However, it could, in theory, be developed so as to relate to the difficulty of the task for this particular trader.[223]

---

[216] UCTA, s. 11(1); UTCCR, Regulation 6(1); and Draft Bill, Clause 14(1)(b).
[217] *Smith* v. *Bush, supra,* 531–532.
[218] *Ibid.*
[219] Preamble to the UTD, Recital 16.
[220] Draft Bill, Clauses 14(1) and 14(4)(c) respectively.
[221] *Smith* v. *Bush, supra,* 531–532.
[222] *Ibid.*
[223] It would be unlikely ever to be taken to include subjective difficulties that the consumer could not be aware of but might plausibly be taken to include those that the consumer was or should have been aware of.

Then there is the question as to the impact of the term on consumers (or the impact on traders of not being able to use it) in terms of the abilities of the parties to bear the relevant loss and the associated question of insurance. Here, again, the picture is mixed. Certainly, in *Smith* v. *Bush* the House of Lords appear to have taken at least a partially contextual approach to the position of the particular consumers; the decision that the term was unreasonable being influenced by the fact that young first time buyers such as these could not be expected to pay for a separate structural survey.[224]

Smith v. *Bush* also suggests the potential for contextual factors relating to the stronger than average financial position of the particular consumer to be taken into account. Lord Griffiths said that, although the exclusion of liability was unreasonable in cases such as this, involving houses of modest value, it might not be in the case of more valuable property:

> I expressly reserve my position of valuations of quite different types of property for mortgage purposes, such as industrial property, large blocks of flats or very expensive houses. In such cases it may well be that the general expectation of the behaviour of the purchaser is quite different. With very large sums of money at stake prudence would seem to demand that the purchaser obtain his own structural survey to guide him in his purchase and, in such circumstances with very much larger sums of money at stake, it may be reasonable for the surveyors valuing on behalf of those who are providing the finance either to exclude or limit their liability to the purchaser.[225]

Strictly, Lord Griffiths relates the possibility of the term being reasonable in different circumstances to the matter of the value of the subject matter. The gist is that the greater the risk involved in the purchase, the more reasonable it is to expect alternative protection to be taken out. However, it might be suggested that one of the reasons that Lord Griffiths believed that this would be more reasonable to expect in cases of expensive property is that those buying more expensive property are likely to have greater financial resources to spend on such alternative protection.

More generally, under UCTA it has been emphasized that the question of reasonableness turns on the circumstances of the particular case. In *Phillips* v. *Hyland*[226] Slade LJ said that the question was not whether the exclusion of liability for negligence by a plant owner was reasonable in general in contracts with plant hirers but whether it was

---

[224] *Smith* v. *Bush, supra,* 531–2.
[225] *Ibid.*
[226] [1987] 2 All ER 620, CA.

reasonable in the particular contract in question.[227] It was clear that on the facts this involved a contextual approach in the sense of taking into account matters related to the substantive impact of the term (and the related question as to the availability of insurance) on the plant hirer in question in the particular circumstances. So it counted against the term that the hirer would not have had time to arrange insurance and that the hirer had no control over the use of the plant.[228] However, these particular circumstances relate to the party against whom the term is being used. So this case does not tell us how much attention would, in practice, be paid to particular circumstances affecting the party using the term (whether these are practical circumstance arising on the facts of the case – such as the lack of time to arrange insurance – or factors related to the particular financial strengths or weaknesses of the party, including their ability to pay for insurance). In other words it does not tell us whether the greater than average size and wealth of a business would lead to the conclusion that a term that would otherwise be reasonable should be treated as unreasonable on the basis that the business is wealthy enough to bear a greater than normal burden of the risks under the contract or pay for insurance that would be regarded as too expensive normally. Neither does it tell us whether the small and poor nature of a business might lead to the conclusion that a term that would otherwise be treated as unreasonable should be treated as reasonable on the basis that this trader is too poor to accept the risks of not being able to use the term in question and too poor to pay for insurance that would normally be regarded as reasonably priced for the average trader. However, there *is* actually specific statutory guidance that is relevant to the particular circumstances of traders. Section 11(4)(a) provides that where a party limits liability to a particular sum regard should be had to 'the resources which he could expect to be available to him for the purpose of meeting the liability should it arise'. This appears to leave scope to say that a term that might be reasonable when used by the 'average' trader, is unreasonable because the trader in question is particularly well-off; and equally that a term that might otherwise be unreasonable, is reasonable because it is being used by a trader who has very limited resources. Certainly, there is evidence of the former approach (or at least of the considerable resources of a trader being a factor counting against a term)

---

[227] *Ibid.*, at 628.

[228] *Ibid.*, at p. 672–9; for a critique of this approach see H. Beale, Unfair Contracts in Britain and Europe (1989) Current Legal Problems 197, at 208 (the view of Beale being that – although contextual factors might be taken into account in coming to the conclusion that a term that might otherwise be unreasonable is reasonable on the facts – it should not usually be taken into account so as to reach the conclusion that a term is unreasonable where 'the clause is a fair one for the normal run of contracts').

in *St Albans City and District Council* v. *ICL*.[229] In that case the considerable resources of the defendant (along with their superior bargaining power and the small amount of liability accepted relative to the possible loss that might be suffered by the plaintiffs) counted against the reasonableness of their limitation of liability clause. By contrast, I cannot find significant evidence of terms being found to be fair based on the particularly limited resources of the trader using it.

Most of the law under the UTCCR is being developed by the regulatory decisions of the OFT. Here there are no individual consumer circumstances to consider. In theory, the OFT could consider whether the trader in question is in a stronger or weaker position than average to bear the risks in question, although there does not appear to be significant evidence of such an approach. In theory, also, the OFT could consider the position of the particular categories of consumers faced with the term and ask whether they are more or less able than normal to bear the risks involved; but, again, there does not seem to be significant evidence of such an approach.

Under the UTCCR the 'high level of protection' goal might certainly push for an interpretation that takes into account the particular weaknesses of certain consumers and their inabilities to bear certain losses. Having said this, the more recent Unfair Commercial Practices Directive actually makes a point of distinguishing explicitly between the level of protection to be given to average consumers and vulnerable consumers.[230] This could be taken to suggest that no such distinction was intended under the UTD as it was not made explicit as it has been under the UCPD. Equally, it might simply be that the UCPD is making more explicit and clear what was thought to be implicit in the UTD and other directives affecting consumers. Certainly, there is evidence in other jurisdictions of taking a contextual approach that shows particular sensitivity to the vulnerability of certain classes of consumers. In a Norwegian case[231] it has been held that a term providing financial penalties for breaking a contract for education was unfair in particular because of the socially deprived status of the students. Of course, this may be a decision that reflects a view as to UTD[232] or it may be simply reflect the traditional Norwegian (and broader Scandinavian) approach which is consistently described by Scandinavian commentators as being

---

[229] [1995] FSR 686.

[230] 2005/29/EC; and compare Article 5(2)(b) and Article 5(3).

[231] CLAB Europa Database, Case 000148.

[232] Even though Norway is not a member it may be that the agenda is to reflect the standards of the UTD.

concerned with using contract law as a tool for protection of the most vulnerable in society.[233]

Of course, whatever the requirements of the UTD, it is open to the Member States to provide for a higher level of protection, e.g. by setting higher fairness standards for more vulnerable consumers. What evidence is there as to the approach thought to be appropriate under the UTCCR? The *First National Bank* decision on the facts did not turn on any such issue. However, there is dicta to the effect that contextual factors relating to the weaknesses of the consumer are indeed relevant. The House of Lords refer to 'necessity' and the importance of the trader not taking advantage of it.[234] We have already seen[235] that it is not clear what is meant by 'advantage taking' in this context and we shall be returning to this issue in the discussion of procedural fairness below. However, here the issue is the idea of 'necessity' and what this might mean in relation to the substantive features of terms. In other words, the question is whether the use of the word 'necessity' suggests that a term that might otherwise not be regarded as particularly substantively prejudicial in substance, should be regarded as more substantively prejudicial where certain consumers (i.e. those suffering from 'necessity') are concerned. The problem is that it is simply not clear what Lord Bingham meant when he referred to 'necessity' It could be taken to be a description of the position *most* consumers are in where many goods and services are concerned. Consumers *need* food, clothing, housing and other things in order to live a normal life. It may be that all that is being said is that traders should not use terms that (judged by the standard of the average consumer who has these needs) are unfair based on the normal analysis of (for present purposes) substantive issues that would apply to all consumers. Then there are cases where consumers are in particular *need* due to pressing emergency circumstances. So, for example, the consumer may be stranded due to a breakdown; or may need to organize finance in a hurry, in order to pay for something. The trader in question may impose terms that are harsher than normal and the consumer may not feel that he has any choice but to accept.[236] This sort of term might be unfair in most

---

[233] See T. Wilhelmsson, Social Contract Law and European Integration, Ashgate, 1995, 202.

[234] [2001] 3 WLR 1279, Lord Bingham at 1308.

[235] See above at 5.5.4.2(iii).

[236] This is a situation that might, depending on the precise circumstances, fall within rules on unconscionability or a suggested category of 'lawful act duress' (see M. Chen-Wishart, Contract Law, OUP, 2005, 342 and 375–391) the consumer being in a particularly weak bargaining position based on the particular emergency circumstances and this being taken advantage of to impose particularly harsh terms –

cases anyway and it would be even more clearly unfair here. But the real question is whether a term that would otherwise be fair in substance (and is being used in circumstances where there is no greater procedural unfairness than normal) will be more likely to be unfair because it has been used against a consumer that is more needy than average. In other words is there more likely to be violation of good faith on substantive grounds based on the more needy position of the consumer in question (more needy than average in terms of his ability to bear the substantive consequences of it)?

Such an approach does seem to be possible. 'Necessity' could (whatever else it covers) include being generally in a 'needy' position, i.e. being poor or at least poorer than average. The idea could be that being in a particularly needy position should be taken into account in assessing the substantive features of the term; i.e. that a term that might be fair when used against the average consumer might be viewed as unfair when used against a particularly poor/needy consumer. There certainly does not appear to be anything in the text to prevent such an approach being taken. Having said this, it might often be difficult to know where to draw the line as between the average and the poor consumer. It may therefore be that the courts would only be inclined to make a distinction in the most clear-cut of cases, i.e. where the consumer is clearly in an extremely vulnerable position.

What the *First National Bank* decision does not do is to provide any indication as to whether contextual factors relating to the *strengths* of that consumer should be taken into account under the UTCCR (in other words whether a term that would otherwise be found to be unfair can be found to be fair on the basis that the consumer is particularly well-off and therefore in a position to bear the loss in question). Neither is there any indication as to whether the *strengths or weaknesses* of the particular trader should be taken into account (so whether the greater than average size and wealth of a business should sometimes lead to the conclusion that a term that would otherwise be fair should be treated as unfair on the basis that the business is wealthy enough to bear a greater than normal burden of the risks under the contract, or whether the small and poor nature of a business should sometimes lead to the conclusion that a term that would otherwise be treated as unfair should be treated as fair on the basis that this trader is too poor to accept the risks of not being able to use the term in question).

The picture, then, in broad terms, seems to be that contextual factors can, in theory, be taken into account under both regimes. In practice, under UCTA the strongest evidence relates to the particular financial

---

see The Port Caledonia [1903] PC 184 and more generally on unconscionability see further below at 8.1.2.

vulnerability of the consumer being taken into account with a view to setting a higher standard than might otherwise be set; and taking into account the greater than average resources of the trader with the same result. There is less evidence of account being taken of contextual factors as to the weak position of traders or the strong position of consumers with the result that the standard is lowered. Under the UTCCR there is no significant evidence of account being taken of any contextual factors in actual application of the law to particular terms. However, there are dicta in *First National Bank* suggesting a contextual approach focused on the particular vulnerabilities of some consumers might be possible.

6.3.9.3 Should Contextual Factors be Taken into Account?

The next interesting question is whether contextual factors (for the moment we will stick to discussing those factors related to the substance of the contract) *should* be part of the regime. One advantage might be said to be that the there is a purer form of individualized justice if we take into account all the facts that might affect the way in which the term might impact upon the particular parties; rather than simply considering how the typical trader and consumer would be affected. Putting this in another way, we might say that there is a more comprehensive fairness analysis, if we take into account all of the circumstances affecting both parties.[237] There is also the opportunity to practice an element of redistributive justice or minimal welfarism and protect the interests of the more vulnerable consumers, i.e. by taking into account the particular financial vulnerability of these consumers and setting a higher standard of fairness in these cases.[238]

---

[237] On the view that this might be more in keeping with English common law tradition of concern with the facts of a case and notions of personalized justice than with Italian legal tradition see P. Nebbia, Unfair Contract Terms in European Law, Hart, 2007, 67–68.

[238] Generally on welfarism see below at 7.1. Maximal welfarism simply protects the interests of those (consumers in general) who are regarded as weaker within the contractual relationship, i.e. relative to the other party (traders in general). This can also be associated with commutative justice. The injustice is represented by terms that do not properly take account of the interests of parties falling into the consumer category, i.e. those buying goods and services in the private sphere of life; and the agenda is to correct this injustice by preventing/disallowing such terms. By contrast, minimal welfarism begins by focusing upon the position of the parties in the overall social order. The agenda is to redistribute resources to those who are most in need. There must, therefore, be discrimination in favour of those consumers who are weakest within the overall social order (see generally T. Wilhelmsson, Consumer Law

However, it might be desirable to go no further than giving extra protection to the most vulnerable consumers and perhaps expecting higher standards of fairness from the most financially well-off traders, i.e. it might be that we should not allow forms of contextualism that *reduce* the level of protection available based on the greater than average resources of the consumer in question or the lower than average resources of the trader in question. As we have seen, there is no particular evidence of such an approach being taken in any case; although it might be wise to make it clear that this approach should not be taken. One reason would simply be to maintain a high level of consumer protection and generate consumer confidence. Although the language of the text of the UTD *could* be read to allow for such trader weaknesses and consumer strengths to be taken into account,[239] there must be a serious question as to whether this was intended, given the consumer confidence and high level of protection goals of the UTD. In addition, there is the problem of the uncertainty that might be caused. It is clear that there is less predictability where contextual factors related to the any of the particular characteristics of the parties are taken into account. This may, again, hamper the harmonization goals of the UTD, making it more difficult for individuals from other Member States to ascertain the precise scope of their rights.[240] However, this certainty argument does not seem to apply with the same force to a contextual approach that gives extra protection based on particular consumer weakness or trader strength. For the purposes of the UTD, the certainty issue is about consumers being able to ascertain their rights. Consumers are most compromised in terms of knowing their rights, if the protection that might otherwise be available can be reduced based on the weakness of the trader; not so much if their own (i.e. consumer) rights can only get better based on their own weaknesses or trader strengths. So, preserving this element and dispensing with the trader sided contextual element might be the best approach. It is true that this does affect the certainty interests of the trader – the interest in being able to draft terms and predict whether they will stand up; but taking account of the particular financial vulnerability of some consumers will surely not have a major impact here as we are only talking of otherwise fair terms being found to be unfair in these limited number of cases where particular financial vulnerability is involved.

---

and Social Justice, in I. Ramsay (ed.), Consumer Law in the Global Economy, Ashgate, 1997, 217).

[239] Article 4(1) refers to taking into account '*all* the circumstances' and Recital 16 to the Preamble refers to good faith as involving 'an *overall* evaluation of the *different* interests involved'.

[240] See P. Nebbia, Law as Tradition and the Europeanization of Contract Law: A Case Study, (2004) Yearbook of European Law, 363, at 381–2.

6.4 Procedural Fairness

6.4.1 Introduction

Above we have discussed the ways in which the general fairness concepts measure fairness in substance. Now we must consider the way in which procedural fairness is measured. The idea of procedural fairness, of course, is that consumers should be placed in a better position to protect themselves against any unfairness in the substantive terms.[241] So, where there is procedural fairness the idea may be that the consumer has had a better chance to look after his own interests and that it is therefore logical that the terms should be more likely to be treated as fair. Equally, if there is a lack of procedural fairness, this may suggest that the consumer was not in a position to protect his interests and that the term should be more likely to be found to be unfair. We have already discussed the approaches taken to procedural fairness in the legislation and the courts. We now seek to further unpack the issues with particular reference to the work of the OFT and the proposed new legislation.

6.4.2 Transparency

6.4.2.1 Unpacking the Different Elements – Introduction

So far we have seen that transparency issues are not set out in UCTA guidelines aimed at consumers but that some of them had been mentioned in UCTA case law.[242] There is no explicit mention of transparency in the UTD or the UTCCR under the general unfairness test (although the indicative list does contain an example of a term 'irrevocably binding the consumer to terms with which he had no real opportunity of becoming acquainted before the conclusion of the contract'[243] and there is the separate provision on plain and intelligible language[244]). However, as we saw, transparency was clearly indicated to be vital to good faith by the House of Lords in the *First National Bank* case.[245] Lord Bingham referred to good faith as requiring 'fair and open dealing'. He said that 'openness' meant that terms should be 'expressed fully, clearly and legibly'; not containing 'concealed pitfalls or traps'; and being given 'appropriate prominence' where they might 'operate disadvantageously'

---

[241] See above at 2.4.3.4.
[242] See above at 4.6.1.
[243] Paragraph 1(i).
[244] Regulation 7.
[245] See above at 5.5.4.2(iii).

to the consumer.[246] We must now seek to unpack some of the more specific aspects of transparency that seem to be relevant, taking into account OFT practice and the proposed new legislation.

6.4.2.2 Availability of Terms and Time for Reflection

In the general introduction to procedural issues facing consumers, availability and time for reflection were mentioned.[247] Availability and time for reflection are not expressly addressed by the UCTA guidance. In fact UCTA makes no reference to transparency in relation to consumer contracts. The only reference to transparency issues comes in relation to commercial contracts; and then only in the case of terms excluding or restricting the liability of a seller of goods for breach of the implied terms as to description, quality and fitness for purpose. In the case of such terms account is to be taken of whether the consumer knew of or ought to have known of existence or extent of the term.[248] This is clearly affected by whether or not the term is available to be read and how much time there is to read and digest it (as well as by other aspects of transparency); and there is nothing to prevent the courts taking this and other transparency issues into account under the reasonableness test in consumer cases. However, for whatever reason, no great play has ever been made of availability, time for reflection or indeed other transparency issues in any of the UCTA consumer case law.[249]

In relation to the UTCCR, the idea that the terms should be available seems to be captured by the House of Lords reference in *First National Bank* to terms being expressed 'fully'. [250] In addition, as we have just seen (6.4.2.1 above), the indicative list actually contains an example of a term 'irrevocably binding the consumer to terms with which he had no real opportunity of becoming acquainted before the conclusion of the contract'.[251] In other words, if there is no real chance to become acquainted with the terms (due to unavailability and/or limited time for reflection and/or general lack of transparency) the term (e.g. on a ticket or notice) seeking to incorporate these terms may be unfair and so not

---

[246] [2001] 3 WLR 1279, 1308.

[247] See above at 2.3.2.1.

[248] See s. 11(2) and Schedule 2, para. (c).

[249] For the approach taken in commercial contracts see The Zinnia [1984] 2 Lloyds Rep 210; *AEG (UK) Ltd* v. *Logic Resource Ltd* [1996] CLC 265 and *Britvic Soft Drinks* v. *Messer UK Ltd* [2002] EWCA Civ 548, [2002] 2 All ER (Comm) 321.

[250] [2001] 3 WLR 1279, 1308.

[251] Paragraph 1(i).

binding. As such, the terms themselves would not form part of the contract and will therefore not be binding on the consumer.

The OFT approach to this issue is to emphasize that the terms need not necessarily all be in one document. Indeed, they emphasize that communicating with the consumer solely by reference to one document full of lengthy terms is problematic in itself[252] (for the obvious reason that a lengthy complex contract may deter consumers from trying to read and understand it). The OFT seek to encourage face to face explanations; brochures; and executive summaries. They also emphasize that such means should seek to draw attention to the most important terms; and in general consumers should be effectively alerted to all terms significantly affecting their legitimate interests.[253] So, in some cases, where there is a term incorporating other provisions but containing no detail as to what these other terms contain, the OFT approach is to simply require deletion of the incorporating term.[254] In other cases, where it is practicable, the approach is to require the incorporating term to actually spell out the precise scope of any exclusion, restriction or onerous term.[255] Another possible approach, where the terms being incorporated are not available at the time of conclusion of the contract, is to insist upon there being a cooling-off period.[256] This is obviously to provide for the opportunity to access and read the terms as this opportunity did not present itself at the time of conclusion of the contract. It should be noted here that the OFT take the view that this approach may be appropriate whenever the terms are not communicated to the consumer at the time of the conclusion of the contract.[257] Very often this will involve contracts that would be covered by the Consumer Protection (Distance Selling) Regulations.[258] However, the OFT clearly intend that even where the contract falls outside these regulations (either because, although it is made at a distance, the trader did not make exclusive use of distance communication prior to the contract[259], or because the contract was not concluded at a distance at all) there should be provision for a cooling-off period where the terms are not available.

All of this is a significant step forward from the common law position where all that is generally important is whether there is 'reasonable

---

[252] 2001 guidelines, 9.3.

[253] *Ibid.*

[254] See, for example, the Global Internet term at p. 111, OFT Guidance, 2001, Annex A.

[255] See, for example, the Time Computer Systems term, *ibid.*

[256] 2001 guidelines, 9.4.

[257] *Ibid.*

[258] 2000, SI 2000/2334 (which contain a legal cancellation right).

[259] See the definition of what is covered by the regulations in Regulation 3(1).

notice' of the term which acts to incorporate the other terms.[260] All that this usually means is that this incorporating term must do what is reasonable to make the consumer aware that terms *exist*.[261] It does not usually matter whether there is any notice as to their actual content. There is an exception in the case of terms that are 'particularly onerous or unusual.' Such terms must be drawn to the attention of the consumer.[262] However, this will only apply to those terms that are extremely unfair in substance, and not to less extreme terms that may nevertheless be significantly prejudicial to the consumer.[263]

Under the Law Commission proposals, the issues of availability and time for reflection would be explicitly addressed. Transparency would be one of the main factors to be taken into account in assessing whether the term is fair and reasonable.[264] Transparency would then be defined to require, *inter alia*, that the term be 'readily available to [the consumer]'.[265]

In addition, the proposed test would include reference to 'all the circumstances existing at the time [the term] was agreed'.[266] These circumstances would then be defined to include 'the knowledge and understanding of the party affected by the term' (i.e. the consumer).[267] In turn, in determining such knowledge and understanding, guidance notes would make reference to 'the information given to the [consumer] about the transaction before the contract was made'[268]; 'how the contract was explained to the [consumer]'[269]; 'whether the [consumer] had a reasonable opportunity to absorb any information given'[270]; and 'whether the [consumer] had a realistic opportunity to cancel the contract without charge'.[271]

---

[260] See *Parker* v. *SE Ry Co. Ltd* (1877) 2 CPD 416.

[261] See *Thomson* v. *LMS Ry Co. Ltd* [1930] 1 KB 41.

[262] *Interfoto Picture Library Ltd* v. *Stiletto Visual Programmes Ltd* [1989] QB 433.

[263] See further below at 6.4.2.3.

[264] Draft Bill, Clause 14(1)(a).

[265] *Ibid.*, Clause 14(3)(d).

[266] *Ibid.*, Clause 14(1)(b).

[267] *Ibid.*, Clause 14(4)(h).

[268] *Ibid.*, n. 44(f).

[269] *Ibid.*, n. 44(h).

[270] *Ibid.*, n. 44(i).

[271] *Ibid.*, n. 44(k).

6.4.2.3 Giving Prominence to Certain Terms

Availability and time for reflection is not much use if the consumer does not know what to look for, especially given the volume and complexity of terms and issues they deal with. One thing which this suggests is that there should be some degree of discrimination in presentation. In particular, the degree of transparency required should vary depending upon the substantive features of the terms in question. This is recognized at common law. As we have already noted, the common law requires a greater degree of prominence to be given to 'particularly onerous or unusual terms'.[272] According to the House of Lords in *First National Bank*, good faith in the UTCCR requires that the contract should be structured in such a way that the more important and onerous terms are given a degree of prominence. It has been said that, 'Appropriate prominence should be given to terms which might operate disadvantageously to the consumer'.[273]

It was also said that there should be 'no hidden pitfalls or traps'.[274] Although it is not made explicit, the suggestion is that a greater degree of transparency is required the more the term is substantively detrimental. The reference to 'terms operating disadvantageously' must be a reference to terms that are substantively disadvantageous. In addition, the idea of 'pitfalls or traps' suggests terms that are not sufficiently prominent given the detriment they cause in substance. This seems to go further than the *Interfoto* approach. First of all, of course, this is only *one* of various transparency issues that may be important under the good faith test; whereas if the appropriate degree of prominence is given under the *Interfoto* rule then the term will satisfy the common law test and be part of the contract. Secondly, according to the *Interfoto* rule a term must be given prominence where it is 'particularly onerous or unusual'. However, a term might be 'disadvantageous' without being 'particularly onerous or unusual'. 'Particularly onerous' has tended to mean that the term excludes some particularly important liability (e.g. implied terms as to quality etc or liability for death or injury[275]) or imposes an extremely onerous obligation or liability (e.g., as in *Interfoto*, a charge of nearly £4,000 for late return of photographic transparencies[276]). There is no suggestion by the House of Lords in *First National Bank* that a term need be so substantively unfair in order to be regarded as 'disadvantageous' and

---

272 *Interfoto Picture Library Ltd* v. *Stiletto Visual Programmes Ltd* [1989] QB 433.

273 [2001] 3 WLR 1297, Lord Bingham at 1308.

274 *Ibid.*

275 *Spurling* v. *Bradshaw* [1956] 1 WLR 461 and *Thornton* v. *Shoe Lane Parking* [1971] 2 QB 163.

276 *Interfoto Picture Library Ltd* v. *Stiletto Visual Programmes Ltd* [1989] QB 433.

therefore deserving due prominence under the good faith concept. In addition, under the common law 'unusual' means not typical in the sector in question (in *Interfoto* the charge was many times greater what was normal for other similar traders). The House of Lords in *First National Bank* simply referred to whether the term was disadvantageous, not whether it was unusual at all, far less 'particularly' unusual.

The proposed new regime does not explicitly mention giving prominence to disadvantageous or unusual terms; and it is arguable that this should be made explicit, given the special mention given to this issue by the House of Lords in *First National Bank* and the fact that the consumer interest in being made aware of these terms is strongest. The proposals do, however, hint at the problem of unusual terms. As we have already noted the 'knowledge and understanding' of the consumer would be relevant.[277] In assessing knowledge and understanding a relevant factor would be 'what a person other than the [consumer], but in a similar position, would usually expect in the case of a similar transaction'.[278] The idea here seems to be that if a term is out of step with what consumers would reasonably expect then it may be possible to assume that consumers will have limited knowledge and understanding of it. However, if it is clearly expressed and given an appropriate degree of prominence, then it will be easier to argue that it is likely to be known of and understood.

The first point here is that the mention of terms that the consumer *does not reasonably expect* (without mentioning terms that are *disadvantageous* more generally) might tend to increase the risk that the message does not come through clearly that *disadvantageous* terms (whether or not they reflect reasonable expectations as such and whatever expectations there may or may not be) should be prominent. So, this seems to reinforce the point that there should be an explicit reference to *disadvantageous* terms. The second point is that if good faith requires that terms that are out of step with reasonable expectations are given prominence (as it surely does[279]), then it might be preferable if the new law made this explicit; i.e. by saying simply that such terms should be prominent, rather than dealing with the issue via the 'knowledge and understanding' route. Finally, there is the question as to exactly what concept of reasonable expectations is being used here. The *Interfoto* notion of a 'particularly unusual' term seems, in the main, to be aimed at

---

[277] Draft Bill, Clause 14(4)(h).

[278] *Ibid.*, n. 44(d).

[279] It has already been argued (above at 5.7.6) that terms that do not reflect reasonable consumer expectations cause significant imbalance. It has also been argued (above at 2.4.3.4(ii) and 5.5.4.2(iii)) that whenever a term is detrimental in substance (i.e. when it causes a significant imbalance) it should usually be transparent.

terms that are unusual by comparison with the type of terms used by other traders in the market. It must be intended under the good faith test in the UTCCR that (whatever else) *this* sort of term is to be viewed as out of step with what consumers would reasonably expect. However, we must remember that under the good faith concept (especially in the light of the goals of the UTD[280]), the reasonable expectations of consumers are not simply to be viewed as being determined by what the formal terms say and whether they are in common use. The point has already been made that the general lack of 'true consent' to standard terms (no matter how transparent) is such that they cannot have a major role in determining the reasonable expectations of consumers.[281] These expectations are often fixed not by what the terms say, but by the way in which the goods or services are advertised and presented and the fact that transactions normally pass off successfully with no recourse to the formal terms.[282] On this approach to reasonable expectations, many terms that are in perfectly normal use may allow for something to happen that the consumer would not necessarily expect. This will include those terms already discussed which define the obligations of the trader so as to allow the trader to perform in ways that do not reflect the reasonable expectations of the consumer; and that define the obligations of the consumer such as to require him to perform in ways that he would not reasonably expect.[283] However, it will surely also include terms that deviate from the default position (to the detriment of the consumer) to a greater degree than the consumer might reasonably expect. Indeed, we know that this is the concept of reasonable expectations that should be relevant to the procedural side of good faith; as it is the concept that appears to be relevant to significant imbalance concept and to the substantive side of good faith.[284] Terms of these types cause significant imbalance and are likely to violate the substantive aspect of good faith. In general, terms causing significant imbalance should be transparent.[285] So, it is presumably terms of this nature that we have in mind when discussing reasonable expectations for the purposes of transparency standards.[286] However, it would be better if the guidance was to spell this

---

[280] That is, in generating consumer confidence and setting a high level of protection.

[281] See above at 5.7.6.3.

[282] *Ibid.*, and see also above at 4.4.3.

[283] See above at 5.7.6.1–2.

[284] See above at 5.7.6 and 6.3.2.

[285] See above at 2.4.3.4(ii) and 5.5.4.2(iii).

[286] Certainly, the OFT view is that a minimum requirement for terms allowing for compromise of the reasonable expectations by allowing changes to terms and to the characteristics of the product or service (paras 1(j) and 1(k) on the list) is that the

out, so as to avoid any danger that traders routinely argue (and some lower courts accept) that only terms that are unusual require to be given prominence.

6.4.2.4 Size of Print

A further transparency problem is often caused by the use of small print. In many standard form contracts, the size of the print is significantly below average. Even if the terms are available and there is time to read them, small print may deter the consumer from doing so. This was recognized as relevant under UCTA.[287] It is clearly relevant to good faith. The Office of Fair Trading have commented that,

> ... if they are to have an opportunity to examine the terms of the contract, consumers must have time to read them and the document must be reasonably legible. Some documents are so printed (tiny, pale green print on pink translucent paper was one example brought to our notice), that we can only conclude that the terms were not intended to be read at all.[288]

The House of Lords in *First National Bank* also, of course, covered the issue, saying that 'terms should be expressed ... clearly and legibly'.[289] The proposed new legislation also refers to legibility and clarity,[290] clearly addressing small, and in other ways illegible, print.

6.4.2.5 Language and the Overall Structure of the Contract

A further transparency problem relates to the language used and the overall structure of the contract. Plain language and clearly structured contracts that are well cross-referenced and easy to follow are surely vital to transparency. Interestingly, however, despite the well-known importance of transparency in EC consumer policy[291] (and the obvious relevance of transparency to the concept of good faith in civilian jurisprudence both in general and in particular to the fairness of contract

---

term specify clearly the circumstances in which changes can be made: see 2001 Guidance, 10.3 and 11.4.

[287] The Zinnia [1984] 2 Lloyds Rep 210.

[288] Unfair Contract Terms Bulletin 4, 1997.

[289] [2001] 3 WLR 1297, Lord Bingham at 1308.

[290] Draft Bill, Clause 14(3).

[291] See above at 3.4.4.

terms[292]), there is no reference to these issues under the auspices of the unfairness test in the UTD (or the UTCCR). However, the UTCCR (following the UTD) do make a separate reference to plain and intelligible language. Regulation 7 (following Article 5 of the UTD) says that 'a seller or supplier shall ensure that any written term of a contract is expressed in plain, intelligible language, and if there is a doubt about a written term, the interpretation most favourable to the consumer shall prevail'. No explicit mention is made in the main text of the UTD or in the UTCCR as to the connection between the good faith/fairness test and this separate provision on plain and intelligible language. The plain and intelligible language provision is in fact backed by an interpretation rule; which is clearly intended to have its own independent force.[293] The basic idea seems to be that, in individual cases, if a term is not in plain and intelligible language, then the interpretation most favourable to the consumer will be one either that renders the term harmless in substance or at least less unfair to the consumer; or one that makes the term patently unfair so that it can be set aside and the consumer protected in this way[294] (the approach taken should be that which is most plausible/possible in the circumstances). In proactive control, this rule does not apply.[295] However, as we saw above,[296] the approach taken seems to be to interpret the term in the *least* favourable way that it might be understood by the consumer; and (to the extent that this is an interpretation that involves the term causing significant imbalance) to find the term to be unfair on this ground allied with the lack of transparency (which violates the good faith requirement).

However, here we are dealing not with the plain and intelligible language requirement and the associated interpretation rule as such. The question is the relevance of plain language to good faith under the test of unfairness. Given that the subject matter of the UTD/UTCCR is 'unfair terms' it seems plausible to suggest that the plain and intelligible language requirement can also be seen as supportive of the general agenda to promote good faith and fairness; and that, notwithstanding the separate significance of the plain language/interpretation rule, plain language is itself relevant to good faith. This is clearly the view of the House of Lords who have said that 'terms should be expressed fully,

---

[292] See above at 3.5.5.2.

[293] See above at 5.10.

[294] See E. MacDonald, Exclusion Clauses and Unfair Contract Terms, Butterworths, 1999, at 183–4; and see E. Ferrante, Contractual Disclosure and Remedies Under the Unfair Contract Terms Directive, in G. Howells, A. Jaansen and R. Schulze (eds), Information Rights and Obligations, Ashgate, (2005), 115 at 123.

[295] Regulation 7(2).

[296] See above at 5.10.

clearly and legibly with no concealed pitfalls or traps'.[297] It is also the view of the OFT who always look to whether language is plain and intelligible in applying the general test of unfairness.[298] The new regime would refer explicitly to plain language as being relevant to transparency.[299]

It is fairly obvious that when we talk about language being plain and intelligible, we are talking about the words and phrases that are employed, and the overall construction of sentences and paragraphs. The words and phrases should be appropriate to convey what the overall sentence purports to convey. The sentences and paragraphs should not be overly convoluted or long, should not contain too much complex cross-referencing and should be constructed in a manner which is grammatically correct. The OFT seems to support such an approach.[300] However the language must surely be looked at from the viewpoint of the average consumer.[301] This must be appropriate in a measure which seeks to develop consumer confidence. This means that legal and technical jargon should generally be viewed as compromising intelligibility. Legal jargon would include words and expressions such as 'condition', 'warranty', 'indemnify', 'waiver', 'lien', '*force majeure*', 'consequential loss' and 'time of the essence'.[302] By technical jargon I mean the language associated with the operation of a particular product or service which would only be understood by a specialist in the product or service in question. The main contract can surely replace such legal and technical jargon with phraseology which is understandable to the average consumer. If the legal and technical jargon is viewed as necessary for completeness and to help resolve disputes, then it can be placed in a separate annex. Alternatively, the technicalities in the main contract can be explained in the contract or in a separate brochure provided along with the contract. This is something that is encouraged by the OFT and indeed could be said to be necessary for fairness in any situation in which the terms themselves are expressed in technical language.[303]

---

[297] [2001] 3 WLR 1297, Lord Bingham at 1308.

[298] See OFT Guidance, 2001, (IV) Analysis of Terms Breaching Regulation 7 – Plain English and Intelligible Language, para. 19.

[299] Draft Bill, Clause 14(3).

[300] Bulletin 4, 1997, p. 15 and OFT, Guidance, 2001, (IV) Analysis of Terms Breaching Regulation 7 – Plain English and Intelligible Language, 19.7.

[301] *Ibid.*, Bulletin 4, p. 14 and OFT, Guidance, 2001, (IV) Analysis of Terms Breaching Regulation 7 – Plain English and Intelligible Language, 19.3.

[302] *Ibid.*, Bulletin 4.

[303] OFT Guidance, 2001, (IV), Analysis of Terms Breaching Regulation 7 – Plain English and Intelligible Language, 2001, 19.9.

It is also arguable that the overall structuring of the contract is relevant to the issue of plain and intelligible language. The meaning and effect of a particular word, phrase, sentence or paragraph may only be able to be fully understood if read along with another section of the contract.[304] For example, a section discussing the exclusion or limitation of liabilities can only be understood properly if the consumer understands which primary obligations must be broken before these liabilities come into play. If these primary obligations are set out in a different section of the contract from the section dealing with the liabilities, then there must be clear cross-referencing between the two sections. If there is no such clear cross-referencing then the language describing the exclusion or limitation of the liabilities is arguably not really plain and intelligible.[305] It may also help if the contract is broken up as much as possible into easily understood sub headings dealing with recognizably similar issues. Indeed, we may be able to take this reasoning further to encourage disclosure of certain information about the legal rights of the consumer independent of the contract. The disclosure of information is not a positive requirement of the good faith test which, as we know, focuses on the fairness of terms and is not a direct vehicle for supplementation of contracts or the disclosure of information (as good faith can be in other contexts[306]). However, we have already seen that summaries and explanations (in brochures or other documents) are often required where the terms are complex, lengthy, unavailable or where legal or technical jargon is involved. So, although we are still dealing with a rule that is focused on the clarity of terms that the trader chooses to use, we begin to insist on a form of more positive disclosure (albeit disclosure that relates purely to better explaining the meaning and effect of terms that the trader chooses to use). However, we engage in a broader form of disclosure if we ask not only that there be explanatory material, but also that information as to the broader legal context be disclosed. Yet, it is arguable that this could be justified in some instances within the good faith/unfairness test we have here. Suppose, for example, that a contract term provides that liabilities are excluded or limited to a fixed sum. The consumer surely has a legitimate interest in knowing what obligations the

---

[304] I am grateful to Hugh Beale for earlier discussions on this point.

[305] OFT, Bulletin 4, at p. 15.

[306] Of course there is the 'utmost good faith' based duty of disclosure in insurance contracts on which see D. Friedmann, The Transformation of Good Faith in Insurance Law, in R. Brownsword, N. Hird and G. Howells, Good Faith in Contract: Concept and Context, 1999, 31. See also T. Wilhelmsson, Good Faith and the Duty of Disclosure in Commercial Contracts, in R. Brownsword *et al.*, *ibid.*, 165 and U. Reifner, Good faith: Interpretation or Limitation of Contracts? The Power of German Judges in Financial Services Law, in R. Brownsword *et al.*, *ibid.*, at 304–5.

trader is seeking to restrict his responsibility for. Some of these may be expressly undertaken obligations which are also set out in the contract. In the case of these obligations the necessary transparency involves these obligations being clearly expressed and there being a clear cross-reference to them. However, what if there are obligations that arise as a matter of law under a general default rule or under an implied term? In the introduction to fairness ideas, the point was made that surely in such a case the consumer has a legitimate interest in knowing what obligations the trader is seeking to restrict his responsibility for[307] (perhaps even more so than with express terms, as the terms derived from the general law will tend to be based on an attempt to reflect the interests of the consumer as well as those of the trader). It could, therefore, be argued that the *lack* of any provision outlining these obligations is a violation of the good faith requirement on the broad grounds that it means that proper account has not been taken of the legitimate interests of the consumer.[308] More specifically, it might be argued that failure to disclose these obligations compromises the intelligibility of the language which describes the exclusions and limitations. Without knowing of the obligations existing in the absence of the exemption clause, the consumer is less able to assess what is being taken from him by the exemption clause and this, arguably compromises the intelligibility of the exemption clause itself.

However, as we have already seen, even if the good faith concept might require such disclosure (i.e. of the nature of obligations that are being excluded or restricted by a term) it appears that the House of Lords do not believe that there needs to be disclosure of other types of information as to the legal framework. So, in the *First National Bank* case the view of the Court of Appeal was that for the term allowing for contractual interest to be charged after judgement in addition to the judgement debt to be fair, information should be provided to the consumer as to the right to have the court review the amount of interest to be paid and the time over which it must be paid.[309] However, the House of Lords did not believe that this form of disclosure was required.[310] We shall return to this issue below when considering the general level of transparency that seems to be required.

---

[307] See above at 2.4.3.4(iii).

[308] Recital 16 of the Preamble to the Directive says that good faith involves 'dealing fairly and equitably with the consumer whose legitimate interests [the trader] must take into account'.

[309] See above at 5.5.3.

[310] See above at 5.5.4.2(iv)(d).

6.4.2.6 Complexity, Cancellation and Advice under the Proposed New Law

The proposed new Explanatory Notes provide useful further factors (not currently mentioned) that are relevant to assessing the extent of transparency that it might be reasonable to demand. First, in considering the knowledge or understanding of a term under Clause 14(4)(h), attention would be directed to 'the complexity of the transaction'.[311] This is a useful context within which to view the other criteria. The level of complexity will affect how much information and explanation is needed and the extent to which questions of availability, time, explanation, clarity, plain language etc matter. Secondly, and also in assessing knowledge and understanding, attention would be directed to 'whether the [consumer] took professional advice or it was reasonable to expect the [consumer] to have done so'.[312] Again, this might affect how much to expect from the trader in the way of transparency. Certainly, if it is normal to take advice, this must to some extent lower the level of transparency that is needed, given that lawyers will be explaining the terms to consumers.

6.4.2.7 Better Legislative Guidance on Transparency

A serious limitation in the current approach to transparency is the lack of legislative guidance over what is such an important element of the fairness standard. Currently we need to 'eke out' the relevance and elements of transparency from general jurisprudence; from references in the legislation to different elements of transparency that are not knitted together; and by relying on the OFT work for detail on transparency criteria.

However, as we have seen, under the Law Commissions' proposals transparency would be one of the main factors to be taken into account in assessing whether the term is fair and reasonable.[313] Transparency would then be defined along the lines identified above, covering plain language, legibility, clarity and availability[314]; along with the various other guidelines mentioned above.

This is a massive improvement in terms of *legislative* 'transparency' and contributes to the Law Commission policy of achieving clearer and

---

[311] Explanatory Notes, 44(e).

[312] *Ibid.*, 44(j).

[313] Draft Bill, Clause 14(1)(a).

[314] *Ibid.*, Clause 14(3).

more accessible legislation.[315] Above we mentioned one or two transparency issues that might also be given attention in the new legislation and there is no need to repeat these here. However, what has not yet been mentioned is the question as to the *importance* of transparency within the fairness test. It is clear from reading the goals of the UTD in the light of EC consumer policy[316] that transparency is fundamental to fairness. This seems to have been accepted by the House of Lords in *First National Bank* where there was reference to good faith involving both fair *and* open dealing,[317] the latter requiring transparency. In this light there might be a case for actually providing in the legislation that a reasonable level of transparency is a requirement if terms are to pass the fair and reasonable test (rather than simply providing, as has been suggested, that transparency is a relevant factor in fairness). There might need to be a slightly different approach to this issue in preventive control and individual litigation. In the case of preventive control there *can* surely be an absolute requirement of the transparency in the case of any term that is in any way substantively prejudicial. However, in individual litigation we might wish to provide that, while the *prima facie* position is that there is such an absolute requirement, a lack of transparency can be excused if it can be shown that the consumer would have been content to agree to the substantive term if he had known of/understood it.

6.4.2.8 Level of Transparency

So far, then, we have considered the general principles of transparency along with some more detailed criteria. However, it is one thing to know what factors make up transparency, but what of the *level* of transparency that is required on the various aspects – e.g. availability, prominence, clarity etc? This is partly dependent on some of the variables already mentioned – complexity, whether advice normally taken and whether there is a right to cancel; but more generally how high should standards of transparency be to satisfy the general tests of fairness, in particular the good faith requirement?

In general, we must bear in mind EC context. First, then, there must be a sufficiently high level of transparency to generate consumer confidence[318] and this must be viewed in the light of the central role

---

[315] See Law Commission Report at 4 and see above at 3.2.

[316] On which see above at 3.4.4.

[317] [2001] 3 WLR 1297, Lord Bingham at 1308.

[318] A key goal of the UTD – see Recitals 5, 6 and 7 to the preamble and see above at 3.4.3.

transparency has in EC consumer policy; so it cannot just be about avoiding extreme lack of transparency or presenting the terms according to the standards of transparency that are normal in the trade sector; it must surely be a level of transparency that would make it reasonably possible for the average consumer to fully assess the risks. (Of course, it cannot be guaranteed that they will take up the opportunity, but the standard must surely be one that places them in a position such that this would be possible.) As we have seen, the ECJ have not articulated a view of transparency in the context of the test of unfairness.[319] However, it remains possible that the ECJ will indicate that transparency is vital and that there must be a high level of transparency.[320] There is, as we have said, another dimension to the EC context, i.e. the ECJ jurisprudence on consumers as it has been developed in the variety of contexts in which EC law bears on the consumer interest. What has emerged is that the ECJ operates on the basis of the 'average consumer' who is regarded as 'reasonably well-informed and circumspect' and who is regarded as being reasonably capable of looking after his own interests.[321] However, it has already been argued that such a consumer is surely in need of a fairly high level of transparency given the nature of standard terms.[322] In other words, whatever the 'reasonably well-informed and circumspect' model means in other contexts, I would suggest that it should not be taken to suggest anything other than a high level of transparency where standard terms are concerned. However, it remains unclear exactly what the ECJ would say as to the appropriate level of transparency in relation to contract terms.

Turning now to the attitude of the OFT, even from the above discussion as to the *type* of criteria that are relevant, it seems apparent that the OFT require quite a high standard. For example, there seems to be a strong policy against legal and technical jargon; and there seem to be quite high expectations in terms of general presentation, structure and the use of explanations and guidance.[323]

What of the view of the House of Lords? As we know, a range of criteria were mentioned and these have all been set out above along with other transparency criteria. Nothing was said expressly on the level of transparency required on the various issues. There was no criticism in relation to the level of transparency displayed by the term itself. As a term doing no more than explaining that interest was payable, it was probably as clear as could be expected, so little can be taken from this as to the

---

[319] See above at 3.5.5.2.
[320] *Ibid.*
[321] *Ibid.*
[322] *Ibid.*
[323] See above at 6.4.2.2–6.

level required. The real problem, however, was that consumers may not have expected to have to pay interest at the contractual rate *in addition to* the judgement debt.[324] The term said that interest would 'continue to be payable before, as well as after, any judgement (such obligation to be independent of, and not to merge in, the judgement)'. There must be some question as to whether this would be entirely clear to the average consumer. Essentially, the issue here is about legal 'jargon' and the failure to more fully explain to consumers the full implications of the term. Would the average consumer know what was meant by a 'judgement', i.e. would they connect it to a court order for payment of a debt, given that there is no reference to courts or going to court in the other parts of the term? In addition, would the reference to the fact that the 'obligation' would not 'merge in the judgement' really mean a great deal to the average consumer? It is arguable, at least, that more could have been done to explain exactly what the effect would be on consumers, e.g. to say something like: 'If we take you to court over non-payment of this loan and the court orders you to pay a sum of money (a 'judgement debt') you will still, in addition to this sum, be required to pay interest at x% of this sum until it is paid off. For example, …'.

It might then be said that if the House of Lords were insisting on a high level of transparency that they would have insisted that the term spelt out the issues along the lines I have suggested. However, it may be hard to draw general conclusions from the failure to insist on this. The House of Lords may have thought that no matter how prominent an explanation of this issue at the time of the contract there was, it would have been unlikely to register with the consumer at this stage; and that it would (at this stage) always be very hard for the consumer to work out what the implications might be. This may have been why Lord Bingham focused on the letter sent at time of judgement warning of the need to continue to pay interest at the contractual rate in addition to paying the judgement debt.[325] There are, of course, some issues as to the legitimacy of taking this letter into account[326] and we shall turn to these shortly. However, the question for now is whether there is any substance in a view that making the *term* clearer would not make any difference. Of course it is true that we must be sceptical about how likely consumers are (and how reasonable it is to expect them) to read terms even where they are transparent.[327] However, it is not obvious that a consumer would be any less likely to be able to focus on a term of the type at issue in *First National Bank* than any other type of term. Yet the OFT seem to insist

---

[324] See above at 5.5.

[325] See above at 5.5.4.2(iv)(d) and (e).

[326] *Ibid.*

[327] 2.4.3.4(iv).

that terms excluding liabilities and those imposing liabilities or allowing for changes, price increases etc., should spell out fairly rigorously how they will operate.[328] So, again, the conclusion may be that the House of Lords do not insist upon as high a level of transparency as the OFT.

We now turn to the attitude of the House of Lords to the letter itself. As suggested above,[329] it is not clear how much of a difference the letter made, i.e. whether, without the letter, the House of Lords would have regarded there as being a violation of good faith. If the letter *was* viewed as making a real difference then, as suggested above, this does, at least, indicate that some form of transparency was viewed as important by the House of Lords. However, as also suggested, the question is whether a rather limited degree of transparency was accepted. Just as the term might have done more to spell out the amount of interest that might be payable and to give an example to emphasize the point, surely the letter might have been expected to do the same.[330] So, again, the fact that this was not insisted upon might suggest that the House of Lords do not insist upon the very highest levels of transparency.

It is also arguable that the House of Lords in *First National Bank* could have insisted upon a higher level of transparency in another way, i.e. in relation to the legal context of the term. Above it was suggested that good faith might sometimes require disclosure of the full nature of the rights that a term is taking away from the consumer.[331] The *First National Bank* case did not involve an issue as to this precise type of disclosure. The issue was whether the lender should have been obliged to draw the attention of consumers to the right to have the court review matters at the time of the judgement.[332] I have already made the argument that this may be a particularly important type of transparency in enabling consumers to protect their interests.[333] This form of transparency was insisted upon by the Court of Appeal but not by the House of Lords. The House of Lords did not insist upon this partly because of the view that the letter just discussed helped to put consumers in the picture.[334] As we have seen, this may be questionable. Disclosure of the right to ask for review was not thought necessary also because it was not customary and

---

[328] See generally the OFT 2001 Guidance and see above at 6.3.2.1(i)(e).

[329] See above at 5.5.4.2(iv)(d) and (e).

[330] *Ibid.*

[331] See above at 6.4.2.5.

[332] *Ibid*; and for a general discussion, see E. MacDonald, Scope and Fairness of the Unfair Terms in Consumer Contracts Regulations: *Director General of Fair Trading v. First National Bank* (2002) 65 Modern Law Review 763, at 770–2.

[333] See above at 2.4.3.4(ii) and (iii).

[334] See above at 5.5.4.2(iv)(d).

because it was not required by law.[335] Again, this could suggest a standard of transparency that is not particularly high. The connection with what is customary suggests an over reliance on market norms. In addition, the idea that transparency standards should extend no further than existing mandatory requirements does not amount to a particularly ambitious approach to transparency.[336]

So, on all these counts (the attitude to the term itself, the attitude to the letter and the attitude to whether the lender should inform as to the review powers of the court) it might be said that the House of Lords was not setting a particularly high standard of transparency in *First National Bank* (and it is possible that the ECJ might insist upon a higher standard[337]). However, it must be remembered that the House of Lords did not believe that the term was actually unfair in substance (i.e. they did not believe that it caused a significant imbalance).[338] The view was that the real problem lay in the law: the *legal* inability of the court to award statutory interest (making it necessary for lenders to provide for contractual interest to continue to accrue)[339] and the lack of a proper *legal* process that would ensure that the consumer was warned at the time of the judgement of the need to pay contractual interest and the possibility of applying for a review by the court.[340] Given that transparency is, in part, aimed at enabling consumers to self protect, it is logical to insist upon a higher level of transparency the more unfair the term is in substance. So, if the view was that the term was not unfair in substance at all then (whether or not we agree with this view), from one point of view, it may not be surprising that a high level of transparency was not demanded; and, conversely, it might be supposed that if a term is viewed as more detrimental in substance then the House of Lords would insist upon a higher level of transparency (possibly involving disclosure of aspects of the legal context where appropriate).

However, the decision remains worrying in relation to the attitude to appropriate levels of transparency. As we have said, the view that a more substantial degree of transparency was not needed was partly premised on the view that the limitations of the law were the real cause of the problem. However, it could be argued that this, in itself, was a rather narrow view of the 'cause' of the unfairness. It is easy to accept that the legal context is indeed a very important part of the problem. However, it is also quite

---

[335] *Ibid.*

[336] See above at 5.5.4.2(iv)(e).

[337] See above at 5.5.4.2(iv)(f).

[338] See above at 5.5.4.2(iv)(a).

[339] *Ibid.*

[340] See above at 5.5.4.2(iv)(d).

plausible to suggest that the term plays its part too.[341] As MacDonald suggests, the issue is the 'interaction of the term and the legislation'.[342] After all, a term has a particular impact (in this case a continuing obligation to pay interest that may not be expected) not only because of what the law says but because of what the term itself provides; and the trader uses a term in the knowledge that what it provides for will have a particular effect within the legal context in question. Viewed in this light, we might have expected the House of Lords to insist upon more in the way of transparency; and the fact that they did not might be in fact be indicative of a general attitude that would extend beyond the confines of the peculiar facts of *First National Bank*. Again, however, it is difficult to know how much to read into *First National Bank* in terms of the general attitude of the House of Lords to requiring disclosure of legal rights. It is unclear whether this suggests a general reluctance to insist on disclosure of legal rights or just a particular reluctance in this case (this reluctance being explained (1) by the view that the term was fundamentally legitimate in substance and (2) the view that the *law* should be changed to ensure that a review process takes place and that requiring *the Bank* to tell people of their rights might weaken the case for a change in *the law*.

6.4.2.9 Disclosure of Facts?

So far we have been focusing upon the transparency of the terms and also on transparency in relation to the legal context of these terms. However, apart from such questions, there are questions as to disclosure of *facts*.

It is interesting to question whether good faith requirement might require disclosure of facts in some circumstances. If we think of good faith in the general sense expressed by Lord Bingham in the *Interfoto* case in terms of 'laying ones cards face upwards on the table'[343] there would certainly seem to be scope for a principle that demands more than the terms themselves being transparent. Good faith in certain civilian jurisdictions often involves the requirement that the parties disclose at least some factual information which would influence the other party's decision to enter the contract.[344] The precise type of information that

---

[341] See above at 5.5.4.2(iv)(d).

[342] E. MacDonald, Scope and Fairness of the Unfair Terms in Consumer Contracts Regulations: *Director General of Fair Trading* v. *First National Bank* (2002) 65 Modern Law Review 763, at 772.

[343] See above at 3.5.5.2.

[344] See the comparative overview (including discussion of English law) by J.H.M. Van Erp, The Pre-Contractual Stage, in A. Hartkamp *et al.*, (eds), Towards A European Civil Code, Kluwer, 3rd edn, 2004, 363; R. Sefton-Green, Duties to Inform versus

should be disclosed varies. So, it can be material facts about a product being bought or sold.[345] It can be material facts about a risk of some kind that is not related to the tangible features of a product.[346] In particular, of course, even in the common law, utmost good faith in the context of insurance contracts requires the disclosure of material facts that would affect the decision of the prudent insurer. In addition, the common law recognizes a variety of discrete situations in which there is a departure from the general rule against requiring disclosure.[347] In addition, there is a debate as to whether a general duty of disclosure based on a good faith principle would be a good thing.[348] Of course, we are not dealing here

---

Party Autonomy, in G.A. Janssen and R. Schulze (eds), Information Rights and Obligations, Ashgate, 2005, 171; R. Sefton-Green, Mistake, Fraud and Duties to Inform in European Contract Law, CUP, 2004; J. Ghestin, The Pre-contractual Duty to Disclose Information, in D. Harris and D. Tallon (eds), Contract Law Today: Anglo-French Comparisons, OUP, 1989; and T. Wilhelmsson, Good Faith and the Duty of Disclosure in Commercial Contracting, in R. Brownsword, N. Hird and G. Howells, Good Faith in Contract: Concept and Context, 165.

[345] See T. Wilhelmsson, Good Faith and the Duty of Disclosure in Commercial Contracting, in R. Brownsword, N. Hird and G. Howells, Good Faith in Contract: Concept and Context, 165, at 174.

[346] For example, information about the risks of acting as a guarantor – undue influence being found where there is not such disclosure; and some might say that there is an underlying principle of good faith at work here – see A.D.M. Forte, Good Faith and Utmost Good Faith: Insurance and Cautionary Obligations in Scots Law, in A.D.M. Forte (ed.), Good Faith in Contract and Property Law, 77, 87–96.

[347] See the review in E. McKendrick, Contract Law, Palgrave Macmillan, 6th edn, 2005, Ch. 12.

[348] See E. McKendrick, *ibid.*, at 464–9; and see P. Legrand, Pre-contractual disclosure and information: English and French law compared (1986) 6 Oxford Journal of Legal Studies 322; B. Nicholas, English Report, in D. Harris and D. Tallon (eds), Contract Law Today: Anglo-French Comparisons, OUP, 1989; Ghestin, The Pre-Contractual Duty to disclose Information, in D. Harris and D. Tallon (eds), Contract Law Today: Anglo-French Comparisons, OUP, 1989; S. Waddams (1991) 19 Canadian Business Law Journal 349; A.M. Rabello, The Culpa in Contrahendo Theory and the Israeli Contracts Law (general part) 5773–1973 Pre-contractual Liability in Israeli Law, in A.M. Rabello (ed.), Essays on European Law and Israel, Hamacabbi Press, 1996, 245, 287 *et seq*; T. Wilhelmsson, Good Faith and the Duty of Disclosure in Commercial Contracting, in R. Brownsword, N. Hird and G. Howells (eds), Good Faith in Contract: Concept and Context, 165 at p. 176; H. Collins, Law of Contract, Butterworths, 2004, at179–220 and in particular at 216–220; J.H.M. Van Erp, The Pre-Contractual Stage, in A. Hartkamp *et al.*, (eds), Towards A European Civil Code, Kluwer, 3rd edn, 2004, 363; and R. Sefton-Green, Mistake, Fraud and Duties to Inform in European Contract Law, CUP, 2004.

with this question; but simply whether, in the context of the fairness of consumer contract terms, a broader disclosure duty would be feasible. There certainly appears to be a logic to such an approach within general good faith thinking as this applies to the contract terms issue. Good faith involves a notion of respect for the interests of the other party and placing accordant limits on pursuit of ones own interest. In our case good faith is (in part) about the transparency of terms to enable the consumer to exercise a degree of self-protection through informed consent at the procedural stage and sometimes also to self-protect post-contractually. The information that I have already suggested may need to be disclosed – explaining the terms and putting them in their legal context – is essentially about better informing the consumer as to the risks posed by the terms; the argument being that this is needed in order to properly protect ones interest in relation to the terms. For this reason it is relevant to fairness and good faith in relation to the terms. I am sticking to the same theme, i.e. whether information as to risks posed by the terms is needed. The question is simply whether sometimes such information may come in the form of *facts* related to the performance of the contract where these facts might make agreement to the term a greater risk than normal.

It can certainly be argued that, in addition to having a legitimate interest in knowing of and understanding the terms of the contract, there may be some cases in which consumers also have a legitimate interest in knowing of the trader's motives and intentions in relation to the use of particular terms (or at least in knowing important facts related to the use of the term). Of course in most cases the trader may simply be using the term as a standard means of allocating risks which have an average chance of coming into play. So, for example, a trader excludes liability for late delivery, this being something that happens relatively rarely, and certainly no more than is average in the sector in question. The term should be transparent to the consumer, so that the consumer knows what the trader purports not to be liable for. The consumer is then in a position to weigh up the risks involved and in doing so he may make the assumption that the risk of late delivery is fairly small; and if this is true it is therefore unnecessary for the trader to inform the consumer of this. But what if the risk is large and the trader knows this? What if the trader or traders generally in this sector are having difficulties with labour, sub-contractors, transport or some other matter? What if this is generally known to traders but not generally know to consumers? It is surely arguable that consumers have a legitimate interest in knowing this background to the use of the term. In order to give fully informed consent to a term which excludes liability for a particular type of breach, a consumer must know if there is an above average likelihood of this event happening. It is arguable, then, that in such circumstances a trader's failure to disclose such information should be a factor which adds weight to an argument that the term violates the good faith requirement.

In fact, this argument may be strengthened by a particular reference in the *First National Bank* case. Lord Bingham said that the concept of good faith had a pedigree in English law as Lord Mansfield had been its 'champion'.[349] He did not go on to elaborate as to his view of Lord Mansfield's vision of good faith. However, it is clear that Lord Mansfield's notion of good faith included disclosure of material facts to the other party. Although Lord Mansfield's notion of disclosure of facts has come to be associated with the duty of disclosure in insurance contracts we have already seen that the matter was expressed more broadly than this by Lord Mansfield himself. He said that: 'The governing principle is applicable to all contracts and dealings. Good faith forbids either party from concealing what he privately knows, to draw the other party into a bargain, from ignorance of that fact, and his believing to the contrary'.[350]

We can see here that, for Lord Mansfield, good faith is not just about disclosure of material facts in an insurance contract. It applies 'all contracts and dealings' and it is about disclosure of 'what he (for our purposes the trader) privately knows'. So, to the extent that Lord Bingham thought it appropriate to build the current good faith rule on the general foundations laid by Lord Mansfield, it may be that this allows for an approach in which there should be disclosure of key facts where these have an impact on the risk involved in agreeing to the terms. This is not ruled out either by the further comments as to good faith made by Lord Bingham. He said that good faith required that the trader should 'deliberately or unconsciously take advantage of the ... unfamiliarity with the subject matter'.[351] 'Subject matter' could be interpreted narrowly just to refer to the main subject matter, so that Lord Bingham could be taken simply to be referring to consumers being unused to buying particular types of goods and services; and therefore being more likely to be taken by surprise, for example, as to the standard terms of contracts being used. However, unfamiliarity with the subject matter could be interpreted more broadly to include a lack of awareness as to the likelihood of the contract being performed properly. This being the case it is surely to 'take advantage' of this not to inform consumers that there is a high probability of non-performance.

This argument is also surely strengthened by the moral/ethical elements of good faith. Even though good faith in our present context appears to be an objective standard which can be violated despite the

---

[349] [2001] 3 WLR 1297, at 1308.
[350] *Carter* v. *Boehm* [1766] 3 Burr. 1907, 97 Eng. Rep. 1162 (K.B.).
[351] [2001] 3 WLR 1297, at 1308.

absence of bad motive on the part of the trader,[352] it is surely even more likely to be violated where there *is* an element of bad motive or at least where there is an element of opportunism. Such bad motive or opportunism might be found in acquiescing in consumer expectations of successful performance that one knows are quite likely to be frustrated; (i.e. the use of a term that is being treated as a mere formality, when in fact there is quite a high likelihood of it being invoked due to the high likelihood of failure to perform).[353]

However, it does need to be borne in mind that there is a need to have a clear trigger for the disclosure obligation. In the case of other situations the issue often is whether there is an awareness that the other is in error as to a specific fact (this triggering the obligation to disclose it[354]). What is the trigger here that is certain enough to make the duty workable? It cannot be simply that the trader has to inform the consumer in all cases of the precise likelihood of non-performance. This would be unrealistic. It would be more realistic and workable to say that if there is a significant exclusion and a greater than average likelihood of failure to perform (which the trader must be aware that the consumer is unaware of) then the trader should make this clear to the consumer.

It might be useful to highlight this issue in the guidance to the new legislation.

6.4.2.10 From the Same Broad Legal Standard to the Same Language and Structure

All of the above discussion of transparency must be set in the context of the reality that transparency will often have little impact upon consumers. There are a variety of reasons for this and these reasons have been set out above.[355] However, one particular problem is that the terms used by different traders are expressed and structured in different ways. There is therefore an argument for seeking to standardize the way in which the terms are expressed and structured within particular trading sectors.[356]

---

352 On this see further below at 6.7.

353 On good faith and morality see U. Reifner, Good Faith: Interpretation or Limitation of Contracts? The Power of German Judges in Financial Services Law, in R. Brownsword, N. Hird and G. Howells, Good Faith in Contract: Concept and Context, 269, 277–286.

354 See *Hartog* v. *Colin and Shields* [1939] 3 All ER 566.

355 See above at 2.4.3.4(iv).

356 *Ibid.*, and see T. Wilhelmmson, Cooperation and Competition Regarding Standard Contract Terms in Consumer Contracts, (2006), European Business Law Review, 49, at 55.

This may at least mean that if terms are read it they may be slightly easier to understand as consumers are used to seeing the information presented in this way. It may therefore mean that there is a greater possibility of informed consent and that it is easier to make comparisons and therefore more likely that competitive pressure will result.

Of course the general good faith standard can only play one part in achieving this. It does, as we have seen, lead to the OFT developing quite detailed policies on language and structure which traders are expected to comply with. The redrafting done by traders may then produce contracts which (following the OFT guidance) are fairly similar. However, the contracts will only be exactly the same in terms of language and structure where the whole trade sector produces contracts which are then used by all members. This does appear to be taking place to some extent via the work of the OFT. The OFT has agreed model contracts with trade associations in a variety of sectors.[357]

6.4.2.11 Contextualism and Transparency

(i) Introduction

We talked above of contextualism in relation to measuring unfairness in substance, i.e. taking account of the weaknesses and strengths (in terms of loss bearing abilities) of particular traders in such a way that we view as fair/unfair in substance (as the case may be) what we might otherwise think of as unfair/fair; and the weaknesses and strengths (in terms of loss bearing abilities) of particular consumers such that we view as unfair/fair in substance (as case may be) what we might otherwise think of as fair/unfair. In relation to transparency the question also arises as to whether there is a role for a degree of contextualism. First let us consider the consumer side of the equation.

(ii) Consumers

The above discussion is really about abstract standards of transparency, i.e. standards for the typical/average consumer; whether the one that comes before the court or the one that the regulatory bodies have in mind when they look at terms in the abstract. They are the abstract standards that are focused principally on the terms themselves: are the terms available, clear etc. (from the point of view of the average consumer)?

---

[357] For example the Association of Letting Agents, the Residential Landlords Association and the Royal Institute of Chartered Surveyors (see: http://www.oft.gov.uk/News/Press+releases/2003/PN+54-03.htm).

However, possibly, as with substance, there is scope for a contextual approach. First, this might mean *increasing* the standard (i.e. finding the level of transparency that would otherwise be regarded as reasonable to be insufficient) if a particular consumer is unaware/did not understand due to his particular vulnerability/lack of education/language skills etc. Under UCTA it is said that the assessment of reasonableness should take account of 'the circumstances which were or ought reasonably to have been in the contemplation of the parties when the contract was made'.[358] As we have already said,[359] the word 'circumstances' is clearly very open textured and could be given a broad or narrow interpretation. However, as we already know, the courts have made it clear under UCTA that in principle they take account of the circumstances surrounding the conclusion of the particular contract.[360] So, this could clearly mean taking into account the particular weaknesses we have mentioned (if the trader knew or should have known of them). Then there is the reference in UCTA Schedule 2 to 'whether the consumer knew or ought reasonably to have known of the existence and extent of the term (having regard to any custom of the trade and any previous course of dealing between the parties'.[361] Of course this is not aimed at consumer contracts[362]; although it is generally thought to be broadly applicable to such contracts (of course this does not necessarily need to mean in every nuance). However, it provides no definite guidance on the question at hand. Even if the consumer does not know of or understand the term, the implication is that this should not matter if he should have known; but this begs the question as to whether what he should have known is to be judged by the standards of the average consumer, or by reference to his own weaknesses. The suggestion is that particular circumstances – trade custom and previous course of dealing – could mean that a party is treated as having knowledge of terms when the term is itself not transparent (and we shall turn to this issue below), but this does not tell us whether particular weaknesses should be taken into account when the term *is* transparent. There is no particular guidance from the courts on the issue. However, in the arguably analogous situation of applying the reasonable notice test for incorporation of terms at common law, the view appears to be that if a consumer is known by the trader to have particular difficulties understanding a term (e.g. due to illiteracy or problems understanding

---

[358] Section 11(1).

[359] See above at 6.3.9.2.

[360] *Phillips Products* v. *Hyland* [1987] 2 All ER 620 (above at 6.3.9.2).

[361] Paragraph (c).

[362] It is aimed at application of the reasonableness test to exclusion or restriction of the implied terms as to description, quality and fitness in contracts for the supply of goods where the buyer is not buying as a consumer (see ss 6(3) and 7(3)).

English) then greater than normal steps are required for their to be reasonable notice.[363]

Under the UTCCR the criteria simply refer to 'all the circumstances attending the conclusion of the contract'.[364] Again, of course, the word 'circumstances' could be read broadly or narrowly. However, the UTD consumer confidence and high level of protection goals must surely push for an interpretation that takes into account particular weaknesses in relation to understanding. Indeed, there is a particularly strong case for this where the issue is that the consumer is from another EC country and does not speak English. The agenda, after all, is to generate consumer confidence in cross-border shopping. Also, it must surely be correct to read the provisions of a directive in the light of the general EC law principle of equal treatment. Parties who speak a different language, or have serious difficulties understanding terms for other reasons, are arguably not treated equally if they are not provided with assistance to overcome these constraints. It may also be that these factors outweigh the disadvantages of taking into account particular difficulties of understanding. So, for example it is clear that there is greater uncertainty for traders if this approach is taken. However, this may be outweighed by the advantages of taking into account such factors.

Interestingly the UTCCR test, unlike UCTA, says nothing of actual or constructive knowledge of the parties in relation to the circumstances. It seems unlikely, however, that it was intended that traders are to be expected to make particular provision for difficulties of which they could not be aware.

An approach that takes into account particular weaknesses in relation to understanding seems to have support from House of Lords in *First National Bank*, where Lord Bingham referred to good faith requiring that the trader not taking advantage of the 'indigence' of the consumer.[365] This reference to 'indigence' could be taken to refer simply to the position of the average consumer relative to the trader. In other words, this could simply be confirmation that terms should be sufficiently transparent for the average consumer; the standard of transparency simply reflecting that the average consumer is a non-expert, private individual and in this sense, relative to the trader, is 'indigent'. However, reference to 'indigence' may go further than this. The idea could be that those consumers that are more indigent than average should be given protection that the average consumer would not receive. So, terms that are regarded as sufficiently transparent where most consumers are concerned might be thought to be insufficiently transparent where particularly indigent

---

[363] *Geier* v. *Kujawa Weston and Warne Bros (Transport) Ltd* [1970] 1 Lloyds Rep 364.

[364] Regulation 6(1).

[365] [2001] 3 WLR, at 1308.

consumers are concerned. The same points can be made in relation to the 'inexperience' and 'unfamiliarity with the subject matter' criteria. (It will be recalled that Lord Bingham said that good faith required that these factors should not be taken advantage of by the trader.[366]) Consumers who are particularly inexperienced or unfamiliar with the subject matter may need terms to be made especially transparent. There is no particular indication from other cases or from the work of the OFT as to the issue.

The new statutory rules may or may not recognize particular vulnerabilities. It would, as we have said, be relevant to consider 'the knowledge and understanding of the party affected by the term' (i.e. the consumer).[367] In turn, in determining such knowledge and understanding, guidance notes would make reference to a number of factors including whether the consumer knew of the term and understood its meaning and implications.[368] Again, as with these criteria under UCTA, this begs the question as to whether it is to be said that whether a consumer should have known of the terms is something to be judged by reference to his particular weaknesses.[369] However, in the light of the arguments made above as to the requirements of the UTD, it might be a good idea to emphasize that problems of understanding faced by particular consumers should be taken into account.

We now turn to the other side of the coin. Giving a broad reading to the relevance of 'circumstances' in both UCTA, the UTCCR and the new regime could mean that we should take into account circumstances that *lower* the standard of transparency that is normally required. Indeed, we have already noted that this seems to be specifically contemplated in UCTA Schedule 2 in relation to trade customs and previous courses of dealing (either of which might mean that a party is treated as having knowledge of terms when the term is itself not transparent). This pattern is followed in the criteria proposed for new regime. There are criteria that seem to allow terms that may not be transparent by the standards of the average consumer, to be justified if the particular consumer has more knowledge in the circumstances. As we have just seen, the consumer's 'knowledge and understanding' is one of the relevant circumstances to be

---

[366] *Ibid.*

[367] Draft Bill, Clause 14(4)(h).

[368] Explanatory Notes, 44(b) and (c).

[369] The same point could be made in relation to other factors that would be made relevant to determining the consumer's knowledge and understanding, i.e. 'the information given to the [consumer] ... before the contract was made' (Explanatory Note, 44(h)); 'how the contract was explained to the consumer' (Note 44(h)); and 'whether the [consumer] had a reasonable opportunity ... to absorb any information given' (Note 44(i)). These matters could all be judged from the point of view of the average and/or the more vulnerable consumer.

taken into account in assessing fairness.[370] Knowledge and understanding itself is then to be assessed by reference to a range of factors. One of these is the question as to whether there has been a previous course of dealing. Presumably this factor is supposed to be relevant in a similar way to the way in which it is relevant at common law and, as we have mentioned, under UCTA. There, it can operate as a kind of substitute for actual notice/reasonable transparency of the term in the context of the particular contract. Despite the absence of actual notice amounting to reasonable notice, the existence of a previous course of dealing may suggest that the consumer was aware of the term and it may therefore be concluded that the consumer had reasonable notice in the context of the contract at hand. Presumably the idea under the proposed new regime is similar, i.e. that if the term is not transparent (by the standards normally required in the legislation) then, while this would normally count against a finding of fairness, this may not be the case where a previous course of dealing suggests that the consumer was in fact aware of the term.

The next factors (already mentioned above) would be simply whether the consumer knew of the term[371] and understood its meaning and implications.[372] It was said above that it was unclear as to whether these factors are intended to require a *higher* standard where a consumer is particularly weak (does this mean he should not have been aware of a term that others should have been aware of?). However, it seems more obvious that these criteria *are* intended to operate as a substitute for the level of transparency that would normally be required. It does seem to be intended that the lack of transparency will not count against the term if there is evidence that, despite the lack of transparency, the party affected by the term was actually aware of the term and understood its meaning and implications (or should have been aware of the term based, for example, on specialist knowledge or independent advice which he took or should have taken – the latter is also mentioned as an independent factor[373]). (In other words these factors could result in a *lower* standard of transparency being acceptable.) Of course, these factors could operate in other ways. For example, evidence that the consumer was aware of and understood the term might be evidence that it was in fact transparent by the standards of the average consumer. Alternatively, evidence that he did not know of or understand it, may help support the argument that it was not transparent by the standards of the average consumer. But the fact is that the criteria could operate to lower the standard in the way described.

---

[370] Draft Bill, Clause 14(4)(h).

[371] Explanatory Notes, 44(b).

[372] *Ibid.,* 44(c).

[373] Explanatory Notes, 44(j).

These forms of contextualism, which allow for standards to be lowered based on the experience/expertise of the particular consumer, are problematic. Taking account of the greater than average knowledge of the particular consumer based on previous experience/greater general expertise than normal (being a lawyer etc), might be a fair balance as between the two particular parties, but it could undermine the certainty needs of consumers and the protection and confidence goals of the UTD. There will be uncertainty as to whether a term lacking transparency can be challenged or whether it will be viewed as acceptable based on the knowledge of the consumer. Of course, it is probably the case that the Law Commission envisages these factors being much more relevant in the commercial contracts to which the same guidance applies.[374] These contractors are much more likely to have experience and expertise in relation to terms than consumers are; and it may be that it is envisaged that the courts would hardly ever, if at all, apply these criteria to consumer cases. However, there is always the risk that the courts *will* give undue weight to such factors in consumer cases. In addition, there is the problem of traders raising experience/expertise arguments routinely with all consumers even where these arguments have no substance. Such arguments are, in practice, likely to deter many consumers from taking the issue further. All of this is particularly problematic given the fundamental importance of transparency to EC consumer policy generally and to the good faith concept in particular.

Another point is that 'good faith' seems to focus on what *the trader* does. This obviously includes the transparency (or lack thereof) of terms he uses for consumers generally and could be said to include the transparency (or lack thereof) of terms that he uses in contracts with particularly ill-informed or ignorant consumers. However, when we are talking about the extra knowledge that some consumers may have, based on experience or expertise, these are factors that could be said not really to be relevant to a concept such as good faith that is focused on the practices of the trader. In the light of all this, there may be a good case (for the purposes of consumer contracts) for removing the references to previous courses of dealing, or at least making it clear that a previous course of dealing cannot reduce the standard of transparency required in consumer cases.

(iii) Traders

The next question is whether a contextual approach might be taken to raise the standard based not (as above) on the particular position of the consumer, but rather on the particular position/actions of the trader. So,

---

[374] Draft Bill, Clauses 9–11.

for example, the trader might be regarded as having an obligation to make terms more transparent than normal because he has the resources to achieve this and/or because he has advertised in such a way as to raise expectations as to his general straightforwardness, paternalistic approach etc or, even more specifically, as to how easy to understand the contract will be. Again, it is clear, in general, that the 'circumstances' existing at the time of the contract could be said to include such factors. In addition, the idea of taking such factors into account fits better with the good faith concept's focus on what the trader does. It also recognizes the importance of transparency to good faith, to achievement of the goals of the UTD and to broader EC consumer policy.

Finally, there is the question as to whether the particular weaknesses of the trader (e.g. limited resources to invest in making contracts transparent) or particular steps taken by the trader in this case (e.g. explanations given, key issues pointed out), can mean that terms that would otherwise be viewed as unfair based on intransparency, will be viewed as fair. As to particular weaknesses of the trader, it seems that (just as with lowering the standard based on special knowledge possessed by the consumer) there is a real danger of undermining the goals of the UTD; and in particular losing sight of the fundamental importance of a high standard of transparency.

(iv) Transparency, Contextualism and the First National Bank Case

A particular issue arises in relation to the facts of the *First National Bank* case. It has been argued that the House of Lords applied a particular form of contextualism to the transparency concept (in this case possibly to lower the standard of transparency that might otherwise have been required of the term itself). In *First National Bank*, as we have seen, the House of Lords took the view that the term allowing for interest to continue to be payable at the contractual rate after judgement was fair, at least in part, because the bank had the practice of sending a letter to consumers after judgement pointing out the implications of the term.[375] (As we saw above, there was not thought to be any need for the term itself to spell out the issue in greater detail or to point out that the consumer was entitled to ask the court for a review of the interest rate and for time to pay; the letter being viewed as doing as much as was required to enable consumers to protect their interests.) The argument is that the letter is a contextual factor, as it is not something that can be assessed as at the time

---

[375] See above at 5.5.4.2(iv)(d).

when the term was drafted.[376] The argument also made is that taking into account such a factor may cause uncertainty.[377] There is also the point that the test is only supposed to take into account circumstances existing at the time of the conclusion of the contract; yet the letter is sent after the conclusion of the contract. However, the point has already been made above that if there is an obligation at the time of the contract to do something post-contractually (whether it be the sending of this letter or the provision of information to the consumer as to the right to ask the court for a review) then the thing that is to be done post-contractually may be argued to be a factor that exists at the time of conclusion of the contract.[378] Indeed, it has also been argued that post-contractual information may often be particularly helpful to the consumer. In particular it has been argued that information as to the right to ask the court to review matters would have been helpful.[379] Viewed in this light, the problem with the letter is not when it is sent. The problem, rather, is that (as suggested above[380]) the contents of the letter do not spell out with sufficient clarity to consumers the implications of the continuing accrual of contractual interest.

6.4.3 Procedural Fairness and Choice

6.4.3.1 Introduction

The agenda of a fairness-oriented approach is to maximize the ability of the consumer to protect his interests in the agreement process. I have argued above that transparency is fundamental to this agenda. However, even if there is transparency, the ability of the consumer to protect his interests may be compromised by lack of choice.[381] Even where terms are sufficiently transparent for the consumer to be aware of their meaning and implications it may be that no real choice is available. Of course, lack of choice can mean a number of different things; and we are not dealing here with problems of choice being removed by physical or economic duress.

As suggested above, the more likely problem is thus. The trader has put forward a term or set of terms. One or more of the terms is in some

---

[376] P. Nebbia, Law as Tradition and the Europeanization of Contract Law: A Case Study, (2004) Yearbook of European Law, 363, 380; and P. Nebbia, Unfair Contract Terms in European Law, Hart, 2007, 158.

[377] *Ibid.*, at 381–2.

[378] See above at 5.5.3.

[379] *Ibid.*

[380] See above at 5.5.4.2(iv)(d).

[381] See above at 2.4.3.4(iv).

way substantively unfavourable to the consumer e.g. because it excludes the trader's liability in the event of negligence or breach of contract. The consumer may be concerned about the implications of the exclusion and may wish to have some form of choice or alternative. For example, the consumer may be prepared to pay a higher price or submit to other less favourable terms if the trader is prepared to accept all or some of the liability in question. However, the trader's standard terms may not have such a choice built in. Equally the trader may not be prepared to depart from his normal terms and offer such a choice 'on the spot'. In addition, there may be no other reasonably accessible trader whose terms offer anything different from those of the first trader, or who is prepared to make special provision in order to provide a choice. So, if the consumer wishes to obtain the goods or services in question he may have little real alternative but to agree to the term in question.

So a fairness regime may wish to say that if there is a term that is in some way unfair in substance the question becomes whether there was a choice of a more favourable term. The idea then is that the lack of such a choice should count against a finding of fairness. The availability of a choice might be said to weigh in favour of a finding of fairness as the choice can be said to enhance procedural fairness. The consumer is, for example, offered services by trader X subject to a term excluding all liability for defective performance. At the same time trader X or another trader, Y, offers the same services while accepting some liability as long as the consumer pays a higher basic price. If this happens, the first advantage in terms of fairness is that the alternative package (whether from trader X or from trader, Y) enhances the basic transparency of the no liability package in that this no liability package is put into some perspective. Then there is the choice issue itself. The consumer can now choose whether to take the risk of agreeing to the no liability package, or pay a higher price in exchange for the trader accepting more liability.

As has already been said,[382] there are a number of points to be made as to applying this choice criterion. First of all, the question of choice only becomes an issue if the term under scrutiny is in some way substantively prejudicial (it being unrealistic to expect there to be a choice where the term are not detrimental in substance). Second, in deciding whether there was a reasonable choice or alternative, it is clear that the substantive features of the alternative package must be assessed. A choice or alternative means something different. If the primary focus is a term significantly compromising the substantive interests of the consumer, then a meaningful choice or alternative can only be offered by a term which, by comparison, is significantly less compromising of the substantive interests of the consumer. So, as in the example above, the

---

[382] See above at 2.4.3.4(v).

alternative to a term excluding all liability must be one which, by comparison, accepts a fair degree of liability.

Third, it is surely not only the substantive features of the alternative package that must be taken into account. There is also the matter of the accessibility of the alternative. In part this brings us back to transparency. If the alternative is offered by the trader whose term is under scrutiny then the existence of the alternative must be transparent to consumers. If the alternative is offered by another trader then, taking into account questions of communication, geography and other relevant factors, it must be practicable for the consumer to know of and take advantage of the alternative. Fourth, the point of taking choice into account is that it affects the ability of the consumer to protect his substantive interests. So, the extent to which a lack of choice (or an inadequate or inaccessible choice) counts against the term must surely be dictated by the extent to which the term under scrutiny is substantively prejudicial. The lack of choice will take on greater significance the more substantively prejudicial the term under scrutiny is.

Finally, unlike with transparency, it cannot be said that choice is fundamental to fairness. As a matter of principle, the ability to give informed consent must be more fundamental than the existence of choice as to what to agree to. The most that can be expected is that choice should be a factor to be taken into account along with all of the other relevant factors, in particular the degree of unfairness in substance and whether the consumer could or could not have bargained for a more favourable term.

6.4.3.2 The Choice Issue in Practice

As we have seen, it does seem that choice is relevant to the reasonableness test under UCTA. In *Smith* v. *Bush*[383] the House of Lords asked whether the consumer had the choice of seeking alternative protection. Of course, here, the House of Lords was referring to a different type of choice, i.e. the choice to take out a separate survey in addition to the valuation. In other words this was choice in the sense of a 'second opinion'. However, in another UCTA case the court did consider the type of choice that we have been discussing here. In *Woodman* v. *Photo Trade Processing*[384] a term excluding liability for negligence in developing film was thought to be unreasonable partly because the developer did not offer an alternative full liability package at a higher price. This was thought to be particularly damning of the term because

---

[383] [1989] 2 All ER 514, Lord Griffiths at 530.
[384] (1981) New Law Journal 935.

such an alternative was recommended by the Trade Association in question.

There is no explicit mention of choice in the test of unfairness or anywhere in the UTCCR. However, (as already suggested) [385] it is certainly arguable that the EC context suggests a concept of procedural fairness that goes beyond transparency and includes choice. Given the limitations on transparency as a concept that can guarantee informed consent, it is difficult to see how we can be guaranteed a high level of protection and consumer confidence simply by focusing on transparency. This, of course, is not to say that choice is to be treated as a prerequisite of fairness, simply that it should be a factor to be taken into account.

In addition, the German conception of good faith involves consideration of whether choices were available to the consumer[386]; and the argument has already been made that the ECJ might decide to draw upon the jurisprudence of other Member States in developing an autonomous notion of unfairness.[387] It seems logical, then, that the question of choice might be considered relevant to good faith in the Directive given that good faith in the Directive is supposed to involve an 'overall evaluation of the different interests involved'.[388] It is clear that at the stage of agreeing to terms the consumer has an interest in having some form of choice, so an evaluation of the interests of the parties surely involves consideration of whether choices were available. It may be then that a similar approach to that taken under UCTA is appropriate, i.e. that the existence of a choice should count in favour of a finding of fairness, while the lack of a choice should count against a finding of fairness.

No explicit mention was made of choice by the House of Lords in *First National Bank*. There does not, in fact, appear to have been much choice in relation to the term in question. It was noted that it was used as standard by lenders in general.[389] However, as we saw from the discussion above, the House of Lords did not take the view that the term caused a significant imbalance or was substantively unfair to the consumer. Indeed it was thought that it would be unfair to expect lenders not to have a term providing for interest to be charged after judgement.[390] It would hardly be logical, then, to condemn the term used by *First*

---

[385] See above at 3.4.4.

[386] See H.-W. Micklitz, La Loi Allemand relative au régime fundique des conditions générales des contrats du 9 Decembre 1976 (1989) Rev. Int. Droit Comparé 101 at 109; H.-W. Micklitz, The Politics of Judicial Co-operation in the EU, CUP, 2005, at 374.

[387] See above at 3.5.5.

[388] Preamble, Recital 16.

[389] [2001] 3 WLR 1297, Lord Millett at 1319.

[390] See above at 5.5.4.2(iv)(a).

National Bank on the basis that other lenders used the same term and that there was therefore no choice for the consumer. So *First National Bank* does not necessarily suggest that choice is not to be considered relevant. There does not appear to have been any significant discussion of choice in other cases under the UTCCR.

6.4.3.3 New Regime

Under the proposed new regime the question as to the relative bargaining positions of the parties would be treated as encompassing questions as to choice. One of the three core criteria (along with substance and effect[391] and transparency[392]) would be 'the circumstances existing at the time [the term] was agreed'.[393] The 'strength of the parties' bargaining positions' would be identified as one of these 'circumstances existing at the time [the term] was agreed'.[394] The 'strength of the parties' bargaining positions' would then be described in the explanatory notes as involving a variety of questions.[395] Some of these are specifically relevant to the question of choice that we are discussing here. So it would be relevant to consider whether the consumer 'was offered a choice over a particular term'[396] (presumably from the trader using the term under scrutiny). It seems that the type of choice contemplated here could be the type we have been discussing, i.e. a choice between agreeing to the term under scrutiny and agreeing to an alternative term. It would also be relevant to consider whether it was reasonable, 'given [the consumer's] abilities, for him to have taken advantage' of any such choice.[397]

In addition, it would be relevant to consider whether a choice was available elsewhere. Account would be taken of 'whether [the consumer] had a realistic opportunity to enter into a similar contract with other persons, but without the term'.[398] So, this broadly accommodates the kind of approach described.

---

[391] Draft Bill, Clause 14(1)(b).
[392] *Ibid.*, 14(1)(a).
[393] *Ibid.*, 14(1)(b).
[394] *Ibid.*, 14(4)(i).
[395] Explanatory Notes, 45.
[396] *Ibid.*, 45(b).
[397] *Ibid.*, 45(f).
[398] *Ibid.*, 45(d).

6.4.3.4 Contextualism and Choice

Again, there is an issue as to the role of contextualism. The factors mentioned above can be considered purely in the abstract. Alternatively, a more contextual approach could be taken. So, for example, it could be that there is a case where no choice is usually available, i.e. no choice is offered as standard by the trader in question and there is no choice available in the market. This would usually count against a finding of fairness. However, on the facts of a particular case the trader offers a choice to the particular consumer. The question is whether this should be treated as a case in which there is no choice (as it will be in proactive control) or alternatively treated as a case in which a choice was available to the individual concerned. In other words should the term be more likely to be fair?

Equally, in cases where there is a choice (whether always or in the specific case), there is a question as to whether to refuse to count this in favour of the term where the consumer doesn't take it up due to his particularly vulnerable position. For example, suppose that due to indigence or unfamiliarity with the subject matter, the consumer does not realize there is a choice. Alternatively, the choice for the consumer in question – given their more vulnerable financial position – is still not a good choice, though it would have been for most.

On the trader side of the equation, similar questions arise. Is it relevant to consider factors (whether related to resources or other matters) that affect the particular trader and make offering a choice more or less difficult than normal?

As with transparency the existing criteria under UCTA and the UTCCR are somewhat ambiguous. 'Circumstances' existing at the time the contract is made[399] could clearly include all of the contextual factors just mentioned.

Certainly, taking into account financial limitations facing particular consumers was recognized in *Smith* v. *Bush* (at least in the context of the type of choice at issue there) where, as we have seen, it was held that the choice of paying twice for the same advice was not a reasonable choice to expect a poor first time buyer to take up.[400]

As to the new regime, the general reference to 'circumstances existing at the time' of the term being agreed to could, again, be read broadly to include all of the forms of contextualism mentioned. More specifically, contextualism that is focused purely on the position of the

---

[399] This being the general formulation used in both UCTA and the UTCCR to describe what should be taken into account – see UCTA, s. 11(1) and UTCCR, Regulation 6(1).

[400] [1989] 2 All ER 514, Lord Griffiths at 530.

consumer seems to be accommodated by the particular choice related criteria proposed. There is reference to whether 'that party' had a 'realistic' opportunity to enter into a similar contract with other persons but without the term.[401] The idea here may be to recognize limitations on what is realistic depending on the characteristics of the consumer in question and possibly also based on the substantive nature of the choice. For example, a choice that might be realistic for most consumers is not realistic for a particular consumer, as it is inaccessible to those (like this consumer) with no car, or it is too expensive for poor consumers like this one. Equally, if the question is whether 'that party' had a choice available elsewhere then it seems that if there was not a choice for most consumers but (perhaps through contacts, geography etc.) there is a choice for this consumer then this may count in favour of the term.

Also para. (b) refers to whether 'the complaining party' (i.e. the particular consumer) was offered a choice over a particular term. So, even if a choice was not available normally, if it was made available to this consumer then this seems to count in favour of the term. Equally, even if a choice was available, para. (f) refers to whether it was reasonable to take up such a choice offered by the trader 'given that party's abilities'. This seems to recognize the problems that might be faced by more vulnerable parties in relation to appreciating/weighing up choices. If we interpret the word 'abilities' to include financial solvency then para. (f) also recognizes the *Smith* v. *Bush* problem, i.e. that the choice might be too expensive for the particular consumer.

Finally, we turn to the question as to whether (and when) contextualism is a good (or valid) practice. As with contextualism in relation to the substantive interests of the parties and in relation to transparency, the strongest case for contextualism surely applies when the consequence is that the standard of fairness is increased. This, as we have seen, might happen if we take account of the particular strengths of traders or particular weaknesses of consumers in assessing the question of choice. Such an approach may accord with the consumer protection and confidence goals of the UTD. However, there must, again, be disquiet over the possibility of lowering the standard of protection on the basis of consumer strengths and trader weaknesses. In particular there must be a concern that the level of protection aimed at intended by the UTD would be undermined.

Having said this, there may be a case for at least taking into account choices offered to the particular consumer. If a choice is offered to this particular consumer for whatever reason and if the term in question and the choice were transparent, then the consumer has at least had the benefits of both informed consent and choice; and, on the trader side of

---

[401] Explanatory Notes, 45(d).

the equation, there is a reasonable argument that this is indicative of good faith by the trader. This actually contrasts with the idea of lowering the standard of transparency based on the particular knowledge of the consumer. In that case the trader has done no more than he always does (i.e. use a term that lacks transparency); and the suggestion is that he should be excused because it happens as a matter of chance that the consumer has some knowledge of the term in the particular case. Having said this, there remains a danger that, in practice, if choices offered to individual consumers are viewed as a legitimate way to justify certain terms, then some traders will routinely raise the argument to deter consumers from taking action (and that this will include cases in which the choice is not really one that a court would consider to be good enough).

6.4.4 Inequality of Bargaining Power

6.4.4.1 Introduction

We have said[402] that traders will not normally be prepared to bargain over terms and that, even if they do bargain, the consumer will often be in a weaker position as a result of lesser skill and expertise and resources and the fact that the individual consumer will simply not be important enough to the trader for the trader to need to bend to his requests.[403] This means that the consumer is to some extent restricted in his ability to protect his interests in the bargaining process. So, a fairness regime may wish to say that if a term is detrimental in substance then (as with lack of choice) the weaker bargaining power of the consumer should count against a finding of fairness. As in the case of the choice issue, the enquiry into bargaining strength cannot be a purely procedural one. It is unrealistic to question the enforceability of any term irrespective of the substantive features simply because there is an inequality of bargaining power. The bargaining power issue should only be taken into account where a term significantly compromises the substantive interests of the

---

[402] See above at 2.4.2.2.

[403] See generally H. Beale, Inequality of Bargaining Power (1986) 6 Oxford Journal of Legal Studies 123; H. Beale, Unfair Contracts in Britain and Europe (1989) Current Legal Problems 197; R. Brownsword, General Themes, in Furmston (ed.), Butterworth's Common Law Series, *The Law of Contract*, 2nd edn, 2003, at pp. 40–55; and Thal, The Inequality of Bargaining Power Doctrine: The Problem of Defining Contractual Unfairness, 1988, 8 Oxford Journal of Legal Studies 17; and Tjittes, Unfair Terms, in H. Beale, A. Hartkamp, H. Kotz and D. Tallon (eds), Cases, Materials and Text on Contract Law, 2002, at p. 527.

consumer (i.e. deviates from a default rule to the detriment of the consumer or allows for compromise of the reasonable expectations of the consumer – see above).

Again, as with other aspects of procedural fairness, the *degree* to which the term compromises the substantive interests of the consumer (e.g. extent of deviation from the default position, the importance of consumer interests affected etc) is relevant to the assessment of the bargaining power issue, i.e. the more the term compromises the substantive interests of the consumer, the more it should count against the term that the consumer is in a weaker bargaining position. This is because the whole point of taking account of the bargaining power issue is that the weaker bargaining power of the consumer affects his ability to protect his interests in the context of the agreement process. This becomes more significant the more substantively prejudicial the term in question is.

Of course, even where the issue of bargaining strength is being taken into account, transparency remains fundamental. If the term is insufficiently transparent, the term should be unfair irrespective of the consumer's bargaining strength. This is because transparency is a fundamental right; and because the consumer cannot bargain successfully over terms that are not transparent. In addition, the bargaining strength issue seems to share with the choice issue a second tier importance in relation to procedural fairness, by comparison with the transparency issue. While informed consent is often fundamental to a fairness model as a matter of principle, the same surely cannot be said of being in an equal bargaining position to the trader. The fact that the consumer agreed to a term compromising his substantive interests while in a weak bargaining position, will be a factor counting against the term. However, the overall determination as to fairness will need to take into account other factors including of course the degree of unfairness in substance, along with the issue of choice.

6.4.4.2 Inequality of Bargaining Power in Practice

We have seen that the weaker bargaining power of the consumer is relevant under UCTA, i.e. the typically weaker position of the consumer counts against terms. This was a factor that the House of Lords in *Smith* v. *Bush* said should always be taken into account.[404] We have also said that the precise relationship between bargaining power and the substantive features of the term was not made explicit by the House of Lords in *Smith* v. *Bush*.[405] However, it seems fairly obvious that the

---

[404] [1989] 2 All ER 514, Lord Griffiths at 530.

[405] See above at 4.6.2.3.

relationship must be along the lines described above, i.e. that there must be some substantive detriment before we become concerned with bargaining power; and then that the greater the substantive detriment the more the disparity of bargaining strength will count against the term. The relative bargaining positions of the parties is clearly relevant to the test of fairness in the UTCCR. The Preamble to the Directive says expressly that in deciding whether there has been a violation of good faith regard should be had to this factor.[406] The relevance of bargaining power to the test of fairness under the UTCCR has also been recognized by the House of Lords. As we have seen, Lord Bingham said that the trader should not *take advantage* of the weak bargaining position of the consumer.[407] We also saw that there was some confusion as to what exactly was meant by this;[408] and whether there was a suggestion that the trader must be acting in bad conscience and/or that the consumer must be weaker than the average consumer (rather than simply weak relative to the trader) and/or that the resulting terms must be extremely unfair in substance. However, it is to be hoped that he did not intend any bad conscience requirement and simply meant that consumers in general are taken to be in a weaker bargaining position; and also that traders will be likely to be treated as having taken advantage of this the more detrimental the terms are in substance (but there being no requirement of extreme unfairness in substance). Certainly there is no suggestion from court or OFT practice that the issue of bargaining power should be dealt with in any other way.

This said, on the facts of *First National Bank* the (accepted) weaker bargaining position of the consumer did not seem to count against the term. However, as with the issues of transparency and choice, this may have been because the House of Lords took the view that the term was fair in substance, and based on this conclusion, the view must have been that the weaker bargaining position of the consumer had not been 'taken advantage' of.

Under the new regime, as already indicated, one of the three core criteria (along with 'substance and effect' and 'transparency') would be 'the circumstances existing at the time [the term] was agreed'.[409] The 'strength of the parties' bargaining positions' would then be identified as one of relevant 'circumstances existing at the time [the term] was agreed'. The 'strength of the parties' bargaining positions' would then be described in the explanatory notes as involving a variety of questions. These would include the choice issues discussed above. However, they would also include other issues. First, whether the transaction was

---

[406] Recital 16.

[407] [2001] 3 WLR 1279, at 1308.

[408] See above at 5.5.4.2(iii).

[409] Draft Bill, Clause 14(1)(b).

unusual for either of the parties.[410] This is clearly a logical factor to consider. The ability of either party to bargain will clearly be affected by how familiar he is with the type of transaction in question. This, as we have seen, is already recognized by House of Lords who referred to the extent to which the consumer was familiar with the subject matter and the experience (or inexperience) of the consumer.[411] The idea, then, seems to be that it will continue to count against a term where, as will be common, the transaction is less common for the consumer than the trader. Also listed would be 'whether [the consumer] had a reasonable opportunity to seek a more favourable term'.[412] This seems to mean that where there is no reasonable opportunity to bargain for an improvement (e.g. because of the simple refusal of the trader to bargain, or, if bargaining does take place, because of the more limited skill and expertise of the consumer), this should count against the term.

6.4.4.3 Contextualism and Bargaining Power

Some factors affecting the bargaining position of the parties might be viewed from some perspectives as being abstract, i.e. assessable as at the time the trader drafts the terms (e.g. whether the trader is a monopolist).[413] However, the approach I have taken[414] involves viewing the market position of the particular trader as contextual. Certainly, most of the questions as to bargaining power (e.g. skill, expertise, experience and other factors affecting the bargaining position of the parties) are by their nature contextual (i.e. dependent on the particular parties and the market circumstances surrounding the conclusion of the particular contract). In both individual cases and where preventive action is concerned an abstract approach could be taken and these contextual elements ignored. So, the particular strengths and/or weaknesses of the parties could be ignored and broad assumptions to the effect that consumers are in a weaker position could be made (as we saw in the *First National Bank* case).

However, in individual cases it is clear that (while an abstract approach could be taken) a contextual approach could also be taken. In other words, the question could be the bargaining power of the particular parties. On such an approach, again, it is possible that in the case of the

---

[410] Explanatory Notes, 45(a).

[411] [2001] 3 WLR 1279, Lord Bingham at 1308.

[412] *Ibid.*, para. (c).

[413] See P. Nebbia, Law as Tradition and the Europeanization of Contract Law: A Case Study, (2004) Yearbook of European Law, 363, at 367.

[414] See above at 2.4.3.6.

term in question, the average consumer would not have had the bargaining power to get a change, though this particular consumer did have bargaining power, i.e. he had more bargaining power than average; so the factor could count in favour of the term and might result in a term that would otherwise be unfair being fair. Equally, there might have been opportunities to bargain that would have been sufficient for the average consumer to possibly get a term removed or amended. However, this particular consumer may be vulnerable and this may explain why he did not get a change; so this may count against the term, making unfair a term that might otherwise have been fair.

Again, on the trader side, the particularly strong bargaining position of the trader could count even more strongly against a term; and conversely, the weaker than average bargaining position of the trader might count in favour of the term.

But is such a contextual approach supposed to be taken? Again, the general reference in UCTA, the UTCCR and the proposed new regime to the 'circumstances' at the time of the contract[415] could be read broadly to include these contextual elements. Both the UCTA guidelines (though these are aimed at commercial contracts) and the preamble to the UTD refer to the strength of the bargaining positions of the parties.[416] Again, this could mean that we are supposed to consider the *particular* bargaining positions of the parties in question.

It certainly seems that the House of Lords recognize that (under the UTCCR) a particularly weak bargaining position might be relevant in the way described, i.e. in strengthening the case for a finding of unfairness.[417] However, there was no indication as to whether a particularly strong consumer bargaining position should be able to save a term that might otherwise be unfair. Neither was there any indication as to the approach to be taken where the trader is stronger or weaker than normal.

There is certainly no doubt that the new guidelines appear to allow for a contextual approach. The criteria refer to whether 'that' party (for our purposes, the consumer) had a reasonable opportunity to seek a more favourable term.[418] Of course this might be read as no more than an indication that the *typical* inability of the consumer to seek a more

---

[415] UCTA, s. 11(1); UTCCR, Regulation 6(1); and Draft Bill, Clause 14(1)(b).

[416] Recital 16.

[417] As we have seen, Lord Bingham said that the trader should not take advantage of the 'necessity, inexperience, indigence, unfamiliarity with the subject matter or weak bargaining power of the consumer' (para. 17). This may mean that where the consumer is particularly weak in these respects this should count especially strongly against the term.

[418] Paragraph (c).

favourable term should be taken into account. However, it seems very plausible that what is also intended is that particular opportunities (that do or do not arise) should be taken into account. It may of course be that this is aimed more at commercial contracts. However, if applied to consumer contracts, it would mean that the weaker than average bargaining position of a consumer should count particularly strongly against a term; while the stronger than average position of the consumer should count in favour of the term.

The guidelines also seem to allow for a degree of contextualism on the trader side. There is, as we have seen, reference to 'whether the transaction was unusual for either or both of [the parties]'.[419] This, of course, confirms that if the consumer is in a particularly weak position (due to the transaction being an unusual one for him) then this should count against the term. However, to the extent that it is intended to apply to consumer contracts in practice, it also seems to mean that if the transaction is unusual for the trader then this should be taken into account (possibly lessening what is expected in terms of fairness).

As in the case of the transparency and choice issues, there might be a good case for being cautious about reading the UTD to allow for contextualism where it *reduces* the level of protection (given the extent to which it might allow for a compromise on a high level of protection and produce greater uncertainty). We must also be alert to the practical danger that if terms can in theory be justified on the basis of stronger than average consumer bargaining power, then traders will routinely raise the argument to deter consumers from taking action; and that this will include cases in which the consumer did not really have any bargaining power or opportunities to make a significant difference.

6.5 Disallowing Terms with Certain Substantive Features

I argued above[420] that the form of fairness that moves furthest from a freedom-oriented approach is one in which the law refuses to enforce terms which have certain substantive features (i.e. irrespective of questions of procedural fairness or overall substantive fairness). There are various rationales for such an approach. There is the fact that the terms are unacceptably unfair in substance, taking away important rights or imposing an unacceptably onerous obligation or liability on the consumer. It might also be presumed that, notwithstanding the existence of a reasonable level of procedural fairness, consumers may still not read terms; and that, even if they do, they may still not understand their

---

[419] Paragraph (a).
[420] See above at 2.4.3.5(i).

meaning and how the terms might affect them in practice. This undermines the prospects for informed consent and for the terms to be subjected to competitive discipline. In addition, if terms are not read and/or understood, then clearly the value of there being a choice, or the consumer being in a stronger than average bargaining position, is reduced; there being limited knowledge of the need to consider choices and bargain for better terms. Even, if the consumer *is* aware of the risks, there may still be good reasons (e.g. habit, poor consumer education, the belief that terms are officially sanctioned and cannot be changed) why consumers do not take up choices or bargaining opportunities that could have protected their interests.

Another reason for setting substantive standards that apply irrespective of matters of procedural fairness or overall substantive fairness is to actually get more benefit from procedural fairness. The limitations on transparency being of use to consumers (which we have just outlined) may actually be exacerbated by the differences in the presentation and substance of the terms used by different traders.[421] So, rather than placing emphasis on using transparency to enable consumers to identify differences, choose between traders and stimulate competition over these terms, it may make more sense to focus simply on improving informed consent. The chances of this may be improved by standardizing both the *presentation* and *substantive* features of the terms. We have already discussed standardized presentation.[422] The issue for now is standardization of the substantive terms. The point is that standardization of the substantive terms necessarily involves setting substantive standards which are to apply irrespective of matters of procedural fairness (shortly we shall turn to whether such standardization is taking place).

The final rationale for disallowing terms with certain substantive features is the need to promote certainty where important consumer interests are concerned.

We saw that some terms are actually banned by UCTA.[423] However, the question now is whether the general UCTA and UTCCR tests allow for terms to be found to be unfair despite a reasonable level of procedural fairness. This approach does seem to accord with the legal and policy background to the UTD.[424] A 'high level of protection' would appear to require protection of the interests of consumers in at least some cases where the compromise of these interests has been made transparent to the consumer. Broader procedural fairness may be needed. But a 'high level of protection' may also surely involve protection of the most important

---

[421] See above at 2.4.3.4(iv).

[422] See above at 6.4.2.10.

[423] See above at 4.2.6.

[424] See above at 3.5.5.3.

substantive interests of the consumer even where there has been a reasonable level of procedural fairness. Article 153 (the old 129a) and the 1975 Consumer Protection and Information Policy Programme, mention information separately from the protection of health and safety and economic interests.[425] In addition, the Preamble to the Directive refers separately to the importance of information and plain language, and the importance of protection against one-sided standard contracts and the exclusion of essential rights.[426] So, all of these sources distinguish between transparency and other forms of protection that are thought to be needed. This could, of course, simply be a reference to the need for there to be broader procedural fairness. However, if there is to be a high level of protection, it seems plausible to read these sources as suggesting that the most substantively unfair terms should be controlled even where there is a reasonable degree of procedural fairness.

In addition, both the reasonableness test and the good faith test seem to be flexible enough to allow for a full departure from freedom of contract where the substantive problem is sufficiently severe. Dealing first with UCTA, there is no reason to suppose, when the legislation refers to 'reasonableness', that there is any intention to exclude this possibility. Even if there is procedural fairness, a term can surely be unreasonable based on its substantive features, if the impact of the substantive features is sufficiently compromising of the interests of the consumer. Indeed, there is nothing in the UCTA case law to suggest that this is not possible. Turning to good faith, the Preamble to the UTD refers to an 'overall evaluation of the different interests'.[427] There seems no reason why the compromise of certain (substantive) interests could not be so great as to result in a lack of good faith despite other (procedural) ways in which these interests have been protected (especially when we recognize the possible difficulties in practice in taking advantage of procedural fairness). In other words there seems nothing to prevent a finding of unfairness in the case of a term which is very substantively unfair but which has nevertheless been agreed to in circumstances of procedural fairness.[428] This accords with Treaty of Rome's aspiration to

---

[425] See OJ 1975 C91/2, paras (d), (a) and (b) respectively.

[426] Recitals 9 and 20.

[427] Recital 16.

[428] This approach would fit with the view taken by some that good faith will often be an ancillary issue. This is a view apparently having support from the European Commission – see M. Tenreiro, The Community Directive on Unfair Terms and National Legal Systems (1995) 3 European Review of Private Law, 273, 279; and M. Tenreiro and E. Ferioli, Examen Comparatif des legislation nationals transposant le Directive 93/13/EEC in H.-W. Micklitz, The Unfair Terms Directive: Five Years On, Office for Official Publications of the European Communities, 2000. The point about

a high level of consumer protection in measures such as the Directive adopted under Article 100a (now Article 95). The ECJ approach is to say that if a term is sufficiently detrimental in substance and there are no countervailing substantive benefits then they (the ECJ) are prepared to view that term as unfair *per se*.[429] This appears to be irrespective of whether the term is transparent. However, if there is some form of countervailing substantive benefit the ECJ passes the issue back to national courts for a full assessment based on all the circumstances. So, to this extent, the ECJ seem to view it as being for the national courts to decide whether any favourable substantive provision can justify use of the term. However, it must also be remembered that much may depend on the way in which the ECJ measures whether or not there has been a sufficient substantive benefit in the first place. We do not really know whether in the case of some types of term the ECJ will take the view that purportedly beneficial terms are simply not sufficiently beneficial to count as a benefit (the consequence of such a conclusion being that the term is viewed as unfair *per se* by the ECJ).

What of the attitude of the UK courts? In the Court of Appeal Peter Gibson LJ cited the following comment by Hugh Beale which very clearly indicates that terms can be unfair despite the existence of procedural fairness:

> I suspect good faith has a double operation. First it has a procedural aspect. It will require the supplier to consider the consumer's interests. However, a clause which might be unfair if it came as a surprise may be upheld if the business took steps to bring it to the consumer's attention and to explain it. Secondly, it has a substantive content: some clauses may cause such an imbalance that they should always be treated as being contrary to good faith and therefore unfair.[430]

What is slightly less clear is whether the Court of Appeal also took the view that a term can be unfair on the basis of its substantive effects irrespective of the existence of a beneficial term that results in there being overall substantive fairness. The above statement by Beale (and therefore

---

this view is that good faith is viewed as ancillary in the sense that where there is significant imbalance in many cases this will also amount to a violation of good faith. So, if the significant imbalance is caused by the substantive features of the term this means that the violation of good faith is also so caused (and that any procedural fairness has been insufficient to prevent there being a violation of good faith).

[429] See above at 3.5.4.

[430] From H. Beale, Legislative Control of Fairness: The Directive on Unfair Terms in Consumer Contracts, in J. Beatson and D. Friedmann, Good Faith and Fault in Contract Law, OUP, 1995, 232, 245, [2000] 2 All ER 759 at 769.

the attitude of the Court of Appeal that can be surmised from the approval of this statement) is ambivalent on this issue. He refers to clauses that '*cause* such an imbalance that they should always be treated as being contrary to good faith and therefore unfair'. This could mean that he views some terms as always causing such a substantive imbalance based on their own substantive effects or it could mean that he regards the question as to whether the term has actually caused such a substantive imbalance as always dependent on whether there is a favourable term that redresses the imbalance. It is submitted that Beale's view is the former as elsewhere in the article from which the quotation comes he refers to the idea of consumers having certain 'irreducible rights', and it seems that he is referring here to rights that cannot be taken away by a term (irrespective of procedural fairness or beneficial terms). Of course, it is unclear whether the Court of Appeal intended to endorse this view in so far as it applies to beneficial terms.

The House of Lords position is unclear also. There is a reference to whether a term causes significant imbalance 'in manner or to an extent which is contrary to good faith'.[431] Given that significant imbalance is caused, or can be caused, by the substantive features of a term, the implication appears to be that violation of good faith can also be so caused. Of course, the violation of good faith may only be caused partly by the substantive elements, with procedural unfairness also playing a part. However, the excerpt seems to suggest that a violation of good faith could be caused wholly by the substantive features of the term. Further, there is the judgement of Lord Steyn where it is said: 'Any purely procedural or even predominantly procedural interpretation of the requirement of good faith must be rejected.'[432]

Again, the suggestion seems to be that the procedural issues can be emasculated by substantive issues where appropriate. What of the House of Lords' attitude to the question as to whether some substantively terms are so unfair that they cannot be balanced out by a beneficial term? It is certainly not possible to draw any definite conclusions. The idea that a term might cause a significant imbalance 'in manner or to an extent which is contrary to good faith' suggests (as noted) that the violation of good faith can be based purely on substance but it does not tell us whether this can be based purely on the substantive features of the term or whether it is always based on the existence of overall substantive unfairness.

The OFT certainly seem to view certain terms as unfair irrespective of matters of procedural or overall substantive unfairness. It has been pointed out that the OFT do often refer to good faith in terms of

---

[431] [2001] 3 WLR, Lord Bingham at 1307.
[432] Lord Steyn, *ibid.*, at 1313.

transparency.[433] However, in practice, it seems that fairness in substance is often required *in addition to* transparency, so that transparency is often viewed as necessary but not sufficient. In general, where a term is described on the list in a quite specific way the OFT view seems to be that such a term is unfair on the basis of its substantive features. For example, above[434] we focused on terms excluding or hindering consumer access to justice; requiring consumers to pay for goods or services not received; allowing for alteration of the terms or performance without valid reasons; transfer of consumer rights without consent; imposition of excessive charges and costs; automatic extension of contracts where the deadline expressed for the consumer to express a desire not to extend is too early; and price escalation clauses where there is no consumer right to cancel. In all of these cases the essential focus of the OFT appears to be on the substantive features of the term. There is no suggestion that these terms are fair as long as they are transparent.

Of course, as we saw, certain paragraphs on the list describe categories of term such as exemption clauses. Clearly, this encompasses a vast range of terms and some will be much less unfair in substance than others. Some restrictions of liability (and even some exclusions) may be able to be justified if they are made sufficiently transparent. However, even in the context of exemption clauses, it is clear that the OFT view many as unfair however they are presented. So, above[435] we said that the OFT generally views as unfair terms that completely exclude a particular liability that would otherwise arise; and terms significantly restricting or limiting of liability (e.g. limitation of the damages claimable so as not to cover consequential losses). The extent to which a limitation is acceptable also appears to depend upon whether the effect is to allow the trader to escape liability in cases where there is an element of fault. We also saw that limitation of liability for delays seems generally to be viewed as unfair if the limitation applies in circumstances that were within the control of the trader. None of these approaches appear to be qualified by any notion that the term is acceptable as long as it is transparent.

Of course none of this is to say that *overall substantive balance* is not viewed by the OFT as justifying some terms. It is clear, for example, that in the case of price escalation clauses that the view is that they can be fair as long as the consumer has the concrete protection of being entitled to cancel in response to the rise and being entitled to compensation for losses caused.[436] However, where there is no particular way of another term offering *concrete* protection against the term under scrutiny (e.g. in

---

[433] H.-W. Micklitz, The Politics of Judicial Co-operation in the EU, CUP, 2005, 395.

[434] At 6.3.3.

[435] At 6.3.2.

[436] See above at 6.3.3.2(2)(b).

the case of exemption clauses) there has been no particular suggestion that the term can always be used as long as there is a benefit in the nature of a low price or the like.

In addition, the Law Commissions take the view that under the existing test a term can be unfair 'because of its substance, whatever the circumstances in which the contract was made'.[437] This clearly suggests that procedural fairness will not always help. In addition the reference is the substance of the *term*, so that the suggestion seems also to be that the unfair substantive effect of the term may be enough for unfairness whatever the substantive effects of the other terms may be.

This approach also seems to be accepted as possible under the new test as well. The Law Commissions believe that the new 'fair and reasonable' test continues to allow for this.[438]

6.6 Standardising the Substance of Terms

It has been argued above[439] that there is a case for standardising both the presentation and substance of terms within particular trading sectors.[440] This may at least mean that if terms are read they may be slightly easier to understand, as consumers are used to seeing these substantive terms and used to seeing them presented in this way. We have already dealt with the issue of standardized presentation.[441] We now turn to the issue of standardization in relation to substance.

The issue mirrors that in relation to standardized presentation, in that the general good faith standard can only play one part in doing the job. The general standard, as we have seen, has led to the OFT developing quite detailed policies on particular types of term. The redrafting done by traders may then produce contracts which (following the OFT guidance) are fairly similar in substance. However, the contracts will only be exactly the same in substance where the whole trade sector produces contracts which are then used by all members. As we have already noted, this does appear to be taking place; the OFT having agreed model contracts with trade associations in a variety of sectors.[442]

---

[437] Law Com Rep, para. 3.93.

[438] *Ibid.*

[439] 2.4.3.4(iv).

[440] *Ibid.*, and see T. Wilhelmmson, Cooperation and Competition Regarding Standard Contract Terms in Consumer Contracts, (2006), European Business Law Review, 49, at 55.

[441] See 6.4.2.10.

[442] *Ibid.*

6.7 Conscience, Fairness and Good Faith

6.7.1 No Good Conscience Defence

If a term is viewed as unfair (based on the above analysis of its substantive features and procedural issues), is there a defence based on the 'good conscience' of the trader? As we have already seen, there was no suggestion of this in the background to UCTA and certainly it would be contrary to the goals of the UTD.[443] The UCTA reasonableness test has never been interpreted in this way. However, good faith does have these connotations in certain contexts.[444]

Violation of good faith (or at least outright bad faith) *is* often thought of as taking place only where the contractor pursues his own interests in a way that is unconscionable. The conscience of the contractor is in some way bound not to act in the way that he has acted.[445] This could involve the contractor being dishonest, contradictory, exploitative etc.[446] These sorts of approaches might suggest a need to establish that the trader has intentionally or recklessly exploited the consumer. It might at least be possible for the trader to establish good faith by establishing that he reasonably believed himself to have acted fairly e.g. by establishing that he reasonably believed that there was procedural fairness and that the terms were fair in substance; or perhaps by establishing that there was no bad motive either for the use of the term in question or the way in which the procedure leading to the contract was conducted.[447] All of these elements may have a role to play in some operations of good faith. The good faith concept in the Principle of European Contract Law (PECL)[448] certainly appears to require no more than (subjective) honesty and fairness in mind. Article 1.201 (formerly Article 1.106) requires that 'in exercising his rights and performing his duties each party must act in accordance with good faith and fair dealing'. The European Contract Commission (who drafted the PECL) has said that good faith means 'honesty and fairness in mind, which are subjective concepts'.[449] So,

---

[443] See above at 3.4.2.2–3.

[444] For example, the 'good faith purchaser' concept in UK contract and sales law is a subjective concept. See M. Hesselink, The New European Private Law, p. 1.

[445] J. Stapleton, Good Faith in Private Law (1999) 52 Current Legal Problems, 1, at 7–8.

[446] *Ibid.*, at 8.

[447] See R. Brownsword, Positive, Negative and Neutral: the Reception of Good Faith in English Contract Law, in R. Brownsword, N. Hird and G. Howells (ed.), Ashgate, 1999, 13, at 17.

[448] O. Lando and H. Beale (eds), Principles of European Contract Law Parts I and II, Kluwer, 2000.

[449] Principles of European Contract Law Part 1, 1995, at p. 55.

while this requires subjective honesty and subjective fairness (which might include good motive) it is not an objective standard.

Turning to the UTD/UTCCR, the Preamble to the Directive provides the only direct guidance as to the meaning of good faith. In assessing good faith it is said that regard shall be had to 'the strength of the bargaining positions of the parties, whether the consumer had an inducement to agree to the term and whether the good or services were sold or supplied to the special order of the consumer'. These are clearly purely objective questions requiring no enquiry into the behaviour or knowledge of the trader. Other aspects of the guidance are perhaps more ambiguous. It is said that the good faith question involves an 'overall evaluation of the different interests involved' and also that 'the requirement of good faith may be satisfied by the seller or supplier where he deals fairly and equitably with the other party whose legitimate interest he has to take into account'. An overall evaluation of the different interests, whether the trader has taken consumer interests into account and whether he has dealt fairly and equitably, could suggest a purely objective analysis as to the substantive features of the term and matters of procedural fairness. At the same time (although only perhaps at a push) it might be suggested that a trader has dealt fairly and equitably if he does not exploit the consumer and if he honestly believes the term to be fair (or even that he had a good motive).

However, as suggested above,[450] we must read such ambiguity as may exist in the light of the aims of the UTD. The aims of the UTD would be at risk of being undermined if there was a requirement of exploitation, lack of honest belief by the trader in the fairness of the term or bad motive. Consumers would have little protection or confidence in a regime which allowed traders to argue that the terms were fair because they had not acted exploitatively or because they reasonably believed that they were fair. It would not be enough for the consumer to establish that the term was unfair in substance and/or that there was a lack of transparency or choice or that he was in a weak bargaining position etc. The trader could defend an assertion that the term was unfair on the basis that he had not exploited the consumer or that he honestly believed the term to be fair or had a good motive. In addition, if courts and regulatory bodies were to take account of such subjective issues, this would lead to inconsistency and competitive distortions. The same substantive term agreed to in the same procedural circumstances would be treated differently based on these subjective issues. This would mean inconsistency in the treatment of terms within and between Member States. Indeed the job of proactive control in particular would also be made be made very difficult if not impossible. Clearly there is no specific

---

[450] See above at 3.4.1–3.

transaction to consider in the context of proactive control. Bodies such as the OFT could look for evidence of bad motives and exploitation in the general use of terms by traders. However, this would make it extremely difficult to fix general standards of fairness that are applicable to the vast majority of consumers.[451]

It must, then, surely be the case that the good faith requirement is concerned with whether (from an objective point of view) the term is fair in substance and was agreed to in circumstances of procedural fairness. It is surely not necessary to establish that the trader has behaved exploitatively (nor is it a defence for the trader to show that he did not so behave); nor is good faith for our purposes concerned with the perceptions of the trader as to how he has behaved or what his motives were.

An objective approach (i.e. one that does not require bad conscience by the trader for a finding of unfairness) is also supported by the way in which the good faith concept has been used in many continental civilian systems for the control of unfair contract terms. We have already set out the way in which good faith in civil law systems has involved transparency and other aspects of procedural fairness along with control over the substance of the terms;[452] and it is clear that these are objective standards.[453] These objective conceptions of good faith are significant in the context of interpreting the concept of good faith in the UTD. As already suggested above, the ECJ is likely to draw from the traditions of the Member States in constructing the meaning of good faith in the Directive. It is clear that, to the extent that the UK legal systems have a tradition of understanding good faith in a more subjective sense, this tradition is in a minority within the European Union.

The objective approach to the good faith concept in the test of fairness is also well accepted within the relevant academic literature.[454] The OFT also take the view that good faith is an objective concept not requiring any 'dishonest and deceptive conduct'[455] In addition, in the

---

[451] See E. MacDonald, Scope and Fairness of the Unfair Terms in Consumer Contracts Regulations: *Director General of Fair Trading* v. *First National Bank* (2002) Modern Law Review MLR 763, at 769.

[452] See above at 3.5.5.2–3.

[453] H. Beale, Legislative Control of Fairness in J. Beatson and D. Friedman (eds), Good Faith and Fault in Contract Law, OUP, 1995, 231, 243–244.

[454] See H. Beale, *ibid*; R. Brownsord G. Howells and T. Wilhelmson, Between Market and Welfare, in C. Willett (ed.), Aspects of Fairness in Contract, Blackstone, 1999, 25, at 39–40; C. Willett, Good Faith in Consumer Contracts: Rule, Policy and Principle, in A. Forte (ed.), Good Faith in Contract and Property Law, Hart, 1999, 181, at 199.

[455] P. Edwards, The Challenge of the Regulations, in OFT Bulletin 4, at 23.

House of Lords an objective approach seems to have been taken. Lord Steyn talks of good faith as an 'objective criterion'.[456] Lord Bingham refers to good faith as a principle of 'fair and open dealing', emphasising that the trader should not take advantage of the necessity, inexperience, indigence, unfamiliarity with subject matter or weak bargaining power of the consumer, 'whether deliberately or unconsciously'.[457] The 'unconscious' reference suggests objectivity. However, the reference to 'advantage taking' in conjunction with the consumer weaknesses mentioned is perhaps unfortunate.

Above, we discussed the possibility that the reference to advantage taking might have meant (or be taken to mean) that (*for any term to be viewed as unfair*) there does need to be some form of exploitation (advantage taking), even if unconscious; and that there is only deemed to be exploitation if the term is agreed to by a consumer who is particularly (i.e. more than averagely) weak.[458] However, we concluded that such an approach would not only be deeply damaging to the goals of the UTD, but was almost certainly wrong. Lord Bingham seemed to have meant that the consumer should be inexperienced, indigent, unfamiliar with the subject matter and weak in bargaining power by comparison with the trader. Indeed this must surely be the case. Lord Bingham also said that: 'It may however be assumed that any borrower is in a much weaker bargaining position than a large bank contracting on its own standard form.'[459]

This suggests that the consumer does not need to be particularly weak, but simply weak relative to the trader (and that this is assumed where the average consumer is concerned). The advantage taking then arises automatically where the trader uses terms that are (objectively) unfair in substance against the weak (i.e. the average) consumer.

Of course, as we suggested above, it is also possible that, when Lord Bingham refers to taking advantage of consumer weaknesses, he is indeed referring to particularly vulnerable consumers but that that he views this as an *extra* dimension to good faith.[460] There is a violation of good faith in the case of the average consumer where (from an objective point of view) there is unfairness in substance and procedure. However, good faith also requires that traders should not take advantage of the most vulnerable consumers.

---

[456] [2001] 3 WLR, at 1313.

[457] *Ibid.*, at 1308.

[458] See above at 5.5.4.2(iii).

[459] [2001] 3 WLR, at 1305.

[460] See above at 6.3.9.3.

6.7.2 Conscience and Objective Good Faith

It seems, then, that in the context of controlling consumer contract terms, many civilian systems, the UTD and now UK law have adopted an objective concept of good faith. Of course, under the new regime the test would be whether the term is fair and reasonable[461] (also clearly an objective standard). However, the idea here is to use language with which the UK courts are more familiar; it still being very clear that, to the extent that the notion of good faith requires a particular nuance to be given recognition in the test, then this must be done – compliance with good faith being a requirement of the UTD. So the good faith concept will remain of importance even if the new regime is implemented. So, good faith (a standard which in English law, at least, has many subjective, conscience-based connotations) underpins an objective fairness standard. It might be said that this is an unfortunate development; that a concept traditionally associated with subjective, conscience based responsibility should not be used to set objective fairness standards. However I would suggest that the development is more logical than it may appear at first sight. It is arguable that the nature of the trader-consumer relationship means that there has never been any need to search for bad conscience (in the sense of subjective knowledge of the unfairness or positive exploitation) on the facts. Violation of good faith does indeed suggest a lack of good conscience,[462] but in the context of the trader-consumer relationship this lack of conscience is established simply by failure to meet objectively fair standards in relation to substance and procedure. I have already argued that the consumer is in a weaker position both procedurally and in his ability to bear the consequences of harsh terms.[463] By operating in a business capacity and entering relationships for profit with private consumers (and possibly by sending more specific signals of fair treatment) the trader raises expectations of fair treatment.[464] It is surely this that binds the conscience of the trader to behave in an objectively fair way.[465] This is what makes it reasonable for the consumer to expect (objectively determined) fair treatment from the trader. So, in order to violate good faith in this context, it is quite logical to say that there does not need to be any evidence on the facts that the

---

[461] Draft Bill, Clause 4(1).

[462] See J. Stapleton, Good Faith in Private Law (1999) 52 Current Legal Problems, 1, at 7–8.

[463] See above at 2.4.2.

[464] See above at 4.4.4.

[465] See C. Willett, Good Faith and Consumer Contract Terms, in R. Brownsword, N. Hird and G. Howells (eds), Good Faith in Contract: Concept and Context, Ashgate, 1999, 67, at 76–78.

trader has acted unconscionably. Due to the nature of the relationship, he has by definition acted unconscionably (and so acted contrary to good faith) if he does not practice sufficient procedural fairness and/or if he uses terms that are unfair in substance. Indeed, if we analyse the good faith concept in this way, we not only escape any notion that the trader needs to be shown to have acted unconscionably (a requirement that would lower the standard of protection); but we may also insist upon a high level of protection. The fact that the conscience of the trader is bound by the nature of the relationship may help to provide a moral justification for the setting of quite high standards of fairness.

Also, of course, good faith (and the conscience element it contains) may help to justify the idea that what is normally fair (based on an objective analysis) might not be fair where the trader is dealing with a particularly vulnerable party (a fairer term being required for the trader to be acting in good conscience).

Chapter Seven

A Broader View of the Fairness Regimes Described

7.1 Welfarism

We said above that fairness can be associated with certain values of the Welfare State.[1] This is because the agenda is to protect certain social and economic interests of weaker parties in the context of economic exchanges. Protection of these interests is certainly an important part of the maintenance of a minimum level of material well being, and the maintenance of a minimum level of well being is the aim of the Welfare State. Two types of welfarism in contract regulation that have been identified by Brownsword, Howells and Wilhelmsson are maximal and minimal welfarism.[2] Maximal welfarism seeks to protect the position of those who are weaker within contractual relationship. The weakness may be caused by the sort of problems I have identified above.[3] So, consumers are weaker than the trader at the procedural stage and in their ability to bear the consequences of the substantive terms. Therefore, a fairness-oriented approach that seeks to address these problems can be viewed as maximally welfarist. Of course, we should emphasize that maximal welfarism is primarily triggered by the weakness of one of the parties within the relationship. It is not primarily triggered by the notion that one of the parties is weak within the context of the overall social order. So the starting point is not whether one of the parties is *particularly* weak in procedural terms (e.g. because he is poorly educated), or because he is particularly weak in terms of bearing the consequences of substantively harsh provisions (e.g. because he is poor). Maximal welfarism will give protection to consumers who are well educated and well-off financially, on the grounds that (these factors notwithstanding) the consumer is weak in terms of protecting himself procedurally and in bearing the

---

[1] See above at 2.4.1; and see R. Brownsword, G. Howells and T. Wilhelmsson, Welfarism in Contract Law, Dartmouth, 1994; T. Wilhelmsson, Varieties of Welfarism in European Contract Law (2004) 10 European Law Journal 712.

[2] R. Brownsword, G. Howells and T. Wilhelmsson, Between Market and Welfare, in C. Willett (ed.), Aspects of Fairness in Contract, Blackstone, 1996, 25, at 50–54.

[3] See above at 2.4.2.

consequences of the substantive terms. We have seen that, in the main, the regime described sets abstract standards aimed at protecting those who are consumers, whatever their individual circumstances. There may be some scope to reduce the standard of fairness in relation to those consumers who are better able than most to look after themselves procedurally and better able than most to bear the consequences of substantively detrimental terms. However, to the extent that this is possible at all, it must surely only be possible in the most extreme cases. As such the regime can be characterized in the main as being maximally welfarist.

Of course, this is not to say that the regime fully achieves maximal welfarism. A major limitation on achieving maximal welfarism is the exclusion of price terms from the review of fairness. Without such control traders are free to increase prices in response to controls over the ancillary terms.[4] Of course, as we have seen, there may still be control over prices by market forces; and this will be most likely in the case of price terms that genuinely reflect what the consumer reasonably expected to pay and that are clearly presented. Such terms reflect one of the core issues upon which purchasing decisions are based. As such, if (on all other counts) there are the conditions for a working market, there is some prospect of these terms being disciplined by market forces.[5] So, by only excluding from the test of fairness terms that genuinely reflect what the consumer reasonably expected to pay and that are clearly presented, there is a contribution to the maximally welfarist agenda. However, this breaks down if the market is, for whatever reason, not working properly. In these circumstances the lack of a direct control over price means that the regime is not full-bloodedly maximally welfarist.

By contrast with maximal welfarism, minimal welfarism begins by focusing upon the position of the parties in the overall social order. The agenda is to redistribute resources to those who are most in need. There must, therefore, be discrimination in favour of those consumers who are weakest within the overall social order.[6] It is, therefore, primarily concerned to protect those who are the weakest in society, whether in terms of poor education or financial vulnerability. Given that the fairness regime outlined is prepared to protect the better off it is clearly not primarily motivated by the values of minimal welfarism. However, we have seen that it is possible that there can be special protection for those

---

4   See above at 5.8.2; and see T. Wilhelmsson, Social Contract Law and European Integration, Dartmouth, 1995, 143–4.

5   See above at 2.3.2.1.

6   See R. Brownsword, G. Howells and T. Wilhelmsson, Between Market and Welfare, in C. Willett (ed.), Aspects of Fairness in Contract, Blackstone, 1996, 25, at 50.

that are more procedurally or substantively weaker than average[7] and to this extent there could be said to be some scope for minimal welfarism.

However there are serious limitations on the role of the regime in pursuing minimal welfarism. First, it can only help in the context of transactions actually entered into. General social justice and material wellbeing is clearly affected by a range of other factors and wellbeing must, in particular, be secured via the tax and social security systems. Contract law can, at best, play a supporting role. Second, even in the context of contractual relationships, there is considerable doubt as to whether the rules against unfair terms can be trusted to provide systematic protection that is concordant with the needs of vulnerable parties. It may be very difficult in many cases to distinguish between those consumers who are not vulnerable enough to be protected against certain terms and those that are. Thirdly, the protection of the most economically vulnerable might be said to require that the price of the goods or services be controlled directly. As we have already observed, the regime does not control price as long as it reflects what the consumer reasonably expected to pay and is clearly presented. This may mean that prices are controlled by market forces, but this will not always be the case. This will have the severest impact upon those who are most vulnerable. Fourthly, traders are generally free to respond to special protection given to vulnerable parties by refusing to offer the relevant goods or services to these parties in the first place. Although this removes the risk of the terms of the contract compromising the interests of the vulnerable parties, the lack of access to the goods or services itself may contribute to social exclusion by reducing the ability to participate meaningfully in society.

These points notwithstanding, there does, at least, seem to be congruence between a fairness-oriented approach to consumer contract terms and broader social justice and Welfare State goals. The rules on unfair terms surely follow other aspects of modern contract law in being grounded in 'similar ideals of social justice' as those underlying the Welfare State.[8]

7.2 Fairness, Markets and Community

7.2.1 Fairness, Efficiency and European Market Building

A question often posed in relation to fairness rules is as to their relationship with the market. To what extent do they simply track the values, standards or morality of the market and to what extent do they

---

7   See above at 6.3.9.3, 6.4.2.11, 6.4.4.4 and 6.4.5.3.
8   H. Collins, Law of Contract, Butterworths, 2003, 9.

deviate from market rationality?[9] We should be clear here that just because the rules described above are broadly fairness, rather than freedom, oriented does not mean that they do not still retain elements of market rationality. Rules can deviate from a traditional freedom-oriented approach in the interests of a degree of fairness (and in this sense deviate from one version of market morality – i.e. a wholly self-interested, self-reliant notion of market morality) but remain connected to market rationality, e.g. in seeking to improve the operation of the market.

It is clear, for example, that there is this mixed agenda in the case of the UTD. First, it contains rules that seek to achieve *fairness* as between the parties (in the sense that there is a balancing of the procedural and substantive interests of the parties); while the *constitutional* goal of these rules is the building/development of the European *market*.[10] This constitutional goal is to be achieved by measures that set fairness standards, but that do so in order to eradicate competitive distortions in the European market and improve consumer confidence in that market.

It is clear also that transparency rules (whether as part of the fairness test or the rule requiring main subject matter and price terms to be transparent) are fairness rules in the sense that they seek to protect the interests of consumers by facilitating more informed consent;[11] but they are also intended to improve the working of the market. Generally, such rules may have the effect of disciplining traders to compete with each other, possibly resulting in greater choice and an improvement in substantive fairness.[12] More specifically, of course, transparency is intended to help to build the European market by generating consumer confidence and by forming a part of a harmonized standard that helps to eradicate competitive distortion.[13]

Where rules disallow terms on purely substantive grounds the position is more controversial. Clearly, these rules are about fairness in the sense of protection of consumers from the most detrimental terms (and possibly they are also about presumed procedural unfairness).[14] From one perspective, such rules are not market rational as they deviate from the freedom-oriented values of the market.[15] However, from another perspective, it could be said that such rules are market rational. They can

---

9   On market rationality see T. Wilhelmsson, Varieties of Welfarism in European
      Contract Law (2004) 10 European Law Journal 712, at 718–9 and 726–7.
10   See above at 3.4.3.
11   See above at 2.4.3.4(i).
12   *Ibid.*
13   See above at 3.4.3.
14   See above at 2.4.3.5.
15   Varieties of Welfarism in European Contract Law (2004) 10 European Law Journal
      712, at 719.

be viewed as recognising the existence of transaction costs and the reality that, even with transparency, market discipline cannot be guaranteed.[16] As such, these rules are simply imposing risk allocations (based on default rules or reasonable expectations) that would otherwise have been agreed; and in this sense they represent efficient (and therefore market rational) outcomes.

Apart from whether disallowing on substantive grounds alone can be viewed as being market rational in the sense of being in line with general efficiency, this approach can be viewed as being market rational in another sense. Disallowance of the most substantively unfair terms is needed in order to secure a high level of protection and generate consumer confidence and these are viewed as necessary in order to contribute to the market integration goals of the UTD.[17]

7.2.2 Market or Community Norms

7.2.2.1 The Possible Approaches

Another question as to the relationship between fairness rules and the market is whether the rules basically follow the practices/norms of the market. To reiterate, we are not talking here about practices and norms that are market-oriented in the sense of being necessarily based on values of self-interest and self-reliance. We are talking, rather, of standards that do not necessarily maximize self-reliant freedom and may well constrain the pursuit of self-interest. The question, however, is whether the constraint on self-interest – the process of interest balancing – is nevertheless shaped (first and foremost) by market norms. On such an approach, the fairness concern only kicks in when there is a significant deviation from what is normal trade practice in the market. Given that it is the trader that fixes the market norms by the terms he drafts and/or the practices that he follows in relation to these terms, such an approach can be characterized as involving setting fairness standards by reference to 'trader dominated' market norms.[18]

---

16 See above at 2.4.3.4(iv).

17 See above at 3.4.4.

18 An approach that tracks market norms may do so based on various motivations. It may be thought that it is to expect too much of traders to raise their standards of behaviour from what has traditionally been accepted market practice. Alternatively, tracking market standards (at least in relation to the substantive terms) may be done on the basis of an agenda to use overall substantive fairness as the benchmark; whether a term (along with the other terms, including price) reflects market norms being *one way* of measuring overall substantive fairness (see above at 2.4.3.3).

Essentially, then, the question is whether, in substance and procedure, the level of fairness matches up to (or does not deviate too significantly from) what is normal for traders in that sector; or whether it represents an independent standard not dominated by trader dominated market norms but influenced by broader fairness values.

The former model (we shall call it the 'market model') accommodates two sub-models. Within one of these, the issue is whether it is normal *to use a term* having the substantive effects in question; and whether the level of procedural fairness *displayed by the term* matches up to what is normal. So, for example, in relation to transparency the question would be whether the term is expressed in as clear language as is normal in standard terms used in that market sector. The other sub-model sets a potentially higher standard. Within this sub-model the issue is whether *relying* on a term with these substantive effects reflects normal *practice*. It may be normal to use a term having certain substantive effects, but normal market practice may be that it is not relied upon, or at least not relied upon in full. On the procedural side, the question, again, is whether what has been done matches up to normal *practice*. So, for example, even although the term is expressed on paper in the same way as most others in the market sector, there may be an accepted practice whereby this sort of term is explained verbally to consumers. However, this practice may not be followed by the trader in question; and on this basis the term may be thought of as unfair.

The market model (and more particularly the second sub-model) seems to be close to what has been described as a 'good faith *requirement*'[19] the essence of which is that fairness is determined by reference to the standards that are recognized in the particular contracting context (for our purposes, the particular market sector). We have already encountered the point that in many commercial contracting contexts both parties will have considerable experience of the process and practice of contracting (including formation, performance and dispute resolution) in that particular context.[20] Shared expectations are likely to develop as to the conduct of the relationship, including how disputes will be resolved.[21] It may be that the shared expectation is that the relationship is conducted entirely on the basis of what the formal terms provide. Often (if not usually), however, the shared expectation (based on experience and practice) is that other standards of behaviour will apply. The practice, for

---

[19] See R. Bradgate, R. Brownsword and C. Twigg-Flesner, The Impact of Adopting a General Duty to Trade Fairly, DTI, 2003, 59.

[20] See above at 2.4.2.2 and see J. Wightman, Beyond Custom: Contracts, Contexts and the Recognition of Implicit Understandings, in D. Campbell, H. Collins and J. Wightman, Implicit Dimensions of Contract, Hart, 2003, 169–70.

[21] *Ibid.*

example, may not be for a seller of goods to rely on the broad exemption clause that he always uses, but, rather, to adopt a more cooperative approach and to accept at least some of the liability that is actually excluded by the term. If this is the case then, within a regime dominated by the good faith *requirement*, it may be unfair for a seller to seek to rely on the exemption clause in a particular case as to do so may be to flout the standards of behaviour that are expected in that sector. In other words, in many commercial contexts a good faith *requirement* may actually mean not enforcing the term, as it does not reflect normal *practice* and shared expectation. (This, in other words, is sub-model two in action.)

However, the difficulty, as we have seen, is that in the consumer contracting context there may actually be very few shared expectations either as to what the terms actually provide for or as to how they will be approached in practice. There may be a shared understanding as to what normally happens in the routine supply of particular goods and services, i.e. that they are routinely supplied according to the general gist of what has been agreed to. However, there is much less of a sense of a shared understanding either as to what the terms provide for or as to what will happen in those cases where the terms themselves actually come into play, i.e. those cases where there is some form of dispute as to the performance/liabilities of either of the parties. As suggested above, a shared understanding as to what it is reasonable to expect in such cases is possible in many commercial contracting contexts where the parties form a part of the same contracting community and have dealt with each other (or at least in this community) sufficiently often to develop common understandings as to what it is reasonable to expect where disputes arise. However, consumers are often not sufficiently frequent buyers of goods or services from particular categories of traders so as to enable them to develop an understanding that is shared with the trader as how theses issues will be dealt with. This might lead us to the conclusion that applying a good faith requirement (i.e. an approach that essentially tracks trader dominated market norms – what is normal in the sense of what the terms provide or what is normal in the sense of how terms are normally applied in practice) is unsuitable in consumer contracts; and that it is preferable to adopt an approach that sets independent (usually higher) standards that are not dominated by market norms but are more influenced by broader fairness values. This appears to be broadly in congruence with what Brownsword calls a good faith *regime*.[22] By contrast with his good faith requirement, that tracks market norms, a good

---

22   R. Bradgate, R. Brownsword and C. Twigg-Flesner, The Impact of Adopting a General Duty to Trade Fairly, DTI, 2003, 59.

faith regime involves a 'critical morality of mutuality and cooperation'[23] (which seems to mean rules that set independent and high standards).

7.2.2.2 Where Do We Stand?

So what do we, in fact, have in the regimes under discussion? The good faith standard was described by Lord Steyn as one intended 'to enforce community standards of decency fairness and reasonableness'.[24] Lord Bingham said that good faith 'looks to good standards of commercial morality and practice'.[25] We can see here the potential for a conflict. Lord Steyn's notion of a community standard makes no reference to market norms and therefore contains no positive suggestion of being tied to trader dominated market norms. By contrast, Lord Bingham refers to 'commercial' morality and practice. This might suggest a standard at least more closely connected (whether or not dominated by) market norms.

The idea of 'community standards' is a common theme in good faith thinking. An important source for this reference to community standards is the US restatement which excludes conduct violating 'community standards of decency, fairness or reasonableness.'[26] The same formulation is used in the PECL.[27] 'Community standards' are indeed a theme in many discussions of good faith.[28]

In general, the tension as to how independent from the market the values are often exists in the measures and the literature. How closely tied to the standards of the market is any given 'community' standard? Alternatively, to what extent is it a broader social notion reflecting the morals of the broader community? Both views emerge in relation to the US good faith concept[29] In general however the US notion of good faith

---

[23] *Ibid.*

[24] [2001] 3 WLR 1279, 1313 (quoting the commentary to O. Lando and H. Beale, Principles of European Contract Law, Parts I and II, at 113).

[25] *Ibid.*, at 1308.

[26] See commentary to the US Second Restatement of Contracts.

[27] O. Lando and H. Beale, Principles of European Contract Law, Parts I and II, at 113.

[28] D. Hutchinson, Good Faith in the South African Law of Contract, in R. Brownsword, N. Hird and G. Howells (eds), Good Faith in Contract: Concept and Context, Ashgate, 1999, 213, at 230; B. Reiter, Good Faith in Contracts (1983) 17 Valparaiso University Law Review, 705, at 716–7; R. Zimmerman, An Introduction to German Legal Culture, in W.F. Ebke and M.W. Finkin (eds), Introduction to German Law, The Hague, 1996, at 18.

[29] See J. Nehf, Bad Faith Breach of Contract in Consumer Transactions, in R. Brownsword, N. Hird and G. Howells (eds), Good Faith in Contract: Concept and Context, Ashgate, 1999,115, at 121; B. Reiter, *ibid*; and M. Bridge, Good Faith in

may be of limited help in assessing what a community standard implies. This is because of the large significance of *motive* in US good faith. This subjective dimension somewhat confuses the issue. Having said this, if the need for bad motive is part of a 'community standard' then perhaps it is not a very high standard.

All in all, then, Lord Steyn's reference to community standards could be read either way. At the same time, Lord Bingham's reference to 'commercial' morality and practice does not necessarily mean to suggest a standard that is based on the market norm in the sense of what is typical, average or common. It might be a reference to the best or highest standards of morality and practice in the sector in question. It might, indeed, measure what is the best or highest standard by reference to the business community as a whole; so that all sectors are expected to aspire to the very best. In fact, the language does not even necessarily mean that he contemplates a standard emerging from commercial practice at all. He could simply have been saying that commercial entities (i.e. traders) should exercise good standards of morality and practice (by reference to the broader standards of the community as a whole).

All in all, the goals of the UTD seem to demand (and the actual practice seems to involve) a standard reflecting the standards and morals of the community as a whole; rather than simply trader dominated market norms (although possibly containing some resonance of the latter). The same could surely be said of the UCTA.

The UTD aims at setting high levels of consumer protection and generating consumer confidence. These goals point to the need for a level of protection that is not constrained by market norms. There is certainly no guarantee that the market norm will be a high standard or will be one that generates consumer confidence. Indeed, the market norm may set be quite a low standard.[30] In addition, the UTD aims at eradicating competitive distortions. Surely, this cannot necessarily be achieved by standards that track market norms given that these market norms may differ as between the Member States.

In relation to UCTA, there was never any suggestion that the agenda was simply to track market norms. The Law Commissions, as we saw, referred to unfairness in process and substance and to inefficiency.[31] They did not relate any of this to market norms.

Commercial Contracts, in R. Brownsword, N. Hird and G. Howells (eds), Good Faith in Contract: Concept and Context, Ashgate, 1999,139, at 142.

[30] See J. Wightman, Good Faith and Pluralism in the Law of Contract, in R. Brownsword, N. Hird and G. Howells (eds), Good Faith in Contract: Concept and Context, Ashgate, 1999, 41, at in B *et al.*, 45.

[31] See above at 3.3.

Then we turn to the actual practice of the courts (and, under UTCCR, the regulatory bodies). Neither under UCTA or the UTCCR does the primary issue seem to be whether there is unfairness by reference to trader dominated market norms. It is true that the question as to whether the term was normal was said to be relevant in the *First National Bank* case,[32] but this term was thought to be fair for more general reasons and there was no strong suggestion that being normal in the market could save a term that was unfair on other criteria. Indeed, terms that are, in substance, perfectly normal and/or that are agreed to in procedural circumstances that are perfectly normal, are routinely found to fail to satisfy both tests. So, for example, the OFT has negotiated with trade associations for the removal of terms that are used as standard across the sector.[33] Under UCTA the term in *Smith* v. *Bush* excluding liability for a negligent valuation was a common one in the trade sector and yet was held to fail the test of reasonableness.[34]

As we have said, another way of putting this may be that the dominant element in assessments of fairness is an element that draws on what Brownsword calls a good faith regime. By contrast with his good faith requirement, that tracks market norms, a good faith regime involves a 'critical morality of mutuality and cooperation'.[35] Indeed, we might be more specific in the connection between the type of standards set by the law and Brownsword's model. First of all, the standards may be said to be 'critical' in the sense that they are critical or correcting of the standards of the market. Secondly, the balancing of the substantive interests (via default rules, reasonable expectations standards, mirror image balancing etc.) could be linked to the idea of mutuality. The reasonable expectations standard can also be associated with a cooperative agenda. One aspect of cooperation surely involves contributing to the attainment of the purposes of the contract. The reasonable expectations standard seeks to keep terms (and what they allow the trader to do or what they allow the trader to require of the consumer) in line with what the consumer reasonably expected under the contract. In other words, these standards can be said to require the cooperation of the trader in achieving the purposes of the contract as these would reasonably be understood by the consumer.

Finally, the procedural standards might also be linked to at least one form of cooperation. The trader must, for example, cooperate by using terms that are transparent; the consequence of the terms not being transparent being that the term may not stand. The consumer (at least in

---

32 [2001] 3 WLR 1297, Lord Millett at 1318.

33 See above at 6.4.2.10.

34 See above at 4.6.2.1.

35 R. Bradgate, R. Brownsword and C. Twigg-Flesner, The Impact of Adopting a General Duty to Trade Fairly, DTI, 2003, 59.

cases where transparency is all that is required) has an incentive to cooperate by taking advantage of the transparency to become familiar with the terms (where transparency is all that is required, he will obtain no further protection).

Of course, paradoxically in some ways, the need for standards that are not wedded to market norms flows from the need to achieve the *market* integration goals of the UTD – this is viewed as requiring consumer confidence and a high level of protection, neither of which can actually be achieved by standards that are wedded to trader dominated market norms.

The ongoing development of the standards (and their precise relationship with market norms) will be shaped by, the EC legal/policy matrix of market integration, consumer protection and confidence and possibly the flow of influences from other jurisdictions; and the mix of these elements with national court and regulatory traits and traditions in relation to fairness.[36] The precise standard that will apply in particular cases will be influenced by a variety of factors such as these.

Taking a broad view of the regime, then, it is clearly based more on broader community values than market norms. However, this is not to say that sometimes, market norms may not have a stronger role to play. It has been suggested that there will inevitably be an extent to which business practice plays a part in construction of the standard (therefore importing an element of the so called 'good faith requirement' approach).[37] This may surface for particular reasons. For example, it may have been that one reason that market norms were discussed in *First National Bank* was that the term in question, although not technically being a core term, was very close to being a core term. The aspect of the term under scrutiny did deal with a post-default scenario and on this basis (along with the general agenda to give a restrictive interpretation to the core exclusion) was held not to be a core term.[38] However, it comes very close to being a core term in the sense that it was a term dealing with the obligation to pay the basic rate of interest.[39] The view may have been that the closer we get to a core term the greater the emphasis should be placed on the traditional freedom of contract ethic *and* on what is accepted practice in the market.

The whole question as to the part that should (or should not) be played by trader dominated market norms may also be affected by the language used in expressing the concept of (un)fairness. The good faith concept seems to be the vehicle for the broad review of fairness under UTCCR. If the UCTA and UTCCR regimes are merged into one, the test

---

36   *Ibid.,* and see 3.4–6 above.
37   R. Bradgate, R. Brownsword and C. Twigg-Flesner, The Impact of Adopting a General Duty to Trade Fairly, DTI, 2003, 59, at 63.
38   [2001] 3 WLR 1297 and see above at 5.8.3.1.
39   See 5.8.3.1 above.

will be a 'fair and reasonable' one, but it will still need to be understood in the context of good faith. Good faith (as intended by the UTD) will need to be the minimum achieved by the fair and reasonable test. Now, we have seen that good faith brings a variety of protective nuances to the idea of fairness in relation to contract terms. However, one feature of good faith is that, even although it clearly sets an objective standard in relation to contract terms and even although this clearly involves taking into account the interests of the consumer, the expression 'good faith' focuses on the behaviour and practice of the trader. There may be a risk that this allows us to slide into focusing on what traders normally do and how other traders would judge the fairness of what they do. By contrast, a 'reasonable expectations' standard focuses more squarely on the consumer perspective and what consumers would think was fair (whether based on what normally happens, how the contract was presented, background signals including advertising etc). It is, of course, true that these elements are already part of the law. We have seen that deviation from reasonable expectations triggers the broad reviews of fairness under the reasonableness test and the good faith test; and that the extent of deviation from reasonable expectations is part of these broad reviews. The point simply is that the emphasis on the consumer perspective (and a downplaying of trader dominated market norms) might be better achieved by giving more prominence to an express concept of reasonable expectations in the future.[40]

A final factor that should be borne in mind is that, in the future, market norms may become a more reliable guide to what is fair. This may happen as the work of the regulatory bodies continues to improve the standards of fairness actually practiced. As this happens what is fair may get closer to what is normal.

7.3 Autonomy and Expectation

7.3.1 Fairness-Oriented Autonomy

The fairness regime described obviously deviates from the self-reliant, self-interested approach associated with a traditional freedom-oriented approach. However, it can still be associated with certain notions of freedom or autonomy; albeit different notions of freedom and autonomy

---

[40]   For a discussion of the role of giving a greater role for reasonable expectations in EC consumer law and policy generally see G. Howells and T. Wilhelmsson, EC consumer law: has it come of age? (2003) 28 European Law Review 370, at 384–5.

from those self-reliant, self-interested notions associated with a traditional freedom-oriented approach.[41]

The traditional freedom-oriented approach is about self-reliant freedom or autonomy; this self-reliance principle being non-contextual.[42] It is non-contextual in the sense that it takes limited account of the real practical limits facing the consumer in exercising self-reliance. In other words, it takes little account of the position of the consumer and the nature of the contracting process that make it difficult for the consumer to really look after his own interests in the bargaining process.

By contrast, the fairness approach is contextual and recognizes these difficulties.[43] In response, it requires terms to be transparent. Part of the agenda here can be argued to be enabling a more free and autonomous choice to be made by the consumer. However, this is clearly a particular version of freedom or autonomy. It is about *assisted, informed consent*; not about pure self-reliance.[44] In addition, of course, the trader pays a price in the sense that there is a restriction on his freedom or autonomy to present his terms as he likes.

Even where some terms are disallowed in cases where there is a reasonable degree of procedural fairness, there can be argued to be an agenda to secure a form of freedom or autonomy. Clearly it is not the orthodox non-contextual, self-reliant and self-interested version of freedom. Neither is it the assisted, informed consent model described above (on such a model a term is enforceable as long as there was a

---

41   As suggested above (at 2.3.2.2) there is a considerable spectrum of what we might regard as 'freedom' or an exercise in 'voluntariness' – see A. Kronman, Contract Law and Distributive Justice, 1980, 89 Yale Law Journal, 472; D. Kennedy, Distributive and Paternalist Motives in Contract and Tort Law, with Special Reference to Compulsory Terms and Unequal Bargaining Power (1982) 41 Maryland Law Review 563 at 582; R. Brownsword, Contract Law: Themes for the Twenty-First Century, 2nd edn, OUP, 2006, 65–66 and R. Barnett, A Consent Theory of Contract (1986) 86 Columbia Law Review 269, at 300–319 in particular.

42   See 2.2–3 above.

43   See 2.4 above.

44   The idea here is that consumers are not really 'free' unless they are free from restrictions at the procedural stage that obstruct their ability to protect their interests. However, this version of freedom is not the self-reliant, non-contextual version, but is a notion of freedom infused with fairness concerns. More generally on the relationship between the different 'ethics' with which we can infuse a concept such as freedom see R. Brownsword, Contract Law: Themes for the Twenty-First Century, 2nd edn, OUP, 2006, 65–66; R. Barnett, A Consent Theory of Contract (1986) 86 Columbia Law Review 269, at 300–319 in particular; C. Willett, Autonomy and Fairness: The Case of Public Statements, in G. Howells, A. Jaansen and R. Schulze, Information Rights and Obligations, Ashgate, 2005, 1; and see 2.4.1 above.

reasonable degree of transparency – such that the consumer has been given some assistance to exercise informed consent – along with a choice of terms or the bargaining power to obtain a change to or deletion of the term). Clearly, also, disallowance of terms even where there is a degree of procedural fairness restricts the freedom *of the trader*. The type of freedom or autonomy that can be regarded as being promoted when terms are disallowed despite a reasonable level of procedural fairness is the *post-contractual* freedom or autonomy *of the consumer*.[45] So, for example, the result of disallowing a term may be that the consumer is free to pursue a claim when the trader does not perform as promised or as reasonably expected (something which the term may have prevented the consumer from doing). Alternatively, the result of disallowing a term may be that the consumer is free from an onerous obligation or free from a contract being renewed, which contract would impose upon him a longer term obligation.

This approach seems to be in congruence with what Collins is referring to when he talks of a 'revised notion of autonomy'.[46] This involves placing restrictions on autonomy where the exercise of autonomy results in the party in question making choices that are not worthwhile. The choices may be defined as not being worthwhile because they do not contribute to meaning in the life of the party in question.[47] Here, the choices made at the time of entering the contract are not worthwhile in the sense that they restrict the post-contractual freedoms described. So, on this revised approach to autonomy, autonomy at the pre-contractual stage is sacrificed in order to preserve post-contractual freedom or autonomy.

7.3.2 Fairness-Oriented Expectation

The fairness approach also departs from a traditional freedom-oriented approach to expectation; but, again (and as we have already seen to an extent), can be viewed as instating a fairness-oriented view of expectation. On the freedom-oriented approach to expectation, one of the reasons that it is just to enforce what has been freely agreed to is because this is what both parties would expect.[48] The freedom-oriented approach to expectation holds that the consumer expects the trader to perform

---

[45]   On restrictions on traditional freedom of contract securing future freedom see S. Smith, Future Freedom and Freedom of Contract (1996) 59 Modern Law review 167.

[46]   See H. Collins, Law of Contract, 4th edn, 2004, at 29 and S. Smith, *ibid.*

[47]   See H. Collins, *ibid.*, and D. Kimmel, Neutrality, Autonomy and Freedom of Contract (2001) 21 Oxford Journal of Legal Studies, 473 at 487–93.

[48]   See generally Fried, Contract as Promise, Harvard University Press, 1981.

according to what he has promised in the formal terms and to be liable for non-performance, again as stipulated for in the terms.[49] Equally, within the freedom-oriented approach to expectation, the consumer expects to be held to his own obligations and liabilities as laid down in the terms. However, this is, of course, a non-contextual vision of expectations, at least of the expectations of the consumer. It does not recognize the limited role that the formal terms may actually have in forming consumer expectations and the more significant role that may be played by other factors.

By contrast, the fairness approach to expectation is based on recognising exactly this. A fairness-oriented approach to expectation is not necessarily about enforcing what is in the formal terms. The formal terms are not seen as the source of consumer expectations. Consumer expectations should be shaped by reference to other criteria, including (in general) the social conditions and realities of the situation. So, as a basic starting point, it might be said that a private consumer can reasonably expect fair treatment when dealing with a party operating as a business. This is essentially a normative concept of expectation. The expectation is primarily based on the fact that consumers operating in the private sphere of life should be given a basic threshold level of protection against their lack of autonomy in the bargaining process and against financial and other losses. What I am positing here is a general social expectation of fair treatment. This is an expectation that is justified by reference to the community standards referred to above. If consumers are viewed as having come to the relationship as weaker parties (both in relation to the process leading to the agreement and in their ability to bear the consequences of substantively unfair terms) then community standards of social justice might be said to hold that consumers can reasonably expect a degree of protection from unfair terms; especially where these terms may have a significant impact upon the private sphere of life.

Of course, more specific expectations of fair treatment may be generated by the extra contractual signals received by consumers that we have been discussing throughout the book. As we have seen, consumers do not tend to have much experience of the detail of standard terms or as to how they are interpreted and applied in practice. This is the type of experience that often generates expectations as to the conduct of the

---

49 This is what has been described as an 'institutional' approach to expectation, i.e. an approach based on the expectations being generated by the institution of the contract – see C. Mitchell, Leading a Life of its Own? The Roles of Reasonable Expectation in Contract Law, Oxford Journal of Legal Studies, Vol. 23, No. 4 (2003), 639, at 647–654. Of course, it can also be viewed as being underpinned by a *normative* choice, i.e. the freedom-oriented, self-reliant based notion that it is the institution of the contract that consumers *should* focus on in forming their expectations.

relationship. If the terms themselves are not particularly transparent and are unlikely to be read at the point of contract, then what they say will have little impact on consumer expectations at this stage. Consumers seem much more likely to be influenced by *extra* contractual signals of a variety of types. These signals may raise specific expectations that are then compromised by terms allowing the trader to exercise some form of discretion.[50] However, the individual and cumulative effect of such signals might be said to fortify the broader normative expectation of fair treatment described above.

We have talked of the sources of these expectations throughout the course of the book. To summarize briefly, it seems that they come first of all from advertising, marketing and the general 'consumption culture'. A general expectation may be argued to be raised to the effect that the purchase of goods and services will be 'life enhancing', that it facilitates more meaningful participation in society.[51] Expectations of reasonably fair treatment will also come from the simple fact that this is what normally happens. The vast majority of consumer experiences of purchasing goods and services will tend to be successful. This experience signals to the consumer that the basic goods or services asked for will be successfully supplied, that any other elements of the performance given emphasis will also be successfully carried out, and that the consumer will successfully carry out his obligation(s). There is, therefore, limited consumer experience of the terms being used to deprive the consumer of redress when the trader fails to perform properly. There is limited consumer experience of the terms being used to impose onerous obligations and liabilities on him (the consumer) when he is in some way in default.

Finally, of course, there are the more specific expectations in particular situations that the goods or services will be as suggested by the basic 'gist' of the deal agreed between the parties and that there will not be scope for variation at the discretion of the trader.

The fairness approach concretizes these general expectations of fair treatment by reference to the various standards of fairness in substance and procedure.

But how does all of this square with the autonomy/freedom and expectations of the trader? Protection of a reasonable consumer expectation of fairness clearly undermines the trader's freedom/autonomy to make agreements and compromises the trader's expectations that these

---

50   These expectations are empirically based to the extent that they are grounded in particular signals that are received by consumers. However, the choice to focus on these signals rather than insisting on only respecting expectations raised by the formal terms seems to be a normative choice. On these issues see above at 4.4.

51   See I. Ramsay, *Advertising, Culture and the Law*, Sweet and Maxwell, 1996, p. 2.

agreements will be enforced. However within a fairness approach this is justified. The different positions of the parties, and the more vulnerable position of the consumer, make it less reasonable for the trader to expect maximum freedom to contract. In a society concerned (at least to some extent) with welfarism, the trader must expect his freedom to assert his interests over a private party to be limited. In addition, we must remember the role of traders in generating expectations by extra contractual signals (the 'encouraged expectation' element). As already suggested, the fact that traders play this role in generating expectations lends weight to the view that, in terms of the justice of the relationship between the trader and the consumer, the consumer is entitled to these expectations; they are reasonable expectations that the trader should, in some sense, be held to.

It must also be remembered in this connection that without the help of contract law (and the process of administration of justice which backs contract law), the trader does not in fact have an effective liberty or autonomy to enforce any agreement which pleases him. As Smith (referring to the terminology of Hart) says: 'Contract Law ... [is] a power-conferring legal doctrine ... it helps people to do things they could not do otherwise or not do as easily'.[52]

So, if, in a modern society, a trader chooses to bring about economic exchanges with a weaker party, he cannot reasonably expect the law to help him unreservedly. He must expect that the law will place some limits on the degree of help which it is prepared to give to him. These limits will be determined, by the values of that modern society. These values include the maintenance of a certain degree of welfarist-type protection for weaker parties in relationships.[53]

This type of approach has echoes of the social contract theories of Hobbes, Locke and Rousseau.[54] We may speak in terms of a 'contract' between the State and the business community. In exchange for the help of the State in enforcing agreements, traders must accept certain restrictions on their autonomy. Put another way, the help being given means that it is not reasonable for traders to expect untrammelled freedom or autonomy when the interests of a weaker party are at stake.

---

[52] S. Smith, In Defence of Substantive Fairness (1996) 112 LQR at 145.

[53] See Brownsword, Howells and Wilhelmsson, *Welfarism in Contract Law*, 1994, Dartmouth; Wilhelmsson, *Social Contract Law and European Integration*, Dartmouth, 1995.

[54] See Buchanan, The Limits of Liberty: Between Anarchy and Leviathan, 1975; Buchanan, The Reason of Rules: Constitutional Political Economy, 1985; Rules and Choice in Economics, 1994; Brennan and Hamlin, Constitutional Economics, in Newman (ed.), The New Palgrave Dictionary of Economics and the Law, Vol. 1, 1998; S. Grundman, W. Kerber and S. Weatherill (eds), Party Autonomy and the Role of Information in the Internal Market, Gruyter, 2001.

Chapter Eight

The Transformation

8.1 The Basic Conceptual Transformation – Introduction

Taking the UCTA and the UTCCR together (or thinking purely of the proposed new regime), we can identify a transformation in approach from that taken by the common law and equity. It is not that common law and equity did not recognize any of the fairness problems described or take any steps to address them. In *Suisse Atlantique SA* v. *Rotterdamsche Kolen Centrale* Lord Reid recognized the procedural problems arising in standard form contracts. He said that:

> In the ordinary way the customer has no time to read [the standard terms], and if he did read them he would probably not understand them. And if he did understand and object to any of them, he would generally be told he could take it or leave it. And if he went to another supplier the result would be the same. Freedom to contract must surely imply some choice or room for bargaining.[1]

The problem was that the tools at hand (or that the courts were prepared to develop) were inadequate in various respects. Essential to the current legislative approach (taking both regimes together) are three components. First, there is a broad review of procedural and substantive fairness applicable to all or most terms that either exclude or restrict the obligations or liabilities that would otherwise be owed by the trader; add to those that would otherwise be owed by the consumer; or provide for either party to perform in a way that does not reflect the reasonable expectations of the consumer. Terms do not get to fall through the net on arbitrary grounds. These fairness benchmarks provide a bit of focus and certainty. At the same time the tests are flexible enough to catch existing and previously unnoticed mischiefs or future types of term that develop. The second key feature of the regimes is that, although the standards may sometimes be in congruence with the market they are not dominated by the market. The idea is not to follow market practice in relation to fairness, but to set independent and usually high standards of fairness that reflect the morality of the community as a whole. This means, for

---

[1] [1967] 1 AC 361, at 406.

example, that there is no need for extreme deviation from the default position or deviation that is greater than what is normal in the market; and that the standards of procedural fairness are based on what is needed to allow the average consumer to protect his interests, not what is normal practice. The third essential element is that a term is not made fair by the good conscience of the trader. The standard is an objective one, based on an objective analysis of substance and procedure.

Common law and equity failed on one or more of these requirements. This can be seen by consideration of several packages of rules related to consumer contract terms.

8.1.1 Agreed Remedies

First of all there is a package of rules relating to terms providing for agreed remedies – specifically terms providing for penalties to be imposed on the consumer and for retention (by the trader) of deposits and part-payments made by the consumer.[2] Essentially, these rules can (in common with the UTCCR[3]) prevent reliance on a term enabling the trader to obtain unduly onerous compensation when the consumer is in breach. A term cannot stipulate for the innocent party to recover losses that exceed a reasonable pre-estimate of his loss (the rule against 'penalties');[4] a deposit may be returnable to the party in breach if the deposit is unreasonable;[5] as is a part-payment, if the party in breach is ready and willing to perform).[6] However, a fundamental problem with these rules is

---

[2] On these rules see H. Collins, Fairness in Agreed Remedies, in C. Willett (ed.), Aspects of Fairness in Contract, 1996, 97.

[3] See above at 5.7.4.2.

[4] *Dunlop Pneumatic Tyre Co. Ltd* v. *New Garage and Motor Co.* [1915] AC 79.

[5] Traditionally it seems that a term allowing a deposit to be retained in these circumstances would have been enforceable, as the rule was that a deposit, being 'an earnest to bind the bargain' (*Howe* v. *Smith* (1884) 27 Ch. D89) was non-returnable to the party in breach (*Howe* v. *Smith, ibid*; and *Union Eagle Ltd* v. *Golden Achievements Ltd* [1997] 2 All ER 215; and see Law Commission, Working Paper, No. 61, para. 53). However, there is now authority to the effect that a deposit must be reasonable; and that if it is not reasonable then it will be recoverable by the party who is in breach – see *Workers Trust & Merchant Bank Ltd* v. *Dojap Investments Ltd* [1993] 2 All ER 370 (PC) and also see H. Beale, Unreasonable Deposits (1993) 109 Law Quarterly Review 524.

[6] See H. Collins, Fairness in Agreed Remedies, in Willett (ed.), Aspects of Fairness in Contract, 1996, at 112; *Rover International Ltd* v. *Cannon Film Sales Ltd* [1989] 1 WLR 912 CA; *Stockloser* v. *Johnson* [1954] 1 QB 476 CA; Re Dagenham (Thames)

one of (limited) breadth of coverage. First of all, of course, they only cover terms relating to the liability *of the consumer*. They do not cover terms dealing with the obligations and liabilities *of the trader*. But, even within this ambit, the focus of the rules is on terms imposing *liabilities* on the consumer (i.e. terms that impact when the consumer is in breach) rather than terms imposing primary *obligations* on the consumer. This, for example (as we have already seen), has allowed traders to avoid the penalty rules by drafting terms such that they technically impose a primary obligation to pay a sum rather than imposing a liability for breach.[7] This means that even although the term, in substance, requires the consumer to make payments that exceed a reasonable pre-estimate of the losses of the trader and exceed what the consumer would reasonably expect to have to pay in the due performance of the contract, the term is not controlled. This is because what is in substance a default is not described as such. It is simply depicted as an event that triggers a fresh consumer obligation to pay a sum of money.

However, even within the ambit of consumer *liabilities* for breach, the rules do not form part of a general principle requiring terms imposing such liabilities on consumers to be fair. Terms will be caught if they impose a financial liability that does not represent a reasonable pre-estimate of the losses likely to be suffered by the trader or if they allow for financial liabilities to be imposed by enabling the trader to retain certain deposits or advance payments. However, there is no *general* rule allowing for control of terms that impose *other* types of liability or give the trader rights of some other kind when the consumer is in breach. There is no general principle to the effect that if such liabilities or rights are detrimental to the consumer by comparison with the default position or if they allow for compromise of reasonable expectations, then an enquiry into fairness should be triggered.

Sometimes there is a further problem with these rules in relation to the *level* of fairness required. In the case of the rules on penalties, there does appear to be what qualifies as a 'community' standard of fairness (or a good faith 'regime'). The benchmark is effectively the default position on damages, i.e. that damages are intended to put the innocent party in the position he would have occupied if the contract had been performed. The breach means that the innocent party is not in this position. The difference between the position that they are now in and the position that they would be in if the contract had been performed represents their loss. This is what is recoverable under the default rule. The rule on penalties essentially says that the term should only provide for compensation that

---

Dock Co, *ex parte* Hulse v (1873) 8 Ch App 1022 and *Kilmer* v. *British Columbia Orchard Lands Ltd* [1913] AC 319.

7   See above at 5.7.4.2.

represents a reasonable pre-estimate of that loss. In this sense the rule on penalties represents a community standard of fairness. However, the same may not be able to be said of the rules on deposits and part-payments. The problem is that the level of fairness provided for by the rules on deposits and part-payments may be quite low. It may be that where the rules on deposits are concerned the standard of fairness is dictated by market norms. The judgement of Lord Browne-Wilkinson in the *Workers Trust* case[8] suggests that what is reasonable may be based on customary norms; and a sum may be reasonable even although it is in excess of what would be a genuine pre-estimate of the loss likely to be suffered by the party not in breach.[9] In relation to part-payments, the suggestion seems to be that the jurisdiction would apply where the sum being retained was out of all proportion to the damage caused by the breach[10] and it was unconscionable to allow retention of the money.[11] Again, this may involve a fairly low standard of fairness. The sum in question needs to be *out of all proportion* to the losses of the other party and be *unconscionable*.

So, in relation to both the rules on deposits and those on part-payments, there appears to be a lower level of fairness than is required when such terms are tested for fairness under the UTCCR. There the standard, as we have seen, is a community standard, informed by the EC market building goals of consumer confidence and a high level of protection. We have seen that these standards are not usually based on trader dominated norms such as what is customary; and do not require the extreme levels of unfairness that might be suggested by the notion of a sum being out of all proportion to the losses of the trader and being unconscionable. Indeed, the indicative list of terms in the UTCCR deals with terms requiring the consumer to compensate the trader when he is in breach and simply refers to a 'disproportionately high sum',[12] saying nothing of the sum being *out of all proportion* and certainly not of it being *unconscionable*. We shall see below that 'unconscionability' tends to involve a fairly severe degree of unfairness in both substance and procedure.

Of course, a further point is that the reference to unconscionability brings the question of bad conscience into the equation. Either this was viewed as something that could be assumed automatically from the amount being retained (in which case this serves to further confirm that quite a high level of unfairness in substance is required) or there is a

---

8   [1993] 2 All ER 370 (PC).
9   *Ibid.*, Lord Browne-Wilkinson at 373b.
10   At 490.
11   At 484.
12   Paragraph 1(e).

distinct requirement of bad conscience (in which case there is a further departure from the type of standard required under the UTCCR, which, as we have seen, contains no such requirement).

8.1.2 Unconscionability

As we have seen, a major limitation with the rules on agreed remedies is that they only apply to particular categories of term. We now turn to the equitable unconscionability rules.[13] These do, in theory, apply to any type of term; and involve a general review of procedural and substantive unfairness. However, what seems, effectively, to be required is extreme procedural and substantive unfairness: terms sufficiently unfair in substance as to be described as 'overreaching and oppressive'[14] (with extreme deviation from the market norm being one possible way of showing this); procedural unfairness that is extreme in the sense that the weaker party is in an extremely vulnerable position;[15] and some evidence of bad conscience in the sense that the stronger party has brought about the contract by exploiting the other's weakness.[16] Putting this in another way, the unconscionability rules seem to fall far short of setting a 'community standard' of fairness which takes mutuality and cooperation seriously. There never seems to have been any appetite to nuance the unconscionability rules so as to deal with the more routine types of unfair term in consumer contracts. However, the courts in other EC countries seem to have been more relaxed about adapting general principles from their codes to control unfair terms in standard contracts before specifically nuanced legislative regimes were introduced. For example, in Germany standard terms were controlled by the general good faith principle in Article 242 of the BGB.[17] In Holland, standard terms were controlled by Article 6 of the BW which requires reasonableness and equity.[18]

---

13 For recent discussions see D. Capper, Undue Influence and Unconscionability: A Rationalisation (1998) 114 Law Quarterly Review 479; Sir Anthony Mason, Contract, Good Faith, and Equitable Standards in Fair Dealing (2000) 116 Law Quarterly Review 66 at 87–90; and M. Chen-Wishart, Contract Law, OUP, 2005, 375–381.

14 See the discussion by Mr Peter Millet QC (as he then was sitting as a deputy High Court Judge) in *Alec Lobb (Garages) Ltd* v. *Total Oil (Great Britain) Ltd* [1983] 1 WLR 87 at pages 94–95; see also *Boustany* v. *Piggott* (1995) 69 p & C.R. 298 which adopted a similar analysis.

15 Alec Lobb, *ibid.*

16 *Ibid.*

17 See case BGH, 4 June 1970, BGHZ 17, 1, 3.

18 See Saladin/HBU, Hoge Raad, 19 May 1967.

8.1.3 The Suggested Inequality of Bargaining Power and Fair and Reasonable Tests

At one stage, Lord Denning did suggest recognition of a general principle of inequality of bargaining power which he seems to have intended should be applicable to any type of term.[19] However, once again, it seems that this was probably essentially focused on the more extreme forms of substantive and procedural unfairness; and was not what could be described as a community standard, aimed at the more routine unfairness to be found in consumer contracts. In any event, the principle was never accepted by the House of Lords.[20] He also suggested a broad reasonableness review of exemption clauses.[21] This may well have been intended to control much more routine unfairness. However, by the time of this suggestion, statutory control of exemption clauses had begun in the shape of the original ban on excluding liability for breach of the implied terms in contracts for the sale and supply of goods[22] and Lord Denning's suggested principle was never developed.

8.1.4 Agreement Rules

The other common law tools were also ineffective. First, there are the general agreement rules. Of course, these are also rules of general application, i.e. they are not restricted in the way the rules on agreed remedies are. The rule that a term must have been agreed to (more specifically that there must be reasonable notice of it[23]) is a rule applicable to all terms. However, it only deals with one aspect of fairness, i.e. transparency, and the actual standard of transparency required is low. Where unsigned documents are concerned, the general rule is that there should be reasonable notice.[24] However, this means simply that the consumer should be made aware of the *existence* of terms. It does not generally matter whether the terms are in plain language, decent sized print, well structured and cross-referenced etc; whether (given subject matter and complexity) there is time to read and understand them; or whether particularly onerous, unusual or important terms have been drawn to the attention of the consumer (all of the things that are required under the good faith concept in the UTCCR). Of course, as we have

---

19 *Lloyds Bank* v. *Bundy* [1975] QB 326 at 329.
20 See *Morgan* v. *National Westminster Bank* [1985] AC 686.
21 *Gillespie Bros & Co. Ltd* v. *Roy Bowles Transport Ltd* [1973] 1 QB 400 at 416.
22 See the Supply of Goods (Implied Terms) Act 1973.
23 *Parker* v. *SE Ry Co* (1877) 2 CPD 416.
24 *Ibid.*

already seen, in the case of unsigned documents, there *is* a higher standard of transparency (i.e. a requirement of prominence) in some cases.[25] However, this is only triggered where there is quite extreme unfairness in substance or the term is unusual (i.e. out of step with market norms).[26] In addition, this higher standard of transparency does not even apply to signed documents where the rule is still that the consumer is bound by virtue of the signature,[27] irrespective of the intransparency of the terms.

8.1.5 Construction Rules

Then there are the rules on construction. Under the auspices of these rules the courts often sought to construe exemption clauses narrowly so as to prevent them covering the liability they sought to exclude or restrict. In particular, there was evidence of a clear distaste for terms excluding liability for negligence. In addition, there is the 'main purpose' rule of construction. Under this rule a term seeking to avoid liability can be construed narrowly in the light of the main purpose of the contract.[28] There is a connection here with the idea of reasonable expectations discussed above.[29] Rather than reading the term in isolation, it might be said to be being read in the light of the background expectations of the parties as to the main purpose of the contract. Of course, the difference between rules of construction and the statutory regimes discussed above (whether in relation to terms excluding liability for negligence or seeking to allow the trader to perform in ways out of step with the background expectations of the parties) is that, under the rules of construction, if the terms clearly have the effect in question then the matter ends there. The term is enforceable. So, at best, some consumers are protected (i.e. in those cases where the trader does not make the term clear enough to escape a restrictive construction). In addition, traders generally have an incentive to draft more clearly. However, this is not about transparency in general, but simply about stating in a sufficiently unambiguous fashion that a certain liability is not accepted. By contrast, under the statutory regimes if a term excludes a liability or allows for compromise of

---

25 *Interfoto Picture Library Ltd* v. *Stiletto Visual Programmes Ltd* [1989] QB 433 and see above at 6.4.2.3.

26 See above *ibid.*

27 See *L'Estrange* v. *Graucob* [1934] 2 KB 394 and *Peninsula Business Services* v. *Sweeney* [2004] IRLR 49.

28 See *Glynn* v. *Margetson* [1893] AC 351, in particular Lord Halsbury at 357; and see discussion by B. Coote, Exception Clauses, Sweet and Maxwell, 1964, 94–98.

29 See above at 4.4.

reasonable expectations, it is subject to a broad review of fairness. This, as we have seen, covers much more in the way of transparency than simply whether the term is unambiguous. In addition, it covers other matters of procedural fairness and also matters of substantive fairness.

8.1.6 Fundamental Breach

Finally, we turn to the idea of a fundamental breach of contract or breach of a fundamental term. For some time during the 1950s and 1960s it appeared that there might actually be a rule of law to the effect that it was impossible for a party to exclude liability for fundamental breach of contract or for breach of a fundamental term. This possibility arose in particular out of the judgements of the Court of Appeal in cases such as *Karsales (Harrow) Ltd* v. *Wallis*[30] and *Charterhouse Credit Ltd* v. *Tolley*.[31] In the *Karsales* v. *Wallis* case, the defendant, having inspected a car (which at that time was in good order), entered into a hire purchase contract for the car. When the car was ultimately delivered to him (late at night) it was little more than a 'shell' which had a broken cylinder head, burnt out valves, and two broken pistons. The contract contained a clause excluding all express or implied conditions and warranties as to roadworthiness or fitness for purpose. It was held that the claimants were not entitled to rely on the exemption clause since there had been a fundamental breach of contract.

Parker LJ said that: 'not every defect which renders a car temporarily unusable would necessarily amount to a fundamental breach, but where as here a vehicle is delivered incapable of self-propulsion except after a complete overhaul … it is abundantly clear that there is a breach of a fundamental term.'[32]

This approach is linked to the idea that deviation from default rules should be viewed with suspicion (the default position being that the car comply with the implied terms as to quality and fitness for purpose). Of course, the fundamental breach 'rule' was only applied to attempts to exclude the legally determined remedies for the most serious (i.e. fundamental) breaches of contract. So terms excluding the legally determined remedies in the case of less serious breaches were not covered by the 'rule'. The fundamental breach 'rule' also sought to pay some heed to the reasonable expectations of the consumer. A consumer can surely reasonably expect that the trader will be liable for breaches that go to the very root of the contract. Clauses that deny this surely compromise such a

---

[30] [1956] 2 All ER 866.
[31] [1963] 2 QB 683.
[32] At p. 871.

reasonable expectation. However, this is a very 'thin' concept of reasonable expectations. Consumers surely reasonably expect traders to be liable for less serious breaches as well as the most fundamental breaches.

In any event the 'rule' did not last long. In 1967 in the case of *Suisse Atlantique Société D' armement Maritime SA* v. *Rotterdansche Kolen Centrale NV*[33] the House of Lords held that there was no absolute rule of law that a person was not entitled to exclude liability for fundamental breach of contract. It was held rather to be a matter of construction of the clause. If the clause was clearly enough worded as to cover the breach in question then it would be effective to exclude liability. However it later appeared that the Court of Appeal were still treating the fundamental breach concept as a rule of law, rather than as a rule of construction, and it was not until 1980 in the case of *Photo Production Ltd* v. *Securicor Transport Ltd*[34] that it was finally settled that if an exclusion clause was sufficiently clearly worded then it could cover liability for fundamental breach.

8.2 From Formal to Substantive Reasoning

One author has also identified the UCTA and UTCCR regimes as representing another form of transformation. This is a transformation from rules based on formal reasoning to rules based on more substantive/discretionary type reasoning.[35] Niglia characterizes common law rules as being based on 'formal' reasoning which contains very limited discretion for the decision maker.[36] So, for example, as we have seen, a term is incorporated on the basis of reasonable notice or signature; if it is a penalty it is invalid; the parties are presumed not to intend to allow for exclusion of liability in relation to fundamental breach or for non-performance of the main purpose of the contract. By contrast, Niglia highlights the way in which under the more discretionary legislative regimes there is a more 'substantive' approach that may allow a term to stand depending on the degree of fairness in substance; on the degree of transparency; and on whether the term makes economic sense.[37] It is certainly true that, although the legislative tests do cast the fairness net

---

[33] [1967] AC 361.

[34] [1980] AC 827; and see more recently *Edmund Murray* v. *BSP International Foundations* (1993) 33 Con LR.

[35] See L. Niglia, The Fall of Formalism in English Contract Law (2004) Journal of Contract Law, 193.

[36] *Ibid.*, at 194–5.

[37] *Ibid.*, at 201, *et seq.*

more broadly by catching terms that would have escaped control at common law, these regimes may also allow terms to stand that a more formal approach might not allow to stand. For example, a formal approach to the term in *First National Bank* would arguably have disallowed it on the basis that it deviated from the common law default position (which is that contractual interest merge in the judgement and does not continue to accrue in addition to the judgement); and also that it might be said to have 'deviated' from the general statutory regime that does not allow the court to award statutory interest. On such a formal approach it would not have been relevant to consider the question as to whether Banks would not lend without such a term or the question as to whether the Bank warned the consumer as to the situation in the letter sent at the time of the judgement. It is also true that the OFT do not always require outright deletion of unfair terms but sometimes require that they be revised so as to make them fairer in substance. In other words we can see the issue being assessed very much as a matter of degree; this, as we have seen, being characteristic of what Niglia describes as 'substantive' reasoning.[38]

However, I would suggest that we should be careful not to overstate the extent of the shift away from formal reasoning, particularly in relation to the approach of the OFT. For example, as we have seen, where terms are described quite specifically on the indicative list, the OFT appears quite ready to take the view that these are unfair without significant questions being asked about whether there is overall substantive fairness or whether there is procedural fairness. This seems to be the case in relation to terms excluding or hindering consumer access to justice; requiring consumers to pay for goods or services not received; allowing for alteration of the terms or performance without valid reasons; transferring consumer rights without consent; imposing excessive charges and costs; automatically extending contracts where the deadline expressed for the consumer to express a desire not to extend is too early; allowing for price escalation clauses where there is no consumer right to cancel. Indeed even in the context of exemption clauses it is clear that the OFT view many as unfair whenever they significantly restrict or limit liability.

8.3 The Transformation in Enforcement

The UTCCR have also brought a transformation for the UK in terms of enforcement. Detailed discussion of enforcement is beyond the scope of this book. However, several points are worthy of mention. First of all, the proactive enforcement powers in the UTCCR have meant that the

---

[38] *Ibid.*, at 202.

standards set out above have become more of a reality in practice than they would ever be within a wholly private law enforcement scheme. Under UCTA the only form of enforcement is via private litigation.[39] This only affects the use of the term in question as between the two parties to the action. Even if the term is set aside, there is nothing to prevent the trader continuing to use the term in contracts with other consumers. It is fairly self-evident that this form of enforcement will only ever have a very limited impact on the use of unfair terms. This was indeed the case under UCTA. Before the UTCCR, large numbers of terms that may well have failed the UCTA reasonableness test (and many that were in theory wholly ineffective) continued to be used. However, as we have seen, the UTCCR give powers to a variety of bodies to seek injunctions to prevent the continued use of unfair terms.[40] In addition, short of seeking an injunction, the OFT may seek undertakings from traders that they will remove or amend terms.[41] These powers were introduced pursuant to the UTD, Article 7 of which requires Member States to:

1. ... ensure that, in the interests of consumers and of competitors, adequate and effective means exist to prevent the continued use of unfair terms in contracts concluded with consumers by sellers or suppliers.

2. The means referred to in paragraph 1 shall include provisions whereby persons or organizations, having a legitimate interest under national law in protecting consumers, may take action according to the national law concerned before the courts or before competent administrative bodies for a decision as to whether contractual terms drawn up for general use are unfair, so that they can apply appropriate and effective means to prevent the continued use of such terms.

3. With due regard for national laws, the legal remedies referred to in paragraph 2 may be directed separately or jointly against a number of sellers or suppliers from the same economic sector or their associations which use or recommend the use of the same general contractual terms or similar terms.

---

[39] The various provisions of UCTA provide that a term is either of no effect in all cases (s. 2(1) and ss 6(2) and 7(2)) or is of no effect where the terms fails to satisfy the requirement of reasonableness. The only proactive action that could be taken was in the case of those terms excluding or restricting liability for breach of the implied terms as to description, quality etc (ss 6(2) and 7(2)). Such terms are criminalized under the Consumer Transactions (Restrictions on Statements) Order 1976.

[40] Regulation 12.

[41] Regulation 10(3).

This clearly required that Member States would allow for some form of proactive action to be taken against unfair terms; and seems to have been based on the continental tradition of allowing consumer and bodies to act against the use of unfair terms.[42] This was necessary to achieve the goals of the UTD as it is obvious that there will not be a high level of consumer protection or consumer confidence if large numbers of terms remain in use (as would be the case where the system is wholly dependent on private litigation). Indeed, the proactive controls were also necessary for the eradication of competitive distortions. The idea is to eradicate the competitive distortions caused by differing regimes on unfair terms which would allow use of different terms. However, these competitive distortions obviously stand little chance of being eradicated if the standards are not enforced effectively and in a broadly similar way.

These powers have been a foundation for the OFT in particular to persuade traders to remove or amend large numbers of terms.[43] The OFT have also issued a considerable body of guidance on unfairness which has informed their approach to enforcement.[44] This has presumably aided traders and their advisers in understanding and complying with the law;[45] presumably also aided consumers and their advisers in recognising breaches of the law; and, as we have seen, contributed hugely to the jurisprudence on unfairness. A further point that can be made as to the

---

[42] See generally U. Bernitz, Consumer Protection and Standard Contracts (1973) 17 Scandinavian Studies in Law, 11; E. Hondius, Unfair Terms in Consumer Contracts, Molengraff Institute for Private Law, 1987, 224–228; and T. Wilhelmsson, Control of Unfair Terms and Social Values (1993) 16 Journal of Consumer Policy, 435. The approach has more recently been extended to apply to a variety of practices affecting consumer interests – see the Injunctions Directive (98/27/EC) and the Enterprise Act Part 8 and see also P. Rott, The Protection of Consumers' Interests after the Implementation of the EC Injunctions Directive into German and English Law (2001) 24 Journal of Consumer Policy 401.

[43] See the Unfair Contract Terms Bulletins 1–29 covering cases dealt with from the passing of the initial 1994 Unfair Terms in Consumer Contracts Regulations until September 2004; and see the lists of Unfair Terms cases with Undertakings that replaced the bulletins and run from October 2004 to the most recent in March 2006 (available on the Consumer Regulations Website – http://www.crw.gov.uk).

[44] The most notable general guidelines are those contained in the OFT Guidance of 2001.There have also been guidelines for particular sectors, e.g. consumer entertainment contracts (2003), care home contracts (2003), home improvement contracts (2005), holiday caravan contracts (2005) and package holiday contracts (2004).

[45] This is of particular importance given the traditional concerns as to the uncertainty caused by broad standards of fairness. Any such uncertainty may not only be a cost for businesses but may also make it more difficult for businesses to comply.

role of the OFT is that its role seems to make it (*de facto*) the most significant standard setter in the whole process. In addition, the vast amount of work that the OFT has done on unfair terms must have the effect of infusing its standard setting and enforcement role with a considerable degree of expertise based on experience.

As we have already seen, injunctive powers are also available to a range of other bodies.[46] Providing a role for bodies other than the OFT clearly broadens the experience and expertise base and can also be seen as important to the democracy of the process. Of course it is also important that a system based on a multiplicity of enforcement bodies should be properly coordinated. This is vital if there is to be consistency and appropriate targeting in enforcement (consistency and targeting being principles of 'good regulation' that the government has committed itself to[47]). This coordination is provided for, in part, by provisions in the UTCCR requiring communication between the qualifying bodies and the OFT;[48] but in much more detail by the 'enforcement concordats' that set out the way in which enforcement should be managed as between the various regulatory bodies.[49] However, in practice it does not appear that the other bodies have done anything like the amount of work on unfair terms as the OFT.

8.4 Other Sanctions?

Even with the above enforcement in place, it is of course inevitable that the market will still contain many unfair terms. At best these will cause inconvenience to consumers who are put to the trouble of challenging these terms. At worse (and this will often be the case), consumers will not challenge unfair terms and will suffer the effects of the term. At present,

---

[46] These are set out in Schedule 1 – The information Commissioner, The Gas and Electricity Markets Authority, The Director General of Electricity Supply for Northern Ireland, The Director General of Gas for Northern Ireland, The Office of Communications, The Director General of Water Services, The Office of Rail Regulation, every weights and measures authority in Great Britain, The Department of Enterprise, Trade and Investment in Northern Ireland, the Financial Services Authority and the Consumers Association.

[47] See the Better Regulation initiative of the DTI; and see S. Weatherill (ed.), Better Regulation, (forthcoming) Hart, 2007.

[48] See Regulations 14 and 15.

[49] See, for example, the concordats between the OFT and OFTEL, the Consumers Association and LACOTS in Unfair Contract Terms Bulletin 12, 2000, at 55–84 and also the concordat between the OFT and the Financial Services Authority, available at http://www.fsa.gov.uk/pubs/other/concordat_fsa_oft.pdf.

all that a trader has to fear is that a consumer challenges the term and it is set aside; so that it is ineffective against the consumer in question (and possibly also that the term is reported to one of the regulatory bodies who take action to prevent it's continued use). The limitations of this system have been highlighted by The European Commission. As the Commission says in its 2000 report on the implementation of the directive:

> Indeed the only risk (and it is a minor one) run by a professional when a consumer challenges a term before the courts is that this term may be declared invalid. Besides, where action for an injunction is brought against the professional the only risk he runs is that he may have to replace the offending term with another one. In both cases the professional is ultimately in a situation pretty similar to the one which would have existed if he had never used the unfair term. However he can make the most of the term in respect of all consumers who do not have the information or wherewithal to react. In the case of injunctions the penalty is not dissuasive enough to the extent that it does not penalise the prior use of the unfair term, but simply means that the professional may not use it in the future.[50]

One question which has been raised by the European Commission (in the light of such concerns) is whether or not there should be improved civil, or indeed criminal, penalties to provide more effective protection for consumers and to deter traders from using unfair terms in the first place.[51] There certainly seems to be a case for some form of liability that would deter traders from using unfair terms, while also compensating the consumer for the trouble and inconvenience of challenging the term.

If it was thought appropriate to award such compensation, then it should obviously be able to be claimed by the consumer in the context of the same action as that being taken as between the parties in relation to the fairness of the term. However, the numbers of claims for compensation (and consequently the pressure to remove terms) might also be increased by empowering regulatory bodies to take representative actions on behalf of consumers. Perhaps they could be given power to act on behalf of individual consumers or groups of consumers, both to have terms set aside, and to obtain compensation for the trouble and inconvenience of the initial dispute.

---

50   COM2000 248 final, at p. 20.

51   *Ibid*; currently, damages are not available under the UTCCR when a trader uses an unfair term. The effectiveness principle in EC law can result in damages being available for breach of a Community obligation. However, as the UTD is not directly applicable it is hard to see how this would be possible at present without substantial development of the law by the ECJ.

Let us now look at the sort of specific circumstances in which compensation might be made available. It is easy enough to justify awarding compensation where the trader knew that the term was considered to be unfair. This would clearly include cases where that trader has already been instructed by a court not to use the term (i.e. where there is an injunction); or where he has given an undertaking to an enforcement body not to use it. The point of these regulatory measures is to declare that, from the point of view of the body in question, the term is unfair whenever it is used in a consumer contract. If the trader has nevertheless used the term (and the court agrees that it is unfair), then a case could be made for awarding compensation to consumers who are put to the trouble and inconvenience of challenging the term.

What of the situation where the term has already been found to be unfair in private litigation between the trader in question and a consumer, but has not been the subject of any form of action by a regulatory body? The function of the court in the context of private litigation is to make an assessment as to the fairness of the term in all the circumstances of the particular case. An important question therefore, may be whether there is any significant difference between the circumstances of the case in which the term was found to be unfair and the circumstances in which the trader is now using the term. Is it the same term in substance? Is it presented in the same way? Is the position the same on choice (or lack of choice)? Is the position the same on relative bargaining strength? If so, then it might be legitimate to award compensation to consumers who are put to the trouble and inconvenience of challenging the term. Given that the circumstances are the same or substantially the same as when the term was previously held to be unfair, it can be argued that the trader should have known that the term would be unfair again.

It also seems possible to justify compensation where the term used against a consumer is substantially the same (and being used in substantially the same circumstances) as a term found to be unfair in previous litigation against another trader. Of course this would imply that traders are to be expected to keep themselves informed as to court decisions under the UTCCR, and to assess the applicability of these decisions to their own terms. However this may be an acceptable burden to impose on traders in the interests of consumer protection, at least in the context of civil liability to the consumer.

It is perhaps more difficult to justify an award of compensation simply on the grounds that a trader has used a term which reflects one of those described on the indicative list. The list often describes terms in fairly general and open textured ways. Considerable further analysis may be needed in order to determine precisely which sorts of terms (used in which sorts of ways) are likely to be unfair. A trader might reasonably believe that the term which he has used (taking into account the way in which it has been used) is fair. Civil liability might therefore be harsh, although it could perhaps be justified in the interests of strong consumer protection; especially where the term being used is closely analogous to one on the indicative list and particularly if it is presented in an intransparent manner.

Another possibility would be to have a criminal sanction for at least some terms. Here the local authority could prosecute and the courts could have power to declare terms invalid and award compensation for any trouble and inconvenience. The difficulty with criminal liability is that there is a hard choice to make. On the one hand the approach could be to only criminalize certain specifically defined terms. This was the approach taken under the FTA Part II. Powers available under Part II of the Fair Trading Act 1973 have been used to criminalize the use of certain terms. Under Article 3 of the Consumer Transactions (Restrictions on Statements) Order 1976 it is an offence to use a term which is ineffective under ss 6 and 7 of UCTA, i.e. a term which excludes or restricts liability for breach of the implied terms as to title, description, quality and fitness for particular purpose. However, these powers no longer exist, having been repealed by the Enterprise Act.[52]

The alternative is to take a much broader and more flexible approach, i.e. to criminalize the use of a term that the trader knows, or should know, is unfair. This would avoid all of the trouble of carefully defining each term to be criminalized. Of course, there is the risk of exposing traders to an unacceptably uncertain and vague criminal regime.

---

[52] Section 10.

Chapter Nine

Reviewing the Rules on Unfair Terms in Consumer Contracts and Surveying the Bigger Picture

9.1 Introduction

This chapter reviews the themes already discussed and emphasizes the questions that remain open (including the question as to the harmonizing effects of the UTD). It then turns to the broader picture. It notes that the terms of a consumer contract are only one aspect of the consumer-trader relationship and considers the ways in which fairness is (and might be) secured in other aspects of the relationship. Finally, it considers the question of the role of fairness in commercial contracts.

9.2 Where We Seem to Be in Relation to Unfairness and Consumer Contract Terms

The fairness regimes that have been the subject of this book have been introduced in pursuit of a variety of goals related to fairness; efficiency; protection of specific substantive interests and EC market building. These goals have shaped (and will continue to shape) the approach to fairness.

It appears that (in broad terms) the regimes use (and the new regime would continue to use) default rules and reasonable expectations as benchmarks of fairness. In assessing fairness in substance there then appears to be consideration of a range of factors: the degree of deviation from the default position or reasonable expectations; the type of interests involved (including a range of economic and other interests and possibly also interests of particular importance in relation to services of general interest and human rights interests); questions as to insurance; and questions of overall substantive fairness (including, possibly whether the consumer is given 'mirror image' rights).

The above substantive issues are considered in the light of matters related to procedural fairness. Procedural fairness is mainly intended to allow the consumer to self-protect pre-contractually. As such the degree of procedural fairness required varies depending upon the degree of unfairness in substance. It stands to reason, also, that the greater the degree of procedural fairness the more likely it is that the term will be viewed as fair (and vice versa). Transparency is the first priority in relation to procedural fairness. Transparency involves terms being available; in plain language and decent sized print; the overall contract being clearly structured; highlighting (and possibly explanation) of terms where appropriate (depending on how detrimental the term is in substance); and possibly disclosure of facts known to the trader that make reliance on detrimental terms significantly more likely than normal. However, procedural fairness extends beyond transparency and takes account of whether there was a choice available to the consumer and the weaker bargaining position of the consumer.

The rules also have a complex relationship with other social, economic and theoretical issues. So, there is a broad congruence with the values of the Welfare State. There is also a connection with market values. There is, for example, congruence with market values in the sense that fairer terms are sometimes more efficient terms and in the sense that the unfairness concept deriving from the UTD aims at EC market building. At the same time fairness is constructed more by reference to independent community based notions than trader dominated market norms. The rules clearly deviate from traditional, self-reliant notions of autonomy and expectation. However, they remain connected to concepts of autonomy and expectation, albeit more fairness-oriented versions of these concepts.

All of this represents a transformation from the approach at common law and in equity. Common law and equity pursued certain fairness agendas. However, they were limited either by the failure to take a consistent approach that covered all of the types of terms that might be unfair; by setting too low a level of fairness, in particular by being too closely linked to market norms; or by allowing issues of conscience to enter the equation.

The UTCCR have also brought a transformation in relation to enforcement. The powers of regulatory bodies, in particular the OFT, have made a real difference in removing terms from the market – something that could never be achieved by private law means alone. The work of the OFT has also contributed hugely to the jurisprudence on fairness and provided enormous guidance to all concerned as to the practical application of the unfairness concept.

9.3 Remaining Questions

However, notwithstanding the above points, there remain a number of difficult questions. First of all, the only case to reach the House of Lords could be said to set quite a low level of fairness by comparison with the approach of the OFT and the Court of Appeal; an approach more at the freedom-oriented end of the spectrum. It seems that only time will tell whether this is indicative of a real schism between the House of Lords and the key regulatory body (and between the House of Lords and the Court of Appeal) or whether the decision is very much one based on its own facts. Of particular importance, in relation to the *First National Bank* case, we are left with a degree of uncertainty as to whether the decision undermines the general idea that a term is under strong suspicion when it deviates from a default rule to the detriment of the consumer. The OFT approach and the Court of Appeal decision seemed to be based on the idea that such a term is indeed under strong suspicion; while the House of Lords seemed much more understanding as to why lenders would choose to deviate from the default position. As suggested it is unclear whether the House of Lords decision tells us a great deal about their attitude to default rules in general or was simply very much about the particular term and default rule in question, so that no general conclusion can be drawn from the House of Lords decision. The *First National Bank* case also leaves open the question as to just what level of transparency the House of Lords is inclined to require. The issue of transparency can be raised in relation to the term itself, the House of Lords not appearing to have expected much in the way of spelling out the full implications of the term. The transparency issue also arose in relation to explanation/disclosure of background legal rights. The question is whether the House of Lords would be prepared to accept the idea that good faith may require disclosure of background legal rights that affect the consumer in the context of the term in question. The Court of Appeal took the view in the case that lenders should be required to explain certain rights to the consumer at the time of a judgement to enable the consumer to be better protected against the effects of the term under scrutiny; while the House of Lords did not believe that such an explanation was incumbent on the lenders. What, if anything, does this suggest more generally about the attitude of the House of Lords to disclosure/explanation of background legal rights? A final question arising from *First National Bank* is whether the House of Lords accept that certain terms can be unfair on essentially substantive grounds, irrespective of procedural fairness. The OFT clearly take this view and it seems that this view is shared by the Court of Appeal. This is really a vital practical and theoretical question. At a practical level, if terms can be removed on purely substantive grounds, then they can be removed more readily and without arguments as to levels of transparency (or other questions of procedural fairness). There can also be standardization of the substantive features of terms across a trading sector, arguably allowing transparency to have more effect in practice. At a theoretical level, if terms can be unfair on substantive grounds, this represents a more radical version of fairness and a clear departure from freedom-oriented values. It also has a broader significance. There is an ongoing debate as to whether EC consumer law should rely on an 'information paradigm', i.e. whether information is all that is needed to protect consumers or whether more is needed.[1] Much of this debate revolves around the themes that were raised in this book as to how much use consumers can, in practice, make of information. The UTD is a central part of the EC consumer and contract law *aquis*. So the position taken in this context in relation to information and its limits is significant for our understanding of the theoretical basis of EC consumer and contract law.

A further question is as to the appropriate role for a contextual approach to the concept of unfairness. We saw above that such an approach might be problematic in terms of causing uncertainty and in reducing the level of protection (i.e. if the level of fairness is adjusted downwards based on the particular strengths of the consumer or the particularly weak position of the trader). Of course, the other side of this coin is whether a contextual approach should be taken so as to provide extra protection for the most vulnerable consumers (i.e. to adjust upwards the level of fairness required in cases involving more vulnerable consumers).

Currently, there exists the ideal opportunity to address these difficult questions and to try to lay down clear markers. This is because the proposed new regime on unfair terms is nothing more than an idea at present and there is therefore the chance to clarify these issues in the final drafting of the new regime. In addition, there is a general review at national and EC level of the consumer *aquis* and this includes the Unfair Terms Directive,[2] so that there is an opportunity to consider these issues in the contexts of these reviews.

But this brings us to a further issue. We may now be about to enter a new era in which the unfair terms regimes merge into one. Above we saw that the new regime would appear to bring a number of advantages: removal of the confusion caused by the existence of two overlapping regimes with differences in terminology, concepts and effects; a test that

---

[1]   See G. Howells and T. Wilhelmsson, Has EC Consumer Law Come of Age? (2003) 28 European Law Review 370, 380–382.

[2]   See the Action Plan on a More Coherent European Contract Law, COM(2003) 68, 12 February 2003 and European Contract Law and the Revision of the *Acquis*: The Way Forward, COM(2004) 251, on which see S. Weatherill, EU Consumer Law and Policy, Elgar, 2005, 151–5 and R. Bradgate, C. Twigg-Flesner and A. Nordhausen, Review of the Eight EU Consumer *Acquis* Minimum Harmonisation Directives and Their Implementation in the UK and Analysis of the Scope for Simplification, Report for the DTI, 2005.

is triggered by a term causing 'detriment' rather than the higher (and otherwise more problematic) threshold of significant imbalance; a 'fair and reasonable' test that is more familiar and easier to apply in the UK than the existing test in the UTCCR and that appears to be flexible enough to provide at least the same level of protection as the test in the UTD; the provision of much more guidance as to the application of the test; and the improved expression (and exemplification) of the paragraphs on the indicative list. However, the proposed new regime is not entirely unproblematic. There is some question as to whether, as a matter of EC law, the Member States are obliged to use exactly the language as that used in the UTD; and whether this would prevent the use of the 'fair and reasonable' test in place of the existing test from the UTD. There appears to be some risk of this.[3] However, it seems to be only a very limited risk and one that the Law Commissions believe is worth taking; given all of the advantages offered by the proposed new approach.

Finally, there is the role of the ECJ in fleshing out the concept of unfairness. We know that the ECJ is prepared to interpret the test of unfairness from the UTD and provide something of an autonomous EC conception of unfairness. Thus far it appears that this notion of unfairness involves various aspects. First of all, there is the idea that assessing the unfairness of a term involves a general notion of interest balancing (taking into account all of the terms). Second, there is the idea that a detrimental term can be balanced out by some provision that is beneficial to the consumer. If such a provision exists the ECJ will pass the matter back to the national court to make its own assessment on the facts of the case and within the national legal context. Finally, where there is no such balance the ECJ will view the term as unfair *per se*. This, in turn, seems to mean that the ECJ view is that (at least in such circumstances) a term can be unfair irrespective of procedural fairness. However, what is as yet unclear is how much further the ECJ will be prepared to go in fleshing-out the meaning of the unfairness concept. In particular, what more might the ECJ have to say about their concept of benefit (i.e. as to what counts as a sufficiently beneficial provision to prevent the ECJ deciding that the term is unfair *per se*)? In this connection, would the ECJ share (what may have been the view of the House of Lords) that use of the interest after judgement term in *First National Bank* brought a benefit to consumers in guaranteeing access to loans that would not otherwise be provided?

---

3   It has been argued that more needs to be done to prove that the effect of the fair and reasonable test is the same as the god faith/significant imbalance test (P. Nebbia, Unfair Contract Terms in European Law, Hart, 2007, 147). However, the same author also concedes that a lot may turn on whether the UTD can be said, as such, to be aimed at embedding good faith in the legal systems of all Member States so as to further harmonization, something which is not clear (at 148).

Finally, we do not know to what extent the ECJ will develop transparency as a vital part of the autonomous unfairness concept. If they were to do so would they set a higher level of transparency than the House of Lords may be inclined to set?

9.4 Harmonization

The fundamental objective of this book has been to develop a better understanding as to the fairness standards existing in the UK. Of course, some of these fairness standards have a European context which we have already addressed. There remain important questions as to the success or otherwise of the harmonization agenda that led to the UTCCR in the first place; and the extent to which there is (and will be) a cross-fertilization of fairness ideas as between the Member States. A detailed discussion of this is beyond the scope of this book.[4] However, several points can be made. First of all, the scope for harmonization is clearly limited by the UTD being a minimum directive, allowing for example, some Member States to control main subject matter and price terms while others choose not to; and allowing more protective approaches to be taken to the unfairness concept than whatever is regarded as the minimum acceptable level of protection. Second, a proper sense as to how similarly the provisions are being approached would require a detailed comparative study. The CLAB database provides help in this regard and there has already been academic work which surveys the CLAB initiative and seeks to draw conclusions as to its influence, which seems to have been quite limited in practice.[5] In addition, there is the 'Consumer Compendium' project,[6] the review of the consumer *aquis* and the work on a Common Frame of Reference (CFR) for European contract law.[7] These initiatives provide an opportunity to better judge the success of harmonization and could conceivably lead to amendment of the UTD (or guidance in a CFR). Third, apart from any such legislative changes, addressing any serious differences will be partly dependent on whether cases actually get referred to the ECJ and how prescriptive they choose to be in setting out an autonomous concept of

---

[4] On this see P. Nebbia, Unfair Contract Terms in European Law, Hart, 2007, 165–171.

[5] H.-W. Micklitz and M. Radeideh, CLAB Europa – The European Database on Unfair Terms in Consumer Contracts (2005) 28 Journal of Consumer Policy 325.

[6] See H. Schulte-Nölke, EC Consumer Law Compendium – A Comparative Analysis, University of Bielfield, 2006, available at:
http://ec.europa.eu/consumers/cons_int/safe_shop/acquis/comp_analysis_en.pdf.

[7] See the Action Plan on a More Coherent European Contract Law, COM(2003) 68, 12 February 2003 and European Contract Law and the Revision of the *Acquis*: The Way Forward, COM(2004) 251.

unfairness. We have seen that something of such a concept is beginning to develop. However, the House of Lords passed up a chance in the *First National Bank* case to obtain a view from the ECJ and at the same time to provide the ECJ with an opportunity to further develop an autonomous EC notion of unfairness. Fourth, despite the House of Lords passing up the opportunity to obtain ECJ guidance, the *First National Bank* judgement did recognize the importance of interpreting the unfairness test in the light of the goals of the UTD. In addition, Lord Bingham chose to draw upon Article 138 of the German BGB in approaching the test. Both of these factors provide grounds for optimism in relation to harmonization prospects. Fifth, harmonization is always likely to be constrained in practice at least to some extent by the distinctive national legal cultural approaches that will inevitably influence interpretation of the unfairness concept.[8] Sixth, the last point notwithstanding, it cannot be denied that on certain issues there is more convergence than there was before. For example, previous UK law (UCTA) did not subject to a general fairness review terms imposing obligations on consumers. It does now. Italian law did not (but now does[9]) use a general test of fairness but relied on formal notification requirements.[10] In this core respect both these traditions are now more in line with German tradition which did previously subject all non-core standard terms to a general fairness test.[11]

Finally, questions as to whether whatever harmonization that has taken place, has actually resulted in improved confidence (business and consumer) resulting in more cross-border purchases – depends on empirical studies, including the Consumer barometer etc. studies.

---

[8] On this see in particular the discussion of the radically different traditions in English and Italian law to the question of abstract versus contextual adjudication by P. Nebbia, Unfair Contract Terms in European Law, Hart, 2007, 67–68 and 159–163.

[9] Article 33, Italian Consumer Code; although there is some question as to whether the good faith concept used is the objective one required by the UTD – see P. Nebbia, Unfair Contract Terms in European Law, Hart, 2007, 145–6.

[10] P. Nebbia, Unfair Contract Terms in European Law, Hart, 2007, 31–34.

[11] AGB-Gesetz, 1976, Articles 8–11.

9.5 A Broader View of Fairness in Consumer Contracts

9.5.1 Introduction

This book has been about what fairness means in the context of the *terms* of a consumer contract; and how this has been operationalized by general reasonableness and fairness/good faith standards. It is now appropriate to look more broadly at fairness in consumer contracts (i.e. to look at issues not related to the fairness of the *terms* as such); and to consider how the law does and should react to problems of unfairness that may arise.

First of all it is important to point out that, in relation to rules concerned to promote the consumer interest, there is a distinction, though certainly also an overlap, between rules of a more positive nature that impose obligations on traders and/or give rights to consumers; and rules of a more negative nature that constrain what traders can do. In the first category are disclosure rules; cancellation rights; implied terms, default rules and any other form of obligation imposed on the trader in favour of the consumer where the obligation is of a positive nature (e.g. to provide goods that are in conformity with a contract of sale); along with consumer remedies that apply when the trader is in breach of one of the obligations described above. In the second category are *vitiation* rules, i.e. rules that allow contracts or terms to be set aside on the basis of misrepresentation, duress, undue influence, unconscionability, mistake or (as in the case of the rules in this book) on the basis that the terms are unfair. Also in this second category are implied terms and default rules that have the effect of obliging traders *not* to take certain action; as are rules on enforcement and remedies that are aimed at preventing the trader from achieving certain outcomes, e.g. preventing traders recovering losses that are too remote or that are not based on the trader having mitigated his losses. Finally, in this second category, are the various criminal and administrative rules controlling false, misleading and aggressive practices.

Of course, a full understanding as to whether the law promotes fairness requires consideration of both categories. Fairness, as we have seen, can be described in the broadest terms as being about balancing the interests of the parties and in particular protecting the interests of the consumer. It is obvious that the interests of the parties (and in particular the consumer) are affected both by rules of a more positive nature imposing positive obligations and outcomes and by rules of a more constraining nature. In addition, understanding some of the rules falling into the second category requires understanding of some of the rules falling into the first category. For example, as we have seen, a term comes under suspicion as being unfair (under the category two rules on unfair terms) because it tries to take away something that is granted by default rules (default rules falling into category one).

This book has been about rules falling into the second category, i.e. rules that provide that it is unfair for the trader to use certain terms. As we have seen, the law has developed such that these rules are now based on general standards of fairness and are not restricted to particular types of term. It therefore fits with the focus of the book to stay (for the moment) with this second category of rules (i.e. rules that – in the interests of fairness – constrain what can be done by traders). The question is whether in the context of other rules in this second category (i.e. rules dealing with aspects of the relationship not covered by rules on unfair terms) we are (and/or should be) moving to an approach that (in common with that taken where contract terms are concerned) is based (at least to some extent) on a general notion of fairness rather than based on specific doctrines.

The particular standards that have been discussed so far do not apply to other aspects of the relationship, i.e. they only apply where what is at issue is the fairness of the term itself. Of course, this (as we have seen) may be affected by what is done pre-contractually. So, for example, the way in which a term is explained to the consumer (and the question as to whether the consumer was misled as to the particular effect of the term) may affect whether the term is viewed as fair or not. If there has been pressure to agree to the particular term this would also affect whether the term is viewed as fair or not. However, if the consumer has been misled or pressurized not in relation to the particular term but more generally in relation to the decision to enter the contract then the main issue is not the fairness of a particular term, but the fairness of the whole contract (and the remedial issues relate to the validity of the whole contract and compensation for the losses caused by entering the whole contract). So, even if any misleading activity or pressure might be said to be relevant to whether particular terms of the contract are fair or not, this is not the key issue. Having the term set aside on the basis of its unfairness (and even compensating the consumer for losses caused by the use of the unfair term) does not deal with the real issue.

In addition, just as what happens pre-contractually may affect the fairness of the terms, the rules on the fairness of terms may affect what can happen in the course of performance or enforcement of a contract. The terms play a part (along with general rules of law) in determining how the contract should be preformed and enforced. So, performance and enforcement can be controlled, in part, by rules on the fairness of the terms. However, this control has limits. For example, the question as to whether the term is fair is assessed based on the circumstances existing at the time of the contract.[12] So, a term may have provided for performance that was considered to be fair based on the circumstances existing at the

---

[12]   UCTA s. 11(1) and UTCCR, Regulation 6(1).

time the contract was made. However, due to changing circumstances, it may now be arguable that it is unfair to perform in this way. So, the authority for acting in the unfair manner in question is derived from the term, yet the unfairness is not controlled by the rules on unfair terms. In other cases the term may not give any such authority to act unfairly in a post-contractual setting, so that the unfairness may have no connection at all with questions as to the fairness of a term. So, for example, the issue may be pressure or misleading tactics employed by the trader to force the consumer to perform in a particular way, pay something allegedly owed or not pursue a claim against the trader.

9.5.2 Existing Law and the Unfair Commercial Practices Directive – A Sketch

Currently, where the issue is not the fairness of a term as such, rules constraining what can be done by traders come in the form of:

(1) (in private law) the various vitiation rules in contract law (misrepresentation, duress, mistake, undue influence etc), any relevant implied terms restricting what trader can do, rules on remedies restricting what the trader can do or claim (e.g. rules on remoteness, mitigation, penalties, limits on termination, specific performance etc), but, importantly, there is no general principle disallowing unfairness;

(2) criminal legislation, which, again, is based on specific offences (e.g. the Trade Descriptions Act 1968 controlling false statements in relation to good and services and the Consumer Protection Act 1987 Part 2 controlling misleading prices), and not on a broad prohibition of unfair trading;

(3) rules in the Enterprise Act 2002 (allowing for injunctions to be granted against traders on the basis of their breach of criminal provisions and various contractual and other duties or acts or omissions making agreements void or unenforceable to any extent.[13] This seems (broadly) to track the private and public law standards discussed at (1) and (2) above;[14] and (therefore) is clearly not based on a general principle against unfairness;

---

[13] Section 211.

[14] However, there is some question as to whether it always covers all of the same ground. It is not clear, for example, that it covers duress and undue influence which make an agreement *voidable* as opposed to void or unenforceable. Having said this, the provision refers to agreements being void or unenforceable 'to any extent' (s.

(4) the rules in the Misleading Advertisement Regulations allowing action to be taken against misleading advertising.[15]

However, to this we must now add the Unfair Commercial Practices Directive.[16] The Directive applies to 'unfair business-to-consumer commercial practices before, during or after a commercial transaction in relation to a product'.[17] A 'commercial practice' is defined as 'any act or omission, course of conduct or representation, commercial communication including advertising and marketing, by a trader, directly connected with the promotion, sale or supply of a product to consumers'.[18]

211(2)(e)) which might be construed broadly to include cases in which a contract is voidable.

[15] Control of Misleading Advertisement Regulations 1988, SI 915, Regulations 4–6.

[16] 2005/29/EC and see generally VIEW. The Feasibility of a General Legislative Framework on Fair Trading, available at:

http://www.europa.eu.int/comm./consumers/cons int/safe shop/fair bus pract/green pap comm./studies/sur 21 sum en.pdf; R. Schulze and H. Schultz-Nolke, Analysis of National Fairness Laws Aimed at Protecting Consumers in Relation to Commercial Practices, available at http://www.europa.eu.int/comm./consumers/cons int/safe shop/fair bus pract/green pap comm./studies/unfair practices en.pdf; R. Brownsword, R. Bradgate and C. Twigg-Flesner, The Impact of Adopting a General Duty to Trade Fairly, DTI, 2003; H. Collins (ed.), The Forthcoming EC Directive on Unfair Commercial Practices: Contract, Consumer and Competition Law Implications, Kluwer, 2004; C. Twigg-Flesner, D. Parry, G. Howells and A. Nordhausen, An Analysis of the Application and Scope of the UCP Directive, DTI, 2005; G. Black, The Unfair Commercial Practices Directive (2005) Scots Law Times 183; C. Willett and A. Nordhausen, A Broader View of Fairness in Consumer Contracts, Regional Consumer Law Conference, Malta, March 2006, available at http://www.mcmp.gov.mt/pdfs/consumers/March05Seminar/Chris%20Willett%20Spe ech.pdf; G. Howells, Unfair Commercial Practices Directive – A Missed Opportunity?, Regional Consumer Law Conference, Malta, March 2006, available at http://www.mcmp.gov.mt/pdfs/consumers/March05Seminar/Geraint_Howells.pdf; C. Poncibo and R. Incardona, The Average Consumer Test in the Unfair Commercial Practices Directive, Regional Consumer Law Conference, Malta, March 2006, available at:

http://www.mcmp.gov.mt/pdfs/consumers/March05Seminar/Poncibo_Incardona.pdf; G. Howells, H.-W. Micklitz, T. Wilhelmsson, European Fair Trading Law: The Unfair Commercial Practices Directive, Ashgate, 2006; T. Wilhelmsson, The Informed Consumer v. The Vulnerable Consumer in European Unfair Commercial Practices Law – A Comment, (2007), 1 Yearbook of Consumer Law, 211.

[17] Article 3(1).

[18] Article 2(d).

We should notice two things in particular here. First of all, there is the point that the provisions cover practices at all stages of a transaction; so, for example, prior to any contract being entered into by the consumer and after any such a contract has been made, but while it is being performed or enforced ('before, during or after a commercial transaction'). Secondly, we should note that for a practice to be covered it does not need to have taken place before, during or after an actual *contract* between the trader using the practice and the consumer. All that is required is that the act, omission, course of conduct or representation is 'directly connected with the sale or supply of a product to consumers'. Clearly this covers practices carried out by the party who seeks to actually contract to supply the goods or services to the consumer and practices carried out by such a party in the course of performance or enforcement of his contract with the consumer. However, it also seems to cover practices carried out by a party such as a manufacturer (including, for example, in the context of advertising) which are intended to induce consumers to enter contracts with other parties (i.e. retailers). Also, because the provisions cover practices before, during or after a transaction, they would seem to catch practices carried out by manufacturers that are related to the post-contractual use of the product or service and the way in which the contract between the retailer and consumer is performed or enforced.

Member States are required to empower persons or organisations 'regarded under national law as having a legitimate interest in combating unfair commercial practices' to take 'legal action' against such practices 'and/or to bring such practices before an administrative authority competent either to initiate complaints or to initiate appropriate legal proceedings'.[19] All in all this seems to contemplate administrative type control (e.g. the use of injunctions); and it is open to question as to whether it also contemplates criminal sanctions (this possibly being covered by the reference to the relevant persons or organizations 'taking action').[20]

The Directive prohibits 'unfair commercial practices' (Article 5(1)). A commercial practice will be unfair if 'it is contrary to the requirements of professional diligence, and it materially distorts or is likely to materially distort the economic behaviour with regard to the product of the average consumer ...'.[21] 'Professional diligence' is defined as 'the standard of special skill or care which a trader may reasonably be

---

[19] Article 11(1).

[20] See discussion by C. Twigg-Flesner, D. Parry, G. Howells and A. Nordhausen, An Analysis of the Application and Scope of the unfair Commercial Practices Directive (Report for the DTI), 2005, at Ch. 5.

[21] Article 5(2).

expected to exercise towards consumers, commensurate with honest market practice and/or the general principle of good faith in the trader's field of activity'.[22]

More particularly a commercial practice will be viewed as unfair if it is 'misleading' or if it is 'aggressive'.[23]

A practice will be 'misleading' both where it involves a misleading action (which includes both false information and information that is not false but is likely to deceive)[24] and where it involves a misleading omission of material information[25] (in both cases where the result is or is likely to be that a consumer takes a transactional decision he would not otherwise have taken[26]).

A practice will be 'aggressive' where it involves 'harassment, coercion, including the use of physical force or undue influence' and 'significantly impairs or is likely to significantly impair the average consumer's freedom of choice or conduct with regard to the product and thereby causes or is likely to cause him to take a transactional decision that he would not have taken otherwise'.[27]

It is clear, then, that there will need to be new standard of fairness applied at public law level. One possibility is to achieve this by amending the Enterprise Act; such that it provides that action can be taken on the basis of a breach of the new unfairness standard(s) described, rather than simply (as at present) where there is a breach of a contractual or other duty. In addition, because the Directive is a *maximum* Directive[28] it will need to be clear that action can *only* be taken on the basis of a breach of the new unfairness standard(s) described.

9.5.3 A Broader Fairness Standard than Currently Existing

It is clear that in several respects the unfairness concept moves the UK system closer to what could be described as a general clause on fairness. It seems clear that the unfairness concept in the Directive is broader than existing triggers for action under the Enterprise Act (breach of a criminal provision or of a contractual or non-contractual duty or acts or omissions making agreements void or unenforceable). The following points can be made:

---

22 Article 2(h).
23 Article 4.
24 Article 6.
25 Article 7.
26 Articles 6 and 7.
27 Article 8.
28 Article 4.

1. Clearly what would count as a misleading or aggressive practice would often cover what counts as misrepresentation or duress or undue influence in the common law and equity. However, the Directive expects these standards to be enforced in public law. As we have already seen public law enforcement currently comes under the Enterprise Act. The point is that the Enterprise Act covers breaches of contractual and other duties and acts or omissions making agreements void or unenforceable and it is not obvious that this covers the common law concepts of duress and undue influence (as suggested above, the problem is that the effect of duress and undue influence is to make a contract voidable – not void or unenforceable).

2. Even if the Enterprise Act covers misrepresentation, duress and undue influence these concepts are probably not always as broad as their rough comparators in the Directive ('misleading' and 'aggressive' practices). In particular, for example, we can see from the above outline that misleading omissions are covered. Of course, it must be remembered that despite the apparent narrowness of the 'false statement of fact' misrepresentation formula, this *can* cover failure to disclose information where conduct or previous statements suggest something different.[29] Nevertheless, the UCPD formulation still appears to be broader. First of all, according to the Directive, there is a misleading omission when the information in question is material information that the average consumer needs according to the context in order to make an informed transactional decision.[30] It is then provided that, in the case of an invitation to purchase, the following is material information: information as to the main characteristics of the service or product; the identity and address of the supplier; the price (and all other freight, delivery or postal charges) inclusive of taxes or the way in which the price or these other charges are calculated; arrangements for payment, delivery, performance and complaint handling (if they deviate from the professional diligence standard); and any right of withdrawal or cancellation that exists.[31] It simply could not be said that the failure to provide information of the types described would necessarily amount to a misrepresentation as it is currently understood in English law. A second more general way in which the test in the UCPD is

---

[29] See *Spice Girls Ltd* v. *Aprilia World Service BV* [2002] EMLR 27 and *With* v. *O'Flanagan* [1936] Ch. 575.

[30] Article 7(1).

[31] Article 7(4)(a)-(e); and see H. Collins, EC Regulation of Commercial Practices, in H. Collins (ed.), The Forthcoming EC Directive on Unfair Commercial Practices: Contract, Consumer and Competition Law Implications, Kluwer, 2004, at 38 on why specification of the obligation to disclose such matters is important.

broader is that the *starting point* under the UCPD is that omissions are covered. By contrast, even if the cases in which these are treated as misrepresentations are not 'exceptions' as such, they do appear more like incremental developments relative to a starting point. This starting point is that there should be a false statement of fact and that there is not a general duty of disclosure. Especially given the restrictions imposed by the doctrine of precedent, it is difficult to say with confidence just how broadly the courts would be prepared to cast the net in relation to omissions under the general law of misrepresentation.

There is also the point that misrepresentation is focused on false (rather than misleading) statements and, although this may sometimes slide into covering more generally misleading statements, it seems clear that 'misleading' is broader. For example, we should recall that the test in relation to misleading omissions under the UCPD is whether the information in question is material information that the average consumer needs according to the context in order to make an informed transactional decision. I am not aware that a modern court has expressed the law on misrepresentation in these terms, i.e. with the focus squarely on the information that is *needed by the consumer*.[32]

Then, there is the point that a statement of intention is not treated as a misrepresentation[33] unless it can be shown that there was actually a misrepresentation as to the intention in question, i.e. that

---

[32]   Of course, it is true that judges in recent times have sometimes approached traditional common law doctrine in ways that draw upon broader civil law notions of good faith. So, in relation to incorporation of terms there is the well known approach taken in *Interfoto Picture Library Ltd* v. *Stiletto Visual Programmes Ltd* [1989] QB 433 where a higher than normal degree of prominence was insisted upon for there to be 'reasonable notice' of a term due to its onerous and unusual nature; and this was associated by Lord Bingham (at 443) with civil law notions of good faith, in particular 'coming clean' and 'putting one's cards face upwards on the table'. However, although Lord Bingham drew inspiration from these sources which might (if applied to misrepresentation) tend to lead us to a broader approach to disclosure, he also made the point that the tradition of the common law is to adopt more 'piecemeal solutions' (*ibid.*). So, notwithstanding that there may be judges such as Lord Bingham who are inclined to a broader, more civil law-oriented approach, as long as the courts are influenced to some extent by the 'piecemeal' tradition, it obviously could not be said with any confidence that the courts in general would be prepared to approach the misrepresentation concept in ways reflecting the misleading concept in the UCPD.

[33]   See *Wales* v. *Wadham* [1977] 1 WLR 199.

the maker of the statement did not have the intention in question.[34] By contrast, it is at least possible that a statement of intention which is not later fulfilled could be said to be misleading under the UCPD. We should recall that all that is required is that the statement is likely to deceive the average consumer; and it seems that, at least in some circumstances, a consumer would be deceived by a statement of intention that is not fulfilled.

Indeed, this brings us back to a further point about omission of information. Following the logic of the rule that a statement of intention is not a misrepresentation, it is also clearly established that if a party makes a statement of intention and then changes his intention prior to conclusion of the contract failure to disclose this change of intention does not amount to a misrepresentation.[35] Yet, such a change of intention is surely something that the average consumer needs to be aware of in order to make an informed transactional decision. So failure to communicate it is surely misleading under the UCPD.

Moving to 'aggressive' practices the form of aggression based on 'coercion' does not appear to require the unlawful threat that would usually be required at common law for duress. First of all, there is no explicit mention of such a requirement. In addition, the Directive contains a list of five guidelines to determine whether the practice is aggressive.[36] One of these guidelines is whether there has been a threat to take action that cannot legally be taken. The fact that this is only one of the criteria certainly suggests it is not an essential requirement for an aggressive practice in general. In addition, the Directive contains a list of practices that are always regarded as aggressive.[37] Some of the practices do not involve an unlawful threat. One of these involves requiring a consumer seeking to make an insurance claim to produce documents that could not reasonably be considered relevant to the validity of the claim.[38] Another involves systematically failing to respond to correspondence in order to dissuade a consumer from pursuing contractual rights.[39] Then there is a practice involving informing the consumer that if he does not buy a product or service that the livelihood of the trader will be in jeopardy.[40]

---

[34] See *Edgington* v. *Fitzmaurice* (1885) 29 Ch. D459.
[35] See *Wales* v. *Wadham, supra.*
[36] Article 9.
[37] Annex 1.
[38] Paragraph 27.
[39] *Ibid.*
[40] Paragraph 30.

Of course, it is possible that duress now catches at least subjectively bad faith threats that are lawful.[41] However, even if this is the case the Directive still appears to go further in that it is not obvious that any *subjective* bad faith is required.

A further way in which the UCPD may be broader is that it covers 'harassment'. Not only does this not appear to require any type of unlawfulness (as-traditionally-does duress); but it does not appear to involve any requirement of a relationship of dependence (as does equitable *presumed* undue influence[42]); and the concept of harassment could plausibly involve less in the way of pressure than traditional *actual* undue influence.[43]

3. We now turn to the general clause on professional diligence. The most obvious comparison here is with the existing equitable concept of unconscionability; the vitiating factor which covers ground beyond the realms of the undue influence and duress concepts. Again it appears that the Directive is broader. By contrast with unconscionability,[44] the Directive has no explicit requirement of any kind of substantive unfairness in relation to any transaction resulting from the practice. All that is required on the consumer side is that a transactional decision results that would not have been taken otherwise. Even if substantive unfairness will normally be the result (or even be used evidentially to help with the conclusion that the trader behaviour was contrary to professional diligence) it does not appear to be the extreme type required under unconscionability. The Directive also seems to be broader on the procedural side. Unconscionability is usually focused on a case where the consumer is particularly weak; while here (although particularly weak consumers are covered), so is the average consumer.

There is then the question as to whether or not the Directive is also broader on another aspect of the procedural issue, i.e. whether the 'honest market practice' and 'diligence' concepts are linked (like unconscionability) to market norms, i.e. whether the practice is only

---

41 See *CTN Cash and Carry* v. *Gallaher Ltd* [1994] 4 All ER 714 and *DSDN Subsea Ltd* v. *Petroleum Geo-Services ASA* [2000] BLR 530, Dyson J at 545.

42 See, most recently, *Royal Bank of Scotland* v. *Etridge (No 2)* [2002] 2 AC 773.

43 See, for example, *Williams* v. *Bayley* (1866) 1 LRHL 200 HL, 200; noting that such instances of actual undue influence are now increasingly regarded as being better understood under the auspices of 'lawful act duress' – see P. Birks and N.Y. Chin, On the Nature of Undue Influence, in J. Beatson and D. Friedman (eds), Good Faith and Fault in Contract Law, OUP, 1995, 63–5 and D. Capper, Undue Influence and Unconscionability: A Rationalisation (1988) 114 Law Quarterly Review 479, at 484 and 493.

44 See above at 8.1.2.

unfair if it is less fair than what is normal. Where unconscionability is concerned the market norm concept seems to dominate in the sense that the exploitation needed is evidenced by taking advantage of procedural disparities/weaknesses that are greater than normal. The question is whether (even though such procedural disparities are not required under the Directive), the *practice* needs to be in some way out of step with market norms to be contrary to professional diligence. The question, in other words, is whether a trader has acted with professional diligence as long as the practice is a common one in the market sector or (perhaps to set a higher standard) represents the average standard for the market sector.[45] A standard in some way closely tied to market norms might be suggested by the references to 'skill and care' and 'diligence'. Both of these are often associated with the avoidance of fault and this in turn is often associated with reaching the standard of care that is normal in one's field.

Such a standard would be of concern as it would hardly provide strong consumer protection. Certainly it is arguable that such a standard would not set the 'high level of protection' aimed at by the Directive and would do little to generate consumer confidence. We should also bear in mind that even if practices are standard they do not necessarily represent what the consumer reasonably expects. The basic expectations of the consumer tend not to extend far beyond the basic price and main subject matter of the contract. If anything else consumers are likely to base their expectations on what normally actually happens, i.e. smooth performance with no potentially unfair behaviour by the trader; this being reinforced by advertising (which may actually suggest particularly fair, paternalistic treatment). Failure to reflect reasonable consumer expectations is surely a good measure of fairness. In addition, if the practices are not what consumers are used to dealing with then it will be less likely that we can rely on market forces to control them.

In one way, the reference to 'honest' market practice could be even more worrying, possibly suggesting nothing more than a subjective 'pure heart and empty head' standard. However, there is a more positive way to read the relationship between the standards of the market and the question of 'honesty'. The idea could at least be that even if a practice is normal it is unfair where it is not honest, i.e. where there is bad motive or conscience.[46]

---

[45] See the discussion above at 7.2 on this question in relation to the rules on contract terms.

[46] See C. Twigg-Flesner, D. Parry, G. Howells and A. Nordhausen, An Analysis of the Application and Scope of the Unfair Commercial Practices Directive (Report for the DTI), 2005, at 2.15.

However, there are more optimistic readings of the standard. The reference after all is to 'special' skill and care; possibly suggesting that even if market norms are a guide it is the highest or 'best' practice that should be achieved. In addition, the standard of special skill or care is that which 'may reasonably be expected'. Of course it is true that it is not specified that the reasonable expectations in question are those of consumers; but at the least the expectations are not associated in particular with traders and the suggestion does appear to be that the expectations of consumers must play a role in determining the level of skill and care to be expected of traders. (Such a standard would also allow courts to draw upon the strong signals of fair and even paternalistic treatment sent out in advertising. The power of advertising and the strong reliance on brand in modern patterns of consumption must mean that these signals play a significant role in determining the reasonable expectations of consumers.) A standard more focused on the reasonable expectations of consumers would certainly seem to accord more with the aims of the Directive to set a high level of protection and generate consumer confidence. In addition, as we have already noted, the maximum nature of the Directive means that Member States cannot set a higher standard; so that it might be imagined that the standard in the Directive itself was intended to allow for a reasonably high level of protection so that Member States would not feel the need to exceed this standard.

The idea of a standard focused more on the reasonable expectations of consumers might also be suggested by reading the 'professional diligence' limb of the test along with the 'transactional decision' limb. The question, we should recall, is whether the practice is one that 'contrary to the requirements of professional diligence ... materially distorts or is likely to materially distort the economic behaviour with regard to the product of the average consumer ...'. It is true that the two limbs could be read wholly disjunctively. However, it is not implausible to read them as being overlapping. In other words, it could be said that whether a practice is contrary to the requirements of professional diligence should be determined at least in part by whether it is the sort of practice likely to materially distort the economic behaviour of the consumer.

A further element in the equation is that whether a practice is contrary to professional diligence can be determined by whether it is 'commensurate with ... the general principle of *good faith* in the trader's field of activity'. So, what can be taken from the reference to good faith? There is no definition of good faith in the Directive. One question then is whether the ECJ would be inclined to take a similar approach to the concept as in the Unfair Terms Directive. There, it is clear that good faith is an objective standard requiring respect for the legitimate interests of the consumer. More particularly it is clear that terms that allow traders to perform in ways (or require consumers to perform in ways) that are contrary to the reasonable expectations of the consumer are likely to violate the good faith requirement. In addition, as for the UK, although the House of Lords has made some references to paying heed to market norms in assessing whether there has been a violation of good faith, this does not seem to have been a dominant factor in the House of Lords analysis of good faith. It has certainly not played any significant role in the vast jurisprudence on good faith that has emerged from the OFT.

So, in conclusion, the professional diligence standard does not appear to be tied to market norms in the way unconscionability is; and appears to be an independent objective standard of fairness paying at least some heed to the reasonable expectations of consumer.

4. A further point is that (again, even if we assume that the Enterprise Act covers misrepresentation, duress and undue influence) these concepts only apply where the result is that a contract between the parties comes about. However, as we have seen, the Directive applies whenever the result is that a 'transactional decision' is taken or is likely to be taken. This could clearly be *something short of a contract*. Indeed, it might be a decision *not* to enter into a contract with trader X based on what trader Y has said or the pressure that he has exerted. Alternatively, the 'transactional decision' could be a *post-contractual* decision to pay what the trader claims is owed or not to take further action against the trader; this decision not being able to be construed to be a fresh contract as such.

5. Finally, the Directive, as we have seen, covers practices carried out by parties such as manufacturers which do not necessarily result in the consumer entering into a relationship with such parties. UK law would cover this under the Misleading Advertisement Regulations only where a misleading *advertisement* is concerned (not where a misleading practice comes in any other form, nor where the practice happened to be aggressive). The Enterprise Act would only cover cases where there is a breach of duty (see above). However, the scope for such a duty is very limited in English law. The manufacturer would not usually be in a contractual relationship with the consumer. There is now Regulation 15 of the Sale and Supply of Goods to Consumers Regulations 2002 which – following Article 6 of the Consumer Sales Directive – makes manufacturer's guarantees contractually binding under the conditions laid down in the guarantee and the associated advertising. Clearly, then, failure to honour the guarantee is already a practice that can be controlled by the Enterprise Act as it would be a breach of contract. However, what is

less clear is exactly the significance of the reference to conditions laid down in the 'associated advertising'. Does this simply refer to anything that might be said in the advertising as to *procedures for enforcing* the guarantee, time limits etc? Alternatively, can the word 'conditions' be construed to include statements as to the characteristics of the goods such that if the goods do not possess these characteristics the repair/replacement etc promises etc. under the formal guarantee are triggered? If this is the case then the failure to fulfil these promises where the goods do not conform to the characteristics promised in the advertising would amount to a breach of contract and action could be taken under the Enterprise Act.

However, this possibility apart (and also ignoring cases in which the manufacturer actually makes a clear promise to pay a sum of money or perform an act[47]) the English courts have been very reluctant to find a contractual relationship between the manufacturer and the consumer.[48] Turning to tort, there has also been considerable reluctance to impose a duty of care in relation to the veracity of manufacturer's statements.[49]

Then, in relation to aggressive statements, English law has never really contemplated a duty of care in tort not to carry out such practices against consumers.

In conclusion, the Directive seems to impose a broader duty on manufacturers than could currently be enforced at public law level in UK law.

9.5.3.1 Some Implications of a General Clause

Clearly, as in the case of a general clause on terms, a general clause on practices has the advantage of flexibility in leaving less scope for existing and developing practices to 'slip through the net'. However, general clauses will always tend to attract concerns as to uncertainty, lack of focus etc. Certainly, the last time that such a general clause was considered seriously for trade practices in the UK these were concerns.[50] Part of the challenge is to ensure not only that traders are not put to unnecessary trouble by vague and possibly unmeritorious challenges, but also that the position is sufficiently clear so as to enable traders to comply with the rules routinely. So, when there is a general clause, the use of guidance and examples is invaluable. Indeed, such guidance and example

---

[47] See *Carlill* v. *Carbolic Smoke Ball Co.* [1893] QB 256.
[48] See *Lambert* v. *Lewis* [1982] AC 225.
[49] *Ibid.*
[50] Report on Trading Malpractices, OFT, 1990.

is not only important in aiding efficient and effective enforcement of the actual standards laid down in the UCPD. These standards will be enforced, ultimately, by bodies such as the OFT and Trading Standards Authorities and occasionally the issues will be played out in the courts. As Collins has suggested, there is always the possibility that the nuances developing in the context of such actions will spill over into the approach taken by the courts in contract law.[51] So, for example, concepts such as misrepresentation, duress and undue influence may be affected by the approach taken in public law enforcement of the UCPD standards. Undue 'irritation' to these concepts might at least be minimized if there is as much guidance as possible as to what exactly is aimed under the UCPD standard.

We have already seen that Article 7(4) provides a number of instances of information that must be included if there is not to be considered to be a misleading omission in cases of invitations to purchase; and such guidance is clearly helpful.[52] However, one concern in this regard is that it is not made clear as to whether this is an exhaustive list and there is clearly a risk that, even if it is not exhaustive, it might be read as being exhaustive by traders and enforcers. Another aid to concretization of the general clause is the list of practices that are always to be regarded as misleading and the list of those always to be regarded as aggressive.[53] This technique obviously follows the use of the 'indicative list' used in the UTD. However, there are two differences. First, this is a 'blacklist' in the sense that these practices are always unfair (by contrast with the list in the UTD which only describes terms that 'may' be regarded as unfair – and in this sense tends to be described as a 'greylist').

The second difference is that (unlike in the case of the list in the UTD) the list in the UCPD is not said to be non-exhaustive. Now it is pretty clear that it is non-exhaustive, as the main provisions of the Directive clearly contemplate that the overriding question is whether there is an unfair commercial practice as defined in Article 5. It is obvious from reading Articles 5(1)–(4) together that misleading and aggressive practices are only *types* of unfair practice (albeit the main types). It is

---

51 H. Collins, EC Regulation of Commercial Practices, in H. Collins (ed.), The Forthcoming EC Directive on Unfair Commercial Practices: Contract, Consumer and Competition Law Implications, Kluwer, 2004, at 36–9. In addition, see below at 9.5.5 on the possibility of formal provision being made for private law enforcement of the UCPD general clause in consumer contracts.

52 See H. Collins, EC Regulation of Commercial Practices, in H. Collins (ed.), The Forthcoming EC Directive on Unfair Commercial Practices: Contract, Consumer and Competition Law Implications, Kluwer, 2004, at 38.

53 See Article 5(1) and Annex 1.

obvious from Article 5(5) that the list of misleading and aggressive practices in Annex 1 are only *types* of misleading and aggressive practice. The reference in Article 5(5) is to practices which shall 'in *all* circumstances be regarded as unfair'. There would be no need to use the phrase 'all circumstances' if it were not intended that other practices would be regarded as unfair in *some* circumstances, i.e. on the basis of the general criteria of unfairness (including the misleading and aggressive categories). However, the problem, as Collins has said, is that if the list is not said explicitly to be non-exhaustive, there may be a tendency for enforcers to treat it as such in practice, thereby reducing the benefits inherent in the flexible general clause.[54] If there had also been a greylist of terms this would not only have emphasized that the other list is not exhaustive but also have provided a further stock of examples.[55]

9.5.4 Restrictions on the Scope of the Fairness Standard in the UCPD

However, notwithstanding the above observations as to the greater coverage of the Directive by comparison with existing UK law, the 'transactional decision' requirement certainly appears (in some respects) to cut down the scope of the Directive. First, as we saw above, in order to be unfair the practice must be one that 'materially distorts or is likely to materially distort the economic behaviour with regard to the product of the average consumer ...'.[56] This appears to be an objective test, meaning that it does not cover cases where the average consumer would not be caused by the practice to make a transactional decision. By contrast, for example, the law of misrepresentation may still treat a misrepresentation as actionable purely based on subjective inducement.[57]

This is of particular importance given that the Directive is a maximum one. This of course means that (within the scope of coverage of the Directive) Member States are not allowed to exceed the level of protection provided for in the Directive. This has been subjected to vigorous criticism.[58] It means that Member States must lower their existing standards to the extent that they exceed the protection provided

---

[54] H. Collins, EC Regulation of Commercial Practices, in H. Collins (ed.), The Forthcoming EC Directive on Unfair Commercial Practices: Contract, Consumer and Competition Law Implications, Kluwer, 2004, at 28.

[55] H. Collins, *ibid.*

[56] Article 5(2).

[57] See discussion by E. McKendrick, Contract Law, 6th edn, Palgrave Macmillan, 2005, 276–8.

[58] See for example, G. Howells and T. Wilhelmsson, EC Consumer Law: Has it Come of Age? (2003) 28 European Law Review 370, at 375–385.

by the Directive in question. Now, I have made the point above that the fairness concept may often cover a broader range of practices than are currently covered in UK law. However, as we have now seen, it may also be *narrower* than some existing doctrines as a result of the need for the practice to have caused the 'average consumer' to make or be likely to make a transactional decision. The maximum character of the Directive may therefore mean that the existing public law controls may need to be adjusted downwards to take this into account.

The second point relates to the very existence of the 'transactional decision' requirement. A general clause covering all possible forms of unfairness would surely catch unilateral action which is in some way unfair to the consumer; 'unilateral' in the sense that it does not involve inducing (or being likely to induce) any particular action or inaction by the consumer, but is simply an action of the trader in the course of performance or enforcement that impacts (or may impact) unfairly upon the consumer.

Such unilateral unfairness might arise in various ways. First of all, there might be a term that was fair given the circumstances at the time of the contract. However, circumstances may have changed in some way such as to affect one or both of the parties; the result being that it is now unfair for the trader to rely upon the term. The unilateral unfairness then involves the trader in fact *relying* on such a term. Of course, this is not caught by the rules on unfair contract terms, which assess fairness as at the time of conclusion of the contract.[59] This is not the case in all jurisdictions. In the Nordic countries, for example, the fairness of terms is assessed also by reference to post-contractual circumstances.[60] The question as to whether this should be the case in UK law has been raised before (e.g. in the 1975 Reports on Exemption Clauses by the Scottish and English Law Commissions). The English Law Commission favoured taking into account such circumstances; but the Scottish Law Commission were against the idea, largely on the grounds of uncertainty (the idea being that the parties should be able to determine, at the time of the contract, whether a term is likely to be enforceable).[61] There is clearly some merit in this argument, although perhaps less so in consumer contracts where protection should arguably prevail over certainty concerns; and even less so if we can identify the types of post-contractual circumstances that we have in mind. Certainly, it seems possible to identify some possible scenarios in which changing circumstances might be said to make reliance on a term unfair. One possibility is that the trader

---

[59] UCTA, s. 11(1) and UTCCR, Regulation 6(1).

[60] See T. Wilhelmsson, *Social Contract Law and European Integration*, Dartmouth, 1995, 27–28.

[61] See Law Commission No. 69, paras 170–183.

may have excluded a particular liability. When the contract was concluded it may have been particularly difficult for the trader to obtain insurance against this liability. Perhaps the insurance policy in question was not available on the market or was not available at a reasonable price. However, after the contract is made and before the liability has arisen, it does become feasible for the trader to insure against the loss in question. There might be circumstances in which it would be reasonable to expect the trader to take out the insurance; so that even if he has not done so it might now be considered unreasonable for him to rely on the exclusion clause. If he has now in fact taken out insurance the argument that it is unfair to rely on the exemption clause is surely even stronger.

Another possibility is that there are changed circumstances affecting the consumer, meaning that the term will now cause the consumer particular hardship. This is the 'social *force majeure*' situation that seems to be given some recognition in Nordic law.[62]

A second form of unilateral fairness might arise in relation to a term providing the trader with discretion of some kind (whether in relation to performance of his own obligations or in relation to what he can demand of the consumer). The typical scenario here is that the term allows the trader discretion, i.e. to perform or get the consumer to perform in ways that are different from what would reasonably have been expected by the consumer – by offering different goods/services, changing the price etc. Such terms are, of course, controlled to a large extent by the rules on unfair terms. If, as at the time of the contract, the term allows too much discretion to the trader, then it is likely to be unfair. So, for such terms to avoid being unfair, they must normally provide, for example, that changes are only allowed where the reason for change in delivery dates is outside the control of the trader.[63] So the scope of the discretion will already be narrowed by the rules on unfair terms. However, there may still remain some discretion and therefore some scope for the trader to exercise this discretion unfairly.

These forms of unfairness would often not be caught by the UK system. There is no general rule requiring good faith or fairness in performance. Certainly, in the 'changing circumstance' cases there is no recognized implied term stipulating that the trader should not rely on terms where changed circumstances have made this unfair. There being no such term there would be no breach upon which to ground public law action under the Enterprise Act. So, if the UCPD does not cover such a situation then (although this might be unfortunate in not broadening the

---

62   T. Wilhelmsson, Social Force Majeure – A New Principle in Nordic Consumer Law (1990) 13 Journal of Consumer Policy 1.

63   See, for example, the discussion by the Law Commission, Report No. 292 (Unfair Terms in Contracts), p. 191, example 11.

scope of fairness as it currently applies in UK law) at least it does not take away any protection that currently exists (i.e. the limited coverage of the UCPD does not cause a 'maximum harmonization' problem).

Turning to the situation involving unfair exercise of discretion by the trader the courts *have* shown willingness to imply a term that controls the exercise of such discretion.[64] However, the standard of fairness seems to be quite low. The approach generally appears to be that he must not act capriciously or as no other trader would have acted.[65] It may be, then, that if the UCPD does not cover such a situation then provision for control of it under the Enterprise Act (as a practice that involves a breach of contract) would need to be removed.[66]

So what exactly is the position under the UCPD? Certainly at first sight the requirement for the practice to result or be likely to result in a 'transactional decision' appears to rule out coverage of the above forms of unilateral unfairness (on the basis that they have not led to a transactional decision). The only way around this would appear to be to argue that traders who carry out such unilaterally unfair practices also act unfairly by not disclosing this to consumers when they enter the contract in the first place. Then it could be said that this unfair omission has led to a transactional decision, i.e. the decision to enter the contract with the trader. This might just about be a plausible interpretation. However, at best, it would catch practices that are routinely carried out. If the trader enters the contract in the knowledge that he may, later, carry out the practice in question, then the failure to indicate that this practice might be carried out could (as suggested) be said to amount to a misleading omission that leads to the consumer entering the contract. However, if the practice in question has never been carried out before, then it is hard to see how failure to mention it prior to entering the contract can be construed as a misleading omission that has led to the consumer entering the contract.

A further point is that, even if the trader is required to disclose unfair post-contractual practices pre-contractually, this is where the control ends

---

64 *Paragon Finance plc.* v. *Nash* [2002] 1 WLR 685.

65 For a full analysis of the control of contractual discretion see H. Collins, Discretionary Power in Contracts, in D. Campbell, H. Collins and J. Wightman, Implicit Dimensions of Contract, Hart, 2003, 219.

66 Indeed, there is a broader point here. To the extent that the UCPD only allows for public law control of a practice that leads to a 'transactional decision' does it not prevent control under the Enterprise Act of any practices by traders involving breaches of contract or torts where there is no resulting 'transactional decision' by consumers (other than where the control is mandated by the Injunctions Directive (98/27/EC) on the basis that the breaches in question are breaches of obligations provided for in other consumer protection directives)?

on the model in the UCPD. As long as the practice is disclosed there is no unfairness, as there has been no misleading omission leading to a transactional decision. The practice itself (as we have already seen) escapes the coverage of the UCPD as it does not lead to a transactional decision as such.

9.5.5 Private Law Enforcement of the Standards

9.5.5.1 Introduction

The Directive only requires that public law measures be introduced to prevent such practices. However, although the directive is a maximum measure contract law is outside its scope,[67] as are any forms of individual actions brought by those affected by an unfair commercial practice.[68] It seems clear then that applying similar (or even higher) standards in private contract law would not be treated as exceeding the level of protection fixed by the Directive; and in fact the DTI have now proposed that the standards from the Directive should be able to be enforced in private law.[69]

This would certainly increase private law consumer rights in relation to existing practices and provide the flexibility to give redress in relation to developing practices.[70] As we have seen above, the unfairness concept

---

[67] Article 3(2).

[68] Recital 9 to the Preamble.

[69] See DTI Consultation on Implementation of the UCPD, December 2005, Ch. 10. The DTI more recently reported that this proposal had received very favourable responses from academic commentators, the OFT, consumer bodies and trading standards authorities; but a very negative response from businesses – see Summary of Responses to the Consultation on Implementing the EU Directive on Unfair Commercial Practices and Amending Existing Consumer Legislation, DTI, June 2006 (summary of response to question 23).

Even more recently the DTI have said that the measures implementing the UCPD will not contain any provision for private law enforcement. This is because it is thought prudent that there be full and careful consideration of the implications of such a move. It is suggested that the Law Commission be asked to investigate the issue (Government Response to the Consultation Paper on Implementing the Unfair Commercial Practices Directive, DTI, December 2006, p. 7).

The remainder of the discussion here seeks to contribute to the debate on this issue.

[70] This is one of the reasons given by the DTI for this suggestion and see also R. Brownsword, R. Bradgate and C. Twigg-Flesner, The Impact of Adopting a General Duty to Trade Fairly, DTI, 2003, at 55.

in the UCPD is broader than the existing private law package of rules (albeit that it may be narrower on certain specific points, e.g. in relation to the requirement that practices should be such that they would, viewed objectively, affect the decision of the average consumer). It certainly appears strangely incoherent to apply such a general clause in public law; but not to allow consumers to benefit from the same general clause in private law. Then there is the issue of the *internal* coherence of private law. This book has been about the general fairness clauses applied to consumer contract terms (under UCTA and the UTCCR). The effect of the UTCCR in particular, as we have seen, is that a general clause applies a combined analysis of procedural and substantive fairness to all terms in consumer contracts except those positively excluded. This means that UK law now organizes the way it thinks about consumer contract terms around this concept of fairness. We have moved away from often arbitrary and piecemeal decisions to regulate some terms and not others. This approach now lies at the heart of the private consumer law of contract. However, the overall coherence of the private law of consumer contracts is arguably in question if such a principle is applied to consumer contract *terms* but not to other aspects of the relationship.

9.5.5.2 Equivalence or at Least Getting There By Traditional Common Law Means?

One argument that is often made against adoption of a general clause against unfairness is the so called 'equivalence' argument.[71] The equivalence argument holds that the existing common law rules often achieve the same results as a general clause by different means. This is often shown to be the case;[72] but it does not appear to be the case here. Of course it is true that there *is* often doctrinal flexibility in the common law concepts that often allow them to reach same results as a general clause. There is no space here to consider in any detail the prospects for developing existing doctrines. However, it is clear that quite a few steps would be needed:

-   developing doctrines such as misrepresentation, duress and undue influence to cover the broader 'misleading' and 'aggressive' concepts;

---

[71]   See R. Brownsword, R. Bradgate and C. Twigg-Flesner, The Impact of Adopting a General Duty to Trade Fairly, DTI, 2003, at 52.

[72]   For example, on a number of the issues analysed in the comparative study by Whittaker and Zimmerman, Good Faith in European Contract Law, CUP, 2000.

- developing such doctrines so that they can apply even where a contract has not resulted (the practice only having resulted in a 'transactional decision' short of a contract);
- adjusting notions of damages and rescission to deal with situations in which the result of the unfair practice is not actually a contract, but some transactional decision short of this;
- developing the law on negligent mis-statement and/or the law of contract so as to allow a remedy against a manufacturer for misleading statements – a step the courts have not been prepared to take thus far[73] (s. 2(1) of the Misrepresentation Act cannot be so developed as it only applies to situations in which the misrepresentation is made by a party X to induce party Y to contract with him, not where the resultant contract is with another party, and certainly not where what results is a transactional decision short of a contract);
- developing a new doctrine to deal with aggressive behaviour by manufacturers that brings about transactional decisions with sellers or any other party;
- adjusting existing doctrines or developing new doctrines in order to reflect the general professional diligence standard.

It hardly needs saying that this would all be rather challenging. At the very least it would take time and be subject to the accidents and vagaries of litigation. In the interim (50 years?!) it would be very difficult for consumer advisers to know how to frame actions and for traders to know how to defend them and how exactly to comply with the law. The effect would be that consumers would go unprotected.

The primary point of the above discussion is to show that the existing doctrine would not find it easy to adapt to a point where the equivalent of a general clause reflecting the UCPD is achieved. However, there is another point. It would be very surprising if the existence of the general clause in public law did not exert a pressure on private law to take a similar path.[74] Academics and some practitioners and judges would inevitably seek to argue for developments of the existing doctrine. However, apart from this taking time and leaving consumers unprotected in the interim, the danger would be that violence would be done to existing doctrines (which might affect the stability of their application to commercial and private relationships); covert means might be used to seek to achieve what precedent prevented in relation to the substantive

---

73 See *Lambert* v. *Lewis* [1982] AC 225.

74 The point has already been made – at 9.5.3.1 above – that the general clause would inevitably be likely to have an influence on the private law contract law rules applicable to both consumer and commercial contracts.

doctrines); and the law would become less certain. This chimes in with an argument that has been made in relation to the development of a general good faith principle in the law of contract, i.e. that it may actually lead to greater calculability in the law by dealing openly and rationally with fairness concerns that will inevitably form part of legal discourse in any event.[75]

9.5.5.3 The Relationship of the General Duty to Existing Rules

The implication of the above analysis, then, is that if a general duty was to be introduced at private law level then it should be done by introduction of a distinct regime providing for remedies to be available where there is an unfair practice (whether within the meaning of the Directive or on the basis of some broader concept of unfairness – on which see below). This appears to the DTI suggestion. They have suggested remedies for breach of statutory duty[76] (the Statute presumably being the one introducing the public law framework implementing the Directive). Of course, there are means short of this that could be adopted. So, there could be a positive obligation on courts to interpret and develop existing rules in the light of the concept of unfairness. However, this would suffer from the flaws identified above as to the substantive difficulties in achieving this, time, uncertainty and impact on the doctrines in their application to other contractors.

Another alternative would be only to introduce a general private law duty in some non-mandatory fashion, e.g. by encouraging ombudsmen schemes and other ADR schemes to apply the general duty and/or build these principles into the criteria for the approval of codes of practice. It is surely right in any case that we should take such steps even if a legal duty is introduced as such soft law regimes may often provide more effective practical protection. However, what we are talking about here is the possibility of *only* introducing the general duty via these soft law avenues. Such means could be used as a means of providing better protection for consumers and testing out how a general duty would work. However, we

---

75 See R. Brownsword, Positive, Negative and Neutral: The Reception of Good Faith in English Contract Law, in R. Brownsord, N. Hird and G. Howells, Good Faith in Contract: Concept and Context, Ashgate, 1999, 13, at 26.

76 DTI Consultation on Implementation of the UCPD, December 2005, at para 192; and this seems to have been supported by the OFT, academic commentators, trading standards and consumer bodies that responded – see Summary of Responses to the Consultation on Implementing the EU Directive on Unfair Commercial Practices and Amending Existing Consumer Legislation, DTI, June 2006 (summary of response to question 25).

might find a very uneven application of the duty, depending upon the sectors in which there are ombudsmen schemes and effective codes of practice.

The best option, then, appears to be imposition (by legislation) of a general duty. This would avoid all of the above problems. In particular it would make the duty transparent to consumers and their advisers, better empowering them to frame claims and enforce the duty (transparency of rights and improving enforcement are particular priorities of the DTI and are distinct reasons given for the introduction of a duty of this nature[77]). It would also reduce uncertainty and aid compliance by traders if there was a distinct statement of the duty. The DTI also focus on the prospect that a clear obligation would encourage traders to seek to resolve the issue by other means.[78] This is emphasized as a consequence of the DTI policy to encourage informal resolution of disputes.[79]

A further question is as to whether the duty should exist alongside existing doctrines with which it overlaps) or whether it should 'swallow up' these doctrines. The former approach would ensure that the any extra protection offered by existing doctrines would be retained. If the new duty is modelled exactly on the Directive then, as we already know, it would, in some respects be narrower (in a protective sense) than existing doctrines. On the other hand the existence of a new duty alongside existing doctrines (with which it would substantially overlap) might cause uncertainty for all concerned; and, in particular, reduce the practical consumer protection effects. This, as we have seen, has been a concern in relation to the two regimes currently existing for unfair terms; and the response has been to seek to create a single regime that adopts the most protective effects of both regimes. The same approach might be taken here (which would also provide an opportunity to better draw upon existing jurisprudence, while also untangling any uncertainties in this existing jurisprudence). Having said this, there may also be arguments for allowing the common law doctrines to develop unhindered. This is the view of the Law Commission in relation to the unfair terms proposals where the idea is to bring the two statutory regimes together but leave the common law rules on unfair terms to develop outside the new statutory regimes.[80] Of course, there is a difference between the unfair terms scenario and this one. In the case of unfair terms the main protective provisions (and those with most in common in terms of the standards set) are those contained in the statutes; while the common law contains

---

[77] *Ibid.*, at paras 186–7.
[78] *Ibid.*, at para 179.
[79] *Ibid.*, at para 178.
[80] See Law Commission Consultation Paper on Unfair Terms in Contracts, No. 166, 4.31.

wholly different tools and sets a lower level of protection (and therefore might be said to be of residual importance). Here, it is the common law rules on misrepresentation, duress and undue influence that provide similar and substantially overlapping protection to that offered by any duty modelled on the Directive.

9.5.5.4 Uncertainty Problems

One question raised by the DTI is as to whether a general duty would cause undue uncertainty in private law; and in particular, whether it would give rise to spurious claims; although they do not consider that this would be likely.[81] However, it is clearly desirable (to reduce the scope for spurious claims, to facilitate efficient framing of claims and to facilitate effective compliance) that it is introduced in such a way that the maximum calculability is retained. Lack of certainty/calculability is a common concern about general clauses.[82] This is not just about the general uncertainty as to what the clause means. It is about the idea that even if courts give a meaning to the clause if this is in the context of a particular set of facts (as it will be in private litigation) it will not necessarily be clear how it will apply to other fact situations. This is exacerbated by the fact that only a relatively small number of cases will be privately litigated, so that the potential for a comprehensive and rigorous jurisprudence based on private litigation will be extremely limited. The consequence may be that there is limited guidance for consumer advisers in framing actions, for traders in seeking to comply and for the courts in the future (isolated) cases. The conclusion is often that regulation by private law means simply will not work.[83]

The first important point in this context is that the suggested private law standard (at least in so far as it simply replicated the standard in the Directive) would not be operating in isolation. As in the case of the unfair terms regime, the private law regime would operate against the backdrop of the public law regime used to enforce the standards of the Directive. In the case of unfair contract terms we have seen that the public law regime (in particular the work of the OFT) has played a huge role in providing and disseminating a jurisprudence on unfairness. This has been a key function of the OFT along with the actual enforcement function. In this light we can see the courts in private litigation not as our primary source of guidance, but more as providing a check on the standards being set and

---

[81] *Ibid.*, at para 182.

[82] See discussion above at 9.5.3.1.

[83] On all this see R. Brownsword, R. Bradgate and C. Twigg-Flesner, *The Impact of Adopting a General Duty to Trade Fairly*, DTI, 2003, at 67–8.

also, importantly, as an avenue for individual consumers to obtain corrective justice. Providing a detailed jurisprudence on the standards can only be a secondary expectation of the courts in the context of private litigation. The primary source of guidance and jurisprudence must be the work of the regulatory bodies in enforcing the general standard at public law level.

The work of regulatory bodies and (in the context of individual litigation) the courts would (at least in the context of standards based on the Directive) also be able to draw upon the blacklist of practices that are always regarded as unfair under the Directive (and this list could be supplemented so as to cover unilateral unfairness scenarios if these were to be covered by the private law standard). In addition, the limitations in guidance identified above[84] could be addressed. So, it could be made clear that the list is not exhaustive. In addition, an attempt could be made to draft a 'greylist' of practices that might be deemed to be unfair depending on the circumstances. It could also be made clear that the list of types of information that must be disclosed in invitations to purchase (under Article 7(4)) is not exhaustive.

9.5.5.5 Going Further then the Directive?

A separate question to which we now turn is whether a private law duty should mirror exactly the duty in the Directive or whether it should go further. The DTI idea is that the duty would mirror that in the Directive and (as indicated above) that private law rights would arise on the basis of a breach of statutory duty (presumably a provision to this effect would simply be inserted in the provision implementing the Directive). However, if a general duty was to be adopted in private law, the fact that private law is outside the scope of the Directive would allow introduction of a higher standard than that in the Directive. This could involve: missing out any requirement of a transactional decision having to be the result (so allowing coverage of unilateral unfairness); in cases where the practice does result in a transactional decision, missing out any requirement that this needs to be a decision that the average consumer would have taken (i.e. allowing for a remedy where (judged subjectively) the consumer was induced to make the transactional decision by the practice); and basing the unfairness standard on failure to respect the legitimate interests or expectations of the consumer (thereby clearly signalling a standard not based on market norms).

---

[84] See above at 9.5.3.1.

Going beyond the Directive in these ways would provide extra protection to consumers and be a means of escaping at least some of the shackles of maximum harmonization.

9.5.5.6 Remedies

(i) Damages

The DTI suggest a damages remedy for breach of any new duty[85] and ask whether damages should also be able to be recovered via a representative action.[86]

The suggestion is that damages be available for the economic losses caused by the unfair practice.[87] Before we go any further it is worthwhile mapping out the kind of situations in which there would be a damages remedy where one does not exist already. The situations seem to be as follows:

- damages for a broader category of misleading practices than would currently amount to false statements of fact (a false statement of fact being the first requirement of the current misrepresentation regime);
- damages for misleading practices where the result is not that the consumer enters a contract with the party responsible for the practice, but that the consumer makes a transactional decision short of a contract in the context of his relationship with the party responsible for the practice (currently not covered by the Misrepresentation Act which requires a contract between the two parties to have resulted[88] and only covered in tort if the party responsible for the practice owed a duty of care);
- damages for a misleading practice by trader X where the result is that the consumer *does not* enter a contract to buy from trader Y (currently not covered by the Misrepresentation Act for the reason given above and only covered in tort where trader X owes a duty of care and there is a form of loss recoverable in tort);
- damages for a misleading practice carried out by a party such as a manufacturer where the result is that the consumer enters a contract with a seller or makes some other form of transactional decision in the context of his relationship with the seller (currently only covered in the restricted circumstances in which there is found to be a

---

85 Consultation document, *supra*, para 180.
86 *Ibid.*, para. 194.
87 *Ibid.*, para. 180.
88 Section 2(1).

unilateral contract between the manufacturer or the manufacturer is held to have owed – and be in breach of – a duty of care to the consumer);

- damages for a misleading practice carried out by a seller where the result is that the consumer enters a contract with a third party such as an insurance or finance company (currently only covered where the seller is found to have made some form of binding contractual promise or where the seller is found to owe – and be in breach of – a duty of care);

- damages for aggressive practices carried out by any party where the result is that the consumer makes any form of transactional decision (whether to enter a contract with the party responsible for the practice or with another party; not to enter a contract with another party; or to make a transactional decision short of a contract in relation to the party carrying out the practice or some other party) (currently not covered at all by rules on duress or undue influence as these do not ground a damages remedy and only conceivably covered where the party responsible for the practice was under a duty of care or where the practice amounts to one of the economic torts, e.g. the tort of inducing a breach of contract or interfering with a contract);

- damages for an unfair unilateral practice causing loss to the consumer (currently only covered if the practice amounted to a breach of contract or breach of a duty of care in tort).

The above list illustrates that the introduction of a damages remedy for unfair practices would significantly expand the range of situations in which damages would be available. However, they all appear to be situations in which there would be a legitimate consumer interest in at least being compensated for reliance loss, i.e. to be put in the position he would have occupied if the practice had not been carried out – meaning the recovery of expenses and other losses caused by having made the transactional decision in question or being at the wrong end of the unilateral unfairness carried out by the trader.

These are the sorts of loss which (at least in the case of practices covered by the Directive) the DTI suggests allowing recovery of. There are various further issues that arise. First of all, there is the question as to whether any new regime should make distinctions (for the purposes of measuring damages) between misleading/false statements depending on whether they have been made innocently, negligently or fraudulently. Clearly there is a case for such distinctions to be made so as to reflect differing degrees of culpability. If the new regime was to be based on breach of statutory duty and distinctions were to be made depending on culpability then clearly it would need to be said specifically that the damages available would depend upon the level of culpability. This is because the 'misleading', 'aggressive' and general 'unfairness' concepts in the UCPD do not as they stand contain any obvious elements that relate to culpability. The question is simply whether the practice is misleading, aggressive or unfair. So if damages were simply said to be available in such circumstances there would be no distinction between degrees of culpability on the part of the trader.

Of course, if the availability of damages *was* to vary depending on culpability then the opportunity should arguably be taken to consider whether this new statutory regime should take a different approach to that taken under the Misrepresentation Act. So there would be the chance to consider whether it is appropriate (as is done under the Misrepresentation Act) to make no distinction between damages for negligent misrepresentation under s. 2(1) of the Misrepresentation Act 1967 and damages for fraud.[89] If a distinction *was* to be made between the measure of damages in cases where the misleading practice was fraudulent and cases where it was negligent then it would need to be decided what the distinction should be. So, it might be said that while all losses flowing from entry into the contract are recoverable in cases of fraud even if these losses are unforeseeable, only foreseeable losses are recoverable where negligence is involved. There would also be the opportunity to consider the appropriate approach to take in a new statutory regime to cases where there is no fraud or negligence. In such cases (under the Misrepresentation Act) there is confusion over the appropriate measure of damages[90] and a new regime presents the opportunity to reflect on an approach that compensates for the misrepresentation but recognizes the lack of culpability of the trader. There would also be the opportunity to reflect on the basic availability of damages in cases of innocent misrepresentation. Currently, these are only available when the court exercises its discretion to award damages in lieu of rescission;[91] however, there is uncertainty as to whether this discretion can be exercised when the consumer has already lost the right to rescind the contract. The answer probably is that damages can only be awarded in lieu of rescission where

---

[89] *Royscot Trust Ltd* v. *Rogerson* [1991] 2 QB 297. This failure to distinguish between fraud and negligence is controversial – see R. Hooley, Damages and the Misrepresentation Act 1967 (1991) 107 LQR 547; and J. Poole and Devenney (forthcoming) Journal of Business Law.

[90] See generally *Thoams Witter Ltd* v. *TBP Industries* [1996] 2 All ER 573; *William Sindall plc.* v. *Cambridgeshire County Council* [1994] 3 All ER 932, per Hoffmann LJ; and Beale Damages in Lieu of Rescission for Misrepresentation (1995) 111 LQR 60.

[91] See Misrepresentation Act, s. 2(2).

the right to rescind still exists.[92] However, there are certainly respectable arguments to the effect that there should be no such restriction. Given that the right to rescind can be lost through no fault of the consumer, why should the consumer not be given damages as an alternative remedy – assuming this would be less onerous for the trader – when the right to reject has been lost? Why is it not appropriate to award damages in such a situation but appropriate to do so in cases when the right to reject has not been lost but the court considers rescission too onerous a remedy for the trader?.[93]

Of course, a statutory regime might make no distinctions based on culpability at all. It might simply provide that reliance damages are available whenever a misleading practice leads to a transactional decision. This would certainly have the advantage of simplicity. However, the choice would then need to be made as to what the single measure of damages should be used. Should it be the measure currently available for an innocent misrepresentation? Should it be the more generous measure allowed for fraud and negligence? Should unforeseeable losses be recoverable? Clearly consumer protection and deterrence increases the more generous the measure.

Another issue is how to measure (the new availability of) damages for aggressive practices. They should clearly be based on the reliance costs of having entered the contract; but should the inherent culpability in an aggressive practice be reflected in recovery of unforeseeable losses (given that the culpability involved in fraud seems to be the justification for such losses being available in that situation)?

A further opportunity arises to consider whether there may be circumstances in which expectation losses might be justifiable. There is no space to develop these arguments at present. However, one particular issue might be raised. The DTI expressly say that they would not allow for damages for distress.[94] However, it is arguable that this might be justified where there has been a misleading statement as to goods or services and this focused expressly on the reliability or freedom from hassle or stress that could be gained by a particular purchase. Such a statement might generate strong expectations to this effect and if the

---

[92]   In *Thomas Witter Ltd v TBP Industries Ltd* [1996] 2 All ER 573 at 590 it was suggested, obiter, that the right to rescind did not need still to exist. However, later authority suggests that the right to rescind does need still to exist – see Judge Humphrey Lloyd in *Floods of Queensferry Ltd* v. *Shand Construction Ltd* [2000] BLR 81, at 93; Judge Raymond Jack QC in *Government of Zanzibar* v. *British Aerospace (Lancaster House) Ltd* [2000] 1 WLR 2333 at 2341–4; and Rex Todd QC (obiter) in *Pankhania* v. *Hackney LBC* [2002] NPC 123.

[93]   See, generally, H. Beale, Points on Misrepresentation (1995) 111 LQR 385.

[94]   DTI Consultation document, para. 180.

statement was incorrect in this respect and distress did result then it is arguable that damages should be available. It is also arguable that by its very nature an aggressive practice causes distress and that there might therefore be an argument for allowing damages to reflect this. However, consideration of the issue of distress damages would need to take place in the context of a full consideration and review as to when damages for distress should be available in general.

As suggested above the DTI also asked whether damages should be available via representative actions. Again, there is no space to develop this issue here. However, we can say that such actions clearly may enable more efficient disposal of claims and allow consumers to be compensated where they might be deterred by a range of factors (including cost and inconvenience) from taking individual action. One possible way of approaching the issue would be to provide that in cases where an enforcement body obtains an injunction against a trader using an unfair practice the court has power to award damages to compensate the consumers who have been affected by this practice thus far.[95]

(ii) Other Remedies

The DTI also ask whether other remedies should be available.[96] There does seem to be a case for other remedies to be available. First, there seems to be a case for a rescission remedy.[97] Such a remedy is already available for misrepresentation, duress and undue influence and it would be strange if it was not available for practices that cover the same ground; and which, even when they cover broader ground are regulated for broadly the same reason, i.e. that the consumer did not make (in the case of a misleading practice) a properly informed decision or (in the case of an aggressive practice) a fully autonomous decision. In addition, if a consumer has been induced to enter a contract as a result of an unfair practice there does not appear to be any justification for confining the consumer to a damages remedy and requiring the consumer keep and maintain goods or continue to receive a service. (Of course, it would be

---

[95]   Summary of Responses to the Consultation on Implementing the EU Directive on Unfair Commercial Practices and Amending Existing Consumer Legislation, DTI, June 2006 (summary of response to question 26).

[96]   *Ibid.*, para 193.

[97]   And this seems to have been supported by at least some of those responding to the DTI consultation-Summary of Responses to the Consultation on Implementing the EU Directive on Unfair Commercial Practices and Amending Existing Consumer Legislation, DTI, June 2006 (summary of response to question 26).

logical to apply the same restrictions on the right to rescind as currently apply.[98])

There also seems to be a good case for remedies appropriately analogous to the repair and replacement remedies available for goods that are in breach of express terms or the implied terms as to description, quality or fitness for particular purpose.[99] If goods have been purchased on the strength of a misleading statement there seems no good reason why the supplier and manufacturer should not be responsible for bringing the goods into conformity with the statement or supplying goods that are in conformity with the statement (subject to the rules on possibility and proportionality that apply where the goods are in breach of express terms or the implied terms as to description, quality or fitness for particular purpose[100]). As to services, there seems no good reason why a similar approach should not be applied (and, indeed, logically extended to cases where there is a breach of contract). Such remedies would certainly enhance the protection available under English law. Although repair and replacement are now available in sale and supply of goods contracts[101] (in order to meet the requirements of the Directive on Consumer Sales and Associated Guarantees[102]), the general rule (applicable to service contracts) is that damages is the primary remedy for breach of contract (with termination being available for serious breaches). The only way of achieving some form of cure or replacement remedy is currently via the remedy of specific performance. However, specific performance in English law is not available as a matter of routine.[103]

9.5.6 The Consumer Credit General Clause

The new Consumer Credit Act 2006 represents a further move in the direction of a general clause that may well be aimed at routine (rather than extreme) unfairness. The Act introduces the concept of an 'unfair relationship'. There may be such an unfair relationship based on the terms of the contract.[104] This overlaps with the regimes on fairness of terms but extends beyond these in catching the interest rate (a term that would be a

---

[98] The right to rescind for misrepresentation is lost by affirmation, lapse of time, the intervention of third party rights and where *restitutio in integrum* is impossible.

[99] See Sale of Goods Act, 1979, ss 48B and 48C.

[100] *Ibid.*

[101] See Sale of Goods Act, 1979, ss 48B and 48C.

[102] 99/44/EC, Article 3.

[103] For a discussion see E. McKendrick, Contract Law, 6th edn, Palgrave Macmillan, 2005, at 21.9.

[104] Section 140(1)(a).

core term under the Unfair Terms in Consumer Contracts Regulations). However, there can also be an unfair relationship based on (1) the way the lender has exercised or enforced his rights or (2) anything done or not done by the lender before or after the agreement.[105]

Both categories (1) and (2) seem to have the potential to catch virtually any type of pre- or post-contractual fairness mentioned above (i.e. misleading or aggressive practices leading to a transactional decision or wholly unilateral unfairness); and in this sense they represent general clauses. So, any form of misleading, aggressive or non-cooperative or otherwise unfair behaviour arising pre-contractually or post-contractually would seem to be caught. So, for example, there might be tactics to pressure the consumer to pay what the lender claims is owed, which tactics might be argued to be unfair, e.g. giving a misleading impression as to the amounts owed; not giving clear breakdowns as to what is owed so as to deter the consumer from making a calm assessment of the position; or refusing to cooperate with consumer attempts to resolve the issue.

Where there is found to an unfair relationship the court has a wide variety of powers including ordering repayment of money by the creditor; requiring the creditor to do (or cease to do) anything in connection with the agreement; reducing or discharging money owed by the debtor or a surety; requiring the return of property to a surety; setting aside any duty owed by the debtor or a surety owed under this or a related agreement; altering the terms of the agreement; or directing accounts to be taken.[106]

Of course, in relation to this new fairness principle in consumer credit contracts, we need to consider what level of fairness is aimed at and its relationship to market standards. This is necessary in order to assess how powerful and significant the standard would be; but certainly the standard does seem to be an attempt to increase the level of protection from the old 'extortionate bargain' general clause[107] so there is at least some suggestion that the provisions are aimed at more routine unfairness.

9.6 The Future European Picture

The UTD and the UCPD form part of a bigger European picture of harmonized law that sets standards that can be associated with fairness values. Above I drew a distinction between fairness rules of a more

---

[105] Section 140(1)(b) and (c) respectively.

[106] Section 140(b)(1).

[107] The extortionate bargain provisions have been repealed by s. 70 of the new Act. This was always taken only to be aimed at the most extremely unfair situations, in particular extremely high interest rates.

positive nature that impose obligations on traders and/or give rights to consumers; and rules of a more negative nature that constrain what traders can do. The UTD and UCPD fall into the latter category. In the former category are the various Directives requiring disclosure of information to consumers;[108] along with the Directive on Consumer Sales and Associated Guarantees which sets substantive conformity standards and provides remedies for breach of these standards.[109] However, these Directives cannot be viewed as the end of the European fairness story in relation to consumer contracts. As part of the ongoing European Commission work on the future of European private law[110] I have already mentioned the ongoing review of this EU consumer *acquis* and the work on developing a so called Common Frame of Reference (CFR).[111] This could lead to changes in any of the existing Directives affecting the degree of fairness-orientation of the various rules. So, there could be changes in the approach to the concept of unfairness applicable to contract terms. Equally, there could be changes to other rules making up the consumer *acquis*; and there might be significant development of the consumer *acquis*.[112] In the context of this work, debates that we have seen in the context of the rules on unfair terms will continue to be important (both in relation to unfair terms rules and in relation to other rules affecting consumers). Key among these debates will be the utility of

---

[108] See, for example, the various disclosure requirements in 85/677/EEC (doorstep selling), 90/314/EEC (package travel), 94/47/EEC (timeshare) and 97/7/EEC (distance selling).

[109] 99/44/EC, Articles 2 and 3.

[110] Communication on Contract Law, 2001, COM(2001) 398; Action Plan on a More Coherent European Contract Law, 2003, COM(2003) 68; and European Contract Law and the revision of the *acquis*: the way forward, 2004, COM(2004) 651, final.

[111] European Contract Law and the revision of the *acquis*: the way forward, *ibid.*

[112] European Contract Law and the revision of the *acquis*: the way forward, *ibid.*, 4; J. Karsten and G. Petri, Towards a Handbook on European Contract Law and Beyond: the Commission's 2004 Communication 'European Contract Law and the Revision of the *Acquis*: the Way Forward' (2005) 28 Journal of Consumer Policy 31, 40–41; Report from the Commission – First Annual Progress Report on European Contract Law and the *Acquis* Review, COM(2005) 456 final, 9–10; M. Kenny, The 2003 Action Plan on European Contract Law: is the Commission Running Wild? (2003) 28 European Law Review 538; M. Kenny, The 2004 Communication on European Contract Law: Those Magnificent Men in Their Unifying Machines (2005) 30 European Law Review, 724; M.W. Hesselink, The Politics of a European Civil Code (2004) 10 European Law Journal 67; and see the academic work done in developing principles from the existing *acquis* in R. Schulze, European Private Law and Existing Law, and Pre-contractual Duties and Conclusion of Contract (2005) 13 European Review of Private Law, 3–19, 841–866.

general clauses as a means of protection; the extent to which protection in the form of information is sufficient or whether more substantive controls are required; the general level of protection to provide;[113] and the extent to which rules should give special protection to the most vulnerable consumers.[114] There will also be debates as to the implications of maximum harmonization,[115] in particular the risk that maximum harmonization suppresses national traditions of and/or ambitions for higher levels of protection.[116] The outcomes of all of these debates are apt to affect the nature and content of rules affecting consumer contracts and (in the case of the minimum/maximum harmonization debate) the relationship between EC and national law standards. There will also be debates as to the *competence* of the EC to legislate for further harmonization[117] and decisions on the appropriate legal basis of action may affect the *form* of future EC measures (whether directives, regulations or some form of soft law measure[118]). This, in turn, may affect the *content* of the rules in question.[119]

---

[113] European Contract Law and the Revision of the *Acquis*: the Way Forward, COM(2004) 651 final, 4; and for a recent overview of the issues in EC consumer law see H. Schulte-Nölke, EC Consumer Law Compendium – Comparative Analysis, University of Bielefeld, 2006 (available at:

http://ec.europa.eu/consumers/cons_int/safe_shop/acquis/comp_analysis_en.pdf.

[114] Thomas Wilhelmsson, Varieties of Welfarism in European Contract Law (2004) 10 European Law Journal 712; S. Weatherill, The Constitutional Competence of the EU to Deliver Social Justice (2006) 2 European Review of Contract Law 136.

[115] Maximum (or predominantly maximum) harmonization may be the European Commission's preferred future direction for new and consolidating measures – see Consumer Policy Strategy 2002–2006, COM(2002) 208 final and D. Staudenmayer, The Way Forward in European Contract Law (2005) 13 European Review of Private Law 95 at104.

[116] See H.-W. Micklitz *et al.*, EU Treaty Revision and Consumer Protection (2004) 27 Journal of Consumer Policy 367, 387; T. Wilhelmsson, The Abuse of the 'Confident Consumer' as a Justification for EC Consumer Law (2004) 27 Journal of Consumer Policy, 317, 325; and G. Howells, The Rise of European Consumer Law – Whither National Consumer Law? (2006) 28 Sydney Law Review, 63.

[117] S. Weatherill, EU Consumer Law and Policy (2005), 12–17; S. Weatherill, The Constitutional Competence of the EU to Deliver Social Justice (2006) 2 European Review of Contract Law 136.

[118] N. Reich, A European Contract Law – Ghost or Host for Integration? (2006) 24 Wisconsin International Law Journal 425–470.

[119] Generally on the relationship between consumer law and the development of European contract law see R. Schulze, Consumer Law and European Contract Law (2007) Yearbook of Consumer Law, 153.

9.7 Fairness in Commercial Contracts

A final issue to be considered is the potential impact of the fairness regime beyond the sphere of consumer contracts. Under UCTA a reasonableness regime already applies to many exemption clauses in commercial contracts.[120] However, UCTA does not cover terms imposing obligations and liabilities. While such terms are covered by the UTCCR, the UTCCR does not apply to commercial contracts. Certain terms imposing obligations and liabilities (e.g. deposits, penalties and forfeiture clauses) are controlled at common law, equity or under statutory provisions.[121] However, if a term falls outside these categories (e.g. a term allowing for an unfair price rise) there is no general fairness rule in common law or equity that can be called upon routinely to control the term. (The general unconscionability jurisdiction existing in equity will only catch the most extreme cases.[122]) In addition, there is no general principle of fairness or good faith that can be applied to other aspects of the contractual relationship between commercial contractors, e.g. to the pre-contractual stage, or to performance or enforcement. Of course, the common law is capable of achieving similar results in many cases by the application of existing, accepted rules. So, for example, the party who is aggrieved that another party has 'unfairly' withdrawn from negotiations prior to the conclusion of a contract may sometimes have a claim in restitution. A degree of procedural fairness is able to be achieved via rules on misrepresentation, duress and undue influence. The implied term device can impose obligations or constrain the exercise of rights if not openly in the name of fairness then at least in ways that limit the unbridled pursuit of self-interest.[123] Rules on mitigation of loss involve a degree of balancing the interests of the parties in the context of the recovery of damages for breach of contract. However, these common law rules may not be broad enough to catch all instances of unfairness that might be caught by a general fairness or good faith principle.

---

[120] Terms excluding or restricting liability for negligence causing loss other than death or injury (s. 2(2)); terms in one party's written standard terms whereby this party excludes or restricts liability for breach of contract or seeks to offer a contractual performance substantially different from that reasonably expected or no performance at all (s. 3); terms excluding or restricting liability for breach of the implied terms as to description, quality and fitness in contracts for the sale and supply of goods (ss 6(3) and 7(3)); and terms excluding or restricting liability for misrepresentation.

[121] See above at 8.1.1 and see H. Collins, Fairness in Agreed Remedies, in C. Willett (ed.), Aspects of Fairness in Contract, Blackstone, 1996, 97.

[122] See above at 8.1.2.

[123] See H. Collins, Discretionary Power in Contracts, in D. Campbell, H. Collins and J. Wightman (eds), Implicit Dimensions of Contract, Hart, 2003, 219, at 242–5.

A considerable volume of recent academic writing has been devoted to the question as to whether a general principle of fairness or good faith should be applied to commercial contract law.[124] This writing has been inspired by a number of factors, e.g. an increased interest in globalization and comparative law (good faith often having a more important role to play in other legal systems); a more specific interest in the possible harmonization of private laws within Europe (good faith again having a more significant role to play in many continental systems than in the legal systems of the UK[125]); an interest in trust, cooperation and reasonable expectations in contract (which, from some perspectives, are enhanced by fairness and/or good faith rules[126]); and an interest in economic efficiency (which again, from some perspectives, may be enhanced in some cases by fairness and/or good faith rules). However, it seems that the development of fairness rules in *consumer contracts* has, often in interaction with some of the above factors, been influential in stimulating debate as to the potential for fairness and/or good faith in commercial contracts. Arguments can be made to the effect that certain rationales for the instatement of fairness in consumer contracts apply also in the context of commercial contracts. So, for example, it might be argued that similar weaknesses may apply to some commercial contractors and that standard form commercial contracts may involve transaction costs that leave scope for (unregulated) terms to be inefficient.[127] It might also be argued that just as a general clause on fairness in consumer contracts may produce greater certainty and rationality by addressing fairness concerns openly,

---

[124] See for example J. Beatson and D. Friedmann (eds), Good Faith and Fault in Contract Law, OUP, 1995; R. Brownsword, N. Hird and G. Howells (eds), Good Faith in Contract: Concept and Context, Ashgate, 1999; A. Forte (ed.), Good Faith in Contract and Property Law, Hart, 1999; J. Stapleton, Good Faith in Private Law (1999) 52 Current Legal Problems 1; and most recently see R. Brownsword, Contract Law: Themes for the Twenty-First Century, OUP, 2006, Chs 3–7 in particular.

[125] See in particular S. Whittaker and R. Zimmerman (eds), Good Faith in European Contract Law, CUP, 2000.

[126] See R. Brownsword, Contract Law, Co-operation and Good Faith: The Movement from Static to Dynamic Market-Individualism, in S. Deakin and J. Michie (eds), Contracts, Co-operation and Competition, OUP, 1997 255; T. Wilhelmsson, Good Faith and the Duty of Disclosure in Commercial Contracting, in R. Brownsword, N. Hird and G. Howells (eds), Good Faith in Contract: Concept and Context, Ashgate, 1999, 165, at 181–3; and most recently, R. Brownsword, Contract Law: Themes for the Twenty-First Century, OUP, 2006, 67–8.

[127] See for example (specifically in relation to proposals to protect small business customers from terms other than exemption clauses) the discussion by the Law Commission (Unfair Terms in Contracts, No. 292, at 5.12–24).

the same may be true in commercial contracts.[128] In the EC context it might be suggested that just as the achievement of Treaty of Rome integration goals is said to necessitate a degree of harmonization of consumer contract law the same goals may require a degree of harmonization of commercial contract law,[129] and (given the importance of good faith as an existing principle in many civil law systems) that good faith may have an important role to play in this process[130]. Of course, arguments can be made against the instatement of a fairness/good faith principle in commercial contracts, e.g. that commercial contracting is and should be premised on an adversarial ethic, freedom-oriented autonomy, certainty, and a strong focus on particular contracting contexts; and that general fairness/good faith principles and rules are corrosive of all of these values.[131]

This is not the place for an evaluation of the respective pros and cons of instating a general principle of fairness or good faith in commercial contracts. The key point here is simply that there is at least something of a movement in this direction.

The developments in terms of fairness in commercial contracts have not been confined to academic commentary. As mentioned above, under UCTA a reasonableness regime already applies to many exemption clauses in commercial contracts. While working on consolidation of UCTA and the Regulations the Law Commission has proposed that a 'fair and reasonable' test should apply not only to exemption clauses but also to other (non-negotiated) terms in commercial contracts when these terms are used against small businesses.[132]

---

[128] See R. Brownsword, Positive, Negative and Neutral: The Reception of Good Faith in English Contract Law, in R. Brownsword, N. Hird and G. Howells (eds), Good Faith in Contract: Concept and Context, Ashgate, 1999, 13, at 26.

[129] See S. Vogenauer and S. Weatherill, The European Community's Competence to Pursue the Harmonisation of Contract Law – an Empirical Contribution to the Debate, in S. Vogenauer and S. Weatherill, The Harmonisation of European Contract Law, Hart, 2006, 105.

[130] On good faith in various European countries see S. Whittaker and R. Zimmerman (eds), Good Faith in European Contract Law, CUP, 2000 and M. Hesselink, The New European Private Law.

[131] See, for example, M. Bridge, Good Faith in Commercial Contracts, in R. Brownsword, Positive, Negative and Neutral: The Reception of Good Faith in English Contract Law, in R. Brownsword, N. Hird and G. Howells (eds), Good Faith in Contract: Concept and Context, Ashgate, 1999, 139.

[132] See Law Commission, Unfair Terms in Contracts, No. 292, Part 5 and see H. Beale, Unfair Terms in Contracts: Proposals for Reform in the UK (2004) 27 Journal of Consumer Policy 289, at 308–313.

I have already mentioned the question as to whether there is a case for EC harmonization of commercial contract law (this harmonized code possibly containing a general good faith clause). This, of course, is a discussion that has gone well beyond academic circles. There is of course already a good faith test (reflecting the one in the UTD) in the (non-mandatory) Principles of European Contract Law (PECL).[133] There have also now been a series of papers from the European Commission on the issue,[134] and based on these papers there is now work ongoing towards the development of a 'Common Frame of Reference'.[135] The idea appears to be that this would provide a set of common, model principles. The avowed intention of the Commission at present is that these would be non

---

[133] O. Lando and H. Beale (eds), Principles of European Contract Law Parts I and II, Kluwer, 2000, Article 1: 106.

[134] Communication on Contract Law, 2001, COM(2001) 398; Action Plan on a More Coherent European Contract Law, 2003, COM(2003) 68; and European Contract Law and the revision of the *acquis*: the way forward, 2004, COM(2004) 651. An enormous volume of academic literature has emerged in the wake of these various proposals. Most recently see S. Weatherill, The European Commissions' Green Paper on European Contract Law: Context, Content and Constitutionality (2002) 24 Journal of Consumer Policy, 339; T. Wilhelmsson, Private Law in the EU: Harmonised or Fragmented Europeanisation? (2002) 10 European Review of Private Law, 77; S. Grundmann and J. Stuyck (eds), An Academic Green Paper on European Contract Law, Hammicks, 2002; S. Grundmann (2004) The Optional European Code on the Basis of the *Acquis* Communautaire – Starting Point and Trends, 10 European Law Journal 698; D. Staudenmayer, The Way Forward in European Contract Law, (2005) 13 European Review of Private Law, 95; J. Karsten and G. Petri, Towards a Handbook on European Contract Law and Beyond: the Commission's 2004 Communication 'European Contract Law and the Revision of the *Acquis*: the Way Forward' (2005) 28 Journal of Consumer Policy 31; H. Heiss and N. Downes, Non-Optional Elements in an Optional European Contract Law – Reflections from a Private International Law Perspective (2005) 13 European Review of Private Law, 693; J. Smits (ed.), The Need for a European Contract Law, Europa Law Publishing, 2005; H.-W. Micklitz, The Concept of Competitive Contract Law (2005) 23 Pennsylvania State International Law Review, 549; H. Beale, The European Commission's Common Frame of Reference Project (2006) 2 European Review of Contract Law, 303; N. Reich, Protection of the Consumer's Economic Interests by EC Contract Law – Some Follow Up Remarks (2006) 28 Sydney Law Review, 37; S. Vogenauer and S. Weatherill (eds), The Harmonisation of European Contract Law, Hart, 2006.

[135] See European Contract Law and the revision of the *acquis*: the way forward, 2004, *ibid.*

mandatory;[136] although it is hard to deny the possibility that they could sew the seeds of a European civil code.[137]

Even if we go no further than non-mandatory rules at European level for commercial contracts (containing a general good faith clause) along with the existing mandatory general clause applicable to consumer contract terms (and the general clause enforceable in public law – and possibly also in private law – applicable to commercial practices aimed at consumers) it is hard to believe that all of this will not have an influence on the approach of the courts to the development of the general common law of contract. So, it is hard to imagine that at least some judges will not be inclined to seek to develop common law doctrine in ways that are more shaped by 'general clause' thinking.[138] Of course, even if this is the case, a general principle of good faith or fairness in the commercial law of contract is likely to be grounded in a less protective ethic than that developing on consumer law. So, for example, it seems likely to be more dominated by transparency and what is normal and accepted practice in the market sector in question. Indeed this possibility seems to be what has prompted certain scholars interested in the role of contract law in promoting social justice to make the case for the inclusion of a strong social justice ethic to be embedded in the developing principles of European contract law.[139]

---

[136] *Ibid.*, at p. 8.

[137] See S. Weatherill, EU Consumer Law and Policy, Elgar, 2005, at p. 155.

[138] For a discussion of the potential for this see R. Bradgate, R. Brownsword and C. Twigg-Flesner, The Impact of Adopting a General Duty to Trade Fairly, DTI, 2003, Ch. 6.

[139] See (2004) 10(6) European Law Journal, 649–803.

Index

CCA = Consumer Credit Act
ECJ = European Court of Justice
OFT = Office of Fair Trading
UCPA = Unfair Commercial Practices
    Directive
UCTA = Unfair Contract Terms Act
UTCCR = Unfair Terms in Consumer
    Contracts Regulations
UTD = Unfair Terms Directive

abstract approach 10, 311, 344
    and freedom of contract 21, 32
    and testing for unfairness 71–3
autonomy 11
    and concepts of fairness 13, 388–90
    and freedom of contract 22, 388–9
Avoidance of Liability Bill 84

bargaining 25–6, 358–63
    and conceptions of unfairness 43–6
    and contextual approach 361–3
    and freedom of contract 27–31
    and testing for unfairness 62–5
    see also under House of Lords,
        OFT, proposed new regime,
        UCTA, UTCCR, UTD
Beale, Hugh 181, 229–30, 366–7
Bingham Lord 13, 112, 189–98 passim,
    207, 208, 210, 211, 215, 222,
    225, 230–31, 241, 317, 321,
    336, 339, 342, 346–7, 360, 373,
    384–5, 417
Browne-Wilkinson, Lord 398
Buckley, Judge 176

Charterhouse Credit Ltd v. Tolley 402
choice (consumer) 23–5, 351–8
    and conceptions of unfairness 43
    and contextual approach 356–8
    and freedom of contract 27–31
    and testing for unfairness 62–5

see also under House of Lords,
    OFT, proposed new regime,
    UCTA, UTCCR, UTD
CLAB European Database on unfair
    terms 13, 118, 416
Cofidis case 99
commercial contracts, fairness in 14,
    453–7
Commission v. Netherlands 97
Commission v. Spain 97–8
Commission v. Sweden 98–9, 103
Common Frame of Reference for
    European contract law 14, 416,
    451, 456
Consumer Compendium project 416
consumer contracts 15–16
    aspects of fairness in 418–20
        other than for terms 418–20
        and CCA 449–50
        and UCPD 420–49
    for terms, see fairness regimes,
        procedural fairness/unfairness,
        substantive fairness/unfairness,
        testing for unfairness
    defined 3
Consumer Credit Act (CCA) (1974)
    178, 183, 184–5, 200, 202, 206,
    207, 247
Consumer Credit Act (CCA) (2006)
    208–9, 247, 449–50
Consumer Protection Act (1987) 420
Consumer Protection (Distance Selling)
    Regulations 323
Consumer Protection and Information
    Policy Programme (1975) 365
Consumer Sales Directive 430
Consumer Transactions (Restrictions on
    Statements) Order (1976) 410
contextual approach 10, 12, 311–20,
    344–50, 356–8
    and fairness approach to contract
        philosophy 33
    and freedom of contract 20–21, 32

and testing for unfairness 71–3
contractual relationships, stages of 1–3
County Courts (Interest on Judgements)
    Order (1991) 178–9, 184, 188,
    202, 226
Court of Appeal
    and disallowing certain substantive
        features 366–7
    and *First National Bank* case 9, 58,
        162, 179–89, 216, 413
    and default rules 182
    and good faith 180, 184, 186–7,
        188, 205–6, 244
    and procedural fairness/interests
        180–81, 185, 187
    transparency 58, 162, 180, 185,
        209, 244, 332, 337
    and reasonable expectations 180,
        181–3, 201, 244, 271
    and significant imbalance 9, 180,
        184, 186–7, 188
    and substantive fairness/interests
        180–81, 184, 186, 187–8
    and fundamental breach 402–3
    and human rights 299
    and OFT 18

default rules 47–9, 269–75
    see also under Court of Appeal,
        House of Lords, OFT, proposed
        new regime, UCTA, UTCCR
Denning, Lord 400
Department of Trade and Industry (DTI)
    14, 437–48 *passim*
Directive on Consumer Sales and
    Associated Guarantees 449, 451
Directive on Unfair Terms in Consumer
    Contracts (1993), *see* Unfair
    Terms Directive (UTD)

Enterprise Act (2002) 410, 420, 423,
    424, 430–31, 435, 436
European Commission
    and an autonomous interpretation of
        unfairness 110–11
    and harmonization of contract law
        13–14, 86–92, 214–15, 320,
        416–17, 450–52
European Contract Commission 370
European Convention on Human Rights
    299–301

European Court of Justice (ECJ) 6–7, 9
    and an autonomous interpretation of
        unfairness 110–18, 354, 416–17
    and Cofidis case 99
    Commission v. *Netherlands* 97
    Commission v. *Spain* 97–8
    Commission v. *Sweden* 98–9, 103
    and concepts of unfairness 6–7, 13,
        97–9, 99–109, 415–16
    and disallowing certain substantive
        features 366
    and favourable terms 303, 305
    and *First National Bank* case 162,
        202–5, 209–12, 213–16, 305–6
    Freiburger case 101–9, 110, 203–4,
        305
    and good faith 103, 104, 105, 110,
        116–18, 209–12, 372
    and implementation of UTD 97–9
    and interpretation of UTD 97–109,
        110, 118
    and 'mirror-image' balance 307
    Oceano case 99–101, 103–4
    and procedural fairness/interests
        104, 108
    transparency 107–9, 111–16, 203,
        209–12, 256–7, 262, 335
    and significant imbalance 103, 104,
        105, 202–5, 210, 255, 256–7,
        302
    and substantive fairness/interests
        104–5, 107–9, 203, 209–10, 273
European Union, Council of
    Council Resolution (1975) 92–3
European Union Member States
    and an autonomous interpretation of
        unfairness 110–18, 189–90, 354
    fairness traditions of 6, 110
    good faith traditions of 110, 111–
        12, 116–18, 372
    harmonization of unfairness
        concepts among 13–14, 86–92,
        110–18, 189–90, 214–15, 320,
        416
    and UCPD 422, 425, 433–4
expectation, *see* reasonable expectations

Fair Trading Act (1973) 410
fairness-oriented contract philosophy
    32–6
    and context 33

defined 4, 17–18
and procedural interests 33
and substantive interests 35–6, 311–20
and welfarism 33–4, 35, 377–9
fairness regimes 6, 35–6, 411–12
unresolved questions pertaining to 412–16
see also proposed new regime, testing for unfairness, UCTA, UTCCR, UTD
fairness testing, *see* testing for unfairness
First National Bank v. *Director General of Fair Trading* 9–10, 177–8
see also under Court of Appeal, ECJ, House of Lords, OFT
France
and Cofidis case 99
and good faith 112
Loi Scrivener (1978) 84, 165–6
and transparency 112–13
Freiburger case 101–9, 110, 203–4, 305
freedom-oriented contract philosophy
and context 18–19, 32
defined 3–4, 17–18
freedom from contract 18–19
freedom of contract 19–20
and procedural interests 26–31
and sanctity of contract 20–21, 32
and substantive interests 31–2, 311–20

George Mitchell v. *Finney Lockseeds* 154, 158
Germany
Civil Code (BGB – Bürgerliches Gesetzbuch) 13, 101, 102, 194–5, 196, 257–8, 272, 399, 417
Court of Appeal 169
and good faith 112, 117, 399
and individually negotiated terms 165, 169
Standard Contracts Act (AGBG) (1976) 84, 101–2, 165, 230
and transparency 112, 257–8, 262, 263
Gibson, Peter, Lord Justice 366
good faith 9, 294–301
and an autonomous interpretation of unfairness 110, 111–12, 116–18

and community norms 384–5, 387
and conscience 370
and human rights 299–301
and market norms 382–5, 386–8
and services of general interest 295–8
traditions of Member States 110, 111–12, 116–18
see also under Court of Appeal, ECJ, House of Lords, UTCCR, UTD
Griffiths, Lord 309–10, 314

High Court
and *First National Bank* case 179
high courts, *see* Court of Appeal, House of Lords
House of Lords
and contextual approach 317–18, 362
and default rules 232–3
and disallowing certain substantive features 367
and favourable terms 303
and *First National Bank* case 9–10, 13, 48, 58, 162, 179, 184, 189–202, 204, 205–9, 211–16, 413, 417
and consumer interests 276–7
and contextual approach 317–18, 346–7, 350
and default rules 48, 232, 233, 240
and ECJ 190, 197, 202–5, 209–12, 213–16, 417
and favourable terms 305
and good faith 193–9, 205–9, 222, 240, 257
and indicative list 197
and insurance 293
and market norms 386, 387
and procedural fairness/interests 192–3, 194–5, 198–9, 208
bargaining 194–5, 197, 360
choice 198, 354–5
transparency 58, 193–4, 207–9, 211, 257, 321–50 *passim*
and reasonable expectation 182–3, 199, 201, 271
and significant imbalance 191–3, 199–202, 222, 226, 230, 232, 233, 240, 241, 254–5, 257

and substantive fairness/interests
179, 184, 191–3, 195–7, 198–9,
208
and UTCCR 189, 249, 251
and UTD 189–90, 196–7, 417
and fundamental breach 402–3
and good faith 112, 222, 225, 299,
373
and human rights 299
and insurance 293
and OFT 216–18
and procedural fairness/interests
222
bargaining 155, 157, 359–60, 362
choice 155, 157, 353
transparency 58, 112, 114, 116,
162
and significant imbalance 9, 222,
225, 232–3, 302
and substantive fairness/interests 12,
222, 225
and trader interests 310–11
and UCTA 153–8, 216–17
and UTCCR 189, 216–17
and UTD 189–90
Human Rights Act (HRA) (1998) 299

individually negotiated terms 165–71
insurance 50, 154, 213, 292–4
Interfoto Picture Library Ltd. v. *Stilleto
Visual Programs* 112, 325–6,
339

Jessell, Sir George, MR 19

Karsales (Harrow) Ltd v. *Wallis* 402

law, changes in relation to fairness
issues 11, 395–410
and agreed remedies 396–9
and agreed rules 400–401
and compensation 408–10
and construction rules 401–2
and enforcement 404–7
and fundamental breach 402–3
and good faith 206
and procedural fairness/interests
bargaining 400
transparency 400–401
and proposed new regime 395
and reasoning 403–4

and unconscionability 399
and UTCA 395, 403, 405
and UTCCR 12, 395, 403, 404–5
and UTD 405–6
Law Commission
and background to UCTA 81–4,
137, 139
and banned terms under UCTA 131,
132–3
and commercial contracts 14
and exclusion of core terms 247–8,
253–4
report (1969) 75, 81
report (1975) 75, 81–2, 137, 139
see also proposed new regime
lower courts
and *First National Bank* case 9
and proposed new regime 218–19
and significant imbalance 9
and UCTA 154, 158–9, 218–19
and UTCCR 175–6, 216–19

Mansfield, Lord 193–4, 342
market values 10
and contract fairness 36, 379–88
and freedom of contract 22, 380–81
Member States, *see* European Union
Member States
Millet, Lord 199, 209, 271, 274
'mirror-image' balance 51, 254, 306–9
Misleading Advertisements Directive
114–15
Misleading Advertisements Regulations
421, 430
Misrepresentation Act 439, 444, 446
Molony Committee 132–3

Netherlands
BW (Civil Code) 399
Commission v. *Netherlands* 97
and good faith 116, 117
Hoge Raad 116

Oceano case 99–101, 103–4
Office of Fair Trading (OFT) 10, 12
and consumer interests 278, 284–92
passim
and contextual approach 316, 347
and default rules 238, 262–3, 270,
272

and disallowing certain substantive
features 367–9
and enforcement 406–7
and favourable terms 304
and *First National Bank* case 9, 162,
178–9, 184, 214, 413
and good faith 297, 372
and higher courts 216–18
and individually negotiated terms
170
and insurance 293
and market norms 386
and 'mirror-image' balance 307,
308
and procedural fairness/interests
176
bargaining 175, 360
choice 175
transparency 161, 175, 257, 262–
3, 323, 328, 330, 333, 335, 336–
7, 344, 347
and reasonable expectations 271–2
and reasoning 404
and significant imbalance 9, 231,
257, 302
and substantive fairness/interests
175–6, 184, 369
and trader interests 310–11
and UCPD 432, 442
and UTCCR 161–2, 173, 174–6,
216–19, 407
options (consumer), *see* choice

Parker, Lord Justice 402
Philips v. *Hyland* 314–15
Photo Production Ltd v. *Securicor
Transport Ltd* 403
Principles of European Contract Law
(PECL) 370, 384
and commercial contracts 14, 456
Printing and Numerical Registering Co.
v. *Samson* 19
procedural fairness/unfairness
conceptions of 39–46
defined 2
and market norms 386–7
presumed 67–70
testing for 55–65
see also bargaining, choice,
transparency, *and under* Court
of Appeal, ECJ, House of Lords,

OFT, proposed new regime,
UCTA, UTCCR, UTD
procedural interests
defined 4
and fairness-oriented contract
philosophy 33
and freedom-oriented contract
philosophy 26–31
see also bargaining, choice,
transparency
proposed new regime 6, 76, 414–15
and commercial contracts 455
and consumer interests 277–92
passim, 309
and contextual approach 319–20,
347–9, 356–7, 362–3
and default rules 134–6, 237, 239–
40, 244, 263–4, 271
'detriment' trigger 134–5, 151, 239–
40, 244
and disallowing certain substantive
features 369
and exclusion of core terms 247–8,
253–4
fairness tests 219–21
and good faith 374, 387–8
and individually negotiated terms
169–71
and insurance 294
and procedural fairness/interests
bargaining 360–61, 362–3
choice 355, 356–7
transparency 253–4, 263–4, 324,
326–7, 328, 333–4, 343, 347–9
and reasonable expectations 9, 150–
51, 244, 253–4
and substantive fairness/interests
134
and trader interests 310
and UCTA 7, 10, 80–81, 134–6,
150–51, 170–71, 239
and UTCCR 8, 10, 80–81, 151, 239,
415
and UTD 80–81, 253–4, 415

reasonable expectations 11, 49, 269–75
and conceptions of unfairness 41
fairness-oriented approach to 390–
93
freedom-oriented approach to 390–
91

and market norms 383, 386, 388
see also under Court of Appeal,
House of Lords, OFT, proposed
new regime, UCTA, UTCCR
reasonableness test, *see under* UCTA
Reid, Lord 395

Sale of Goods Act (1979) 15, 133
Sale and Supply of Goods to Consumers
Regulations (2002) 430
SAM Business Systems case 150
sanctity of contract 20–21
Scandinavia
and contextual approach 316–17
and good faith 112
and transparency 112
Scottish Law Commission 434
significant imbalance 85, 301–2
defined 9
and favourable terms 254–8
see also under Court of Appeal,
ECJ, House of Lords, OFT,
UCTA, UTCCR, UTD
Slade, Lord Justice 314–15
Smith v. *Bush* 124, 153–4, 156–7, 212,
213, 275, 292, 303, 309–11,
313, 314, 353, 356, 357, 359,
386
social contract theories 393
Spain
Commission v. *Spain* 97–8
St Albans City v. *ICL* 316
Stenna Sealink 137–8
Steyn, Lord 137, 189, 191, 197–9, 222,
225, 367, 373, 384–5
substantive fairness/unfairness 12
and abstract approach 311
conceptions of 37–9
and contextual approach 311–20
and default rules 47–9, 269–75
defined 2
and favourable terms 301–6
and good faith 294–301
and insurance 50, 154, 292–4
and market norms 386
and 'mirror-image' balance 306–9
and reasonable expectations 49,
269–75
and significant imbalance 301–2
and standardization 369
testing for 49–55, 65–71

and trader interests 309–11
and types of consumer interest 275–
92
see also under Court of Appeal,
ECJ, House of Lords, OFT,
proposed new regime, UCTA,
UTCCR, UTD
substantive interests
abstract approaches to 311
contextual approaches to 311–20
defined 4
and fairness-oriented contract
philosophy 35–6, 311–20
and freedom-oriented contract
philosophy 31–2, 311–20
*Suisse Atlantique Société D'armement
Maritime SA* v. *Rotterdamsche
Kolen Centrale NV* 395, 403
Supply of Goods and Services Act
(1982) 15
Sutherland Report (1992) 88
Sweden
Commission v. *Sweden* 98–9, 103

testing for unfairness
and abstract fairness 71–3
and contextual fairness 71–3
default rules 47–9
disallowing certain substantive
features 65–71, 363–9
for consumer protection 70–71
and freedom of contract 71
and presumed procedural
unfairness 67–70
and social rights 66–7
and transparency 70
possible approaches to 4–6, 10
procedural issues 55–65
bargaining 62–5
choice 62–5
transparency 55–62
reasonable expectations 49
substantive issues 49–55
see also abstract approach,
contextual approach, default
rules, fairness regimes,
procedural fairness/unfairness,
reasonable expectations,
substantive fairness/unfairness
Trade Descriptions Act (1968) 420
Trading Standards Authorities 432

transparency 22–3, 321–2
and advice taking 333
and an autonomous interpretation of
unfairness 111–16
availability of terms 322–4
better legislative guidance on 333–4
and complexity 333
and conceptions of unfairness 39–43
and contextual approach 344–50
and contract structure 328–32
disclosure of facts 339–43
and freedom of contract 26–7, 30–
31
giving certain terms prominence
325–8
and language 328–32
level of 334–9
limits of 59–62, 70
and market integration 380
and market norms 386–7
and reasonable expectations 144–6,
326–7
size of print 328
and standardization 343–4
and testing for unfairness 55–62
and legal rights 57–8
limits of 59–62
and substantive fairness/interests
56–7, 61–2, 70
time for reflection 322–4
see also under Court of Appeal,
ECJ, House of Lords, OFT,
proposed new regime, UCTA,
UTCCR, UTD
Treaty of Rome 455
Article 95 of 86, 90, 91, 92, 365–6

Unfair Commercial Practices Directive
(UCPD) 13, 113, 316, 420–23,
450–51
and the concept of a general clause
431–2, 437–9
and current UK fairness standards
424–31, 434–7
and private law enforcement 437–49
Unfair Contract Terms Act (1977)
(UCTA) 3
application 76–8
background to 81–4
and commercial contracts 14, 453,
455

and community norms 385
concepts and terminology 79
and consumer interests 275–92
passim, 309
and contextual approach 311–20
passim, 345–6, 347, 356, 362
default rules under 7, 49, 234–9,
269
interest balancing 121–3, 235, 236
limits of 128
misrepresentation 126–7
obligations 121–6, 234–5, 236–9
overview 119–21
reasonableness 128, 235
transfer of information 123–7, 235
wholly ineffective terms 129–34,
235
and disallowing certain substantive
features 364, 365
effects 78–9
and enforcement 405
fairness tests 7, 10, 36, 119–20
and favourable terms 303
and individually negotiated terms
166, 170–71
and insurance 292
and market norms 385–6
overview 75–9
and procedural fairness/interests
128–9, 130, 131–3, 146, 152–3,
155–6, 157–8
bargaining 81–2, 130, 132, 133,
155, 157, 359–60, 362
choice 130, 131, 155, 157, 353–4,
356
transparency 144–6, 321, 322,
328, 345–6, 347
reasonable expectations under 7,
269, 272
and community values 138–42
compared to other concepts of
146–7
compared to UTCCR 148–50,
226, 242–3
content of 143–4
and core exclusion 248–53
limits of 148–50
'no performance at all' rule 147–8
overview 136–7
and significant imbalance 240–43,
248, 252

and trader discretion 137–8, 146–
7
and transparency 144–6, 243–4
reasonableness test under
in the higher courts 153–8
in the lower courts 154, 158–9
and procedural fairness/interests
152–3, 155–6, 157–8, 243
and substantive fairness/interests
152–3, 154–5, 156, 157–8, 243
and substantive fairness/interests
128–9, 130–31, 132, 146, 152–
3, 154–5, 156, 157–8, 243
and trader interests 309–10
and UTCCR compared 7–8, 76–9,
128, 161, 163, 216–17, 234–9
Unfair Terms in Consumer Contracts
Regulations (1994) (UTCCR) 6,
75
Unfair Terms in Consumer Contracts
Regulations (1999) (UTCCR) 3,
13
application 76–8
and commercial contracts 453
and community norms 386
concepts and terminology 79
and consumer interests 275–92
passim, 309
and contextual approach 73, 311–20
passim, 346, 349, 350, 356, 362
and default rules 8, 48, 49, 128,
227–33, 234–9, 258–65, 269
and disallowing certain substantive
features 364
effects 78–9
and enforcement 404–5
and exclusion of core terms 246
fairness tests 7–8, 10, 35, 36, 85,
162–5, 219–21
and favourable terms 302–3
and first instance cases 176–7
and good faith 7–8, 79, 85, 112,
172, 174, 222, 223–5, 243, 248,
294, 298, 371, 387
indicative list of unfair terms 171–2,
221–2, 231, 235, 242, 249, 277–
91 *passim*, 297, 306–8, 398, 432
and individually negotiated terms
165–71
and insurance 293
and market norms 386

and procedural fairness/interests
161–4, 177
bargaining 168–9, 360, 362
choice 168–9, 354, 355, 356
transparency 112, 114, 161, 162,
164–5, 168, 243–4, 256–8, 258–65,
321–9 *passim*, 346, 349, 350
overview 75–9
and reasonable expectations 8–9,
148–50, 226, 242–3, 248–53,
269, 272
and significant imbalance 7–8, 36,
79, 85, 172, 174, 221–6, 227–
33, 234–5, 240–44, 254–8
sources of interpretation of 173–6
and substantive fairness/interests
161–4, 169, 172, 177, 221–5,
243–4, 254–8
and trader interests 310–11
and UCTA compared 7–8, 76–9,
128, 161, 163, 216–17, 234–9
unfair terms defined by 7
see also First National Bank case
Unfair Terms Directive (UTD) 12, 414–
15
background to 84–5, 86–92, 92–3
and Cofidis case 99
and commercial contracts 14
and *Commission* v. *Netherlands*
case 97
and *Commission* v. *Spain* case 97–8
and *Commission* v. *Sweden* case 98–
9
and community norms 385
conceptions of unfairness 86–92,
92–7
and consumer interests 276
and contextual approach 316–17,
320, 357, 362, 363
and disallowing certain substantive
features 364, 365–6, 380–81
and enforcement 405–6
and exclusion of core terms 245–7,
253–4
fairness tests 13, 85–6, 92–7, 219–
21
and favourable terms 302–3
and *First National Bank* case 13
and *Freiburger* case 101–9
and good faith 85, 103, 116, 223,
294–301, 371–2, 374

implementation of 97–9, 408
and individually negotiated terms
   165–6
and insurance 293–4
interpretation of 97–101
and market integration 11, 86–92,
   379, 381, 385, 387
and market norms 385, 387
and *Oceano* case 99–101, 103–4
Preamble to 85–6, 87, 88, 93, 116,
   166, 224, 253, 270, 278, 295–7,
   302–3, 310, 360, 365
and procedural fairness/interests 91,
   93, 95, 104, 108, 117
   bargaining 85–6, 360, 362, 363
   choice 85–6, 354, 357
   transparency 85–6, 92–7, 117,
      258, 262, 321, 327, 329, 333
and significant imbalance 85, 103,
   223, 258

and substantive fairness/interests 83,
   93–6, 104–5, 107, 117, 223,
   258, 273
and trader interests 310
unfairness, conceptions of
   for consumers 37–46
   and procedural interests 39–46
   and substantive interests 37–9
unfairness testing, *see* testing for
   unfairness
United States
   good faith concept in 384–5

welfare state 10
   and contract fairness 33–4, 35, 377–9
Westminster Building Co. v. *Director
   General of Fair Trading* 177
Woodman v. *Photo Trade Processing*
   153, 276, 353–4
Workers Trust case 398